The Best Aires in France 2021/ 22

by

Alan Russell

www.motorhomingfrance.co.uk

Index

The regions are listed in geographical order from West to East & North to South.

THE AIRES

listed by **REGION/ former region** & DEPARTMENT (with number)

NORTHERN FRANCE

SOUTHERN FRANCE

Cover Photo La Mailleraye sur Seine

<u>REGIONS OF FRANCE MAP (pre 2016)</u>

The former (& smaller) regions of France are used for clarity

The new larger regions incorporate the former regions
with the name changes as follows:

NORTHERN FRANCE

Lower Normandy & Upper Normandy are now **NORMANDY**
Picardy & Nord-Pas-de-Calais are now **HAUTS DE FRANCE**
Champagne-Ardenne, Lorraine & Alsace are now **GRAND EST**
Burgundy & Franche-Comte are now **BURGUNDY-FRANCHE COMTE**

SOUTHERN FRANCE

Poitou Charente, Limousin & Aquitaine are now **NOUVELLE AQUITAINE**
Auvergne & Rhone Alpes are now **AUVERGNE-RHONE ALPES**
Midi-Pyrenees & Languedoc-Roussillon are now **OCCITANIE**

DEPARTMENTS OF FRANCE MAP

FOREWORD

France is one of the best countries to visit in a motorhome, RV or campervan (rather than use all three terms each time, I will simply describe your vehicle as a motorhome). The roads often have little traffic, the parking is mainly free, and unlike in the UK, overnight parking in a motorhome is subject to few restrictions. In addition to the above, France is the most visited tourist destination in the world, with many historic towns and villages, great beaches, picturesque mountain scenery and much more.

However one of the things that makes France great for motorhomes are the number of aires. These are places that are specifically created for motorhomes to stop in order to refill/ empty their tanks, recharge the battery & possibly stay the night – many of these are either free or charge a minimal amount. A more detailed explanation of aires is found in the next chapter.

This guide only deals with **Aires de Services** which are parking places that allow a stopover but also have some of the aforementioned service facilities. There are also Aires de Stationnement which are places where one can park (with no services) but since it is possible to park almost anywhere in France, these are too numerous to include.

There are almost 4,000 aires in France & obviously their quality can vary widely, not only in their location/ ambience/ price but also in their maintenance & available facilities. Many times I have visited different aires only to find that they were either dirty, expensive, noisy, had broken service points or were in an unpleasant location. I therefore wanted to produce a guide that would allow people to avoid staying in what may be a dirty, noisy car park aire with no shade & instead stay at an aire in hopefully a more pleasant, quieter environment.

I have been managing my French aires website www.motorhomingfrance.co.uk since 2006 & in selecting the 547 'Best Aires in France' I have not only used my own judgement & experience but have taken into account the opinions of various motorhomers / 'camping-caristes' who have visited these aires over a period of time. This guide will be a bi-annual review as aires often close, are relocated, change their prices, suffer from a lack of maintenance or new ones open.

The brief local directions given to the aires are suggested routes; please check individual roads for any width/ weight restrictions that may apply to your vehicle as variations to the routes can often be taken. GPS coordinates (in Decimal Degrees) are also given for the aires as these are sometimes difficult to find due to the lack of signage in many locations.

Abbreviations/ words used in the guide:

AireServices: Type of service point
Artisanal: Custom made service point
Autoroute: French motorway
Borne: Service point for water/ electric/ drainage
C: Century
APR: AireParkReservation (Aires company)
CCP: Camping Car Park (Aires company)
Ehu: Electric hook up
Euro-Relais: Type of service point

Flot Bleu & Urba Flux: Types of service point
ha: Hectare
km: Kilometre
Jeton: Token used at a service point
Mairie: Town hall
m: metre
OT: Office de Tourisme

HOW TO USE THE GUIDE

The file on each aire contains the following information:
NAME: This is the name of the commune or the nearest town to where the aire is located
ADDRESS: The road/ route where the aire is located
TYPE OF AIRE: Municipal – owned by the town or commune.
Private – owned by an individual, campsite or company
FACILITIES: Water – Fresh potable water supply Grey
Drainage – Drain for waste water from the grey tank
Black Drainage – Toilet cassette emptying point
Electric: Electric point for recharging the battery or possibly a 24 hour supply with a higher amperage that allows you to connect up your 240V appliances.
Toilets: Public toilets nearby (sometimes with showers)
Rubbish: Waste disposal/ recycling point
Wifi: Internet availability
LOCATION: Rural, Urban, next to a Lake/ River/ Canal
NO. OF SPACES: Number of pitches available for motorhomes
PRICES: Price for 24 hours of parking Services:
Price for electric, water, wifi, showers, etc.
OPENING TIMES: Period of the year when the aire is open. GPS:
GPS coordinates in decimals.
DIRECTIONS: Brief directions usually from the town/ village.
SITE DESCRIPTION: A description of the location, parking surface, environment, facilities, shade, service point & distance from town centre.
REVIEW: An opinion based on a one night stopover is not really a fair opinion so I have compiled an average review taken from various motorhomers (British & French) who have actually stayed at the aire for at least 1 or 2 nights over the past year. Comments include noise levels, ambience, shops nearby, leisure facilities, access, maintenance of services, etc.
MAPS: The region maps each have enlarged sections for clarity. Aires that were included in the previous guide but have not been included in this edition for reasons of either falling standards or closure are shown as deleted in the key, whilst new aires are shown with their reference number underlined on the map.

NOTE : In the case of small private aires, a phone number is given & it is advisable to check that there are vacancies, especially in high season, as often there are only half a dozen pitches available. Please add 0033 & ignore the first zero if you are using a UK mobile. If the number commences with 06 or 07 then it is a French mobile number & you can send a text if you are not happy speaking French.

TYPES OF SERVICE POINT FOUND AT AIRES

Above: A Euro Relais service point

Below : AireServices service point

Right: Flot Bleu service point

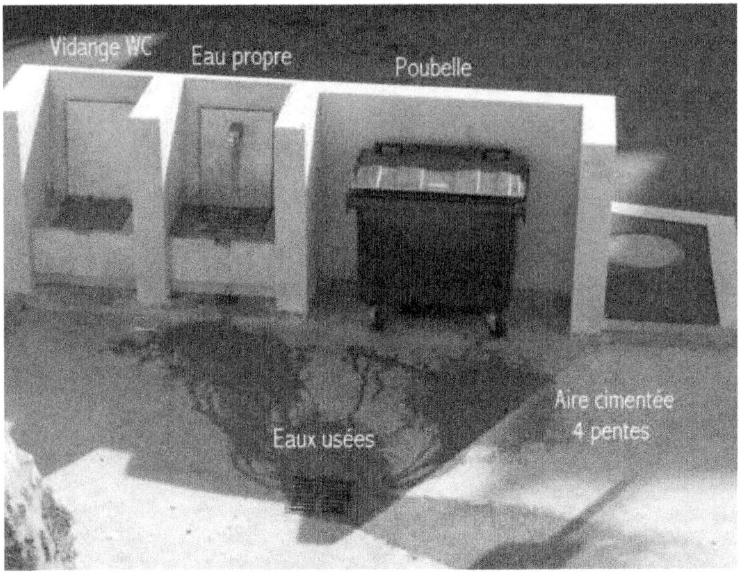

Above: A well designed Artisanal service point

STAYING AT THE AIRES DE SERVICES

What are they?

There are two main types of aire – Aire de Services and Aire de Stationnement. An Aire de Stationnement is basically a parking area with no services (water, drainage or electricity) but overnight parking is usually allowed here. An Aire de Services is a stopping place for motorhomes that can offer a few options – ranging from just being able to fill up with fresh water or empty wastewater, to stopping for a few days, filling/emptying your various tanks, access to toilets and possibly hooking up to an electricity supply (and maybe even a wifi connection). Aires de Services generally fall into the following categories:

1) Municipal Aire – Run by the town/village commune and usually provided as an encouragement to visitors to stop in the area and spend some money on local goods/ services (something it is wise not to forget when making use of these facilities). Although these stops are often free, a charge may sometimes be made - for parking, for using an electrical hook-up, or for refilling the fresh water tank. Emptying of the grey tank or chemical toilet is usually free. The permitted length of stay typically varies from 1 to 3 days, although this is seldom policed. Payment (if required) is often at the Mairie (town hall) or the Office de Tourisme (OT), or at a nearby ticket machine – it is useful to keep a supply of euro coins for this purpose.
2) Private Aire - Privately owned, these may be provided by a local business, such as a supermarket or garage, and are often just a service point (although parking for a night may be allowed on the car park). Others are sometimes run by an individual, often along the lines of a small campsite, with a charge made for the parking and/ or the services.

3) Aire de Services on a Campsite - Run by campsites but often located outside, these allow you to stay overnight but obviously for less than the cost of a night's stay on a site pitch. You would be able to able to use the various emptying/filling facilities, and possibly the campsite showers/ toilets. Many campsites run a scheme called Stop-Accueil Camping Car, allowing you to stay inside the site on a pitch for a reduced price, so long as you arrive after 18.00pm and leave before 10.00am.
4) Autoroute Aire - These often have the same facilities as private aires but are located in the motorway service areas. Whilst these may be useful for either refilling or emptying, and for a short break, they are not to be recommended for an overnight stay due to the various security problems (not to mention the noise) that have often occurred at these aires in the past – especially those in the South of France.
5) Aires on Farms/vineyards – These are similar to CL's in the UK, but availability of services can vary from just a place to stay to having those similar to that of a good private aire. The France Passion scheme allows motorhomes to stay on French farms and vineyards overnight, for a one-off annual fee of 30 euros, at more than 2,000 stopover places in France. The disadvantages are that there may be no facilities provided, apart from a pitch for overnight parking, and it's not possible to book these pitches in advance (on average these are limited to 2 to 5 places per farm) - you just have to turn up and ask if there is a space. If you intend to use these farm stopovers, it's advisable to make your motorhome self-sufficient due to this possible lack of facilities. Advantages include; the low price, usually a nice rural location, the possibility of purchasing fresh farm produce, and often many of these locations can offer some basic services.
6) Sani Station – These are just a space - often in garages or supermarket car parks - where you can refill/ empty your tanks and possibly recharge your battery, but they do not normally allow you to park overnight.

Aires can vary in what they present to the traveller, from a fairly unpleasant car park stopover to a beautiful location next to the coast, or tranquillity in the heart of a medieval walled town. They can also vary from offering just a couple of parking places to possibly having over 100 or more spaces. Increasingly, towns are finding that Municipal campsites are becoming too expensive to operate & many communes are turning these campsites into unmanned aires with automatic barriers for entry. Many of these 'campsite aires' however have retained some or all of the campsite facilities such as toilets, showers, washing-up sinks & individual ehu's, etc. These aires thus represent excellent value & the 67 listed in this guide are noted in the map indices in **bold** (see also the note on 'campsite aires' in the CampingCarPark section below).

Facilities available

Once again these vary but are usually either a couple, or possibly all, of the following:

- **Drinking Water** – a tap with a supply of drinking water (eau potable or eau propre) for refilling your fresh water tank – there may be a charge involved.
- **Waste Water** – either a drive over gully/ drainage platform, or just a grid where you can empty the waste water (eau vidange or usee) out of your motorhome's grey tank; this is usually a free service. The process may involve using a hose if there is no gully or if you cannot get close enough.
- **Chemical Toilet** – A compartment or covered grid with a flushing arrangement in which to empty the contents of your cassette (WC Chimique), again this is usually a free service.

- **Electricity** – An electrical connection (often at a low 3A amperage) for recharging your battery for an hour or so, a service that is usually charged for but is occasionally free. The socket is normally the standard European socket but may occasionally be a French socket.
- **Public Toilets** – Availability and standards vary depending on the location, often these are only available in service areas or town car parks.
- **Rubbish disposal** – Provision of recycling bins or waste bins (poubelles) for your waste, once again it is normally free.
- **Wifi** is becoming increasingly available, especially on campsites and private aires, and many Offices de Tourisme offer this facility as well.

The first four of the above services are often contained within a post arrangement or 'borne' which usually consists of 4 main types:

Euro-Relais or Raclet – This is a factory made service point built into a stainless steel or white triangular/square shaped unit, with separate taps for refilling water and rinsing, an integral drain for black waste and usually a separate grid or drainage platform for grey waste. There may also be electricity hook up sockets for recharging the leisure battery – these types of bornes are often operated by tokens (jetons), coins or credit card.

Flot Bleu – Another purpose built service point, usually blue in colour, with similar facilities as the Euro-Relais but often without a separate grey drain – the integral grey drainage point often requires a hose to use it. These are once again usually controlled by jetons or coins, although an increasing number are operated by credit cards.

AireServices or UrbaFlux – variations of the above, either oval shaped or a post arrangement.

Artisanal: These are custom made service points and can vary greatly in both quality and ease of use; they mainly consist of 1 or 2 fresh water taps, grey and black drainage points of some form and possibly an electric socket. Often the artisanal service point may only have a single tap for drinking and rinsing - care should obviously be taken with these with regard to hygiene. These 'bornes' are often free or are operated by coins or jetons.

Payment

As stated before, if you are lucky, all of the above may in some instances be free but there may be a charge (2 to 4 €) for the electricity and possibly the water, although the drainage facilities are usually free (gratuit). Don't forget your euro coins: if a payment is due for any of the previous services (and also possibly for the overnight stay), they are generally paid for by a ticket (billet) issued at a machine (horodateur) on site, or at the town hall or the tourist information office. Alternatively, it's possible that someone will call round to collect a fee. Frequently, it is required to buy a jeton for the service point, with instructions usually found on a sign nearby as to where you can buy them – usually from the OT (Office de Tourisme), Town Hall (Mairie) or the local shops. In many cases now, payment is only possible by credit card (Carte Bancaire or CB) and the machines generally accept UK cards without any problem. If for some reason your card isn't accepted, the only alternative I have found is to ask a friendly Frenchman if they will pay using their card and reimburse them in cash – they'll often oblige! Once again don't forget how much you would pay in the UK for these facilities (if you could get them) and be sure to spend some euros locally in the shops as a thank you.

Finding aires other than those listed in this guide

If you are lucky, you may come across a blue motorhome sign, which would indicate the exact location of an aire. However the easiest way to find them is either to consult the various aires sites online or buy a guide that lists Aires de Services. The most complete guidebook to Aires in France, the book '*LE GUIDE NATIONAL DES AIRES DE*

SERVICES CAMPING-CARS,' is published annually and lists around 4,000 various aires in France. This is available from www.amazon.fr or in decent bookshops/ supermarkets in France. They are however on a limited print run and often sell out well before the end of the summer, so make sure you get your copy soon after the March issue date. This book is, of course, in French – it is however fairly easy to translate and since most of the listings tend to have similar facilities, it is fairly easy to follow. The guide also comes with a map section showing the location of the aires. The main problem with the guide is that the directions to the aires are pretty minimal & there is no review but given that the aires tend not to be signposted until you are within close proximity (often making them difficult to find) the GPS coordinates given are essential.

Staying at an Aire

There are few differences in the practicalities between staying at a campsite or at an aire. The main difference will probably be regarding the spacing (if it is busy) – vans stopped at an aire will be closer together, whereas on a campsite you still have all of the pitch to yourself. Putting up your awning at an aire is usually frowned upon by other 'camping-caristes' (French motorhomers), as it limits the available spaces, unless the aire is quite empty. If you require electricity you could find that a longer hook-up cable is required, as you may not be able to get as close to the connection as you would like. You may also need a hose for the wastewater tank, due to the arrangement of the emptying facility – it is sometimes built into the servicing post. Hose connectors may also be required for the freshwater connection – as these may vary from aire to aire. The length of your stay at an aire is obviously determined by the regulations on the site; this is commonly a maximum of 3-nights (although this is often not enforced), whereas there is usually no limit at a campsite.

Winter Use

In winter you may often find that the service point at an aire is unavailable, as the water has been turned off as a precaution against freezing, and you may have to visit several aires before you find one with the water connected (failing that you may have to find a campsite that is open).

In conclusion, I think that the biggest noticeable difference between aires and campsites will be the cost!

CampingCarPark Aires

CampingCarPark are a French company that own over 200 private aires in France & access into their aires is controlled by an automatic barrier operated by their membership card. The card is topped up with credit either over the internet or at one of the terminals located at the aire. If you wish to use one of these aires then you will need to purchase one of their cards. Go to: **www.campingcarpark.com** to buy a card (with map), cost is around 5€. The company have also started introducing their 'Mon Village' aires – these are former Municipal campsites that they have taken over & converted into an aire but still retaining most of the original campsite facilities e.g. toilets/ showers, etc. Spaces can be booked online at any of their aires but they charge extra for this facility.

AireParkReservation is another French company owned by the service point manufacturer 'AireServices' who also own or manage over 1,500 aires throughout France & Europe. Many of the aires run by APR are still owned by local towns but are managed & maintained by APR. Their aires offer many of the same facilities as CCP aires & are run along the same lines although a membership card is not required to gain access (usually done by credit card) but it is also possible to reserve a pitch online at many of their aires via their website: **www.aireparkreservation.com**. Details, locations & prices of their aires can also be found on their website.

NORTHERN FRANCE
BRITTANY

Brittany region is made up of four departments;
Cotes-d'Armor (22)
Finistere (29)
Ille-et-Vilaine (35)
Morbihan (56)

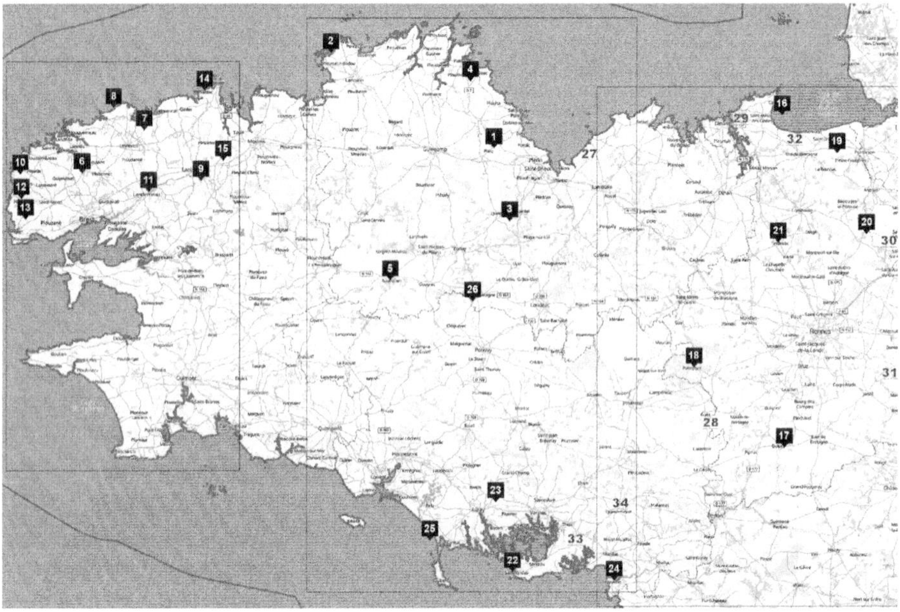

Key to enlarged Brittany Maps (on next 3 pages)

Former campsites that are now aires are noted in ***bold***

1) CHATELAUDREN -2) ILE GRANDE – 3) LANFAINS – ***4) PLEHEDEL***
5) ROSTRENEN – 6) BOURG BLANC – 7) GOULVEN – 8) KERLOUAN
9) LAMPAUL GUIMILIAU – 10) LAMPAUL PLOUARZEL – ***11) LANDERNEAU***
12) PLOUARZEL – 13) PLOUMOGUER – 14) SANTEC – 15) ST THEGONNEC
16) HIREL - 17) MESSAC – 18) PAIMPONT – 19) SAINS
20) ST BRICE EN COGLES – 21) TINTENIAC – 22) ARZON – 23) BADEN
24) PENESTIN – 25) PLOUHARNEL – 26) ST AIGNAN – ***27) PLANGUENOUAL***
28) COMBLESSAC – ***29) ST MALO*** *– 30) FOUGERES –* ***31) LE PERTRE***
32) LE VIVIER – 33) SURZUR – 34) QUESTEMBERT

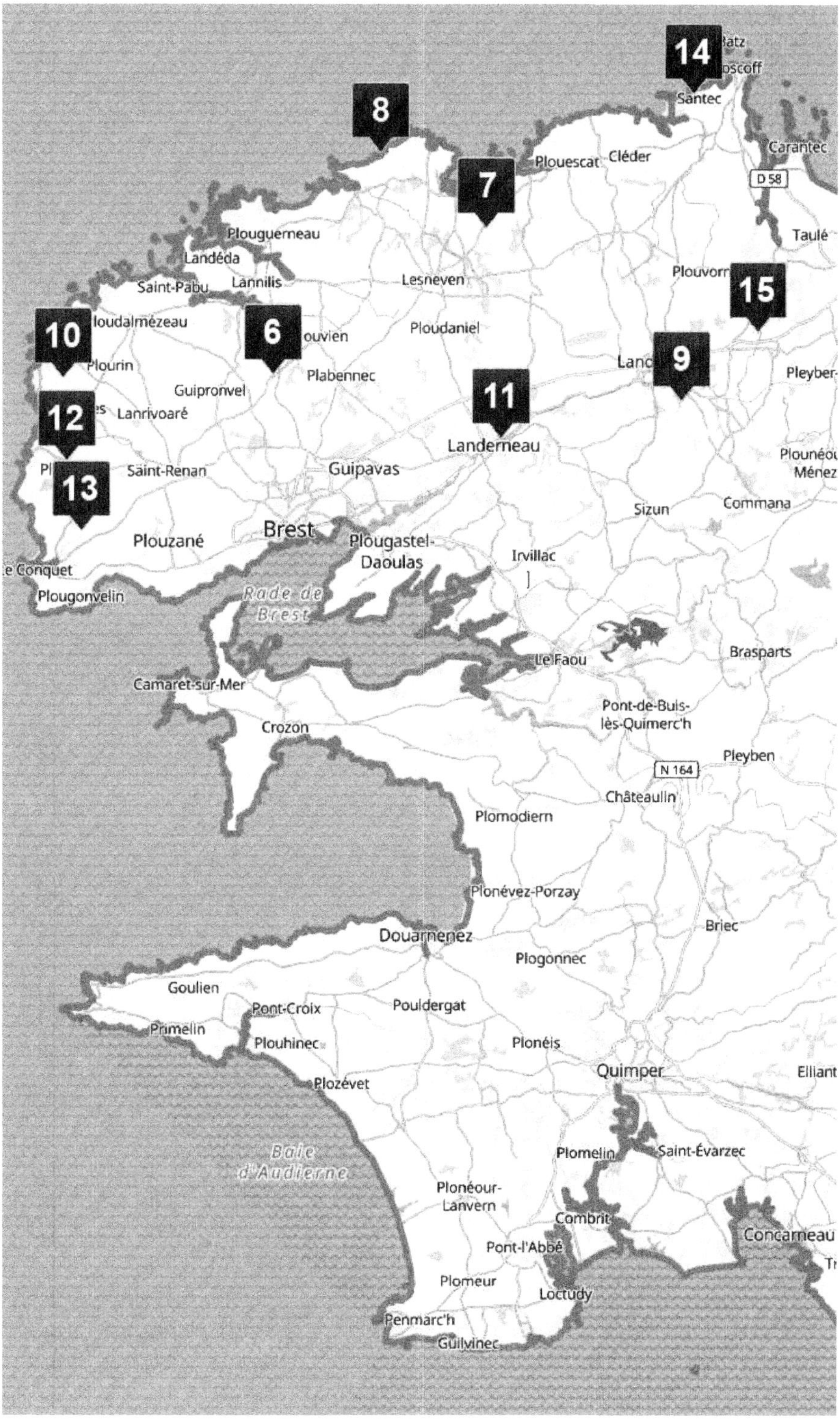
14
Santec
8
7
Plouescat
Cléder
Carantec
D 58
Plouguerneau
Landéda
Lannilis
Saint-Pabu
Lesneven
Taulé
15
10
6
Ploudaniel
Plourin
Plabennec
9
Guipronvel
Lanrivoaré
11
Pleyber-
12
Landerneau
13
Saint-Renan
Guipavas
Sizun
Commana
Plouzané
Brest
Plougastel-
Daoulas
Irvillac
Plougonvelin
Rade de
Brest
Le Faou
Brasparts
Camaret-sur-Mer
Pont-de-Buis-
lès-Quimerc'h
Crozon
Pleyben
N 164
Châteaulin
Plomodiern
Plonévez-Porzay
Briec
Douarnenez
Plogonnec
Goulien
Pont-Croix
Pouldergat
Primelin
Plouhinec
Plonéis
Quimper
Plozévet
Baie
d'Audierne
Plomelin
Saint-Évarzec
Plonéour-
Lanvern
Combrit
Concarneau
Pont-l'Abbé
Plomeur
Loctudy
Penmarc'h
Guilvinec

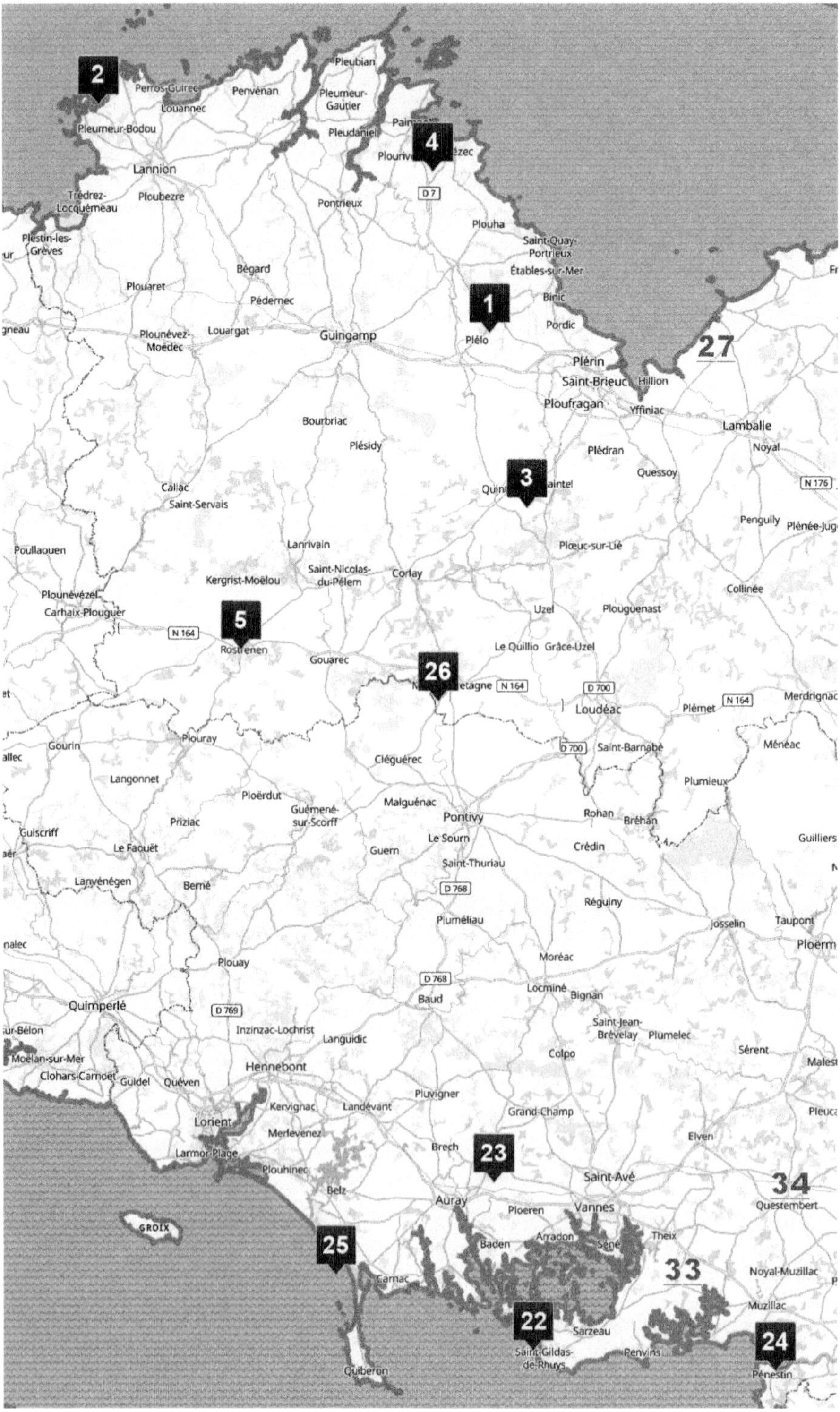
2
Perros-Guirec
Louannec
Penvénan
Pleubian
Pleumeur-Gautier
Pleudaniel
4
Pleumeur-Bodou
Lannion
Trédrez-Locquémeau
Ploubezre
Pontrieux
D 7
Plouha
Saint-Quay-Portrieux
Étables-sur-Mer
Plestin-les-Grèves
Bégard
Plouaret
Pédernec
1
Binic
Pordic
Plounévez-Moëdec
Louargat
Guingamp
Plélo
27
Plérin
Saint-Brieuc
Hillion
Ploufragan
Yffiniac
Lamballe
Bourbriac
Plésidy
Plédran
Noyal
3
Quessoy
N 176
Callac
Saint-Servais
Penguily
Poullaouen
Lanrivain
Plœuc-sur-Lié
Saint-Nicolas-du-Pélem
Corlay
Kergrist-Moëlou
Plounévézel
Collinée
Carhaix-Plouguer
5
Uzel
Plouguenast
N 164
Rostrenen
Le Quillio
Grâce-Uzel
Gouarec
26
N 164
D 700
Loudéac
Plémet
N 164
Gourin
Plouray
D 700
Saint-Barnabé
Ménéac
Cléguérec
Langonnet
Plumieux
Ploërdut
Malguénac
Guémené-sur-Scorff
Pontivy
Rohan
Priziac
Bréhan
Guiscriff
Le Sourn
Guilliers
Le Faouët
Guern
Crédin
Saint-Thuriau
Lanvénégen
Berné
D 768
Réguiny
Pluméliau
Josselin
Taupont
Moréac
Plouay
D 768
Locminé
Bignan
Quimperlé
Baud
D 769
Saint-Jean-Brévelay
Plumelec
Inzinzac-Lochrist
Languidic
Moëlan-sur-Mer
Colpo
Sérent
Hennebont
Clohars-Carnoët
Guidel
Quéven
Pluvigner
Kervignac
Landévant
Grand-Champ
Lorient
Merlevenez
Elven
Brech
23
Larmor-Plage
Plouhinec
Saint-Avé
34
Belz
Auray
Ploeren
Vannes
Questembert
GROIX
Arradon
Séné
Theix
25
Baden
33
Carnac
Noyal-Muzillac
Muzillac
22
Sarzeau
24
Saint-Gildas-de-Rhuys
Penvins
Quiberon
Pénestin

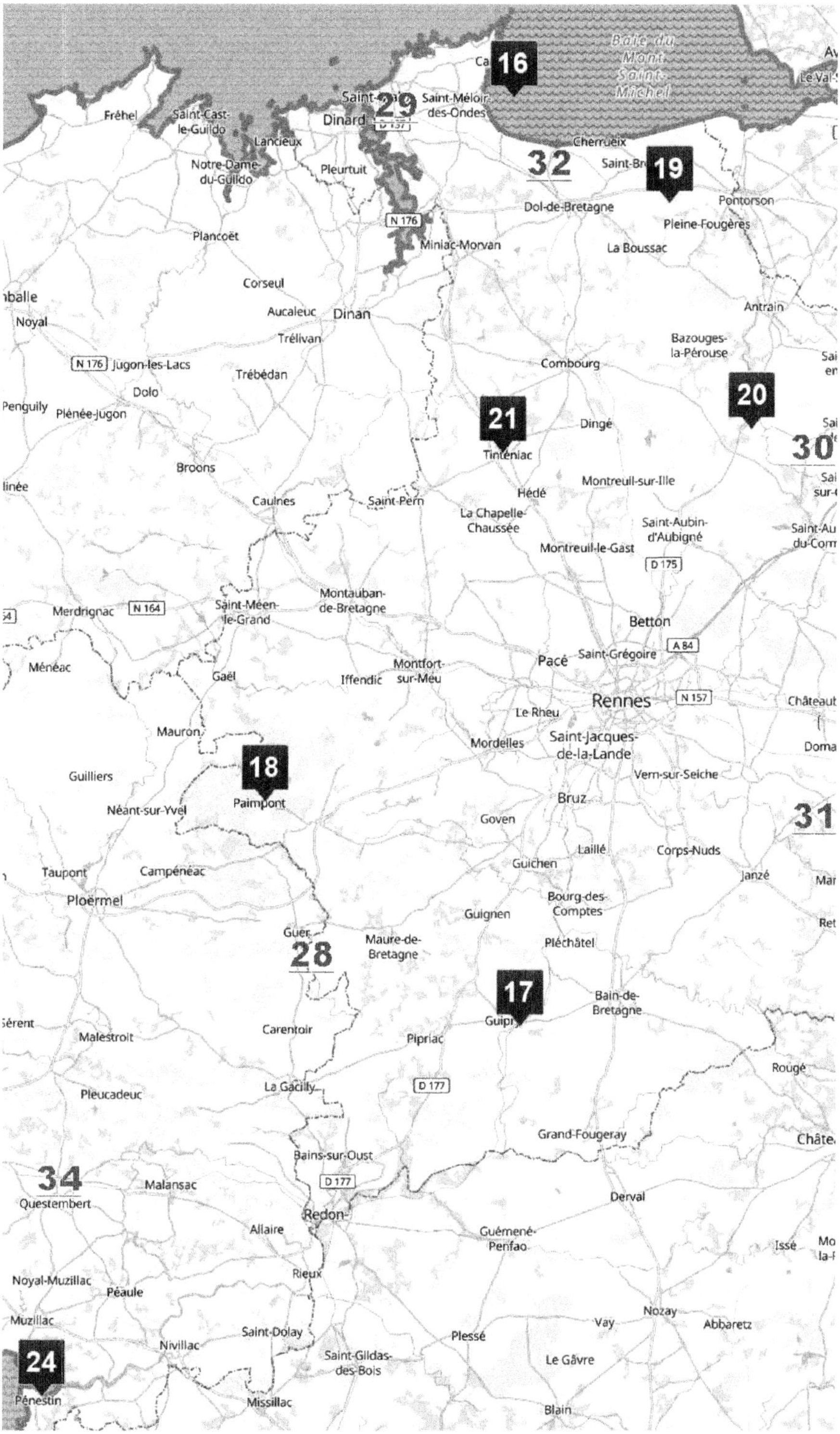

Baie du Mont Saint-Michel
16
29
Saint-Méloir-des-Ondes
Dinard
D 137
Fréhel
Saint-Cast-le-Guildo
Lancieux
Notre-Dame-du-Guildo
Pleurtuit
Cherrueix
32
19
Dol-de-Bretagne
Pontorson
Pleine-Fougères
N 176
Miniac-Morvan
La Boussac
Plancoët
Corseul
Aucaleuc
Dinan
Antrain
Noyal
Trélivan
Bazouges-la-Pérouse
N 176
Jugon-les-Lacs
Trébédan
Combourg
Dolo
20
Penguily
Plénée-Jugon
21
Dingé
Tinténiac
30
Broons
Hédé
Montreuil-sur-Ille
Caulnes
Saint-Pern
La Chapelle-Chaussée
Saint-Aubin-d'Aubigné
Montreuil-le-Gast
D 175
Montauban-de-Bretagne
Merdrignac
N 164
Saint-Méen-le-Grand
Betton
A 84
Ménéac
Gaël
Pacé
Saint-Grégoire
Iffendic
Montfort-sur-Meu
Rennes
N 157
Le Rheu
Mauron
Mordelles
Saint-Jacques-de-la-Lande
18
Guilliers
Vern-sur-Seiche
Néant-sur-Yvel
Paimpont
Bruz
Goven
31
Laillé
Corps-Nuds
Taupont
Campénéac
Guichen
Janzé
Ploërmel
Bourg-des-Comptes
Guignen
Guer
Maure-de-Bretagne
28
Pléchâtel
17
Bain-de-Bretagne
Malestroit
Carentoir
Pipriac
Rougé
La Gacilly
D 177
Pleucadeuc
Grand-Fougeray
Bains-sur-Oust
34
Malansac
D 177
Questembert
Redon
Derval
Allaire
Guémené-Penfao
Issé
Noyal-Muzillac
Péaule
Rieux
Muzillac
Nozay
Saint-Dolay
Vay
Abbaretz
Nivillac
Plessé
Saint-Gildas-des-Bois
24
Le Gâvre
Pénestin
Missillac
Blain

22 COTES D'ARMOR

CHATELAUDREN

ADDRESS: RUE DE LA GARE, D7 **TYPE OF AIRE:** MUNICIPAL
FACILITIES: WATER /GREY & BLACK DRAIN/ ELECTRIC/ TOILETS/ WIFI
LOCATION: URBAN/ LAKE **NO. OF SPACES:** 17
PRICES: PARKING: 8-11€/ 24 Hrs **SERVICES**: INCL
OPENING TIMES: ALL YEAR **GPS :** N48.53888 W02.97045
DIRECTIONS: From town take D7 SOUTH, CAMPING/AIRE is on LEFT after 300m.
SITE DESCRIPTION *The aire is located on the south side of this small town, outside the campsite, where there are up to 17 spaces with ehu's/ wifi in a small park like area, spaces on either a gravel parking area or on grass but having little shade. UrbaFlux service point with drainage platform.*
REVIEW: *A very nice lakeside aire with level spaces. Very quiet with a short 300m level walk into town - reasonable range of shops/ eating-places & a supermarket. Higher rate payable from 01/ 05 – 30/09 when the adjacent campsite (with toilets/ showers) is open. An interesting 'Small Town of Character' that's well worth a visit.*

Chatelaudren

LANFAINS

ADDRESS: ETANG DU PAS, D7 **TYPE OF AIRE:** MUNICIPAL
FACILITIES: WATER /GREY & BLACK DRAIN/ TOILETS
LOCATION: RURAL/ LAKE **NO. OF SPACES:** 6
PRICES: PARKING: FREE **SERVICES**: FREE
OPENING TIMES: ALL YEAR **GPS:** N48.36375 W02.87901
DIRECTIONS: From QUINTIN take D7 SOUTH 5kms to LAKE & AIRE is adjacent.
SITE DESCRIPTION *The aire is located a few kms east of this small village in a small tarmac car park where there are half a dozen level spaces, surrounded by grass areas & next to a lake. There is shade in places, parking on tarmac or grass but no lighting. Artisanal service point with drainage grid & black drain in the small toilet block.*
REVIEW: *A remote, rural, lakeside location but close to some houses so fairly secure. Very quiet spot with picnic tables, boules & play area adjacent.*

Lanfains

ILE GRANDE

ADDRESS: OUTSIDE CAMPING, RUE DE TOUL AR STANG **TYPE :** PRIVATE
FACILITIES: WATER /GREY & BLACK DRAIN/ ELECTRIC
LOCATION: RURAL/ SEASIDE **NO. OF SPACES:** 10
PRICES: PARKING: 7€/ 24Hrs **SERVICES**: 3€ WATER or ELEC.
OPENING TIMES: ALL YEAR **GPS:** N48.79889 W03.58333
DIRECTIONS: From LANNION take D21 NORTH thru PLEUMEUR-BODOU & on to ILE GRANDE. Continue due WEST to AIRE.
SITE DESCRIPTION: *This small private aire is nicely located outside the Municipal campsite of the small village of Dourlin on the western side of the Ile Grande. The parking is in a small grass parking area, 100m from the beach, enclosed by a low wall but no shade & quite exposed in winter. A separate Euro-Relais service point with drainage grid is opposite. Tel: 02 96 91 98 38*
REVIEW: *An excellent little aire in a superb beach side location, very quiet, lots of birds & wildlife, level parking on grass & with nice coastal walks around the island. A few shops are within 400m & a small café (seasonal) is opposite. If the aire is full, the adjacent municipal campsite is open 05/04 – 30/09 & has 200 pitches.*

PLANGUENOUAL

ADDRESS: RUE BASSIERES, D59 **TYPE OF AIRE:** PRIVATE
FACILITIES: WATER /GREY & BLACK DRAIN/ ELECTRIC
LOCATION: RURAL **NO. OF SPACES:** 30
PRICES: PARKING: 10€/ 24 Hrs **SERVICES**: INCL
OPENING TIMES: APRIL – NOV **GPS :** N48.54823 W02.59711
DIRECTIONS: From PLANGUENOUAL take D59 NORTH bear RIGHT to AIRE at ST MARC.
SITE DESCRIPTION *This private aire managed by AireParkReservation is located in the former Municipal campsite of the fishing village of La Cotentin where there are 30 level spaces on grass with ehu's, separated by high hedges & accessed by a tarmac track. Aire is on south side of this small coastal village close to walks & 400m from the coast. Lighting at night with shade in places. Access is via an automatic barrier (credit card) with an AireServices service point & platform drain.*
REVIEW: *A very pleasant conversion of a campsite into an aire, well maintained, quiet with good walks & nice surroundings. Possible to reserve a space online.*

Planguenoual

PLEHEDEL

ADDRESS:L'HERMITAGE,OFF D21 **TYPE OF AIRE:** MUNICIPAL
FACILITIES: WATER /GREY & BLACK DRAIN/ ELECTRIC / TOILETS
LOCATION: SEMI-RURAL/ LAKE **NO. OF SPACES:** 15
PRICES: **PARKING**: 10€/ 24 Hrs **SERVICES**: INCL
OPENING TIMES: 01/04 – 31/10 **GPS:** N48.69250 W03.00635
DIRECTIONS: From SOUTH take D21 to PLEHEDEL, as you enter village turn LEFT to AIRE (signposted).
SITE DESCRIPTION *An aire on the site of the former municipal campsite where there are 15 level spaces bordered by grass areas & shaded by trees. The aire is located south of the village, accessed by automatic barriers with a credit card & is only 10 minutes walk from the village centre. Artisanal service point with large drainage platform, ehu's, toilets & showers. 1 space reserved for handicapped parking.*
REVIEW: *A very nice, well laid out aire next to a lake with very large level spaces, each with ehu, on hardstanding. Toilet block with shower & sinks. Short walk into a pretty village where there is a small selection of shops/ bars. Quiet location, secure. Drainage & water included in tariff.*

Plehedel

ROSTRENEN

ADDRESS: RUE P. LE BALPE, D790 **TYPE OF AIRE:** MUNICIPAL
FACILITIES: WATER /GREY & BLACK DRAIN/ ELECTRIC
LOCATION: URBAN **NO. OF SPACES:** 15
PRICES: PARKING: FREE **SERVICES**: 2€ WATER or ELEC.
OPENING TIMES: ALL YEAR **GPS:** N48.23405 W03.32011
DIRECTIONS: AIRE is in town on D790, opposite Football Stade.
SITE DESCRIPTION *This Municipal aire is located on the south western edge of town, where there is a purpose built area with spaces separated by low kerbs, backing onto woodland & bordered by grass verges with picnic tables, some shade under trees, street lighting. Raclet service point with drainage platform.*
REVIEW: *Well located & maintained aire with 15 individual spaces, picnic tables. Short walk to picturesque town centre where there is a good range of shops /services in town as well as a Leclerc supermarket/ service station nearby. A drive-thru service point that is easy to access & use. Some traffic noise from adjacent road during day but quiet at night. Jetons from OT, Mairie or tabac.*

Rostrenen

29 FINISTERE

BOURG BLANC

ADDRESS: RUE DE BREST **TYPE OF AIRE:** MUNICIPAL
FACILITIES: WATER /GREY & BLACK DRAIN/ TOILETS
LOCATION: SEMI-RURAL/ LAKE **NO. OF SPACES:** 20
PRICES: PARKING: FREE **SERVICES**: FREE
OPENING TIMES: ALL YEAR **GPS:** N48.49208 W04.50184
DIRECTIONS: From SOUTH take D13 into town & at R/bout take 2nd exit. AIRE is 200m on LEFT.
SITE DESCRIPTION *The aire is located on the southern outskirts of this small town in a large gravel parking area, next to a large leisure lake & the Centre Nautique. Mature trees provide shade & the aire is about 500m from the town centre & its shops. Artisanal service point with drainage grid.*
REVIEW: *A very nice aire next to a lake with 20 level spaces on tarmac surrounded by grass & trees. Quiet spot with modern child's play area, walks around lake & picnic tables. Small Carrefour nearby & shops/ eating places in town. Well maintained aire with toilets.*

Bourg Blanc

GOULVEN

ADDRESS: OFF D10 **TYPE OF AIRE:** MUNICIPAL
FACILITIES: WATER /GREY & BLACK DRAIN/ ELECTRIC/ TOILETS
LOCATION: RURAL **NO. OF SPACES:** 15
PRICES: PARKING: 6€/ 24 Hrs **SERVICES**: 2€ WATER
OPENING TIMES: 15/04 – 30/10 **GPS:** N48.63102 W04.30827
DIRECTIONS: From WEST on D10, at GOULVEN, take 1st exit at large R/bout, bear RIGHT & take 2nd LEFT to AIRE.

SITE DESCRIPTION *This Municipal aire is located 500m to the west of the small seaside village in a pleasant location surrounded by farmland yet only a short walk to the village & the beach. There are 15 large spaces on gravel bordered by grass verges with mature trees giving shade. There is a toilet block with a large shower, sink & washing-up sink, as well as an Artisanal service point with drainage grid. The aire has an ehu for each pitch - included in the parking fee.*

REVIEW: *An 'aire naturelle' on this famous coast, 500m from the village where there is a cafe/ tabac/ newsagent/ grocer & a restaurant. Aire is managed & maintained by volunteers, quiet & secure with hot showers, electric & services. Council official calls each evening for the parking fee.*

Goulven

KERLOUAN

ADDRESS: MENEHAM, C4 **TYPE OF AIRE:** PRIVATE
FACILITIES: WATER /GREY & BLACK DRAIN/ ELECTRICITY/WIFI/ LAUNDRY
LOCATION: SEMI-RURAL/BEACH **NO. OF SPACES:** 50
PRICES: PARKING: 9€/ 24 Hrs **SERVICES**: 2€ WATER, 3.5€ ELEC.
OPENING TIMES: ALL YEAR **GPS:** N48.66831 W04.36738
DIRECTIONS: From KERLOUAN take C32 to MENEHAM, AIRE is on C4 on LEFT.
SITE DESCRIPTION: *This private aire is located 2kms north of the village of Kerlouan. The aire is open 7 days a week and is situated next to Camping 'Plage de Meneham'. It offers 50 flat, hard-standing pitches bordered by hedges, a service point, ehu's, wifi, showers, laundrette and video surveillance. AireServices service point with drainage platform.*
REVIEW: *Well equipped aire on the "Coast of Legends" near the historic village of Menehan and its inn, in a peaceful, secure location with CCTV. Bar/ restaurant within 300m. From the pitches you can walk 200m directly to a beautiful sandy beach surrounded by granite rocks and the GR34 marked coastal path. Shops, restaurants and a market are located in Kerlouan with watersports at the Centre Nautique.*

Kerlouan

LAMPAUL GUIMILIAU

ADDRESS: ROUTE ST JACQUES **TYPE OF AIRE:** MUNICIPAL
FACILITIES: WATER /GREY & BLACK DRAIN
LOCATION: SEMI-RURAL **NO. OF SPACES:** 20
PRICES: PARKING: FREE **SERVICES**: FREE
OPENING TIMES: ALL YEAR **GPS:** N48.49411 W04.03865
DIRECTIONS: From EAST take D111 into village & take 1st RIGHT, AIRE is on LEFT.
SITE DESCRIPTION *A Municipal aire located on the north side of town in a large flat gravel parking area, bordered by grass areas & surrounded by mature trees. The aire is*

about 300m from the town centre, bordered by woodland /farmland. Artisanal service point with drainage platform.
REVIEW: *A nice, quiet aire in a large shaded, grassy parking area with picnic tables & lit at night. Clean & well designed services. Short walk into town where there are a small selection of shops & eating places.*

LAMPAUL PLOUARZEL

ADDRESS: RUE DE BEG AR VIR, OFF D5 **TYPE OF AIRE:** MUNICIPAL
FACILITIES: WATER /GREY & BLACK DRAIN / TOILETS / ELECTRIC
LOCATION: RURAL/ SEASIDE **NO. OF SPACES:** 50
PRICES: PARKING: 7€/ 24 Hrs **SERVICES**: 2€ WATER or ELEC.
OPENING TIMES: ALL YEAR **GPS:** N48.44692 W04.77742
DIRECTIONS: In LAMPAUL take D5 WEST, turn RIGHT into RUE DE BEG AR VIR & AIRE.
SITE DESCRIPTION: *The aire is in a large area of open grassland next to the coast with pitches on grass (not marked) & accessed by a gravel track. Parking is very open, with no trees or shrubs, giving good views of the sea & plenty of open space. The aire has picnic tables, bbq & direct access to the beaches. AireServices borne with drainage channel & WC block.*
REVIEW: *A very pleasing, quiet location next to good beaches with a lovely view - nice out of season although can be exposed to the elements. Restaurant opposite & plenty of good walking routes & about 1km from the town. Aire pictured below.*

LANDERNEAU

ADDRESS: RUE DU CALVAIRE **TYPE OF AIRE:** MUNICIPAL
FACILITIES: WATER /GREY & BLACK DRAIN / ELECTRIC
LOCATION: SEMI-RURAL/ RIVERSIDE **NO. OF SPACES:** 25
PRICES: PARKING: 7€/ 24 Hrs **SERVICES**: 3€ WATER or ELECTRIC
OPENING TIMES: ALL YEAR **GPS:** N48.44728 W04.25793
DIRECTIONS: From SOUTH on D29 to LANDERNEAU, continue straight over R/bout then next LEFT into RUE du CALVAIRE & AIRE on LEFT.
SITE DESCRIPTION: *Situated in a large parking area in the former Municipal campsite & on the south bank of the river with tall poplars providing some shade. Pitches are large (60 - 90m2), on gravel or grass, separated by hedges, accessed by*

automatic barrier. The aire is about ½ km from the town centre, across the river. AireServices borne with drainage channel.
REVIEW: *A former Municipal campsite transformed into an aire for camping-cars. Very agreeable & quiet with picnic tables, on the banks of the Elorn river with a childrens' play area/ tennis courts nearby & pleasant walks along the river. Grass pitches can become very soft in wet weather. Town with good range of services.*

Landerneau

PLOUARZEL

ADDRESS: ROUTE DU RUSCUMUNOC **TYPE OF AIRE:** MUNICIPAL
FACILITIES: WATER /GREY & BLACK DRAIN/ ELECTRIC/ WIFI/ TOILETS
LOCATION: RURAL/ COASTAL **NO. OF SPACES:** 30
PRICES: PARKING: 6€/ 24 Hrs **SERVICES**: 2€ WATER or 3€ ELECTRIC
OPENING TIMES: ALL YEAR **GPS:** N48.42195 W04.78490
DIRECTIONS: From PLOUARZEL take ROUTE TREZIEN to WEST & AIRE is on RIGHT 150m before sea.
SITE DESCRIPTION: *An aire within 150m of the beach in a very rural location with fine sea views, near the hamlet of Roscumunoc, 5km west of Plouarzel. The large aire is well arranged with parking spaces mainly on grass, although there is a small hard standing area, & surrounded by hedges, there is little shade but a very peaceful spot. AireServices borne with platform drain, WC block with showers & washing up sinks.*
REVIEW: *Super place, excellent beaches, play area & great walks along the coast, hot showers & toilets plus wifi, parking is free from Sept till June. Total quiet apart from the sound of the sea. Creperie within walking distance in Trezien & a few shops/ bars in Plouarzel plus a Super U with fuel at Menez Crenn. GR34 hiking trail adjacent.*

Plouarzel

PLOUMOGUER

ADDRESS: RUE DU STADE, D28 **TYPE OF AIRE:** MUNICIPAL
FACILITIES: WATER /GREY & BLACK DRAIN/ ELECTRIC/ TOILETS
LOCATION: SEMI-RURAL **NO. OF SPACES:** 30
PRICES: PARKING: 4€/ 24 Hrs **SERVICES**: 2€ WATER or ELEC
OPENING TIMES: ALL YEAR **GPS :** N48.40510 W04.72397
DIRECTIONS: In village take D28 NORTH & turn RIGHT after 200m to AIRE.
SITE DESCRIPTION: *Aire is about 200m from the centre of this rural village with individual spaces on tarmac/ grass separated by grass verges & surrounded by hedges – accessed by a tarmac track. The aire has adjacent picnic tables & is quietly situated on the north side of the village next to the sports fields & adjoining farmland. Artisanal service point with drainage grid & toilets, laundry facilities & showers .*
REVIEW: *The aire has good toilet/ laundry facilities (available 01/04- 31/10) & spaces separated by small hedges, grassy & wooded surroundings, clean toilets & showers. Short walk to a boulangerie, pharmacy, newsagent, epicerie & Poste in the village.*

Ploumoguer

SANTEC

ADDRESS: 247 RUE MECHOUROUX **TYPE OF AIRE:** PRIVATE
FACILITIES: WATER /GREY & BLACK DRAIN/ ELEC./ WIFI
LOCATION: URBAN **NO. OF SPACES:** 12
PRICES: PARKING: FREE **SERVICES**: 2€ WATER, 5€ ELECTRIC
OPENING TIMES: ALL YEAR **GPS:** N48.70139 W4.03888
DIRECTIONS: AIRE is signposted off D75 (towards Mechouroux).
***SITE DESCRIPTION**: This private aire is owned by the restaurant 'Bistrot a Crepes' & is in a large field to the west of Santec with parking on grass/ gravel, behind the Bistrot, close to the centre of the village. Quiet location but little shade. An Artisanal service point with a drainage grid & separate electric points (long lead may be required).*
***REVIEW:** A quiet spot, numerous large spaces available & the first night is free for customers. Nice welcome from the owners at the bar/ restaurant (traditional Breton cuisine). Wifi available (code from the bar). Basic borne, clean & easy to use - jetons are 2€. Shops (boulangerie, Proxi epicerie, butcher & several eating places) are nearby & beach is about 100m away, a nice village with 17km of coast adjacent & 14km of beach.*

Santec

ST. THEGONNEC

ADDRESS: AVE PARK AN ILIZ **TYPE OF AIRE:** MUNICIPAL
FACILITIES: WATER /GREY & BLACK DRAIN/ ELECTRIC/ TOILETS
LOCATION: SEMI-RURAL **NO. OF SPACES:** 15
PRICES: PARKING: FREE **SERVICES**: FREE
OPENING TIMES: ALL YEAR **GPS:** N48.52231 W03.94594
DIRECTIONS: From WEST on D712, turn LEFT at MAIRIE to AIRE on LEFT.
***SITE DESCRIPTION**: The aire is in a purpose built large gravel parking area on the northern edge of the village, 250m from the centre & near to open farmland. The large parking spaces are separated by hedges but there is little shade. A Raclet service point with drainage grid.*
***REVIEW:** A well laid out aire, with good sized spaces (slightly sloping) separated by hedges & fairly close to the shops. A quiet location but near the good range of shops in the village, an interesting old church & a market every 4th Wednesday of the month. Aire is clean & services are easy to use with jetons from the shops.*

Saint Thegonnec

35 ILLE-ET-VILAINE

COMBLESSAC

ADDRESS: CHATEAU DE CRAON, D50 **TYPE OF AIRE:** PRIVATE
FACILITIES: WATER /GREY DRAIN/BLACK DRAIN/ ELEC./ TOILETS/ WIFI
LOCATION: RURAL **NO. OF SPACES:** 6
PRICES: **PARKING**: 16€/ 24 Hrs **SERVICES**: INCL
OPENING TIMES: ALL YEAR **GPS :** N48.88889 W01.59098
DIRECTIONS: From GUER, take D50 SOUTH & AIRE is on LEFT (signposted).
SITE DESCRIPTION *A modern private aire located midway between Guer & Comblessac, south west of Rennes in the grounds of a chambre d'hote. The aire is in a small tarmac parking area where there are half a dozen level spaces with some shade from tall trees. Lighting at night. Artisanal service point with drainage grid, ehu's & laundrette.*

REVIEW: *A very rural aire, well maintained & very quiet but not near to any facilities. Good range of services provided; washing machine, dryer, shower, toilets, wifi & electric which is reflected in the price.*

Comblessac

FOUGERES

ADDRESS: OFF BVD J.FAUCHEUX **TYPE OF AIRE:** MUNICIPAL
FACILITIES: WATER /GREY DRAIN/BLACK DRAIN/ TOILETS
LOCATION: URBAN **NO. OF SPACES:** 20
PRICES: PARKING: FREE **SERVICES**: FREE
OPENING TIMES: ALL YEAR **GPS :** N48.35517 W01.21115
DIRECTIONS: Entering town from the WEST on N12 - turn LEFT at R/bout next to CHATEAU, AIRE is on RIGHT.
SITE DESCRIPTION: *A pleasant Municipal aire located just east of the centre of this old & interesting town. The aire is located in a large tarmac/ gravel parking area near to the Chateau of Fougeres & bordered by mature trees giving good shade in places with lighting at night. Artisanal service point with drainage platform & rubbish bins.*
REVIEW: *A nice quiet aire, close to the old quarter but still on edge of town & close to large lake/ park area. All shops & services in town, tourist train & well preserved château to visit. Aire is well frequented but there is additional (unshaded) parking in a car park adjacent. Market on Saturday morning.*

HIREL

ADDRESS: RUE BORD DE MER, D155 **TYPE OF AIRE:** MUNICIPAL
FACILITIES: WATER /GREY & BLACK DRAIN/ ELECTRIC
LOCATION: RURAL/ BEACH **NO. OF SPACES:** 80
PRICES: PARKING: 8€/ 24 Hrs **SERVICES**: 2€ WATER or ELECTRIC
OPENING TIMES: ALL YEAR **GPS:** N48.60812 W01.82048
DIRECTIONS: From HIREL take D155 WEST, turn LEFT just after WINDMILL to AIRE.
SITE DESCRIPTION: *This large Municipal aire is located about 500m to the west of Hirel, close to an old restored windmill. The aire is in a large level parking area close to the sea with up to 80 large spaces on grass accessed by a gravel track, trees provide a little shade. 2 x AireServices service points with drainage grids.*
REVIEW: *A well maintained aire with ample room overlooking the sea, a short walk to the beach. Very quiet but a bit remote – nearest shops are at Hirel. Boulanger calls in mornings & council employee calls am & pm for parking fee. Restaurant nearby. Parking is free during day.*

Hirel

LE PERTRE

ADDRESS: RUE DE BANA **TYPE OF AIRE:** PRIVATE
FACILITIES: WATER /GREY & BLACK DRAIN/ ELECTRIC/ WIFI/ TOILETS
LOCATION: URBAN/ LAKE **NO. OF SPACES:** 29
PRICES: PARKING: 10€/ 24HRS **SERVICES**: INCL
OPENING TIMES: ALL YEAR **GPS :** N48.03288 W01.03962
DIRECTIONS: In village follow signs for 'Camping/ Lac'.
SITE DESCRIPTION: *This 'Camping Village' aire, run by CampingCarPark, is situated in the campsite 'Chardonneret', south side of the village & next to a lake. Pitches are on grass (most shaded) separated by high hedges each with 6A ehu & wifi accessed by a tarmac track with toilets (open 15/06-15/09). Artisanal service point with drainage platform. Access by automatic barrier with CCP card.*
REVIEW: *A pleasant location close to a large leisure lake with path around, 400m from the village centre, quiet with good pitches & picnic tables. Shops in village & a château/ gardens to visit.*

Le Pertre

LE VIVIER SUR MER

ADDRESS: RUE DE L'ABRI FLOTS **TYPE OF AIRE:** PRIVATE
FACILITIES: WATER /GREY & BLACK DRAIN/ ELECTRIC/ WIFI/ RUBBISH
LOCATION: SEASIDE/ URBAN **NO. OF SPACES:** 52
PRICES: PARKING: 11-13€/ 24HRS **SERVICES**: INCL
OPENING TIMES: ALL YEAR **GPS :** N48.60292 W01.77253
DIRECTIONS: From WEST take D155 into village & follow signs for 'Le Port', AIRE is on LEFT.
SITE DESCRIPTION *This private aire run by Camping Car Park is located on the northern side of Le Vivier, next to the sea in a large parking area reserved for motorhomes. The aire is in the former Municipal Camping & has 52 large (50m^2) spaces on grass/ hard standings each with 4A ehu & wifi, accessed by a tarmac track, bordered by grass with shade & 100m from the village centre. Access is via an automatic barrier, CCP card required. Euro Relais service point with drainage platform.*
REVIEW: *The aire has good sized pitches, all services & is just 150m from the town's shops /restaurants with a cycle track adjacent running along the coast. Nothing much of interest in the town apart from the beach.*

Le Vivier

MESSAC

ADDRESS: MARINA, RUE DE LA RESISTANCE **TYPE :** MUNICIPAL
FACILITIES: WATER /GREY & BLACK DRAIN/ RUBBISH
LOCATION: SEMI-RURAL/ RIVERSIDE **NO. OF SPACES:** 15
PRICES: PARKING: FREE **SERVICES**: FREE
OPENING TIMES: ALL YEAR **GPS:** N47.82574 W01.81430
DIRECTIONS: From WEST take D772 to MESSAC, cross RIVER, turn 1st LEFT & follow this road 1km to MARINA & AIRE on LEFT.

***SITE DESCRIPTION**: The aire is in a nice position next to a small river basin with moorings for yachts on the Vilaine river, with open grassy areas either side of the parking, although it is also close to the railway line that runs alongside the river. Parking is on grass or tarmac next to the yacht basin, about 500m from the village centre, but there is no shade & no lighting. A modern Artisanal service point with drainage platform.*

***REVIEW:** Very pleasant spot next to river despite being near the adjacent railway line although there were only 3 trains between 11pm & 6am. Nice grassy areas with picnic tables & the borne was practical & clean. Good walks alongside the river & fishing is possible here. Boulangerie, pharmacy & eating places in village. 55 space campsite on opposite bank (open Apr – Oct)*

Messac

PAIMPONT

ADDRESS: RUE L'ENCHANTEUR MERLIN, D71 **TYPE :** MUNICIPAL
FACILITIES: WATER /GREY & BLACK DRAIN / RUBBISH/ TOILETS/ WIFI
LOCATION: SEMI-RURAL/ LAKE **NO. OF SPACES:** 65
PRICES: **PARKING**: 5€/ 24 Hrs **SERVICES**: INCL
OPENING TIMES: ALL YEAR **GPS:** N48.02285 W02.17091
DIRECTIONS: In village take D71 NORTH then 2nd LEFT to AIRE.
***SITE DESCRIPTION**: The aire is in a very large parking area next to the village sports facilities and the parking benefits from shade under trees in places. A nice location close to a large lake with ample spaces on tarmac or grass with picnic tables. AireServices borne with a drainage grid & rubbish bin, free wifi with access by automatic barrier.*
***REVIEW:** This aire is well maintained & laid out resulting in the fact it is always busy. The lakeside village is very pleasant with nice walks in the vicinity, mini-mart & boulangerie. Very quiet & there is a WC available in the Sports Stadium. Set in the forest of Broceliande, near to the Abbey of Notre-Dame & Tomb of Merlin.*

Paimpont

SAINS

ADDRESS: RUE DE PUIT RIMOULT, D89 **TYPE OF AIRE:** MUNICIPAL
FACILITIES: WATER /GREY & BLACK DRAIN / ELECTRIC/ TOILETS
LOCATION: URBAN **NO. OF SPACES:** 8
PRICES: PARKING: 6€/ 24 Hrs **SERVICES**: INCL
OPENING TIMES: ALL YEAR **GPS:** N48.55221 W01.58666
DIRECTIONS: Take D89 NORTH out of village, AIRE is on RIGHT.
***SITE DESCRIPTION**: Aire is on north side of the village with individual spaces on hard standings, surrounded by grass & shaded by small trees, hedges also adding to the privacy of the spot. Picnic tables adjacent. Euro-Relais service point & drainage grid, toilets nearby.*
***REVIEW:** This aire is clean & quiet whilst the small village is very pleasant but has no shops although there is a restaurant & a bread machine. Good walk to a large lake. Council official collects fee.*

ST BRICE EN COGLES

ADDRESS: RUE DE NORMANDIE, D102 **TYPE OF AIRE:** MUNICIPAL
FACILITIES: WATER /GREY & BLACK DRAIN/ TOILETS/ ELECTRIC
LOCATION: URBAN **NO. OF SPACES:** 8
PRICES: PARKING: FREE **SERVICES**: 2€ WATER or ELECTRIC
OPENING TIMES: ALL YEAR **GPS:** N48.41158 W01.36291
DIRECTIONS: From NORTH take D102 to ST BRICE, as you enter village turn LEFT to AIRE (next to GENDARMERIE).
***SITE DESCRIPTION**: This aire is situated in a large tarmac car park on the eastern side of the village, 300m from the centre, next to the cemetery & the Gendarmerie - backing onto open farmland. There are 8 large spaces reserved for motorhomes & separated by shrubs with a modern toilet block adjacent, not much shade but lit at night. Modern Artisanal service point has a large platform drain & 2 ehu's.*
***REVIEW:** A modern & well maintained aire with spaces designed for motorhomes & separated by hedges. Securely located next to the Gendarmerie with clean toilets, some noise from road but quiet at night. Very pleasant little village with several shops & SuperU 2kms away. A handy stopover if you are using the A84 autoroute (Jcn 30).*

St Brice

ST MALO

ADDRESS: D201, ROTHENEUF **TYPE OF AIRE:** MUNICIPAL
FACILITIES: WATER /GREY DRAIN/BLACK DRAIN/ ELECTRIC/ WIFI
LOCATION: URBAN **NO. OF SPACES:** 120
PRICES: PARKING: 9-13€ / 24HRS **SERVICES**: INCL
OPENING TIMES: ALL YEAR **GPS :** N48.68071 W01.96282
DIRECTIONS: Entering town on D201 from EAST, AIRE is on LEFT as you enter ROTHENEUF (signposted 'Les Ilots').
***SITE DESCRIPTION** The aire is in a very large former campsite on the eastern edge of town, shade in places & lighting with large pitches on grass accessed by a tarmac track. The aire is about 2km from the old town, but there is a shuttle bus (No.8) from the aire into town. It has a Euro-Relais borne with large drainage platform, ehu's & wifi.*
***REVIEW:** The aire is quiet & 50m from the large beach 'du Havre'. Shops within walking distance as well as the Rock Sculpture gardens & St Malo is a very nice old town with good shops, cathedral, old fort, museum & ramparts. Pitches can become quite soft/ muddy in wet weather.*

St Malo

TINTENIAC

ADDRESS: QUAI DE LA DONAC **TYPE OF AIRE:** MUNICIPAL
FACILITIES: WATER /GREY & BLACK DRAIN/ RUBBISH
LOCATION: SEMI-RURAL/ CANAL **NO. OF SPACES:** 8
PRICES: PARKING: 4€/ 24Hrs **SERVICES**: INCL
OPENING TIMES: ALL YEAR **GPS:** N48.33171 W01.83198
DIRECTIONS: From EAST take D20 to TINTENIAC, turn RIGHT immediately before CANAL (signposted "Musee") to AIRE 100m on RIGHT.
SITE DESCRIPTION: *This aire is located on the northern edge of this small town on the banks of the canal, next to the Musee de l'Outil where there are 8 level spaces on tarmac, bordered by grass with a little shade. Aire is about 400m from the town centre & its shops. AireServices service point with drainage platform.*
REVIEW: *A pleasant little aire next to the canal & farmland in a quiet location with easy access. Short level walk into town with a good selection of shops/ services as well as a SuperU. Tool museum adjacent (summer only). Nice walks along canal towpath & 25km of cycle paths.*

Tinteniac

56 MORBIHAN

ARZON

ADDRESS: AVE DE KERLUN **TYPE OF AIRE:** MUNICIPAL
FACILITIES: WATER /GREY & BLACK DRAIN / ELECTRIC/ WIFI
LOCATION: URBAN/ SEASIDE **NO. OF SPACES:** 49
PRICES: PARKING: 10€ / 24 Hrs **SERVICES**: INCL
OPENING TIMES: ALL YEAR **GPS:** N47.53915 W02.88054
DIRECTIONS: Take D780 WEST towards ARZON, take last exit @ 1st R/bout & 1st exit @ next R/bout. Follow road to RIGHT & AIRE is on LEFT.
SITE DESCRIPTION: *Aire is in a large, fenced tarmac parking area, on east side of the town, with marked spaces but little shade, illuminated at night & surrounded by hedges. It is close to the beach (300m) & a supermarket (500m). Access is via security barriers, there is a Euro-Relais borne with a large platform drain outside the site.*
REVIEW: *Nicely located close to a good beach with a footpath giving direct access, a quiet spot with wifi, picnic tables & electric but only 15 ehu's for 49 pitches. Pleasant aire but busy in summer. SuperU & shops nearby. Cycle tracks into town & harbour.*

Arzon

BADEN

ADDRESS: RTE PORT BLANC, KERILIO **TYPE OF AIRE:** PRIVATE
FACILITIES: WATER /GREY & BLACK DRAIN/ ELECTRIC/ WIFI/ TOILETS
LOCATION: SEMI-RURAL **NO. OF SPACES:** 49
PRICES: PARKING: 11 -15€ /24Hrs **SERVICES**: 2€ WATER
OPENING TIMES: ALL YEAR **GPS:** N47.60588 W02.87283
DIRECTIONS: From BADEN take D101 & D316A WEST to KERILIO, AIRE is on LEFT.
SITE DESCRIPTION: *The private 'Aire des Iles' is located 3kms to the west of Baden, close to the coast in a semi-rural location. The aire is well-equipped with toilets (inc disabled), showers, laundrette, ehu's & wifi. 49 level spaces on gravel with shade in places under trees. 2 x EuroRelais service points with drainage grid.*
REVIEW: *A modern, well kept aire located in a very pleasant & quiet spot close to the Gulf of Morbihan & near to the ferry to the adjacent islands. Good, clean facilities;*

showers /toilets (open April - Oct) & wifi as well as ehu's on every pitch. Bread machine outside & fast food van in summer but no shops or services nearby. Bike hire available

Baden

PENESTIN

ADDRESS: ALLEE DES COQUELICOTS **TYPE OF AIRE**: PRIVATE
FACILITIES: WATER /GREY & BLACK DRAIN/ RUBBISH/ ELECTRIC/ WIFI
LOCATION: URBAN/ BEACH **NO. OF SPACES:** 20
PRICES: **PARKING**: 11 –14€/ 24 Hrs **SERVICES**: INCL
OPENING TIMES: ALL YEAR **GPS:** N47.47035 W02.48527
DIRECTIONS: From PENESTIN follow signs for 'Mine d'Or', AIRE is signposted.
SITE DESCRIPTION: *A private aire, run by AireParkReservation, located to the south of this small town, where there are 20 level spaces in a medium sized gravel parking area bordered by hedges/ trees & close to the beach. The parking has some shade & lighting at night, access by automatic barrier. AireServices service point with a double drainage platform, ehu's & wifi.*
REVIEW: *A nice modern aire, close to the beach with a direct footpath, play area adjacent & not too far from Penestin centre. Ehu's & wifi included in the parking fee, payable by credit card. 14 nice beaches in the area as well as good walks. Penestin has a few small shops & a cafe. Bike hire depot nearby.*

Penestin

PLOUHARNEL

ADDRESS: AVE DE QUIBERON, D768 **TYPE OF AIRE:** MUNICIPAL
FACILITIES: WATER /GREY & BLACK DRAIN/ ELECTRIC
LOCATION: RURAL/ BEACH **NO. OF SPACES:** 40
PRICES: PARKING: 12€/ 24 Hrs **SERVICES:** 4€ ELECTRIC
OPENING TIMES: ALL YEAR **GPS:** N47.57378 W03.12425
DIRECTIONS: From PLOUHARNEL take D768 SOUTH, turn LEFT after 2kms to 'Les Sables Blancs' (signposted). AIRE is just before Camping.
SITE DESCRIPTION: *The aire here is next to the entrance to the campsite, 'Les Sables Blancs' where there are about 40 level spaces on grass overlooking the sea. There is lighting but little shade & the aire is accessed via an automatic barrier. Artisanal service point, ehu's & drainage grid.*
REVIEW: *A well located aire for the beach with good views but a bit remote & exposed to the wind/ sun. Quiet spot with walks & cycle tracks adjacent, 40 good size pitches but only 20 have hook ups available. Managed by adjacent campsite.*

Plouharnel

QUESTEMBERT

ADDRESS: OFF D1C **TYPE OF AIRE:** MUNICIPAL
FACILITIES: WATER /GREY DRAIN/ BLACK DRAIN / ELECTRIC/ WIFI
LOCATION: SEMI-RURAL **NO. OF SPACES:** 27
PRICES: **PARKING:** 8€/ 24 Hrs **SERVICES:** INCL
OPENING TIMES: ALL YEAR **GPS :** N47.66252 W02.46988
DIRECTIONS: Entering town from WEST on D1C, the AIRE is LEFT as you enter town.
SITE DESCRIPTION: *The aire, managed by AireParkReservation, is sited in a former Municipal campsite on the west side of town, 400m from the shops/ town centre. The parking is on grass opposite a large lake, there is good shade here, lit at night & a quiet location with an AireServices borne, drainage platform & ehu's, access via automatic barrier with CCTV surveillance. Possible to reserve spaces online.*
REVIEW: *This aire is handy as a stopping place if you want to visit the beaches (15kms) & the Gulf de Morbihan, whilst there is also a 50km cycle-path along a former railway line. Interesting historic town with many ancient buildings, a good range of shops/ services & a large market.*

Questembert

ST AIGNAN

ADDRESS: BEHIND CHURCH, D31 **TYPE OF AIRE:** MUNICIPAL
FACILITIES: WATER /GREY & BLACK DRAIN/ TOILETS
LOCATION: URBAN/ RIVER **NO. OF SPACES:** 10
PRICES: PARKING: 6€/ 24 Hrs **SERVICES**: INCL
OPENING TIMES: ALL YEAR **GPS:** N48.18278 W03.01278
DIRECTIONS: In village, AIRE is immediately behind CHURCH.
SITE DESCRIPTION: *An aire located in a large tarmac car park (shared with cars) behind the village church, backing onto farmland & bordered by mature trees offering shade, lit at night. The aire is on the east side of this small rural village, Artisanal service point with drainage grid & small toilet block.*
REVIEW: *A nice, quiet little aire with basic facilities & plenty of level spaces in a car park with good shade, 50m from centre, with a canal/ river adjacent & a large fishing lake 200m to the north. Numerous walks around the lake, along the river Blavet/ canal or through the forest. 3 Restaurants & a grocer (with bread) in village as well as a Museum of Electricity. Parking payable April – Oct. 50 space, 2* Campsite just north of village next to Lac de Guerledan.*

St Aignan

SURZUR

ADDRESS: ALLEE DU PETIT TRAIN **TYPE OF AIRE:** PRIVATE
FACILITIES: WATER /GREY & BLACK DRAIN/ ELECTRIC/ RUBBISH
LOCATION: URBAN **NO. OF SPACES:** 43
PRICES: PARKING: 8-12€ / 24 Hrs **SERVICES**: INCL
OPENING TIMES: ALL YEAR **GPS :** N47.58313 W02.63285
DIRECTIONS: In SURZUR follow signs for AIRE.
SITE DESCRIPTION: *The aire is in a nice location, a former Municipal camping, which is 600m north of the town centre. Parking is in a large wooded area with good shade in places & lit at night, 17 of the pitches are on hard standing & 26 on grass with some larger spaces for long vehicles. Access is via automatic barrier. AireServices borne with platform drain, electric hook-ups, laundrette & rubbish bin.*
REVIEW: *Very enjoyable place, quiet, well laid out & maintained with large spaces separated by hedges each with ehu & access to a free laundrette with tourist info. Close to the Gulf de Morbihan with a supermarket, boulangerie, pharmacy, butcher & Poste in town. Play area & sports ground within 200m. Voted 'Aire of the Year 2019'.*
Reservation possible on Tel/ Text: 06 31 40 19 26.

Surzur aire below

NORMANDY

Normandy region is made up of Upper & Lower Normandy.

Lower Normandy consists of 3 departments;

Calvados (14)
Manche (50)
Orne (61)

Lower Normandy Map

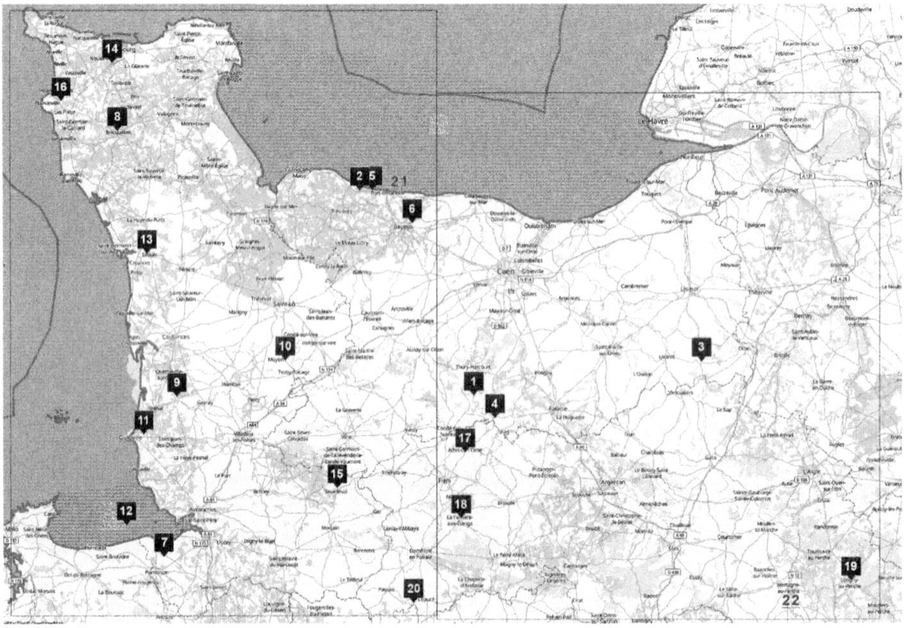

Key to Lower Normandy maps (below)

Former campsites that are now aires are noted in ***bold***

1) CLECY – 2) COLLEVILLE MONTGOMERY – 3) NOTRE DAME DE COURSON
4) PONT D'OUILLY - 5) STE HONORINE-DES-PERTES
6) ST VIGOR LE GRAND – 7) ARDEVON – 8) BRICQUEBEC – 9) CERENCES
10) FERVACHES – 11) GRANVILLE – 12) LE MONT ST MICHEL & LE MONT ST MICHEL/ BEAUVOIR – 13) LESSAY – 14) ~~SIDEVILLE~~
15) SOURDEVAL 16)TREAUVILLE – 17) ATHIS DE L'ORNE
***18) LA FERRIERE AUX ETANGS** 19) LONGNY AU PERCHE*
20) ST FRAIMBAULT - 22) PORT EN BESSIN - 23) MORTAGNE AU PERCHE

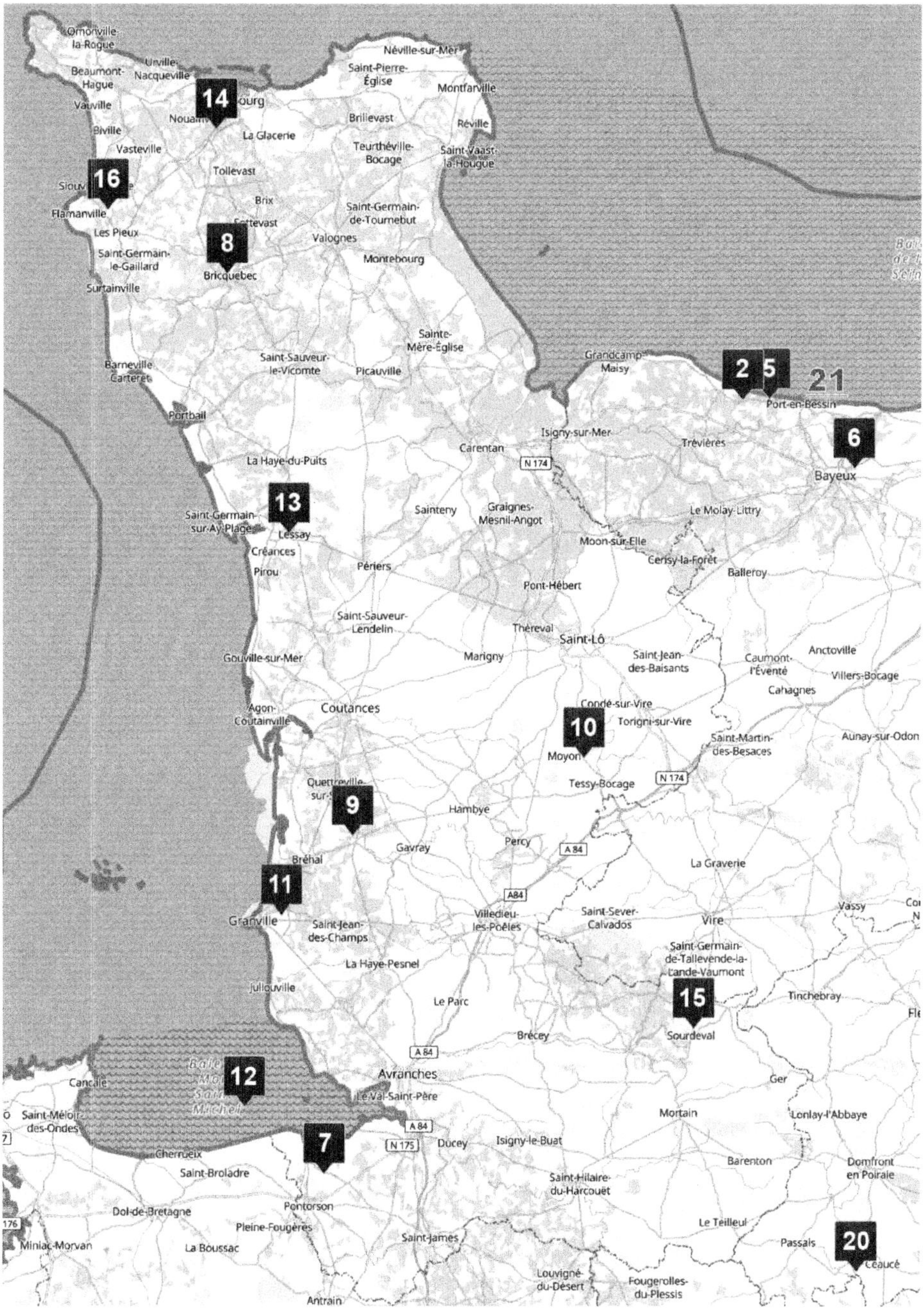
Omonville-la-Rogue
Urville-Nacqueville
Beaumont-Hague
Néville-sur-Mer
Saint-Pierre-Église
Montfarville
14
Vauville
Biville
La Glacerie
Brillevast
Réville
Vasteville
Teurthéville-Bocage
Saint-Vaast-la-Hougue
Tollevast
16
Brix
Flamanville
Saint-Germain-de-Tournebut
Les Pieux
8
Valognes
Saint-Germain-le-Gaillard
Montebourg
Bricquebec
Surtainville
Sainte-Mère-Église
Barneville-Carteret
Saint-Sauveur-le-Vicomte
Picauville
Grandcamp-Maisy
2
5
21
Port-en-Bessin
Portbail
Isigny-sur-Mer
Trévières
6
Carentan
N 174
Bayeux
La Haye-du-Puits
13
Sainteny
Graignes-Mesnil-Angot
Le Molay-Littry
Saint-Germain-sur-Ay-Plage
Lessay
Moon-sur-Elle
Créances
Cerisy-la-Forêt
Pirou
Périers
Balleroy
Pont-Hébert
Saint-Sauveur-Lendelin
Thèreval
Saint-Lô
Gouville-sur-Mer
Marigny
Saint-Jean-des-Baisants
Caumont-l'Éventé
Anctoville
Villers-Bocage
Cahagnes
Coutances
Agon-Coutainville
Condé-sur-Vire
10
Torigni-sur-Vire
Saint-Martin-des-Besaces
Aunay-sur-Odon
Moyon
Tessy-Bocage
N 174
9
Hambye
Gavray
Percy
A 84
Bréhal
La Graverie
11
A84
Villedieu-les-Poêles
Saint-Sever-Calvados
Vassy
Vire
Granville
Saint-Jean-des-Champs
Saint-Germain-de-Tallevende-la-Lande-Vaumont
La Haye-Pesnel
Jullouville
15
Le Parc
Tinchebray
Brécey
Sourdeval
A 84
12
Cancale
Avranches
Ger
Le Val-Saint-Père
Saint-Méloir-des-Ondes
Mortain
Lonlay-l'Abbaye
7
A 84
N 175
Ducey
Isigny-le-Buat
Cherrueix
Barenton
Domfront en Poiraie
Saint-Broladre
Saint-Hilaire-du-Harcouët
Pontorson
Dol-de-Bretagne
Le Teilleul
Pleine-Fougères
Saint-James
Passais
20
Miniac-Morvan
La Boussac
Céaucé
Louvigné-du-Désert
Fougerolles-du-Plessis
Antrain

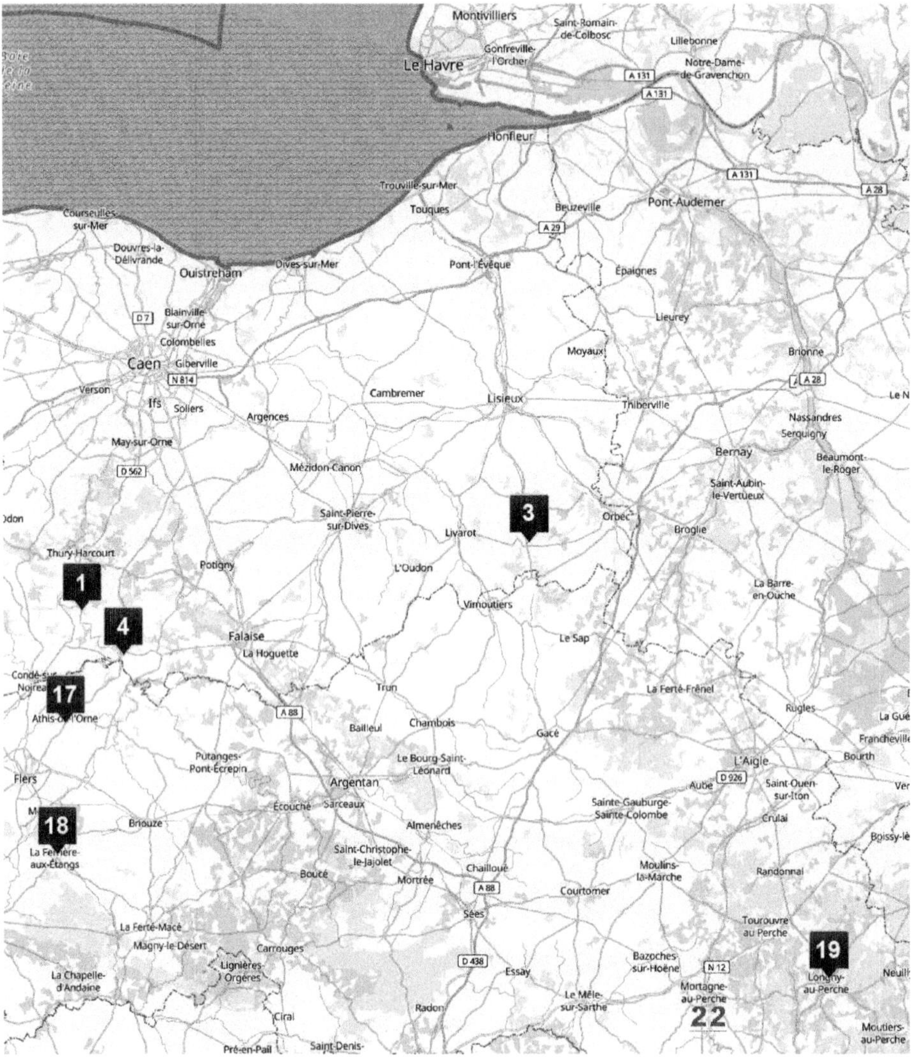

14 CALVADOS

CLECY

ADDRESS: RUE DU STADE **TYPE OF AIRE:** MUNICIPAL
FACILITIES: WATER / BLACK & GREY DRAIN/ RUBBISH
LOCATION: SEMI-URBAN **NO. OF SPACES:** 5
PRICES: PARKING: FREE **SERVICES**: 2€ WATER
OPENING TIMES: ALL YEAR **GPS:** N48.91925 W00.48098
DIRECTIONS: Follow signs for 'STADE' in village & AIRE is next to Tennis Courts.

SITE DESCRIPTION: *This small aire is located on the north side of the village in a residential area, next to the tennis courts, 250 m north of the village centre. The aire has 5 spaces available on tarmac bordered by grass verges, overlooking farmland but with little shade or lighting. Mini Flot Bleu service point & drainage platform. Jetons from Cocci superette.*

REVIEW: *A pleasant, quiet little aire with nice views in a quaint village. Play area adjacent, short walk into village; boulangerie, superette, butcher, café /bar, bank & OT. Canoe hire on river nearby & model railway museum.*

COLLEVILLE-MONTGOMERY

ADDRESS: RUE SAINT-AUBRIN, D35 **TYPE OF AIRE:** MUNICIPAL
FACILITIES: WATER /GREY & BLACK DRAIN
LOCATION: SEMI-RURAL **NO. OF SPACES:** 9
PRICES: PARKING: 6€/ 24 Hrs **SERVICES**: INCL
OPENING TIMES: ALL YEAR **GPS:** N49.27115 W0.29919
DIRECTIONS: Entering village from SOUTH on D35, AIRE is on LEFT (signposted).
SITE DESCRIPTION: *The aire is in an enclosed parking area with pitches on gravel, divided by high hedges giving good privacy. The spaces are a bit narrow however with a little shade but good location next to sports field & open countryside. Raclet borne with platform drain.*
REVIEW: *A nice well laid out aire outside the village sports ground with individual spaces separated by hedges, clean & well maintained. Pleasant village is only a short walk away with a reasonable selection of shops & supermarket, good cycle routes nearby. Council official collects fee. Additional free parking is available next to aire in gravel car park of sports ground, but a bit noisier as this is alongside road.*

NOTRE DAME DE COURSON

ADDRESS: RTE DE LIVAROT, D4 **TYPE OF AIRE:** MUNICIPAL
FACILITIES: WATER /GREY & BLACK DRAIN/ ELECTRIC
LOCATION: RURAL/ RIVER **NO. OF SPACES:** 8
PRICES: PARKING: FREE **SERVICES**: 2€ WATER or ELECTRIC
OPENING TIMES: ALL YEAR **GPS:** N48.99018 E00.25893
DIRECTIONS: Take D4 to village & AIRE is signposted on WEST side of village.
SITE DESCRIPTION *A pleasant rural aire in a gravel parking area 150m west of the small village, with 8 level spaces on gravel separated by grass but no shade or lighting. The aire is surrounded by grass areas and farmland, it is accessed off the main road by means of a tarmac track. Flot Bleu service point with drainage grid & 16A ehu's.*
REVIEW: *A quiet little aire next to the hamlet with 8 separate spaces on hard standing surrounded by grass, next to a small river with a sheltered picnic table, also possible to park on grass. Short walk into the village where there is just a boulangerie, restaurant & a cider producer.*

Notre Dame de Courson

PONT D'OUILLY

ADDRESS: RUE DE LA LIBERATION, D167 **TYPE :** PRIVATE
FACILITIES: WATER /GREY & BLACK DRAIN/ ELECTRIC
LOCATION: RURAL/ RIVERSIDE **NO. OF SPACES:** 50
PRICES: PARKING: 12€/ 24Hrs **SERVICES**: INCL
OPENING TIMES: 01/02 – 30/11 **GPS:** N48.87792 W00.41262
DIRECTIONS: Enter from NORTH on D167, AIRE is on RIGHT.
SITE DESCRIPTION: *A very large aire in a rural location alongside the river where there are 50 spaces on gravel, each space is separated by hedges, has a 4A ehu & is adjacent to large grassy areas with picnic tables & bbq. The aire is on the northern edge of the town accessed off the main road by means of a gravel track, entry by automatic barrier. Flot Bleu service point with drainage grid.*
REVIEW: *Excellent private aire, prices include electric, each of the 50 spaces has a hook up, western spaces overlook river with views over farmland. Short level walk into town & its shops. Fishing in river, walks nearby. Well maintained by the proprietor who visits daily. Also a Municipal campsite south of town. Aire is pictured on next page.*

Pont d'Ouilly

PORT EN BESSIN-HUPPAIN

ADDRESS: RUE DU 11 NOVEMBRE **TYPE OF AIRE:** MUNICIPAL
FACILITIES: WATER /GREY DRAIN/BLACK DRAIN
LOCATION: RURAL/ RIVERSIDE **NO. OF SPACES:** 33
PRICES: PARKING: 10-12€/ 24 HRS **SERVICES**: 2€ WATER
OPENING TIMES: ALL YEAR **GPS :** N49.34568 W0.75829
DIRECTIONS: Entering TOWN from WEST on D514, turn 1st left to AIRE.
SITE DESCRIPTION: *A large modern aire in a semi-rural location alongside farmland where there are 33 large marked spaces on concrete, separated by grass verges with shade in places but no lighting. The aire is on the western edge of the town, 300m from the centre, accessed by an automatic barrier off the main road. Raclet service point with drainage platform.*
REVIEW: *Pleasant, quiet spot overlooking farmland yet only a 400m walk into the fishing port & the harbour. Reasonable selection of shops, eating places and a SuperU supermarket as well as a listed Vauban tower.*

Port en Bessin

STE HONORINE-DES-PERTES

ADDRESS: GARAGE DES DIVETTES, D514 **TYPE:** PRIVATE
FACILITIES: WATER /GREY & BLACK DRAIN/ ELECTRIC
LOCATION: SEMI-RURAL **NO. OF SPACES:** 20
PRICES: PARKING: 10€/ 24Hrs **SERVICES:** INCL

OPENING TIMES: ALL YEAR **GPS:** N49.34833 W00.81682
DIRECTIONS: Take D514 WEST thru village & GARAGE is on LEFT before leaving.
SITE DESCRIPTION: *This private aire is owned by the village petrol station (Elan) & is located behind the garage in a large parking area with spaces on grass accessed by a gravel track, bordered by farmland but offering little shade. The garage is ½ km west of the village centre, on the D514 road but the village has few facilities. The spaces each have an ehu included in tariff. Euro-Relais service point with double drainage platform & toilet.*
REVIEW: *An aire behind a garage doesn't sound very inviting, but this private aire is well worth a stopover – a pleasant spot next to open countryside & quietly situated behind the garage. Garage owner is very friendly & aire is well positioned on the coast road for visiting the various WWII sites & it's possible to walk to the coast from the aire (about 1km). Pitches have electric & lighting plus a good borne with gas & accessories in the garage shop.*

Ste Honorine

ST VIGOR LE GRAND

ADDRESS: RUE DE MAGNY, OFF D153 **TYPE OF AIRE**: PRIVATE
FACILITIES: WATER /GREY & BLACK DRAIN/ ELECTRIC
LOCATION: RURAL **NO. OF SPACES:** 18
PRICES: PARKING: 13€ / 24 Hrs **SERVICES**: INCL
OPENING TIMES: ALL YEAR **GPS:** N49.29918 W0.67459
DIRECTIONS: Take D516 NORTH from BAYEUX, turn RIGHT onto D153 & AIRE is signposted LEFT after 500m.
SITE DESCRIPTION: *A rural aire in a tarmac parking area next to a farm & within 3km of the centre of Bayeux. 6 separate, large, level spaces with ehu's but no shade, bordered by grass area & surrounded by farmland. The aire is accessed off the main road by means of a gravel track. Artisanal service point with drainage platform.*
REVIEW: *A pleasant aire between Bayeux & Arromanches, in the grounds of the dairy farm 'Les Peupliers' with 18 level spaces on hard standing surrounded by grass. Bit remote from any shops but the farm sells meat & milk. Very quiet with boules pitch, picnic tables, good walks & cycle tracks nearby. Tel/ Text: 0643449659*

Picture on next page

St Vigor

50 MANCHE

ARDEVON

ADDRESS: LA BIDONNIERE, RTE DE LA RIVE **TYPE OF AIRE:** PRIVATE
FACILITIES: WATER /GREY & BLACK DRAIN/ ELECTRIC/ SHOWERS/ TOILETS/ WIFI
LOCATION: SEMI-RURAL **NO. OF SPACES:** 50
PRICES: PARKING: 12-13€ / 24Hrs **SERVICES**: INCL, 3€ SHOWER
OPENING TIMES: ALL YEAR **GPS:** N48.60351 W01.47680
DIRECTIONS: From MONT ST MICHEL take D275 EAST for 1km & then D280 SOUTH to ARDEVON & AIRE on RIGHT.
SITE DESCRIPTION: *This modern purpose-built private aire is located about 5km south of Mont St Michel in the small village of Ardevon where there is a large level tarmac parking area bordered by farmland. The parking is on the northern edge of the village & has little shade but there are good facilities including ehu's, wifi, toilets, showers as well as an artisanal service point with platform drain. Access is by an automatic barrier, closed 10pm – 9am.*
REVIEW: *A well equipped & maintained aire with hook ups (4A)/ wifi included in price, plenty of spaces, modern toilet & shower block (unisex) all within sight of Mont St Michel. No shops in village but bread can be ordered the night before & drinks/ local produce for sale on site. Only 30 ehu's for the 50 pitches. 10 mins by bike to the Abbey, 45 mins on foot.* *Ardevon*↓

BRICQUEBEC

ADDRESS: RTE DU CHERBOURG, D900 **TYPE :** MUNICIPAL
FACILITIES: WATER /GREY & BLACK DRAIN/ ELECTRIC
LOCATION: SEMI-RURAL **NO. OF SPACES:** 12
PRICES: PARKING: FREE **SERVICES**: 5€ WATER or ELECTRIC
OPENING TIMES: ALL YEAR **GPS:** N49.47379 W01.64675
DIRECTIONS: From BRICQUEBEC take D900 NORTH, AIRE is on LEFT after LAKE.

SITE DESCRIPTION: *Aire is situated on the northern side of the village, next to a fishing lake & a small park, but also next to the D900. There is ample parking space on gravel hard standings surrounded by trees with lighting at night but little shade. AireServices borne with a large drainage platform.*

REVIEW: *A good aire in a pleasant location, surrounded by farmland, convenient for Cherbourg but suffering from road noise during the day though quiet at night. Plenty of spaces but slightly sloping, large grass areas with picnic benches, rubbish bins & an adjacent fishing lake. The aire is 400m from the village centre where there are shops, eating places & 2 supermarkets as well as a ruined château with museum.*

Briquebec

CERENCES

ADDRESS: RUE DE L'HOTEL, D33 **TYPE OF AIRE:** MUNICIPAL
FACILITIES: WATER /GREY & BLACK DRAIN / TOILETS
LOCATION: SEMI-RURAL **NO. OF SPACES:** 6
PRICES: PARKING: FREE **SERVICES**: 2€ WATER
OPENING TIMES: ALL YEAR **GPS:** N48.91332 W01.43502
DIRECTIONS: From village, take D33 EAST & AIRE is 2nd RIGHT.

SITE DESCRIPTION: *A small modern aire on the eastern edge of this little village, located 200m from the centre of the village in a tarmac car park with 6 spaces separated by hedges, lit at night but little shade. Urbaflux service point with a drainage platform. Jetons from shops.*

REVIEW: *A pleasant small aire close to the village where there are some shops; boulangerie, butcher, supermarket, butcher & bars with a market on Thursdays. Quiet spot with picnic tables (one under shelter) & a play area.*

Picture on next page

FERVACHES

ADDRESS: LA VALLEE **TYPE OF AIRE:** MUNICIPAL
FACILITIES: WATER /GREY & BLACK DRAIN/ WIFI
LOCATION: SEMI-RURAL **NO. OF SPACES:** 8
PRICES: PARKING: FREE **SERVICES**: 3€ WATER
OPENING TIMES: ALL YEAR **GPS:** N48.99551 W01.08255
DIRECTIONS: In village follow signs to AIRE.
SITE DESCRIPTION: *The aire is situated on the eastern side of this small rural village, next to farmland, where there are 8 parking spaces on tarmac separated by hedges & surrounded by trees / grass but little shade. A modern Artisanal borne with a drainage platform.*
REVIEW: *The aire is well laid out & maintained in a pleasant location, large spaces with adjacent grass areas, covered picnic table, bbq and only 200m from the village where there is a bar/ tabac/ epicerie. Wifi code from the bar (closed Wed pm). Walks alongside the nearby Vire river.*

Fervaches

GRANVILLE

ADDRESS: , RUE DU ROC **TYPE OF AIRE:** MUNICIPAL
FACILITIES: WATER /GREY & BLACK DRAIN/ ELEC./ TOILETS
LOCATION: URBAN/ COASTAL **NO. OF SPACES:** 25
PRICES: PARKING: 10€/ 24 Hrs **SERVICES**: 3€ WATER or ELECTRIC
OPENING TIMES: ALL YEAR **GPS:** N48.83521 W01.60939

DIRECTIONS: In town, follow signs for AQUARIUM to the western end of town & AIRE.

SITE DESCRIPTION: *The aire is located next to the harbour at the extreme western side of the town on a promontory in a large tarmac car park that has little shade but is lit at night. Large central AireServices borne with drainage channels either side & multiple ehu's.*

REVIEW: *A popular but expensive aire above the harbour on the Point Roc promontory in a parking area surrounded by a high wall on 3 sides – so no views but quiet. The aire is next to the Aquarium & about 1/2km from the centre of the old town with its ramparts & 3 museums to visit. There are plenty of hook ups available but you need very long cables if you are near either end of the parking. There are a few bars/ eating places within 300m in the old town but for shopping you need to go into the main town where there is a large shopping centre. There is a good coastal path starting from the lighthouse, within a short distance of the aire.*

Granville

LE MONT ST MICHEL 1

ADDRESS: LA CASERNE, OFF D275 **TYPE OF AIRE:** PRIVATE
FACILITIES: WATER /GREY & BLACK DRAIN / TOILETS/ WIFI/ ELECTRIC
LOCATION: URBAN **NO. OF SPACES:** 90
PRICES: PARKING: 16€/ 24 Hrs **SERVICES**: INCL
OPENING TIMES: 05/04 – 28/09 **GPS:** N48.61464 W01.50973
DIRECTIONS: Take D776 into LE MONT ST MICHEL & AIRE/ Camping is on RIGHT opposite the restaurant.

SITE DESCRIPTION: *This private aire is really a small campsite 'Mont St Michel' but is mainly used by motorhomes visiting the Mont, with pitches on tarmac, under trees & separated by hedges. Each pitch is 100m² in size, has a 20A ehu, wifi & there is a service point with 2 platform drains as well as toilets & laundry on site. Reservation preferred on Tel: 02333602210*

REVIEW: *This is the closest aire to the Abbey, in a quiet environment with large pitches, a play area for kids & great views of Le Mont. Clean showers & WC's with shops & eating places within 50m, The Abbey is 2km away, along the causeway so best to bring bikes if you are visiting Le Mont or there are shuttle buses every few minutes in season, bus stop is within 100m.* *Picture on next page*

Le Mont St Michel, La Caserne

LE MONT ST MICHEL 2 – BEAUVOIR

ADDRESS: AIRE BEAUVOIR, D776 **TYPE OF AIRE:** PRIVATE
FACILITIES: WATER /GREY & BLACK DRAIN/ ELECTRIC/ WIFI
LOCATION: SEMI-RURAL **NO. OF SPACES:** 180
PRICES: **PARKING**: 14 -17€ /24Hrs **SERVICES**: INCL
OPENING TIMES: ALL YEAR **GPS :** N48.59443 W01.51242
DIRECTIONS: From SOUTH on D776, AIRE is on LEFT in village.
SITE DESCRIPTION: *A very large purpose-built aire with many level spaces on tarmac of 100 sq m, all with 20A hook ups & wifi, rows are separated by grass strips lit at night but little shade. The aire is about 2kms from the departure point of the shuttle buses for Mont St Michel - 4kms from the Mont. There is a restaurant & boulangerie adjacent as well as a cycle hire depot. AireServices borne with drainage platform.*
REVIEW: *A vast aire but very convenient for visiting Mont St Michel – well equipped with electric & wifi. There is a green lane that runs alongside the Couesnon river from the aire directly to the Mont, a pleasant level walk or cycle ride or free shuttle buses run every few minutes from village centre in season. Shops & restaurants nearby. Low & high season parking rates.*

Le Mont St Michel, Beauvoir

LESSAY

ADDRESS: PLACE ST CLOUD, D72 **TYPE OF AIRE:** MUNICIPAL
FACILITIES: WATER /GREY & BLACK DRAIN/ RUBBISH
LOCATION: SEMI-URBAN **NO. OF SPACES:** 12

PRICES: PARKING: FREE **SERVICES**: FREE
OPENING TIMES: ALL YEAR **GPS:** N49.21868 W01.53634
DIRECTIONS: From LESSAY take D72 WEST & last exit at R/bout.
SITE DESCRIPTION: *The aire is located in a medium size tarmac parking area about 150m west of the town centre, spaces on grass or tarmac bordered by grass areas with little shade but lit by street lights. Artisanal borne with platform drain with toilets near to Abbey.*
REVIEW: *A quiet open aire with probably upto 20 spaces available, very convenient for the good selection of shops, supermarket, laundrette & eating places in this pleasant little town & a 12th C Abbey adjacent.*

Lessay

SOURDEVAL

ADDRESS: RUE JEAN BAPTISTE JANIN, OFF D82 **TYPE:** MUNICIPAL
FACILITIES: WATER /GREY & BLACK DRAIN/ ELECTRIC
LOCATION: URBAN **NO. OF SPACES:** 10
PRICES: PARKING: FREE **SERVICES**: FREE
OPENING TIMES: ALL YEAR **GPS:** N48.72592 W00.92232
DIRECTIONS: In SOURDEVAL take D82 WEST & turn 1st RIGHT.
SITE DESCRIPTION: *The aire is in a small tarmac parking area next to the cemetery, 200m north of the centre of town, 10 individual spaces separated by shrubs & shaded in places by small trees with picnic tables available. Euro Relais service point with a small drainage platform.*
REVIEW: *A modern purpose-built aire on the edge of this small town, with level separate spaces next to a small park with tennis courts. A little shade, quiet but only 2 ehu's for 10 spaces. Cycle track along former railway line adjacent. A few small shops & a pizzeria nearby, market in town on Tuesday.*

Sourdeval→

TREAUVILLE

ADDRESS: LA CHAUSSEE **TYPE OF AIRE:** PRIVATE
FACILITIES: WATER /GREY & BLACK DRAIN/ ELECTRIC
LOCATION: RURAL **NO. OF SPACES:** 10
PRICES: PARKING: 7€/ 24 Hrs **SERVICES**: INCL
OPENING TIMES: ALL YEAR **GPS:** N49.54450 W01.83497
DIRECTIONS: From LES PIEUX take D23 NORTH & AIRE is signposted RIGHT after LA VIEILLE FORGE.
SITE DESCRIPTION: *A private aire on a farm, about 3kms north of Treauville, with spaces on sand/gravel separated by grass strips each with an ehu, next to the farm where some pitches are shaded by trees. A rural location surrounded by fields with good views. An Artisanal service point next to the farm buildings. Tel: 0233526445*
REVIEW: *Very nice stopover place, rural France at its best with a friendly welcome from the farmer. Peaceful at night, but not convenient for any shops/ services.*

61 ORNE

ATHIS DE L'ORNE

ADDRESS: FERME DES BOIS, D20 **TYPE OF AIRE:** PRIVATE
FACILITIES: WATER /GREY & BLACK DRAIN/ ELECTRIC
LOCATION: RURAL **NO. OF SPACES:** 4
PRICES: PARKING: 10€/ 24Hrs **SERVICES**: INCL
OPENING TIMES: ALL YEAR **GPS:** N48.81118 W00.53894
DIRECTIONS: From ATHIS take D20 WEST, turn LEFT after 3kms.
SITE DESCRIPTION: *The aire is situated on a farm in a small parking area next to the farm & about 3km west of the village. The large spaces are on hard standing & back onto open farmland, with grass separating the spaces, but no shade or lighting. Artisanal service point with drainage grid.*
REVIEW: *A very quiet, clean & well maintained place on a dairy farm with bike hire, bbq & picnic tables. Friendly welcome, price includes water/ drainage & 1 hour of electric, dogs welcome, but remote from village. Tel/ Text: 0683170860*

Athis de l'Orne

LA FERRIERE AUX ETANGS

ADDRESS: RUE DE L'ETANG, OFF D18E **TYPE OF AIRE:** MUNICIPAL
FACILITIES: WATER /GREY & BLACK DRAIN / ELECTRIC
LOCATION: SEMI-RURAL/ LAKE **NO. OF SPACES:** 25
PRICES: PARKING: FREE **SERVICES**: 4€ WATER or ELECTRIC
OPENING TIMES: ALL YEAR **GPS:** N48.65949 W0.51725
DIRECTIONS: From village take D18E SOUTH over D21 & then 1st RIGHT.
SITE DESCRIPTION: *Situated on the south side of the village, in the former municipal campsite next to a large lake, this aire is about 400m from the centre. There is shade available in places under trees, lighting, large pitches on grass or gravel. Modern AireServces service point with platform drain.*
REVIEW: *A very quiet position in a nice location, not far from pleasant village centre where there is just a boulangerie, pharmacy, bank & a Cocci superette. The aire is well maintained & next to a fishing lake, with tennis & petanque nearby.*

La Ferriere aux Etangs

LONGNY AU PERCHE

ADDRESS: ROUTE DE MONCEAUX, D111 **TYPE:** PRIVATE
FACILITIES: WATER /GREY & BLACK DRAIN/ ELECTRIC/ WIFI
LOCATION: SEMI-RURAL **NO. OF SPACES:** 25
PRICES: PARKING: 11€/ 24Hrs **SERVICES**: 2€ WATER
OPENING TIMES: ALL YEAR **GPS:** N48.51508 E00.73947
DIRECTIONS: From LONGNY take D111 SOUTH 1km to AIRE.
SITE DESCRIPTION: *This private aire is located about 1km south of a large village, in a medium size tarmac parking area outside the Monaco Park campsite where there are two dozen level spaces for motorhomes. Access is via an automatic barrier & the aire is bordered by small trees & a grass verge. Artisanal service point/ drainage grid outside aire.*
REVIEW: *A large, well equipped aire outside the village camping with large spaces (not much shade), picnic tables, bbq, table tennis & ehu's, but wifi is extra. Quiet but not very close to the village, a footpath takes you to the centre where there is a small range of shops, restaurants & a small InterMarche. Adjacent campsite is open all year with a restaurant.* *Picture on next page*

Longny au Perche

MORTAGNE AU PERCHE

ADDRESS: CHEMIN FOLLE ENTERPRISE **TYPE** : MUNICIPAL
FACILITIES: WATER /GREY & BLACK DRAIN / ELECTRIC
LOCATION: SEMI-RURAL/ LAKE **NO. OF SPACES:** 8
PRICES : PARKING: FREE /24 Hrs **SERVICES**: 2€ WATER or ELECTRIC
OPENING TIMES: ALL YEAR **GPS :** N48.51856 E0.52928
DIRECTIONS: Entering MORTAGNE from west on D612, turn RIGHT @ SuperU & 2nd RIGHT to AIRE.
SITE DESCRIPTION: *A semi-rural lakeside aire to the west of this small town. Parking is in individual spaces separated by grass verges/ hedges, lit at night but no shade. The shops in the town centre are about 500m away. Euro-Relais service point with a platform drain, 2€ coins required.*
REVIEW: *A nice quiet spot overlooking a fishing lake just outside the town, with 8 spaces for motorhomes. The aire is clean & well maintained but a bit remote, seasonal restaurant nearby. There is a good range of shops & eating places in town including SuperU & Aldi supermarkets, free wifi at OT. Museum & Convent with cloisters in town, Abbey at Soligny.*

Mortagne au Perche

ST FRAIMBAULT

ADDRESS: CEMETERY, OFF D24 **TYPE OF AIRE:** MUNICIPAL
FACILITIES: WATER /GREY DRAIN/BLACK DRAIN/ ELECTRICITY/ TOILETS/ WIFI
LOCATION: SEMI-RURAL **NO. OF SPACES:** 12
PRICES: PARKING: 2€/ 24Hrs **SERVICES**: 2€ WATER, 6€ ELECTRIC
OPENING TIMES: ALL YEAR **GPS:** N48.48799 W00.69603
DIRECTIONS: From village, take D24 EAST & turn RIGHT at CEMETERY to AIRE.
SITE DESCRIPTION: *The aire is located 300m east of this small floral village, behind the cemetery & surrounded by woodland, the individual pitches on gravel are separated by hedges & shaded by mature trees. The parking is in a large parking area controlled by an automatic barrier. Artisanal service point/ drainage platform & 4x6A ehu's, wifi available, small toilet block with sinks.*
REVIEW: *A well maintained & quiet aire close to the nice village centre where there are a few shops; boulangerie, superette, news, butcher & restaurant. Jetons from the Mairie needed for water & to operate the barrier if you need to come & go, also ask there for ehu connection. Boules, tennis & a lake with fishing/ pedalos nearby. Village is famous for its floral displays.*

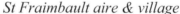

St Fraimbault aire & village

Upper Normandy consists of 2 departments;

Eure (27)
Seine-Maritime (76)

<u>Upper Normandy Map</u>

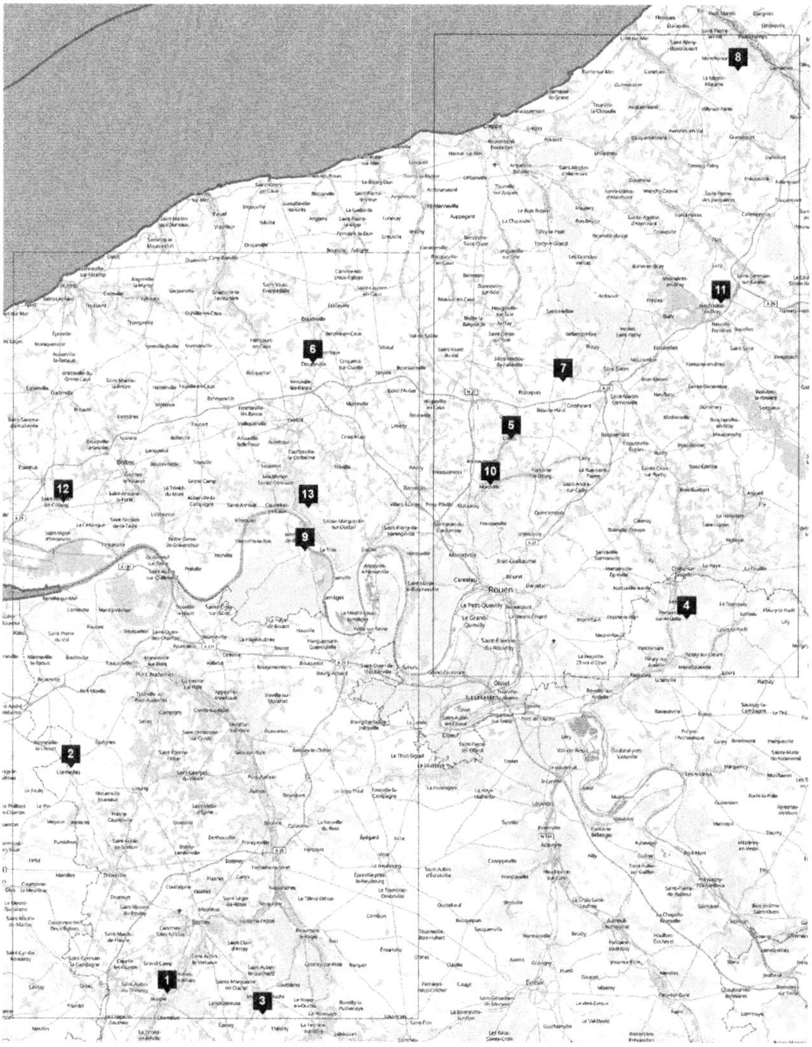

<u>Key to enlarged Upper Normandy Maps (on next 2 pages)</u>

1) BROGLIE – 2) CORMEILLES – 3) GISAY LA COUDRE
4) ~~LES HOGUES~~ – 5) CLERES – 6) ETOUTTEVILLE
7) GRIGNEUSEVILLE – 8) INCHEVILLE – 9) LA MAILLERAYE SUR SEINE
10) MONTVILLE – 11) NEUFCHATEL-EN-BRAY – 12) ST ROMAIN DE COLBOSC
13) ST WANDRILLE RANCON – 14) HERTEAUVILLE

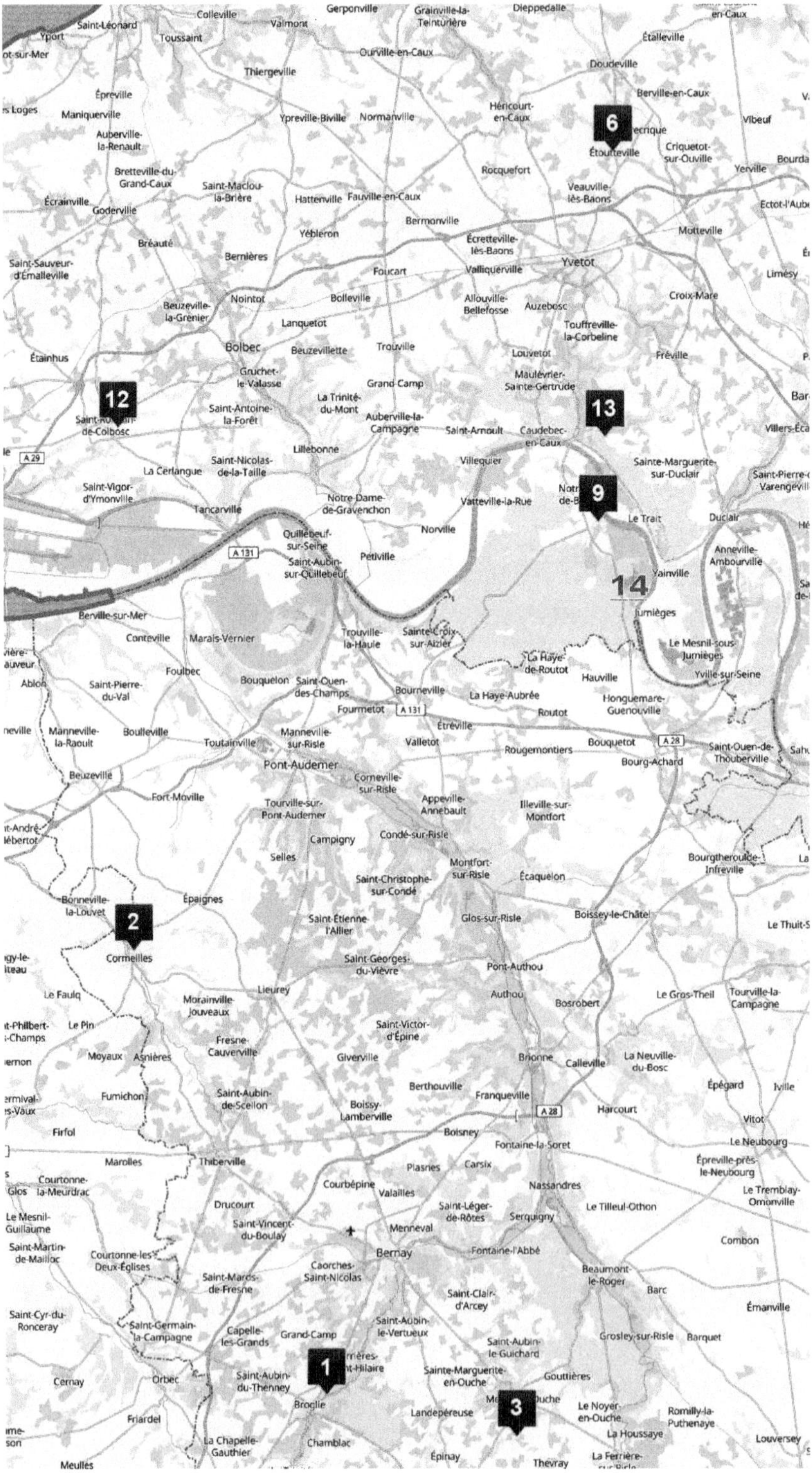

Colleville
Gerponville
Grainville-la-Teinturière
Dieppedalle
Saint-Léonard
Valmont
Toussaint
Ourville-en-Caux
Étalleville
Doudeville
Thiergeville
Berville-en-Caux
Épreville
Maniquerville
Ypreville-Biville
Normanville
Héricourt-en-Caux
6
Vibeuf
Auberville-la-Renault
Étoutteville
Criquetot-sur-Ouville
Yerville
Bretteville-du-Grand-Caux
Saint-Maclou-la-Brière
Rocquefort
Veauville-lès-Baons
Écrainville
Goderville
Hattenville
Fauville-en-Caux
Ectot-l'Auber
Bermonville
Motteville
Yébleron
Écretteville-lès-Baons
Bréauté
Bernières
Yvetot
Saint-Sauveur-d'Émalleville
Foucart
Valliquerville
Limésy
Nointot
Bolleville
Allouville-Bellefosse
Auzebosc
Croix-Mare
Beuzeville-la-Grenier
Lanquetot
Touffreville-la-Corbeline
Bolbec
Beuzevillette
Trouville
Louvetot
Fréville
Étainhus
Gruchet-le-Valasse
Maulévrier-Sainte-Gertrude
12
Grand-Camp
La Trinité-du-Mont
13
Saint-Antoine-la-Forêt
Auberville-la-Campagne
Saint-Arnoult
Caudebec-en-Caux
Villers-Écalles
de-Colbosc
A 29
Lillebonne
Villequier
Sainte-Marguerite-sur-Duclair
La Cerlangue
Saint-Nicolas-de-la-Taille
Saint-Pierre-de-Varengeville
Saint-Vigor-d'Ymonville
9
Vatteville-la-Rue
Tancarville
Notre-Dame-de-Gravenchon
Le Trait
Duclair
Norville
Quillebeuf-sur-Seine
Anneville-Ambourville
A 131
Petiville
Saint-Aubin-sur-Quillebeuf
Yainville
14
Jumièges
Berville-sur-Mer
Conteville
Marais-Vernier
Trouville-la-Haule
Sainte-Croix-sur-Aizier
Le Mesnil-sous-Jumièges
La Haye-de-Routot
Hauville
Foulbec
Yville-sur-Seine
Saint-Pierre-du-Val
Bouquelon
Saint-Ouen-des-Champs
Bourneville
La Haye-Aubrée
Honguemare-Guenouville
Fourmetot
A 131
Routot
Manneville-la-Raoult
Boulleville
Étréville
Toutainville
Manneville-sur-Risle
Valletot
Rougemontiers
Bouquetot
A 28
Saint-Ouen-de-Thouberville
Pont-Audemer
Bourg-Achard
Beuzeville
Corneville-sur-Risle
Fort-Moville
Appeville-Annebault
Illeville-sur-Montfort
Tourville-sur-Pont-Audemer
Campigny
Condé-sur-Risle
Selles
Montfort-sur-Risle
Bourgtheroulde-Infreville
Saint-Christophe-sur-Condé
Écaquelon
Bonneville-la-Louvet
Épaignes
2
Saint-Étienne-l'Allier
Glos-sur-Risle
Boissey-le-Châtel
Cormeilles
Saint-Georges-du-Vièvre
Pont-Authou
Le Faulq
Lieurey
Authou
Bosrobert
Le Gros-Theil
Tourville-la-Campagne
Morainville-Jouveaux
Le Pin
Saint-Victor-d'Épine
Fresne-Cauverville
Moyaux
Asnières
Giverville
Brionne
Calleville
La Neuville-du-Bosc
Fumichon
Saint-Aubin-de-Scellon
Berthouville
Franqueville
Épégard
Boissy-Lamberville
A 28
Harcourt
Firfol
Boisney
Vitot
Fontaine-la-Soret
Le Neubourg
Marolles
Thiberville
Carsix
Plasnes
Épreville-près-le-Neubourg
Courtonne-la-Meurdrac
Courbépine
Valailles
Nassandres
Le Tremblay-Omonville
Drucourt
Saint-Léger-de-Rôtes
Le Tilleul-Othon
Le Mesnil-Guillaume
Saint-Vincent-du-Boulay
Serquigny
Menneval
Combon
Saint-Martin-de-Mailloc
Bernay
Fontaine-l'Abbé
Courtonne-les-Deux-Églises
Caorches-Saint-Nicolas
Beaumont-le-Roger
Saint-Mards-de-Fresne
Barc
Saint-Clair-d'Arcey
Émanville
Saint-Cyr-du-Ronceray
Saint-Germain-la-Campagne
Capelle-les-Grands
Grand-Camp
Saint-Aubin-le-Vertueux
Saint-Aubin-le-Guichard
Grosley-sur-Risle
Barquet
1
Sainte-Marguerite-en-Ouche
Cernay
Orbec
Saint-Aubin-du-Thenney
Gouttières
Broglie
3
Le Noyer-en-Ouche
Romilly-la-Puthenaye
Friardel
Landepéreuse
La Houssaye
La Chapelle-Gauthier
Chamblac
Louversey
Épinay
Meulles
Thevray

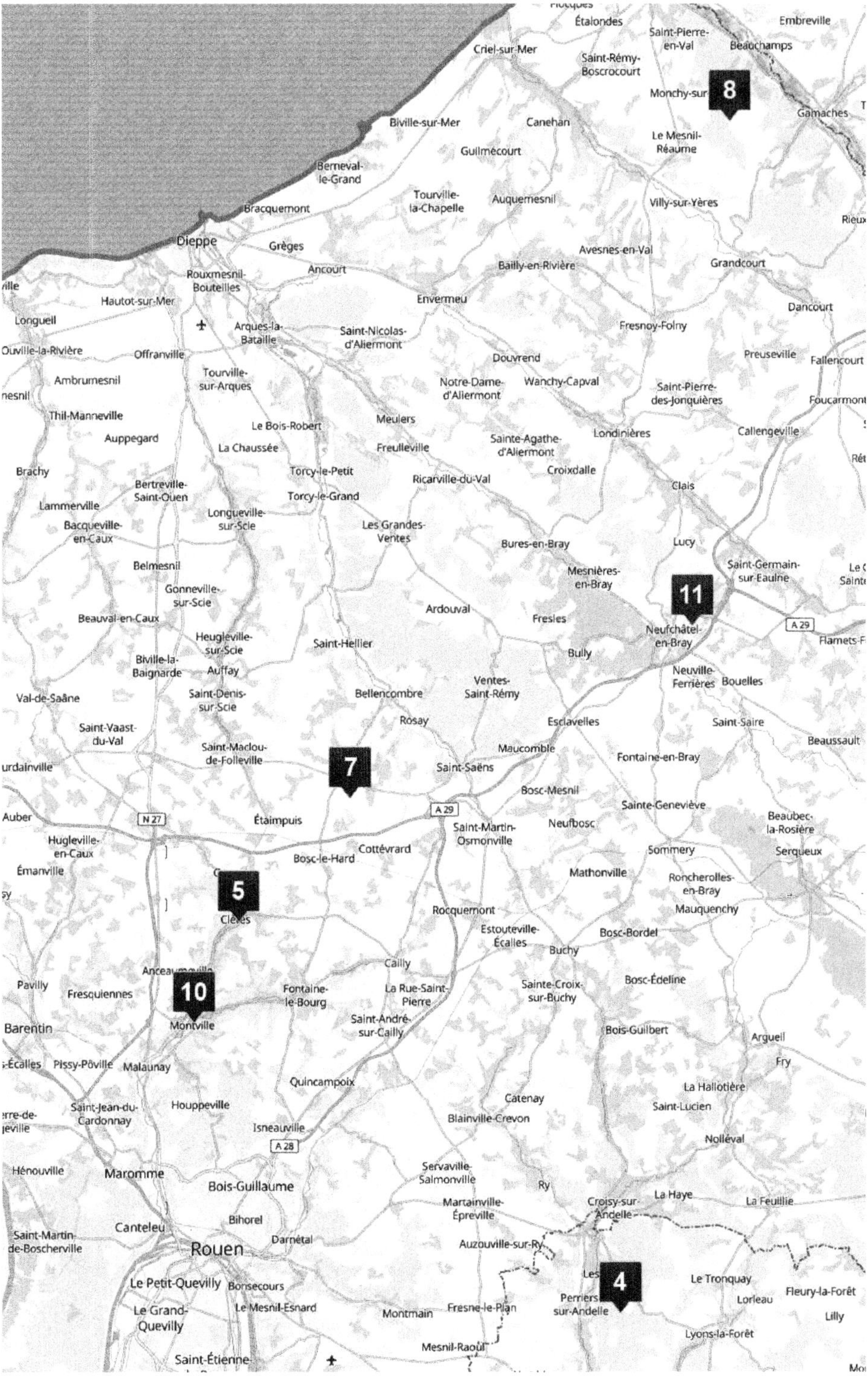
Étalondes
Embreville
Saint-Pierre-en-Val
Beauchamps
Criel-sur-Mer
Saint-Rémy-Boscrocourt
8
Gamaches
Biville-sur-Mer
Canehan
Le Mesnil-Réaume
Guilmécourt
Berneval-le-Grand
Tourville-la-Chapelle
Auquemesnil
Villy-sur-Yères
Bracquemont
Dieppe
Grèges
Avesnes-en-Val
Ancourt
Bailly-en-Rivière
Grandcourt
Rouxmesnil-Bouteilles
Hautot-sur-Mer
Envermeu
Dancourt
Longueil
Arques-la-Bataille
Saint-Nicolas-d'Aliermont
Fresnoy-Folny
Ouville-la-Rivière
Offranville
Douvrend
Preuseville
Fallencourt
Tourville-sur-Arques
Notre-Dame-d'Aliermont
Wanchy-Capval
Saint-Pierre-des-Jonquières
Ambrumesnil
Foucarmont
Thil-Manneville
Meulers
Le Bois-Robert
Sainte-Agathe-d'Aliermont
Londinières
Callengeville
Auppegard
La Chaussée
Freulleville
Brachy
Torcy-le-Petit
Croixdalle
Ricarville-du-Val
Bertreville-Saint-Ouen
Torcy-le-Grand
Clais
Lammerville
Longueville-sur-Scie
Bacqueville-en-Caux
Les Grandes-Ventes
Bures-en-Bray
Lucy
Belmesnil
Saint-Germain-sur-Eaulne
Mesnières-en-Bray
11
Gonneville-sur-Scie
Ardouval
Fresles
Beauval-en-Caux
A 29
Neufchâtel-en-Bray
Heugleville-sur-Scie
Saint-Hellier
Bully
Biville-la-Baignarde
Auffay
Neuville-Ferrières
Bouelles
Ventes-Saint-Rémy
Val-de-Saâne
Saint-Denis-sur-Scie
Bellencombre
Rosay
Esclavelles
Saint-Saire
Saint-Vaast-du-Val
Beaussault
Saint-Maclou-de-Folleville
Maucomble
Fontaine-en-Bray
7
Saint-Saëns
Bosc-Mesnil
Auber
N 27
A 29
Sainte-Geneviève
Étaimpuis
Saint-Martin-Osmonville
Neufbosc
Beaubec-la-Rosière
Hugleville-en-Caux
Cottévrard
Sommery
Serqueux
Bosc-le-Hard
Émanville
Mathonville
Roncherolles-en-Bray
5
Mauquenchy
Rocquemont
Clères
Estouteville-Écalles
Bosc-Bordel
Buchy
Cailly
Pavilly
Sainte-Croix-sur-Buchy
Bosc-Édeline
Fresquiennes
10
Fontaine-le-Bourg
La Rue-Saint-Pierre
Barentin
Montville
Saint-André-sur-Cailly
Bois-Guilbert
Argueil
Pissy-Pôville
Malaunay
Fry
Quincampoix
La Hallotière
Catenay
Saint-Jean-du-Cardonnay
Houppeville
Saint-Lucien
Blainville-Crevon
Isneauville
Nolléval
A 28
Hénouville
Maromme
Servaville-Salmonville
Bois-Guillaume
Ry
La Haye
Croisy-sur-Andelle
La Feuillie
Martainville-Épreville
Bihorel
Canteleu
Saint-Martin-de-Boscherville
Darnétal
Rouen
Auzouville-sur-Ry
4
Le Petit-Quevilly
Bonsecours
Le Tronquay
Fleury-la-Forêt
Lorleau
Perriers-sur-Andelle
Le Grand-Quevilly
Le Mesnil-Esnard
Montmain
Fresne-le-Plan
Lilly
Lyons-la-Forêt
Mesnil-Raoul
Saint-Étienne-

27 EURE

BROGLIE

ADDRESS: RUE DU 11 NOVEMBRE, D49 **TYPE :** MUNICIPAL
FACILITIES: WATER /GREY & BLACK DRAIN/ / ELECTRIC / TOILETS
LOCATION: SEMI-RURAL/ RIVERSIDE **NO. OF SPACES:** 12
PRICES: PARKING: 7€/ 24 Hrs **SERVICES**: 2.5€ WATER or ELECTRIC
OPENING TIMES: ALL YEAR **GPS:** N49.00615 E00.53007
DIRECTIONS: From BROGLIE take D49 EAST over RIVER to AIRE.
SITE DESCRIPTION*: The aire is in a purpose built parking area next to the town's old railway station – pitches are on gravel separated by grass with access via a tarmac track. Pleasantly located next to the river, trees providing shade in places and only 200m to the town centre. A Raclet service point with drainage platform but only 2 ehu's, rubbish bins & toilets. Aire is locked at night, council official looks after aire, pay cash only.*

REVIEW: *An excellent aire, south of the town, well spaced pitches in a pleasing location, quiet, & shops; boulangerie, butcher, epicerie, etc are nearby as well as an Aquatic Park. Plenty of walks in area as well as the old railway line now a 20km cycle track from Broglie, north to Bernay. Jetons from Mairie or from guardian. Barrier is open till 10pm, but closes at 7pm in winter.*

CORMEILLES

ADDRESS: D111 **TYPE OF AIRE:** MUNICIPAL
FACILITIES: WATER /GREY DRAIN/ BLACK DRAIN / ELECTRIC
LOCATION: SEMI-RURAL **NO. OF SPACES:** 12
PRICES: PARKING: FREE **SERVICES**: 2€ WATER or ELECTRIC
OPENING TIMES: ALL YEAR **GPS:** N49.24929 E0.37387
DIRECTIONS: From town take D96 WEST & then RIGHT after 100m to AIRE on RIGHT.

***SITE DESCRIPTION**: A purpose built aire in a semi-rural location, adjacent to a park with walks along the river. The parking is bordered by hedges/ grass but with little shade, lit at night, 12 spaces on tarmac separated by hedges, all within a short walk of the town. Raclet service point with drainage platform.*
***REVIEW:** A pleasant quiet spot on the northern side of the pretty town next to farmland with a picnic area adjacent. Nice town with range of old buildings, half-timbered houses & interesting church. Good range of shops/ services (market on Fri) within 200m of aire plus an OT (sells jetons).*

Cormeilles

GISAY LA COUDRE

ADDRESS: LA VILLETTE, OFF D159 **TYPE OF AIRE:** MUNICIPAL
FACILITIES: WATER /GREY DRAIN/ BLACK DRAIN / ELECTRIC
LOCATION: RURAL/ LAKESIDE **NO. OF SPACES:** 8
PRICES: PARKING: FREE **SERVICES**: 2€ WATER or ELECTRIC
OPENING TIMES: ALL YEAR **GPS :** N48.94889 E00.63329
DIRECTIONS: From GISAY take D159 1km EAST to AIRE on LEFT
***SITE DESCRIPTION**: This aire has nice far-reaching views and is next to a small lake in a medium sized tarmac parking area, surrounded by farmland but not much shade. Raclet service point with drain as well as a rubbish bin.*
***REVIEW:** A lovely, tranquil situation but a bit remote for some, alongside a small lake that can be fished (for a fee). Aire is about 1km from the village, surrounded by grass with picnic tables available. Jetons are from 'the La Tortue' bar/ restaurant in village.*

76 SEINE-MARITIME

CLERES

ADDRESS: RUE E. SPALIKOWSKI, D6 **TYPE OF AIRE:** MUNICIPAL
FACILITIES: WATER /GREY & BLACK DRAIN / ELECTRIC
LOCATION: SEMI-RURAL **NO. OF SPACES:** 18

PRICES: PARKING: FREE **SERVICES**: 5€ ELECTRIC or WATER
OPENING TIMES: ALL YEAR **GPS:** N49.60181 E01.11659
DIRECTIONS: Take D6 WEST to CLERES turn RIGHT at AIRE sign
SITE DESCRIPTION: *The aire is on the eastern edge of town, 500m from the centre, next to the Sports Hall & surrounded by farmland. Parking is in a gravel area with large double spaces separated by high hedges giving a good degree of privacy & some shade. 3 terminals each with 4 ehu's & a Euro-Relais service point with platform drain. Jetons from OT & shops.*
REVIEW: *A good stopover with a super village only a short walk away – good restaurants, shops, Zoological gardens, Automobile museum.& a leisure area. Parking is quiet & free with large shaded pitches, well maintained & easy to find.*

Cleres

ETOUTTEVILLE

ADDRESS: RUE DE LA BRUYERE, D53 **TYPE OF AIRE:** MUNICIPAL
FACILITIES: WATER /GREY & BLACK DRAIN / ELECTRIC
LOCATION: URBAN **NO. OF SPACES:** 6
PRICES: PARKING: FREE **SERVICES**: 2€ WATER or ELECTRIC
OPENING TIMES: ALL YEAR **GPS:** N49.67605 E0.79055
DIRECTIONS: In village take D53 EAST & AIRE is on RIGHT.
SITE DESCRIPTION: *The aire is in a small tarmac parking area, east of the village centre; 6 spaces on concrete separated by shrubs lit at night but no shade. Close to the village centre (200m), next to the sports field & a small lake. Modern Euro-Relais borne with platform drain & ehu's.*
REVIEW: *A quiet spot on the edge of this small rural village, good size spaces with picnic tables & play area, ideal for a stopover. 2 points each with 4 ehu's available for 6 spaces. Marked walks in area. No shops nearby. Handy for Le Havre & Dieppe.*

GRIGNEUSEVILLE

ADDRESS: RUE DE LA PLAINE, OFF D96 **TYPE :** PRIVATE
FACILITIES: WATER /GREY & BLACK DRAIN / ELECTRIC
LOCATION: RURAL **NO. OF SPACES:** 7
PRICES: PARKING: 8€/ 24Hrs **SERVICES**: 3€ ELECTRIC
OPENING TIMES: ALL YEAR **GPS:** N49.64398 E01.19901
DIRECTIONS: From village take D96 SOUTH, turn LEFT @ 2nd crossroads to AIRE.
SITE DESCRIPTION: *The aire is in the large grounds of a Chambre d'Hotes 'Relais Bray-Caux' where there are 7 large (50m²) level spaces on gravel separated by grass/ hedges, shade in places, with a large lawned area, picnic tables, play area, games room & a sheltered picnic area. Artisanal service point with drainage platform, ehu's.*
Tel/Text: 0682607675
REVIEW: *A handy stopover off the A29 (Jcn 10), accessed up a farm track in a pleasant, quiet location, surrounded by fields, although you could hear the autoroute when the wind was in the wrong direction. Well maintained with friendly owner, enclosed pitches, but remote from village - bike hire & meals available.*

Grigneuseville

HERTEAUVILLE

ADDRESS: RUE DU VILLAGE **TYPE OF AIRE:** PRIVATE
FACILITIES: WATER /GREY & BLACK DRAIN/ ELECTRIC
LOCATION: RURAL/ RIVER **NO. OF SPACES:** 20
PRICES: PARKING: 8€/ 24HRS **SERVICES**: 4€ ELECTRIC
OPENING TIMES: 01/ 04 – 30/11 **GPS :** N49.44765 E00.81377
DIRECTIONS: From NORTH take D65 to HERTEAUVILLE & AIRE is on LEFT.
SITE DESCRIPTION *The aire is in the large grounds of a private residence which is located on the banks of the Seine river where there are 20 individual, level spaces on gravel, accessed by a gravel track, separated by grass verges, lit but little shade. The aire is located at the northern end of the village in a secure, fenced & gated terrain. Artisanal service point with drainage platform.*
REVIEW:
A very well maintained & equipped private aire in a large terrain on the side of the Seine, with 6 of the pitches having good views of the river. Quiet with nice owners, large 50m² pitches bordered by grass, picnic tables but only 12 ehu's. Bread available to order. Level walk into village but no shops or facilities. Tel/ Text: 0618912010

Herteauville

INCHEVILLE

ADDRESS: RUE MOZART **TYPE OF AIRE:** MUNICIPAL
FACILITIES: WATER /GREY & BLACK DRAIN/ ELECTRIC
LOCATION: RURAL **NO. OF SPACES:** 12
PRICES: **PARKING**: 10€/ 24Hrs **SERVICES**: INCL
OPENING TIMES: ALL YEAR **GPS:** N50.01389 E01.50438
DIRECTIONS: From INCHEVILLE take D2 EAST & turn 1st RIGHT after RAILWAY to AIRE.
SITE DESCRIPTION: *Aire is in a large tarmac parking area, bordered by grass & trees, where there are 12 large spaces for motorhomes, next to a lake, about 600m east of the village centre & close to the 190 space campsite. Access is by an automatic barrier operated by credit card. AireServices service point with drainage platform & ehu's.*
REVIEW: *A well appointed, quiet aire with good service point, spacious level pitches, lit at night & ehu's available. Walks around the large lake, play area & forest nearby. Small range of shops/ supermarket/ services in village.*

Incheville

LA MAILLERAYE SUR SEINE

ADDRESS: QUAI PAUL GIRARDEAU **TYPE OF AIRE:** MUNICIPAL
FACILITIES: WATER /GREY & BLACK DRAIN / ELECTRIC
LOCATION: SEMI-RURAL/ RIVERSIDE **NO. OF SPACES:** 30
PRICES: PARKING: 6€/ 24 Hrs **SERVICES**: 3€ WATER or ELECTRIC
OPENING TIMES: ALL YEAR **GPS:** N49.48449 E0.77325
DIRECTIONS: In village centre take D913 EAST to river & AIRE.
SITE DESCRIPTION: *On the banks of the Seine with parking on grass or gravel alongside & overlooking the river, 400m east from the village. Parking has little shade*

but is lit by street lights, accessed by a tarmac track & an automatic barrier, with picnic tables nearby. Raclet service point with a large platform drain.
REVIEW: *A popular position on the banks of the river Seine watching the boats pass by, quiet & a short walk from a selection of shops, supermaarket & a bar. Grass verges slope & can become soft in wet weather.*

La Mailleraye

MONTVILLE

ADDRESS: RUE DOCTEUR MATHIEU **TYPE OF AIRE:** MUNICIPAL
FACILITIES: WATER /GREY & BLACK DRAIN / ELECTRIC
LOCATION: URBAN/ LAKESIDE **NO. OF SPACES:** 8
PRICES: PARKING: FREE **SERVICES**: 5€ WATER OR ELECTRIC
OPENING TIMES: ALL YEAR **GPS:** N49.54749 E01.07248
DIRECTIONS: In town centre, AIRE is between CHURCH & LAKE.
SITE DESCRIPTION: *An aire found in the towns Leisure area parking (in a motorhome only section) where parking is on a gravel surface bordered by grass/ hedges & only 200m from the town centre. Euro-Relais service point with a platform drain is in the adjacent car park.*
REVIEW: *A pleasant, quiet location next to a lake/ swimming pool (indoor) with a restaurant (L'Hexagone - open from 15/3 – 31/10) adjacent as well as a play area, boules, tennis, mini-golf & pedaloes on the lake. Fire engine museum in the town & shops, etc.*

Montville

NEUFCHATEL-EN-BRAY

ADDRESS: RUE GRANDE FLANDRE **TYPE OF AIRE:** MUNICIPAL
FACILITIES: WATER /GREY & BLACK DRAIN/ ELECTRIC/ WIFI/ TOILETS
LOCATION: SEMI-RURAL **NO. OF SPACES:** 14

PRICES: PARKG: 12€/ 24 Hrs **SERVICES**: INCL, SHOWERS 2€
OPENING TIMES: ALL YEAR **GPS:** N49.73782 E01.42941
DIRECTIONS: From NORTH take D1 to town, turn 1st RIGHT to AIRE.
SITE DESCRIPTION: *Aire is located on the north side of the town next to Camping Ste-Claire where there are 14 large hard standing spaces (100m^2) separated by hedges & grass. Ehu's, water, drainage & wifi are included in price. Artisanal service point & drainage grid.*
REVIEW: *Very large parking spaces in a quiet, well maintained location but no shade, access is via an automatic barrier. The aire is 1km from the town centre & its large range of shops/ supermarkets & services. Restaurant, showers, laundrette & cycle hire in adjacent campsite, open April – Sept. Handy stopover 3km from A28 (Jcn 9).*

Neufchatel

ST ROMAIN DE COLBOSC

ADDRESS: ROUTE D'OUDALLE **TYPE OF AIRE:** MUNICIPAL
FACILITIES: WATER /GREY & BLACK DRAIN/ ELECTRIC
LOCATION: RURAL **NO. OF SPACES:** 13
PRICES: PARKING: FREE **SERVICES**: FREE
OPENING TIMES: ALL YEAR **GPS:** N49.52078 E00.34699
DIRECTIONS: From ST ROMAIN take D6015 WEST to R/bout, take last exit to AIRE, on RIGHT at next R/bout.
SITE DESCRIPTION: *The aire is located in a rural spot about 1km south west of the town centre, next to a château & its park, surrounded by a grass area with little shade but lit at night. The parking has 13 large level spaces on concrete, an AireServices service point with drainage platform & ehu's.*
REVIEW: *A modern aire located next to a minor road (slight noise, quiet at night) with large individual spaces separated by hedges each with an ehu. A very rural situation surrounded by farmland, Chateau Gromesnil is adjacent with its nice park area. The electricity is free but is limited to 3A & is only available from 01/ 04 – 30/09, water is also free. The aire is within 1km of the town centre shops & eating places, handy for Le Havre.*

Picture on next page

St Romain de Colbosc

ST WANDRILLE RANCON

ADDRESS: RTE DU ETAINTOT **TYPE OF AIRE:** PRIVATE
FACILITIES: WATER /GREY & BLACK DRAIN/ ELECTRIC
LOCATION: RURAL **NO. OF SPACES:** 4
PRICES: PARKING: 8€/ 24Hrs **SERVICES**: 2€ ELECTRIC or SHOWER
OPENING TIMES: ALL YEAR **GPS:** N49.54058 E00.76699
DIRECTIONS: From Village take D33 NORTH & next RIGHT for 2kms & then turn LEFT to FERME DE LA MARE.
SITE DESCRIPTION: *A modern aire located on a farm about 2 kms north of the rural village. The aire has 4 level spaces on gravel separated by grass verges, no shade or lighting. Artisanal service point with drainage grid & 6A ehu's. Tel/Text: 0609853103*
REVIEW: *A very quiet & rural situation on a farm (below), close to a waymarked walk with nice gravel pitches, picnic benches, showers & ehu's - a secure location with views & farm produce for sale. Remote from the village with its Abbey to visit, that lies on the banks of the Seine, where there are a couple of eating places, reasonable range of shops, Lidl supermarket & a creperie close to Abbey.*

St Wandrille

PICARDY

Picardy region is made up of 3 departments;
Aisne (02)
Oise (60)
Somme (80)

Picardy Map

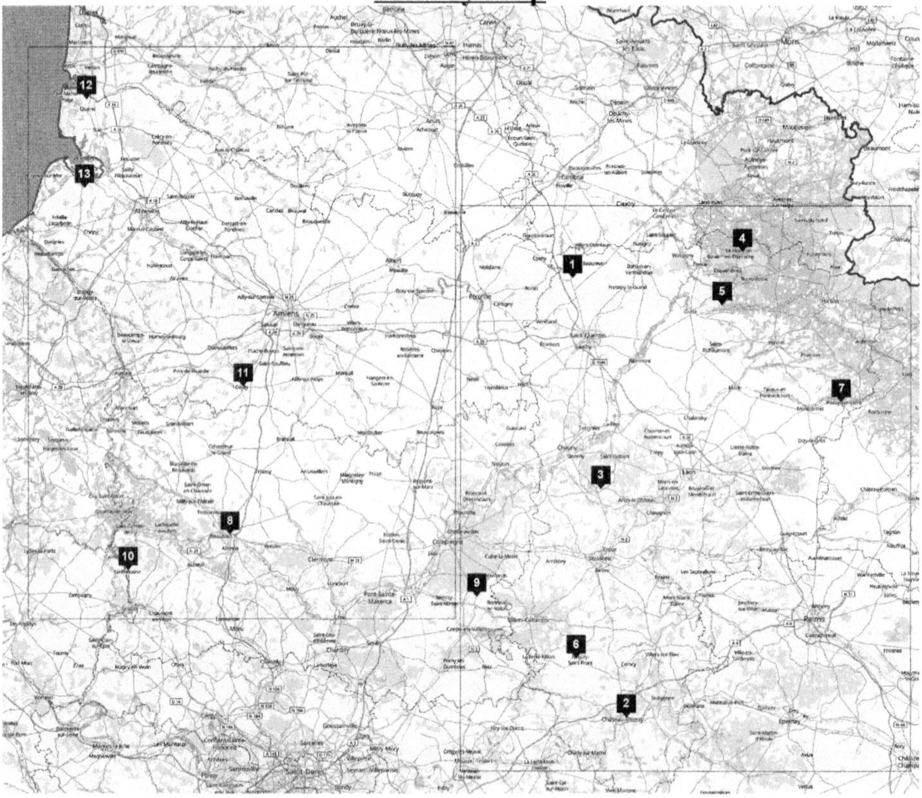

Key to enlarged Picardy Maps (on next 2 pages)

Former campsites that are now aires are noted in ***bold***

1) BELLICOURT – 2) CHATEAU THIERRY
3) COUCY LE CHATEAU AUFFRIQUE – 4) LE NOUVION EN THIERACHE
5) MALZY – 6) NEUILLY ST FRONT – 7) ROZOY SUR SERRE
8) BEAUVAIS *– 9) MORIENVAL – 10) SERIFONTAINE – 11) CONTY*
12) QUEND – 13) ST VALERY-SUR-SOMME – 14) ST GOBAIN – 15) SONGEONS
16) LONG – ***17) CAPPY***

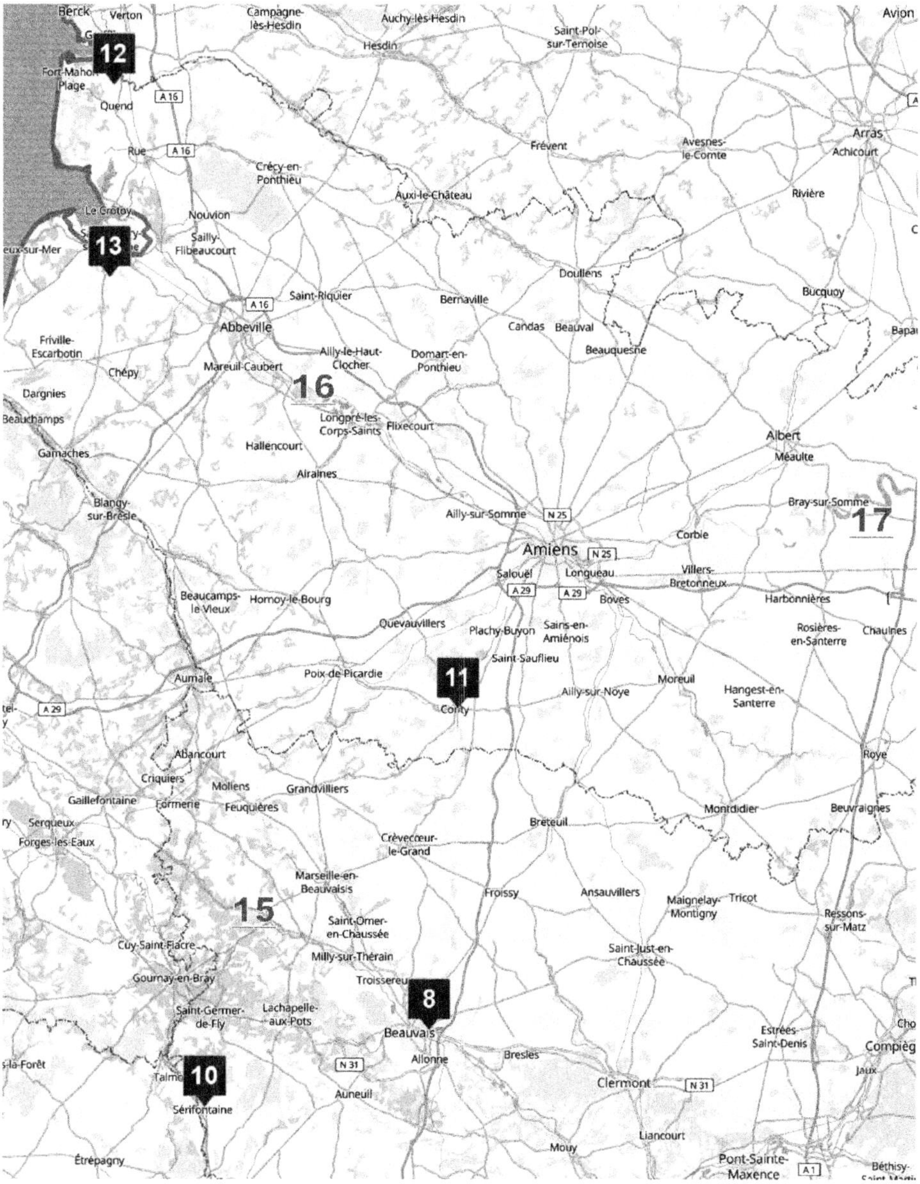
Berck
Verton
Campagne-lès-Hesdin
Auchy-lès-Hesdin
Hesdin
Saint-Pol-sur-Ternoise
Avion
12
Fort-Mahon-Plage
Quend
A 16
Rue
Crécy-en-Ponthieu
Frévent
Avesnes-le-Comte
Arras
Achicourt
Auxi-le-Château
Rivière
Le Crotoy
Nouvion
13
Sailly-Flibeaucourt
Doullens
Bucquoy
Saint-Riquier
Bernaville
Abbeville
Candas
Beauval
Friville-Escarbotin
Ailly-le-Haut-Clocher
Domart-en-Ponthieu
Beauquesne
Mareuil-Caubert
Chépy
16
Dargnies
Beauchamps
Longpré-les-Corps-Saints
Flixecourt
Albert
Gamaches
Hallencourt
Méaulte
Airaines
Blangy-sur-Bresle
Bray-sur-Somme
Ailly-sur-Somme
N 25
17
Corbie
Amiens
Salouël
Longueau
Villers-Bretonneux
A 29
Boves
Harbonnières
Beaucamps-le-Vieux
Hornoy-le-Bourg
Quevauvillers
Plachy-Buyon
Sains-en-Amiénois
Rosières-en-Santerre
Chaulnes
Saint-Sauflieu
Aumale
Poix-de-Picardie
11
Moreuil
Hangest-en-Santerre
Ailly-sur-Noye
Conty
Abancourt
Roye
Criquiers
Moliens
Grandvilliers
Gaillefontaine
Formerie
Feuquières
Montdidier
Beuvraignes
Serqueux
Breteuil
Forges-les-Eaux
Crèvecœur-le-Grand
Marseille-en-Beauvaisis
Froissy
Ansauvillers
Maignelay-Montigny
Tricot
15
Ressons-sur-Matz
Saint-Omer-en-Chaussée
Cuy-Saint-Fiacre
Saint-Just-en-Chaussée
Milly-sur-Thérain
Gournay-en-Bray
Troissereux
8
Saint-Germer-de-Fly
Lachapelle-aux-Pots
Beauvais
Estrées-Saint-Denis
Allonne
Bresles
N 31
10
Jaux
Clermont
Sérifontaine
Auneuil
Liancourt
Mouy
Étrépagny
Pont-Sainte-Maxence
A 1

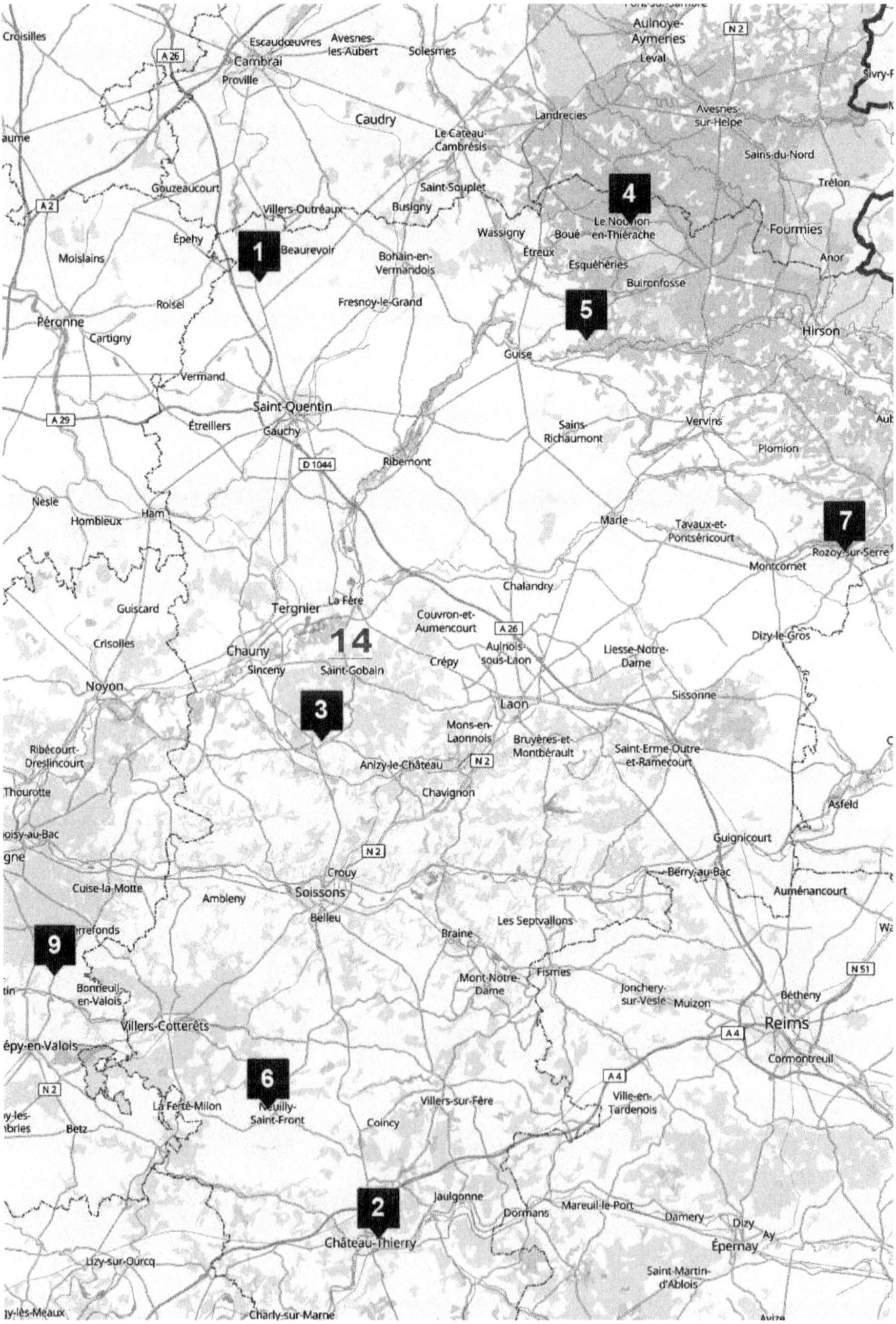
Croisilles
Escaudœuvres
Avesnes-les-Aubert
Solesmes
Aulnoye-Aymeries
Leval
N 2
A 26
Cambrai
Proville
Caudry
Le Cateau-Cambrésis
Landrecies
Avesnes-sur-Helpe
Sains-du-Nord
Trélon
Gouzeaucourt
Saint-Souplet
Busigny
A 2
Villers-Outréaux
4
Le Nouvion-en-Thiérache
Fourmies
Épehy
Wassigny
Boué
Étreux
1
Beaurevoir
Moislains
Bohain-en-Vermandois
Esquéhéries
Anor
Buironfosse
Roisel
Fresnoy-le-Grand
5
Péronne
Cartigny
Hirson
Guise
Vermand
Saint-Quentin
A 29
Étreillers
Gauchy
Vervins
Sains-Richaumont
Plomion
D 1044
Ribemont
Nesle
Hombleux
Ham
Marle
Tavaux-et-Pontséricourt
7
Rozoy-sur-Serre
Montcornet
Chalandry
Guiscard
Tergnier
La Fère
Couvron-et-Aumencourt
A 26
14
Crisolles
Chauny
Aulnois-sous-Laon
Liesse-Notre-Dame
Dizy-le-Gros
Sinceny
Saint-Gobain
Crépy
Noyon
Laon
Sissonne
3
Mons-en-Laonnois
Bruyères-et-Montbérault
Ribécourt-Dreslincourt
Saint-Erme-Outre-et-Ramecourt
Anizy-le-Château
N 2
Thourotte
Chavignon
Asfeld
Guignicourt
N 2
Crouy
Berry-au-Bac
Cuise-la-Motte
Ambleny
Soissons
Aumenancourt
Belleu
Les Septvallons
9
Braine
Fismes
N 51
Bonneuil-en-Valois
Mont-Notre-Dame
Jonchery-sur-Vesle
Muizon
Bétheny
Villers-Cotterêts
Reims
A 4
Cormontreuil
6
A 4
N 2
La Ferté-Milon
Neuilly-Saint-Front
Villers-sur-Fère
Ville-en-Tardenois
Betz
Coincy
2
Jaulgonne
Dormans
Mareuil-le-Port
Damery
Dizy
Ay
Château-Thierry
Épernay
Lizy-sur-Ourcq
Saint-Martin-d'Ablois
Charly-sur-Marne

02 AISNE

BELLICOURT

ADDRESS: RUE DU VIEUX CHEMIN, OFF D1044 **TYPE :** MUNICIPAL
FACILITIES: WATER /GREY & BLACK DRAIN/ ELECTRIC
LOCATION: RURAL/ CANAL **NO. OF SPACES:** 8
PRICES: PARKING: FREE **SERVICES**: 4€ WATER & ELECTRIC
OPENING TIMES: ALL YEAR **GPS:** N49.95123 E03.23498
DIRECTIONS: From BELLICOURT take D1044 SOUTH & RIGHT after 500m onto RUE DU VIEUX CHEMIN to AIRE on LEFT.
SITE DESCRIPTION *The aire is located to the south of Bellicourt in a large tarmac car park, near to a museum & the OT – there are mature trees providing shade in places with grass areas & picnic tables. Service point with drainage platform.*
REVIEW: *A modern well equipped aire, next to a canal in a quiet location but parking has slight slope.. Walks along the canal, not too far from village where there is a boulangerie, restaurant, OT & cafe plus a museum. Jetons from the OT.*

CHATEAU THIERRY

ADDRESS: AVE D'ESSOMES **TYPE OF AIRE:** MUNICIPAL
FACILITIES: WATER /GREY & BLACK DRAIN / ELECTRIC/ TOILETS/ WIFI
LOCATION: URBAN/ RIVER **NO. OF SPACES:** 13
PRICES: PARKING: 9€/ 24 Hrs **SERVICES**: 4€ ELECTRIC
OPENING TIMES: ALL YEAR **GPS :** N49.03768 E03.38552
DIRECTIONS: In CHATEAU THIERRY follow signs for CARREFOUR/ McD, AIRE is opposite.
SITE DESCRIPTION: *This aire is located next to the Marne river on the western side of town with parking on tarmac in large marked spaces separated by hedges/ grass - having lighting & shade. Modern artisanal service point with platform drain & ehu's, access via automatic barrier by credit card.*
REVIEW: *A well equipped modern aire on north bank of river with large spaces & individual electric points plus wifi, reasonably peaceful at night despite McD opposite. Payable by card at machine which issues code, electric is extra, water included. Heated toilets/ showers with washing up sinks. Good range of shops in town & Carrefour opposite, play area nearby.*

Chateau Thierry

COUCY LE CHATEAU AUFFRIQUE

ADDRESS: CHEMIN VAL SERAINN, OFF D937 **TYPE :** MUNIICIPAL
FACILITIES: WATER /GREY & BLACK DRAIN / ELECTRIC/ TOILETS
LOCATION: URBAN **NO. OF SPACES:** 12
PRICES:PARKING: 7€/ 24HRS **SERVICES**: INCL
OPENING TIMES: ALL YEAR **GPS :** N49.52004 E03.31396
DIRECTIONS: From SOUTH take D937 NORTH to village. In village turn LEFT @ 'Plan d'Eau/ Aire' sign & AIRE is 100m on RIGHT.
***SITE DESCRIPTION**: The aire is located in a designated parking area on the western side of the village with parking on tarmac in marked spaces, lit at night but having little shade, picnic table adjacent. The spaces are separated by low hedges & bordered by grass verges, each having an ehu. Urba Flux service point with platform drain & small toilet block adjacent.*
***REVIEW:** A well laid out aire (below) with 12 reserved spaces situated about ½ km from the centre of this small rural village in a quiet spot. The fee, which is paid by credit card at a machine, includes water & 24 hrs of electricity (each space has an ehu) – the machine issues a code allowing use of services as well as access to the toilets. Short walk to leisure lake & 300m from Château/ museum. Grocer, boulangerie, pharmacy & eating places in village.*

LE NOUVION EN THIERACHE

ADDRESS: ALLEE DE LT. F. D'ORLEANS **TYPE OF AIRE:** MUNICIPAL
FACILITIES: WATER /GREY & BLACK DRAIN / ELECTRIC
LOCATION: RURAL **NO. OF SPACES:** 5
PRICES: PARKING: FREE **SERVICES**: 3€ WATER or ELECTRIC
OPENING TIMES: ALL YEAR **GPS:** N50.00549 E03.78116
DIRECTIONS: From LE NOUVION take D26 SOUTH & LEFT to AIRE
***SITE DESCRIPTION**: This Municipal aire is located in a designated parking area next to the Municipal camping, 1.5km south of the village with parking on tarmac in 5 large marked spaces, lit at night but having little shade, picnic table adjacent. Urba Flux service point with platform drain.*
***REVIEW:** A small, modern, well maintained aire next to the campsite with very large level spaces on tarmac in a fenced compound. No shade but a quiet rural spot with forest/ play area adjacent & picnic area, short walk to large lake. Camping open 01 /04 – 30/ 09 (with small shop & bread), jetons sold here or in shops. Village has a few shops & a small Carrefour.* *Picture top of next page*

Le Nouvion

MALZY

ADDRESS: 16 RUE DES MARICHOUX **TYPE OF AIRE**: PRIVATE
FACILITIES: WATER /GREY & BLACK DRAIN / ELECTRIC/ WIFI/ TOILETS
LOCATION: RURAL/ LAKE **NO. OF SPACES:** 4
PRICES: PARKING: 5€/ 24Hrs **SERVICES**: 2€ WATER or ELECTRIC
OPENING TIMES: ALL YEAR **GPS :** N49.90598 E03.72162
DIRECTIONS: From WEST take D462 to MALZ, take 1st LEFT in village & AIRE is 150m on RIGHT.
SITE DESCRIPTION: *This private aire is located in the grounds of a fishing lake 'L'Etang des Sources' on the western side of the small village with parking on grass & having a little shade but no lighting. The aire is adjacent to the lakes with just 4 spaces available. Artisanal service point & toilets nearby. Aire is closed Tues & Fridays unless you make a reservation in advance; Tel/ Text: 06 83 87 88 76*
REVIEW: *Pleasant, quiet, rural spot overlooking lake but will appeal more to anglers with the large trout & carp lakes. Snacks & drinks are available as well as picnic tables & wifi. Fishing is limited from 12/ 03 till 06/ 11. Cycle track is nearby & bikes are available to hire. Short walk into village but no facilities there. Secure spot near to house & gates are closed 19.00 till 07.30.* *Aire pictured below*

NEUILLY ST FRONT

ADDRESS: RUE DE LA CHANTEREINE, OFF D4 **TYPE :** MUNICIPAL
FACILITIES: WATER /GREY & BLACK DRAIN/ ELECTRIC
LOCATION: SEMI-RURAL/ LAKESIDE **NO. OF SPACES:** 15
PRICES: PARKING: FREE **SERVICES**: 3€ WATER or ELECTRIC

OPENING TIMES: ALL YEAR **GPS:** N49.16713 E03.25998
DIRECTIONS: From WEST on D4, carry on into NEUILLY & take 1st RIGHT at GARAGE to AIRE on LEFT.
SITE DESCRIPTION: *The aire is located to the west side of Neuilly in a large wooded park area, near to a lake – there are mature trees providing shade in places with large grass areas. Aire is about 300m from the village centre. AireServices service point with drainage platform.*
REVIEW: *Pleasant aire in a quiet residential location on the edge of this village with ample parking. Picnic tables & fishing lake adjacent. Short walk into village with small range of shops/ eating-places & a Leclerc supermarket 500m away.*

Neuilly St Front ↓

ROZOY SUR SERRE

ADDRESS: RUE DE LA PRAILLE **TYPE OF AIRE:** MUNICIPAL
FACILITIES: WATER /GREY & BLACK DRAIN/ RUBBISH
LOCATION: SEMI-RURAL **NO. OF SPACES:** 5
PRICES: **PARKING**: FREE **SERVICES**: 2€ WATER
OPENING TIMES: ALL YEAR **GPS:** N49.71358 E04.12188
DIRECTIONS: From ROZOY take D977 NORTH, turn LEFT @ GEDIMAT to AIRE.
SITE DESCRIPTION *The aire is located to the north side of Rozoy in a small tarmac parking area, next to a minor road – there is little shade here but it is lit at night & has a picnic table. 5 places are reserved for motorhomes separated by low hedges & bordered by grass verges. Urba Flux service point with drainage platform.*
REVIEW: *A modern, small, rural aire in a quiet location on outskirts of village. Parking is on individual spaces for motorhomes & is a 400m level walk from centre of village where there is a small selection of shops including a superette, a boulangerie & a restaurant. Walks/ cycling along the nearby former railway line. Aire (below) is 4kms from Parfondeval, one of the 'Most Beautiful villages in France'.*

Rozoy→

ST GOBAIN

ADDRESS: IMPASSE DES MARETTES, OFF D13 **TYPE :** MUNICIPAL
FACILITIES: WATER /GREY & BLACK DRAIN/ ELECTRIC/ TOILETS
LOCATION: SEMI-RURAL **NO. OF SPACES:** 5
PRICES : PARKING: 7€/ 24 Hrs **SERVICES**: INCL
OPENING TIMES: ALL YEAR **GPS :** N49.59142 E03.37868
DIRECTIONS: Enter village from SOUTH on D13, AIRE is 1st RIGHT.
SITE DESCRIPTION: *The aire is located to the south side of St Gobain in a small gravel parking area, next to a forest – there is some shade here & it is lit at night. 5 separate spaces each with ehu, UrbaFlux service point with drainage platform & toilets nearby.*
REVIEW: *A well-maintained, small aire in a quiet location Parking is level & the 5 individual spaces are separated by timber platforms. Aire is 250m from centre of the large village where there is a small selection of shops; boulangerie, butcher, Bio-shop, 2 cafes & a mini supermarket (just 50m from the aire). Walks/ cycling in forest.*

St Gobain

60 OISE

BEAUVAIS

ADDRESS: RUE ALDEBERT BELLIER **TYPE OF AIRE:** MUNICIPAL
FACILITIES: WATER /GREY & BLACK DRAIN/ RUBBISH
LOCATION: URBAN **NO. OF SPACES:** 20
PRICES: PARKING: FREE **SERVICES**: FREE
OPENING TIMES: ALL YEAR **GPS:** N49.42431 E02.08013
DIRECTIONS: In town follow signs to 'CAMPING MUNICIPAL', AIRE is in the campsite.
SITE DESCRIPTION: *An aire located in the former Municipal campsite in the southern half of the town, parking on grass, accessed by a tarmac track, bordered by hedges with some trees giving shade & lit at night. Aire is fenced with gates at entrance & looked after by a warden. AireServices borne with drainage platform.*
REVIEW: *An excellent, peaceful, little stop, well looked after, located on a hill (steep access road) overlooking the town, short walk to town centre & shops. Swimming pool nearby, Cathedral, château & museum to visit.*

Beauvais

MORIENVAL

ADDRESS: 32 ROUTE DE PIERREFONDS, D335 **TYPE :** PRIVATE
FACILITIES: WATER /GREY & BLACK DRAIN/ ELECTRIC
LOCATION: RURAL **NO. OF SPACES:** 8
PRICES: PARKING: 8€/ 24Hrs **SERVICES**: 2€ WATER or ELECTRIC
OPENING TIMES: 22/ 03 – 11/ 11 **GPS:** N49.30285 E02.92297
DIRECTIONS: From MORIENVAL take D335 NORTH & AIRE is 400m on RIGHT.
SITE DESCRIPTION: *This privately owned aire is in the residence of a landscape gardener, 400m to the north of the village centre in a secure fenced & gated location with individual spaces on grass, separated by hedges & with trees giving shade in places, lighting at night. Euro-Relais service point with drainage platform & ehu's on pitches.*
REVIEW: *A very secure, well designed & maintained private aire, a short walk from Morienval in peaceful, landscaped gardens. Aire is open 7am – 10pm, March till November & rate is cheaper after 2nd night. Boulangerie, pharmacy & a nice auberge in village as well as an abbey.* ***Note: Access can be awkward for long vehicles due to steep ramp at entrance.***

Morienval

SERIFONTAINE

ADDRESS: RUE DE COCAGNE **TYPE OF AIRE:** PRIVATE
FACILITIES: WATER /GREY & BLACK DRAIN/ ELECTRIC/ SHOWERS/ WIFI
LOCATION: RURAL **NO. OF SPACES:** 14
PRICES: **PARKING**: 11€/ 24Hrs **SERVICES**: INCL
OPENING TIMES: MARCH – DEC **GPS:** N49.35565 E01.78077
DIRECTIONS: In village take RUE COCAGNE, EAST towards CHAMPIGNOLLES & AIRE is on RIGHT as you leave.
SITE DESCRIPTION: *This modern private aire is set in residential grounds to the east of the village in a secure guarded location with individual 100m² spaces on grass, separated by shrubs & trees offering shade in places. The pitches have individual ehu's & there is a small toilet block with handicapped access & shower. Artisanal service point with drainage platform.*
REVIEW: *A very clean, well equipped & maintained aire, a 400m walk from village centre in a peaceful, rural setting. Large level pitches with ehu, wifi, bbq, boules & local tourist info plus toilets with shower. Small selection of shops in village. You can also reserve a space on Tel/ Text: 0679409285.*

Serifontaine

SONGEONS

ADDRESS: RUE DES SORBIERS **TYPE OF AIRE:** MUNICIPAL
FACILITIES: WATER /GREY DRAIN/BLACK DRAIN/ RUBBISH
LOCATION: SEMI-URBAN **NO. OF SPACES:** 6
PRICES: PARKING: FREE **SERVICES**: 2€ WATER or ELECTRIC
OPENING TIMES: ALL YEAR **GPS :** N49.94571 E01.85553
DIRECTIONS: From EAST take D133 into town, turn 1st LEFT then RIGHT to AIRE.
SITE DESCRIPTION: *A Municipal aire located behind the sports complex on the southern edge of the small town, a residential area with individual parking spaces on tarmac bordered by grass verges with mature trees offering shade, lit at night. AireServices borne with large drainage platform.*

REVIEW: *A modern aire with 6 large spaces within 300m of the town centre where there is a reasonable selection of shops & a Cocci minimarket. Good shade, level & quiet with adjacent grass areas. Jetons from shops & OT in Gerberoy. Footpath leads to Gerberoy (20 mins), one of the 'Most Beautiful Villages in France'.*

Songeons

80 SOMME

CAPPY

ADDRESS: RUE DE BANA, OFF D1 **TYPE OF AIRE:** PRIVATE
FACILITIES: WATER /GREY & BLACK DRAIN/ ELECTRIC/ WIFI/ TOILETS
LOCATION: RURAL/ RIVER **NO. OF SPACES:** 27
PRICES: PARKING: 12€/ 24HRS **SERVICES**: INCL
OPENING TIMES: ALL YEAR **GPS :** N49.92823 E02.74028
DIRECTIONS: From CAPPY take D1 across RIVER & turn 1st LEFT to AIRE.
SITE DESCRIPTION *This 'Camping Village' aire, run by CampingCarPark, is situated in the campsite 'les Charmilles', about 1kms west of Cappy & alongside the Somme river. Pitches are on grass (most shaded) separated by high hedges each with 6A ehu & wifi with toilets (open 01/07-30/08). Artisanal service point with drainage platform. Access by automatic barrier, CCP card required.*
REVIEW: *A pleasant, popular location on the Somme river, remote from the village but quiet with good pitches & services (but wifi intermittent). Shops/ restaurants & a Carrefour supermarket in Bray sur Somme (3kms) & a pick-your-own fruit/ veg next to aire. A good area for walking & cycling along Somme.* *Pictured below*

CONTY

ADDRESS: RUE DU MARAIS **TYPE OF AIRE:** MUNICIPAL
FACILITIES: WATER /GREY & BLACK DRAIN / TOILETS / RUBBISH
LOCATION: SEMI-RURAL **NO. OF SPACES:** 50
PRICES: PARKING: FREE **SERVICES**: 3€ WATER
OPENING TIMES: ALL YEAR **GPS:** N49.74388 E02.15618
DIRECTIONS: From centre of CONTY take D920 EAST & turn 1st LEFT to AIRE on RIGHT.
SITE DESCRIPTION: *A large level parking area alongside a minor road with spaces on grass or tarmac accessed by a tarmac track, lighting, some shade from trees & a play area adjacent. Located on the northern edge of village next to farmland, with some lakes nearby & about 300m from the village centre. Artisanal service point with drainage grid & toilets.*
REVIEW: *A very peaceful place, nice walks/ cycle routes around the lakes but grass areas can become soft in wet weather. Notice board on site with local info – restaurants/ walks & map. Short walk into village where there is a small range of shops, bar & restaurant, bread van calls in mornings. Jetons from shops & OT.*

Conty

LONG

ADDRESS:CAMPING, RUE CHASSE A VACHES **TYPE OF AIRE:** MUNICIPAL
FACILITIES: WATER /GREY & BLACK DRAIN / ELECTRIC / RUBBISH
LOCATION: SEMI-RURAL/ RIVER **NO. OF SPACES:** 8
PRICES: PARKING: 5€ /24HRS **SERVICES**: 2€ WATER or ELECTRIC
OPENING TIMES: ALL YEAR **GPS :** N50.03462 E01.98308
DIRECTIONS: From LONG take D32 SOUTH & turn LEFT after RIVER (sign 'Camping'). AIRE is outside campsite.
SITE DESCRIPTION: *A Municipal aire in a medium sized level parking area alongside the Somme with 8 large spaces on grass, lighting, some shade from trees & a campsite adjacent. Located on the southern edge of village next to farmland, with lakes nearby & about 500m from the village centre. Euro Relais service point with drainage grid that is easy to access & 4 ehu's.*
REVIEW: *Pleasant location, next to the Somme river with picnic tables & surrounded on other sides by large fishing lakes but ground quite soft in rain. 500m from Long where there is a cafe & restaurant. Council official collects the parking fee, ehu is available at 2€ /hr but if you need 24 hr electric then the camping (open 15/03 – 15/11) is a cheaper option with ehu's, wifi & showers. Museum, level walking & cycling in area.*

Long

QUEND

ADDRESS: RUE DES MAISONNETTES **TYPE OF AIRE:** PRIVATE
FACILITIES: WATER /GREY & BLACK DRAIN / ELECTRIC/ WIFI
LOCATION: RURAL **NO. OF SPACES:** 10
PRICES: PARKING: 8€ /24hrs **SERVICES**: 4€ ELECTRIC
OPENING TIMES: ALL YEAR **GPS:** N50.32925 E01.61708
DIRECTIONS: From QUEND take D32 WEST, turn RIGHT (sign "Camping") continue to T-junction, FERME is on LEFT (sign).
SITE DESCRIPTION: *The aire is in a very large grass area on the 'Ferme Grande Retz', 2kms north of the village of Quend, surrounded by farmland with large spaces on gravel, accessed by a gravel track with some shade but no lighting. Artisanal borne with drainage grid, ehu's & wifi.*
REVIEW: *Very tranquil, rural location with large spaces & good facilities including free wifi, picnic tables & boules. Remote from any shops/ services & it is 6km to the beach at Quend Plage. Cycle track adjacent to entrance.*

Quend

ST VALERY-SUR-SOMME

ADDRESS: RUE DE LA CROIX L'ABBE **TYPE OF AIRE:** MUNICIPAL
FACILITIES: WATER /GREY & BLACK DRAIN / RUBBISH/ ELECTRIC
LOCATION: URBAN **NO. OF SPACES:** 90
PRICES: PARKING: 13€ /24 Hrs **SERVICES**: INCL
OPENING TIMES: ALL YEAR **GPS:** N50.18308 E01.62945
DIRECTIONS: Entering town on D2 turn RIGHT into RUE LA CROIX L'ABBE & AIRE.
SITE DESCRIPTION: *The aire is in a very large sandy/ gravel parking area with some grass areas & surrounded by woodland, with lighting & small trees but little shade on the aire. Situated on the edge of an interesting town about 800m to the seafront & shops/ restaurants. Artisanal borne with drainage grid & ehu's. Access via automatic barrier.*
REVIEW: *A nice seaside aire in a pleasant town with an old quarter & a château where Joan of Arc was imprisoned. Well looked after, quiet but only 40 ehu's for 90 pitches, not that far from the shops & an InterMarche supermarket in town. It is a good area for cycling – being close to the Somme estuary with all its' associated birds & wildlife, but it does get very busy here in the summer & at weekends.*

St Valery-sur-Somme

NORD-PAS-DE-CALAIS

Nord-Pas-de-Calais region is made up of two departments;
Nord (59)
Pas-de-Calais (62)

Nord-Pas-de-Calais Map

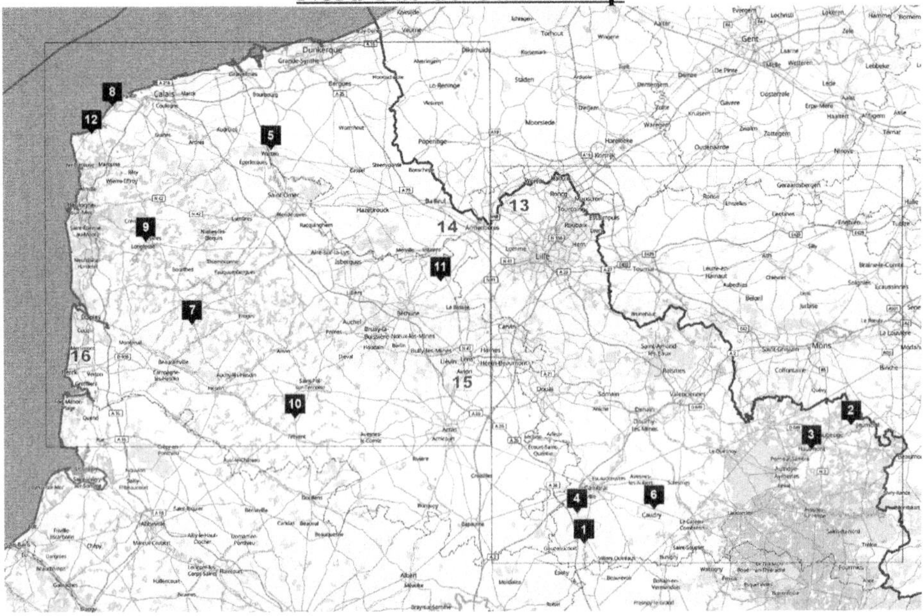

Key to enlarged Nord-Pas-de-Calais Maps (on next 2 pages)

1) BANTEUX– 2) BOUSSOIS – 3) CAUDRY – 4) HAUTMONT
5) MARCOING – 6) WATTEN – 7) EMBRY – 8) ESCALLES
9) LONGFOSSE – 10) NUNCQ-HAUTECOTE – 11) RICHEBOURG
12) TARDINGHEN 13) COMINES – 14) ESTAIRES 15) AVION
16) MERLIMONT

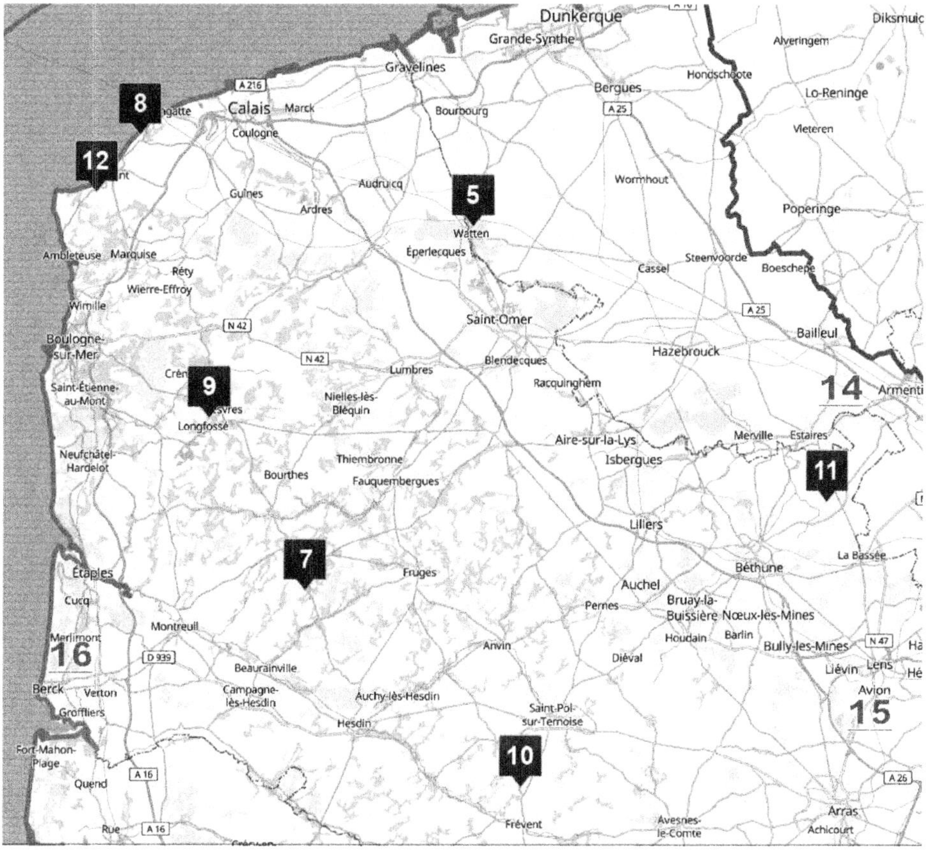

59 NORD

BANTEUX

ADDRESS: DIGUE DU CANAL **TYPE OF AIRE:** MUNICIPAL
FACILITIES: WATER /GREY & BLACK DRAIN / ELECTRIC
LOCATION: URBAN/ CANAL **NO. OF SPACES:** 5
PRICES: PARKING: 5€/ 24Hrs **SERVICES**: INCL
OPENING TIMES: ALL YEAR **GPS:** N50.06244 E03.20098
DIRECTIONS: In BANTEUX, take RUE DU PORT to CANAL/ AIRE.
SITE DESCRIPTION: *The aire is in a small gravel parking area bordered by grass areas next to a canal & between two locks, on the east side of the village. There is some shade from trees & the parking is about 150m from the village centre with an artisanal borne/ drainage grid plus 4 ehu's.*
REVIEW: *A pleasant stopover spot, quietly situated alongside a canal, not close to any shops but a bread van calls each morning. Council official calls each day to collect parking fee which includes water & 24 hr electric. Nice walks along the canal.*

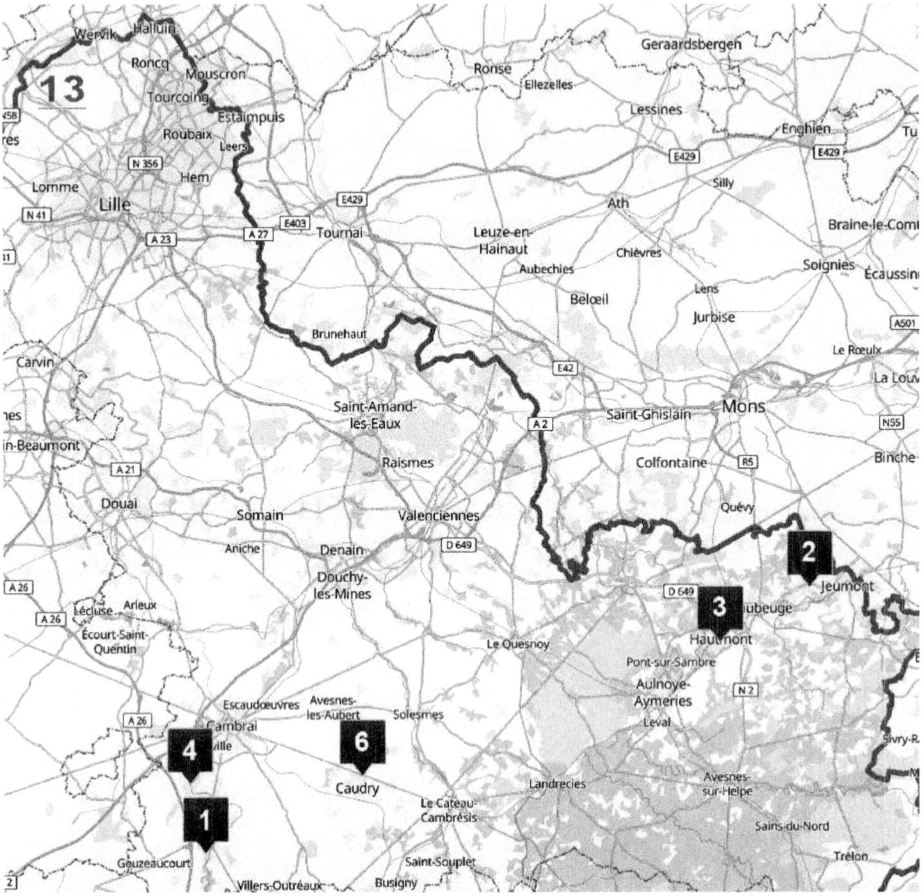
13
Wervik
Halluin
Roncq
Mouscron
Tourcoing
Estaimpuis
Roubaix
Leers
N 356
Hem
Lomme
Lille
N 41
A 23
A 27
E403
E429
Tournai
Ronse
Ellezelles
Geraardsbergen
Lessines
Enghien
E429
Silly
Ath
Leuze-en-Hainaut
Aubechies
Chièvres
Soignies
Lens
Belœil
Jurbise
A501
Le Rœulx
Brunehaut
Carvin
E42
Saint-Amand-les-Eaux
A 2
Saint-Ghislain
Mons
N55
Colfontaine
R5
Binche
A 21
Raismes
Douai
Somain
Valenciennes
Quévy
D 649
2
Aniche
Denain
Douchy-les-Mines
D 649
3
A 26
A 26
Lécluse
Arleux
Écourt-Saint-Quentin
Le Quesnoy
Pont-sur-Sambre
Aulnoye-Aymeries
N 2
Escaudœuvres
Avesnes-les-Aubert
Solesmes
A 26
Cambrai
Leval
4
6
Caudry
Landrecies
Avesnes-sur-Helpe
1
Le Cateau-Cambrésis
Sains-du-Nord
Gouzeaucourt
Saint-Souplet
Trélon
Villers-Outréaux
Busigny

Banteux

BOUSSOIS

ADDRESS: RUE DU RIVAGE **TYPE OF AIRE:** MUNICIPAL
FACILITIES: WATER /GREY & BLACK DRAIN/ RUBBISH
LOCATION: URBAN/ RIVER **NO. OF SPACES:** 4
PRICES: **PARKING**: FREE **SERVICES**: FREE
OPENING TIMES: ALL YEAR **GPS:** N50.28843 E04.04544
DIRECTIONS: Take D959 WEST to BOUSSOIS & turn LEFT in town @ AIRE sign.
SITE DESCRIPTION *The aire is located in a medium sized gravel parking area next to the river, where there are 4 dedicated level spaces on hard standing bordered by grass. Spaces have some shade under trees & lighting at night, the individual spaces are separated by hedges. AireServices service point with drainage platform is situated 80m from parking.*

REVIEW: *A modern aire located on the south side of this small town, next to a school, in a pleasant, quiet spot near to the river, convenient for town centre (250m away) where there are 2 supermarkets & a small selection of shops. Walks/ cycle route along river towpath & fishing.*

CAUDRY

ADDRESS: RUE DE CAMBRAI **TYPE OF AIRE:** MUNICIPAL
FACILITIES: GREY & BLACK DRAIN/ WATER/ ELECTRIC/ WIFI
LOCATION: SEMI-URBAN/ LAKE **NO. OF SPACES:** 6
PRICES: PARKING: 6€/ 24 Hrs **SERVICES**: INCL
OPENING TIMES: ALL YEAR **GPS:** N50.12664 E03.39927
DIRECTIONS: In town follow signs for 'Base Loisirs', AIRE is next to Salle Polyvante.
SITE DESCRIPTION: *This small municipal aire is located on the western edge of the town of Caudry, in a small tarmac parking area next to the village leisure area & lake. The aire is about 600m from the town centre, has 6 individual spaces with ehu's, next to grass areas, no shade but is lit at night. UrbaFlux service point with drainage platform & wifi, access by automatic barrier.*

REVIEW: *A modern well maintained aire in landscaped surroundings, next to a nice park & leisure lake. 24 hour ehu, wifi & water included in price, picnic tables, quiet but a bit cramped if full. 6 reserved spaces monitored by the automatic barrier. Reasonable range of shops, eating places & a supermarket in town.*

COMINES

ADDRESS: 1447 CHEMIN DE L'APOTHICAIRE **TYPE OF AIRE:** PRIVATE
FACILITIES: WATER /GREY & BLACK DRAIN / ELECTRIC
LOCATION: RURAL **NO. OF SPACES:** 6
PRICES : PARKING: 5€/ 24HRS **SERVICES**: 2€ WATER, 3€ ELEC. (24hrs)
OPENING TIMES: ALL YEAR **GPS :** N50.74182 E03.02273
DIRECTIONS: From WEST take D945 to COMINES. At 2nd R/bout take 1st EXIT to AIRE (sign 'Elevage d'Escargots').
SITE DESCRIPTION: *This private aire on a Snail farm is located about 2.5kms to the south of this large town, in a small tarmac parking area bordered by farmland & shaded by small trees but no lighting at night. There are 6 individual spaces on gravel separated by grass spaces with ehu's. It has an AireServices borne & drainage platform.*
Tel/ Text: 06 37 58 77 81

REVIEW: *A pleasant, quiet spot in a very rural location & quite remote from any shops/ services. This well maintained aire is on a snail farm so you have to be prepared to try some! Modern service point & large spaces with ehu's. Good location for visiting Lille.*

ESTAIRES

ADDRESS: RUE AIME COUPET, OFF D946 **TYPE OF AIRE:** MUNICIPAL
FACILITIES: GREY & BLACK DRAIN/ WATER/ ELECTRIC
LOCATION: URBAN **NO. OF SPACES:** 3
PRICES : PARKING: FREE **SERVICES**: 2€ WATER or ELECTRIC
OPENING TIMES: ALL YEAR **GPS :** N50.64341 E02.71889
DIRECTIONS: From WEST take D946 to ESTAIRES & then turn 1st RIGHT to AIRE.
SITE DESCRIPTION *This small aire is located 200m south of the town centre, in a tarmac parking area bordered by grass areas, with a little shade & lighting. The aire has an AireServices service point with drainage platform & ehu's.*
REVIEW: *A pleasantly located aire (below) in a quiet residential area with just 3 spaces on hardstanding separated by hedges, each with a picnic table & ehu, 12 hrs of electric for 4€ payable by 2€ coins. Short walk into town with a reasonable range of shops/ services. Convenient aire for visiting Lille.*

Estaires

HAUTMONT

ADDRESS: BVD DE L'ECLUSE, OFF D95 **TYPE OF AIRE:** MUNICIPAL
FACILITIES: WATER /GREY & BLACK DRAIN/ ELECTRIC/ TOILETS/ WIFI
LOCATION: URBAN/ RIVER **NO. OF SPACES:** 6
PRICES: PARKING: 11€/ 24 Hrs **SERVICES**: INCL
OPENING TIMES: ALL YEAR **GPS:** N50.25173 E03.91482
DIRECTIONS: Take D95 EAST to HAUTMONT. cross RIVER & turn LEFT @ 1st R/bout to AIRE.
SITE DESCRIPTION: *Found on the north bank of the Sambre river, this aire is in a small dedicated tarmac parking area next to the port, just off the nearby D95. Parking has 6 spaces on hard standing bordered by grass with lighting but little shade & is 400m from the town centre. The aire has an Flot Bleu service point with drainage platform, toilets & ehu's.*
REVIEW: *A modern, well-designed aire next to the town marina & only a short level walk into the centre where there is a good selection of shops as well as Lidl & Carrefour supermarkets, markets on Tues & Fri. Quiet, pleasant location with 6 spaces (slight slope), ehu's, toilets, showers & wifi included in fee. Pay at Port office to get access (open 10am-4pm).*

Hautmont

MARCOING

ADDRESS: PLACE DE LA GARE **TYPE OF AIRE:** MUNICIPAL
FACILITIES: WATER /GREY & BLACK DRAIN / ELECTRIC
LOCATION: URBAN/ CANAL **NO. OF SPACES:** 6
PRICES: PARKING: FREE **SERVICES**: FREE
OPENING TIMES: ALL YEAR **GPS:** N50.12101 E03.18204
DIRECTIONS: Take D15 WEST into MARCOING, turn RIGHT before BRIDGE.
SITE DESCRIPTION: *Found next to the old station building and the canal, this aire is in a medium sized tarmac parking area bordered by trees & hedges offering some shade with lighting at night. The site is on the edge of town, 500m east of the town centre. Artisanal service point with drainage grid & 4 ehu's.*
REVIEW: *A nice, quiet aire next to the canal locks (50m away) & close to the former railway station. A reasonable walk into the heart of this residential town where there is just a couple of shops, bank plus a bar/ cafe. Free services including electric which comes on with the street lights.*

Marcoing

WATTEN

ADDRESS: RUE PAUL MORTIER **TYPE OF AIRE:** MUNICIPAL
FACILITIES: WATER /GREY & BLACK DRAIN / TOILETS / ELECTRIC
LOCATION: URBAN/ CANAL **NO. OF SPACES:** 12
PRICES: PARKING: FREE **SERVICES**: 4€ WATER or ELECTRIC
OPENING TIMES: ALL YEAR **GPS:** N50.83142 E02.20885
DIRECTIONS: Take D213 NORTH to WATTEN, turn LEFT just before BRIDGE over canal, then over 2nd bridge to AIRE.
SITE DESCRIPTION: *The aire is located on the western side of Watten where there are a dozen spaces in an extended tarmac parking area shaded by trees & bordered by grass areas, next to the canal. AireServices service point with a drainage platform, jetons from Mairie, Vival, tabac or cafe.*
REVIEW: *Very pleasant & popular spot for a stopover (to Calais or Tunnel) overlooking the canal. Clean, quiet & well maintained, next to a park & a 400m walk to town centre with its small selection of shops/ cafes, supermarket & a Museum.*

Watten

62 PAS-DE-CALAIS

AVION

ADDRESS: RUE DE CITE ST ANTOINE **TYPE OF AIRE:** MUNICIPAL
FACILITIES: WATER /GREY & BLACK DRAIN/ ELECTRIC/ WIFI
LOCATION: SEMI-URBAN **NO. OF SPACES:** 6
PRICES : PARKING: FREE **SERVICES**: 3€ WATER OR ELECTRIC
OPENING TIMES: ALL YEAR **GPS :** N50.41573 E02.83058
DIRECTIONS: Exit N17 (just before A211) to AVION & follow signs 'Parc/ Police National & AIRE'.
SITE DESCRIPTION: *This aire is situated on the northern outskirts of Avion (just south of Lens) in a medium sized tarmac parking area with 6 marked spaces reserved for*

camping cars. The parking being fenced with a gate, bordered by grass areas, lit at night & well shaded by trees. AireServices borne with drainage platform, electric & wifi.

REVIEW : *A pleasant, quiet & shaded aire, in a residential area but close to the good selection of shops in town & next to a large park area with playground, lakes, beach & kiosk – good walks & fishing in lakes. Securely located next to a police station. Good stopover off A26 (Jcn. 7) & for visiting Lens & the Louvre-Lens museum.*

EMBRY

ADDRESS: OFF D108 **TYPE OF AIRE:** PRIVATE
FACILITIES: WATER /GREY & BLACK DRAIN / ELECTRIC / TOILETS
LOCATION: SEMI-RURAL **NO. OF SPACES:** 8
PRICES: PARKING: 8€/ 24 Hrs **SERVICES**: 3€ WATER or ELECTRIC
OPENING TIMES: ALL YEAR **GPS:** N50.49493 E01.96622
DIRECTIONS: From EMBRY, take D108 NORTH & turn LEFT to AIRE.
SITE DESCRIPTION: *This aire is owned by the local auberge and is located in a gravel parking area on the northern outskirts of the village, lit at night & shade in places surrounded by farmland. The facilities include WC's, showers, bbq, picnic tables & ehu's with CCTV in operation. Separate Flot-Bleu service points for water/ drainage & electric as well as a machine for jetons.*

REVIEW: *Nice quality aire in a pleasant location with modern toilets & showers, very quiet. Short walk into the pleasant small village with a good restaurant. Lady calls in evening for fee.*

ESCALLES

ADDRESS: RUE DU CHATEAU D'EAU, D243 **TYPE OF AIRE:** PRIVATE
FACILITIES: WATER /GREY & BLACK DRAIN/ ELECTRIC/ TOILETS/ WIFI
LOCATION: RURAL **NO. OF SPACES:** 27

PRICES: PARKING: 16€ /24 Hrs **SERVICES**: 5€ ELECTRIC
OPENING TIMES: 23/03 – 01/11 **GPS:** N50.91869 E01.72046
DIRECTIONS: From ESCALLES, take D243 EAST & turn RIGHT after 1km to AIRE.
SITE DESCRIPTION: *The aire is located in a very rural location, surrounded by farmland just east of the small village of Escalles & about 2km from the coast. The large terraced pitches (upto 300m^2) are on grass accessed by gravel tracks, shade in places & lighting at night. There is a small toilet/ shower block, laundrette & an artisanal service point with a large platform drain.*
REVIEW: *Very nice 'aire naturelle' with pitches on grass in a quiet environment, all having nice views of the channel & wifi, toilets dated but clean. Nice walks to the coast & a good stopover for Calais.* *Aire pictured below ↓*

LONGFOSSE

ADDRESS: RTE DE WIERRE **TYPE OF AIRE:** PRIVATE
FACILITIES: WATER /GREY & BLACK DRAIN/ ELECTRIC/ RUBBISH
LOCATION: RURAL **NO. OF SPACES:** 18
PRICES: PARKING: 10€ /24Hrs **SERVICES**: INCL
OPENING TIMES: ALL YEAR **GPS:** N50.64672 E01.79059
DIRECTIONS: From LONGFOSSE take D215 WEST & follow 'Chambre d'Hotes' signs.
SITE DESCRIPTION: *The aire is about 2kms to the west of the rural hamlet of Longfosse, located on the dairy farm 'Louvet', where there are ample spaces on gravel with ehu's, picnic tables & shade in places. Artisanal service point & drainage platform.*
REVIEW: *A well managed, friendly aire run by a farm/ Chambre d'Hotes in a quiet rural spot, a bit remote but a pleasant location with nice views. Farm produce for sale & nearest shops & services are 5kms distant.*

MERLIMONT

ADDRESS: RUE D' ESTREES **TYPE OF AIRE:** PRIVATE
FACILITIES: WATER /GREY & BLACK DRAIN/ ELECTRIC/ RUBBISH/ WIFI
LOCATION: SEMI-URBAN **NO. OF SPACES:** 29
PRICES: PARKING: 12-14€/ 24HRS **SERVICES**: INCL
OPENING TIMES: ALL YEAR **GPS :** N50.46361 E01.57965
DIRECTIONS: Take D144 into town & follow AIRE signs.
***SITE DESCRIPTION**: A modern CampingCarPark aire with large spaces on gravel located near to a residential area, to the north of town, about 200m from the centre & about 400m from the fine sand beach/ promenade. Spaces have no shade but lit at night, all with ehu's & wifi. A Euro-Relais service point with platform drain. Access via automatic barrier, CCP card required.*

***REVIEW:** A pleasant quiet aire, not particularly attractive but with good facilities whilst convenient for the beach & the small selection of shops/ OT in the old fortified town.*

NUNCQ-HAUTECOTE

ADDRESS: D916 **TYPE OF AIRE:** PRIVATE
FACILITIES: WATER /GREY & BLACK DRAIN / ELECTRIC /WIFI/ RUBBISH
LOCATION: SEMI-RURAL **NO. OF SPACES:** 6
PRICES: PARKING: 10€/ 24Hrs **SERVICES**: 5€ ELECTRIC
OPENING TIMES: ALL YEAR **GPS:** N50.30555 E02.29298
DIRECTIONS: From NORTH take D916 to village & AIRE is on RIGHT (signposted).
***SITE DESCRIPTION:** A private aire situated in the grounds of a Chambres d'Hotes, 'La Pommeraie', on the northern edge of this small rural village where there are 6 level spaces on tarmac shaded by mature trees & bordered by lawns with a small lake. Euro-Relais service point with a 'drive-thru' drainage platform. Tel: 0321036985*

***REVIEW:** An excellent, well maintained aire in a peaceful location with welcoming owners. Parking is next to the house/ garden which has a barbecue, an indoor pool, wifi & ehu's are available. Small rural village but nearest shops/ services are 2kms away.*

RICHEBOURG

ADDRESS: RUE BRIQUETERIE, OFF D166 **TYPE OF AIRE:** MUNICIPAL
FACILITIES: WATER /GREY & BLACK DRAIN / ELECTRIC / WIFI/ RUBBISH
LOCATION: SEMI-RURAL **NO. OF SPACES:** 12
PRICES: PARKING: FREE **SERVICES**: 2€ WATER or ELECTRIC
OPENING TIMES: ALL YEAR **GPS:** N50.58039 E02.74644
DIRECTIONS: In village follow signs for 'Complexe Sportif' & AIRE.
SITE DESCRIPTION: *The aire is located in a medium sized tarmac car park next to the sports hall on the east side of this small rural village. Several level spaces separated by hedges with little shade but lit at night. AireServices borne with drainage platform.*
REVIEW: *A quiet, well maintained, modern, secure (with CCTV) aire in a semi-rural location 250m from the village centre. Picnic tables, play area, wifi (access code from Mairie), rubbish bins & modern service point. Boulangerie, butcher & supermarket in village & market on Saturday morning. Many WW1 sites to visit locally.*

Richebourg aire below

TARDINGHEN

ADDRESS: FERME D'HORLOGE, D249 **TYPE OF AIRE:** PRIVATE
FACILITIES: WATER /GREY & BLACK DRAIN / RUBBISH/ ELECTRIC
LOCATION: RURAL **NO. OF SPACES:** 25
PRICES: PARKING: 8€ /24 Hrs **SERVICES**: 4€ WATER or ELECTRIC
OPENING TIMES: ALL YEAR **GPS:** N50.86220 E01.64849
DIRECTIONS: From TARDINGHEN take D249 EAST 2kms & Farm is on LEFT.
SITE DESCRIPTION: *This privately owned aire on a farm is found close to Cap Gris Nez in an open grassy area with superb panoramic views. Pitches are on grass/ hard standing next to the farm buildings with ehu's, without shade but they have glorious views to compensate. Artisanal service point next to the barn.*
REVIEW: *Super position – very quiet, plenty of birdsong and great panoramic views over the English Channel & countryside. Owner is very helpful & supplies leaflets about the area, comes in pm or early am to collect fees. Popular area for walking & cycling – quite flat. There is a restaurant/ brasserie in Tardinghen & shops in Wissant (both a short dive away).*

Tardinghen aerial view

ILE-DE-FRANCE

Ile-de-France region is made up of five departments but only one has recommended aires in it;

Seine-et-Marne (77)

Key to Ile-de-France Map (on next page)

Former campsites that are now aires are noted in ***bold***

1) PROVINS
2) ST CYR SUR MORIN
3) SOUPPES SUR LOING

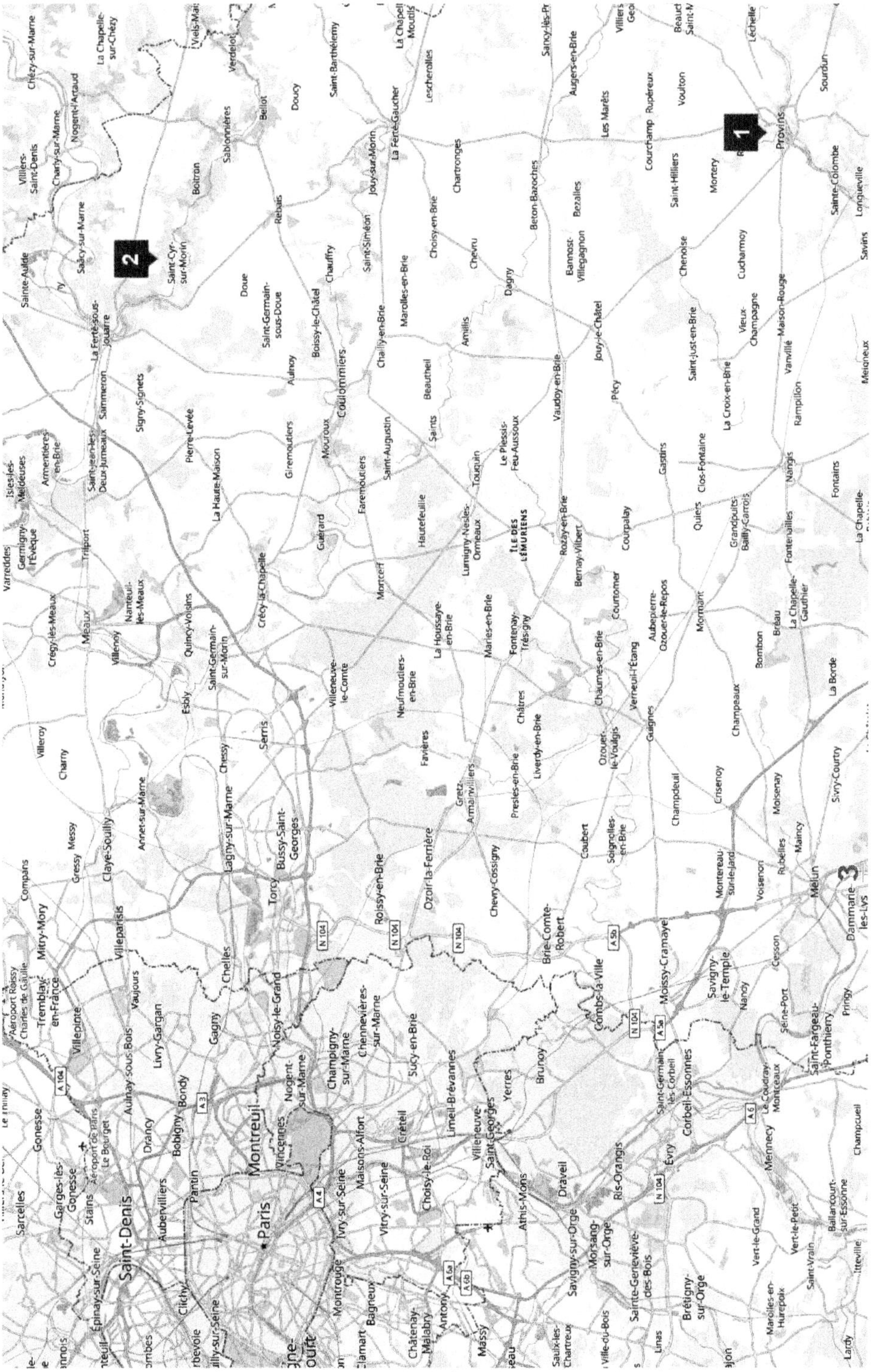

3) Souppes sur Loing is 45kms due south of Melun

77 SEINE-ET-MARNE

PROVINS

ADDRESS: CHEMIN DE PARIS **TYPE OF AIRE:** MUNICIPAL
FACILITIES: WATER /GREY & BLACK DRAIN /TOILETS
LOCATION: SEMI-RURAL **NO. OF SPACES:** 25
PRICES: PARKING: 8€/ 24 Hrs **SERVICES**: INCL
OPENING TIMES: ALL YEAR **GPS:** N48.56139 E03.27965
DIRECTIONS: Take D231 SOUTH to PROVINS then 1st LEFT before R/bout to AIRE.
SITE DESCRIPTION: *The aire is in a large gravel car park on the western outskirts of town, backing onto farmland & next to the OT with trees providing shade in places. A modern UrbaFlux borne with large platform drain. Official collects fee.*

REVIEW: *Aire is in a very large parking area, quiet but not much shade & not very handy for the town's good selection of shops & restaurants as it is about 1km from centre. Provins is a very well preserved, fortified, medieval, UNESCO listed town with ramparts, underground galleries, a Museum & stages large Medieval Festivals from April-November.*

ST CYR SUR MORIN

ADDRESS: AVE DANIEL SIMON **TYPE OF AIRE:** MUNICIPAL
FACILITIES: WATER /GREY & BLACK DRAIN /RUBBISH
LOCATION: URBAN **NO. OF SPACES:** 10
PRICES: PARKING: FREE **SERVICES**: FREE
OPENING TIMES: ALL YEAR **GPS:** N48.90631 E03.18477
DIRECTIONS: In ST CYR on D31, AIRE is between CHURCH & MAIRIE.

SITE DESCRIPTION: *The aire is in a small gravel/ grass parking area screened by hedges, bordered by grass areas, lit at night & with plenty of trees offering shade, pitches are either on gravel or grass. Artisanal service point with a large platform drain.*
REVIEW: *A pleasant little, quiet aire centrally located & next to the river in this small village where there are a few shops (boulangerie, superette, bar/tabac) within a short level walk. Good shaded parking with plenty of room, boules/ play area, way-marked walks & museum in village.*

SOUPPES-SUR-LOING

ADDRESS: CHEMIN DES MARINIERS **TYPE OF AIRE**: PRIVATE
FACILITIES: WATER /GREY & BLACK DRAIN /ELECTRIC/ TOILETS/ WIFI/ SHOWERS
LOCATION: SEMI-URBAN/ RIVER **NO. OF SPACES:** 49
PRICES: PARKING: 13-14€/ 24 Hrs **SERVICES**: INCL
OPENING TIMES: ALL YEAR **GPS :** N48.17971 E02.73022
DIRECTIONS: From SOUTH take D607 to SOUPPES, then 1st LEFT & follow 'Camping' signs to AIRE.
SITE DESCRIPTION: *This is a 'Camping Village' aire run by CampingCarPark in a riverside location on the south side of the village. This former Municipal campsite has 49 pitches, with a gravel access track, separated by hedges, bordered by grass areas & with trees offering shade, parking is on grass. Access by automatic barrier, CCP card required. Artisanal service point with a platform drain, ehu's, toilets, showers, washing-up sinks & wifi.*

REVIEW: *A pleasant, quiet aire located, next to the river, canal & a lake, with toilets/ showers (open 01/04 – 30/09) - 48 ehu's for 49 pitches. 400m from the centre of this small village where there are a few shops as well as a leisure area (500m) with swimming, fishing, canoes & pedaloes on a lake. Good shaded parking with plenty of room. Nearby green lane along the river. 11th C church & a 12th C Abbey nearby whilst the village is famous for its ancient stone quarry.*

CHAMPAGNE-ARDENNE

Champagne-Ardenne region is made up of 4 departments; Ardennnes (08), Aube (10), Marne (51) & Haute-Marne (52)

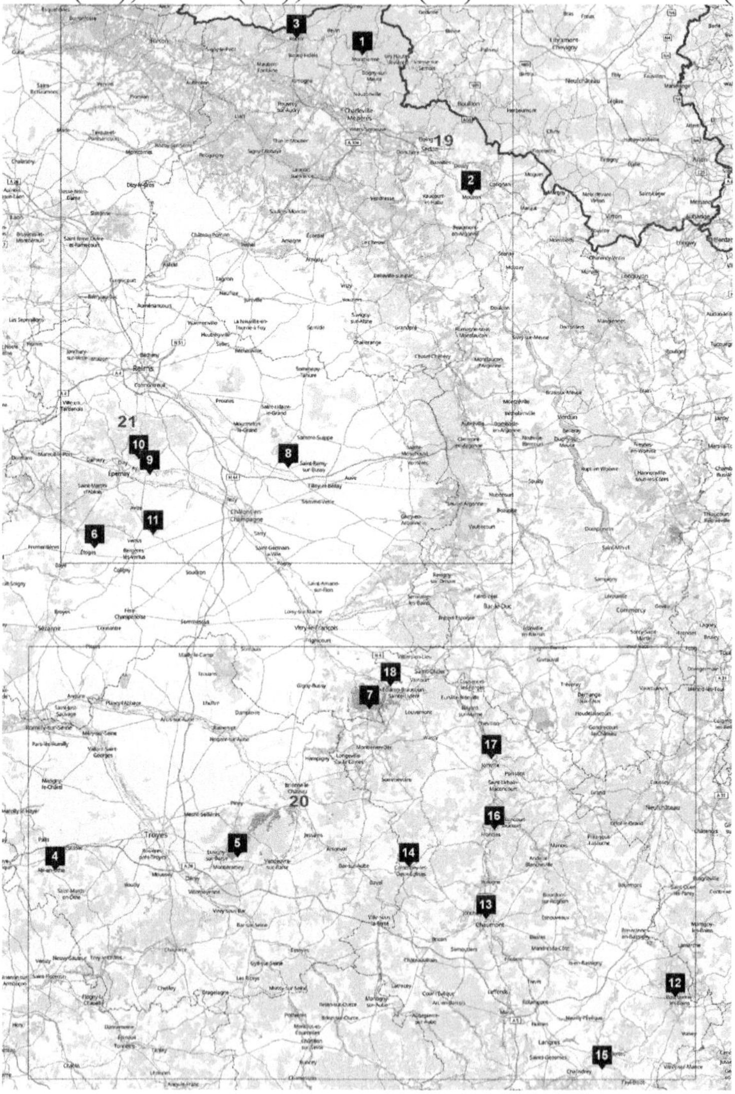

Key to enlarged Champagne-Ardenne Maps (on next 2 pages)

Former campsites that are now aires are noted in ***bold***

1) MONTHERME – 2) MOUZON – 3) ROCROI – 4) AIX EN OTHE – 5) MESNIL ST PERE – 6) BEAUNAY – 7) GIFFAUMONT CHAMPAUBERT – 8) LA CHEPPE – 9) MAREUIL SUR AY – 10) MUTIGNY – 11) VILLENEUVE- CHEVIGNY

12) BOURBONNE LES BAINS – 13) CHAUMONT – 14) COLOMBEY LES DEUX EGLISES – 15) CORGIRNON – 16) FRONCLES – 17) JOINVILLE – 18) STE LIVIERE

***19) SEDAN** – 20) DIENVILLE – 21) ST IMOGES*

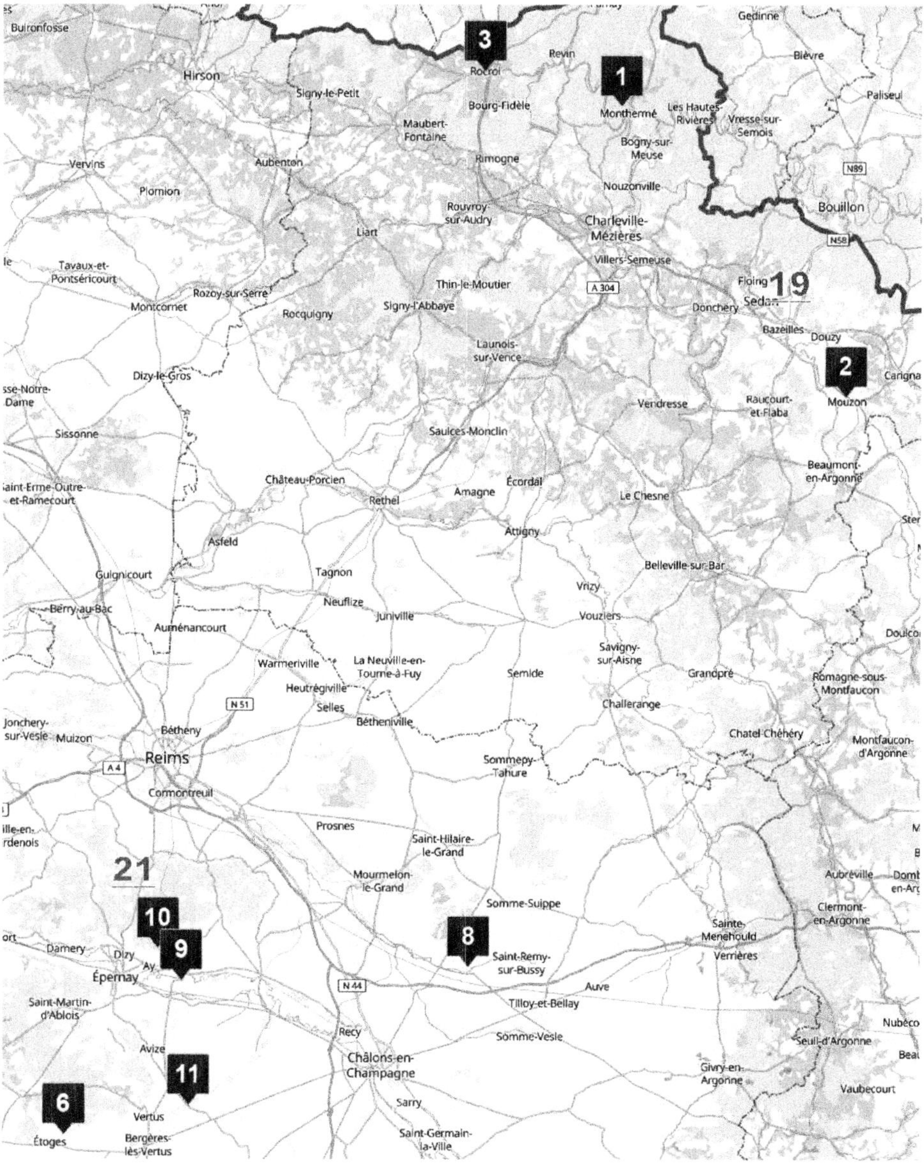
3
1
2
19
21
10
9
8
11
6
Gedinne
Buironfosse
Revin
Rocroi
Bièvre
Hirson
Signy-le-Petit
Paliseul
Bourg-Fidèle
Monthermé
Les Hautes-Rivières
Vresse-sur-Semois
Maubert-Fontaine
Bogny-sur-Meuse
Vervins
Aubenton
Rimogne
N89
Plomion
Nouzonville
Bouillon
Rouvroy-sur-Audry
Charleville-Mézières
Liart
N58
Villers-Semeuse
Tavaux-et-Pontséricourt
Thin-le-Moutier
Floing
Sedan
Rozoy-sur-Serre
A 304
Montcornet
Rocquigny
Signy-l'Abbaye
Donchery
Bazeilles
Douzy
Launois-sur-Vence
Dizy-le-Gros
Mouzon
Vendresse
Raucourt-et-Flaba
Sissonne
Saulces-Monclin
Beaumont-en-Argonne
Château-Porcien
Écordal
Amagne
Rethel
Le Chesne
Attigny
Asfeld
Belleville-sur-Bar
Guignicourt
Tagnon
Vrizy
Neuflize
Berry-au-Bac
Juniville
Vouziers
Auménancourt
Savigny-sur-Aisne
La Neuville-en-Tourne-à-Fuy
Warmeriville
Semide
Grandpré
Romagne-sous-Montfaucon
Heutrégiville
N 51
Selles
Challerange
Jonchery-sur-Vesle
Bétheniville
Bétheny
Chatel-Chéhéry
Muizon
Montfaucon-d'Argonne
Reims
A 4
Sommepy-Tahure
Cormontreuil
Prosnes
Saint-Hilaire-le-Grand
Mourmelon-le-Grand
Aubréville
Somme-Suippe
Clermont-en-Argonne
Sainte-Menehould
Damery
Dizy
Ay
Saint-Remy-sur-Bussy
Verrières
Épernay
N 44
Auve
Tilloy-et-Bellay
Saint-Martin-d'Ablois
Recy
Somme-Vesle
Seuil-d'Argonne
Avize
Châlons-en-Champagne
Givry-en-Argonne
Vaubecourt
Sarry
Vertus
Étoges
Bergères-lès-Vertus
Saint-Germain-la-Ville

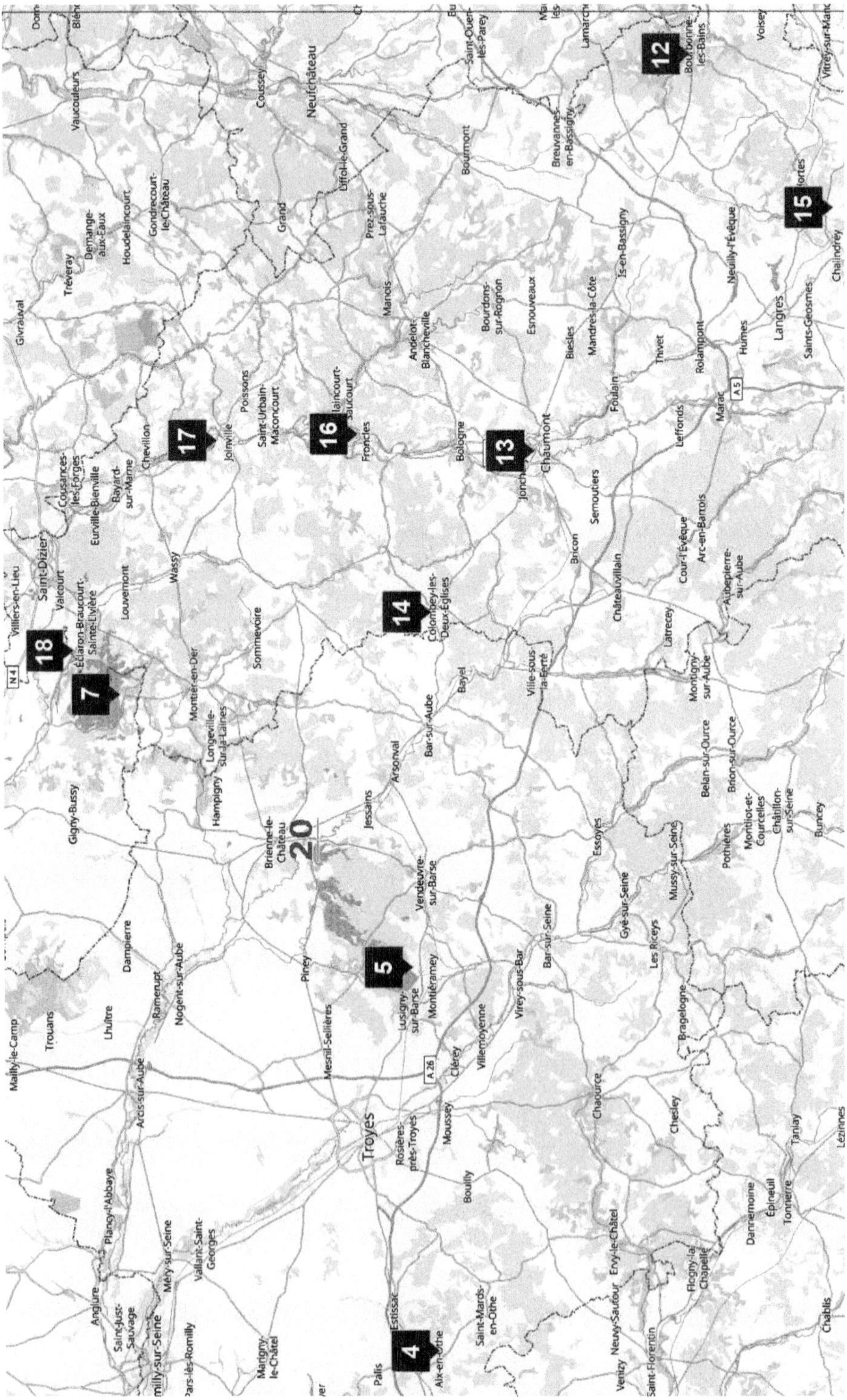
18
7
17
16
13
14
5
20
12
15
4
Saint-Dizier
Villiers-en-Lieu
Valcourt
Eclaron-Braucourt-Sainte-Livière
Louvemont
Wassy
Montier-en-Der
Sommevoire
Longeville-sur-la-Laines
Hampigny
Brienne-le-Château
Jessains
Arsonval
Bar-sur-Aube
Bayel
Colombey-les-Deux-Églises
Vendeuvre-sur-Barse
Piney
Lusigny-sur-Barse
Montiéramey
Mesnil-Sellières
Troyes
Rosières-près-Troyes
Moussey
Clérey
Villemoyenne
Virey-sous-Bar
Bar-sur-Seine
Bouilly
Essoyes
Gyé-sur-Seine
Les Riceys
Mussy-sur-Seine
Chaource
Chesley
Bragelogne
Pothières
Montliot-et-Courcelles
Châtillon-sur-Seine
Buncey
Belan-sur-Ource
Brion-sur-Ource
Montigny-sur-Aube
Latrecey
Aubepierre-sur-Aube
Châteauvillain
Cour-l'Évêque
Arc-en-Barrois
Bricon
Semoutiers
Jonchery
Chaumont
Bologne
Froncles
Saint-Urbain-Maconcourt
Joinville
Poissons
Chevillon
Bayard-sur-Marne
Eurville-Bienville
Cousances-les-Forges
Andelot-Blancheville
Manois
Bourdons-sur-Rognon
Esnouveaux
Biesles
Mandres-la-Côte
Foulain
Leffonds
Marac
Thivet
Rolampont
Humes
Langres
Saints-Geosmes
Chalindrey
Neuilly-l'Évêque
Is-en-Bassigny
Breuvannes-en-Bassigny
Bourmont
Prez-sous-Lafauche
Grand
Liffol-le-Grand
Neufchâteau
Coussey
Saint-Ouen-lès-Parey
Bourbonne-les-Bains
Lamarche
Voisey
Vitrey-sur-Mance
Gondrecourt-le-Château
Houdelaincourt
Demange-aux-Eaux
Tréveray
Givrauval
Vaucouleurs
Mailly-le-Camp
Trouans
Gigny-Bussy
Lhuître
Dampierre
Ramerupt
Nogent-sur-Aube
Arcis-sur-Aube
Plancy-l'Abbaye
Anglure
Saint-Just-Sauvage
Méry-sur-Seine
Vallant-Saint-Georges
Romilly-sur-Seine
Pars-lès-Romilly
Marigny-le-Châtel
Estissac
Aix-en-Othe
Paisy
Saint-Mards-en-Othe
Neuvy-Sautour
Ervy-le-Châtel
Venizy
Saint-Florentin
Flogny-la-Chapelle
Dannemoine
Épineuil
Tonnerre
Tanlay
Lézinnes
Chablis
A 26
A 5
N 4

08 ARDENNES

MONTHERME

ADDRESS: QUAI A. BRIAND, OFF D1 **TYPE OF AIRE:** MUNICIPAL
FACILITIES: WATER /GREY & BLACK DRAIN / ELECTRIC / TOILETS
LOCATION: RURAL/ RIVER **NO. OF SPACES:** 6
PRICES: PARKING: 6€/ 24 Hrs **SERVICES**: 3€ ELECTRIC
OPENING TIMES: ALL YEAR **GPS:** N49.88351 E4.73255
DIRECTIONS: Entering MONTHERME on D1– BORNE is opposite the CEMETERY & PARKING is next to BRIDGE.
***SITE DESCRIPTION**: Situated next to the Meuse River at the western outskirts of the town, this aire is found in a tarmac car park immediately to the east of bridge before the D1 crosses the river. Parking here is next to the river & close to shops across the river. Raclet service point with a drainage grid & rubbish bins is in a separate location opposite cemetery but there is no parking allowed there.*

***REVIEW:** An interesting small town with a tranquil aire, unshaded, next to & overlooking the Meuse river, as well as being convenient for the few shops & restaurants on the opposite bank. Parking is next to boat moorings on the river with walks along the river bank, showers in Harbour office (Apr-Oct).*

MOUZON

ADDRESS: RUE MOULIN LAVIGNE **TYPE OF AIRE:** MUNICIPAL
FACILITIES: WATER /GREY & BLACK DRAIN/ TOILETS/ ELECTRIC/ WIFI
LOCATION: URBAN/ RIVER **NO. OF SPACES:** 8
PRICES: PARKING: 9€/ 24Hrs **SERVICES**: INCL
OPENING TIMES: ALL YEAR **GPS:** N49.60695 E05.07722
DIRECTIONS: Take D964 to MOUZON & cross RIVER on D19, turn 1st RIGHT & bear RIGHT to CAPITAINERIE & AIRE.
***SITE DESCRIPTION:** The aire is located next to the river on the north side of Mouzon, with 8 individual spaces on tarmac overlooking the Meuse river, having little shade but lit at night & only 100m from the centre of the village. There are showers & toilets adjacent on the harbour at the Capitainerie, where electric hook ups are also available with an Artisanal service point.*
***REVIEW:** Clean & quiet with all the necessary services including wifi, overlooking the Meuse river. Showers & toilets are clean but only accessible when the Port office is open, no services are available from Nov till April. Village has an abbey, museum, ramparts with marked walk & remains of a château to see as well as a few shops, supermarket & bars/ cafes. Mouzon is classed as a 'Little Town of Character'.*

Aire pictured opposite top

ROCROI

ADDRESS: RUE TOUR DE VILLE, OFF D877 **TYPE OF AIRE:** MUNICIPAL
FACILITIES: WATER /GREY DRAIN/ BLACK DRAIN / ELECTRIC / RUBBISH
LOCATION: RURAL **NO. OF SPACES:** 15
PRICES: PARKING: FREE **SERVICES:** 2€ WATER or ELECTRIC
OPENING TIMES: ALL YEAR **GPS:** N49.92351 E4.51695
DIRECTIONS: From WEST on the D877, at ROCROI junction – turn 2nd LEFT to AIRE.
***SITE DESCRIPTION**: Situated on the southern outskirts of the small town, the aire is found in a small tarmac parking area. There are individual spaces on tarmac separated by strips of grass, with additional parking on grass, shaded by trees with grass areas & lighting at night, play area nearby. UrbaFlux service point with a drainage grid & rubbish bin.*

***REVIEW:** A pleasant, quiet little aire, slope on the spaces but well shaded & lit, about 400m from the centre of this historic star-shaped fortified town. Small selection of shops in town; butcher, grocer, boulangerie & a few eating places with walks around the ramparts. A Henry II stronghold, later altered by Vauban, & the setting for a battle in 1643 against the Spanish with a museum tracing the history of this conflict.*

SEDAN

ADDRESS: BVD FAUBERT **TYPE OF AIRE:** PRIVATE
FACILITIES: WATER /GREY & BLACK DRAIN/ ELECTRIC/ WIFI/ RUBBISH
LOCATION: SEMI-URBAN/ RIVER **NO. OF SPACES:** 20
PRICES : PARKING: 11-14€/ 24 HRS **SERVICES**: INCL
OPENING TIMES: ALL YEAR **GPS :** N49.69870 E04.93807
DIRECTIONS: From WEST take D8043 into SEDAN, cross river to AIRE on RIGHT.
SITE DESCRIPTION: *This private aire in a former Municipal campsite, run by the Camping Car Park company, is located close to the centre of Sedan on an island in the Meuse river, with parking on grass/ gravel pitches with lighting & reasonable shade – in a semi-rural location bordered by the river. There are 20 spaces all with ehu's and wifi – accessed by a tarmac track. The aire is bordered by grassy areas & has a Euro-Relais service point with a drainage platform. Access is via an automatic barrier operated by the CCP membership card (topped up by credit card).*
REVIEW: *A pleasant, quiet riverside location with shade in places & close to the cycle tracks along the Meuse. Aire is convenient for the town, being 400m from the centre, a good range of shops, a market on Wed & Sat & 1.5km from the chateau,.*

Sedan

10 AUBE

AIX EN OTHE

ADDRESS: RUE DU MOULIN A TAN **TYPE OF AIRE:** PRIVATE
FACILITIES: WATER /GREY & BLACK DRAIN / ELECTRIC/ TOILETS/ WIFI
LOCATION: SEMI-RURAL **NO. OF SPACES:** 40
PRICES: PARKING: 7€/ 24Hrs **SERVICES**: 2.5€ ELECTRIC
OPENING TIMES: 01/04 - 15/10 **GPS:** N48.22901 E03.72302
DIRECTIONS: From NORTH on D374, in village turn RIGHT immediately after 'Subdivision de l'Equipement' sign to AIRE.
SITE DESCRIPTION: *This private aire is not signposted in the village, but can be found on the northern side of this large village in a rural location next to a small river in the grounds of a former mill, about 600m from village centre. There are a few dozen level spaces on grass with shade, accessed by a gravel drive. Artisanal service point & drainage grid with ehu's, toilets & showers.*

REVIEW: *A very well equipped private aire located in a large garden/ field with ample parking space on either grass or hard standing. Equipment includes picnic tables, showers, laundrette, kitchenette, wifi, toilets & washing up sinks. Ehu available for an extra charge. Very quiet, clean, well maintained & welcoming owners. Only open Easter till October. Good range of shops & eating places in village. Came second in CamperContact 'Aire of the Year 2019'. Tel/ Text: 0609425347 to book.*

DIENVILLE

ADDRESS: PORT, OFF D443 **TYPE OF AIRE:** MUNICIPAL
FACILITIES: WATER /GREY & BLACK DRAIN/ ELECTRIC
LOCATION: URBAN/ LAKE **NO. OF SPACES:** 11
PRICES : PARKING: FREE **SERVICES**: 2€ WATER or ELECTRIC
OPENING TIMES: ALL YEAR **GPS :** N48.34695 E04.52762
DIRECTIONS: Take D443 NORTH to DIENVILLE then 3rd exit @ R/bout to PORT & AIRE.
SITE DESCRIPTION: *The modern aire is located next to the lake port on the west side of Dienville, with parking on tarmac overlooking the Lac d'Amance, having a little shade & lit at night. The aire is only 300m from the centre of town where there is a small selection of shops & a restaurant. Euro-Relais service point with platform drain (credit card payment).*

Dienville

REVIEW: *A pleasantly located lakeside aire with 11 large, level spaces on tarmac bordered by grass areas, next to the yacht marina & close to the lake beach with swimming allowed. The beach area has picnic tables, child's play area, bike rental, water sports & a bar/ cafe. Cycling / walks around lake.*

MESNIL ST PERE

ADDRESS: RUE DU LAC **TYPE OF AIRE:** MUNICIPAL
FACILITIES: WATER /GREY & BLACK DRAIN / ELECTRIC/ RUBBISH
LOCATION: RURAL/ LAKESIDE **NO. OF SPACES:** 30
PRICES: PARKING: FREE **SERVICES:** 2€ WATER or ELECTRIC
OPENING TIMES: ALL YEAR **GPS :** N48.25533 04.34090
DIRECTIONS: Pass through village towards LAKE & AIRE is on RIGHT.
***SITE DESCRIPTION**: This aire is located in a very large tarmac car park on the east shore of the Lac d'Orient & near to a large campsite. A quiet location overlooking the lake with shade in places around edges. Euro-Relais service point with 2 drainage grids.*
***REVIEW:** A modern aire, shared with cars, but ample parking in a nice peaceful place next to a large lake with a good beach, fishing & play area. Restaurants/ pizzeria are within a short walk but there are no shops in the village. Walks/ cycling around lake.*

51 MARNE

BEAUNAY

ADDRESS: FERME DE BEL AIR, OFF D618 **TYPE OF AIRE:** PRIVATE
FACILITIES: WATER /GREY & BLACK DRAIN/ ELECTRIC
LOCATION: RURAL **NO. OF SPACES:** 12
PRICES: PARKING: 8€ / 24 Hrs **SERVICES:** INCL
OPENING TIMES: ALL YEAR **GPS:** N48.88190 E03.87499
DIRECTIONS: In BEAUNAY, FARM is off RUE PRINCIPALE.
***SITE DESCRIPTION:** The aire is in a very rural location on a farm, producers of champagne, just west of the village where the parking is in a medium sized gravel area, little shade but it does have lighting & picnic tables. Artisanal service point with drain & ehu's. Tel: 0326593494*
***REVIEW:** A green location with peace & quiet next to the farm. A nice position with good views of the countryside & surrounded by vineyards, no shops but bread can be ordered for next morning. Aire is signposted in village, picnic tables adjacent, champagne for sale. & wine tastings.*

Beaunay

GIFFAUMONT CHAMPAUBERT

ADDRESS: RUE DU PORT, LAC DU DER **TYPE OF AIRE:** MUNICIPAL
FACILITIES: WATER /GREY & BLACK DRAIN/ TOILETS
LOCATION: RURAL/ LAKESIDE **NO. OF SPACES:** 60
PRICES: PARKING: 6€ /24Hrs **SERVICES**: 2.5€ WATER
OPENING TIMES: ALL YEAR **GPS:** N48.55051 E04.76798
DIRECTIONS: From GIFFAUMONT, take D55 SOUTH, then RUE DU PORT to R/bout & AIRE.
SITE DESCRIPTION: *Numerous spaces available close to a large lake & yacht marina, some with shade, on a gravel/ grass car park edged by trees & grass verges but no lighting. There is an AireServices borne with drainage grid. Parking available on parkings P1 & P5.*

REVIEW: *A great place with superb views, aire is quiet at night with lots of parking places, good for bird watching with lots of cranes & there are several beaches if you want to swim in the lake. Walks & cycle tracks in the forests surrounding the lake, the OT is located here as well as a play area, bar, shop & toilets (in season). No shops in the area out of season (nearest are 12km away) but boulanger calls in morning.*

LA CHEPPE

ADDRESS: CAMP D'ATTILA **TYPE OF AIRE:** MUNICIPAL
FACILITIES: WATER /GREY & BLACK DRAIN / ELECTRIC/ TOILETS
LOCATION: RURAL **NO. OF SPACES:** 4
PRICES: PARKING: FREE **SERVICES**: 2€ WATER OR ELECTRIC
OPENING TIMES: ALL YEAR **GPS:** N49.04883 E04.49281
DIRECTIONS: In LA CHEPPE, turn off D366 @ "Camp d'Attila" sign to AIRE.
SITE DESCRIPTION*: The aire here is in a small tarmac parking area next to the Camp d'Attila – the largest Celtic fortress in Europe. The aire is lit at night but not much shade, located on the western edge of the small rural village of la Cheppe & on the eastern side of the fortress. Urbaflux service point with a drainage platform, toilets adjacent.*
REVIEW: *A rural aire next to an interesting iron age fortress, quietly located at the end of a cul-de-sac. Bordered by grass areas with picnic tables, parking spaces are a bit short but well equipped with good service point & clean toilets. Guided walks around the site (2kms). No shops in village.*

La Cheppe

MAREUIL SUR AY

ADDRESS: MARINA, OFF RUE CARNOT **TYPE OF AIRE:** MUNICIPAL
FACILITIES: WATER /GREY & BLACK DRAIN / TOILETS / ELECTRIC
LOCATION: SEMI-URBAN/ CANAL **NO. OF SPACES:** 8
PRICES: PARKING: FREE **SERVICES**: 5€ WATER or ELECTRIC
OPENING TIMES: ALL YEAR **GPS:** N49.04525 E04.03385
DIRECTIONS: Exit D9 @ MAREUIL-SUR-AY & take D111 along canal into village, turn LEFT at PLACE DEGALLE & LEFT to AIRE.
SITE DESCRIPTION: *The village lies on the Marne river & its canal, while the aire is next to & overlooking the canal with parking on tarmac shaded by tall trees, 200m from the village centre. Artisanal borne with a drainage grid, jetons from superette.*
REVIEW: *A quiet position next to the canal with shaded spaces facing the water, a restaurant adjacent & lovely walks along the towpath. The aire (below) is popular in summer & the canal is good for angling, whilst the village has a couple of eating places, a few shops & wine cellars.*

MUTIGNY

ADDRESS: RTE DE MONTFLAMBERT **TYPE:** MUNICIPAL
FACILITIES: WATER /GREY & BLACK DRAIN/ ELECTRIC/ RUBBISH
LOCATION: RURAL **NO. OF SPACES:** 8
PRICES: PARKING: FREE/ 24Hrs **SERVICES**: 5€ WATER & ELECTRIC
OPENING TIMES: ALL YEAR **GPS:** N49.06922 E04.02700
DIRECTIONS: From MUTIGNY, take RTE MONTFLAMBERT, NORTH & AIRE is on LEFT.
SITE DESCRIPTION: *The aire is located about 400m north of the centre of the small rural village, set amongst vineyards & shaded on one side by mature trees. The aire has 8 marked spaces on tarmac & enjoys good views. Two UrbaFlux bornes each with water/ 16A ehu & separate platform drain.*
REVIEW: *A good, modern little aire, slight slope on parking, well marked spaces bordered by grass with walks nearby & fine views over farmland. Bread van calls each morning in summer but no services in village.*

ST IMOGES

ADDRESS: RUE DE LA BRIQUETRIE, off D71 **TYPE OF AIRE:** MUNICIPAL
FACILITIES: WATER /GREY & BLACK DRAIN / TOILETS/ ELECTRIC
LOCATION: RURAL **NO. OF SPACES:** 8
PRICES : PARKING: FREE **SERVICES**: 2€ WATER or ELECTRIC
OPENING TIMES: ALL YEAR **GPS :** N49.10619 E03.97898
DIRECTIONS: From ST IMOGES take D71 EAST to AIRE on RIGHT.
SITE DESCRIPTION: *The modern aire at St Imoges is in a tarmac parking area with individual spaces, grass areas & trees providing a little shade, lit at night. The aire is surrounded by farmland, 1km east of St Imoges (no shops) & 4kms from Epernay with its wide range of shops/ services. Euro-Relais service point with drainage platform.*

REVIEW: *Recommended for an overnight stop or as a location to visit Epernay. Quiet, well maintained with walks/ cycling in area. Restaurant in village, pizza van on Sunday pm & grocery van on Friday mornings.*

VILLENEUVE-CHEVIGNY

ADDRESS: 12 RUE DU PLESSIS **TYPE OF AIRE:** PRIVATE
FACILITIES: WATER /GREY & BLACK DRAIN / RUBBISH / ELECTRIC
LOCATION: SEMI-URBAN **NO. OF SPACES:** 5
PRICES: PARKING: 5€/ 24Hrs **SERVICES**: INCL
OPENING TIMES: ALL YEAR **GPS:** N48.91303 E04.05499
DIRECTIONS: In village, follow signs 'Camping Car' to AIRE.

***SITE DESCRIPTION**: This private aire is in a medium sized tarmac parking area next to the house of a small champagne producer, where there are 5 level spaces away from the road, accessed by a tarmac drive bordered by grass with some shade under trees & lit at night. Artisanal service point with drainage grid.*

***REVIEW:** A good aire for a stopover, next to the vineyards of a friendly wine producer, quiet, clean, secure, well maintained location with a lawn area/ picnic table & a lake opposite. No shops or services in Villeneuve, the nearest facilities are at Vertus (4kms) although a bread van calls each morning. Tasting & sale of champagne.*
Tel/ Text: 0683948025

52 HAUTE-MARNE

BOURBONNE LES BAINS

ADDRESS: RUE DE LA CHAVANNE **TYPE OF AIRE:** MUNICIPAL
FACILITIES: WATER /GREY & BLACK DRAIN/ ELECTRIC
LOCATION: SEMI-URBAN **NO. OF SPACES:** 20
PRICES: PARKING: 10€ /24 Hrs **SERVICES**: INCL
OPENING TIMES: ALL YEAR **GPS:** N47.94955 E05.74767
DIRECTIONS: In town, follow signs for 'CASINO', the AIRE is behind the Casino.
***SITE DESCRIPTION:** The aire is located to the south side of this small thermal spa town in a medium sized tarmac parking area bordered by fields, having ample level spaces with a little shade & lit at night. The aire is about 150m from the town centre. UrbaFlux service point with ehu's & drainage platform, access via automatic barrier.*

REVIEW: *A well equipped aire with 20 spaces, each with ehu & wifi available, services included in parking fee, payable by credit card. A quiet spot with grass areas adjacent. Short walk into this small town with a thermal spa complex, casino & a good range of shops. Arboretum nearby.*

CHAUMONT

ADDRESS: PORT DE LA MALADIERE, OFF D674 **TYPE OF AIRE:** MUNICIPAL
FACILITIES: WATER /GREY & BLACK DRAIN/ ELEC./ TOILETS/ SHOWERS
LOCATION: SEMI-RURAL/ CANALSIDE **NO. OF SPACES:** 12
PRICES: PARKING: 8€/ 24 Hrs **SERVICES**: INCL
OPENING TIMES: 01/04 – 31/10 **GPS:** N48.11822 E05.15419
DIRECTIONS: From CHAUMONT take D417 EAST over CANAL & then 1st LEFT.
SITE DESCRIPTION: *The aire is located next to the Marne canal, east of the town - adjacent to the Port where there are toilets & showers available from April to October. The parking for the aire is in a separate tarmac area which has a little shade & is lit at night, there are ehu's as well as an artisanal service point & drainage grid.*
REVIEW: *A well equipped canal side aire in a peaceful location overlooking the canal & countryside with a picnic area/ tables. During the summer there are showers, laundry, wifi, toilets & 2 ehu's available. Fees are payable at the Capitainerie, open 9am-12 & 4-8pm. The aire is surrounded by countryside but only about 1/2km from the town & its shops/ services.*

Chaumont

COLOMBEY LES DEUX EGLISES

ADDRESS: RUE GENERAL DE GAULLE, D23 **TYPE OF AIRE:** MUNICIPAL
FACILITIES: WATER /GREY & BLACK DRAIN / TOILETS
LOCATION: URBAN **NO. OF SPACES:** 10
PRICES: PARKING: FREE **SERVICES**: FREE
OPENING TIMES: ALL YEAR **GPS:** N48.22320 E04.88621
DIRECTIONS: In village centre, AIRE is next to MAIRIE.
SITE DESCRIPTION: *Located in the centre of this rural village, the aire is in a medium sized gravel parking area next to the Mairie where there are 10 level spaces bordered by grass verges with shade in places under mature trees. Artisanal service point with drainage grid.*

REVIEW: *A pleasant little aire provided mainly for visitors to the nearby tomb & house/ museum of General DeGaulle. Quiet location with some shade, close to shops; boulangerie, restaurants, Poste, grocer & souvenir shops. Service point is basic but free. Petanque pitch, tennis, tourist info, toilets & shower nearby.*

CORGIRNON

ADDRESS: ALLEE DU PARC **TYPE OF AIRE:** MUNICIPAL
FACILITIES: WATER /GREY & BLACK DRAIN / ELECTRIC/ TOILETS
LOCATION: SEMI-RURAL **NO. OF SPACES:** 10
PRICES: PARKING: 7€/ 24Hrs **SERVICES**: INCL
OPENING TIMES: ALL YEAR **GPS:** N47.80715 E05.50303
DIRECTIONS: In CORGIRNON take D311 EAST & AIRE is immediately on the right.

SITE DESCRIPTION: *Located on the north side of this small rural village, this aire has individual spaces on tarmac, separated by hedges, lit at night & well shaded by trees, each pitch has ehu & price includes use of showers/ toilets. Artisanal service point with drainage grid.*

REVIEW: *Warden calls at about 7pm to collect fee, turn on ehu's/ water & provide combination for toilet and shower. Site was very clean, peaceful & well shaded with hot showers (a bit dated). Short walk into village, fishing in lake. Boulangerie van passes each morning except Monday.*

FRONCLES

ADDRESS: HALTE NAUTIQUE, CANAL **TYPE OF AIRE:** MUNICIPAL
FACILITIES: WATER /GREY & BLACK DRAIN/ ELEC./ TOILETS/ SHOWERS
LOCATION: SEMI-RURAL/ CANAL **NO. OF SPACES:** 8
PRICES: PARKING: 3€/ 24 Hrs **SERVICES**: 3.5€ WATER or ELECTRIC
OPENING TIMES: ALL YEAR **GPS:** N48.30003 E05.15198
DIRECTIONS: From FRONCLES take D253 NORTH & turn RIGHT immediately before BRIDGE, continue 350m along single track lane to AIRE.
SITE DESCRIPTION: *An aire located on the side of the canal, next to a boat mooring area on the northern edge of Froncles, where there are spaces on tarmac backing onto grass areas & overlooking the canal – some shade & lit at night. The aire has separate ehu's (2 posts with 4 sockets), toilets, showers, a laundry room as well as an artisanal service point with drainage platform.*

REVIEW: *A quiet, modern & well looked after aire next to the Marne canal. The aire has all the amenities, fees are payable at the Clevacances office (closes at 6pm). There are picnic tables, grass areas & a play area. The aire is about 600m from the town centre where there are shops; superette, boulangeries, tabac, newsagent, pharmacy, Poste, bank & restaurants.*

JOINVILLE

ADDRESS: RUE DES JARDINS, OFF D60 **TYPE OF AIRE:** MUNICIPAL
FACILITIES: WATER /GREY & BLACK DRAIN / ELECTRIC / RUBBISH
LOCATION: SEMI-RURAL/ CANALSIDE **NO. OF SPACES:** 15
PRICES: PARKING: FREE **SERVICES**: 2€ WATER or ELECTRIC
OPENING TIMES: ALL YEAR **GPS:** N48.44587 E05.15007
DIRECTIONS: From JOINVILLE take D60 EAST, cross BRIDGE & take next LEFT to AIRE.
SITE DESCRIPTION: *The aire is located next to the canal, east side of Joinville, with parking on tarmac with marked spaces & next to a grassy area with trees/ picnic tables. A little shade under trees & lighting at night - 5 minute walk to the shops. Modern AireServices borne with a drainage channel & rubbish bins.*

REVIEW: *Pleasant aire (below), on the banks of a canal, well maintained & quiet, nice for watching boats using the canal, with walks, cycling & fishing. To see in town: 12th C church & chapel, Museum, 16th C Court and prison & the Grand Jardin Chateau. Shops/ services & a Carrefour supermarket nearby.*

STE LIVIERE

ADDRESS: RUE STE LIBAIRE **TYPE OF AIRE:** MUNICIPAL
FACILITIES: WATER /GREY & BLACK DRAIN / ELECTRIC / WIFI
LOCATION: URBAN **NO. OF SPACES:** 19
PRICES: PARKING: 8€/ 24 Hrs **SERVICES**: ELECTRIC 3€
OPENING TIMES: ALL YEAR **GPS :** N48.60111 E04.82139
DIRECTIONS: AIRE is well signposted in village.
SITE DESCRIPTION: *This aire is in the heart of the small village in a secure, fenced compound, access by automatic barrier with video-surveillance. There are 19 separate level spaces on concrete with grassed areas adjacent, but not each space having an ehu or shade although it is lit at night. Urba Flux service point with platform drain & wifi.*
REVIEW: *A good quality aire with well maintained facilities, very quiet but no shops in village, boulangerie van calls in morning plus a grocer calls Tues & Friday. The aire is located 2kms from Lac du Der, one of the largest artificial lakes in Europe with a large selection of bird life.*

Sainte Liviere

LORRAINE

Lorraine region is made up of 4 departments;
Meurthe-et-Moselle (54)
Meuse (55)
Moselle (57)
Vosges (88)

Lorraine Map

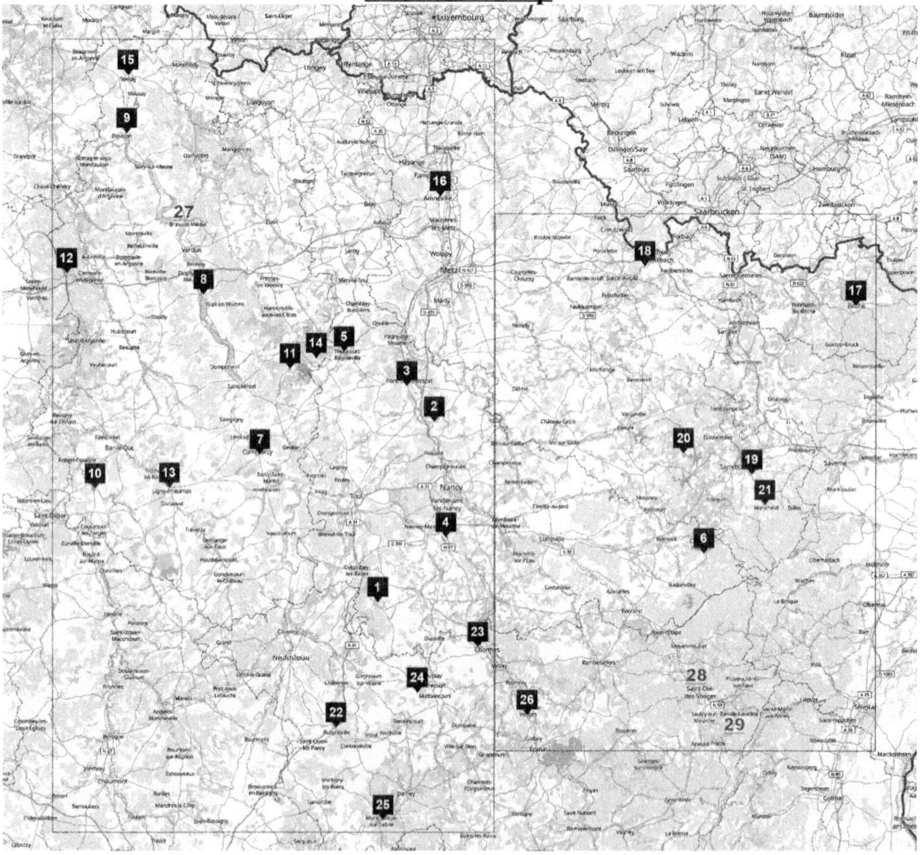

Key to enlarged Lorraine Maps (on next 2 pages)

Former campsites that are now aires are noted in ***bold***

1) FAVIERES – 2) MILLERY – 3) PONT A MOUSSON – 4) RICHARDMENIL ***5) THIAUCOURT*** *– 6) VAL ET CHATILLON – 7) COMMERCY – 8) DIEUE SUR MEUSE – 9) DUN SUR MEUSE – 10)HAIRONVILLE – 11) HEUDICOURT 12) LES ISLETTES – 13) LIGNY EN BARROIS – 14) NONSARD LAMARCHE 15) STENAY – 16) AMNEVILLE – 17) BITCHE – 18) HOMBOURG HAUT 19) NIDERVILLER – 20) RHODES – 21) WALSCHEID – 22) BULGNEVILLE 23) CHARMES – 24) MIRECOURT – 25) MONTHUREUX SUR SAONE 26) THAON LES VOSGES –* ***27) CHARNY*** *– 28) ST DIE – 29) PLAINFAING*

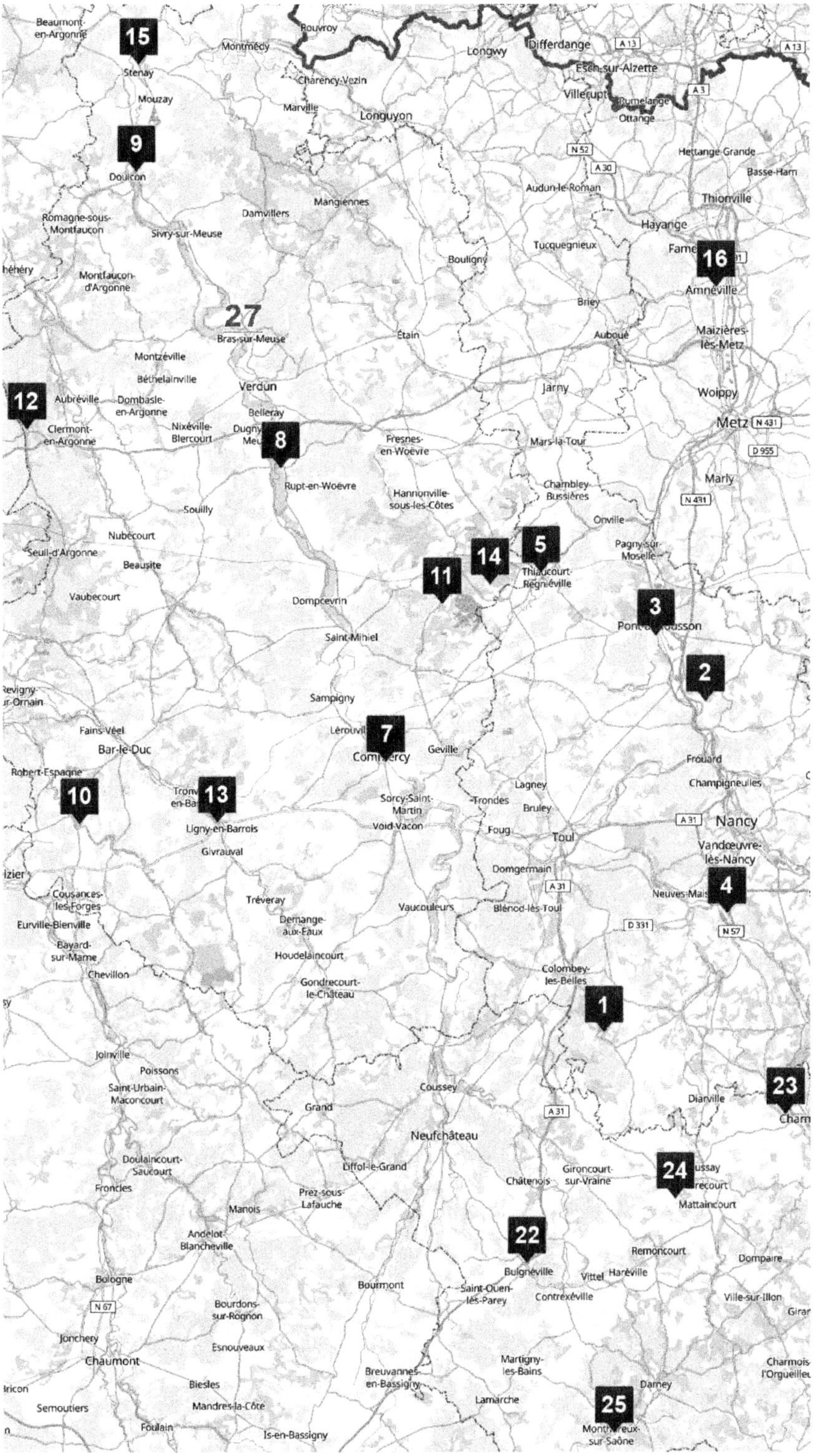
Beaumont-en-Argonne
15
Stenay
Mouzay
Montmédy
Rouvroy
Longwy
Differdange
Esch-sur-Alzette
Charency-Vezin
Villerupt
Ottange
Marville
Longuyon
9
Doulcon
Hettange-Grande
Basse-Ham
Audun-le-Roman
Thionville
Mangiennes
Damvillers
Romagne-sous-Montfaucon
Sivry-sur-Meuse
Hayange
Tucquegnieux
16
Amnéville
Bouligny
Montfaucon-d'Argonne
Briey
27
Bras-sur-Meuse
Étain
Auboué
Maizières-lès-Metz
Montzéville
Béthelainville
Verdun
Jarny
Woippy
12
Aubréville
Dombasle-en-Argonne
Belleray
Metz
Clermont-en-Argonne
Nixéville-Blercourt
8
Fresnes-en-Woëvre
Mars-la-Tour
Rupt-en-Woëvre
Hannonville-sous-les-Côtes
Chambley-Bussières
Marly
Souilly
Onville
Nubécourt
5
14
Pagny-sur-Moselle
Seuil-d'Argonne
Beausite
11
Vaubecourt
Dompcevrin
3
Saint-Mihiel
2
Sampigny
Fains-Véel
7
Geville
Bar-le-Duc
Frouard
Robert-Espagne
Champigneulles
10
13
Sorcy-Saint-Martin
Trondes
Lagney
Bruley
Ligny-en-Barrois
Void-Vacon
Foug
Toul
Nancy
Vandœuvre-lès-Nancy
Givrauval
Domgermain
Tréveray
Vaucouleurs
Blénod-lès-Toul
4
Cousances-les-Forges
Demange-aux-Eaux
Eurville-Bienville
Bayard-sur-Marne
Houdelaincourt
Chevillon
Colombey-les-Belles
Gondrecourt-le-Château
1
Joinville
Poissons
Saint-Urbain-Maconcourt
Coussey
23
Diarville
Grand
Neufchâteau
Doulaincourt-Saucourt
Liffol-le-Grand
Gironcourt-sur-Vraine
24
Froncles
Châtenois
Prez-sous-Lafauche
Mattaincourt
Manois
22
Andelot-Blancheville
Remoncourt
Dompaire
Bulgnéville
Vittel
Haréville
Bologne
Bourmont
Saint-Ouen-lès-Parey
Contrexéville
Ville-sur-Illon
Bourdons-sur-Rognon
Jonchery
Esnouveaux
Chaumont
Martigny-les-Bains
Biesles
Breuvannes-en-Bassigny
Darney
Semoutiers
Mandres-la-Côte
Lamarche
25
Foulain
Is-en-Bassigny
Monthureux-sur-Saône

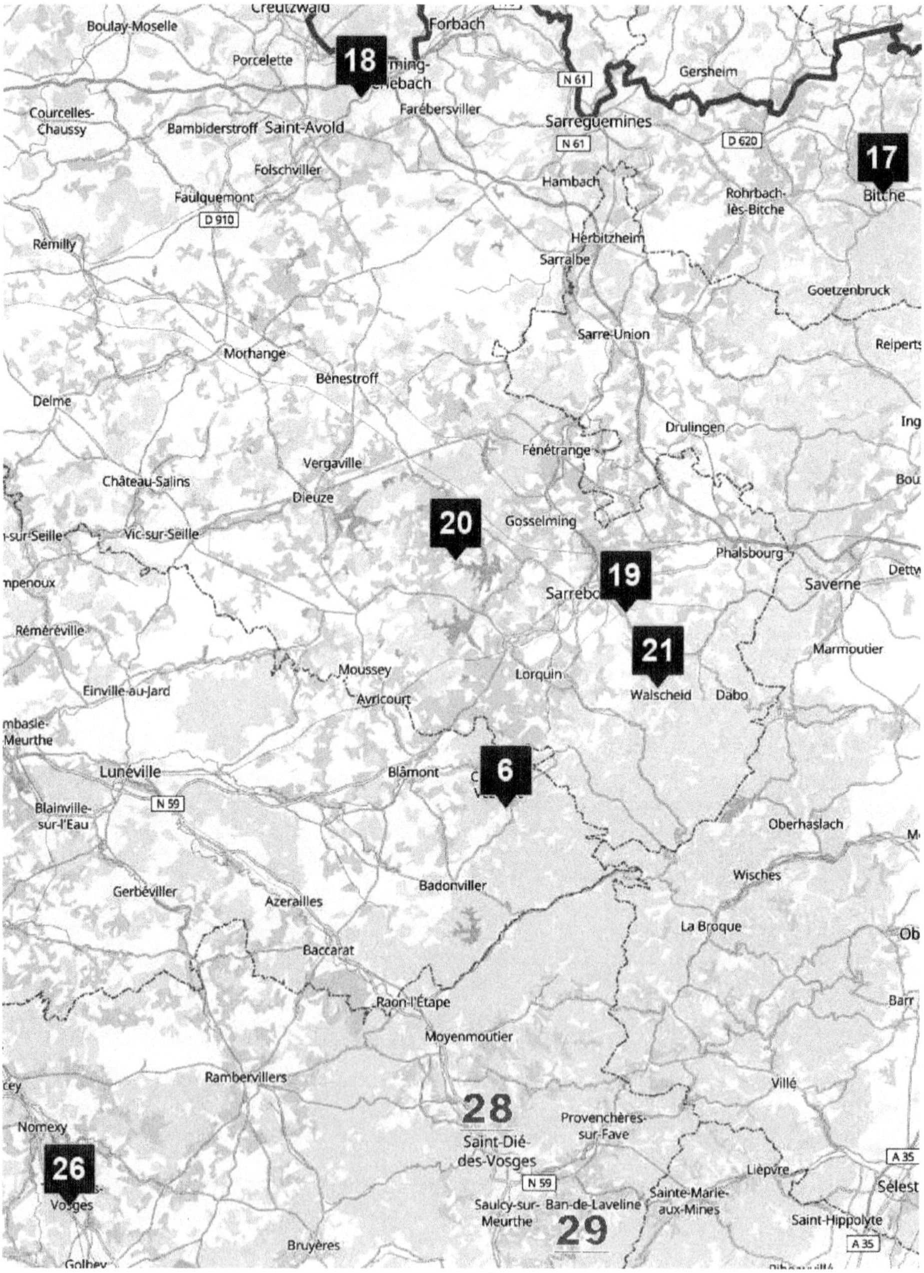
Boulay-Moselle
Forbach
18
Porcelette
Gersheim
N 61
Farébersviller
Courcelles-Chaussy
Bambiderstroff
Saint-Avold
Sarreguemines
N 61
D 620
17
Folschviller
Hambach
Faulquemont
Rohrbach-lès-Bitche
D 910
Herbitzheim
Rémilly
Sarralbe
Goetzenbruck
Sarre-Union
Morhange
Bénestroff
Delme
Drulingen
Fénétrange
Vergaville
Château-Salins
Dieuze
20
Gosselming
Vic-sur-Seille
Phalsbourg
19
Saverne
Réméréville
21
Marmoutier
Moussey
Lorquin
Einville-au-Jard
Avricourt
Walscheid
Dabo
6
Lunéville
Blâmont
Blainville-sur-l'Eau
N 59
Oberhaslach
Badonviller
Wisches
Gerbéviller
Azerailles
La Broque
Baccarat
Raon-l'Étape
Moyenmoutier
Rambervillers
Villé
28
Provenchères-sur-Fave
Nomexy
Saint-Dié-des-Vosges
A 35
26
N 59
Liepvre
Sainte-Marie-aux-Mines
Saulcy-sur-Meurthe
Ban-de-Laveline
Saint-Hippolyte
29
A 35
Bruyères

54 MEURTHE-ET-MOSELLE

FAVIERES

ADDRESS: RTE GELAUCOURT **TYPE OF AIRE:** MUNICIPAL
FACILITIES: WATER /GREY & BLACK DRAIN / ELECTRIC
LOCATION: RURAL **NO. OF SPACES:** 5
PRICES: PARKING: FREE **SERVICES**: FREE
OPENING TIMES: 01/05 - 31/10 **GPS:** N48.46649 E05.96143
DIRECTIONS: From FAVIERES follow signs for GELAUCOURT & 'Base de Loisirs'
SITE DESCRIPTION: *The aire is in a small tarmac parking area bordered by grass areas, next to the village leisure area & a large car park, little shade here but lit at night. The aire is close to a couple of lakes & grass areas, about 300m east of the village centre. AireServices service point with drainage platform.*

REVIEW: *A quiet, rural spot next to the Base de Loisirs & to the east of this little village with plenty of spaces in a car park as well as the 5 large marked camping-car spaces. Good rural views, busy during day in summer with cars but quiet at night. Bar/ restaurant with wifi (open all year), play area, walks, boules, small lakes & cycle tracks nearby with a couple of shops in the village, 10 mins walk away. There is also a small 25 space camping, which is open May – September with ehu's & showers/ toilets.*

MILLERY

ADDRESS: AVE DE LA MOSELLE, D40 **TYPE OF AIRE:** MUNICIPAL
FACILITIES: WATER /GREY & BLACK DRAIN/ ELECTRIC
LOCATION: SEMI-RURAL/ RIVERSIDE **NO. OF SPACES:** 7
PRICES: PARKING: FREE **SERVICES**: 2€ WATER or 5€ ELECTRIC (24 Hrs)
OPENING TIMES: ALL YEAR **GPS:** N48.81587 E06.12705
DIRECTIONS: From NORTH take D40 to MILLERY & AIRE is on RIGHT.
SITE DESCRIPTION: *The recently refurbished aire is situated between the Moselle river & the D40 road, on the east side of the village, in a tarmac car park with individual spaces, shade provided by mature trees & street lighting. Close to the boat moorings on the river. AireServices borne with 2 ehu's & a platform drain.*
REVIEW: *A very picturesque little aire (image on next page) on the side of the river, picnic area & next to a nice village but unfortunately there are no shops or amenities here apart from a restaurant & a boulanger van passes in the morning. Cycle routes along river. Some road noise during day but quiet at night. Handy for a stopover from A31 (Jcn 25).* *Millery opposite top*

PONT A MOUSSON

ADDRESS: PORT, AVE DES ETATS-UNIS **TYPE OF AIRE:** MUNICIPAL
FACILITIES: WATER /GREY & BLACK DRAIN/ ELECTRIC/ TOILETS/ WIFI
LOCATION: URBAN/ RIVERSIDE **NO. OF SPACES:** 40
PRICES: PARKING: 10€/ 24Hrs **SERVICES**: INCL
OPENING TIMES: ALL YEAR **GPS:** N 48.90271 E 06.06105
DIRECTIONS: Enter town from SOUTH on D120, 1st exit @ R/bout & LEFT to AIRE.
SITE DESCRIPTION: *The aire is in a large tarmac parking area with marked spaces next to a marina on the Moselle river & the Capitainerie, edged by grass areas, lit at night but having little shade. There are public toilets, hot showers as well as 5A ehu's, wifi & an artisanal service point with drainage grid. Aire is accessed by automatic barrier, pay at reception (8am-7pm).*

REVIEW: *A clean, modern well maintained & equipped aire in a nice location on the banks of the river with 24 hour electricity, wifi, toilets & showers. The aire has a couple of shops nearby & is within 300m of more shops/ several restaurants across the river. Interesting little town with an ancient abbey, churches & a museum.*

RICHARDMENIL

ADDRESS: RUE DU LAC, OFF D570 **TYPE OF AIRE:** MUNICIPAL

FACILITIES: WATER /GREY & BLACK DRAIN/ ELECTRIC/ RUBBISH
LOCATION: SEMI-RURAL/ CANAL **NO. OF SPACES:** 5
PRICES: PARKING: FREE **SERVICES**: FREE
OPENING TIMES: ALL YEAR **GPS:** N48.59463 E06.16110
DIRECTIONS: In RICHARDMENIL on D570, turn onto RUE DU LAC (one way) & follow road to CANAL & AIRE.
SITE DESCRIPTION: *This aire is located on the western side of this small town, next to the Canal de l'Est, 600m from the small town centre, bordered by woodland with the Moselle river nearby. The aire is in a small tarmac parking area accessed off a one-way road, surrounded by woodland, shaded & lit at night. Artisanal service point with drainage grid & separate ehu's.*

REVIEW: *On the edge of a forest, a pleasant small aire with 5 spaces in a green location, next to a road - quiet at night although a bit remote. Pleasant walks /cycling along canal with shops & restaurant in town.*

THIAUCOURT

ADDRESS: RUE DU STADE **TYPE OF AIRE:** MUNICIPAL
FACILITIES: WATER /GREY & BLACK DRAIN/ ELECTRIC/ RUBBISH
LOCATION: SEMI-RURAL **NO. OF SPACES:** 10
PRICES: PARKING: FREE **SERVICES**: 2€ WATER or ELECTRIC
OPENING TIMES: ALL YEAR **GPS:** N48.95218 E05.86092
DIRECTIONS: In THIAUCOURT, follow signs for 'La Loco' & AIRE.
SITE DESCRIPTION: *The aire is situated next to the tennis courts in a former campsite, on the west side of this small town, in a large tarmac/ gravel car park, with shade provided by mature trees & lighting at night. There is a Flot Bleu borne with a platform drain & separate point with 4 ehu's.*
REVIEW: *A quiet, well maintained aire located near to the village hall, being about 600m from the town centre. A*

pleasant spot, a bit remote but with plenty of spaces on gravel or grass, bordered by large grass areas. Good range of shops/ services & eating places including a small Carrefour.

VAL ET CHATILLON

ADDRESS: LA GRANDE RUE, D993A **TYPE OF AIRE:** MUNICIPAL
FACILITIES: WATER /GREY & BLACK DRAIN / ELECTRIC
LOCATION: URBAN **NO. OF SPACES:** 6
PRICES: PARKING: FREE **SERVICES**: 3€ WATER or ELECTRIC
OPENING TIMES: ALL YEAR **GPS:** N48.56078 E06.96507
DIRECTIONS: In village, AIRE is on WEST side of D933A, behind houses in car park.
SITE DESCRIPTION: *The aire in this small rural village is located in a 7 ha park area with a lake & stream, yet only a short walk from the village centre. There are 6 level spaces on tarmac/ grass, lit at night, separated by shrubs with shade in places bordered by grass areas & a play area for children. AireServices service point with 4 ehu's & a large drainage platform.*
REVIEW: *A modern & well laid out aire, in a pleasant park area within 100m of the village centre. A quiet spot with some shade but no shops in village although bread van passes each morning at 9am & there is a supermarket/ shops within 3kms. Textile museum in village & Abbey of St-Sauveur 4 kms away with way-marked walks nearby.*

Val et Chatillon

55 MEUSE

CHARNY SUR MEUSE

ADDRESS: OFF D115 **TYPE OF AIRE:** PRIVATE
FACILITIES: WATER /GREY & BLACK DRAIN/ ELECTRIC/ WIFI/ RUBBISH
LOCATION: RURAL/ RIVER **NO. OF SPACES:** 50
PRICES: PARKING: 11-13€/ 24 HRS **SERVICES**: INCL
OPENING TIMES: ALL YEAR **GPS :** N49.21121 E05.36599
DIRECTIONS: From NORTH take D964 SOUTH & D115 into CHARNY, cross RIVER then 1st RIGHT to AIRE.
SITE DESCRIPTION: *The private aire, run by the CampingCarPark company, is located close to the centre of Charny next to the Meuse river, with parking on grass pitches with lighting & reasonable shade – in a semi-rural location bordered by farmland, a lake & the river. This former campsite has up to 50 spaces on grass or hard standing with wifi (but only 20 x6A ehu's) & a Euro-Relais service point with a drainage*

platform. Access is via an automatic barrier operated by the CCP membership card topped up by credit card.

REVIEW: *A pleasant, quiet riverside location with shade in places & close to a cycle track along the Meuse to Verdun, the aire is convenient for the village, being 200m north of the centre with shops/ supermarket within 10 mins. Close to the Douaumont Fort & 8 kms from the Verdun memorial/ WWI battle sites.*

COMMERCY

ADDRESS: RUE DU DR. BOYER **TYPE OF AIRE:** MUNICIPAL
FACILITIES: WATER /GREY & BLACK DRAIN / ELECTRIC/ RUBBISH/ WIFI
LOCATION: URBAN/ CANALSIDE **NO. OF SPACES:** 4
PRICES: PARKING: FREE **SERVICES**: 3€ WATER or ELECTRIC
OPENING TIMES: ALL YEAR **GPS:** N48.76377 E05.59608
DIRECTIONS: From EAST take D958 to COMMERCY, cross CANAL & take 1st RIGHT & then 1st RIGHT to AIRE.
SITE DESCRIPTION: *The aire is located in a tarmac parking area next to the canal port on the eastern side of this town, lit at night with a little shade & about 400m to the town centre. There are 4 individual motorhome spaces with a small wooded area adjacent. Flot bleu borne with a platform drain & separate electric point. Jetons from machine or nearby OT.*

Commercy

REVIEW: *A pleasant, modern & well located aire, next to the canal with 4 large, level spaces, quiet but occasional noise from a railway line. Aldi supermarket 200m away & town centre with shops/ restaurants at 400m distance. Walks/ cycling along canal tow path.*

DIEUE SUR MEUSE

ADDRESS: OFF RTE DES DAMES **TYPE OF AIRE:** MUNICIPAL
FACILITIES: WATER /GREY & BLACK DRAIN
LOCATION: URBAN/ CANALSIDE **NO. OF SPACES:** 6
PRICES: PARKING: FREE **SERVICES**: FREE
OPENING TIMES: ALL YEAR **GPS:** N49.06995 E05.42668
DIRECTIONS: Entering village from NORTH on D964 turn RIGHT at 2nd R/bout & LEFT immediately before CANAL to AIRE.
SITE DESCRIPTION: *The aire is located next to the canal, about 250m west of the village centre, with half a dozen level spaces on grass, some shade & lit at night, accessed by a gravel track. Artisanal borne with a small drain.*
REVIEW: *A quiet location (below) overlooking the Canal de l'Est yet close to the shops, supermarket, OT & restaurants in this large village. Parking for several vehicles on grass shaded by mature trees with picnic tables adjacent. Walks/ discovery trails in area.*

DUN SUR MEUSE

ADDRESS: RUE DU VIEUX PORT **TYPE OF AIRE:** MUNICIPAL
FACILITIES: WATER /GREY & BLACK DRAIN / ELECTRIC / TOILETS/ WIFI
LOCATION: URBAN/ RIVER SIDE **NO. OF SPACES:** 12
PRICES: PARKING: 8€/ 24Hrs **SERVICES**: INCL
OPENING TIMES: 01/04 - 30/10 **GPS:** N49.38852 E05.17838
DIRECTIONS: Enter DUN from NORTH on D964 turn RIGHT after 'Dun Agri' to AIRE.
SITE DESCRIPTION: *This modern aire is situated next to & overlooking a mooring basin on the Meuse river, with parking on a dozen gravel spaces bordered by grass verges & small trees, accessed off a tarmac road. Aire is 300m north of the centre of village with nice views, lit at night & some shade, having a WC block, ehu's & an UrbaFlux borne with drainage platform.*
REVIEW: *An excellent, quiet & popular aire on the banks of the Meuse river, next to the marina, which has toilets/ showers, picnic tables, tourist info, laundry & wifi. The spaces (slightly sloping) have ehu's – 3 posts each with 4 sockets (included in fee), 7.5m limit on*

spaces. Short walk into village for shops, supermarket & restaurants as well as a good lakeside campsite. *Dun sur Meuse ↓*

HAIRONVILLE

ADDRESS: OFF RUE CHARLES COLLET, D4 **TYPE OF AIRE:** MUNICIPAL
FACILITIES: WATER /GREY & BLACK DRAIN / ELECTRIC/ RUBBISH
LOCATION: SEMI-RURAL/ RIVER **NO. OF SPACES:** 6
PRICES: PARKING: FREE **SERVICES**: 2€ WATER OR ELECTRIC
OPENING TIMES: ALL YEAR **GPS:** N48.68447 E05.08618
DIRECTIONS: From SOUTH take D4 to HAIRONVILLE & turn RIGHT just before BRIDGE to SALLE DES FETES &AIRE.
SITE DESCRIPTION: *Located outside the village hall, just 250m south of the small rural village centre, with spaces on gravel, lit at night & having some shade. The spaces are in a medium sized gravel car park surrounded by trees/ grass areas & there is an AireServices borne with a drainage platform in a drive-thru arrangement.*
REVIEW: *A fairly modern aire (below) in a pleasant spot off a side road, on the edge of the village, it is quiet at night & overlooks the small river Saulx. There are picnic tables, boulangerie, bar & Proxi grocer nearby with jetons available from shops. Possible noise from Hall at weekends.*

HEUDICOURT

ADDRESS: LAC DE MADINE, OFF D133 **TYPE OF AIRE:** PRIVATE
FACILITIES: WATER /GREY & BLACK DRAIN / TOILETS/ ELECTRIC
LOCATION: RURAL/ LAKE SIDE **NO. OF SPACES:** 40
PRICES: PARKING: 12€/ 24Hrs **SERVICES**: INCL
OPENING TIMES: ALL YEAR **GPS:** N48.93531 E05.71540
DIRECTIONS: From village take D133 EAST to Lac & follow signs for CampingCars.
SITE DESCRIPTION: *The aire is situated next to the large Lac de Madine, with parking on gravel/ grass, lit at night & shaded by trees accessed by a tarmac track & automatic barrier. Aire is 2km from the centre of village, with nice views & good shade. There is a WC block, ehu's, rubbish bins & a Flot Bleu borne with a drainage platform. No services Nov – March.*

REVIEW: *A very pleasant, quiet aire overlooking a large lake although quite remote. Busy in summer & employee comes round to collect fee in morning. Nearest shops/ services 6kms away but bread van calls each morning. Bathing, fishing in lake & walks.*

LES ISLETTES

ADDRESS: CSA, CHEMIN BOIS BACHIN **TYPE OF AIRE:** PRIVATE
FACILITIES: WATER /GREY & BLACK DRAIN / ELECTRIC / TOILETS
LOCATION: RURAL **NO. OF SPACES:** 15
PRICES: PARKING: 7€ /24 Hrs **SERVICES**: INCL
OPENING TIMES: ALL YEAR **GPS:** N49.12139 E05.03678
DIRECTIONS: From LES ISLETTES take D603 EAST, then D2E & D2C NORTH for 5km to Centre Social d'Argonne & AIRE.

SITE DESCRIPTION: *This private aire is located in the Argonne Forest with large spaces on gravel & shaded by trees. It is a fairly remote location, quiet & with plenty of spaces as well as a shower, WC's & picnic tables. There is a separate electric post with about 4 ehu's & a basic Artisanal service point with drainage grid. Tennis court & walks in the vicinity,*

REVIEW: *The site here is very tranquil & well equipped; there are heated showers & toilets, 16A ehu's, picnic tables & payment/ entry is via an automatic barrier. A very welcoming spot, well maintained, secure & clean with nice walks in the surrounding forest with some nearby WWI sites to visit. 10 mins from A4 autoroute, Jcn 29 but no services nearby.*

LIGNY EN BARROIS

ADDRESS: RUE JEAN WILLEMART, OFF N135 **TYPE OF AIRE:** MUNICIPAL
FACILITIES: WATER /GREY & BLACK DRAIN / ELECTRIC / WIFI/ RUBBISH
LOCATION: URBAN/ CANAL SIDE **NO. OF SPACES:** 8
PRICES: PARKING: 2€/ 24 Hrs **SERVICES**: 2€ WATER or ELECTRIC
OPENING TIMES: ALL YEAR **GPS:** N48.68775 E05.31975
DIRECTIONS: From WEST take N135 into LIGNY EN BARROIS, turn 1st LEFT after crossing CANAL to AIRE on LEFT.

SITE DESCRIPTION: *The aire is situated next to a mooring basin on a canal, 300m west of the centre of this small town, with parking on individual marked tarmac spaces bordered by grass verges & small trees, lit at night but little shade. There is wifi & an AireServices borne with drainage platform.*

REVIEW: *The aire here is well positioned & easy to find in a grassy location next to the canal basin. Parking is quiet & close to the shops/ supermarkets & restaurants with walks/ cycle routes along canal. Parking fee is collected by a Port official. Campsite nearby (open 01/06 - 30/09).*

NONSARD LAMARCHE

ADDRESS: OFF RUE BOIS GERARD **TYPE OF AIRE:** MUNICIPAL
FACILITIES: WATER /GREY & BLACK DRAIN/ ELECTRIC/ TOILETS
LOCATION: SEMI-RURAL/ LAKESIDE **NO. OF SPACES:** 40
PRICES: PARKING: 5-12€/ 24 Hrs **SERVICES**: INCL
OPENING TIMES: APRIL - OCT **GPS:** N48.92862 E05.75878
DIRECTIONS: From centre of NONSARD follow signs for 'Base de Loisirs' & AIRE.

SITE DESCRIPTION: *The aire here is situated next to Lac de Madine with ample parking spaces on tarmac or grass, surrounded by grassed areas & some shade from mature trees in places. Flot Bleu service point with platform drain but only 9 ehu's.*
REVIEW: *This is a pleasant spot (below) with nice walks/ cycling around the lake, very quiet & there is a restaurant nearby (open summer only), an OT & a beach but the nearest shops are 5km away. An employee of the campsite calls in the morning to collect the fee. Closed in winter.*

STENAY

ADDRESS: RUE DU PORT, OFF D947 **TYPE OF AIRE:** MUNICIPAL
FACILITIES: WATER /GREY & BLACK DRAIN / ELECTRIC / TOILETS
LOCATION: URBAN/ RIVERSIDE **NO. OF SPACES:** 55
PRICES: PARKING: 10€ / 24 Hrs **SERVICES**: INCL, 2€ SHOWER
OPENING TIMES: ALL YEAR **GPS:** N49.49095 E05.18379
DIRECTIONS: From WEST take D947 to STENAY, cross 2nd BRIDGE & turn 1st LEFT to large AIRE or cross 3rd BRIDGE & turn 1st LEFT to small AIRE.
SITE DESCRIPTION: *There are two aires in town, the large 49 space one is located in a large tarmac/ grass parking area on an island in the river with large trees giving good shade & the small 6 space aire is on the east bank of the river, closer to town but little shade. There are WC's & showers provided for each & there is an automatic barrier as well as an artisanal service point with platform drain & separate ehu's.*
REVIEW: *Very good aires that are both quiet & in a lovely place, with laundrette, clean toilets & hot showers as well as 6A ehu's, wifi & picnic tables. They are conveniently located next to the river yet only 5/ 10 mins walk to the town centre, but unfortunately there is not a lot to do - a small range of shops/ cafes & a Beer Museum (free entry). Market on Friday morning.*

57 MOSELLE

AMNEVILLE

ADDRESS : BEHIND OT, RUE DE L'EUROPE **TYPE OF AIRE:** MUNICIPAL
FACILITIES: WATER /GREY & BLACK DRAIN/ TOILETS/ ELECTRIC/ WIFI
LOCATION: SEMI-RURAL **NO. OF SPACES:** 14
PRICES: PARKING: 12€/ 24 Hrs **SERVICES**: INCL
OPENING TIMES: ALL YEAR **GPS:** N49.24772 E06.13798
DIRECTIONS: In town, follow signs for ZOO, AIRE is behind the OT & Coach park.
SITE DESCRIPTION: *A modern aire next to a Zoo, south of the town centre, with ample large, level spaces on tarmac off a tarmac road shaded by mature trees but little lighting at night. Raclet borne with drainage platform, ehu's, wifi & small modern automatic toilet block adjacent. Access by automatic barrier.*

REVIEW: *A pleasant, quiet (at night) aire located on the edge of a forest area, just behind the OT & next to the Zoo, hence parking can be limited during school holidays. Indoor ski centre, pool, thermal spa, bowling, restaurants are nearby & the town centre with its large range of shops/ eating places is about 800m away. Water & ehu's included in price but not available on all pitches, pay at OT.*

BITCHE

ADDRESS : RUE BOMBELLES **TYPE OF AIRE:** MUNICIPAL
FACILITIES: WATER /GREY & BLACK DRAIN/ TOILETS/ ELECTRIC
LOCATION: SEMI-URBAN **NO. OF SPACES:** 5
PRICES: PARKING: FREE **SERVICES**: 2€ WATER or ELECTRIC
OPENING TIMES: ALL YEAR **GPS:** N49.05431 E07.43382
DIRECTIONS: Take D35 WEST to BITCHE & take last exit @ R/bout & then 1st RIGHT to AIRE.
SITE DESCRIPTION: *A modern aire within 600m of the town centre with 5 reserved level spaces on tarmac for motorhomes separated by hedges, lighting & shaded by trees. The aire is beneath the town Citadel, surrounded by grass areas with picnic tables & further parking spaces adjacent. AireServices borne with drainage platform, 2 ehu's & toilets nearby.*
REVIEW: *A pleasant, quiet aire on the eastern side of the town next to a 17th C fortress built by Vauban with level parking & a footpath to the town centre. A quiet location but not much shade with adjacent lawns/ picnic tables, walks around citadel. Boulanger van calls in morning.*

Bitche

HOMBOURG HAUT

ADDRESS : RUE DES SUEDOIS **TYPE OF AIRE:** MUNICIPAL
FACILITIES: WATER /GREY & BLACK DRAIN/ TOILETS/ ELECTRIC
LOCATION: URBAN **NO. OF SPACES:** 7
PRICES: PARKING: FREE **SERVICES**: 2€ WATER or ELECTRIC
OPENING TIMES: ALL YEAR **GPS:** N49.12421 E06.77919
DIRECTIONS: From SOUTH take D603 to HOMBOURG HAUT, at 1st R/bout take last exit to STADE & AIRE on RIGHT.
SITE DESCRIPTION: *A modern aire located 200m south of the small village centre in a large tarmac parking area between the village hall & the football pitch. There are 7 level motorhome spaces separated by grass, not much shade but with lighting at night. Flot Bleu borne with drainage platform.*

REVIEW: *A quiet location with adjacent grass areas, woods, river, & walks/ cycle paths in area. InterMarche (with laundrette) adjacent & shops in village; butcher, boulangeries, grocers & several restaurants.*
Convenient for stopover off A4 autoroute (Jcn 40).

NIDERVILLER

ADDRESS: CANAL, OFF D45 **TYPE OF AIRE:** PRIVATE
FACILITIES: WATER/ GREY & BLACK DRAIN/ TOILETS/ LAUNDRY/ ELEC./ WIFI/ SHOWERS

LOCATION: SEMI-RURAL/ CANALSIDE **NO. OF SPACES:** 14
PRICES: PARKING: 17€/ 24Hrs **SERVICES**: INCL
OPENING TIMES: ALL YEAR **GPS:** N48.71722 E07.09889
DIRECTIONS: Take D45 SOUTH to NIDERVILLER, cross CANAL & turn 1st RIGHT to AIRE.
SITE DESCRIPTION: *This private aire is located next to the Rhein-Marne canal marina, 500m north of Niderviller in a semi-rural location surrounded by farmland on all sides. There are 14 hard-standing spaces for motorhomes next to the canal or behind the marina offices, all equipped with ehu's. Other facilities include toilets, laundry, showers & wifi but no drainage.*

REVIEW: *A very pleasant (but expensive) spot, located next to the canal with good facilities including wifi but no drainage. Quiet at night but some noise from boats during day, overnight fees payable at marina office. Old church in town & Porcelain factory to visit, museum in Sarrebourg. Superette, tabac, Poste, bank, chemist, restaurant & boulangerie in village.*

RHODES

ADDRESS: OFF RUE DE L'ETANG **TYPE OF AIRE:** MUNICIPAL
FACILITIES: WATER /GREY & BLACK DRAIN/ ELEC. / TOILETS/ SHOWERS
LOCATION: SEMI-RURAL/ LAKESIDE **NO. OF SPACES:** 25
PRICES: PARKING: 20€/ 24 Hrs **SERVICES**: INCL
OPENING TIMES: 01/04 - 31/10 **GPS:** N48.75778 E06.90055
DIRECTIONS: From NORTH take D95 to RHODES, continue to CHURCH & turn LEFT to AIRE.
SITE DESCRIPTION: *The aire is on the banks of a large lake & next to the Municipal campsite, parking is on grass /tarmac overlooking the lake with shade in places & lighting. There is an artisanal borne with a large platform drain & a modern toilet block/ washing up sinks.*
REVIEW: *The aire is part of the campsite (hence price), in a lovely location with quiet parking overlooking the lake/ marina. Price includes 16A hook up & use of borne / toilets/ showers. In summer there are boat trips/ watersports on the lake, fishing, play area for children & an Animal Park (3kms). 200m to small village centre where there is a grocers/ boulangerie & bar/ restaurant (July/Aug). Walks/ cycling around lake. Friendly warden on site 24/7.*

Rhodes

WALSCHEID

ADDRESS : ROUTE D'ALSACE **TYPE OF AIRE:** MUNICIPAL
FACILITIES: WATER /GREY & BLACK DRAIN / RUBBISH
LOCATION: SEMI-RURAL/ LAKE **NO. OF SPACES:** 6
PRICES: PARKING: 5€/ 24 Hrs **SERVICES**: INCL
OPENING TIMES: ALL YEAR **GPS:** N48.64587 E07.15659
DIRECTIONS: Take D96 NORTH to WALSCHEID, in centre turn 1st RIGHT to AIRE.
SITE DESCRIPTION: *A modern aire overlooking a large lake, located about 300m south of the village centre, with 6 marked level spaces on tarmac bordered by grass areas but with little shade nor lighting. Mini-Flot Bleu borne with drainage platform.*

REVIEW: *A pleasant, very quiet aire on the southern side of the small rural village located on the edge of a lake where there are 6 marked spaces, plus more parking, with picnic tables. In the village, there is a restaurant, bar/café, grocer/ tabac & a boulangerie (jetons/ pay here).*

88 VOSGES

BULGNEVILLE

ADDRESS: RUE DES RECOLLETS **TYPE OF AIRE:** MUNICIPAL
FACILITIES: WATER /GREY & BLACK DRAIN/ ELECTRIC/ TOILETS
LOCATION: SEMI-RURAL/ LAKESIDE **NO. OF SPACES:** 10
PRICES: PARKING: 4€/ 24 Hrs **SERVICES**: INCL
OPENING TIMES: ALL YEAR **GPS:** N48.20739 E05.83879
DIRECTIONS: From SOUTH take D164 into village centre, turn RIGHT at HOTEL to AIRE.
SITE DESCRIPTION: *The aire is in a purpose built medium sized tarmac parking area with spaces in a circular arrangement, next to grass areas, no shade but lighting & next to a lake on the eastern side of this village, 400m from the centre. Modern Artisanal borne with a drainage platform, toilets.*

REVIEW: *A nice quiet spot next to the lake & a large landscaped park area with tennis, fishing, boules & picnic tables. There are shops in village including a boulangerie, bars, supermarket, bank & restaurants. Council official collects fee in evening. Good stopover off A31, Jcn 9.*

CHARMES

ADDRESS: PORT DE PLAISANCE **TYPE OF AIRE:** MUNICIPAL
FACILITIES: WATER /GREY & BLACK DRAIN/ ELECTRIC /TOILETS/ WIFI
LOCATION: SEMI-RURAL/ CANALSIDE **NO. OF SPACES:** 70
PRICES: PARKING: 9€/ 24 Hrs **SERVICES**: INCL, SHOWERS 2€
OPENING TIMES: ALL YEAR **GPS:** N48.37392 E06.29467
DIRECTIONS: From NORTH cross RIVER into CHARMES, turn 1st RIGHT, then RIGHT & RIGHT again - under bridge to AIRE on LEFT.
SITE DESCRIPTION: *This popular aire is located alongside the canal with spaces on grass, a little shade under small trees, lighting, accessed off a tarmac road & about 250m from the town centre. Many spaces have ehu's & there is a shower block/ WC adjacent. Artisanal borne with a large platform drain. Access via automatic barrier.*
REVIEW: *A pleasant aire next to a canal in a green location, quiet although it can get very busy, & next to the waters edge with wifi & 6A electric. Close to the town centre where there are restaurants & some shops. Grass parking can be boggy in wet weather.*

Charmes

MIRECOURT

ADDRESS: PLACE THIERRY, OFF D266 **TYPE OF AIRE:** MUNICIPAL
FACILITIES: WATER /GREY & BLACK DRAIN / ELECTRIC/ TOILETS
LOCATION: URBAN/ RIVERSIDE **NO. OF SPACES:** 20
PRICES: PARKING: 7 €/ 24 Hrs **SERVICES**: INCL
OPENING TIMES: ALL YEAR **GPS:** N48.29952 E06.13573
DIRECTIONS: In MIRECOURT, turn into RUE CANON (sign Musee) & then LEFT to AIRE.
SITE DESCRIPTION: *The aire is located next to the river, on the eastern side of this small town, 200m from the town centre. Parking is alongside the river with spaces separated by shrubs on tarmac next to grass verges with young trees, a little shade & lighting at night. WC's nearby & a small park/ play area adjacent. AireServices service point with drainage grid, access by automatic barrier.*

REVIEW: *A nice modern aire next to a river & a small park with picnic tables/ playground, quiet with large spaces. Fee includes one use of either water or electric. Shops/ eating places nearby & 2 museums to visit with plenty of additional parking nearby.*

MONTHUREUX SUR SAONE

ADDRESS: RUE CROIX DE MISSION **TYPE OF AIRE:** MUNICIPAL
FACILITIES: WATER /GREY & BLACK DRAIN/ TOILETS/ RUBBISH/ WIFI
LOCATION: SEMI-RURAL/ RIVERSIDE **NO. OF SPACES:** 10
PRICES: PARKING: FREE **SERVICES**: INCL, 3€ WIFI
OPENING TIMES: ALL YEAR **GPS:** N48.03159 E05.97379
DIRECTIONS: From MONTHUREUX, take D460 NORTH & AIRE is on LEFT .
SITE DESCRIPTION: *The aire is in a small dedicated tarmac parking area with some shade, lit at night & next to the river Saone in a semi-rural location at the northern side of this linear village, 100m from the centre. There are 10 level spaces separated by grass verges with an adjacent toilet block. Artisanal borne with a large drainage grid.*

REVIEW: *A pleasant village aire overlooking the river, toilets adjacent with washing up sinks & wifi available (pay at Mairie). Short walk into pleasant rural village with a boulangerie, butcher, tabac, superette, bank, restaurant, Poste as well as an old church, wash house & remains of a château.*

PLAINFAING

ADDRESS: CROIX DES ZELLES, OFF D23 **TYPE OF AIRE:** MUNICIPAL
FACILITIES: WATER / GREY & BLACK DRAIN/ ELECTRIC/ WIFI
LOCATION: SEMI-URBAN **NO. OF SPACES:** 18
PRICES: PARKING: 6€/ 24 HRS **SERVICES**: INCL
OPENING TIMES: ALL YEAR **GPS :** N48.17101 E07.01368
DIRECTIONS: Entering town from SOUTH on D23, AIRE is on LEFT next to VIVAL.
SITE DESCRIPTION: *The aire here is located just south of the centre of this small town where there are 18 level spaces on tarmac, alongside grass areas in a circular arrangement within a short walk of the shops/etc. The parking has a little shade & is lit at night by street lamps. Artisanal service point with platform drain & ehu's, wifi.*

REVIEW: *A quiet spot yet within a short walk of the town centre, with a Vival superette adjacent. Good facilities including 24 hr electric hook-ups & wifi with a modern service point. Walks nearby.*

ST DIE LES VOSGES

ADDRESS: AVE VANNE DE PIERRE **TYPE OF AIRE:** MUNICIPAL
FACILITIES: WATER /GREY & BLACK DRAIN/ ELECTRIC/ WIFI
LOCATION: SEMI-URBAN/ RIVER **NO. OF SPACES:** 42
PRICES : PARKING: 6€/ 24 Hrs **SERVICES**: INCL
OPENING TIMES: ALL YEAR **GPS :** N48.28631 E06.96579
DIRECTIONS: From SOUTH take D420 to ST DIE, turn RIGHT over river & take 1st RIGHT to AIRE (signposted).
***SITE DESCRIPTION**: The aire here is in a large tarmac/ grass parking area with shade in places, lit at night & next to the river at the eastern edge of town, 1km from the centre & shops. 42 spaces on tarmac or grass, an artisanal borne with a large drainage platform, 16A ehu's & wifi. Access via automatic barrier.*

***REVIEW:** A pleasant, quiet shaded aire on the edge of town & next to the Meurthe river, there are no shops nearby but only 10 min level cycle ride into town centre where there are all amenities. Walks / cycle rides in the area, bowling alley & swimming pool just across river. Unfortunately the town is not very interesting.*

THAON LES VOSGES

ADDRESS: RUE DE COIGNET, OFF D62 **TYPE OF AIRE:** MUNICIPAL
FACILITIES: WATER /GREY & BLACK DRAIN /TOILETS/ SHOWERS
LOCATION: SEMI-RURAL/ CANAL **NO. OF SPACES:** 12
PRICES: PARKING: FREE **SERVICES**: 3€ WATER
OPENING TIMES: ALL YEAR **GPS:** N48.25017 E06.42519
DIRECTIONS: From town centre take D62 EAST over CANAL & 1st RIGHT to AIRE.
***SITE DESCRIPTION:** The aire is located next to a canal, 400m east of the town centre with parking on tarmac, WC's adjacent & a small park/ play area nearby. Modern artisanal service point with drainage platform in a lay by.*
***REVIEW:** A pleasant canal aire with a picnic area, small park/ playground, quiet with WC's /showers whilst the shops are quite close. Pitches are lit at night but there is no shade. Good walks & level cycle track to Epinal.*

ALSACE

Alsace region is made up of 2 departments; Bas-Rhin (67) & Haut-Rhin (68)

Bas-Rhin Map

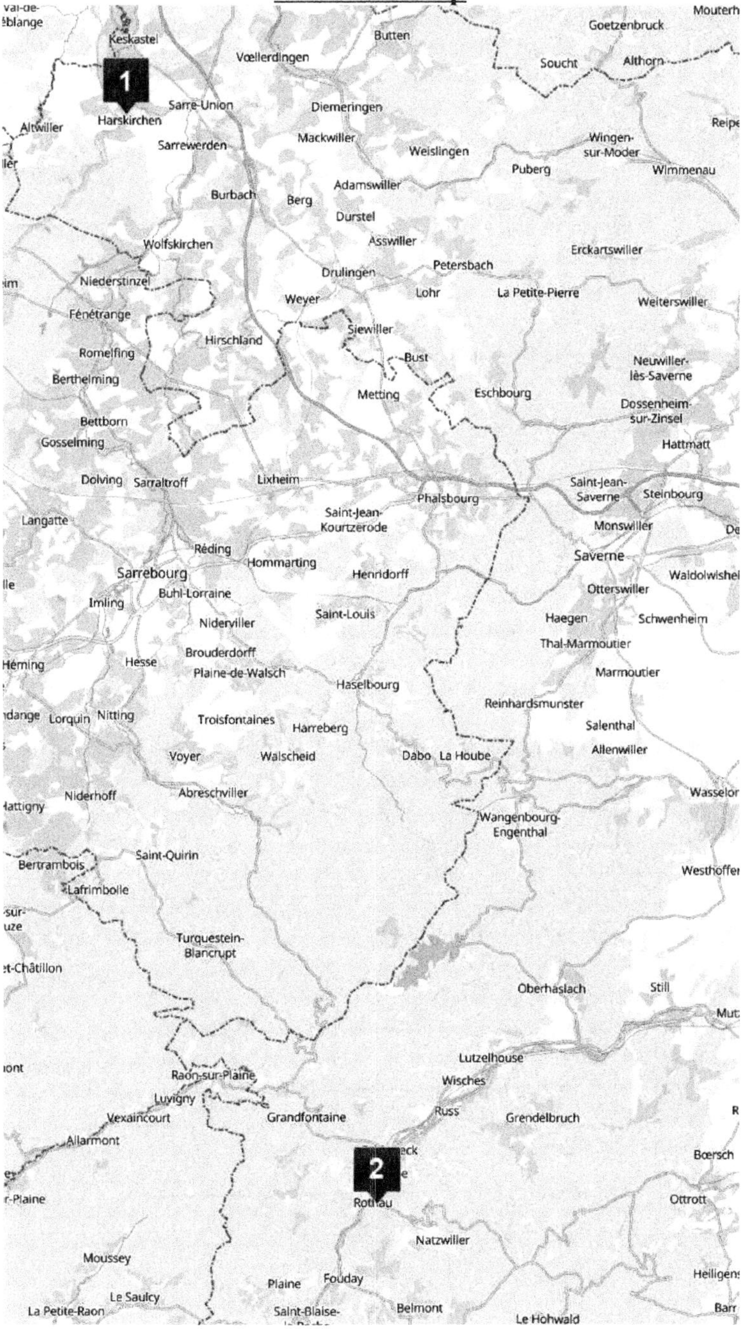

Haut-Rhin Map

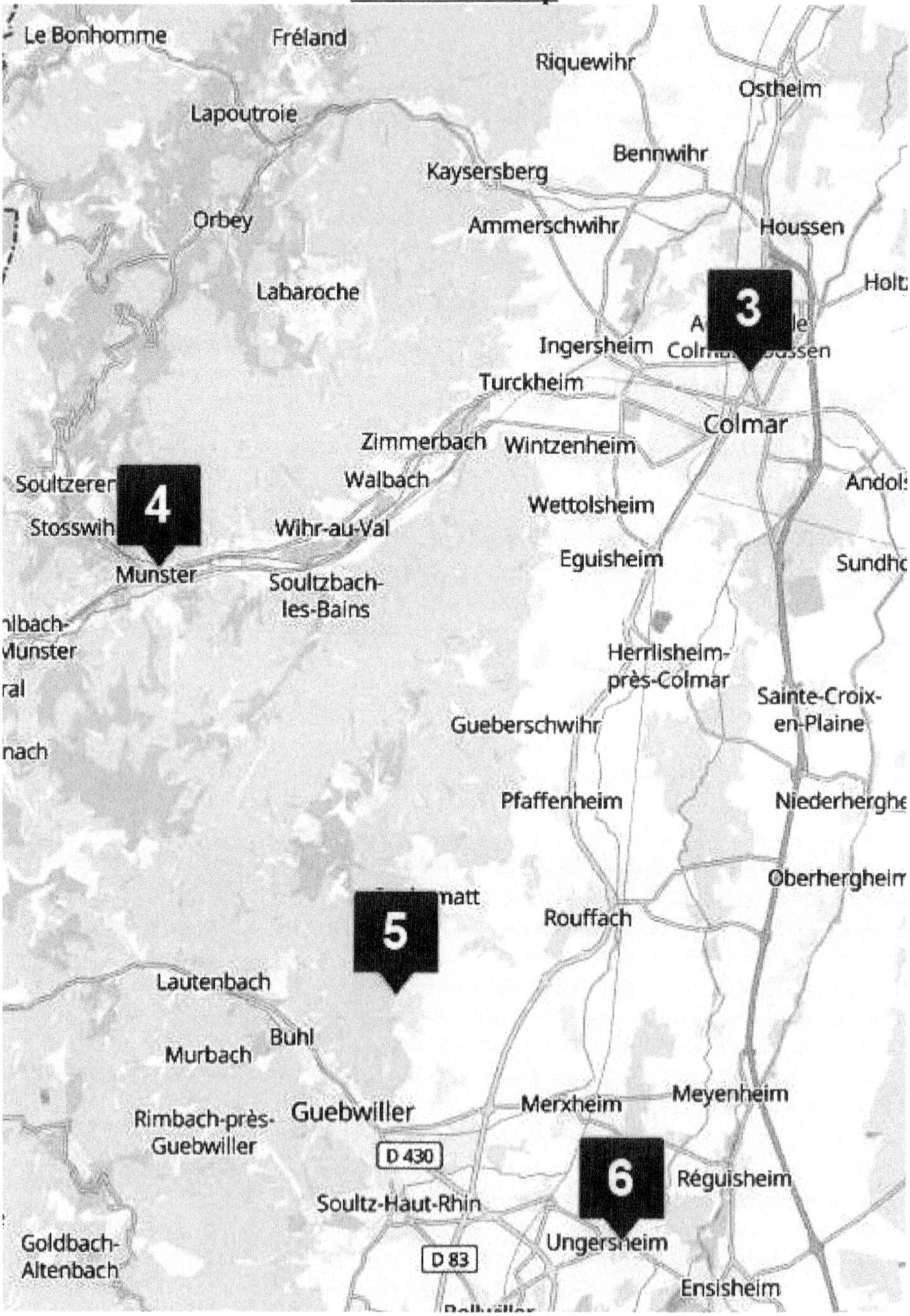

Key to Alsace Maps (above)

1) HARSKIRCHEN – 2) ROTHAU – 3) COLMAR
4) MUNSTER – 5) ORSCHWIHR – 6) UNGERSHEIM

67 BAS-RHIN

HARSKIRCHEN

ADDRESS: RUE DE BISSERT **TYPE OF AIRE:** MUNICIPAL
FACILITIES: WATER /GREY & BLACK DRAIN/ RUBBISH
LOCATION: RURAL/ CANAL **NO. OF SPACES:** 6
PRICES: PARKING: 10€/ 24Hrs **SERVICES**: 1€ WATER
OPENING TIMES: ALL YEAR **GPS:** N48.93906 E07.02808
DIRECTIONS: Take D23 WEST from village, cross CANAL & take 1st RIGHT to AIRE.
SITE DESCRIPTION *This modern aire is located next to the canal on the western edge of this rural village where there are half a dozen spaces on hard standing, bordered by grass, having a little shade & lit at night. The aire is in a quiet location surrounded by farmland with picnic tables available. Artisanal service point with drainage platform.*
REVIEW: *Quiet & clean, with pitches overlooking the canal, no services in winter. Access to toilets/ showers in the canal port is also available March – September. A short walk to the village centre where there are a few shops including a boulangerie & restaurant, with a campsite nearby.*

Harskirchen ↓

ROTHAU

ADDRESS: RUE P. MARCHAL, OFF D1420 **TYPE OF AIRE:** MUNICIPAL
FACILITIES: ELECTRIC /WATER /GREY & BLACK DRAIN/ WIFI
LOCATION: SEMI-RURAL **NO. OF SPACES:** 8
PRICES: PARKING: 8€/ 24 Hrs **SERVICES**: INCL
OPENING TIMES: ALL YEAR **GPS:** N 48.45245 E 07.19879
DIRECTIONS: Take D1420 EAST to ROTHAU, turn 1st LEFT & keep LEFT to AIRE.
SITE DESCRIPTION: *A modern aire, outside the Municipal campsite, on the western outskirts of the town where parking is on tarmac spaces with a grass area & picnic tables adjacent. Pitches are lit at night & shaded in places. Flot Bleu service point with small drain, 8 ehu's (available 5pm-10am) & wifi.*
REVIEW: *A lovely aire, managed by the adjacent 40 space campsite, in a semi-rural location on the edge of Rothau. Quiet with just the sound of the river, enjoyable country walks nearby & 500m to the town centre/ shops. Snack bar open in summer & bread can be ordered for next morning. Electric only available overnight.*

Rothau

68 HAUT-RHIN

COLMAR

ADDRESS: RUE DU CANAL **TYPE OF AIRE:** MUNICIPAL
FACILITIES: WATER /GREY & BLACK DRAIN/ ELECTRIC/ TOILETS/ WIFI
LOCATION: URBAN/ CANAL **NO. OF SPACES:** 30
PRICES: PARKING: 15€/ 24Hrs **SERVICES**: INCL
OPENING TIMES: ALL YEAR **GPS:** N48.08051 E07.37395
DIRECTIONS: Take D418 WEST to COLMAR, turn 2nd RIGHT after LECLERC to AIRE.
SITE DESCRIPTION: *The aire is in a tarmac parking area on the eastern side of the town, next to the canal, about 400m from the centre of the town. The aire has 30 spaces on tarmac or grass in a fenced/ gated enclosure, bordered by grass with trees providing shade in places & picnic tables available with lighting at night. Artisanal service point with grid, toilets adjacent, ehu's & wifi.*

REVIEW: *A pleasant, clean, secure & well maintained aire on the outskirts of the town - next to the canal but only a short walk to the picturesque historic centre with a Leclerc supermarket within 100m. 10A ehu's, free wifi (at the Capitainerie), toilets, bbq, showers & laundrette. Play area opposite, café adjacent & swimming pool nearby.*

MUNSTER

ADDRESS: RUE DU DR HEID **TYPE OF AIRE:** MUNICIPAL
FACILITIES: WATER /GREY & BLACK DRAIN/ ELECTRIC/ WIFI/ TOILETS
LOCATION: URBAN **NO. OF SPACES:** 49
PRICES: PARKING: 8€/ 24Hrs **SERVICES**: 3€ ELECTRIC or WATER
OPENING TIMES: ALL YEAR **GPS:** N48.03779 E07.13308
DIRECTIONS: Take D10 EAST to MUNSTER, then 1st exit @ R/bout & 4th RIGHT.
SITE DESCRIPTION: *The aire is located in a large tarmac parking area at the southern side of the town, 300m from the centre. Aire is lit at night & shaded by trees on the southern side, spaces on hard standing accessed by tarmac road, entry by automatic barrier. AireServices service point with ehu's, pressure washer, drainage platform & modern toilets adjacent.*

REVIEW: *A well equipped aire, close to the centre of this small town. Electric (6A or 16A) available, machine issues jetons for services, free wifi, washing-up sinks with hot water, toilets & showers, picnic tables, bbq & petanque. Some noise from adjacent railway line but quiet at night. 44 large spaces plus 5 extra long spaces. Good range of shops & services, nice rural area surrounding town.*

ORSCHWIHR

ADDRESS: ROUTE DE SOULTZMATT, D5 **TYPE OF AIRE:** MUNICIPAL
FACILITIES: WATER /GREY & BLACK DRAIN / ELECTRIC / RUBBISH
LOCATION: SEMI-RURAL **NO. OF SPACES:** 5
PRICES: PARKING: FREE **SERVICES**: 5€ WATER or ELECTRIC
OPENING TIMES: ALL YEAR **GPS:** N47.93775 E07.23169
DIRECTIONS: Take D5 SOUTH to COLMAR, turn RIGHT @ 1st Zebra crossing.
SITE DESCRIPTION: *This modern aire is found on the northern outskirts of the village next to the tennis courts & surrounded by vineyards. Parking is in marked spaces on tarmac, lighting but little shade & 200m to the village centre. Flot Bleu service point, with a large platform drain.*

***REVIEW:** On the route of the Vins d'Alsace, between the vineyards & the forest, this is a well-made aire in a park area; but there are only 4 or 5 spaces available. A quiet spot with nice views & not far from the village centre where there is a boulangerie & some wine cellars with tastings available.*

UNGERSHEIM

ADDRESS: ECOMUSEE, CHEMIN DU GROSSWALD, **TYPE OF AIRE:** PRIVATE
FACILITIES: WATER /GREY & BLACK DRAIN
LOCATION: URBAN **NO. OF SPACES:** 25
PRICES: PARKING: 7€ / 24 Hrs **SERVICES**: INCL
OPENING TIMES: 06/04 - 03/11 **GPS:** N47.85175 E07.28579
DIRECTIONS: Follow signs for 'ECOMUSEE' & then 'PARKING/ BUS'.
***SITE DESCRIPTION:** A private aire in the grounds of the EcoMusee (an open air museum), about 4 kms south of village, with pitches on gravel/ grass & shaded under mature trees, accessed by a tarmac track but little lighting. Parking is guarded at night. Artisanal service point with drainage platform.*

REVIEW:** The aire is very quiet with nice spaces on grass, in a reserved area with plenty of room but a basic service point & remote from anywhere else. Interesting museum (history of the Alsace region) in a large 25 ha location with over 70 ancient buildings re-erected within the museum grounds, a restaurant, shop & boulangerie. Pay at reception, museum is closed on Mondays.* ***NOTE: The parking area was being redeveloped at time of going to press, now with covered parking under solar panels.

PAYS-DE-LA-LOIRE

Pays-de-la-Loire region is made up of 5 departments; Loire-Atlantique (44), Maine-et-Loire (49), Mayenne (53), Sarthe (72) & Vendee (85)

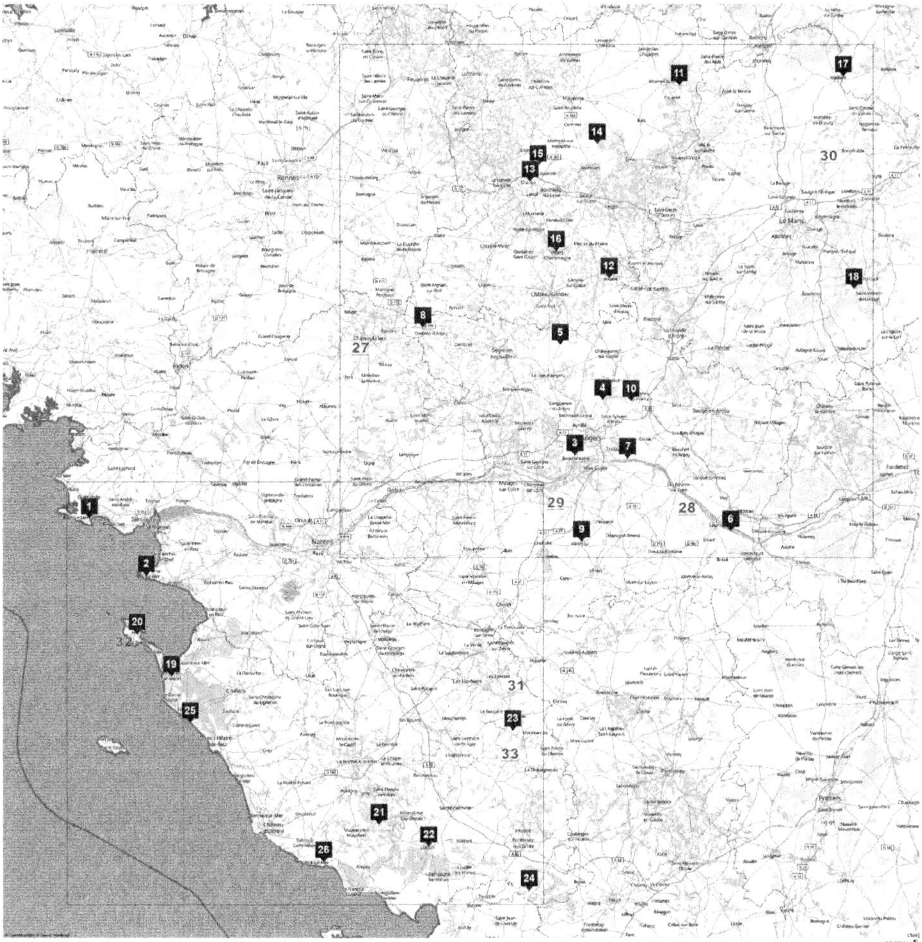

Key to enlarged Pays-de-la-Loire Maps (on next 2 pages)

Former campsites that are now aires are noted in ***bold***

1) LE POULIGUEN – ***2) PREFAILLES*** – ***3) BOUCHEMAINE*** – *4) BRIOLLAY*
5) CHENILLE CHANGE – ***6) DAMPIERE SUR LOIRE*** – *7) LA DRAGUENIERE*
8) POUANCE – 9) VALANJOU – 10) VILLEVEQUE – 11) AVERTON – ***12) BOUERE***
13) ~~CHANGE~~ – 14) DEUX EVAILLES – ***15) ST JEAN SUR MAYENNE***
16) VILLIERS-CHARLEMAGNE – 17) MAMERS – 18) PRUILLE L'EGUILLE

19) LA BARRE DE MONTS – 20) LA GUERINIERE – 21) LE CHAMP ST PERE
22) LUCON – 23) LA MEILLERAIE-TILLAY – 24) MAILLE – 25) ST JEAN-DE-MONTS
*26) ST VINCENT SUR JARD – 27 CHATEAUBRIANT – **28) CHENEHUTTE***
***29) VAL DU LAYON** – 30) BRIOSNE – **31) SEVREMONT** - 32) L'EPINE*
33) MOUILLERON

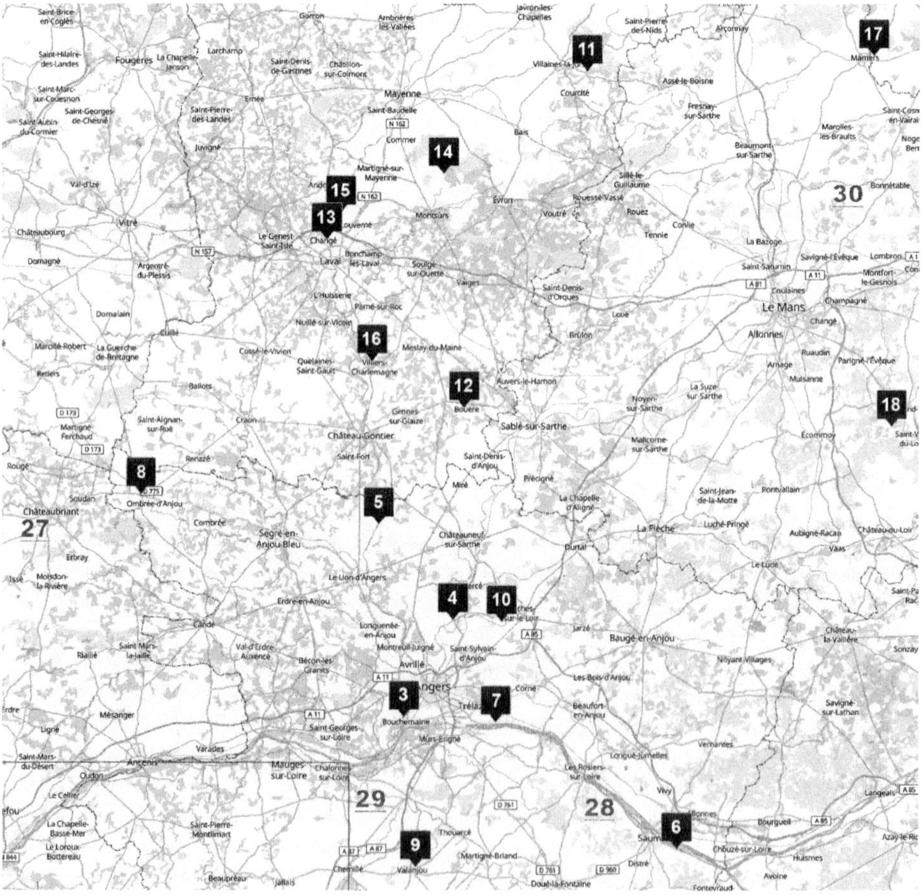

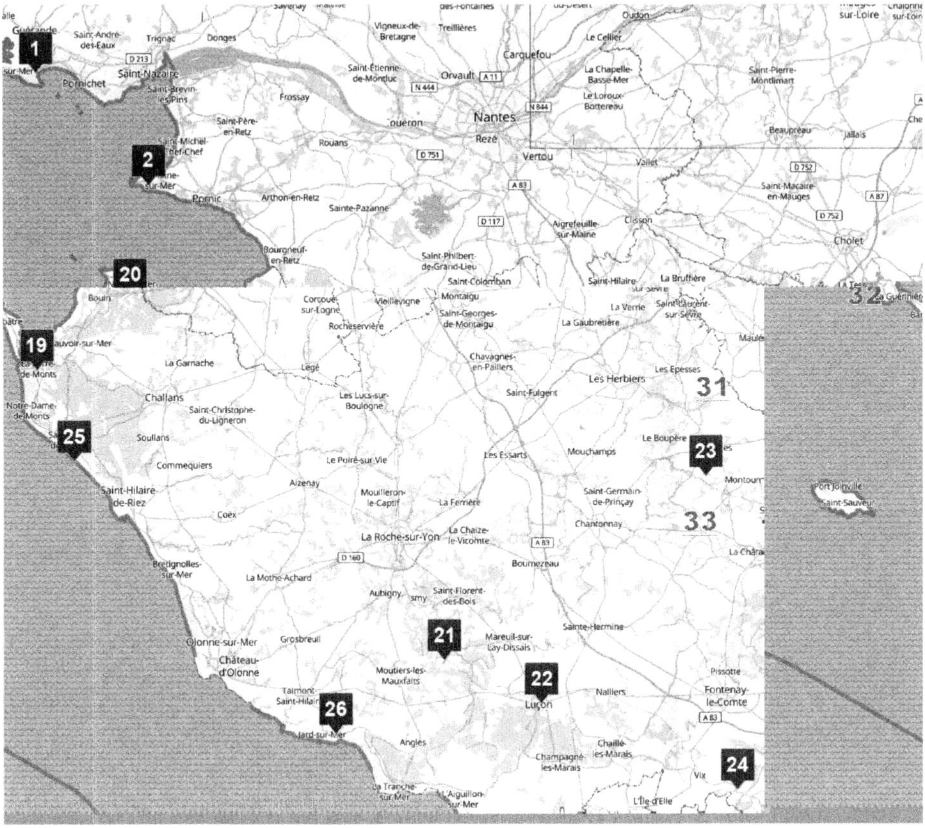

44 LOIRE-ATLANTIQUE

CHATEAUBRIANT

ADDRESS: RUE GUY MOQUET **TYPE OF AIRE:** MUNICIPAL
FACILITIES: WATER /GREY & BLACK DRAIN / ELECTRIC/ RUBBISH
LOCATION: SEMI-RURAL/ LAKES **NO. OF SPACES:** 20
PRICES: PARKING: 10€/ 24 Hrs **SERVICES**: INCL
OPENING TIMES: ALL YEAR **GPS :** N47.73122 W01.37975
DIRECTIONS: Entering town from NORTH on D41, AIRE is on LEFT after lakes.
***SITE DESCRIPTION**: This aire is managed by AireParkReservation, located in a tarmac surface parking area with spaces separated by up-stands, little shade but lit at night, next to large leisure lakes & 1km north of the town centre & it's shops. An AireServices service point with a large platform drain & ehu's on each space. Access is via automatic barrier, reservation possible online.*
***REVIEW:** Nicely located close to 3 large leisure lakes & park areas but some road noise from adjacent D41, although quiet at night. Walks around lakes, play area, aquatic centre nearby. Medieval town with good range of shops, 2 long cycle paths, markets on Wed & Sat. The town also has a second more basic aire at its southern end, outside the municipal campsite.*

Chateaubriant

LE POULIGUEN

ADDRESS: CAMPING, AVE DE L'OCEAN **TYPE OF AIRE:** MUNICIPAL
FACILITIES: WATER /GREY & BLACK DRAIN/ELECTRIC/ TOILETS/ WIFI
LOCATION: URBAN/ BEACH **NO. OF SPACES:** 26
PRICES: PARKING: 11-13€/ 24Hrs **SERVICES**: INCL
OPENING TIMES: ALL YEAR **GPS:** N47.27198 W02.43285
DIRECTIONS: In the town follow signs for 'CAMPING LE CLEIN', AIRE is outside.
SITE DESCRIPTION: *This aire is located at the entrance to the town campsite 'Le Clein' where there are 26 level spaces on grass accessed by a tarmac track & shaded by small trees. The aire is within 200m of the town centre & 250m from the beach. Access is via an automatic barrier (open 7am - 11pm) controlled by a credit card machine that issues a code. AireServices service point with drainage platform, ehu's & toilet block.*

REVIEW: *A well maintained & well located aire within short walks of both the town centre & its beach. Quiet spot with some shade & has access to the campsites toilets/ showers plus wifi, there is also a laundrette & play area. Price includes services but there are only 12 ehu's (6A) for 26 spaces, also the spaces are only 8m in length so not really suitable for long vehicles. Good selection of shops/ restaurants within short walk & cycle routes nearby. Campsite is open 20/03 – 04/ 10 & has 128 spaces.*

PREFAILLES

ADDRESS: RUE DU PORT AUX ANES **TYPE OF AIRE:** PRIVATE
FACILITIES: WATER /GREY & BLACK DRAIN/ ELECTRIC/ WIFI/ RUBBISH
LOCATION: SEMI-RURAL **NO. OF SPACES:** 49
PRICES: PARKING: 11€/ 24Hrs **SERVICES**: INCL
OPENING TIMES: ALL YEAR **GPS :** N47.13873 W02.22213
DIRECTIONS: Take D313 WEST towards La Pointe, follow CCP signs to AIRE on RIGHT.
SITE DESCRIPTION: *This aire, run by Camping Car Park, is located 1km to the north of Prefailles, next to a campsite in a large parking area reserved for motorhomes. The aire is in a former campsite & has 49 large (35m^2) spaces on grass accessed by a gravel track, with shade in places & 1km from the sea. Access is via an automatic barrier, CCP card required. Euro Relais service point with double drainage platforms, all spaces have 4A ehu's as well as wifi. Shops & bar/ restaurant nearby.*

REVIEW: *A nice seaside aire, with large grassy pitches separated by shrubs, no services nearby but there is access to the adjacent campsite facilities (shop/ bar/ restaurant/ play area & pool) from 01/03 – 15/11 when there is also a warden present.*

49 MAINE-ET-LOIRE

BOUCHEMAINE

ADDRESS: RUE CHEVRIERE **TYPE OF AIRE:** MUNICIPAL
FACILITIES: WATER /GREY & BLACK DRAIN / TOILETS/ ELECTRIC/ WIFI
LOCATION: URBAN/ RIVER **NO. OF SPACES:** 40
PRICES: PARKING: 9 - 15€/ 24 hrs **SERVICES**: INCL
OPENING TIMES: ALL YEAR **GPS:** N47.41890 W0.61115
DIRECTIONS: From EAST take D112 over RIVER to BOUCHEMAINE, turn LEFT @ R/bout & AIRE is 400m on LEFT.
SITE DESCRIPTION: *Situated in the former municipal Campsite, south of the town & on the banks of the Maine river, in a large tarmac & grass parking area, the individual spaces are well separated by grass with trees providing shade. WC's & showers are available from 1/03 to 31/10. Previous winner of "Aire of the Year".*

REVIEW: *A nice quiet place with a lovely walk along the river, also good for cyclists. The aire benefits from the facilities of the old campsite; wifi, electricity, showers, WC & washing up sinks. Shops are 10 mins walk away, boulanger calls in summer & there is a bus stop for Angers in front of the aire. No toilets, water or wifi in winter & aire is closed the first weekend in September.*

CHENEHUTTE TREVES CUNAULT

ADDRESS: RUE DE BEAUREGARD, D751 **TYPE OF AIRE:** MUNICIPAL
FACILITIES: WATER /GREY & BLACK DRAIN/ ELECTRIC/ RUBBISH
LOCATION: RURAL/ RIVER **NO. OF SPACES:** 20
PRICES : PARKING: FREE /72 HRS **SERVICES**: 4€ WATER or ELECTRIC (6 hrs)
OPENING TIMES: ALL YEAR **GPS :** N47.32676 W0.19452
DIRECTIONS: AIRE is located on D751, between Treves & Cunault, next to Loire.
***SITE DESCRIPTION**: This aire is situated between the hamlets of Cunault & Treves, next to the D751 road in a former campsite with mature trees providing some shade & lighting at night. There are 20 level spaces on grass overlooking the Loire, accessed by a gravel track. The Euro-Relais service point has a drainage platform & electric point.*

REVIEW: *A pleasant aire with walks along the river, some road noise during day but quiet at night. Ground can be quite soft after rain. Aire is a bit remote with no facilities nearby but very tranquil, shops & eating places in Gennes – 3km away.*

BRIOLLAY

ADDRESS: OFF ROUTE DE TIERCE, D52 **TYPE OF AIRE:** MUNICIPAL
FACILITIES: WATER /GREY & BLACK DRAIN/ TOILETS/ RUBBISH
LOCATION: SEMI-RURAL/ RIVERSIDE **NO. OF SPACES:** 10
PRICES: PARKING: FREE **SERVICES**: 2€ WATER
OPENING TIMES: ALL YEAR **GPS:** N47.56771 W00.50681
DIRECTIONS: From BRIOLLAY take D52 NORTH, turn LEFT just before BRIDGE & 1st RIGHT to AIRE (signposted).

SITE DESCRIPTION: *The aire is in an excellent location on the banks of the Sarthe river, about 200m north of the town centre with parking on gravel/ grass & with small trees providing some shade. A quiet position but the grass areas can get muddy & this area is also liable to flooding during heavy rainfall. AireServices service point with drainage platform & modern toilets.*

REVIEW: *A pleasant aire in a green location, next to the river where it is quiet at night. Parking on gravel with a small park, picnic tables & a playground nearby. Jetons from garage, Mairie or shops in town; boulangerie, superette & bar/ tabac.*

CHENILLE CHANGE

ADDRESS: NEXT TO D78 & RIVER **TYPE OF AIRE:** MUNICIPAL
FACILITIES: WATER /GREY & BLACK DRAIN
LOCATION: SEMI-RURAL/ RIVER **NO. OF SPACES:** 8
PRICES: PARKING: 6€/ 24 Hrs **SERVICES**: INCL
OPENING TIMES: ALL YEAR **GPS:** N47.69940 W0.66718
DIRECTIONS: Take D78 SOUTH from CHENILLE & turn 1st RIGHT to AIRE.

SITE DESCRIPTION: *Aire is situated south of the village, just off the D78 road in a large gravel car park with trees providing some shade & overlooking the Mayenne river. The service point only has water & a grey drainage grid; if you need black drainage & electricity - these can be found in the small 20 pitch campsite adjacent. There are WC's at the nearby Base Nautique.*

REVIEW: *A pleasant basic little aire with walks in the surrounding village, fishing in the river, river cruises (in season) & a picnic area. It is only a short walk from the aire to the centre of this very attractive village with a small river port, ancient houses, 12th C church, water mill, restaurant & cafe (that supplies jetons - closed Wed.), but no shops.*

DAMPIERE SUR LOIRE

ADDRESS: OFF ROUTE DE SAUMUR, D947 **TYPE OF AIRE:** MUNICIPAL
FACILITIES: WATER /GREY & BLACK DRAIN/ TOILETS
LOCATION: RURAL/ RIVERSIDE **NO. OF SPACES:** 70
PRICES: PARKING: 8€/ 24Hrs **SERVICES**: INCL
OPENING TIMES: 01/ 04 – 31/10 **GPS:** N47.24116 W00.02260
DIRECTIONS: From WEST take D947 to DAMPIERE & AIRE is on LEFT.
SITE DESCRIPTION: *The aire is located in a pleasant, shaded riverside location on the northern side of this small village, about 50m from the village centre. There are ample parking spaces on grass, accessed by a tarmac track & bordered by the river Loire - having good shade under mature trees. UrbaFlux service point & platform drain with a small toilet block adjacent.*

REVIEW: *A pleasant large aire, located in a former Municipal campsite close to the centre of a small rural village. The village has no shops but there is a wine producer (who sells wine direct) & 2 restaurants. Bread van calls each morning as well as a pizza van in the evenings. Council official calls to collect fee. Play area & tennis courts nearby. Loire cycle path adjacent that leads to Saumur (5kms).*

LA DAGUENIERE

ADDRESS: PORT MAILLARD, south of VILLAGE **TYPE OF AIRE:** MUNICIPAL
FACILITIES: WATER /GREY & BLACK DRAIN/ TOILETS
LOCATION: SEMI-RURAL/ RIVERSIDE **NO. OF SPACES:** 10
PRICES: PARKING: FREE **SERVICES**: 2€ WATER
OPENING TIMES: ALL YEAR **GPS:** N47.41771 W00.43754
DIRECTIONS: From EAST take D952 WEST to LA DAGUENIERE, at R/bout continue straight on D952 & take next LEFT to AIRE.

SITE DESCRIPTION: *The aire is located on the south side of this little rural village, in a large gravel/ grass parking area, bordered by the river Loire, with trees for shade but no lighting. The aire is about 200m from the village centre, with toilets nearby. Artisanal service point with platform drain is located separately next to the football pitch on the north side of the village on Rue du Stade.*
REVIEW: *A nice location next to the river in a large parking area where there are picnic tables plus bbq provided, access is quite narrow & difficult for large vehicles. The pleasant little village has a boulangerie, grocer & a small restaurant as well as bike hire. Jetons from shops.*

POUANCE

ADDRESS: RUE DE L'HIPPODROME **TYPE OF AIRE:** MUNICIPAL
FACILITIES: WATER /GREY & BLACK DRAIN/ TOILETS/ ELEC./ SHOWERS
LOCATION: RURAL/ LAKE **NO. OF SPACES:** 6
PRICES: PARKING: 6€/ 24Hrs **SERVICES**: INCL
OPENING TIMES: ALL YEAR **GPS:** N47.75247 W01.18003
DIRECTIONS: From POUANCE take D6 NORTH & turn LEFT after 500m to ST AUBIN, cross BRIDGE & AIRE is on LEFT opposite CHURCH.
SITE DESCRIPTION: *The aire is in a small tarmac car park north of Pouance alongside a minor road & overlooking the St Aubin lake with spaces on grass for up to 6 vehicles. A pleasant location bordered by grass areas but there is not much shade nor lighting here. Artisanal borne with drainage platform as well as toilets, rubbish bins & ehu's.*

REVIEW: *A nice small aire in a quiet rural location overlooking a large lake with walks, about 1 km from the town centre. Toilets with showers adjacent, picnic tables & 4 ehu's. Parking fee is only payable when town campsite is open (01/05 – 15/09), free at other times. Small range of shops in town as well as several eating places/ bars, medieval château nearby.*

VALANJOU

ADDRESS: RUE DE LA MAIRIE, D84 **TYPE OF AIRE:** MUNICIPAL
FACILITIES: WATER /GREY & BLACK DRAIN / ELEC. / TOILETS / RUBBISH
LOCATION: URBAN **NO. OF SPACES:** 6
PRICES: PARKING: FREE **SERVICES**: FREE

OPENING TIMES: ALL YEAR **GPS:** N47.21662 W0.60369
DIRECTIONS: From WEST take D84 to VALANJOU & AIRE is signposted to LEFT.
SITE DESCRIPTION: *The aire is surrounded by grass areas in a residential area, only 300m west of the village centre with parking on gravel shaded by the surrounding trees. There are also WC's next to the artisanal service point, 1 ehu & a drainage platform.*

REVIEW: *A comfortable aire, in a green verdant spot, quiet and nicely situated near to a small lake, large grass areas & a play area yet only 5 mins to the shops. Services were all free, picnic tables provided & a modern toilet block.*

VAL DU LAYON

ADDRESS: RUE JEAN DE PONTOISE **TYPE OF AIRE:** PRIVATE
FACILITIES: WATER /GREY & BLACK DRAIN/ ELECTRIC/ WIFI/ TOILETS
LOCATION: RURAL/ RIVER **NO. OF SPACES:** 27
PRICES: PARKING: 11-13€/ 24HRS **SERVICES**: INCL
OPENING TIMES: ALL YEAR **GPS :** N47.32803 W00.67129
DIRECTIONS: Approaching village from WEST on D125, turn 1st RIGHT to AIRE.
SITE DESCRIPTION *This 'Camping Village' aire, run by CampingCarPark, is situated in the former municipal campsite, about 200m south west of the small village centre & next to the river Layon. Pitches are on gravel/ grass (most shaded), lit at night, each has 6A ehu & wifi with toilets (open 01/04-30/09). Artisanal service point with drainage platform. Access by automatic barrier, CCP card required.*

REVIEW: *A pleasant location next to the river yet close to the village & quiet with good shaded pitches but some low branches. Toilets cleaned daily but only open April- Sept. Grocer, cafe & bar in village as well as Anjou wine producers.*

VILLEVEQUE

ADDRESS: RUE DU PORT **TYPE OF AIRE:** MUNICIPAL
FACILITIES: WATER /GREY & BLACK DRAIN/ TOILETS
LOCATION: URBAN/ RIVERSIDE **NO. OF SPACES:** 10
PRICES: PARKING: FREE **SERVICES**: 2€ WATER
OPENING TIMES: ALL YEAR **GPS:** N47.56217 W00.42250
DIRECTIONS: From town take D113 NORTH towards BRIDGE & 1st LEFT to AIRE.
SITE DESCRIPTION: *A well situated aire, in a large gravel car park on the northern edge of the town, next to the Loir river & about 150m from the town centre. The parking is bordered by grass verges & lined with trees providing some shade. Artisanal service point with platform drain & adjacent toilet block. Jetons from shops, Mairie or OT.*

REVIEW: *A very pleasant location, next to & overlooking the Loir river, with an adjacent picnic area with tables. Quiet at night, plenty of spaces, level parking, good walks/ cycling, shops & restaurant are a short walk away. Beach on river with fishing & swimming possible. Nice little museum & château (open every day May to Oct) in town.*

53 MAYENNE

AVERTON

ADDRESS: LES PERLES, OFF D121 **TYPE OF AIRE:** MUNICIPAL
FACILITIES: WATER /GREY & BLACK DRAIN/ ELECTRIC/ TOILETS
LOCATION: RURAL/ LAKE **NO. OF SPACES:** 15
PRICES: PARKING: FREE **SERVICES**: 2.5€ WATER or ELECTRIC
OPENING TIMES: ALL YEAR **GPS:** N48.34753 W00.24441
DIRECTIONS: From VILLAINES take D121 EAST, after 2kms turn RIGHT to LES PERLES & AIRE is on LEFT after 500m..
SITE DESCRIPTION: *The aire is located near to a lake, on the northern side of the hamlet of Les Perles – about 2km north of Averton itself. The pitches are on tarmac, some having shade under trees, only 50m from a large lake. Flot Bleu service point with drainage platform, pay by credit card.*
REVIEW: *Very pleasant spot (opposite) but quite remote from anywhere, with a large 7ha fishing lake, cycling/ walks around it, play area, bbq & sheltered picnic tables. Quiet with ample parking, nearest shops /services are at Villaines-la-Juhel, 2kms west.*

BOUERE

ADDRESS: RUE DES SENCIES, D14 **TYPE OF AIRE:** MUNICIPAL
FACILITIES: WATER /GREY & BLACK DRAIN
LOCATION: SEMI-RURAL/ LAKE **NO. OF SPACES:** 15
PRICES: PARKING: FREE **SERVICES**: 2€ WATER or ELECTRIC
OPENING TIMES: ALL YEAR **GPS:** N47.86333 W00.47611
DIRECTIONS: AIRE is near to the village centre, off D14, opposite BAR/TABAC .
SITE DESCRIPTION: *This municipal aire is located on the site of the former Municipal campsite, on the eastern side of the village – about 150m from the centre. The pitches are well laid out in pairs on grass, separated by high hedges & some having shade under mature trees. Euro-Relais service point with drainage platform. Jetons from shops or Mairie.*

REVIEW: *An excellent address, nice pitches with picnic tables, bbq, quiet yet close to the village centre, only 100m from a large 1.5ha lake with fishing, park & good walks nearby. Shops in the village include a boulangerie, grocer & a café/tabac/bar, there is also a 12th C church, a listed cemetery & some old industrial workings.*

DEUX EVAILLES

ADDRESS: LA PICHARDIERE, OFF D129 **TYPE OF AIRE:** MUNICIPAL
FACILITIES: WATER /GREY & BLACK DRAIN / TOILETS/ RUBBISH
LOCATION: RURAL/LAKE **NO. OF SPACES:** 20
PRICES: PARKING: FREE **SERVICES**: FREE
OPENING TIMES: ALL YEAR **GPS:** N48.20205 W00.52034

DIRECTIONS: From DEUX EVAILLES take D129 NORTH for 1km & turn RIGHT at sign "La Fenderie" to AIRE.
SITE DESCRIPTION: *Situated about 1km north of the small rural hamlet, a large aire next to a large leisure lake. There is shade here from mature trees, with ample parking on grass but just 6 spaces on hard standing, accessed by a tarmac road.. Euro Relais borne with platform drain.*
REVIEW: *A well maintained tranquil aire in a very pleasant location; next to a large leisure lake where you can walk/ cycle, fish or swim with a play area, beach, mini-golf & seasonal restaurant. Toilets adjacent, cleaned daily but remote from any shops/ services. Roman ruins within 4kms. Restaurant & lake below ↓*

ST JEAN SUR MAYENNE

ADDRESS: RUE DU MOULIN, OFF D162 **TYPE OF AIRE:** MUNICIPAL
FACILITIES: WATER /GREY & BLACK DRAIN/ ELEC./ TOILETS/ RUBBISH
LOCATION: URBAN/ RIVER **NO. OF SPACES:** 25
PRICES: PARKING: 11€ /24Hrs **SERVICES**: INCL
OPENING TIMES: 01/04 – 13/11 **GPS:** N48.12781 W00.75250
DIRECTIONS: In village, take D162 SOUTH & turn LEFT before BRIDGE to AIRE.
SITE DESCRIPTION: *The aire is next to the river in a tarmac parking area just south of the village centre. The location is in the former municipal campsite where there are level spaces on tarmac separated by hedges & grass areas shaded by trees & lit at night. Artisanal service point with drainage platform, toilets & ehu's.*

REVIEW: *A well-equipped & maintained aire, facilities include; toilets, hot showers, ehu's, bbq, covered picnic area, washing-up sinks & handicapped access. The aire is*

well laid out with grass areas & direct access to the Mayenne river & its tow-path. Nice village but few facilities; tabac/ bar (sells bread) & visiting pizza/ butchers vans (Tues) plus crêpes van (Thurs). Fee collected daily by council official. Fishing & boat hire on river. Aire is closed Nov-April.

VILLIERS-CHARLEMAGNE

ADDRESS: RUE DES HAIES **TYPE OF AIRE:** MUNICIPAL
FACILITIES: WATER /GREY & BLACK DRAIN / ELECTRIC
LOCATION: SEMI-RURAL/ LAKESIDE **NO. OF SPACES:** 5
PRICES: PARKING: 6€ /24 Hrs **SERVICES**: INCL
OPENING TIMES: ALL YEAR **GPS:** N47.92094 W0.68275
DIRECTIONS: Exit N162 onto D20 to VILLIERS & take 1st RIGHT to AIRE.
SITE DESCRIPTION: *The aire is situated next to a holiday village, 500m from the village centre, centred around a large fishing lake edged by its holiday chalets. The parking is close to the lake with pitches on grass, some with shade under the trees, & these are accessed by a tarmac track. Euro-Relais borne with a drainage grid & 1 ehu.*

REVIEW: *A very nice, tranquil aire, especially if you fish, in a quiet situation on the side of a fishing lake alongside holiday chalets. Picnic area, play area, good walks with Mayenne towpath nearby. Restaurant in village.*

72 SARTHE

BRIOSNE LES SABLES

ADDRESS: RUE DES SABLONS, D83 **TYPE OF AIRE:** MUNICIPAL
FACILITIES: WATER /GREY & BLACK DRAIN/ ELECTRIC/ TOILETS
LOCATION: SEMI-URBAN/ LAKE **NO. OF SPACES:** 10
PRICES : PARKING: FREE **SERVICES**: 2€ WATER or ELECTRIC
OPENING TIMES: ALL YEAR **GPS :** N48.17343 E00.39365
DIRECTIONS: Entering village from SOUTH on D83, AIRE is on LEFT.
SITE DESCRIPTION *This small municipal aire is located on the western edge of the village, 300m from the centre, just off the main D83 road thru the village. The aire is next to the leisure area in a park where a dozen spaces are available on gravel, shaded by trees in places, bordered by grass areas with a little lighting. Euro-Relais service point with drainage platform.*

REVIEW: *There is an adjacent large leisure/ fishing lake, picnic tables, play area & boules pitches all surrounded by farmland. No shops in village apart from a restaurant that also sells bread & jetons.*

MAMERS

ADDRESS: RUE DE LA PISCINE **TYPE OF AIRE:** MUNICIPAL
FACILITIES: WATER /GREY & BLACK DRAIN / ELECTRIC
LOCATION: URBAN/ NEAR LAKE **NO. OF SPACES:** 9
PRICES: PARKING: 8-15€ / 24 Hrs **SERVICES**: INCL
OPENING TIMES: 28/04 - 01/10 **GPS:** N48.35639 E0.37145
DIRECTIONS: From NORTH take D113 off ring-road into town & 1st RIGHT to AIRE.
SITE DESCRIPTION: *The aire is in a medium sized gravel car park, next to the Municipal campsite, enclosed by a chain link fence in a compound with automatic gates (digicode supplied by OT or campsite). Small trees in the compound provide a little shade & the aire is next to a large park,*

lakes, tennis courts, 800m to the town centre. Artisanal borne with a large platform drain.
REVIEW: *The aire is in a gravel car park, with individual (but small) spaces separated by hedges, next to a nice park & some large lakes (fishing possible) – with good walks. The Municipal campsite with snack bar is 100m away & there is a good range of shops/ eating places in town.*

PRUILLE L'EGUILLE

ADDRESS: LA QUELLERIE, D13 **TYPE OF AIRE:** PRIVATE
FACILITIES: WATER /GREY DRAIN/BLACK DRAIN / SHOWERS
LOCATION: RURAL **NO. OF SPACES:** 20
PRICES: PARKING: 8€ / 24 Hrs **SERVICES**: 2€ WATER or ELECTRIC
OPENING TIMES: ALL YEAR **GPS:** N47.82498 E00.42629
DIRECTIONS: From PRUILLE take D13 SOUTH & turn LEFT after 1km into AIRE.
SITE DESCRIPTION: *This 'aire naturelle' is situated in a large flat open field bordered by high hedges & an adjacent forest. Plenty of spaces on grass accessed by a gravel track, no problem manoeuvring but little lighting & some shade next to forest. Artisanal service point with drainage platform, 12 ehu's & small sanitary block.*

REVIEW: *Very quiet rural campsite in a pleasant spot with friendly proprietor. Ehu's available, service point & toilets/ showers (bit dated). Fishing in lake, tennis, signposted walks/ cycling in forest & petanque. A few shops can be found in the small village 1km away.*

85 VENDEE

LA BARRE DE MONTS

ADDRESS: ROUTE DE GRANDE COTE **TYPE OF AIRE:** PRIVATE
FACILITIES: WATER /GREY & BLACK DRAIN / ELECTRIC/ RUBBISH/ WIFI
LOCATION: RURAL/ BEACH **NO. OF SPACES:** 59
PRICES: PARKING: 14€/ 24 Hrs **SERVICES**: INCL
OPENING TIMES: ALL YEAR **GPS:** N46.88540 W02.15151
DIRECTIONS: From village take RTE DE GRANDE COTE, EAST to AIRE.
SITE DESCRIPTION: *The aire is run by CampingCarPark company & is in a large parking area 800m west of the village of Fromentine & 200m from the beach, with shade in places under pine trees & grass areas adjacent. Euro-Relais service point with drainage platform, 6A ehu's & wifi. Access by automatic barrier, CCP card required.*
REVIEW: *A well maintained, quiet aire close to nice beaches & a forest with walks/ good level cycle routes. 40 ehu's for 49 pitches, variable reception for wifi. No shops nearby apart from seasonal shop in adjacent campsite. Fromentine is a port for ferries to Ile d'Yeu.*

La Barre de Monts

LA GUERINIERE

ADDRESS: L'ESCALE'ILE, D38 **TYPE OF AIRE:** PRIVATE
FACILITIES: WATER /GREY & BLACK DRAIN/ ELECTRIC/WIFI
LOCATION: SEMI-URBAN **NO. OF SPACES:** 49-98
PRICES: PARKING: 9-15€/ 24Hrs **SERVICES**: INCL
OPENING TIMES: ALL YEAR **GPS :** N46.96592 W02.21583
DIRECTIONS: Entering the isle NOIRMOUTIER on D38, take last exit at R/bout before village, turn immediately LEFT & LEFT again to AIRE.
SITE DESCRIPTION: *The aire is in the large gravel/ grass parking area outside the campsite "L'Escale d'Ile". It is about 600m east of the centre of town & 300m from the beach, access is via 24/7 automatic barrier operated by credit card, lighting at night but no shade here. Flot Bleu service point with drainage platform, ehu's/ wifi available on all spaces.*

REVIEW: *A large well maintained aire near to the beach, no shade but quiet at night. The aire has 8A ehu's, wifi, CCTV & access to the campsite facilities (bar/restaurant, mini-mart, toilets & pool) when open (mid-April-Sept). Rate is seasonal & 49 additional grass pitches are added in summer making 98 total.*

LE CHAMP ST PERE

ADDRESS: OFF, RUE DE LA NANTE, D12 **TYPE OF AIRE:** PRIVATE
FACILITIES: WATER /GREY & BLACK DRAIN/ELECTRIC/ RUBBISH
LOCATION: URBAN **NO. OF SPACES:** 19
PRICES: PARKING: 9€/24 Hrs **SERVICES**: INCL
OPENING TIMES: ALL YEAR **GPS:** N46.50551 W01.34938
DIRECTIONS: From SOUTH on D12, turn LEFT as you enter LE CHAMP to AIRE.
SITE DESCRIPTION: *This private aire, run by AireParkReservation, is situated 150m from the centre of this small village, just off the main road on the southern side of the village in a medium sized gravel parking area with 19 level spaces. Aire is bordered by grass areas/ trees & backs on to farmland, access is via automatic barrier. Sanistation service point with platform drain & ehu's.*

REVIEW: *A pleasant, secure & quiet location within 200m from the village centre. Large spaces with electric, shade in places, lit at night & picnic tables. Facilities in the village; boulangerie, butcher, bar/ restaurant, Carrefour supermarket & tabac/ news. Short walk to a lake. Reservation possible online.*

L'EPINE

ADDRESS: RUE DES ORMEAUX, OFF D95, **TYPE OF AIRE:** MUNICIPAL
FACILITIES: WATER /GREY & BLACK DRAIN/ ELEC./ TOILETS/ RUBBISH
LOCATION: URBAN **NO. OF SPACES:** 62
PRICES : PARKING: 10€ /24HRS **SERVICES**: INCL
OPENING TIMES: ALL YEAR **GPS :** N46.98063 W02.26414
DIRECTIONS: Take D95 WEST to L'EPINE over R/bout & 1st LEFT to AIRE.
SITE DESCRIPTION: *This large aire is managed by AireParkReservation, located on the eastern edge of L'Epine with salt marshes to the east. Spaces are on tarmac in a large parking area bordered by grass areas, no shade but lighting at night. The aire is about 1km from the sea & 400m from L'Epine centre where there are some shops/ eating places & a market on Saturday mornings. AireServices service point with drainage platform, toilets & ehu's. Reservation possible online.*
REVIEW: *A pleasant aire, parking is quiet at night & services are well maintained. Superette, restaurant & picnic area adjacent. Level walk/ cycle to sea & good beaches. Price reduces for subsequent nights.*

L'Epine

LUCON

ADDRESS: RUE DE LA CLAIRAYE **TYPE OF AIRE:** PRIVATE
FACILITIES: WATER /GREY & BLACK DRAIN/ ELECTRIC/ WIFI
LOCATION: RURAL/ LAKE **NO. OF SPACES:** 25
PRICES: PARKING: 17€/ 24Hrs **SERVICES**: INCL
OPENING TIMES: ALL YEAR **GPS:** N46.43306 W01.18297
DIRECTIONS: In LUCON, take RUE DU PORT, SOUTH & then RUE CLAIRAYE.

SITE DESCRIPTION: *This private aire is located 2kms south of the small town within the 3* Domaine des Guifettes campsite where parking is located in a separate tarmac area with individual spaces separated by hedges & small trees offering some shade. Pitches have individual 16A ehu's, wifi & there is an artisanal service point with drainage grid.*
REVIEW: *A quiet, well equipped lakeside aire with access to the campsite facilities (April - Nov): toilets/ showers, laundrette, restaurant, covered swimming pool, jacuzzi, tennis, play area, large lake (with beach & fishing) & mini golf. Dogs & wifi extra. Nice walks/ cycling around the lake.*

LA MEILLERAIE-TILLAY

ADDRESS: RUE DES OMBRAGES **TYPE OF AIRE:** MUNICIPAL
FACILITIES: WATER /GREY & BLACK DRAIN / TOILETS/ RUBBISH
LOCATION: URBAN **NO. OF SPACES:** 8
PRICES: PARKING: FREE **SERVICES**: FREE
OPENING TIMES: 01/ 04 – 31/10 **GPS:** N46.73892 W00.84527
DIRECTIONS: AIRE is well signposted in village.

SITE DESCRIPTION: *The aire is in a large gravel car park 150m south from the small village centre & next to a park/ play area with a little shade under trees, lit at night & a grass area adjacent. Artisanal service point with a large drainage platform & an adjacent toilet block. Jetons from the Mairie or shops.*

REVIEW: *A well equipped aire in a quiet location, bordered by a park & farmland on 3 sides, a small clean toilet block with hot showers (1€ by jeton) & washing-up sinks. Few facilities in village, just a boulangerie, superette & a couple of eating places.*

MAILLE

ADDRESS: RUE DE LA PETITE CABANE **TYPE OF AIRE:** MUNICIPAL
FACILITIES: WATER /GREY & BLACK DRAIN/ ELECTRIC/TOILETS
LOCATION: RURAL/ CANAL **NO. OF SPACES:** 8
PRICES: PARKING: 9€ /24Hrs **SERVICES**: INCL
OPENING TIMES: ALL YEAR **GPS:** N46.34040 W00.79602
DIRECTIONS: In village head WEST to CANAL & cross bridge to CAMPING, AIRE is adjacent.

SITE DESCRIPTION: *The aire is located 400m from the small rural village centre, in a long gravel parking area, next to the canal & outside the municipal campsite on the western side of the village. There is a toilet block in the camping with showers & washing up sinks, ehu's available. Artisanal service point with drainage platform.*

REVIEW: *A very pleasant & quiet location next to the Canal de Bourneau with picnic tables, shade under mature trees but no lighting. Good walks along canal towpath & level cycle routes. Long lead needed for electric as sockets are in campsite. Few facilities in village, just a bar & boulangerie. Fee payable at Canal office.*

MOUILLERON ST GERMAIN

ADDRESS: RUE DU PAVE **TYPE OF AIRE:** PRIVATE
FACILITIES: WATER /GREY & BLACK DRAIN/ ELECTRIC/ WIFI/ TOILETS
LOCATION: SEMI-URBAN **NO. OF SPACES:** 25
PRICES: PARKING: 11-13€/ 24HRS **SERVICES**: INCL
OPENING TIMES: ALL YEAR **GPS :** N46.67153 W00.84527
DIRECTIONS: Entering village from SOUTH on D89, AIRE is on LEFT.
SITE DESCRIPTION *This 'Camping Village' aire, run by CampingCarPark, is situated in the former municipal campsite 'La Pree du Pave', about 300m south of the village centre close to farmland. Pitches are on gravel/ grass (many shaded) each with 6A ehu & wifi with toilets (open 01/07-30/08). Artisanal service point with drainage platform. Access by automatic barrier, CCP card required.*

REVIEW: *A nice semi-rural location yet close to the village centre & quiet with large pitches. Good toilets/ showers, cleaned daily but only open July & Aug, wifi very poor. Shops in village; boulangerie, grocer, & bar/ eating places. Several walking trails from village.*

ST JEAN-DE-MONTS

ADDRESS: RUE DE LA PAREE DU JONC **TYPE OF AIRE:** PRIVATE
FACILITIES: WATER /GREY & BLACK DRAIN/ ELECTRIC/ TOILETS/WIFI
LOCATION: SEMI-RURAL **NO. OF SPACES:** 30
PRICES: PARKING: 9 - 13€ /24Hrs **SERVICES**: INCL
OPENING TIMES: ALL YEAR **GPS :** N46.80524 W02.11264
DIRECTIONS: From ST JEAN take D38 WEST & follow signs to Camping & AIRE.

SITE DESCRIPTION: *The aire is in a large tarmac parking area with marked spaces in an area of pine forests, 3 km to the north west of St Jean & about 200m from the beaches. The aire has about 30 spaces but has no shade, is surrounded by a high wall & access is via an automatic barrier. The parking area is in a fairly quiet spot next to a campsite (open 04/05 –29/09) but there are few other facilities nearby. There is a drainage grid & hook up on each parking space plus many spaces also have a tap, toilets are nearby.*
REVIEW: *A quiet spot within walking distance of the beach, a well equipped, modern aire with wifi & individual 6A ehu's but no greenery. Slight slope on spaces. Pay for access to campsite facilities (bar/ restaurant & entertainment) when open.*

ST VINCENT SUR JARD

ADDRESS: CHEMIN DES ROULETTES **TYPE OF AIRE:** PRIVATE
FACILITIES: WATER /GREY & BLACK DRAIN / ELECTRIC/ WIFI
LOCATION: URBAN/ BEACH **NO. OF SPACES:** 48
PRICES: PARKING: 13€/ 24 Hrs **SERVICES**: INCL
OPENING TIMES: ALL YEAR **GPS:** N46.41048 W01.54109
DIRECTIONS: In village take D19A to sea & follow road EAST to BEACH & AIRE.

Aire at St Vincent

SITE DESCRIPTION: *The aire is run by CampingCarPark, in a large tarmac parking area with some shade under trees, & 150m from the beach – bordering a residential area & farmland, about 700m south of the village centre. Pitches each have ehu/ wifi with an AireServices borne & drainage platform. Access via automatic barrier, CCP card required.*

REVIEW: *A well located spacious aire next to one of St Vincent's three beaches, large pitches, quiet at night but busy in summer, not very close to the village although it is an easy & level walk or bike ride. There is a market in the village on Friday & Sunday mornings in July/August & the village has a few shops/ restaurants as well as a SuperU (with fuel). Tariff reduces in winter.*

SEVREMONT

ADDRESS: RUE DES PONTS, LA POMMERAIE/SEVRE **TYPE :** MUNICIPAL
FACILITIES: WATER /GREY & BLACK DRAIN/ TOILETS
LOCATION: RURAL **NO. OF SPACES:** 12
PRICES: PARKING: FREE **SERVICES**: FREE
OPENING TIMES: ALL YEAR **GPS :** N46.83785 W00.77477
DIRECTIONS: In LA POMMERAIE, take D43 NORTH & AIRE is on LEFT as you leave village.

SITE DESCRIPTION: *The aire is in a small gravel/ grass parking area, a former campsite, with 12 spaces, bordered by grass areas with good shade, lit at night & near to the river, about 150 m north of the large village centre of La Pommeraie. There is an artisanal borne with a platform drain, water & toilets.*

REVIEW: *A nice basic aire with free services & parking, a short walk into the village where there are a few shops & a restaurant. Quiet spot in a former municipal campsite next to a park area with picnic tables & close to a fishing river. 15Kms from the theme park Puy du Fou.*

CENTRE-VAL DE LOIRE

Centre-Val de Loire region is made up of 6 departments; Cher (18), Eure-et-Loir (28), Indre (36) Indre-et-Loire (37), Loir-et-Cher (41) & Loiret (45)

Centre-Val de Loire Map

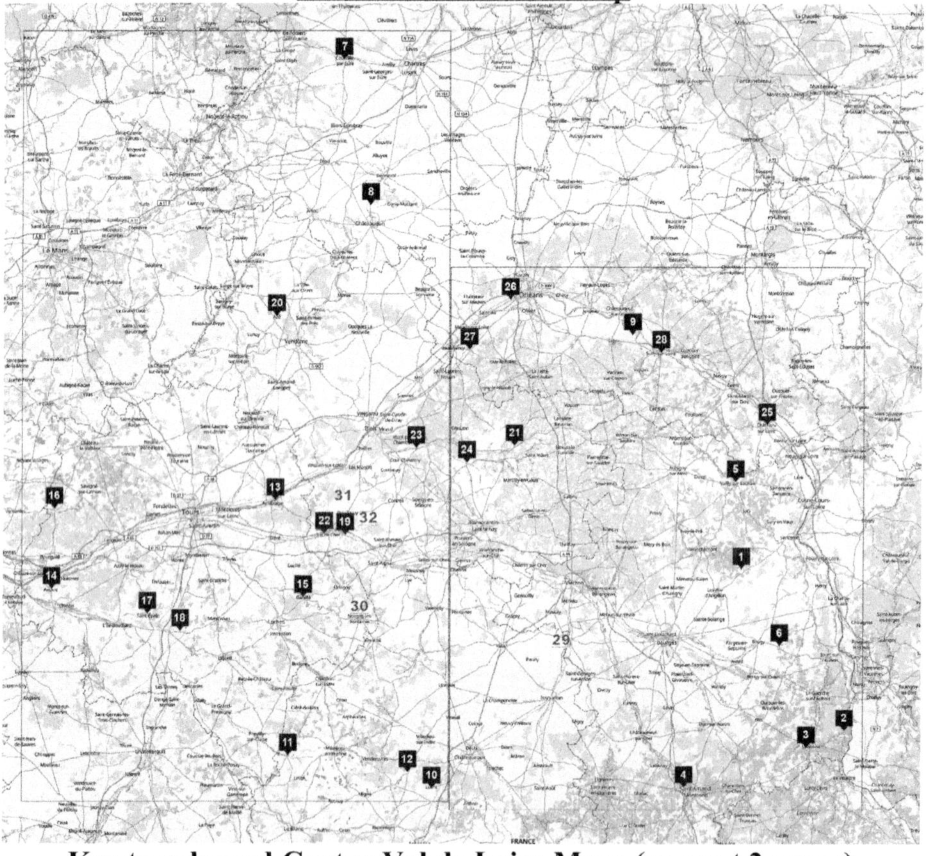

Key to enlarged Centre-Val de Loire Maps (on next 2 pages)

Former campsites that are now aires are noted in ***bold***

1) HUMBLIGNY – 2) NEUVY LE BARROIS – 3) SANCOINS
4) ST AMAND MONTROND – 5) VAILLY SUR SAULDRE – 6) VILLEQUIERS
7) COURVILLE SUR EURE – 8) MARBOUE – 9) GUILLY – 10) LUANT
11) MARTIZAY – 12) NEUILLAY LES BOIS - 13) AMBOISE – 14) AVOINE
15) GENILLE – 16) GIZEUX – 17) ST EPAIN – 18) STE MAURE DE TOURAINE
19) ANGE – 20) AZE – 21) LA FERTE BEAUHARNAIS – ***22) MONTRICHARD***
23) TOUR-EN-SOLOGNE – 24) VERNOU EN SOLOGNE
25) CHATILLON SUR LOIRE – ***26) LA CHAPELLE ST MESMIN***
27) LAILLY-EN-VAL – 28) SULLY-SUR-LOIRE – ***29) REUILLY*** *– 30) NOUANS*
31) PONTLEVOY – ***32) MONTHOU SUR CHER***

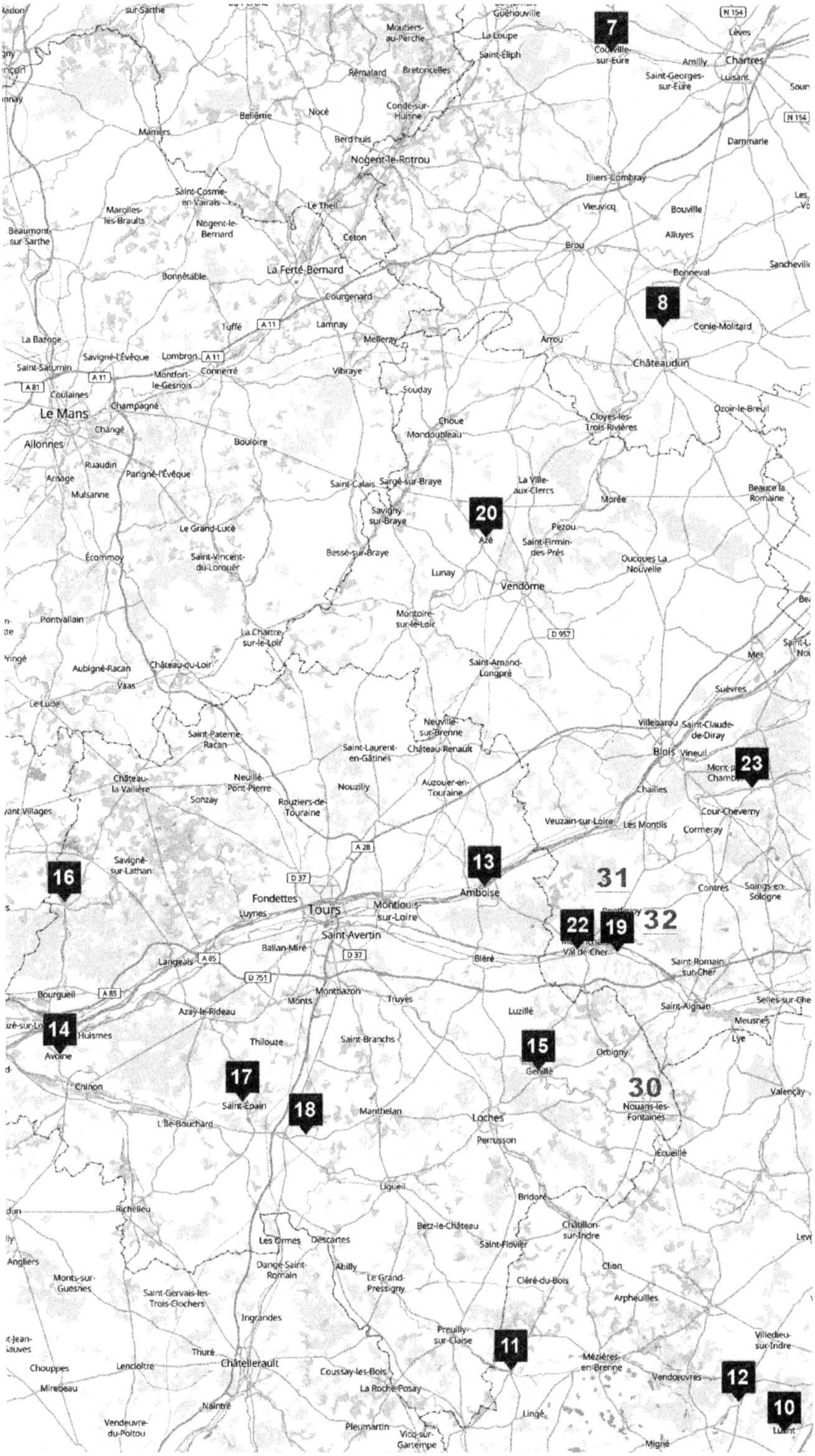
7
Courville-sur-Eure
Guéhouville
Moutiers-au-Perche
La Loupe
Saint-Éliph
Rémalard
Bretoncelles
Amilly
Chartres
Saint-Georges-sur-Eure
Lèves
Luisant
N 154
Bellême
Nocé
Condé-sur-Huisne
Mamers
Berd'huis
Nogent-le-Rotrou
Dammarie
Illiers-Combray
Saint-Cosme-en-Vairais
Marolles-lès-Braults
Le Theil
Nogent-le-Bernard
Vieuvicq
Bouville
Beaumont-sur-Sarthe
Ceton
Alluyes
Brou
Bonnétable
La Ferté-Bernard
Bonneval
Sancheville
Courgenard
8
Tuffé
A 11
Lamnay
Conie-Molitard
La Bazoge
Melleray
Arrou
Savigné-l'Évêque
Lombron
Saint-Saturnin
A 11
Montfort-le-Gesnois
Connerré
Vibraye
Châteaudun
A 81
Coulaines
Souday
Le Mans
Champagné
Ozoir-le-Breuil
Changé
Choue
Cloyes-les-Trois-Rivières
Allonnes
Bouloire
Mondoubleau
Ruaudin
Arnage
Parigné-l'Évêque
Mulsanne
Saint-Calais
Sargé-sur-Braye
La Ville-aux-Clercs
Beauce la Romaine
Morée
Savigny-sur-Braye
20
Azé
Le Grand-Lucé
Pezou
Écommoy
Saint-Vincent-du-Lorouër
Bessé-sur-Braye
Saint-Firmin-des-Prés
Ouques La Nouvelle
Lunay
Vendôme
Pontvallain
Montoire-sur-le-Loir
La Chartre-sur-le-Loir
D 957
Aubigné-Racan
Château-du-Loir
Vaas
Saint-Amand-Longpré
Mer
Le Lude
Suèvres
Neuville-sur-Brenne
Villebarou
Saint-Claude-de-Diray
Saint-Paterne-Racan
Saint-Laurent-en-Gâtines
Château-Renault
Blois
Vineuil
23
Château-la-Vallière
Neuillé-Pont-Pierre
Nouzilly
Auzouer-en-Touraine
Chailles
Sonzay
Rouziers-de-Touraine
Cour-Cheverny
Veuzain-sur-Loire
Les Montils
Cormeray
A 28
Savigné-sur-Lathan
16
13
31
D 37
Amboise
Contres
Soings-en-Sologne
Fondettes
Tours
Montlouis-sur-Loire
Luynes
22
19
32
Saint-Avertin
Val de Cher
Ballan-Miré
Langeais
A 85
D 37
Bléré
Saint-Romain-sur-Cher
D 751
Bourgueil
A 85
Montbazon
Monts
Truyes
Saint-Aignan
Selles-sur-Cher
Azay-le-Rideau
Luzillé
Meusnes
14
Huismes
Thilouze
Saint-Branchs
15
Lye
Avoine
Orbigny
Chinon
17
Genillé
30
Saint-Épain
Valençay
18
Manthelan
Nouans-les-Fontaines
L'Île-Bouchard
Loches
Perrusson
Écueillé
Ligueil
Bridoré
Richelieu
Betz-le-Château
Châtillon-sur-Indre
Saint-Flovier
Les Ormes
Descartes
Angliers
Clion
Monts-sur-Guesnes
Dangé-Saint-Romain
Abilly
Le Grand-Pressigny
Clére-du-Bois
Saint-Gervais-les-Trois-Clochers
Arpheuilles
Ingrandes
Preuilly-sur-Claise
Villedieu-sur-Indre
11
Thuré
Mézières-en-Brenne
Chouppes
Lencloître
Châtellerault
Coussay-les-Bois
12
Vendœuvres
Mirebeau
La Roche-Posay
10
Naintré
Lingé
Vendeuvre-du-Poitou
Pleumartin
Vicq-sur-Gartempe
Migné

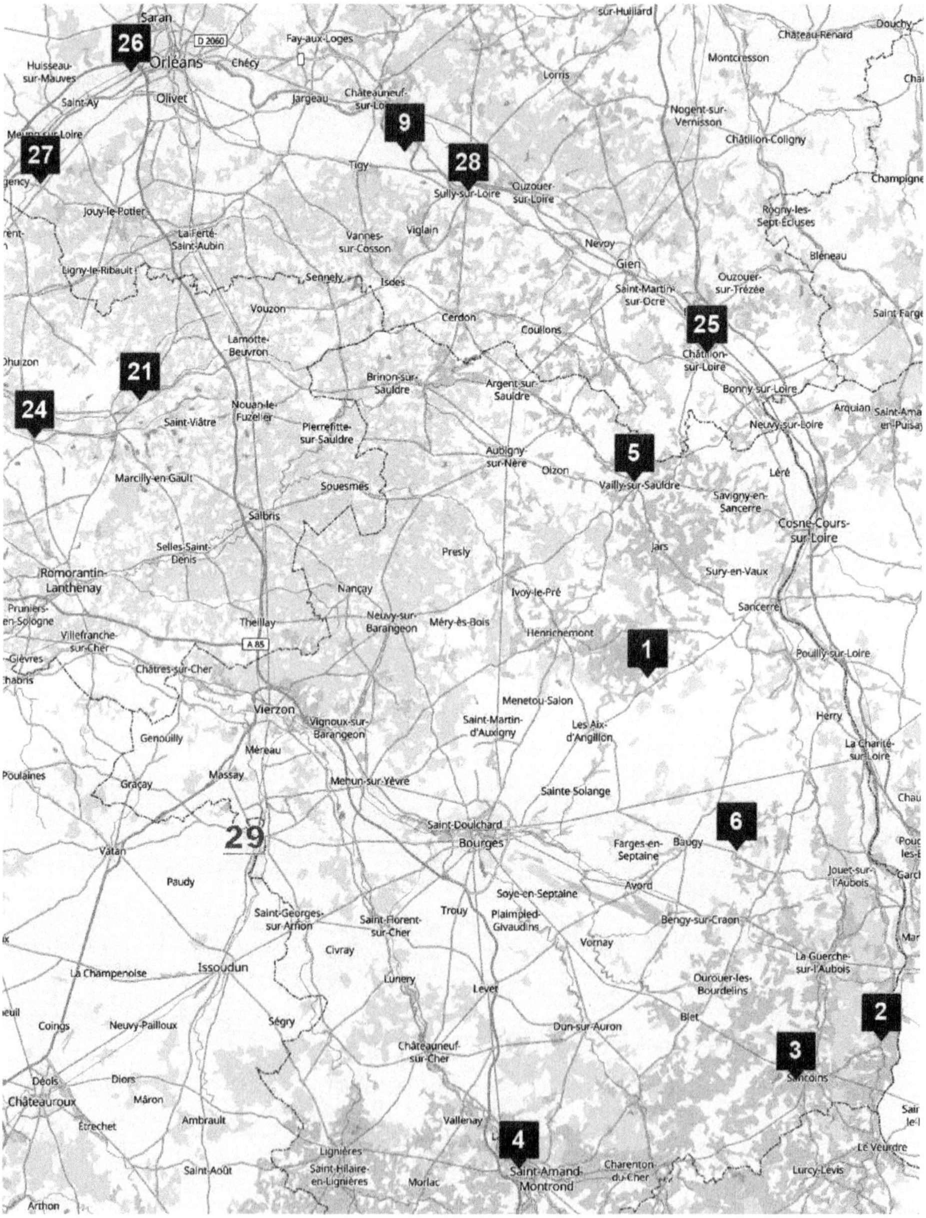

Saran
26
Orléans
Chécy
Fay-aux-Loges
Huisseau-sur-Mauves
Saint-Ay
Olivet
Jargeau
Châteauneuf-sur-Loire
9
Lorris
Montcresson
Château-Renard
Douchy
Nogent-sur-Vernisson
Châtillon-Coligny
27
Tigy
28
Sully-sur-Loire
Ouzouer-sur-Loire
Champignelles
Jouy-le-Potier
La Ferté-Saint-Aubin
Vannes-sur-Cosson
Viglain
Rogny-les-Sept-Écluses
Nevoy
Bléneau
Ligny-le-Ribault
Sennely
Isdes
Gien
Saint-Martin-sur-Ocre
Ouzouer-sur-Trézée
Vouzon
Cerdon
Coullons
25
Saint-Fargeau
Lamotte-Beuvron
Châtillon-sur-Loire
21
Brinon-sur-Sauldre
Argent-sur-Sauldre
Bonny-sur-Loire
24
Nouan-le-Fuzelier
Saint-Viâtre
Pierrefitte-sur-Sauldre
Arquian
Neuvy-sur-Loire
5
Aubigny-sur-Nère
Oizon
Vailly-sur-Sauldre
Marcilly-en-Gault
Souesmes
Léré
Savigny-en-Sancerre
Salbris
Cosne-Cours-sur-Loire
Selles-Saint-Denis
Presly
Jars
Sury-en-Vaux
Romorantin-Lanthenay
Nançay
Ivoy-le-Pré
Pruniers-en-Sologne
Neuvy-sur-Barangeon
Méry-ès-Bois
Sancerre
Theillay
Henrichemont
Villefranche-sur-Cher
A 85
1
Gièvres
Châtres-sur-Cher
Pouilly-sur-Loire
Menetou-Salon
Vierzon
Vignoux-sur-Barangeon
Saint-Martin-d'Auxigny
Les Aix-d'Angillon
Herry
Genouilly
Méreau
La Charité-sur-Loire
Poulaines
Graçay
Massay
Mehun-sur-Yèvre
Sainte Solange
6
Saint-Doulchard
29
Bourges
Farges-en-Septaine
Baugy
Vatan
Jouet-sur-l'Aubois
Paudy
Soye-en-Septaine
Avord
Saint-Georges-sur-Arnon
Saint-Florent-sur-Cher
Trouy
Plaimpied-Givaudins
Bengy-sur-Craon
Civray
Vornay
La Guerche-sur-l'Aubois
La Champenoise
Issoudun
Lunery
Levet
Ourouer-les-Bourdelins
2
Coings
Neuvy-Pailloux
Ségry
Dun-sur-Auron
Blet
Châteauneuf-sur-Cher
3
Sancoins
Déols
Diors
Châteauroux
Mâron
Étrechet
Ambrault
Vallenay
4
Lignières
Saint-Hilaire-en-Lignières
Saint-Août
Morlac
Saint-Amand-Montrond
Charenton-du-Cher
Lucy-Lévis
Le Veurdre
Arthon

18 CHER

HUMBLIGNY

ADDRESS: D44 **TYPE OF AIRE:** MUNICIPAL
FACILITIES: WATER /GREY & BLACK DRAIN/ RUBBISH/ ELECTRIC
LOCATION: RURAL **NO. OF SPACES:** 6
PRICES: PARKING: FREE **SERVICES**: 2€ WATER or ELECTRIC
OPENING TIMES: ALL YEAR **GPS:** N47.25448 E02.65860
DIRECTIONS: From HUMBLIGNY take D44 NORTH & AIRE is on LEFT.
SITE DESCRIPTION *An aire located close to the centre of this small rural village in a medium sized gravel parking area, next to the road where there are half a dozen level spaces on gravel. There is a little shade here, lighting at night & the aire is about 50m from village centre. Aire is bordered by grass with picnic tables adjacent. Euro-Relais service point with drainage grid.*

REVIEW: *A very quiet spot despite being next to a minor road, on the north side of this small isolated hamlet. Pleasant location surrounded by farmland with far reaching views, slight slope, easy to access service point & 2 picnic tables. No facilities in village, jetons from Mairie.*

NEUVY LE BARROIS

ADDRESS: LA PRAIRIE, RTE DE MORNAY, D45 **TYPE OF AIRE:** PRIVATE
FACILITIES: WATER /GREY & BLACK DRAIN/ ELECTRIC/ TOILETS
LOCATION: RURAL **NO. OF SPACES:** 6
PRICES: PARKING: 13€/ 24HRS **SERVICES**: INCL
OPENING TIMES: 01/04 - 30/10 **GPS:** N46.86098 E03.03961
DIRECTIONS: From NEUVY, take D45 SOUTH & AIRE is on LEFT after 500m.
SITE DESCRIPTION *A private aire located in the grounds of a farm, 1/2km south of the small rural village of Neuvy - where there are 6 level spaces on hard standing bordered by grass verges. There is a little shade here in places, lighting at night as well as a toilet block with sinks & showers. Artisanal service point with large drainage platform.*

REVIEW: *A very quiet, well appointed rural aire located behind the barn of a small farm with views over the surrounding countryside. 6 large individual spaces separated by hedges/ trees all with 16A hook ups, adjacent grass area, laundry facilities, good service point & farm produce for sale. No facilities in the nearby small village of Neuvy. Tel/ Text: 0688837475*

SANCOINS

ADDRESS: QUAI DU CANAL, OFF D43 **TYPE OF AIRE:** MUNICIPAL
FACILITIES: WATER /GREY & BLACK DRAIN/ TOILETS/ RUBBISH
LOCATION: SEMI-URBAN/ CANALSIDE **NO. OF SPACES:** 20
PRICES: PARKING: FREE **SERVICES**: 3€ WATER
OPENING TIMES: ALL YEAR **GPS:** N46.83381 E02.91505
DIRECTIONS: From SANCOINS, take D43 WEST, cross CANAL & LEFT to AIRE.
SITE DESCRIPTION: *This Municipal aire is located alongside the Canal du Berry (on the north side of canal & town) in a large gravel parking area shaded on one side by tall trees, with adjacent grass areas & picnic tables next to the canal. The Euro-Relais service point with platform drain is located on the opposite bank of the canal (accessed by a bridge) & there is a small toilet block nearby. Jetons from shops.*

REVIEW: *A very nice, tranquil position next to the canal & close to the centre of town (well signposted) with plenty of level spaces. Good range of shops/ services in town as well as two supermarkets. The aire has open countryside to the west with walks along the towpath.*

ST AMAND MONTROND

ADDRESS: CHEMIN DE VIRLAY, OFF D2144 **TYPE OF AIRE:** MUNICIPAL
FACILITIES: WATER /GREY & BLACK DRAIN/ RUBBISH
LOCATION: SEMI-URBAN/ LAKE **NO. OF SPACES:** 20
PRICES: PARKING: FREE **SERVICES**: 2€ WATER
OPENING TIMES: ALL YEAR **GPS:** N46.73456 E02.48906
DIRECTIONS: From town take D2144 NORTH & take last exit @ INTERMARCHE Roundabout to AIRE.
SITE DESCRIPTION*: The aire is in a large tarmac/ grass parking area, 1km north of the town centre, next to a lake. Ample spaces with picnic tables, grass areas, lighting but little shade. Artisanal service point with large platform drain.*

REVIEW: *A quiet location next to a large lake, a fair way from the large town centre but there is a supermarket & a McDonalds opposite as well as a bus stop if you need to go into town. Good walks around lake. Handy stopover off A71, Jcn 8.*

VAILLY SUR SAULDRE

ADDRESS: RUE DU PONT (D926) **TYPE OF AIRE:** MUNICIPAL
FACILITIES: WATER /GREY & BLACK DRAIN / RUBBISH/ TOILETS
LOCATION: RURAL/ RIVERSIDE **NO. OF SPACES:** 18
PRICES: PARKING: 7€ / 24 Hrs **SERVICES**: 2€ WATER
OPENING TIMES: ALL YEAR **GPS:** N47.45722 E02.64673
DIRECTIONS: From VAILLY, take D926 WEST & AIRE is on RIGHT after bridge.
SITE DESCRIPTION*: In a rural location on the western side of the village, this renovated aire has spaces on tarmac accessed by a gravel track with some shade in places from small trees, lighting & adjacent grass areas. The aire is surrounded by open farmland about 400m from village, in a quiet position next to a river, access is by automatic barrier. Artisanal service point, small toilets (disabled) & drainage platform.*

REVIEW: *This aire is in a lovely open location with excellent shaded pitches & picnic tables close to a nice little village, very welcoming with services easily accessible. Small*

range of shops/ Cocci mini-mart/ bars & eating places in village with a market on Wednesdays & remains of a château to visit.

VILLEQUIERS

ADDRESS: FERME DU PETIT AZILLON, D93 **TYPE OF AIRE:** PRIVATE
FACILITIES: WATER /GREY & BLACK DRAIN / ELECTRIC/ TOILETS/ WIFI
LOCATION: RURAL **NO. OF SPACES:** 6
PRICES: PARKING: 8€/ 24 Hrs **SERVICES**: 3€ WATER
OPENING TIMES: ALL YEAR **GPS:** N47.08750 E02.77533
DIRECTIONS: From VILLEQUIERS, take D93 WEST & FARM is 2km on LEFT.
***SITE DESCRIPTION**: Set on an arable farm in a rural location NW of village with individual parking spaces on gravel separated by grass verges, accessed by a gravel track & having views over open farmland in all directions. This private aire also has wifi, separate hook ups for each pitch & toilets/ showers. Artisanal services with platform drain being located next to a small farm building.*

***REVIEW:** An excellent small aire on a farm outside the village; very clean & well laid out with good walks / cycling in the surrounding countryside but nearest shops are 5kms away. This is a quiet location, lit at night but with little shade. Electric included in price, farm produce for sale. Tel/ Text: 0608308219, English spoken.*

28 EURE-ET-LOIR

COURVILLE SUR EURE

ADDRESS: AVE THIERS, D114 **TYPE OF AIRE:** MUNICIPAL

FACILITIES: WATER /GREY & BLACK DRAIN / ELEC./ RUBBISH/ TOILETS
LOCATION: SEMI-RURAL/ RIVER **NO. OF SPACES:** 14
PRICES: PARKING: FREE **SERVICES**: 2.5€ WATER or ELECTRIC
OPENING TIMES: ALL YEAR **GPS:** N48.44591 E01.24118
DIRECTIONS: From town take D114 SOUTH & AIRE is on LEFT outside CAMPING.
***SITE DESCRIPTION**: The aire is in the medium size tarmac parking area outside the Municipal camping on the southern side of this small rural town. Pitches are on grass separated by hedges or on tarmac with some shade under mature trees, lit at night.. Euro Relais service point with a platform drain & small toilet block.*
***REVIEW:** A very nice, quiet position, just outside the campsite & not far from the town centre (300m), where there is a Super U, a good selection of shops & eating-places. A well maintained aire with level spaces, next to the Eure river & near some small lakes with walks adjacent. Camping open 01/05 – 22/09. Jetons from Camping or shops.*

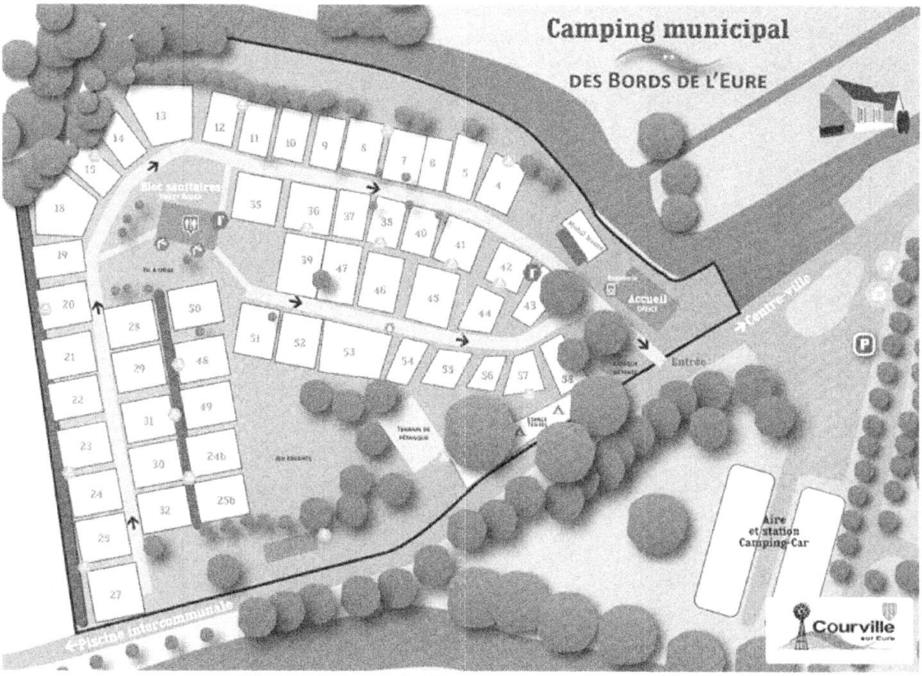

Plan of Aire & Camping at Courville

MARBOUE

ADDRESS: RUE DE CROC MARBOT **TYPE OF AIRE:** MUNICIPAL
FACILITIES: WATER /GREY & BLACK DRAIN / ELEC. / RUBBISH / TOILETS
LOCATION: URBAN/ NEAR RIVER **NO. OF SPACES:** 15
PRICES: PARKING: FREE **SERVICES**: 2€ WATER OR ELECTRIC
OPENING TIMES: ALL YEAR **GPS:** N48.11233 E01.32863
DIRECTIONS: From SOUTH take N10 NORTH to MARBOUE & cross LOIR, take 1st LEFT. AIRE is 200m on RIGHT (one-way road).
***SITE DESCRIPTION**: The aire is in a residential area on the southern side of Marboue, opposite a park & the river Loir. Parking is on gravel accessed directly from a*

tarmac road with good shade, 200m from the centre of town. AirServices service point with platform drainage & WC block.

REVIEW: *A lovely place, opposite an open park area & the river but some slight noise from traffic crossing the Loir bridge. The aire has picnic tables, boules pitch, childrens play area & there is a good boulangerie on the corner of the road. Pizza van calls in evening. Nice walks nearby. Bar/ tabac & cafe in town but little else.*

36 INDRE

GUILLY

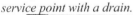

ADDRESS : RUE DU PRIEURE, D34 **TYPE OF AIRE:** PRIVATE
FACILITIES: WATER /GREY & BLACK DRAIN / ELECTRIC/ WIFI
LOCATION: RURAL **NO. OF SPACES:** 4
PRICES: PARKING: 5€/ 24Hrs **SERVICES**: 3€ ELECTRIC
OPENING TIMES: ALL YEAR **GPS:** N47.06077 E01.77155
DIRECTIONS: From GUILLY take D34 WEST, LE PRIEURE is on LEFT after 400m.
SITE DESCRIPTION*: This private aire is located about 400m west of the small rural village of Guilly, in the grounds of "Le Prieure", a Chambre d'Hotes, where there are 4 level spaces available on hard standing but little shade & bordered by hedges. Artisanal service point with a drain.*

REVIEW: *A very pleasant, quiet, rural aire in the grounds of a small B&B where there are just a few spaces available (booking recommended) with hook ups. A short walk to Guilly but there is little there apart from a café, aire is well signposted from the village. Nice proprietors, evening meals available. Nearest shops at Vatan to the East. Tel/ Text: 0661407440*

LUANT

ADDRESS: ETANG DURIS, D80 **TYPE OF AIRE:** MUNICIPAL
FACILITIES: WATER /GREY & BLACK DRAIN/ ELEC./ RUBBISH/ TOILETS
LOCATION: RURAL/ LAKESIDE **NO. OF SPACES:** 12
PRICES: PARKING: FREE **SERVICES**: 2€ WATER or ELECTRIC
OPENING TIMES: ALL YEAR **GPS:** N46.72221 E01.57301
DIRECTIONS: SOUTH on D80 from LUANT, after 2kms turn LEFT to AIRE.
SITE DESCRIPTION: *Located in a medium sized gravel parking area next to a large fishing lake (etang Duris), this aire has some shade from trees but unfortunately is not near to any facilities apart from a restaurant. Euro Relais service point with a large platform drain, toilets nearby. Jetons from Mairie or shops.*

REVIEW: *A very pleasant & peaceful aire overlooking this large lake, nice walk around it & longer waymarked walks nearby. Aire is next to the road but there is very little traffic, there is also a house next to the aire giving added security. It is about 2kms south east of the small village of Luant where there is a small range of shops & a bar. Restaurant next to aire but not open in winter nor Sunday evening/ Mondays. Play area & picnic tables nearby. Good stopping off point on A20, 3kms from Jcn 15.*

MARTIZAY

ADDRESS: NEXT TO RIVER, off D975 **TYPE OF AIRE:** MUNICIPAL
FACILITIES: WATER /GREY & BLACK DRAIN/ TOILETS/ ELECTRIC
LOCATION: SEMI-RURAL/ RIVERSIDE **NO. OF SPACES:** 9
PRICES: PARKING: FREE **SERVICES**: FREE
OPENING TIMES: ALL YEAR **GPS:** N46.80583 E01.03833
DIRECTIONS: Take D975 NORTH to MARTIZAY & turn LEFT immediately before RIVER to AIRE on RIGHT.

SITE DESCRIPTION: *The aire is located next to the river, on the south bank, about 400m from the centre of the village in a park/ leisure area where there are picnic tables, grass areas & a play area. There are 9 spaces on tarmac with some shade & lighting, a pleasant location with open farmland to the west. Artisanal service point with drainage platform & toilets/ sinks adjacent. There are 4 separate ehu's also with water taps.*

REVIEW: *Next to the river Claise & not too far from the small range of shops, a quiet stop at a well equipped aire with hard standings. The village has a small selection of shops; boulangerie, butcher, bar/ café/ news & superette, there is also a market on Wednesday mornings & a museum.*

NEUILLAY LES BOIS

ADDRESS: LAKE, RTE DE BUZANCAIS, D1 **TYPE OF AIRE:** MUNICIPAL
FACILITIES: WATER /GREY & BLACK DRAIN / ELECTRIC / TOILETS
LOCATION: SEMI-RURAL/ LAKESIDE **NO. OF SPACES:** 6
PRICES: PARKING: FREE **SERVICES**: FREE
OPENING TIMES: 01/05 – 26/10 **GPS:** N46.76892 E01.47395
DIRECTIONS: From NEUILLAY take D1 NORTH & RIGHT after 200m to AIRE.
SITE DESCRIPTION*: Located next to a lake on the northern outskirts of the small village, this aire is in a small parking area with the parking on grass or gravel & having some shade under small trees. A pleasant location with a mini Flot Bleu service point, 4x10A ehu's & 200m from the centre of the village.*

REVIEW: *A little gem where everything is free including electric & quietly located next to a fishing lake with a play area, picnic tables & toilets adjacent. There is an epicerie/ bar (not open mornings) in the village.*

REUILLY

ADDRESS: RUE DES PONTS **TYPE OF AIRE:** PRIVATE
FACILITIES: WATER /GREY & BLACK DRAIN/ ELECTRIC/ WIFI/ TOILETS
LOCATION: RURAL/ RIVER **NO. OF SPACES:** 33
PRICES: PARKING: 12€/ 24HRS **SERVICES**: INCL
OPENING TIMES: ALL YEAR **GPS :** N47.08523 E02.05061
DIRECTIONS: Approaching REUILLY from EAST on D918, turn 1st RIGHT after RIVER to AIRE.
SITE DESCRIPTION: *This 'Camping Village' aire, run by CampingCarPark, is situated in the former Municipal campsite, about 500m east of Reuilly & between two rivers. Pitches are on gravel/ grass (most shaded) with 6A ehu & wifi with toilets (open 01/05-30/09). Artisanal service point with drainage platform. Access by automatic barrier, CCP card required.*

REVIEW: *A nice semi-rural location next to the river, close to the village & quiet with good shaded pitches/ services. Toilets cleaned daily but only open May - Sept. Only 20 ehu's for the 33 pitches. Shops in village; boulangeries, pharmacy, Carrefour supermarket & eating places. Several walking trails from village.*

37 INDRE-ET-LOIRE

AMBOISE

ADDRESS: ALLEE CHAPELLE ST JEAN **TYPE OF AIRE:** PRIVATE
FACILITIES: WATER /GREY & BLACK DRAIN/ ELECTRIC/ WIFI
LOCATION: SEMI-RURAL/ RIVER **NO. OF SPACES:** 24
PRICES: PARKING: 13€ /24Hrs **SERVICES**: INCL
OPENING TIMES: ALL YEAR **GPS:** N47.41759 E00.98757
DIRECTIONS: In AMBOISE take BRIDGE over Loire onto island & to AIRE.

SITE DESCRIPTION: *This CampingCarPark aire, situated on the north side of Ile d'Or in the Loire river opposite the Chateau & next to the municipal campsite "L'Ile d'Or", is purpose built for motorhomes & is about 1km from the town centre (across the river). Parking is fenced, on grass with little shade, accessed by a tarmac track with entry to the aire controlled by an automatic barrier, CCP card required. Artisanal service point with drainage platform. Campsite & municipal swimming pool next to aire.*

REVIEW: *A well managed & maintained aire, quiet & in a pleasant spot in the middle of the Loire river, however it may be better to stay at the Municipal campsite next door (which has toilets, showers, shade & 24hour electric) when open (April-Sept). Amboise is about a 15 minute walk across the bridge with a good range of shops in town & market on Sunday morning. Château d'Amboise & Leonardo DaVinci exhibition to see.*

AVOINE

ADDRESS: AVE DE LA REPUBLIQUE **TYPE OF AIRE:** MUNICIPAL
FACILITIES: WATER /GREY & BLACK DRAIN/ ELECTRIC
LOCATION: SEMI-RURAL/ LAKE **NO. OF SPACES:** 11
PRICES: PARKING: 6€/ 24Hrs **SERVICES**: 2€ WATER or ELECTRIC
OPENING TIMES: ALL YEAR **GPS:** N47.21313 E00.17745
DIRECTIONS: From AVOINE take D749 & then D122 NORTH, turn LEFT at R/bout onto AVE REPUBLIQUE & AIRE is 500m on RIGHT.
SITE DESCRIPTION: *This municipal aire is located on the northern edge of the town, close to a lake in a park area where there are 11 large parking spaces, shaded & lit, arranged in a circle, on tarmac bordered by grass areas. Access is by automatic barrier at entrance & the parking is close to a wooded area, backing onto farmland, being about 800m from the town centre. UrbaFlux service point with drainage platform. Previous winner of "Aire of the Year".*

REVIEW: *A very well laid out & maintained aire, but not very close to the town centre. Nice park like area with woodland walks around fishing lake, play area, boules & picnic tables. Fairly quiet, parking& services are paid for at the entrance. Reasonable selection of shops in town, Shopi supermarket, 4 restaurants & café/ tabac plus a swimming pool.*

GENILLE

ADDRESS: RUE DE L'HUILERIE **TYPE OF AIRE:** MUNICIPAL
FACILITIES: WATER /GREY & BLACK DRAIN/ ELECTRIC/ RUBBISH
LOCATION: URBAN **NO. OF SPACES:** 6
PRICES: PARKING: 5€/ 24Hrs **SERVICES**: 2€ WATER
OPENING TIMES: ALL YEAR **GPS:** N47.18450 E1.09225
DIRECTIONS: In village centre, follow signs for "Parc Paysage", AIRE is adjacent.
SITE DESCRIPTION *This Municipal aire is located close to the village centre, on the south side of the village. Parking is on level, gravel spaces bordered by grass verges & trees/ bushes offering some shade. Picnic tables adjacent, boules & childrens play area. Artisanal borne with drainage grid & 6 ehu's, electric included. Euro-Relais service point for drainage & water is located 150m south of the parking. Jetons for water from shops.*

REVIEW: *A nice, quiet aire 150m from the centre of the village next to a small park area. Shops in village include; boulangerie, pharmacy, 8 til 8 mini-mart, news/ tabac, restaurant, pizzeria & bank. Honesty box for parking fee.*

GIZEUX

ADDRESS: RUE DE LAVOIR, D749 **TYPE OF AIRE:** MUNICIPAL
FACILITIES: WATER /GREY & BLACK DRAIN/ TOILETS
LOCATION: URBAN **NO. OF SPACES:** 8
PRICES: PARKING: FREE **SERVICES**: 2€ WATER
OPENING TIMES: ALL YEAR **GPS:** N47.39230 E0.19615
DIRECTIONS: From GIZEUX, take D749 EAST & AIRE is on LEFT after MAIRIE.

SITE DESCRIPTION *This Municipal aire is located close to the village centre, off the D15 road thru the village. Parking is on gravel in level spaces separated by grass verges/ hedges & surrounded by trees /bushes but offering little shade. Picnic tables adjacent. AireServices borne with drainage platform & toilets nearby. Jetons from cafe, boulangerie or Mairie.*

REVIEW: *Spacious pitches in the centre of the nice village next to a pretty park, a quiet spot on the 'Route of the Châteaux of the Loire'. Facilities in village include boulangerie, butcher, café/tabac & garage. Chateau nearby to visit (1/04 – 4/11).*

NOUANS LES FONTAINES

ADDRESS: RUE DE LA PISCINE **TYPE OF AIRE:** MUNICIPAL
FACILITIES: WATER /GREY & BLACK DRAIN / ELECTRIC / RUBBISH
LOCATION: SEMI-URBAN **NO. OF SPACES:** 6
PRICES : PARKING: FREE **SERVICES**: 1€ WATER or ELECTRIC
OPENING TIMES: ALL YEAR **GPS :** N47.13848 E01.30002
DIRECTIONS: From NORTH take D775 SOUTH to NOUANS. AIRE is on LEFT.

SITE DESCRIPTION: *The aire is in a medium sized gravel parking area with 6 individual spaces separated by grass verges, no shade but lit at night. A nice location next to the swimming pool with an adjacent lake, grass areas, picnic & play area, 300m north of the town centre. AireServices service point with drainage platform & 2 ehu's.*

***REVIEW:** Short walk into town where there is a small selection of shops; boulangerie, epicerie, butcher & Poste, jetons available from swimming pool, Mairie or shops. Handy stopover for visiting the nearby "Plus Beaux Village" of Montresor.*

SAINT EPAIN

ADDRESS: RUE DES DENEUX **TYPE OF AIRE:** MUNICIPAL
FACILITIES: WATER /GREY & BLACK DRAIN/ ELEC./ TOILETS/ SHOWERS
LOCATION: SEMI-URBAN/ LAKE **NO. OF SPACES:** 12
PRICES: PARKING: 5€/ 24Hrs **SERVICES**: 2€ ELECTRIC
OPENING TIMES: ALL YEAR **GPS:** N47.14439 E00.53945
DIRECTIONS: From ST EPAIN take D8 NORTH & turn RIGHT to AIRE.

***SITE DESCRIPTION**: The aire is on the eastern side of the village, 200m from the centre, located next to the village leisure lake where there are a dozen level spaces on grass separated by hedges with shade in places. The spaces have hook ups, toilets/ showers, overlook the lake & are accessed by a gravel track with lighting at night. Artisanal service point is next to the road, easy to use & access. Additional tarmac parking opposite.*

***REVIEW:** A very pleasant little 'aire naturelle' next to a large fishing lake with individual pitches each with ehu. Quiet, clean location with childrens play area, fishing in lake. Toilet/ shower block adjacent (key provided after paying at Mairie), phone 0247658021 if arriving after 6pm. Butcher, baker, grocer, bar, tabac & pizza/ creperie in village. Nice walk to ruined château & troglodyte caves.*

STE MAURE DE TOURAINE

ADDRESS: LE BOIS CHAUDRON, OFF D910 **TYPE OF AIRE:** PRIVATE
FACILITIES: WATER /GREY & BLACK DRAIN/ ELECTRIC /TOILETS/ SHOWERS/ WIFI
LOCATION: RURAL **NO. OF SPACES:** 35
PRICES: PARKING: 5€/ 24 Hrs **SERVICES**: 2€ WATER or ELECTRIC or SHOWER
OPENING TIMES: ALL YEAR **GPS:** N47.09332 E00.61282
DIRECTIONS: From STE MAURE, take D910 SOUTH for 1.5km turn LEFT just before industrial area to AIRE (signed).

***SITE DESCRIPTION** This well equipped private aire is located 1.5km south of Ste Maure, just off the D910 in a rural location, bordered by woodland with parking in a* *level grassy field. The parking has shade in places & there are picnic tables adjacent as well as WC's, shower, laundry facilities & wifi. Artisanal service point with platform drainage grid.*

REVIEW: *A very well maintained private aire, the parking/ drainage/ wifi is 5€ & you pay for everything else. Bread can be ordered for morning delivery. Not very convenient for Sainte Maure, where tthere are shops /restaurants as well as a museum & market in town on Wednesday morning. Handy stopover off A10, Jcn 25.*

41 LOIR-ET-CHER

ANGE

ADDRESS: BEHIND MAIRIE, **TYPE OF AIRE:** MUNICIPAL
FACILITIES: WATER /GREY & BLACK DRAIN / RUBBISH / ELECTRIC/ WIFI
LOCATION: SEMI-RURAL **NO. OF SPACES:** 15
PRICES: **PARKING**: 8€/ 24 Hrs **SERVICES**: INCL, 2€ WATER
OPENING TIMES: ALL YEAR **GPS:** N47.33160 W01.24435
DIRECTIONS: In the centre of ANGE, AIRE is behind the MAIRIE.
SITE DESCRIPTION: *This aire is located in a large gravel parking area in this small village, near to the Mairie & surrounded by open farmland, but there is only shade in a couple of places. Access via automatic barrier. Euro Relais borne with drainage grid is lit at night with ehu's & wifi available. Jetons for water from Mairie/ shops (closed Mon.)*
REVIEW: *Aire is fairly quiet (slight road noise) being well positioned close to the village centre – a nice open location with plenty of spaces on grass or gravel in a nice little village. There are just an epicerie & a boulangerie plus a café/bar in the village.*

AZE

ADDRESS: LES PETITES PLACES, OFF D957 **TYPE OF AIRE:** PRIVATE
FACILITIES: WATER /GREY & BLACK DRAIN / ELECTRIC
LOCATION: RURAL **NO. OF SPACES:** 6
PRICES: **PARKING**: 10€ / 24 Hrs **SERVICES**: INCL
OPENING TIMES: ALL YEAR **GPS:** N47.86414 E0.97662
DIRECTIONS: From VENDOME take D957 NORTH & turn RIGHT to LES PLACES.

SITE DESCRIPTION: *This private aire on a dairy farm, to the north of Aze, is in an open grassy area with no shade & spaces on gravel accessed by a gravel track. Artisanal service point with ehu's. Tel: 0254720329*

REVIEW: *A little private aire on an isolated farm with pleasant & welcoming owners, an extremely quiet spot surrounded by fields, lawns & floral displays. Well maintained with picnic tables & farm produce/ wine/ tourist info available. Shops, etc can be found either at Epuisay (4km) or Vendome.*

LA FERTE BEAUHARNAIS

ADDRESS: D922, NORTH of VILLAGE **TYPE OF AIRE:** MUNICIPAL
FACILITIES: WATER /GREY & BLACK DRAIN/ ELECTRIC/ TOILETS
LOCATION: SEMI-RURAL/ LAKE **NO. OF SPACES:** 12
PRICES: PARKING: FREE **SERVICES**: 2€ WATER & ELECTRIC
OPENING TIMES: ALL YEAR **GPS:** N47.54500 E01.84917
DIRECTIONS: From LA FERTE take D922 NORTH & AIRE is on RIGHT after river.
SITE DESCRIPTION: *The aire is situated to the north of this small rural village in a small park area, next to a river/ lake where fishing is possible. Parking is on grass or gravel accessed by a gravel track with some shade surrounded by open countryside, no lighting & is about 200m north of the village centre. AireServices service point with drainage platform & toilets adjacent.*
REVIEW: *A quiet, pleasant location yet only a short walk from the village centre. Ample parking area, good service point with toilets (bit dated). Nice village with several old buildings & a château. Jetons available in the village shops; boulangerie, superette, tabac/ news & an auberge.*

Photo top of next page

MONTHOU-SUR-CHER

ADDRESS: ROUTE PLAN D'EAU **TYPE OF AIRE:** PRIVATE
FACILITIES: WATER /GREY & BLACK DRAIN/ ELECTRIC/ WIFI/ TOILETS
LOCATION: URBAN/ LAKE **NO. OF SPACES:** 25
PRICES: PARKING: 10-14€/ 24HRS **SERVICES**: INCL
OPENING TIMES: ALL YEAR **GPS :** N47.34870 E01.29323
DIRECTIONS: Entering village from WEST on D85, turn LEFT just before RIVER.
SITE DESCRIPTION: *CampingCarPark run this 'Camping Village' aire, situated in the campsite 'Les Anguilleuses', west side of the village & next to a large lake & river. Pitches are on gravel (most shaded) separated by high hedges with 6A ehu & wifi accessed by a tarmac track with toilets/ shower/ sinks (open 01/05-30/09). Euro-Relais service point with drainage platform. Access by automatic barrier, CCP card required.*

REVIEW: *A pleasant location close to a large leisure lake, 200m from the village centre, quiet with large pitches/ picnic tables but only 19 ehu's for the 25 pitches & sanitary block only open May till Sept. Restaurant next to camping, grocery shop in village & play area/ fishing adjacent plus cycle tracks.*

MONTRICHARD

ADDRESS: RUE G. FRIDELOUX **TYPE OF AIRE:** PRIVATE
FACILITIES: WATER /GREY & BLACK DRAIN/ ELECTRIC/ WIFI

LOCATION: URBAN **NO. OF SPACES:** 40
PRICES: PARKING: 12€ /24HRS **SERVICES**: INCL
OPENING TIMES: ALL YEAR **GPS:** N47.33858 E01.17097
DIRECTIONS: Entering MONTRICHARD from WEST on D176, turn 1st RIGHT.
SITE DESCRIPTION: *CampingCarPark run this large aire located on the west side of town, close to the river Cher in a large gravel area with level spaces separated by hedges & with some shade under trees. The aire is 400m from the shops with a Raclet service point, drainage platform, wifi & ehu's.*

REVIEW: *Well positioned aire in a former Municipal campsite, with large separate shaded spaces (40m^2), each with 6A hook-up & wifi. Quiet location with access by automatic barrier, CCP card required. Nice small town on Cher river with ruined château, shops, restaurants & good market on Friday mornings. Walk along river into town.*

PONTLEVOY

ADDRESS: RUE DU PETIT BOIS, OFF D30 **TYPE OF AIRE:** MUNICIPAL
FACILITIES: WATER /GREY DRAIN/BLACK DRAIN/ ELECTRIC
LOCATION: SEMI-RURAL **NO. OF SPACES:** 12
PRICES: PARKING: FREE **SERVICES**: FREE
OPENING TIMES: ALL YEAR **GPS :** N47.38656 E01.25895
DIRECTIONS: From EAST take D30 WEST to PONTLEVOY. As you enter town turn LEFT onto Rue Petit Bois & AIRE is 300m on RIGHT.
SITE DESCRIPTION *The aire is located on the south side of town, 400m from the town centre in a gravel parking area bordered by grass with some shade but little lighting. Euro-Relais service point with drainage platform & ehu's. Jetons from shops.*
REVIEW: *The aire is next to farmland with a view of an abbey but not far from the town, with a footpath leading to the centre. Quiet location with free services, some*

shaded parking & electric points. Pleasant small town with a small selection of shops & eating places.

TOUR-EN-SOLOGNE

ADDRESS: RUE DE LA MAIRIE, D102 **TYPE OF AIRE:** MUNICIPAL
FACILITIES: WATER /GREY & BLACK DRAIN /ELECTRIC/ TOILETS
LOCATION: URBAN **NO. OF SPACES:** 10
PRICES: **PARKING**: FREE **SERVICES**: 2.5€ WATER & ELECTRIC
OPENING TIMES: ALL YEAR **GPS:** N47.53765 E01.50015
DIRECTIONS: AIRE is opposite CHURCH in village, off D102.
SITE DESCRIPTION: *The aire is located in the centre of this small village in a medium sized gravel parking area, near to the church & the Mairie, surrounded by grass areas with shade in places. Euro-Relais borne with platform drain & toilets adjacent. Jetons from Mairie/ boulangerie.*

REVIEW: *A well maintained, clean & quiet aire close to the centre of the village with several level spaces available. Toilet block with washing up sinks & picnic tables on grass. A butcher, boulangerie with some grocery & a restaurant in village.*

VERNOU EN SOLOGNE

ADDRESS: RUE DE BEAUGENCY, D13 **TYPE OF AIRE:** MUNICIPAL
FACILITIES: WATER /GREY & BLACK DRAIN / RUBBISH / ELECTRIC
LOCATION: SEMI-RURAL/ RIVER **NO. OF SPACES:** 12
PRICES: PARKING: FREE **SERVICES**:2€ WATER & ELECTRICITY
OPENING TIMES: ALL YEAR **GPS:** N47.50302 E01.68012
DIRECTIONS: Take D13 SOUTH to VERNOU, cross RIVER & turn 1st RIGHT.

***SITE DESCRIPTION**: This aire is located in a large gravel/ grass parking area at the northern edge of this small village, next to the river & surrounded by open farmland with shade in places. Euro-Relais borne with drainage grid. Jetons from shops or Poste.*

***REVIEW:** A nice little aire, easy to find next to a river in a large flat area with parking on gravel or grass, with shade under mature trees. Quiet at night, some road noise during day. Picnic tables nearby as well as a park/ lake. Short walk into village with just 4 shops; epicerie, boulangerie, butcher & a tabac/bar.*

45 LOIRET

CHATILLON SUR LOIRE

ADDRESS: RUE DU PORT, OFF D50 **TYPE OF AIRE:** MUNICIPAL
FACILITIES: WATER /GREY & BLACK DRAIN/ ELECTRIC/ TOILETS
LOCATION: SEMI-RURAL/ CANAL **NO. OF SPACES:** 8
PRICES: PARKING: 10€/ 24 Hrs **SERVICES**: INCL
OPENING TIMES: ALL YEAR **GPS:** N47.59109 E02.76059
DIRECTIONS: From NORTH take D50 to TOWN, cross LOIRE & CANAL, turn 1st LEFT & AIRE is on RIGHT after 200m.
***SITE DESCRIPTION:** A modern aire located on the eastern outskirts of this small town in a large tarmac parking area of the Port, next to the road where there are 4 double spaces. The aire overlooks the canal marina & has separate ehu's. There is some shade here under mature trees, lit at night & the aire is about 500m from town centre with its good selection of shops/ supermarket. Urbaflux service point with drainage grid.*

REVIEW: *A very pleasant canal & riverside aire, quietly located in a cul-de-sac with large spaces partially shaded by mature trees next to grass areas with picnic tables. Pay at ticket machine which issues code for the water/ electric.* ***NOTE: Height restriction of 2.7m on Loire bridge.***

LA CHAPELLE ST MESMIN

ADDRESS: CHEMIN DES FOURNEAUX **TYPE OF AIRE:** MUNICIPAL
FACILITIES: WATER /GREY & BLACK DRAIN/ ELECTRIC/ WIFI
LOCATION: URBAN/ RIVERSIDE **NO. OF SPACES:** 20
PRICES: PARKING: 6€ /24Hrs **SERVICES**: INCL
OPENING TIMES: ALL YEAR **GPS:** N47.88549 E01.83961
DIRECTIONS: In town on D2152, follow signs for CHATEAU & AIRE.
SITE DESCRIPTION: *The aire located on the south side of this small town, on the banks of the Loire, is a former Municipal campsite. Large (60m²), level spaces on gravel, most with shade & ehu's, with lighting at night. Artisanal service point with drainage grid, access via automatic barrier. Rate reduces for 2/ 3 nights.*

REVIEW: *An excellent former campsite, on the banks of the Loire within sight of the town's château, with walks/ cycle path to Orleans (5kms) adjacent plus play area, mini golf & picnic tables. A quiet location yet the aire is not far from the large town centre where there are shops, eating places & a supermarket with petrol station. Weekly market on Saturday morning.*

LAILLY-EN-VAL

ADDRESS: RUE DE LA MAIRIE **TYPE OF AIRE:** PRIVATE
FACILITIES: WATER /GREY & BLACK DRAIN/ ELECTRIC/ WIFI/ RUBBISH
LOCATION: URBAN/ LAKESIDE **NO. OF SPACES:** 20
PRICES: PARKING: 12€/ 24 Hrs **SERVICES**: INCL
OPENING TIMES: ALL YEAR **GPS:** N47.77033 E01.68557
DIRECTIONS: From WEST, take D19 to LAILLY, turn 1st RIGHT after LAKE & RIGHT again to CHURCH & AIRE.
SITE DESCRIPTION: *The aire, managed by CampingCarPark, is located behind the church & next to a lake on the western side of this small town, in a large gravel parking*

area surrounded by grass areas. There is a little shade here, some pitches are separated by hedges, all with 6A ehu's, wifi & only 100m from the centre of town. Access via automatic barrier, CCP card required. Euro-Relais service point with drainage platform.

REVIEW: *A large aire in a nice quiet location next to a lake with walks around it, a boules pitch, play area & cycle routes/ walks in the town. Shops in town include boulangeries, epicerie, tabac, news, cheese shop, cafes/ restaurants.*

SULLY-SUR-LOIRE

ADDRESS: CHEMIN DE LA SALLE VERTE **TYPE OF AIRE:** MUNICIPAL
FACILITIES: WATER /GREY & BLACK DRAIN/ RUBBISH
LOCATION: RURAL/ RIVER **NO. OF SPACES:** 35
PRICES: PARKING: FREE **SERVICES**: FREE
OPENING TIMES: ALL YEAR **GPS:** N47.77116 E02.38448
DIRECTIONS: From EAST take D951 into town, turn 1st RIGHT @ AIRE sign & follow road for 200m to AIRE.

SITE DESCRIPTION: *This aire is located at the edge of the Loire on the eastern side of this small town in a large gravel parking area surrounded by grass areas. There is a little shade here in places, lit at night & is 1km from the centre of town. Large spaces with grass adjacent, Artisanal service point & drainage platform.*

REVIEW: *A very quiet location in a large gravel parking area, with shade in places & next to a forest with several walks/ cycle trails. Château within 500m & a good range of shops in town as well as some eating places.* ***NOTE: Access is via a narrow 'chicane' bordered by rocks which may present problems to large vehicles (8m+).***

BURGUNDY

Burgundy region is made up of 4 departments;
Cote d'Or (21), Nievre (58), Saone-et-Loire (71) & Yonne (81)

Burgundy Map

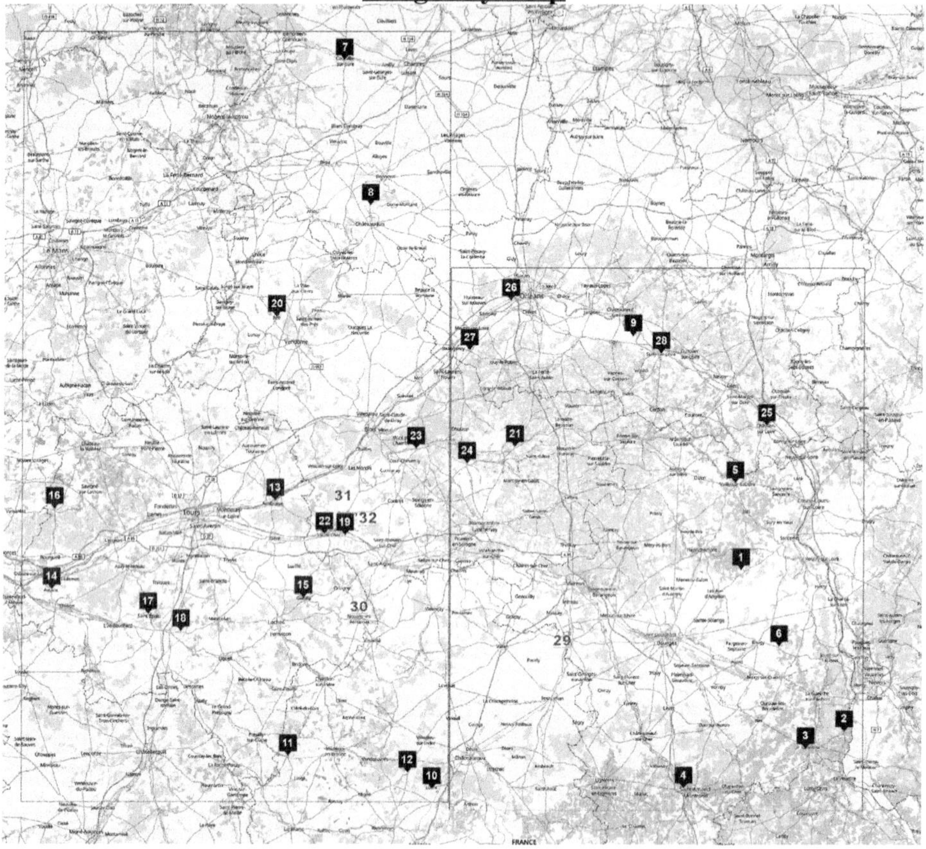

Key to enlarged Burgundy Maps (on next 2 pages)

Former campsites that are now aires are noted in ***bold***

1) FONTAINE FRANCAISE – 2) LAMARCHE SUR SAONE
3) HEUILLEY SUR SAÔNE – ***4) SEURRE*** *– 5) CHAUMOT – 6) IMPHY – 7) ROUY*
8) CHAROLLES – 9) GERMAGNY – 10) LOUHANS
11) ST CRISTOPHE EN BRIONNAIS – 12) ST GENGOUX DE SCISSE
13) ST GENGOUX LE NATIONAL – 14) GRON – 15) GURGY – 16) ST PRIVE
17) ST PIERRE LE MOUTIER – 18) TOULON SUR ARROUX

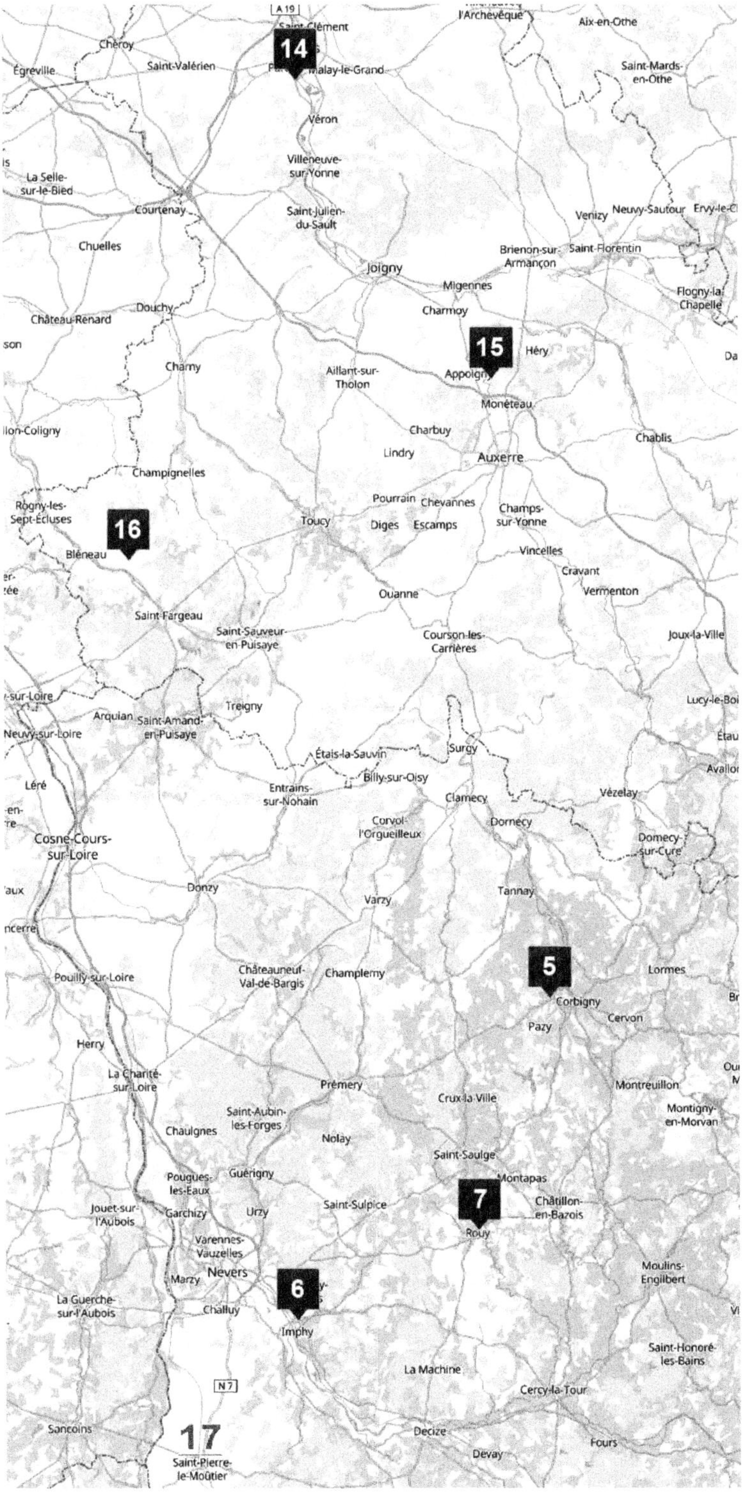
A 19
Saint-Clément
14
Malay-le-Grand
l'Archevêque
Aix-en-Othe
Chéroy
Égreville
Saint-Valérien
Saint-Mards-en-Othe
Véron
Villeneuve-sur-Yonne
La Selle-sur-le-Bied
Courtenay
Saint-Julien-du-Sault
Venizy
Neuvy-Sautour
Chuelles
Brienon-sur-Armançon
Saint-Florentin
Joigny
Migennes
Flogny-la-Chapelle
Château-Renard
Douchy
Charmoy
15
Héry
Charny
Aillant-sur-Tholon
Appoigny
Monéteau
Charbuy
Chablis
Lindry
Auxerre
Champignelles
Pourrain
Chevannes
Rogny-les-Sept-Écluses
16
Toucy
Diges
Escamps
Champs-sur-Yonne
Bléneau
Vincelles
Cravant
Vermenton
Ouanne
Saint-Fargeau
Saint-Sauveur-en-Puisaye
Courson-les-Carrières
Joux-la-Ville
Treigny
Arquian
Saint-Amand-en-Puisaye
Neuvy-sur-Loire
Étais-la-Sauvin
Surgy
Billy-sur-Oisy
Léré
Entrains-sur-Nohain
Clamecy
Vézelay
Corvol-l'Orgueilleux
Dornecy
Cosne-Cours-sur-Loire
Domecy-sur-Cure
Donzy
Varzy
Tannay
5
Lormes
Pouilly-sur-Loire
Châteauneuf-Val-de-Bargis
Champlemy
Corbigny
Cervon
Pazy
Herry
La Charité-sur-Loire
Prémery
Crux-la-Ville
Montreuillon
Montigny-en-Morvan
Saint-Aubin-les-Forges
Chaulgnes
Nolay
Saint-Saulge
Pougues-les-Eaux
Guérigny
Montapas
7
Châtillon-en-Bazois
Jouet-sur-l'Aubois
Garchizy
Urzy
Saint-Sulpice
Rouy
Varennes-Vauzelles
Moulins-Engilbert
Marzy
Nevers
6
La Guerche-sur-l'Aubois
Challuy
Imphy
Saint-Honoré-les-Bains
La Machine
N 7
Cercy-la-Tour
Sancoins
17
Decize
Fours
Devay
Saint-Pierre-le-Moûtier

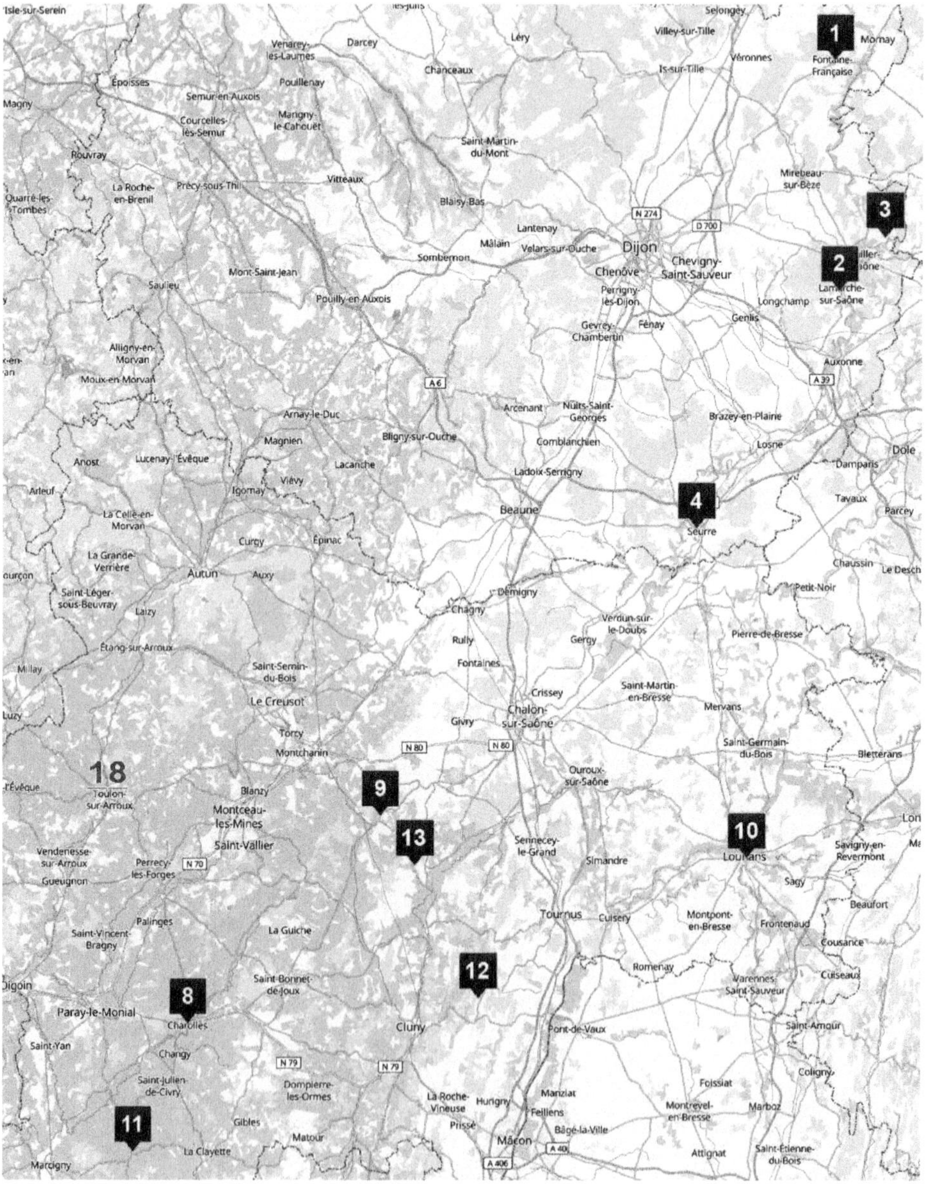
1
2
3
4
8
9
10
11
12
13
18
Selongey
Villey-sur-Tille
Mornay
Véronnes
Is-sur-Tille
Darcey
Léry
Venarey-les-Laumes
Chanceaux
Époisses
Pouillenay
Semur-en-Auxois
Magny
Marigny-le-Cahouët
Courcelles-lès-Semur
Rouvray
Saint-Martin-du-Mont
Mirebeau-sur-Bèze
La Roche-en-Brenil
Précy-sous-Thil
Vitteaux
Quarré-les-Tombes
Blaisy-Bas
N 274
D 700
Lantenay
Mâlain
Velars-sur-Ouche
Dijon
Sombernon
Chenôve
Chevigny-Saint-Sauveur
Mont-Saint-Jean
Saulieu
Perrigny-lès-Dijon
Pouilly-en-Auxois
Longchamp
Genlis
Fénay
Gevrey-Chambertin
Alligny-en-Morvan
Auxonne
Moux-en-Morvan
A 6
A 39
Arcenant
Nuits-Saint-Georges
Brazey-en-Plaine
Arnay-le-Duc
Magnien
Bligny-sur-Ouche
Comblanchien
Losne
Dole
Anost
Lucenay-l'Évêque
Lacanche
Damparis
Ladoix-Serrigny
Viévy
Arleuf
Igornay
Tavaux
Beaune
Parcey
La Celle-en-Morvan
Curgy
Épinac
Seurre
La Grande-Verrière
Chaussin
Autun
Auxy
Le Desch
Saint-Léger-sous-Beuvray
Petit-Noir
Demigny
Chagny
Laizy
Verdun-sur-le-Doubs
Pierre-de-Bresse
Rully
Gergy
Étang-sur-Arroux
Millay
Saint-Sernin-du-Bois
Fontaines
Saint-Martin-en-Bresse
Crissey
Le Creusot
Mervans
Luzy
Chalon-sur-Saône
Givry
Torcy
Saint-Germain-du-Bois
N 80
Montchanin
Bletterans
Ouroux-sur-Saône
Toulon-sur-Arroux
Blanzy
Montceau-les-Mines
Saint-Vallier
Sennecey-le-Grand
Louhans
Savigny-en-Revermont
Vendenesse-sur-Arroux
Perrecy-les-Forges
N 70
Simandre
Gueugnon
Sagy
Beaufort
Palinges
Tournus
Cuisery
Montpont-en-Bresse
Frontenaud
Saint-Vincent-Bragny
La Guiche
Cousance
Romenay
Digoin
Saint-Bonnet-de-Joux
Varennes-Saint-Sauveur
Cuiseaux
Paray-le-Monial
Charolles
Cluny
Pont-de-Vaux
Saint-Amour
Saint-Yan
Changy
N 79
Saint-Julien-de-Civry
Dompierre-les-Ormes
Foissiat
Coligny
La Roche-Vineuse
Hurigny
Manziat
Feillens
Montrevel-en-Bresse
Marboz
Gibles
Prissé
Bâgé-la-Ville
Matour
Mâcon
A 40
Attignat
Saint-Étienne-du-Bois
La Clayette
A 406
Marcigny

21 COTE D'OR

FONTAINE FRANCAISE

ADDRESS: RUE DE BERTHAULT **TYPE OF AIRE:** MUNICIPAL
FACILITIES: WATER /GREY & BLACK DRAIN / ELECTRIC
LOCATION: URBAN/ RIVERSIDE **NO OF SPACES:** 4
PRICES: PARKING: FREE **SERVICES**: 5€ WATER & ELECTRIC
OPENING TIMES: ALL YEAR **GPS:** N47.52501 E05.36749
DIRECTIONS: From EAST take D960 thru village, over bridge & take 1st LEFT.
***SITE DESCRIPTION**: This small aire is located on the west side of this rural village next to a large lake & a small river, in a quiet residential location with shade under trees. AireServices borne with drainage channel.*
***REVIEW:** A nice quiet location close to a lake & the river with picnic table, but the aire is small & access might be difficult for larger motorhomes. There are only 3/ 4 spaces at the aire but there is more parking alongside the river. butcher, boulangerie, tabac & a restaurant in the picturesque village.*

HEUILLEY SUR SAÔNE

ADDRESS: RUE DE CONDE **TYPE OF AIRE:** MUNICIPAL
FACILITIES: WATER /GREY & BLACK DRAIN/ ELECTRIC
LOCATION: SEMI-RURAL / CANAL **NO. OF SPACES:** 25
PRICES: PARKING: FREE **SERVICES**: 3€ WATER or ELECTRIC
OPENING TIMES: ALL YEAR **GPS:** N47.32785 E05.45448
DIRECTIONS: Entering village from WEST turn RIGHT at CHURCH & AIRE is on RIGHT, next to CANAL.

***SITE DESCRIPTION:** This Municipal aire is located on the south side of this small rural village (Pop. 300), 100m from the centre & next to the canal & the River Saone. The aire is located in a large level tarmac/ gravel parking area with no shade, it has farmland to the west & there is a nearby play area. Flot Bleu service point.*
***REVIEW:** A very quiet location but few facilities in village apart from a bar/ tabac that also sells bread. Municipal campsite on other side of canal with 25 spaces, open May till Sept. Fishing in canal & river, walks alongside the canal in both directions, picnic tables & tennis court adjacent to aire. Jetons from the Mairie or Poste.*

LAMARCHE SUR SAONE

ADDRESS: RUE DE LA MARCHOTTE **TYPE OF AIRE:** MUNICIPAL
FACILITIES: WATER /GREY & BLACK DRAIN/ ELECTRIC
LOCATION: URBAN/ RIVERSIDE **NO. OF SPACES:** 20

PRICES: PARKING: FREE **SERVICES**: 3€ WATER or ELECTRIC
OPENING TIMES: ALL YEAR **GPS:** N47.27250 E05.38667
DIRECTIONS: Take D976 NORTH out of village & before leaving turn RIGHT opposite LAKE, AIRE is straight ahead next to river.
SITE DESCRIPTION: *The aire is pleasantly located next to the Saone river in a large parking area with spaces on grass accessed off a gravel track, the parking has a little shade around the edges but no lighting. The parking is next to the moorings on the river, with adjacent grass areas, about 150m north of the village centre. Flot Bleu service point with large drainage platform.*

REVIEW: *A very peaceful position next to the Saone river with parking on grass (which can be a bit soft in wet weather), there are 2 Flot Bleu bornes (for boats & motorhomes) – jetons from Mairie. The aire has the river to the east (with open countryside beyond) & lakes to the west, fishing is possible both in the river or in the nearby lakes (payable by the day). Walks & cycling alongside the river and a 15km cycle path. Shops in village include; boulangerie, grocer/ news, butcher, 2 restaurants & a pizzeria.*

SEURRE

ADDRESS: RUE DE LA PERCHE A L'OISEAU **TYPE OF AIRE:** PRIVATE
FACILITIES: WATER /GREY & BLACK DRAIN/ ELECTRIC/ WIFI
LOCATION: SEMI-RURAL **NO. OF SPACES:** 28
PRICES: PARKING: 14€ /24 Hrs **SERVICES**: INCL
OPENING TIMES: ALL YEAR **GPS:** N47.00226 E05.14494
DIRECTIONS: Entering town on D34 from NORTH, turn 1st RIGHT to 'PORT DE PLAISANCE' & AIRE.

***SITE DESCRIPTION**: A well-placed aire, run by CampingCarPark, next to the Saone River & close to the towns Port – parking is in the former Municipal camping with parking on hard standings or grass, bordered by grass with shade & lighting. Access by automatic barrier (CCP card required), 28 pitches all with ehu's & wifi. The drive-thru Artisanal borne is easy to access (also lit at night).*
***REVIEW:** A very practical aire, in a pleasant location close to the Leisure area with a children's playground. There are nice walks/ cycling along the Saone & the town centre is not too far; an interesting town & worthy of a visit, an ideal halt for discovering the Valley of the Saone. Good range of shops/ eating places & an InterMarche supermarket.*

58 NIEVRE

CHAUMOT

ADDRESS: CANAL, OFF D977 **TYPE OF AIRE:** MUNICIPAL
FACILITIES: WATER /GREY & BLACK DRAIN / ELECTRIC / RUBBISH
LOCATION: RURAL/ CANAL **NO. OF SPACES:** 6
PRICES: PARKING: FREE **SERVICES**: 2€ WATER or ELECTRIC
OPENING TIMES: ALL YEAR **GPS:** N47.25909 E03.64805
DIRECTIONS: From WEST take D977/bis to CHAUMOT, cross CANAL to AIRE on RIGHT.
***SITE DESCRIPTION:** This rural aire is located just north of Chaumot next to the canal marina where there are several spaces on gravel or grass, in a large parking area, 400m from the village centre. The spaces have a little shade, bordered by grass with views over the canal & farmland. Euro Relais borne with platform drain.*

***REVIEW:** Quiet (at night) rural location outside a rural hamlet, next to & overlooking a canal with several level spaces available. Picnic tables & tow path along the canal for walks/ cycling. No services 15/11 – 15/04. Small campsite nearby.*

IMPHY

ADDRESS: CHEMIN DE HALAGE **TYPE OF AIRE:** MUNICIPAL
FACILITIES: WATER /GREY & BLACK DRAIN/ ELEC./ RUBBISH/ TOILETS
LOCATION: SEMI-URBAN/ RIVER **NO. OF SPACES:** 12
PRICES: PARKING: FREE **SERVICES**: 4€ WATER or ELECTRIC
OPENING TIMES: ALL YEAR **GPS:** N46.92211 E03.25969
DIRECTIONS: Take D200 WEST to IMPHY, cross LOIRE & take next RIGHT for 1km to AIRE.

SITE DESCRIPTION: *The aire is located on the south west side of this small town, next to the Loire river where there are a dozen large level spaces on tarmac in a large open grassed area. There is little shade but it is lit at night. Flot Bleu service point with drainage grid & toilets.*

REVIEW: *A well maintained, quiet aire on the banks of the Loire river with large grass spaces, footpaths, picnic tables & children's play area adjacent. The aire is 800m from the town centre shops/ supermarket & services. Swimming pool & boulangerie nearby. Jetons from Mairie/ pool.*

ROUY

ADDRESS: FOYER RURAL, D978 **TYPE OF AIRE:** MUNICIPAL
FACILITIES: WATER/ GREY & BLACK DRAIN
LOCATION: SEMI-RURAL **NO. OF SPACES:** 6
PRICES: PARKING: FREE **SERVICES**: FREE
OPENING TIMES: ALL YEAR **GPS:** N47.02862 E03.53403
DIRECTIONS: Entering ROUY from EAST on D978, AIRE is immediately on RIGHT.
SITE DESCRIPTION: *The aire is located about 300m north of the centre of the small rural village in a medium size gravel parking area next to the Village hall surrounded by open farmland, where there is a drainage platform with an adjacent water tap. No shade but lit at night.*

REVIEW: *A basic but nice free aire with half a dozen large, level parking spaces set back from the road, quiet & a short walk into village with a boulangerie, epicerie, laundrette & an organic farm shop. Picnic table in a shelter & grass areas, possible noise from Hall at weekends.*

ST PIERRE LE MOUTIER

ADDRESS: RUE DE BEAUDRILLON **TYPE OF AIRE:** PRIVATE
FACILITIES: WATER /GREY & BLACK DRAIN/ ELECTRIC/ WIFI
LOCATION: SEMI-URBAN **NO. OF SPACES:** 48
PRICES: PARKING: 12-14€/ 24HRS **SERVICES**: INCL
OPENING TIMES: ALL YEAR **GPS :** N46.78573 E03.11927
DIRECTIONS: Entering village from SOUTH on D272, AIRE is on RIGHT.
SITE DESCRIPTION: *This 'Camping Village' aire, run by CampingCarPark, is situated in the former Municipal campsite, about 400m south of the village centre close to farmland. Pitches are on gravel/ grass (many shaded) with 6A ehu & wifi with toilets (open 15/06-15/09). Euro-Relais service point with drainage platform. Access by automatic barrier, CCP card required.*

REVIEW: *A nice location on the edge of the village yet close to the centre - quiet with large pitches & fishing lake adjacent. Toilets/ showers cleaned daily but dated & only open June to Sept. 42 ehu's for the 48 pitches. Shops in village; boulangerie, grocer & bar/ eating places.*

71 SAONE-ET-LOIRE

CHAROLLES

ADDRESS: RTE DE VIRY, D33 **TYPE OF AIRE:** MUNICIPAL
FACILITIES: WATER /GREY & BLACK DRAIN/ ELECTRIC/ WIFI
LOCATION: SEMI-RURAL/ RIVER **NO. OF SPACES:** 8
PRICES: PARKING: 3€/ 24 Hrs **SERVICES**: 3€ WATER or ELECTRIC
OPENING TIMES: 01/04 - 05/10 **GPS:** N46.43945 E04.28212
DIRECTIONS: From town take D17 & D33 EAST, following CAMPING signs to AIRE.
SITE DESCRIPTION: *The aire is located outside the Municipal campsite, with views over the surrounding countryside, about 1km east from the town centre. There are 8 spaces in a tarmac parking area, some with shade under trees, bordered by grass/ hedges & next to the river. Euro-Relais service point with drainage grid.*
REVIEW: *An aire in a lovely place surrounded by plenty of greenery, quiet at night, next to the river with good sized level spaces. Pay at ticket machine. Nice campsite with pool, modern toilets & showers adjacent - a level walk into town where there is a small Carrefour, shops & a château.*

Charolles

GERMAGNY

ADDRESS: RUE DE LA GUYE **TYPE OF AIRE:** MUNICIPAL
FACILITIES: WATER /GREY & BLACK DRAIN/ TOILETS
LOCATION: RURAL **NO. OF SPACES:** 6
PRICES: PARKING: FREE **SERVICES**: FREE
OPENING TIMES: ALL YEAR **GPS:** N46.67071 E04.59898
DIRECTIONS: In GERMAGNY, turn WEST at Renault Garage & AIRE is on LEFT.
SITE DESCRIPTION: *The aire is located in a small tarmac/gravel car park where there are 6 level spaces located on the western edge of the village, 200m from the village centre. Artisanal service point / drainage platform & small toilet block with sink .*

REVIEW: *A peaceful location surrounded by open farmland next to a quiet minor road but unfortunately no shade or lighting. Few facilities in village apart from grocer, petrol station & restaurant/ pizzeria, although there are more shops 2kms away. Picnic area & a children's play area next to the nearby river.*

LOUHANS

ADDRESS: MARINA, RUE DU PORT **TYPE OF AIRE:** MUNICIPAL
FACILITIES: WATER /GREY & BLACK DRAIN / TOILETS/ WIFI
LOCATION: URBAN/ RIVERSIDE **NO. OF SPACES:** 20
PRICES: PARKING: 6€/ 24Hrs **SERVICES**: 2€ WATER
OPENING TIMES: ALL YEAR **GPS:** N46.62948 E05.21310
DIRECTIONS: In LOUHANS cross RIVER to WEST side & turn 1st RIGHT to AIRE.
SITE DESCRIPTION: *The aire is in a large gravel parking area next to the river on the west side of town; where there are level parking spaces next to grass areas with picnic tables, accessed off a tarmac track. The aire is about 600m from the town centre with a*

modern Flot Bleu service point, wifi & large platform drain, toilets/ showers are available at the Capitainerie.

REVIEW: *A peaceful aire, on the banks of the River Seille with some shade, good services, fishing & walks along the towpath. Good market in town on Monday mornings & a range of shops. An interesting medieval town, the main street is lined with over 150 arcades, 15th C houses & a 17th C hospital.*

ST CRISTOPHE EN BRIONNAIS

ADDRESS: RTE DE L'ALLEE, OFF D989 **TYPE OF AIRE:** MUNICIPAL
FACILITIES: WATER /GREY & BLACK DRAIN/ ELECTRIC/ TOILETS
LOCATION: SEMI-RURAL **NO. OF SPACES:** 6
PRICES: PARKING: FREE **SERVICES**: FREE
OPENING TIMES: ALL YEAR **GPS:** N46.28465 E04.17995
DIRECTIONS: In centre of ST CHRISTOPHE, take RTE DE L'ALLEE to AIRE.
SITE DESCRIPTION: *This small aire is located on the south side of this little rural village, bordered by farmland & only a short 400m walk to the village centre. Parking is in a small gravel parking area, no shade with an adjacent toilet block as well as 4 ehu's. Artisanal service point with platform drain.*

REVIEW: *Excellent little aire, level parking surrounded by farmland with good views, toilets, boules pitch & electric (pay by donation). Quiet & secure with houses nearby, but avoid Wednesdays due to large cattle market in village. Good way-marked walks in area. Village has a butcher, boulangerie, mini-market & 2 restaurants.*

ST GENGOUX DE SCISSE

ADDRESS: RTE DU TACOT **TYPE OF AIRE:** MUNICIPAL
FACILITIES: WATER /GREY & BLACK DRAIN / ELECTRIC / RUBBISH
LOCATION: SEMI-RURAL **NO. OF SPACES:** 4
PRICES: PARKING: FREE **SERVICES**: FREE
OPENING TIMES: ALL YEAR **GPS:** N46.46082 E04.77520

DIRECTIONS: In village, AIRE can be found opposite CEMETERY.
SITE DESCRIPTION: *The aire is situated in a large gravel car park on the south west side & only 350m to the centre of this small rural village. Parking is opposite the cemetery, surrounded by farmland with little shade & no lighting at night. Modern artisanal borne with a large platform drain & adjacent electric point (not working in winter).*

REVIEW: *A pleasant little village with a quiet, well maintained aire, nicely situated surrounded by vineyards with ample parking despite only having 4 authorised pitches. Couple of small shops in village; epicerie/ tabac, bar/ wine cave with picnic areas & a 13km signposted walk around village.*

ST GENGOUX LE NATIONAL

ADDRESS: OLD RAILWAY STATION, OFF D67 **TYPE OF AIRE:** MUNICIPAL
FACILITIES: WATER /GREY & BLACK DRAIN / ELECTRIC / TOILETS
LOCATION: SEMI-RURAL **NO. OF SPACES:** 20
PRICES: PARKING: FREE **SERVICES**: 4€ WATER or ELECTRIC
OPENING TIMES: ALL YEAR **GPS:** N46.60612 E04.66859
DIRECTIONS: From town take D67 SOUTH & 1st LEFT after RAILWAY BRIDGE.

SITE DESCRIPTION: *The aire is situated in the tarmac car park of the old railway station with plenty of spaces available & shaded by trees in places. The aire is about 1km south of the town centre. Modern artisanal borne with a large platform drain & toilets/ sinks.*

***REVIEW:** A very nice aire with a large level car park in a quiet place, where you can cycle along the old railway line to Cluny, bikes can also be hired here. An interesting 11th C church in the town & there is a good range of shops; supermarket, boulangerie, butcher, cave, etc & a brasserie with a Tuesday market. Childs' play area & petanque pitch adjacent.*

TOULON SUR ARROUX

ADDRESS: RTE D'UXEAU **TYPE OF AIRE:** PRIVATE
FACILITIES: WATER /GREY & BLACK DRAIN/ ELECTRIC/ TOILETS
LOCATION: RURAL/ RIVER **NO. OF SPACES:** 68
PRICES: PARKING: 14€/ 24HRS **SERVICES**: INCL
OPENING TIMES: ALL YEAR **GPS :** N46.69423 E04.13261
DIRECTIONS: From TOULON take D985 across RIVER & turn 1st LEFT to AIRE.
***SITE DESCRIPTION:** This large 'Camping Village' aire, run by CampingCarPark, is situated in the former Municipal campsite about 400m west of Toulon & alongside the Arroux river. Pitches are on grass (most shaded), with hedges & each with 6A ehu as well as toilets/ showers (open 15/04-30/10). UrbaFlux service point with drainage platform. Access by automatic barrier, CCP card required.*

***REVIEW:** A pleasant location on the Arroux river, close to the village & quiet with good pitches, toilets are clean but dated & no wifi. Shops in village; boulangerie, butcher, pharmacy & eating places. Walking routes around village.*

89 YONNE

GRON

ADDRESS: RUE DES PETITS PRES **TYPE OF AIRE:** MUNICIPAL
FACILITIES: WATER /GREY & BLACK DRAIN / TOILETS/ RUBBISH
LOCATION: SEMI-RURAL **NO. OF SPACES:** 10
PRICES: PARKING: FREE **SERVICES**: FREE
OPENING TIMES: ALL YEAR **GPS:** N48.15996 E03.25658
DIRECTIONS: Approaching GRON from WEST on D157, turn 1st RIGHT & LEFT into AIRE.
***SITE DESCRIPTION:** The aire is located on the western side of this rural village in a small tarmac parking area, where there are 10 spaces available, lighting but no shade. EuroRelais borne with drainage grid & adjacent small toilet.*
***REVIEW:** A modern, clean aire next to a nice large park with picnic tables, play area & a small toilet block, fairly quiet with a footpath that leads (400m) to the village centre & its small range of shops; boulangerie, butcher, bar-tabac, pharmacy & Poste/ news. Level cycle track along river to Sens.*

Gron

GURGY

ADDRESS: CHEMIN DE HALAGE **TYPE OF AIRE:** MUNICIPAL
FACILITIES: WATER /GREY & BLACK DRAIN / ELECTRIC/ WIFI
LOCATION: SEMI-RURAL **NO. OF SPACES:** 30
PRICES: PARKING: 13€ / 24Hrs **SERVICES**: INCL
OPENING TIMES: ALL YEAR **GPS:** N47.86382 E03.55429
DIRECTIONS: From NORTH take D348 into GURGY, at far end of village turn RIGHT into RUE DU GUE & then LEFT to AIRE.
SITE DESCRIPTION: *This aire is on the banks of the River Yonne at the southern edge of the village, backing onto open farmland, parking is on gravel/ grass with lighting, some trees providing shade & 400m to the centre of the village. Raclet borne with drainage grid & ehu's.*

Gurgy

REVIEW: *A relaxing place, clean & next to a lovely river with good walks or bike rides along its banks. A level walk into village where there is a boulangerie, supermarket, bar/ tabac, pharmacy & a restaurant. Ehu's for all 30 spaces but slight noise during day from the autoroute, Good stopover from A6, Jcn 19. Council official collects parking fee, free in winter but no services.*

Aire at Gurgy

ST PRIVE

ADDRESS: ALLEE R. BARON, OFF D221 **TYPE OF AIRE:** MUNICIPAL
FACILITIES: WATER /GREY & BLACK DRAIN / TOILETS/ ELECTRIC
LOCATION: URBAN/ LAKE **NO. OF SPACES:** 4
PRICES: PARKING: FREE **SERVICES**: 2€ WATER or ELECTRIC
OPENING TIMES: ALL YEAR **GPS:** N47.68395 E02.99627
DIRECTIONS: From ST. PRIVE take D90 WEST, turn LEFT on D221 & then RIGHT.
SITE DESCRIPTION: *The aire is in a small tarmac parking area next to a lake on the western edge of the village, bordered by mature trees & grass areas. Parking is close to the village centre (200m), shaded but little lighting. Modern AireServices service point, drainage platform & small toilet block. Jetons from boulangerie.*

REVIEW: *A pretty little village with a good lakeside aire although spaces would struggle to take anything longer than 7m. Very quiet & a short level walk into village with its boulangerie, cafe & a pizza van calls in village in evening. Play area, fishing in lake, & picnic tables.*

FRANCHE-COMTE

Franche-Comte region is made up of 4 departments; Doubs (25), Jura (39), Haute-Saone (70) & Belfort (90)

Franche-Comte Map

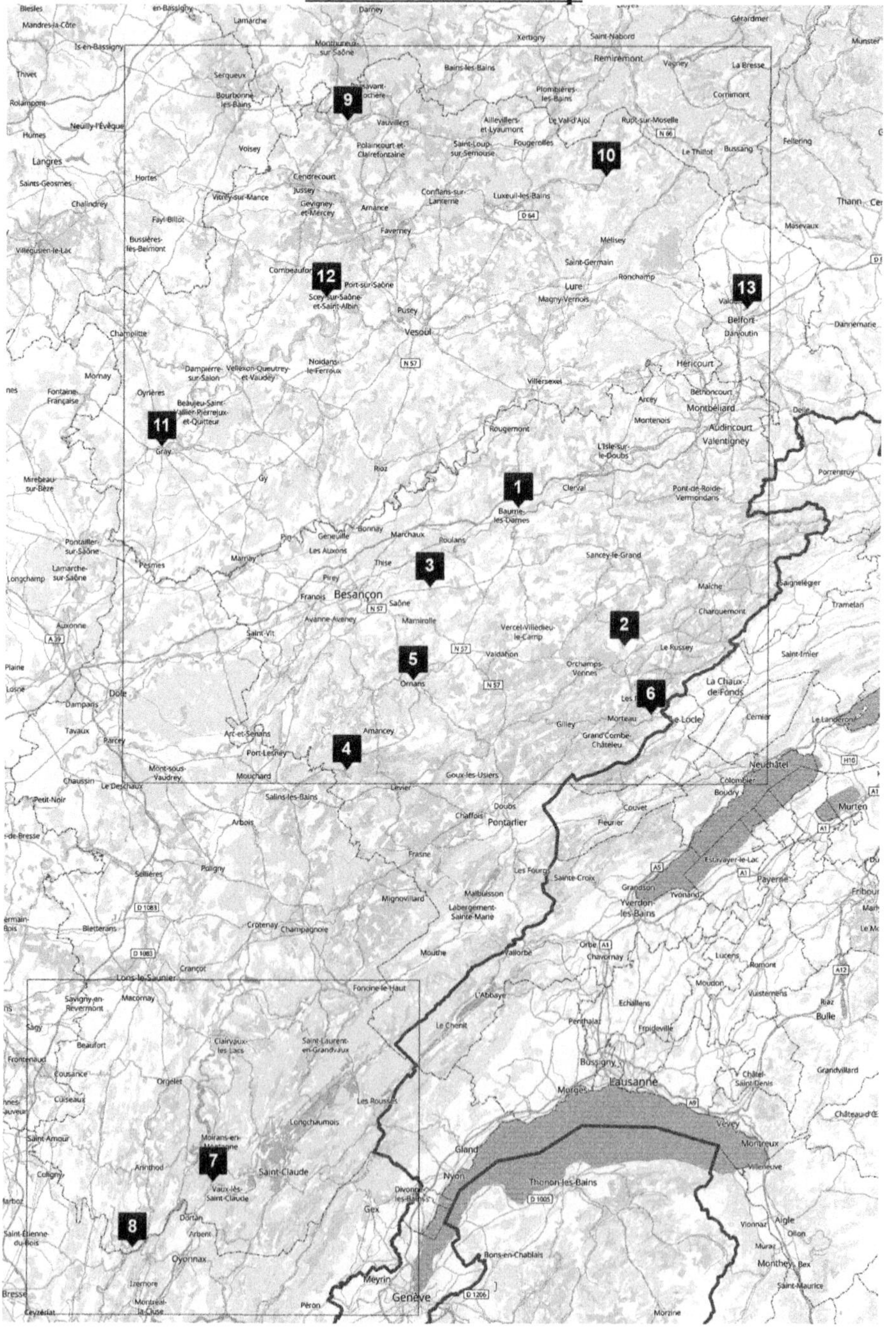

<u>Key to enlarged Franche-Comte Maps (below & next page)</u>

1) BAUME LES DAMES – 2) ~~CONSOLATION-MAISONETTES~~ - 3) NANCRAY
4) NANS SOUS STE ANNE – 5) ORNANS – 6) VILLERS LE LAC – 7) JEURRE
8) THOIRETTE – 9) CORRE – 10) FAUCOGNEY ET LA MER – 11) GRAY
12) SCEY SUR SAONE – 13) BELFORT

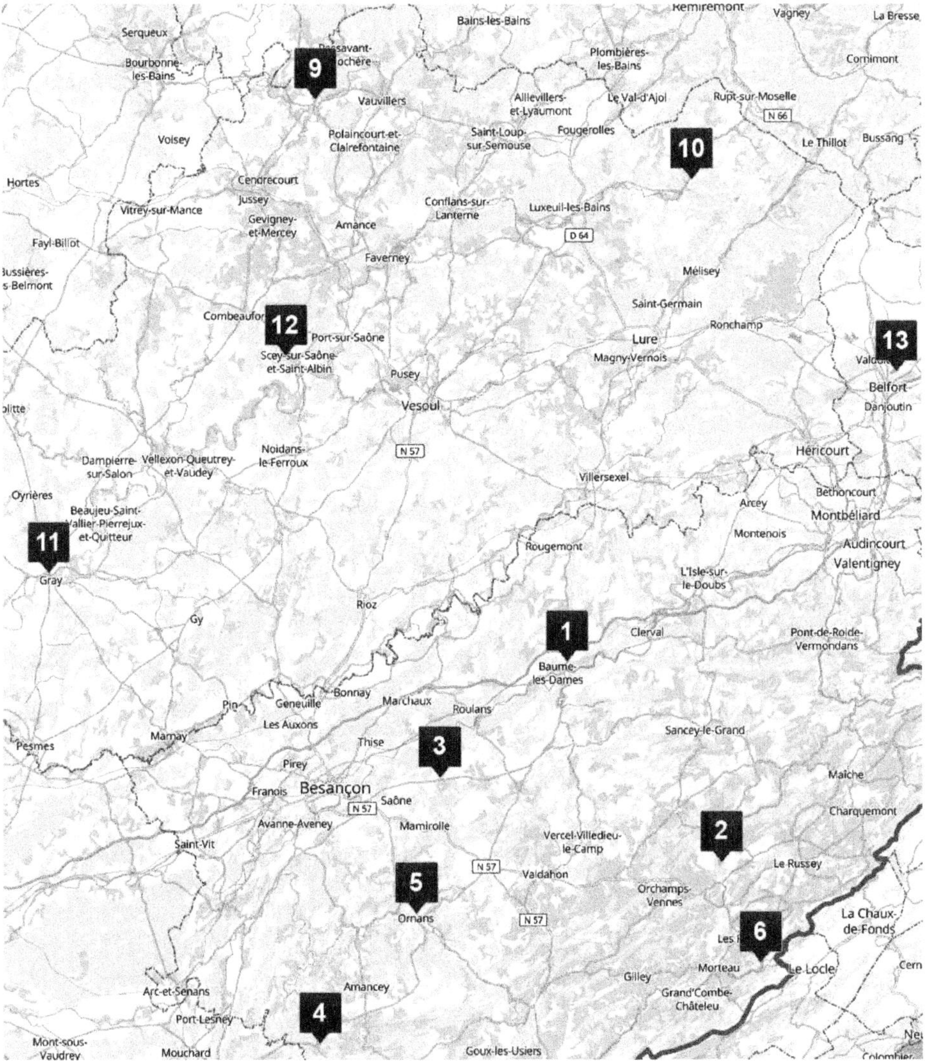

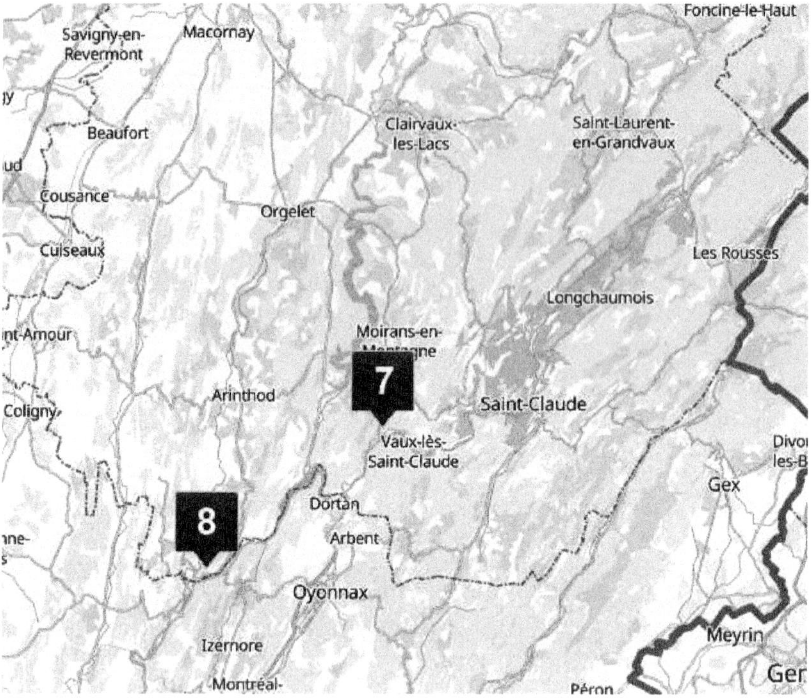

25 DOUBS

BAUME LES DAMES

ADDRESS: QUAI DU CANAL, D277 **TYPE OF AIRE:** MUNICIPAL
FACILITIES: WATER /GREY & BLACK DRAIN / TOILETS / ELECTRIC
LOCATION: SEMI-RURAL/ CANAL **NO. OF SPACES:** 40
PRICES: PARKING: 12€/ 24 Hrs **SERVICES**: FREE
OPENING TIMES: ALL YEAR **GPS:** N47.34021 E06.35778
DIRECTIONS: From BAUME take D50 over RIVER/ CANAL & turn 1st RIGHT.

***SITE DESCRIPTION**: Aire is on a modern purpose built, large tarmac parking area, surrounded by fields & woodland, next to the Doubs River & canal. Parking is laid out in a horseshoe shape with marked spaces separated by grass/ shrubs & is about 1km south from the town centre. Toilets & showers on site in a modern timber building. A good artisanal borne with a large platform drain.*

***REVIEW:** A very nice aire - quiet with electric, services, toilets & showers, all in a lovely spot next to the canal. Good place to spend a night, lit at night but not much shade & well frequented. Boulanger calls in morning, a small auberge is nearby & a 15 min walk to the town with its good range of shops, etc. Walks along canal. Previous winner of "Aire of the Year".*

NANCRAY

ADDRESS: MUSEE, RUE DE MUSEE **TYPE OF AIRE:** MUNICIPAL
FACILITIES: WATER /GREY & BLACK DRAIN/ RUBBISH
LOCATION: RURAL **NO. OF SPACES:** 12
PRICES: PARKING: FREE **SERVICES**: 2€ WATER
OPENING TIMES: 01/04 – 30/10 **GPS:** N47.23952 E06.18471
DIRECTIONS: In NANCRAY follow signs to MUSEE. AIRE is just past Museum.

***SITE DESCRIPTION**: The aire is located in a large gravel car park, next to the museum & 500m south from the village, where there are a dozen level spaces bordered by grass areas, no lighting or shade. UrbaFlux borne with a platform drain.*

***REVIEW:** A very quiet (once the museum is closed), comfortable location surrounded by open farmland on all sides, being about 15mins walk from the village. Slight slope on car park but superb far-reaching views. Walks start from this Country Crafts museum (with various workshops). Range of shops/ services in Nancray including Proxi supermarket with a restaurant/ cafeteria in the museum plus a shop selling local produce. Jetons from museum.*

NANS-SOUS-SAINTE ANNE

ADDRESS: ROUTE TAILLANDERIE **TYPE OF AIRE:** MUNICIPAL
FACILITIES: WATER /GREY & BLACK DRAIN
LOCATION: RURAL **NO. OF SPACES:** 6
PRICES: PARKING: 6€ /24 Hrs **SERVICES**: INCL
OPENING TIMES: ALL YEAR **GPS:** N46.97173 E05.99700

DIRECTIONS: From NANS take GRADE RUE WEST & then 1st LEFT to AIRE.
***SITE DESCRIPTION**: The aire is in a small gravel parking area, south of the small rural village, with 6 spaces reserved for motorhomes separated by hedges but without much shade or lighting. The aire is surrounded by grass area, near to the river & some chalets, about 400m from the village. Artisanal service point with drain is located at the Laiterie in the village.*

***REVIEW:** A very rural location with nice views, divided pitches, extremely quiet near to the river with a cheese producer, restaurant & shop in the village. 1.5km walk to the impressive Source de Lion & its caves/ waterfalls. Pay for parking at Laiterie.*

ORNANS

ADDRESS: CHEMIN DES ESSARTS **TYPE OF AIRE:** MUNICIPAL
FACILITIES: WATER /GREY & BLACK DRAIN/ RUBBISH/ ELECTRIC/ WIFI
LOCATION: URBAN **NO. OF SPACES:** 16
PRICES: PARKING: 5-10€/ 24Hrs **SERVICES**: INCL
OPENING TIMES: ALL YEAR **GPS COORDS:** N47.10755 E06.14790
DIRECTIONS: From EAST take D67 into ORNANS, turn RIGHT into CHEMIN.
***SITE DESCRIPTION**: The aire is located in a medium sized tarmac car park on the north east edge of this small town, near to the river & close to the OT, where there are level spaces each 7x5m plus a large 12x5m pitch – lit at night but little shade. Access by automatic barrier to parking where there is an artisanal borne with a platform drain.*

***REVIEW:** A pleasantly situated aire overlooking this historic little town. Price includes ehu & wifi, payable by credit card only, rate varies according to season. Access road is narrow/ steep. Short walk into town where there are shops, eating places, a museum & the Via Ferrata rock climbing area.*

VILLERS LE LAC

ADDRESS: RUE P. BERCOT **TYPE OF AIRE:** PRIVATE
FACILITIES: WATER /GREY & BLACK DRAIN
LOCATION: SEMI-URBAN/ RIVER **NO. OF SPACES:** 20
PRICES: PARKING: 9€/ 24 Hrs **SERVICES**: 3.5€ WATER
OPENING TIMES: APRIL – OCT **GPS:** N47.05631 E06.67075
DIRECTIONS: At R/bout on D461 take D215 into village, AIRE is 400m on RIGHT.
***SITE DESCRIPTION** This private aire is located in the grounds of the river cruise company "Bateaux du Saut du Doubs" in a large shaded parking area where there are plenty of parking spaces on grass or tarmac shaded by mature trees & alongside the river. Picnic area adjacent. Aire is located at south side of town, 300m from the centre but within 100m of a supermarket. AireServices service point with platform drain.*

***REVIEW:** Easy to find, an excellent aire that is free if you pay for a cruise on the river, with ample quiet parking bordering the river Doubs. Good shade, short walk into town where there are plenty of shops, eating places, a museum as well as supermarkets. Brasserie & bar on site, fishing in river. Cruise is a 2 hour long trip along the Doubs including a 1 hour stop, leaving every hour in peak season.*

39 JURA

JEURRE

ADDRESS: RUE PRINCIPALE, **TYPE OF AIRE:** PRIVATE
FACILITIES: WATER /GREY & BLACK DRAIN / ELECTRIC
LOCATION: SEMI-RURAL **NO. OF SPACES:** 15
PRICES: PARKING: 5€ /NIGHT **SERVICES**: 3€ ELECTRIC, 2€ WATER
OPENING TIMES: 01/05 – 31/10 **GPS:** N46.36625 E05.70665
DIRECTIONS: Take D27 to JEURRE, turn 1st RIGHT into RUE PRINCIPALE & AIRE is immediately on RIGHT.
***SITE DESCRIPTION**: This private aire is off the Rue Principale leading into Jeurre with parking in a large field surrounded by a tall hedge & trees – giving good privacy & shade in places. The artisanal borne is easy to access with platform drainage.*

***REVIEW:** A very nice aire in a pleasant location, parking on grass (slight slope), bread machine but no shops or amenities nearby. Well maintained/ secure with pleasant owners, good walking area with waterfall nearby.*

THOIRETTE

ADDRESS: GRANDE RUE, D936 **TYPE OF AIRE:** MUNICIPAL
FACILITIES: WATER /GREY & BLACK DRAIN/ ELECTRIC/ RUBBISH
LOCATION: SEMI-RURAL **NO. OF SPACES:** 6
PRICES: PARKING: 7€/ 24 Hrs **SERVICES**: INCL
OPENING TIMES: ALL YEAR **GPS:** N46.26942 E05.53502
DIRECTIONS: From SOUTH cross RIVER into village, turn LEFT @ R/bout to AIRE.

***SITE DESCRIPTION**: The aire is located in a small gravel car park, situated at the western side of this small rural village, next to the Ain river. The parking spaces are separated by grass & edged by a grass area with ehu's, lighting but little shade. The aire is 50m from the river & 200m from the village centre. Artisanal service point with drainage platform.*

***REVIEW:** A nice little aire for 6 motorhomes with gravel spaces separated by grass, council official collects the fee. Light traffic noise but quiet at night. The village has an 8 til 8 Mini-market (next to aire), a boulangerie, Poste & a restaurant, there is also a 70 pitch municipal campsite. The village is close to the Ain Gorges & Selignac Abbey.*

70-HAUTE-SAONE

CORRE

ADDRESS: MARINA DE CORRE, D44 **TYPE OF AIRE:** PRIVATE
FACILITIES: WATER /GREY & BLACK DRAIN /ELECTRIC /TOILETS/ WIFI
LOCATION: SEMI-RURAL/ RIVERSIDE **NO. OF SPACES:** 30
PRICES: PARKING: 11€ /24 Hrs **SERVICES**: INCL, 2€ SHOWER
OPENING TIMES: ALL YEAR **GPS:** N47.91385 E05.99333
DIRECTIONS: In village take D44 towards river & 1st LEFT to MARINA & AIRE.

***SITE DESCRIPTION:** A well placed aire in a rural location, next to the Marina on the Saone River, in a large open grassy area with individual large spaces on grass or gravel separated by grass & accessed by a gravel track. Pitches have individual hook-ups & water but no shade. Artisanal service point with a large platform drain, toilets at Capitainerie.*

***REVIEW:** An extremely nice, quiet aire in a lovely place, 400m south of the village, on the banks of the Saone; plenty of boats/ birds/ wildlife, with it's own bar/restaurant & clean/ heated toilets/ showers. Not too far from the shops (superette, boulangerie, pharmacy) in the village, good walks/ cycling along the towpath.*

FAUCOGNEY ET LA MER

ADDRESS: RUE DES CHARS, D72 **TYPE OF AIRE:** MUNICIPAL
FACILITIES: WATER/ GREY DRAIN/ ELECTRIC/ RUBBISH/ TOILETS
LOCATION: SEMI-RURAL **NO. OF SPACES:** 6
PRICES: PARKING: FREE **SERVICES**: 2€ WATER or ELECTRIC
OPENING TIMES: ALL YEAR **GPS:** N47.83722 E06.55996
DIRECTIONS: From SOUTH on D672, in village turn 1st RIGHT to STADE & AIRE.

SITE DESCRIPTION: *A modern, well equipped aire located on the southern side of the village, next to the football pitch, about 1km from the centre. The aire has individual shaded hard standing pitches, separated by grass, together with a picnic table, boules pitch & a small toilet block. AireServices service point with drainage platform.*
REVIEW: *On the "Plateau of 1,000 Lakes", a good aire (below) in a rural location yet within walking distance of a small range of shops/ services. Faucogney is an ancient village, with well kept and preserved 17th C houses and buildings.*

GRAY

ADDRESS: RUE DE LA PLAGE **TYPE OF AIRE:** MUNICIPAL
FACILITIES: WATER /GREY & BLACK DRAIN /ELECTRIC/ RUBBISH
LOCATION: SEMI-RURAL **NO. OF SPACES:** 20
PRICES: PARKING: 11€/ 24 Hrs **SERVICES**: INCL
OPENING TIMES: ALL YEAR **GPS:** N47.45221 E05.60269
DIRECTIONS: Take D67 SOUTH into GRAY, cross RIVER & after 200m turn LEFT .

SITE DESCRIPTION: *The aire is located in a large parking area next to the campsite, on the east side of this small rural town, where there are 20 hard standings with ehu's together with picnic tables next to grass areas, lighting but without shade. Artisanal service point with drainage grid, toilets in campsite. Free when campsite closed but no electric.*
REVIEW: *A pleasant quiet spot close to the Saone river, securely located next to the town campsite with ehu's but a bit remote from the town centre. Good range of shops & eating places in town & a Hyper Casino supermarket across river. Cycle lane nearby.*

SCEY SUR SAONE

ADDRESS: RUE DEUX PORTS, D3 **TYPE OF AIRE:** MUNICIPAL
FACILITIES: WATER /GREY & BLACK DRAIN/ ELECTRIC
LOCATION: RURAL/ RIVER **NO. OF SPACES:** 7
PRICES: PARKING: FREE **SERVICES**: 2€ WATER or ELECTRIC

OPENING TIMES: ALL YEAR **GPS:** N47.65369 E05.97502
DIRECTIONS: From SCEY take D3 SOUTH to MARINA & AIRE.
***SITE DESCRIPTION**: This Municipal aire is located about 1km to the south of this small village, next to the river marina in a gravel parking area bordered by grass & with shade under trees in places. 7 individual level spaces separated by hedges. Flot Bleu borne with platform drain.*

***REVIEW:** A modern aire next to the river port & surrounded by farmland, but a bit remote from the village(15 min walk). Small Carrefour supermarket, boulangerie & a bar/ tabac in village.*

90 BELFORT

BELFORT

ADDRESS: AVE DE LA MOTTE, OFF D83 **TYPE OF AIRE:** MUNICIPAL
FACILITIES: WATER /GREY & BLACK DRAIN /ELECTRIC/ RUBBISH
LOCATION: URBAN **NO. OF SPACES:** 20
PRICES: PARKING: FREE **SERVICES**: FREE
OPENING TIMES: ALL YEAR **GPS:** N47.64201 E06.86599
DIRECTIONS: Entering BELFORT from EAST on D583/ D83, AIRE is signposted to RIGHT (Parking L'Epide).
***SITE DESCRIPTION** The aire here is located in a very large walled tarmac parking area on the north side of this large town, where there are ample hard standings but just 8x16A ehu's. Slightly shaded by adjacent trees & lit at night with an artisanal service point /drainage platform.*

***REVIEW:** A good spot close to the town centre, quiet at night & plenty of spaces but the 8 ehu's are at a premium, grass areas nearby. Good range of shops & eating places in town. Nice town with many old buildings, impressive Citadel & guided walks in town.*

SOUTHERN FRANCE

POITOU-CHARENTE

Poitou-Charente region is made up of 4 departments;

Charente (16), Charente-Maritime (17), Deux-Sevres (79), Vienne (86)

Poitou-Charente Map

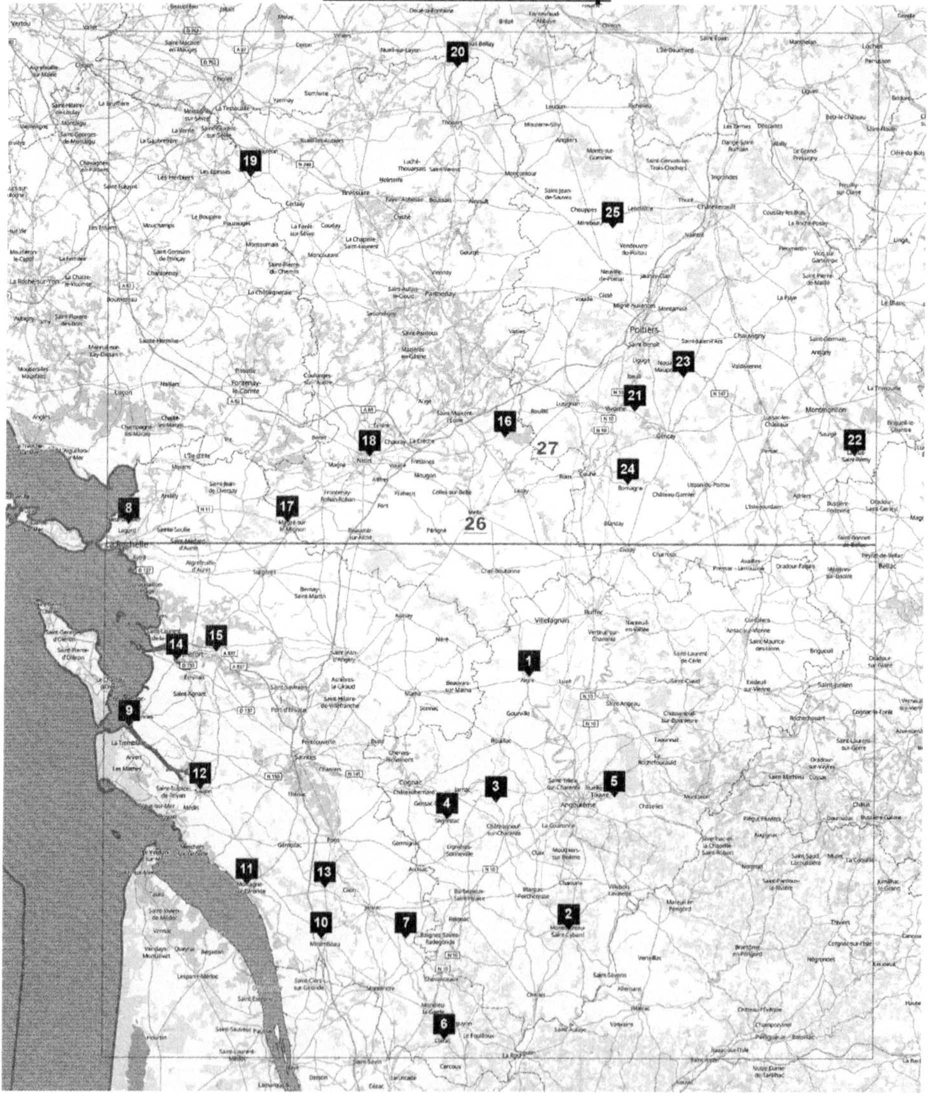

Key to enlarged Poitou-Charente Maps (on next 2 pages)

Former campsites that are now aires are noted in ***bold***

1) AIGRE – 2) MONTMOREAU ST CYBARD – 3) ST SIMON – 4) SEGONZAC

5) TOUVRE – 6) CLERAC – 7) LEOVILLE – ***8) LA ROCHELLE*** *– 9) LA TREMBLADE*

10) MIRAMBEAU – 11) MORTAGNE SUR GIRONDE – 12) SAUJON

13) ST GENIS DE SANTONGE – 14) SOUBISE – ***15) TONNAY CHARENTE***

16) BOUGON – 17) MAUZE SUR LE MIGNON – 18) NIORT
19) ST AMAND SUR SEVRE – 20) ST-MARTIN DE SANZAY
21) CHATEAU LARCHER *– 22) LATHUS-ST REMY – 23) NIEUIL L'ESPOIR24) ROMAGNE – 25) THURAGEAU –* ***26) MELLE – 27) SAINT SAUVANT***

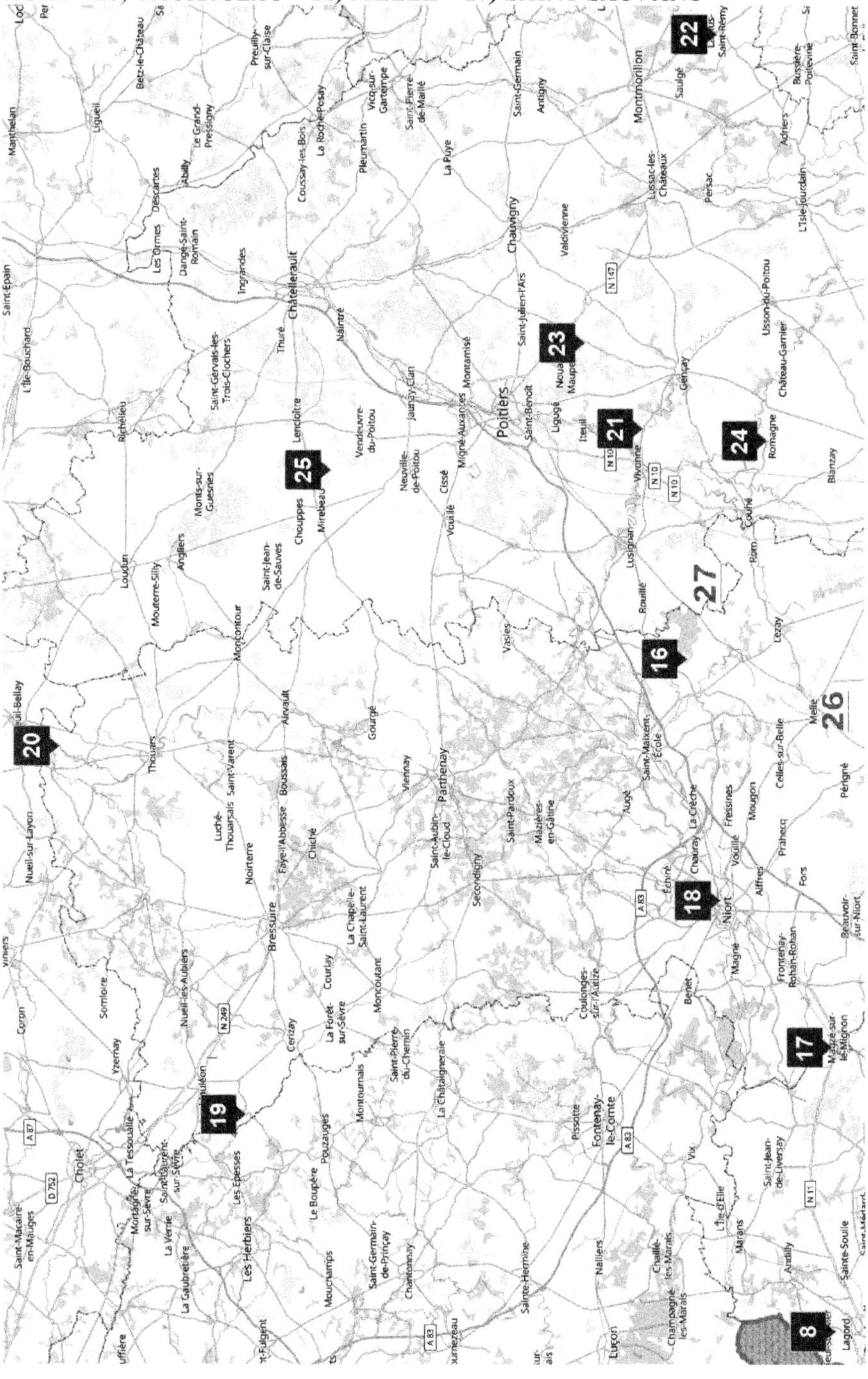

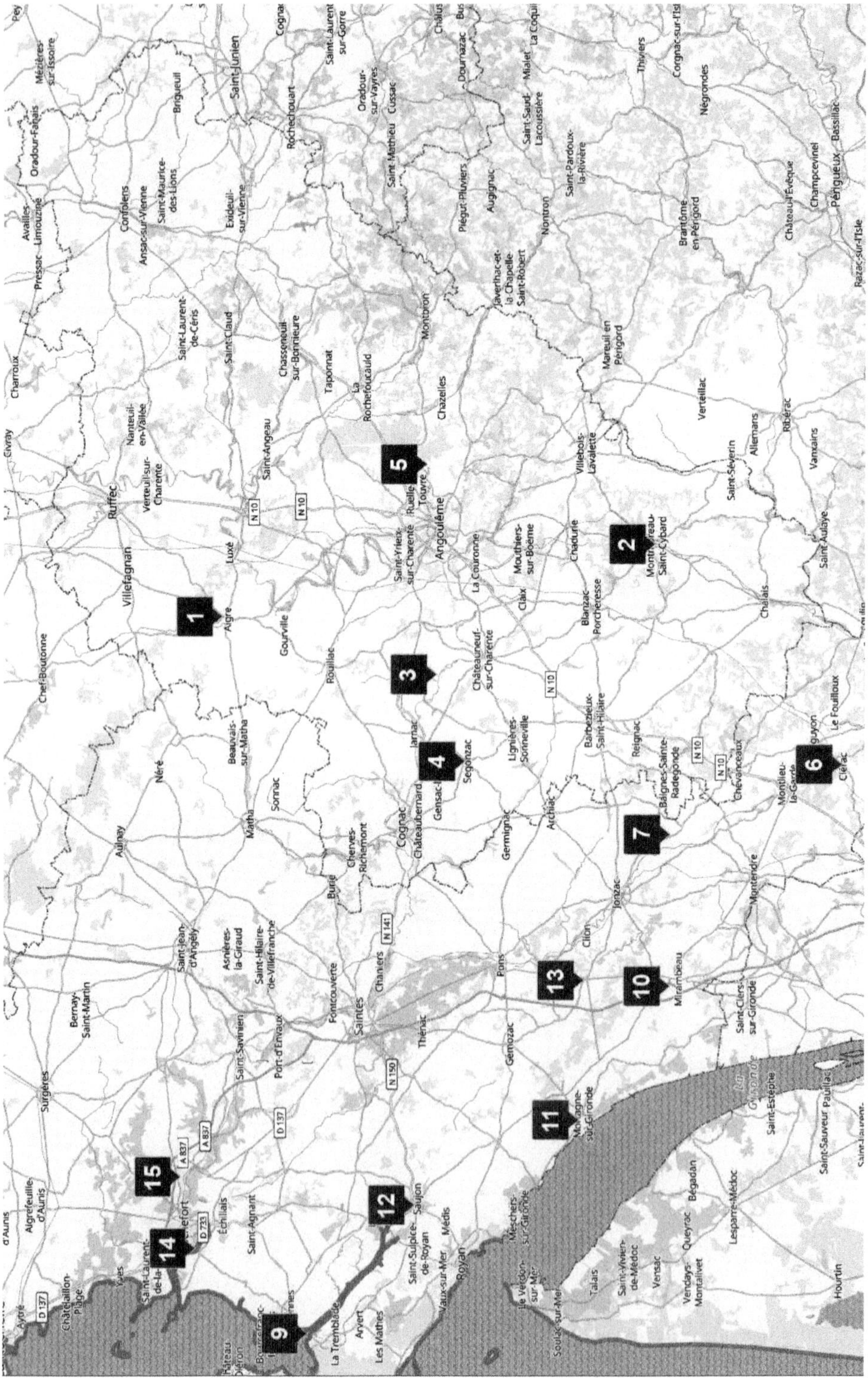
1
2
3
4
5
6
7
9
10
11
12
13
14
15
Charroux
Civray
Ruffec
Villefagnan
Chef-Boutonne
Aulnay
Néré
Surgères
Saint-Jean-d'Angély
Matha
Cognac
Jarnac
Segonzac
Châteauneuf-sur-Charente
Angoulême
La Rochefoucauld
Montbron
Confolens
Saint-Junien
Rochechouart
Nontron
Brantôme en Périgord
Périgueux
Ribérac
Chalais
Barbezieux-Saint-Hilaire
Saintes
Pons
Jonzac
Mirambeau
Montendre
Royan
Saujon
Marennes
Mortagne-sur-Gironde
Le Verdon-sur-Mer
Soulac-sur-Mer
Pauillac
Hourtin
N 10
N 141
N 150
A 837
D 137
D 733

16 CHARENTE

AIGRE

ADDRESS: RUE DES CHARRIERES **TYPE OF AIRE:** MUNICIPAL
FACILITIES: WATER /GREY & BLACK DRAIN/ ELECTRIC/ RUBBISH
LOCATION: SEMI-RURAL **NO. OF SPACES:** 5
PRICES: PARKING: 4€ / 24 Hrs **SERVICES**: INCL
OPENING TIMES: ALL YEAR **GPS:** N45.89343 E00.00556
DIRECTIONS: Leaving village on D739, turn LEFT into RUE DES CHARRIERES & then RIGHT after 100m to AIRE.
***SITE DESCRIPTION**: The aire in Aigre is in a large enclosed tarmac parking area on the western edge of the village, backing onto farmland, with a large adjacent grass area & various trees providing shade. Ample parking on grass or tarmac, about 300m to the village centre. Artisanal service point with drainage grid & 2 ehu's.*

REVIEW:** A good little aire, quiet, clean & easy to use services. Aire is well signposted in village. A lady from the OT calls round in the morning for the fee. Market in village 3 times a week.* ***Note: Rue des Charrieres is one way so you have to enter it off D739.

MONTMOREAU ST CYBARD

ADDRESS: OFF RUE DE LA GARE **TYPE OF AIRE:** MUNICIPAL
FACILITIES: WATER /GREY & BLACK DRAIN / TOILETS
LOCATION: URBAN **NO. OF SPACES:** 10
PRICES: PARKING: FREE **SERVICES**: 2€ WATER
OPENING TIMES: ALL YEAR **GPS:** N45.39913 E00.13274
DIRECTIONS: In town take road opposite CHURCH, EAST & then 1st LEFT to AIRE.

***SITE DESCRIPTION**: There are plenty of spaces on this aire, set in a large tarmac parking area, close to the town centre but also backing onto open countryside. There is*

little shade here but it has a well-designed Flot Bleu service point with a platform drain, WC's & lighting at night.

REVIEW: *A very welcoming aire, well signposted, very large & quiet, despite being close to the SNCF railway line. Picnic tables on a large grassy area, next to the small river (fishing possible). Town centre is about 100m away where there are shops, supermarket & a château.*

SAINT SIMON

ADDRESS: JUAC, JUNCTION OF D22/ D155 **TYPE OF AIRE:** MUNICIPAL
FACILITIES: WATER /GREY & BLACK DRAIN/ ELECTRIC/ RUBBISH
LOCATION: RURAL **NO. OF SPACES:** 6
PRICES: PARKING: FREE **SERVICES**: 2.5€ WATER or ELECTRIC
OPENING TIMES: ALL YEAR **GPS:** N45.65267 W00.08539
DIRECTIONS: From the WEST take D22 to ST SIMON, ½ km before the village turn LEFT into AIRE at JUAC.

SITE DESCRIPTION: *The aire is located on the west side of the small rural village of St Simon, about 700m from the centre, in a small hamlet surrounded by farmland. Parking is in a medium sized tarmac parking area, spaces separated by low hedges with no shade but edged by grass areas. Modern UrbaFlux service point with platform drain,*

REVIEW: *A pleasant, modern aire with 6 allocated spaces, good services & picnic table. Additional parking is adjacent, also used in summer by cars parking for river boat trips. Short walk to Charente river. No facilities in hamlet but St Simon - a small village with old buildings & a port on the river (½ km distant) has a bar/ restaurant.*

SEGONZAC

ADDRESS: RUE GOURRY **TYPE OF AIRE:** MUNICIPAL
FACILITIES: WATER /GREY & BLACK DRAIN/ ELEC./ TOILETS/ RUBBISH
LOCATION: SEMI-URBAN **NO. OF SPACES:** 4
PRICES: PARKING: FREE **SERVICES**: FREE
OPENING TIMES: ALL YEAR **GPS:** N45.61461 W00.22147
DIRECTIONS: Take D736 WEST & before leaving village, AIRE is to LEFT

SITE DESCRIPTION*:* *Aire is clearly signed in village, situated in a medium sized gravel parking area on western edge, with hedge surround, shade from small trees & lit at night. A good artisanal service point, a large platform drain, toilets adjacent & ehu's.*

REVIEW: *A well maintained small aire, quiet with clean toilets & a permanent electricity supply to the 4 ehu's. Village is very nice with good shops, supermarket & walks nearby. Petanque pitch adjacent.*

TOUVRE

ADDRESS: RTE DU PONTIL, OFF D57 **TYPE OF AIRE:** MUNICIPAL
FACILITIES: WATER /GREY & BLACK DRAIN/ RUBBISH
LOCATION: SEMI-URBAN **NO. OF SPACES:** 7
PRICES: PARKING: FREE **SERVICES**: FREE
OPENING TIMES: ALL YEAR **GPS:** N45.66089 E0.25834
DIRECTIONS: In TOUVRE. AIRE is next to MAIRIE (signposted).
SITE DESCRIPTION: *A small tarmac parking area close to the centre of this hamlet, with 7 spaces separated by low hedges & bordered by grass areas, next to farmland. AireServices service point with drainage platform.*

REVIEW: *A pleasant little aire with designated motorhome spaces having a little shade. No shops or services in the village but there are shops at nearby Mornac. At the nearby springs of Touvre, an underground river emerges from the foot of a cliff, there is also a forest with walks/ cycling. Railway line adjacent but little used.*

17 CHARENTE-MARITIME

CLERAC

ADDRESS: ROUTE DES VIGNES, D261 **TYPE OF AIRE:** MUNICIPAL
FACILITIES: WATER /GREY & BLACK DRAIN/ TOILETS
LOCATION: SEMI-RURAL/ LAKE **NO. OF SPACES:** 10
PRICES: PARKING: FREE **SERVICES**: FREE
OPENING TIMES: ALL YEAR **GPS:** N45.17916 W0.22785
DIRECTIONS: From CLERAC take D261 SOUTH & AIRE is alongside LAKE on LEFT.

***SITE DESCRIPTION**: The aire is in a small gravel parking area alongside the lake accessed by a gravel track, on the south side of Clerac. The location is shaded by trees, with a little lighting & is only a short walk from the village centre. The lake here is also a picnic area but fishing isn't allowed. Euro Relais service point with a drain.*

***REVIEW:** A pleasant lakeside aire with picnic tables, very quiet, good shade, only a couple of shops in the village – boulangerie, bar & a mini-market but a Leclerc supermarket is 5 mins drive away at Coutras. Small museum & château in village.*

LA ROCHELLE

ADDRESS: BVD ARISTIDE RONDEAU **TYPE OF AIRE:** MUNICIPAL
FACILITIES: WATER /GREY & BLACK DRAIN / ELECTRIC / RUBBISH/ WIFI
LOCATION: URBAN **NO. OF SPACES:** 150
PRICES: PARKING: 13-15€ / 24 Hrs **SERVICES**: INCL
OPENING TIMES: ALL YEAR **GPS:** N46.16057 W01.18449
DIRECTIONS: In city, follow signs for "Port Neuf" & AIRE.

***SITE DESCRIPTION**: The aire in La Rochelle is in the former Municipal campsite on the western side of city, close to the port, with ample spaces on gravel, lit at night & some having shade. Access is via automatic barrier. No shops or services near to parking & old town centre is about 2km away. AireServices service point with a double platform drain, ehu's & wifi.*

***REVIEW:** The location is a bit remote from the old city centre, nice pitches, wifi but not all have electric & the charge is the same for both. Parking is secure & quiet at night, a little road noise only on spaces near to road. Interesting city/ port for a visit. Also a second aire in city in the Visitors car park on eastern edge of town.*

LA TREMBLADE

ADDRESS: RUE M. GAILLARDON, OFF D14 **TYPE OF AIRE:** MUNICIPAL
FACILITIES: WATER /GREY & BLACK DRAIN/ ELECTRIC/ WIFI
LOCATION: URBAN **NO. OF SPACES:** 49
PRICES: PARKING: 12€/ 24Hrs **SERVICES**: INCL
OPENING TIMES: ALL YEAR **GPS:** N45.78275 W01.15242
DIRECTIONS: Take D25 NORTH to R/BOUT @ LES BRANDES, take 1st exit (D14) & then 1st LEFT – AIRE is 400m on RIGHT.

***SITE DESCRIPTION:** The aire is in a large tarmac parking area reserved for motorhomes, with a little shade in places under young trees & lighting at night, it is on the northern outskirts of the town, about 1km to the estuary & 1km to the town centre. The 49 level space parking is payable by credit card only via a machine on the aire. UrbaFlux service points with twin drainage platform & ehu's on each parking space. Previous winner of "Aire of the Year".*

REVIEW:** A very well managed, clean & modern aire in a large square parking area, but not very convenient for the town centre. Quiet location in a residential area with picnic tables, 16A electric points & wifi – all included in the price. Good fine sand beaches in area plus large forest with good cycle routes. Large selection of eating places & shops in town plus SuperU & InterMarche supermarkets. Camping Les Ombrages nearby as an alternative.* ***Note: Motorhomes are not allowed to park in the town between 11pm & 9am & 3 nights maximum stay allowed at the aire.

LEOVILLE

ADDRESS: LE BOURG, OFF D142 **TYPE OF AIRE:** MUNICIPAL
FACILITIES: WATER /GREY & BLACK DRAIN/ RUBBISH/ TOILETS
LOCATION: RURAL/ RIVERSIDE **NO. OF SPACES:** 10
PRICES: PARKING: FREE **SERVICES**: 1€ WATER
OPENING TIMES: ALL YEAR **GPS:** N45.37935 W00.33526
DIRECTIONS: In village centre turn EAST at crossroads – AIRE is 200m on RIGHT.

***SITE DESCRIPTION**: The aire is next to the river in the village leisure park where there is a large gravel parking area with plenty of available parking spaces. There is some shade/ lighting & it is surrounded by farmland yet convenient for the village. Euro Relais services with a drainage grid & toilet block.*

***REVIEW:** Pleasant & quiet little aire in this very small rural village. Picnic tables, play area, petanque, fishing in river, toilets, bins – a short walk from village centre where there is a boulangerie (sells jetons), butcher, tabac/ news & Poste. Jetons also available in Mairie.*

MIRAMBEAU

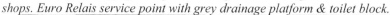

ADDRESS: RUE PARC DE LOISIRS, OFF D137 **TYPE OF AIRE:** MUNICIPAL
FACILITIES: WATER /GREY & BLACK DRAIN/ ELECTRIC/TOILETS
LOCATION: SEMI-RURAL **NO. OF SPACES:** 20
PRICES: PARKING: 8€ /24 Hrs **SERVICES**: INCL
OPENING TIMES: ALL YEAR **GPS:** N45.37885 W00.56849
DIRECTIONS: From NORTH, enter town on D137 & LEFT to "Parc Loisirs"/ AIRE.

***SITE DESCRIPTION**: The aire is in a medium size parking area next to farmland with adjacent grass areas on the northern outskirts of town, close to the town leisure park & within 500m of the town centre. Access is via an automatic barrier operated by credit card. Parking on large grass spaces with good shade, lights & the aire is close to the shops. Euro Relais service point with grey drainage platform & toilet block.*

***REVIEW:** The location is quite attractive, quiet & is within a short walk of the towns' amenities, a reasonable range of shops as well as a SuperU opposite the aire. Picnic tables & play area adjacent as well as a fast food restaurant (seasonal).*

MORTAGNE SUR GIRONDE

ADDRESS: QUAI DES PECHEURS **TYPE OF AIRE:** MUNICIPAL
FACILITIES: WATER /GREY & BLACK DRAIN / ELECTRIC/ TOILETS/WIFI
LOCATION: SEMI-RURAL/ RIVERSIDE **NO. OF SPACES:** 70
PRICES: PARKING: 10€ / 24 Hrs **SERVICES**: INCL.

OPENING TIMES: ALL YEAR **GPS:** N45.47612 W00.79474
DIRECTIONS: In town, take D6 (RUE L'ESTUAIRE) to PORT, AIRE is 3rd RIGHT.
***SITE DESCRIPTION**: The aire is 500m from the centre of town, located on the Port quayside, with spaces being on grass – accessed by a tarmac road & having open countryside on one side (behind the parking) & the quay on the other. Parking is level but most spots have little shade & exposed to the elements in bad weather. Each pitch has a hook up & the tariff includes water & electric. Artisanal service point with drainage platform behind Harbourmaster's office. Previous winner of "Aire of Year".*

***REVIEW:** A top of the range aire but busy in summer, in a lovely spot on the Gironde estuary, quiet at night, ehu's but long lead required for some pitches. Epicerie next to aire, shops/ restaurants in town, bread van passes in the morning. Showers & toilets in yacht marina, pay at ticket machine.*

SAUJON

ADDRESS: ROUTE DES ECLUSES **TYPE OF AIRE:** MUNICIPAL
FACILITIES: WATER /GREY & BLACK DRAIN/ ELECTRIC/ WIFI
LOCATION: URBAN **NO. OF SPACES:** 20
PRICES: PARKING: 12€/ 24 Hrs **SERVICES**: INCL
OPENING TIMES: ALL YEAR **GPS :** N45.67508 W00.93199
DIRECTIONS: In town follow signs for STADE & AIRE is adjacent.

***SITE DESCRIPTION:** The aire is in a tarmac parking area next to the town sports ground, on the western side of town, 100m from the river & about 500m from the town centre/ shops. The aire is in a quiet location, lit at night but has no shade, access by automatic barrier. UrbaFlux service point with drainage platform, ehu's & wifi.*

REVIEW: *A quiet, well equipped aire on the outskirts of town, next to the Sports centre, the Base de Loisirs & with SuperU nearby. Nice cycle path along the river Seudre into the thermal spa town with good shops & a market on Saturday, Leclerc outside town.*

ST GENIS DE SANTONGE

ADDRESS: RUE FANNY (Behind Cinema) **TYPE OF AIRE:** MUNICIPAL
FACILITIES: WATER /GREY & BLACK DRAIN/ ELECTRIC/ TOILETS
LOCATION: URBAN **NO. OF SPACES:** 20
PRICES: PARKING: 7€/ 24Hrs **SERVICES**: 3€ ELECTRIC
OPENING TIMES: ALL YEAR **GPS:** N45.48349 W00.56675
DIRECTIONS: Take D137 SOUTH through town & turn LEFT into RUE FANNY, (50m before Cinema) to AIRE.
SITE DESCRIPTION *The aire is located in a large tarmac parking area, with large marked spaces shaded by mature trees (in places) & next to a grass area with toilets nearby. The aire is accessed by an automatic barrier & the spaces are equipped with ehu's (water included in the fee). Artisanal service point with drainage platform & separate electric sockets.*

REVIEW: *A modern, well appointed purpose-built aire in a quiet location close with plenty of room. It is close to the town centre (150m) & its shops, well signposted in town. Water tap is frost protected making the aire accessible all year.* ***Note: Access road is quite narrow & turning is tight for larger vehicles.***

SOUBISE

ADDRESS: AT PORT ON CHARENTE RIVER **TYPE OF AIRE:** PRIVATE
FACILITIES: WATER /GREY & BLACK DRAIN/ ELECTRIC /TOILETS /WIFI
LOCATION: RURAL / RIVERSIDE **NO. OF SPACES:** 40
PRICES: PARKING: 12-15€/ 24Hrs **SERVICES**: INCL
OPENING TIMES: ALL YEAR **GPS:** N45.92838 W01.00684
DIRECTIONS: In village follow signs for PORT, AIRE is signposted to RIGHT.
SITE DESCRIPTION: *The private aire, run by CampingCarPark, is located in a medium size tarmac/ grass parking area within 350m of the village centre & about 50m from the banks of the Charente River. The aire is in a fairly open location backing onto fields & within a short walk of the Capitainerie where there are toilets & showers available. There is an artisanal service point with platform drain & electric hook up is included in the price, entry via automatic barrier – CCP card required.*
REVIEW: *A well equipped aire with wifi, bbq & ehu's (40 x 6A available) included in the price as well as showers & toilets available. Quiet location with a pleasant outlook & only a short walk to village shops & restaurant. Village has an InterMarche,*

boulangerie, bar/tabac, newsagent & a couple of restaurants & an open air market on Friday morning. Aire pictured below.

TONNAY CHARENTE

ADDRESS: QUAI DES CAPUCINS, D124 **TYPE OF AIRE:** PRIVATE
FACILITIES: WATER /GREY & BLACK DRAIN/ RUBBISH/ ELECTRIC/ WIFI
LOCATION: URBAN/ RIVERSIDE **NO. OF SPACES:** 26
PRICES: PARKING: 12-15€/ 24Hrs **SERVICES**: INCL
OPENING TIMES: ALL YEAR **GPS:** N45.93928 W00.88169
DIRECTIONS: From EAST, take D124 into town. AIRE is on LEFT just before river.
SITE DESCRIPTION: *The aire, run by CampingCarPark, is in a tarmac/ grass parking area of a former campsite next to the town sports ground, on the eastern side of town, 50m from the river & about 500m from the town centre/ shops. The aire is in a quiet location, fenced, with ehu's & has some shade under trees with large grass areas. Artisanal service point with drainage platform.*

REVIEW: *A quiet aire, on the outskirts of town, next to the river Charente where there are ample spaces, shaded with grass areas, play area & picnic tables. 26 spaces with wifi & ehu's, with entry via automatic barrier – CCP card required, toilets open from April till Dec. Not too far to town centre with its shops/ SuperU & a Sunday morning market. Cycle path alongside river. Handy for visiting Rochefort (5kms).*

79 DEUX-SEVRES

BOUGON

ADDRESS: MUSEE DES TUMULUS, OFF D5 **TYPE OF AIRE:** PRIVATE
FACILITIES: WATER /GREY & BLACK DRAIN / ELECTRIC / TOILETS
LOCATION: RURAL **NO. OF SPACES:** 10
PRICES: PARKING: FREE **SERVICES**: FREE
OPENING TIMES: APRIL-OCT **GPS:** N46.37829 W00.06879
DIRECTIONS: From PAMPROUX take D5 2kms SOUTH, turn LEFT to MUSEE.
SITE DESCRIPTION: *The aire is located in the large gravel car park of the excellent Museum des Tumulus; a quiet rural location with some shade under trees & surrounded by farmland – about 1km west of Bougon. The artisanal service point has 2 drainage areas & there is a separate ehu.*

REVIEW: *The aire is very clean & quiet, lit at night, next to the museum with toilets, plenty of parking space, shaded in places, & cycle hire for exploring the area. The museum covers a large area with indoor displays, 5 prehistoric tumuli (over 6,000 years old) & reconstructions of ancient houses, as well as a picnic area & cafeteria (open every day June – Sept).*

MAUZE SUR LE MIGNON

ADDRESS: ROUTE DE ST-HILAIRE, D101 **TYPE OF AIRE:** MUNICIPAL
FACILITIES: WATER /GREY & BLACK DRAIN / ELEC. / TOILETS / RUBBISH
LOCATION: SEMI-RURAL/ RIVERSIDE **NO. OF SPACES:** 12
PRICES: PARKING: FREE **SERVICES**: 4€ WATER or ELECTRIC
OPENING TIMES: ALL YEAR **GPS:** N46.19918 W00.67989
DIRECTIONS: In town take ROUTE ST HILAIRE 1km NORTH then LEFT to AIRE.
SITE DESCRIPTION: *Well signposted in town & situated in a small gravel car park surrounded by grass areas & trees providing shade, close to the campsite, canal & river. There is a small toilet unit & Flot Bleu service point with a large platform drain. Jetons from shops/ camping.*
REVIEW: *A good basic aire in the Marais Poitevin, quiet with shaded hard standings, in the old port area between a canal & the river, surrounded by farmland. There is a good selection of shops, supermarket & restaurants in the pleasant town, about 800m distant.*

MELLE

ADDRESS: RUE DE VILLIERS **TYPE OF AIRE:** PRIVATE
FACILITIES: WATER /GREY & BLACK DRAIN/ ELECTRIC/ WIFI/ TOILETS
LOCATION: SEMI-RURAL/ RIVER **NO. OF SPACES:** 24
PRICES: PARKING: 9-13€/ 24HRS **SERVICES**: INCL
OPENING TIMES: ALL YEAR **GPS :** N46.23178 W00.14397
DIRECTIONS: In town follow 'Camping' signs.
SITE DESCRIPTION: *This 'Camping Village' aire, run by CampingCarPark, is situated in the former municipal campsite 'la Fontaine', about 500m north of the centre of Melle & next to the river. Pitches are on grass (most shaded) each with 6A ehu & wifi with toilets (open 01/07-30/08). Artisanal service point with drainage platform. Access by automatic barrier, CCP card required.*

REVIEW: *A nice semi-rural location next to the river, quiet with large shaded pitches on grass – soft when wet. Toilets cleaned daily but only open July & August. Good range of shops, eating places, Friday market & supermarkets in this 'Small Town of Character' with a medieval quarter, fortifications & silver mine.*

NIORT

ADDRESS: RUE DE BESSAC **TYPE OF AIRE:** MUNICIPAL
FACILITIES: WATER /GREY & BLACK DRAIN/ ELECTRIC
LOCATION: URBAN **NO. OF SPACES:** 16
PRICES: PARKING: 10€ / 24 Hrs **SERVICES**: INCL
OPENING TIMES: ALL YEAR **GPS:** N46.32891 W00.46517
DIRECTIONS: AIRE is next to the PISCINE (Swimming Pool) & signposted in town.

SITE DESCRIPTION: *The aire is a purpose built area on north bank of the river with 16 individual spaces on concrete with grass surrounds & small trees/ walls giving shade/ privacy. Parking is 300m from the town centre. Euro-Relais service point with large platform drain.*

REVIEW: *A modern aire in a good location close to the town centre & shops/ restaurants, next to a pleasant park with picnic tables, swimming pool, playground & footpaths along the river. Quite peaceful considering it is in a town centre location but only 8 x16A ehu's for the 16 spaces.*

ST AMAND SUR SEVRE

ADDRESS: MOULIN DE CHALIGNY **TYPE OF AIRE:** PRIVATE
FACILITIES: WATER /GREY & BLACK DRAIN/ ELEC. / TOILETS/ RUBBISH
LOCATION: RURAL/ RIVER **NO. OF SPACES:** 8
PRICES: PARKING: 10€/ 24Hrs **SERVICES**: INCL
OPENING TIMES: ALL YEAR **GPS:** N46.88374 W00.82623
DIRECTIONS: From ST AMAND take D34 & C1 3kms NORTH (sign 'Treize Vents').

SITE DESCRIPTION: *This aire is located in the grounds of a former mill on the river, about 3km north of St Amand, where there are 8 large pitches on grass under the shade of mature trees, each pitch having an ehu & access to a small (dated) toilet/ shower block. Artisanal service point with drainage platform. Tel: 0549816773*

REVIEW: *Very nice stopover, warm welcome & all the facilities of a small basic campsite. There is a bar/ café in the mill house, toilets with washing-up sinks & hot showers, electric included in price, fishing in river. Fee reduces for subsequent nights. Aire is liable to closure in times of flood & ground is possibly soft in wet weather. No facilities nearby.*

ST-MARTIN DE SANZAY

ADDRESS: LA BALLASTIERE, OFF D158 **TYPE OF AIRE:** MUNICIPAL
FACILITIES: WATER /GREY & BLACK DRAIN/ TOILETS/ ELECTRIC
LOCATION: RURAL/ LAKESIDE **NO. OF SPACES:** 25
PRICES: PARKING: 5€ / 24 Hrs **SERVICES**: INCL
OPENING TIMES: APRIL - NOV **GPS:** N47.09334 W00.20013
DIRECTIONS: From ST-MARTIN take D158 NORTH 1km & turn LEFT to AIRE.

SITE DESCRIPTION: *The aire is located next to a Base de Loisirs,1km north of village, in a medium sized parking area with spaces on grass accessed by a gravel track & shaded by mature trees. The reserved parking area is next to a large lake & surrounded by farmland, it is accessed via an automatic barrier, entry card is available from either the nearby reception (open July & August) or the Mairie in Passay. There is an artisanal service point with platform drain & toilets.*

REVIEW: *A lovely, peaceful place next to the village leisure area with fishing, mini-golf, tennis, a picnic area & a playground. Shops in the village of St-Martin; epicerie, bar/tabac & Poste.*

86 VIENNE

CHATEAU LARCHER

ADDRESS: OFF D88, SOUTH of VILLAGE **TYPE OF AIRE:** MUNICIPAL
FACILITIES: WATER /GREY & BLACK DRAIN/ ELECTRIC/ TOILETS
LOCATION: RURAL **NO. OF SPACES:** 12
PRICES: PARKING: 6€/ 24 Hrs **SERVICES**: INCL
OPENING TIMES: ALL YEAR **GPS:** N46.41470 E00.31547
DIRECTIONS: From CHATEAU LARCHER, take D88 SOUTH 500m & turn LEFT.
SITE DESCRIPTION: *The aire is located, south of the quaint village, in the former village campsite where there are 12 spaces with 6A ehu's on hard standing reserved for motorhomes in enclosed grounds. The spaces are bordered by grass areas & shaded by mature trees, close to a large lake & next to the village football pitch. Artisanal service point with drainage grid.*

REVIEW: *The aire is in a beautiful green setting, overlooked by the ruins of the château, reserved shaded spaces on hard standing with bbq, picnic tables & boulangerie van calls in morning. Aire is start point for walks/ cycling in the area. Parking fee collected by OT official in pm. No shops in the picturesque village, just an Auberge – shops can be found in either Vivonne or Gencay.*

LATHUS-ST REMY

ADDRESS: RTE DE ST REMY, D10 **TYPE OF AIRE:** MUNICIPAL
FACILITIES: WATER /GREY & BLACK DRAIN/ ELEC./ RUBBISH/ TOILETS
LOCATION: SEMI-RURAL/ LAKE **NO. OF SPACES:** 8
PRICES: PARKING: FREE **SERVICES**: FREE
OPENING TIMES: ALL YEAR **GPS:** N46.33240 E00.95727
DIRECTIONS: Take D10 NORTH to LATHUS, as you enter village turn LEFT.

SITE DESCRIPTION: *The aire is located in a leisure area on the south west side of the small village, where there is a large parking area with 8 separate spaces on tarmac for motorhomes. The spaces are separated by hedges, lit at night by nearby street lighting, bordered by grass areas, a little shade & next to a lake. Euro Relais service point with drainage platform, toilets nearby but just 1 ehu.*
REVIEW: *A well equipped, modern aire with individual spaces giving good privacy overlooking a lake & adjacent park, quiet - nearby road is little used. Picnic tables, bbq, fishing in lake, petanque & children's play area. Short walk along footpath to village centre where there are just a few shops; boulangerie, butcher, Spar superette & a restaurant.*

NIEUIL L'ESPOIR

ADDRESS: ALLEE DU CHAMPE DE FOIRE, D1 **TYPE OF AIRE:** MUNICIPAL
FACILITIES: WATER /GREY & BLACK DRAIN / ELECTRIC
LOCATION: SEMI-RURAL/ LAKE **NO. OF SPACES:** 10
PRICES: PARKING: FREE **SERVICES**: 2€ WATER or ELECTRIC
OPENING TIMES: ALL YEAR **GPS :** N46.48511 E00.45412
DIRECTIONS: AIRE is on WEST side of main D1, SOUTH of R/bout.
SITE DESCRIPTION: *The aire is situated in the Base de Loisirs, next to the car park with 10 separate spaces for motorhomes, on gravel, lighting, shaded by trees, a semi-rural spot at the edge of the village. Euro Relais service point with drainage grid, jetons from Mairie.*
REVIEW: *An aire next to a lake in a green & shaded position with nice walks, swimming pool, park, fishing, play area & picnic tables. Aire is within a short walk of the shops; tabac, boulangerie, butcher, Proxi superette, chemist & auberge/ pizzeria. Some road noise from D1.*

Aire pictured top of next page

ROMAGNE

ADDRESS: RUE DU VIGNEAU **TYPE OF AIRE:** MUNICIPAL
FACILITIES: WATER /GREY & BLACK DRAIN/ ELEC. /TOILETS/ RUBBISH
LOCATION: SEMI-RURAL **NO. OF SPACES:** 6
PRICES: PARKING: FREE **SERVICES**: FREE
OPENING TIMES: ALL YEAR **GPS:** N46.26869 E0.30365
DIRECTIONS: In village follow signs for "ROULOTTES", AIRE is on LEFT.
SITE DESCRIPTION: *A semi-rural aire located on the east side of this small village where there are 6 level spaces with 5A ehu's on gravel hard standing separated by low hedges, lighting but no shade. Picnic tables, boules pitch, tennis & toilets nearby. Artisanal service point with drainage platform.*

REVIEW: *Quiet, clean & each pitch has its own ehu as well as a light but electric only on during summer. A Rural Life museum, monkey park & ostrich farm nearby. Restaurant, boulangerie, bar/ tabac & grocer in village (300m).*

ST SAUVANT

ADDRESS: RUE DU FOUR **TYPE OF AIRE:** PRIVATE
FACILITIES: WATER /GREY & BLACK DRAIN/ ELECTRIC/ RUBBISH/ WIFI
LOCATION: SEMI-RURAL **NO. OF SPACES:** 16
PRICES: PARKING: 10-12€/ 24HRS **SERVICES**: INCL
OPENING TIMES: ALL YEAR **GPS :** N46.35896 E00.05023

DIRECTIONS: Entering town from WEST on D29, AIRE is on RIGHT, close to the water tower.
SITE DESCRIPTION: *This CampingCarPark aire is located in the former Municipal campsite, within 500m of the little town centre where a small selection of shops can be found. The 16 individual pitches are on grass, bordered by hedges, accessed by a gravel track, with a little shade & lighting at night. Artisanal service point with drainage platform & wifi/ ehu's on each pitch. CCP card required, access by automatic barrier.*

REVIEW: *This is a very good aire within the old campsite which is located on the west side of the town. Quiet spot with swimming pool adjacent. 16 large pitches each with ehu & wifi. Small range of shops & a restaurant in town. Large forest to the east of the town with walks, play area & picnic tables, Gallo-Roman remains nearby.*

THURAGEAU

ADDRESS: AGRESSAIS, D42 **TYPE OF AIRE:** PRIVATE
FACILITIES: WATER /GREY & BLACK DRAIN
LOCATION: RURAL **NO. OF SPACES:** 8
PRICES: PARKING: FREE **SERVICES**: FREE
OPENING TIMES: ALL YEAR **GPS:** N46.78397 E00.25655
DIRECTIONS: From THURAGEAU take D42 into AGRESSAIS & AIRE is on LEFT.
SITE DESCRIPTION: *The aire is in the grounds of a goat farm/ cheese producer, 3km north of Thurageau in the hamlet of Agressais with parking on gravel/ grass, shaded in places, accessed by a gravel track & surrounded by fields with far reaching views. Artisanal service point with drainage grid. Tel:* 0549506173
REVIEW: *A warm welcome to this well managed & clean aire, not far from Futuroscope theme park. A very quiet rural situation where you purchase cheese from the farm in lieu of a parking fee & visits around the farm /fromagerie are possible.*

<u>LIMOUSIN</u>

Limousin region is made up of 3 departments;

Correze (19), Creuse (23) & Haute-Vienne (87)

<u>Limousin Map</u>

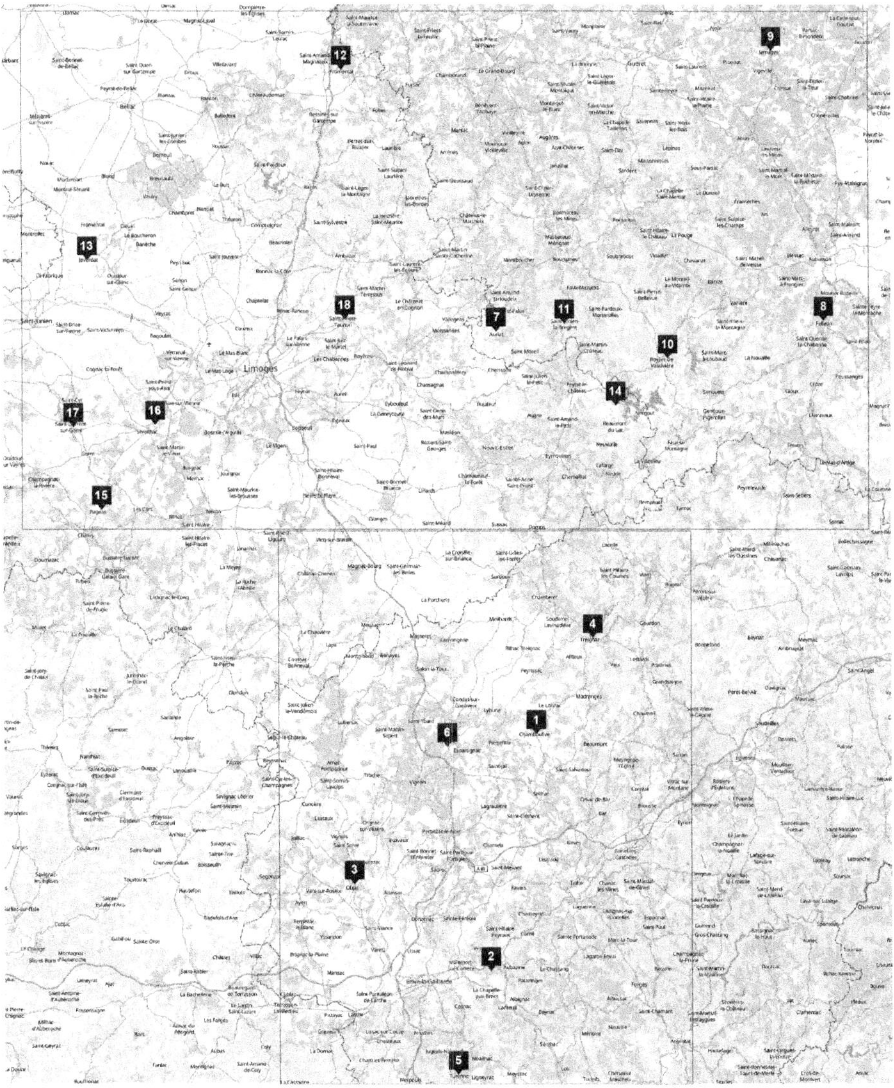

<u>Key to enlarged Limousin Maps (on next 2 pages)</u>

Former campsites that are now aires are noted in ***bold***

__1) CHAMBOULIVE__ – 2) DAMPNIAT – 3) OBJAT – 4)TREIGNAC – 5) TURENNE 6) UZERCHE – 7) AURIAT – 8) FELLETIN – 9) JARNAGES10) ROYERE DE VASSIVIERE – 11) ST JUNIEN LA BREGERE – 12) FROMENTAL – 13) JAVERDAT – 14) LAC DE VASSIVIERE – 15) PAGEAS – 16) SEREILHAC – 17) ST LAURENT SUR GORRE – 18) ST PRIEST TAURION

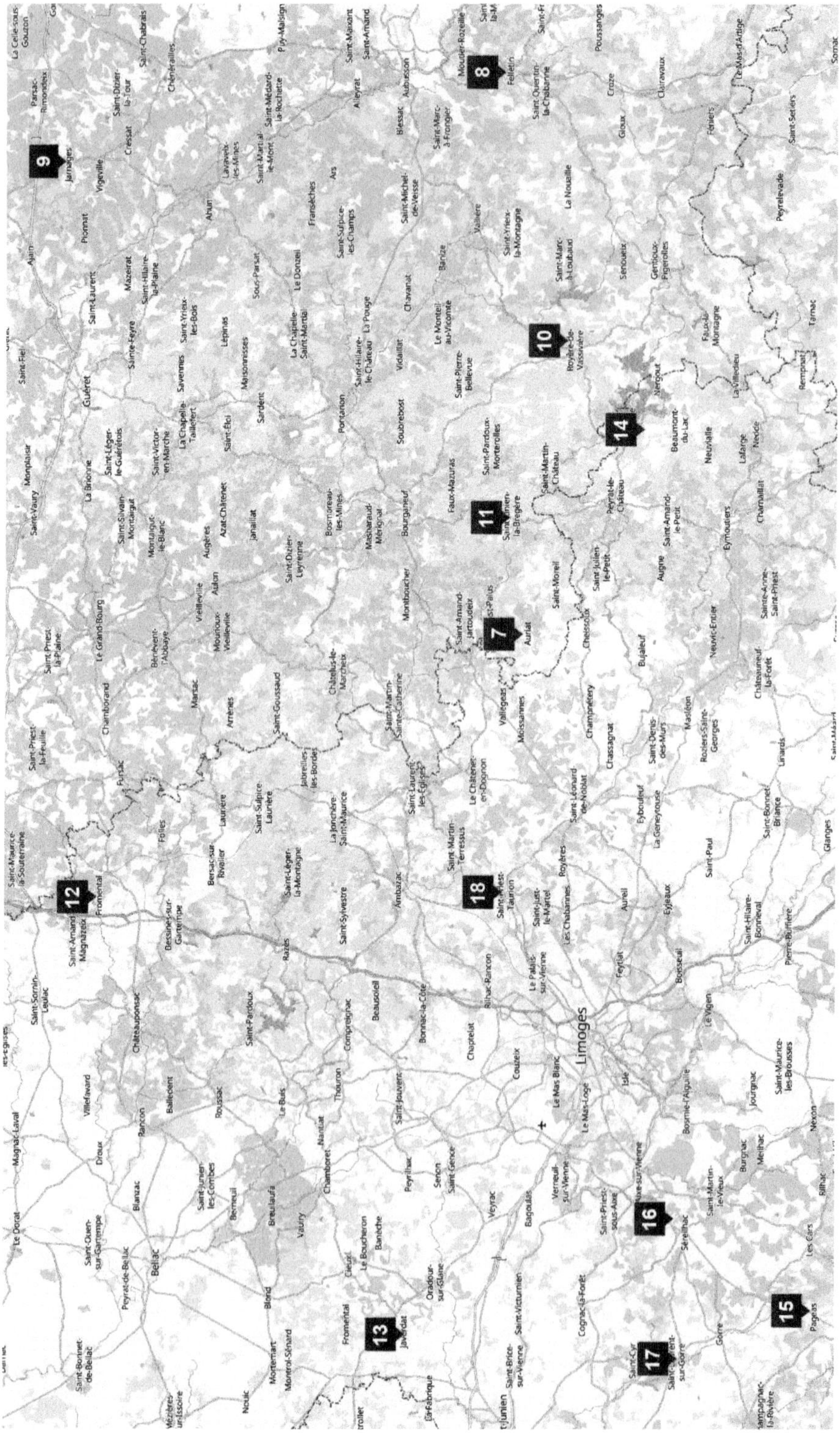
Limoges
7
8
9
10
11
12
13
14
15
16
17
18

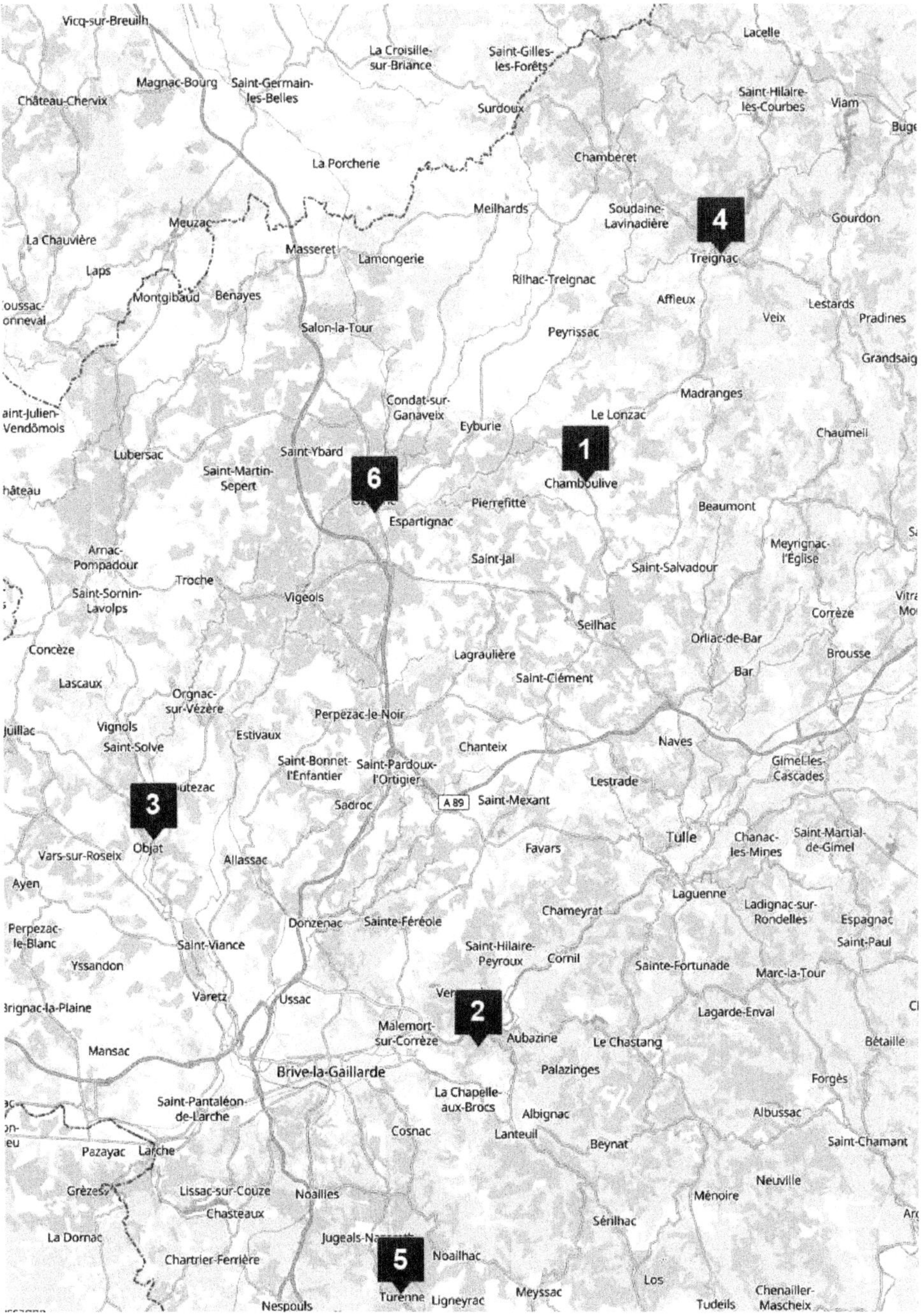
Vicq-sur-Breuilh
Lacelle
La Croisille-sur-Briance
Saint-Gilles-les-Forêts
Magnac-Bourg
Saint-Germain-les-Belles
Château-Chervix
Saint-Hilaire-les-Courbes
Viam
Surdoux
La Porcherie
Chamberet
Meilhards
Soudaine-Lavinadière
4
Gourdon
Meuzac
La Chauvière
Masseret
Lamongerie
Treignac
Laps
Rilhac-Treignac
Montgibaud
Benayes
Affieux
Lestards
Veix
Pradines
Salon-la-Tour
Peyrissac
Madranges
Condat-sur-Ganaveix
Le Lonzac
Eyburie
Chaumeil
Lubersac
Saint-Ybard
1
Saint-Martin-Sepert
6
Chamboulive
Pierrefitte
Beaumont
Espartignac
Arnac-Pompadour
Meyrignac-l'Église
Saint-Jal
Troche
Saint-Salvadour
Saint-Sornin-Lavolps
Vigeois
Corrèze
Seilhac
Orliac-de-Bar
Concèze
Lagraulière
Brousse
Saint-Clément
Lascaux
Bar
Orgnac-sur-Vézère
Perpezac-le-Noir
Vignols
Estivaux
Naves
Saint-Solve
Chanteix
Saint-Bonnet-l'Enfantier
Saint-Pardoux-l'Ortigier
Gimel-les-Cascades
Lestrade
3
A 89
Saint-Mexant
Sadroc
Tulle
Chanac-les-Mines
Saint-Martial-de-Gimel
Objat
Favars
Vars-sur-Roseix
Allassac
Ayen
Laguenne
Ladignac-sur-Rondelles
Chameyrat
Perpezac-le-Blanc
Donzenac
Sainte-Féréole
Espagnac
Saint-Viance
Saint-Hilaire-Peyroux
Cornil
Saint-Paul
Yssandon
Sainte-Fortunade
Marc-la-Tour
Varetz
Ussac
2
Lagarde-Enval
Malemort-sur-Corrèze
Aubazine
Le Chastang
Mansac
Bétaille
Brive-la-Gaillarde
Palazinges
La Chapelle-aux-Brocs
Forgès
Saint-Pantaléon-de-Larche
Albignac
Albussac
Cosnac
Lanteuil
Pazayac
Larche
Beynat
Saint-Chamant
Neuville
Grèzes
Lissac-sur-Couze
Noailles
Ménoire
Chasteaux
Sérilhac
La Dornac
5
Noailhac
Chartrier-Ferrière
Los
Meyssac
Chenailler-Mascheix
Nespouls
Turenne
Ligneyrac
Tudeils

19 CORREZE

CHAMBOULIVE

ADDRESS: OFF D142/E4 **TYPE OF AIRE:** MUNICIPAL
FACILITIES: WATER /GREY & BLACK DRAIN / ELECTRIC
LOCATION: RURAL **NO. OF SPACES:** 12
PRICES: PARKING: FREE **SERVICES**: 2€ WATER or ELECTRIC
OPENING TIMES: 01/03 – 30/11 **GPS:** N45.42267 E01.71642
DIRECTIONS: From CHAMBOULIVE take D940 SOUTH, then LEFT onto D142E4, AIRE is 500m on LEFT.
SITE DESCRIPTION: *The aire is located in the grounds of the former Municipal campsite alongside a minor road & next to a newly created fishing lake, 1km south of the village centre. Spaces are on grass accessed by a tarmac track, shaded by trees but no lighting. AireServices borne with a platform drain & separate ehu's.*

REVIEW: *A pleasant former campsite, converted to an aire, a bit remote from the village but quiet. Picnic tables, fishing lake adjacent, very reasonable 12 hours of electric for 2€. Shops in village; superette, boulangerie, butcher, café/ tabac, restaurant & pharmacy. 3 marked walks around village.*

DAMPNIAT

ADDRESS: LE MAS **TYPE OF AIRE:** MUNICIPAL
FACILITIES: WATER /GREY & BLACK DRAIN /ELECTRIC / RUBBISH
LOCATION: RURAL **NO. OF SPACES:** 4
PRICES: PARKING: FREE **SERVICES**: FREE
OPENING TIMES: ALL YEAR **GPS:** N45.16262 E01.63721
DIRECTIONS: In DAMPNIAT turn EAST at CHURCH & AIRE is next to the Sports Field after 1km.

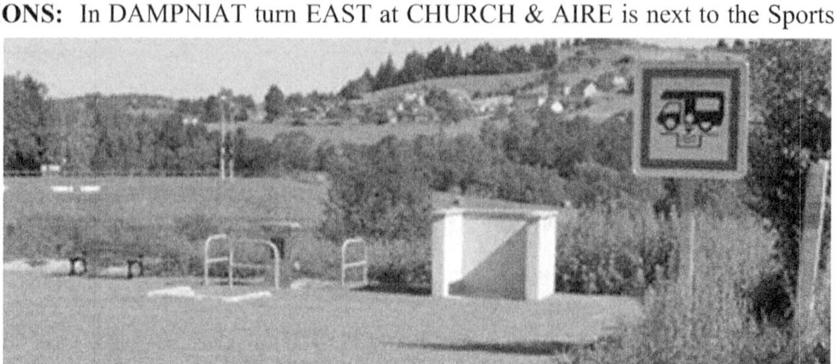

***SITE DESCRIPTION**: Located in a small tarmac parking area next to the village sports field, in a rural position & surrounded by open countryside with fine views. It is a quiet location but there is little shade & no facilities nearby. Modern Euro-Relais service point with a drainage grid & rubbish bin.*

***REVIEW:** A very quiet, compact aire in a nice spot, services including electric & water are free (reasonable usage), rural location but secure with houses opposite. Remote from village where there is just a butcher shop.*

OBJAT

ADDRESS: OFF AVE JULES FERRY, D148 **TYPE OF AIRE:** MUNICIPAL
FACILITIES: WATER /GREY & BLACK DRAIN / ELECTRIC/ TOILETS/ SHOWER/ WIFI
LOCATION: SEMI-RURAL **NO. OF SPACES:** 26
PRICES: PARKING: 8€ /24Hrs **SERVICES**: 2€ WATER OR SHOWER
OPENING TIMES: ALL YEAR **GPS:** N45.27135 E01.41176
DIRECTIONS: In centre of town take D148E, NORTH & AIRE is 1km on RIGHT.

***SITE DESCRIPTION**: The aire is located in an "Espace Loisirs" next to a large lake north of the town centre, with access via an automatic barrier (operated by credit card). A pleasant place with individual pitches on hard standing accessed by a tarmac road & surrounded by grass /trees. Toilets, washing up sinks & showers plus a Euro-Relais service point with drain. Previous winner of 'Aire of the Year'.*

***REVIEW:** A really excellent aire equipped with ehu's, picnic tables, bbq, play area, toilets & hot showers in a quiet environment with clean amenities as well as an Aqua centre only 500m away. Jetons for water or hot shower from OT. Price includes electric but increases in winter to cover extra usage. There are nice walks around the lake/ waterfall & it is not too far to the town centre where there is a good selection of shops, eating places & supermarket.*

TREIGNAC

ADDRESS: PARKING DES RIVIERES, OFF D940 **TYPE OF AIRE:** MUNICIPAL
FACILITIES: WATER /GREY & BLACK DRAIN/ ELEC./ RUBBISH/ TOILETS
LOCATION: RURAL/ RIVERSIDE **NO. OF SPACES:** 40
PRICES: **PARKING**: 1€/ 24 Hrs **SERVICES**: 3€ WATER or ELECTRIC
OPENING TIMES: ALL YEAR **GPS:** N45.54444 E01.80088
DIRECTIONS: From TREIGNAC take D940 NORTH & take 1st exit @ R/bout & AIRE is next to river.

***SITE DESCRIPTION**: This is a rural location next to the river & surrounded by countryside, with some parking under trees in a very large gravel/ grass car park. Not very convenient for the town (2km away) & there are no shops or facilities nearby. Artisanal service point with drainage platform & toilets.*

***REVIEW:** A pleasant place on the banks of the Vezere river with plenty of parking spaces, shaded & peaceful but ground is quite soft in wet weather. Pay for parking at ticket machine, remote but police pass regularly to check parking has been paid. Fishing in adjacent river.*

TURENNE

ADDRESS: CENTRE OF VILLAGE **TYPE OF AIRE:** MUNICIPAL
FACILITIES: WATER /GREY & BLACK DRAIN / ELEC. / TOILETS / RUBBISH
LOCATION: SEMI-URBAN **NO. OF SPACES:** 10
PRICES: PARKING: FREE **SERVICES**: FREE
OPENING TIMES: ALL YEAR **GPS:** N45.05393 E01.57988
DIRECTIONS: Entering village from WEST on D8, take 1st LEFT to AIRE.
***SITE DESCRIPTION**: This aire is in a medium sized gravel parking area edged by small trees (giving some shade) & with superb views over the surrounding countryside, a quiet spot with toilets nearby. Access to the aire however is quite narrow. Euro Relais service point with drainage grid & rubbish bin.*

REVIEW: *A practical aire, nicely located next to one of the 'Plus Beaux Villages de France', a superb place with magnificent views. Aire is close to the centre of village & there is a small Vival mini market nearby with a few eating places, OT & tourist shops in the in the medieval centre as well as a large château overlooking the village. Occasional problems with operation of the service point.*

UZERCHE

ADDRESS: OLD STATION, RUE P. LANGEVIN **TYPE OF AIRE:** MUNICIPAL
FACILITIES: WATER /GREY & BLACK DRAIN /TOILETS/ RUBBISH/ ELEC.
LOCATION: SEMI-RURAL/ RIVERSIDE **NO. OF SPACES:** 30
PRICES: PARKING: FREE **SERVICES**: 2€ WATER or ELECTRIC
OPENING TIMES: ALL YEAR **GPS:** N45.42452 E01.56618
DIRECTIONS: Entering town from EAST on D3, turn LEFT immediately before BRIDGE to Old Station & AIRE.
SITE DESCRIPTION: *The aire is very well situated in the large tarmac parking area of the old railway station (Petit Gare), alongside the east side of the river in a quiet position with good shade provided by large trees. Artisanal service point & WC's – chemical waste disposed of in toilets, some spaces with ehu's, information boards & picnic tables.*

REVIEW: *An excellent aire with plenty of room, on the side of a river & at the base of an interesting medieval town. It is very tranquil & well maintained with clean toilets in the old station building & a nice riverside walk starting from the aire, the town tourist train also starts from here. Close to the town centre & a good selection of shops/ eating places, pizza van parks on aire Thurs. evenings. Interesting old town to visit with 11th C church & many medieval buildings.* ***Note: that there is a fair here on the 20th of each month & the aire is closed from 0600 –1600 on that day, there is also a market here on Saturday mornings.***

23 CREUSE

AURIAT

ADDRESS: ETANG D'AURIAT **TYPE OF AIRE:** MUNICIPAL
FACILITIES: WATER /GREY & BLACK DRAIN / RUBBISH/ TOILETS
LOCATION: RURAL/LAKE **NO. OF SPACES:** 3
PRICES: PARKING: FREE **SERVICES**: FREE
OPENING TIMES: ALL YEAR **GPS:** N45.87832 E01.64292
DIRECTIONS: In village, follow signs to "Etang d'Auriat", AIRE is 400m on LEFT.
SITE DESCRIPTION: *The aire is situated to the north of this small rural village, 600m from the centre, in a small tarmac parking area next to the cemetery, bordered by grass & trees giving shade in places & with lighting at night. There are just 3 spaces on tarmac. Modern Euro-Relais service point & drainage platform with WC cabin adjacent.*

REVIEW: *A pleasant little aire with 3 / 4 spaces separated by hedges in a small parking area next to a fishing lake surrounded by woods, very quiet but a bit remote from the small village where unfortunately there are no shops or services.*

FELLETIN

ADDRESS: AVENUE JOFFRE **TYPE OF AIRE:** MUNICIPAL
FACILITIES: WATER /GREY & BLACK DRAIN / RUBBISH / TOILETS
LOCATION: URBAN **NO. OF SPACES:** 40
PRICES: PARKING: FREE **SERVICES**: FREE
OPENING TIMES: ALL YEAR **GPS:** N45.88294 E02.17585
DIRECTIONS: Entering on D982, pass thru town (1-way) & AIRE is signposted.
SITE DESCRIPTION: *The aire is in a very large tarmac car park, with ample spaces separated by small trees & shrubs, east of the centre of town but close to the shops & services. There is a little shade here, WC's in the car park as well as an information board & parking is lit at night. Euro-Relais borne with a large platform drain.*

REVIEW: *Close to the centre of a picturesque town & its shops; a quiet aire in a spacious car park surrounded by vegetation with heated toilets. Services are very functional. Reasonable range of shops/ restaurants & a supermarket. A medieval town famous for its tapestries with many old buildings & a diamond workshop.*

JARNAGES

ADDRESS: NEXT TO LAKE, D65 **TYPE OF AIRE:** MUNICIPAL
FACILITIES: WATER /GREY & BLACK DRAIN / ELECTRIC
LOCATION: SEMI-RURAL/ LAKE **NO. OF SPACES:** 12
PRICES: PARKING: FREE **SERVICES**: 2€ WATER or ELECTRIC
OPENING TIMES: ALL YEAR **GPS:** N46.18419 E02.08105
DIRECTIONS: In village take RTE DES PROMENCIES (D65) & AIRE is on LEFT.
***SITE DESCRIPTION**: Situated next to the village tennis courts & overlooking a large lake, the parking is on a small tarmac car park or adjacent large grass areas, lighting, a little shade & about 400m to the centre of the village. Euro-Relais service point with drainage grid.*
***REVIEW:** A very nice location next to a pretty lake & only ½ km to the village, quite peaceful but not much shade. Shops in village are: boulangerie, bar/tabac/newsagent, epicerie, bank, Poste & a restaurant.*

ROYERE DE VASSIVIERE

ADDRESS: RUE DE VASSIVIERE, D3 **TYPE OF AIRE:** MUNICIPAL
FACILITIES: WATER /GREY & BLACK DRAIN / TOILETS
LOCATION: URBAN **NO. OF SPACES:** 8
PRICES: PARKING: FREE **SERVICES**: FREE
OPENING TIMES: ALL YEAR **GPS:** N45.84038 E01.91054
DIRECTIONS: From SOUTH on D3, enter village & AIRE is on LEFT.
***SITE DESCRIPTION:** The aire is in the village centre car park, with marked spaces on tarmac, little shade, backing onto a grass/ wooded area & close to the shops. The village is surrounded by woodland & there are public toilets next to the church. There are ample parking spaces in village & a fairly modern Euro-Relais service point with a platform drain.*

REVIEW: *The aire is close to the shops; a Proxi mini-market, butchers, restaurant, OT, Poste, pharmacy & a boulangerie, there is also a market here on Tuesday mornings. Parking not allowed here on Monday night because of market, but there is other parking in village. Large lake nearby (3kms) with fishing, swimming, boating & walks.*

ST JUNIEN LA BREGERE

ADDRESS: RUE DU CHEVALIER, OFF D940 **TYPE OF AIRE:** MUNICIPAL
FACILITIES: WATER /GREY & BLACK DRAIN / RUBBISH
LOCATION: RURAL **NO. OF SPACES:** 3
PRICES: PARKING: FREE **SERVICES**: FREE
OPENING TIMES: ALL YEAR **GPS:** N45.88159 E01.75196
DIRECTIONS: From SOUTH take D940 to village, turn RIGHT & 1st RIGHT to AIRE.
SITE DESCRIPTION: *The aire is located on the south side of this small rural village, in a small tarmac area with 3 separate spaces, bordered by grass with lighting nearby but no shade & backing onto woodland. Artisanal service point with drainage platform.*

REVIEW *A very nice little hamlet with a pleasant aire, quiet & clean. Separate tarmac spaces each with picnic table. Interesting church & way-marked walks in area. No shops or services in village, nearest shops at Bourganeuf (11kms).*

87 HAUTE-VIENNE

FROMENTAL

ADDRESS: AVE JEAN CACAUD, D63 **TYPE OF AIRE:** MUNICIPAL
FACILITIES: WATER /GREY & BLACK DRAIN / TOILETS/ ELECTRIC
LOCATION: URBAN **NO. OF SPACES:** 6
PRICES: PARKING: FREE **SERVICES**: FREE
OPENING TIMES: ALL YEAR **GPS:** N46.15961 E01.39637
DIRECTIONS: AIRE is behind the CHURCH in the village centre.
SITE DESCRIPTION: *A well positioned aire in the centre of the village, in a medium size gravel car park bordered by trees with small grass areas, lit at night but not much shade. AireServices service point with drainage platform, toilets & 4 ehu's.*
REVIEW: *A good little aire in this small rural village between the church & Mairie, with a grocery shop (sells bread) opposite. Quiet at night, picnic tables & free electric but only 4 sockets. Free wifi at library. Short walk into surrounding countryside & Chateau with gardens to visit. Handy stop off A20, Jcn 23.1.*

Aire pictured next page top

JAVERDAT

ADDRESS: RUE DU CEDRE **TYPE OF AIRE:** MUNICIPAL
FACILITIES: WATER /GREY & BLACK DRAIN/ ELECTRIC/ TOILETS
LOCATION: SEMI-RURAL **NO. OF SPACES:** 4
PRICES: PARKING: FREE **SERVICES**: 3€ WATER or ELECTRIC
OPENING TIMES: ALL YEAR **GPS:** N45.95269 E0.98595
DIRECTIONS: In village centre, take road heading SOUTH – AIRE is 50m on RIGHT.
SITE DESCRIPTION: *The aire is located on the south side of this small rural village in a purpose built park area with 4 spaces on hardstanding, separated by hedges & next to a large open grass area with picnic tables & toilets/ washing up sinks. AireServices borne with drainage platform & separate electric point with 4 sockets. Jetons from Mairie or Auberge.*

REVIEW: *4 quiet individual pitches on tarmac, quietly situated with good panoramic views & next to a play area, short walk to village centre where there is a restaurant. Lit by street lights, no shade on pitches but a nicer stopover for visiting Oradour (7kms).*

LAC DE VASSIVIERE

ADDRESS: AUPHELLE, D3A2 **TYPE OF AIRE:** MUNICIPAL
FACILITIES: WATER /GREY & BLACK DRAIN/ TOILETS
LOCATION: RURAL/ LAKE **NO. OF SPACES:** 80
PRICES: PARKING: 6€/ 24 Hrs **SERVICES**: 3€ WATER
OPENING TIMES: ALL YEAR **GPS:** N45.80535 E01.84368

DIRECTIONS: From PEYRAT LE CHATEAU take D13/D222 EAST to LAKE/ AIRE.
SITE DESCRIPTION: *The aire, managed by the adjacent campsite, is located next to the large 1,000ha Lac de Vassiviere where parking is on a large grass area, access via tarmac tracks, with shade under mature trees. Euro-Relais service point with drainage platform & toilets in campsite, where fees are payable (reduced in low season).*

REVIEW: *A lovely, tranquil lakeside aire close to the centre of a small hamlet but no shops, nearest shops/ supermarket in Peyrat. Walks/ cycling around & boating/ watersports on lake. Island in lake with an Art centre to visit.*

PAGEAS

ADDRESS: LE BOURG NORD **TYPE OF AIRE:** MUNICIPAL
FACILITIES: WATER /GREY & BLACK DRAIN / ELEC./ TOILETS/ RUBBISH
LOCATION: SEMI-RURAL **NO. OF SPACES:** 20
PRICES: PARKING: FREE **SERVICES**: 3€ WATER or ELECTRIC
OPENING TIMES: ALL YEAR **GPS:** N45.67745 E01.00217
DIRECTIONS: From NORTH take N21 SOUTH to PAGEAS, take 1st RIGHT to AIRE.

SITE DESCRIPTION: *This aire is in a large grass or gravel parking area 300m east from the centre of the small rural village & 100m from a large lake. The parking is on the east side of the village having views over the neighbouring farmland & some shade. EuroRelais borne with a large drainage platform & adjacent toilets.*

REVIEW: *An excellent aire with mainly grass pitches but no facilities in the pleasant little village apart from an adjacent restaurant (with wifi) & a bread machine. Plenty of spaces with picnic tables, children's play area & several walks in the area. Slight road noise from N21 during day but quiet at night.*

SEREILHAC

ADDRESS: ALLEE C. TABARAUD, OFF N21 **TYPE OF AIRE:** MUNICIPAL
FACILITIES: WATER /GREY & BLACK DRAIN/ ELECTRIC/ RUBBISH
LOCATION: SEMI-RURAL/ LAKE **NO. OF SPACES:** 12
PRICES: PARKING: FREE **SERVICES**: 2€ WATER & ELECTRIC
OPENING TIMES: ALL YEAR **GPS:** N45.76755 E01.07919
DIRECTIONS: In SEREILHAC, on N21, turn WEST opposite Bar/ Cave to AIRE.
SITE DESCRIPTION: *This aire is located on the western side of this rural village, 100m from the centre, in a large tarmac/ gravel parking area with spaces on hard standing, little shade but lit at night & next to a large lake with an open grass area. AireServices borne with drainage platform & toilets nearby.*

REVIEW: *A pleasantly situated aire in a quiet part of the village, parking is large with level spaces bordered by grass & play area/ picnic tables. Bar/ cave & a few shops/ restaurant within a short walk. Jetons from Mairie or tabac.*

ST LAURENT SUR GORRE

ADDRESS: ALLEE LEON DUNAUD **TYPE OF AIRE:** MUNICIPAL
FACILITIES: WATER /GREY & BLACK DRAIN/ WIFI/ ELECTRIC/ TOILETS
LOCATION: SEMI-RURAL/ LAKE **NO. OF SPACES:** 20
PRICES: PARKING: FREE **SERVICES**: 2€ WATER or ELECTRIC
OPENING TIMES: ALL YEAR **GPS:** N45.76533 E00.95644
DIRECTIONS: From ST LAURENT take D34 WEST- follow "Plan d'Eau/ Aire" signs.
SITE DESCRIPTION: *An aire located on the south side of this small village where there are 20 spaces shaded by trees, with ehu's/ wifi, on grass alongside a gravel track, 400m from village centre. Artisanal service point with drainage platform & toilets nearby.*
REVIEW: *A nice aire naturelle, quietly situated next to a large fishing lake with play area, excellent amenities & only 10 mins walk from the village centre where there is a reasonable range of shops & eating places. Toilet block adjacent (washing-up sinks, shower/ handicapped access). Door code for the WC block from the Mairie.*

Aire pictured top of next page

ST PRIEST TAURION

ADDRESS: RUE JEAN GAGNANT, D29 **TYPE OF AIRE:** MUNICIPAL
FACILITIES: WATER /GREY & BLACK DRAIN/ RUBBISH
LOCATION: SEMI-URBAN/ RIVER **NO. OF SPACES:** 10
PRICES: PARKING: FREE **SERVICES**: FREE
OPENING TIMES: ALL YEAR **GPS:** N45.88638 E01.39678
DIRECTIONS: From WEST take D29 to ST PRIEST, cross RIVER & turn 2nd RIGHT.
SITE DESCRIPTION: *The aire is located in the centre of this rural village in a large gravel parking area with spaces on hard standing, little shade but lit at night & next to a large open grass area. The aire is situated behind a sports centre overlooking the river. Artisanal borne with drainage platform.*
REVIEW: *A pleasant river-side aire (below) in a quiet part of the village, set back from the main road with plenty of spaces bordered by hedges & grass areas. Short level walk to the small selection of shops, bar & restaurant. Fishing in river. Conveniently located for visiting Limoges (train station in village) & A20 (Jcn 29).*

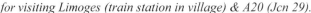

AQUITAINE

Aquitaine region is made up of 5 departments;
Dordogne (24), Gironde (33), Landes (40), Lot-et-Garonne (47) & Pyrenees-Atlantiques (64)

Aquitaine Map

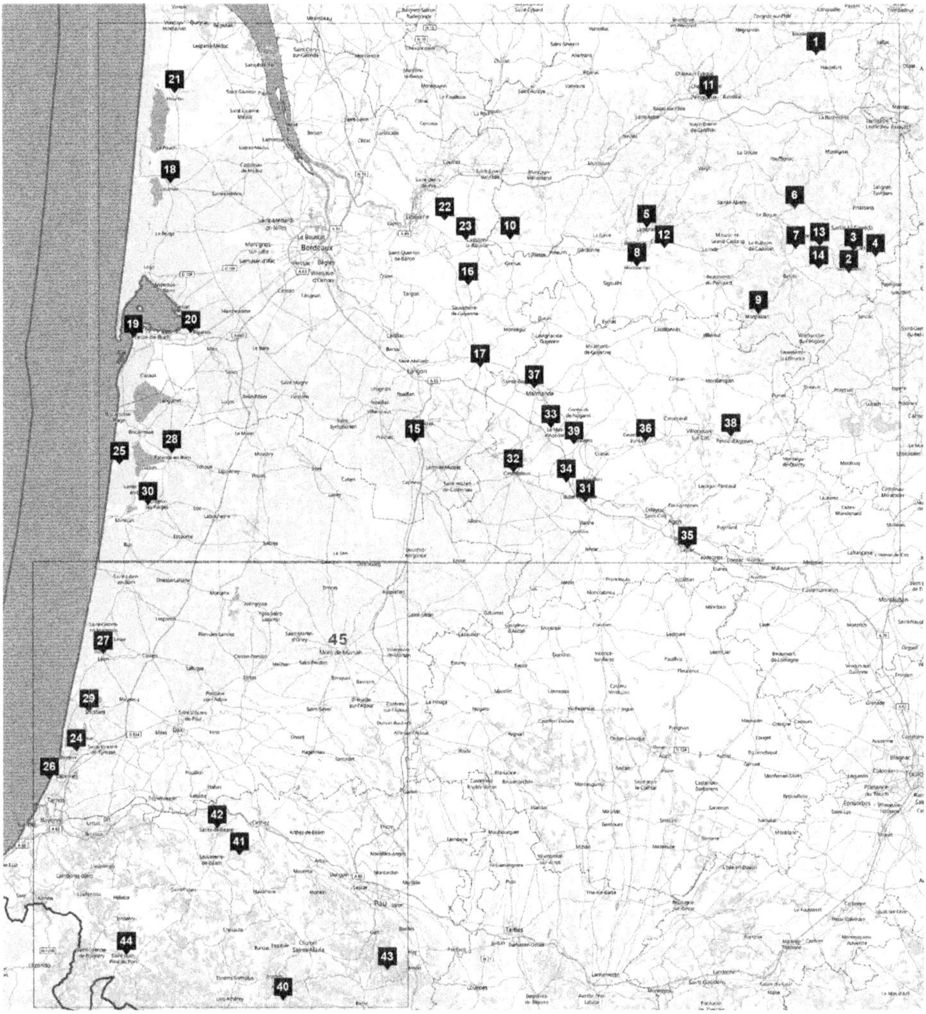

Key to enlarged Aquitaine Maps (on next 2 pages)

Former campsites that are now aires are noted in ***bold***

1) *ANGOISSE – 2) CENAC ET ST JULIEN – 3) DOMME – 4) GROLEJAC*
5) LEMBRAS – 6) LES EYZIES DE TAYAC / SIREUIL – 7) MARNAC
8) MONBAZILLAC – 9) MONPAZIER – 10) MONTCARET – 11) PERIGUEUX
12) ST GERMAIN ET MONS – 13) ST VINCENT DE COSSE
14) VEYRINES DE DOMME – 15) BERNOS BEAULAC – 16) BLASIMON

17) FONTET – 18) LACANAU – 19) LA TESTE DE BUCH – 20) GUJAN MESTRAS
21) HOURTIN – 22) ST EMILION – 23) ST PEY D'ARMENS – 24) CAPBRETON
25) GASTES – 26) LABENNE OCEAN – 27) LEON – 28) PARENTIS EN BORN
29) SOUSTONS – 30) STE EULALIE EN BORN – 31) BUZET SUR BAISE
32) CASTELJALOUX – 33) CAUMONT SUR GARONNE – 34) DAMAZAN
35) LAYRAC – 36) LE TEMPLE SUR LOT – 37) MARMANDE
38) ST SYLVESTRE SUR LOT – 39) VILLETON – 40) ACCOUS/ LHERS
41) ORRIULE – 42) SALIES DE BEARN – 43) SEVIGNACQ MEYRACQ
44) ST JEAN PIED DE PORT – ***45) MONT DE MARSAN***

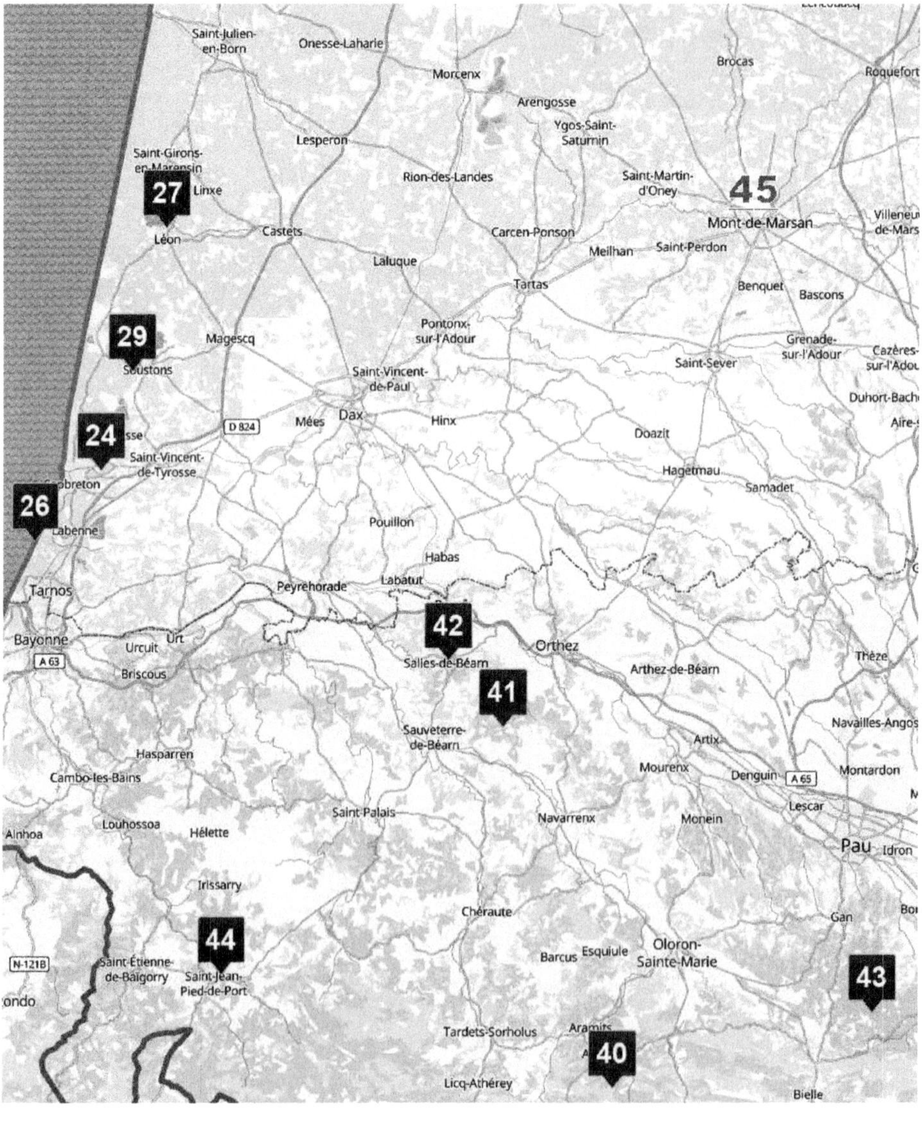

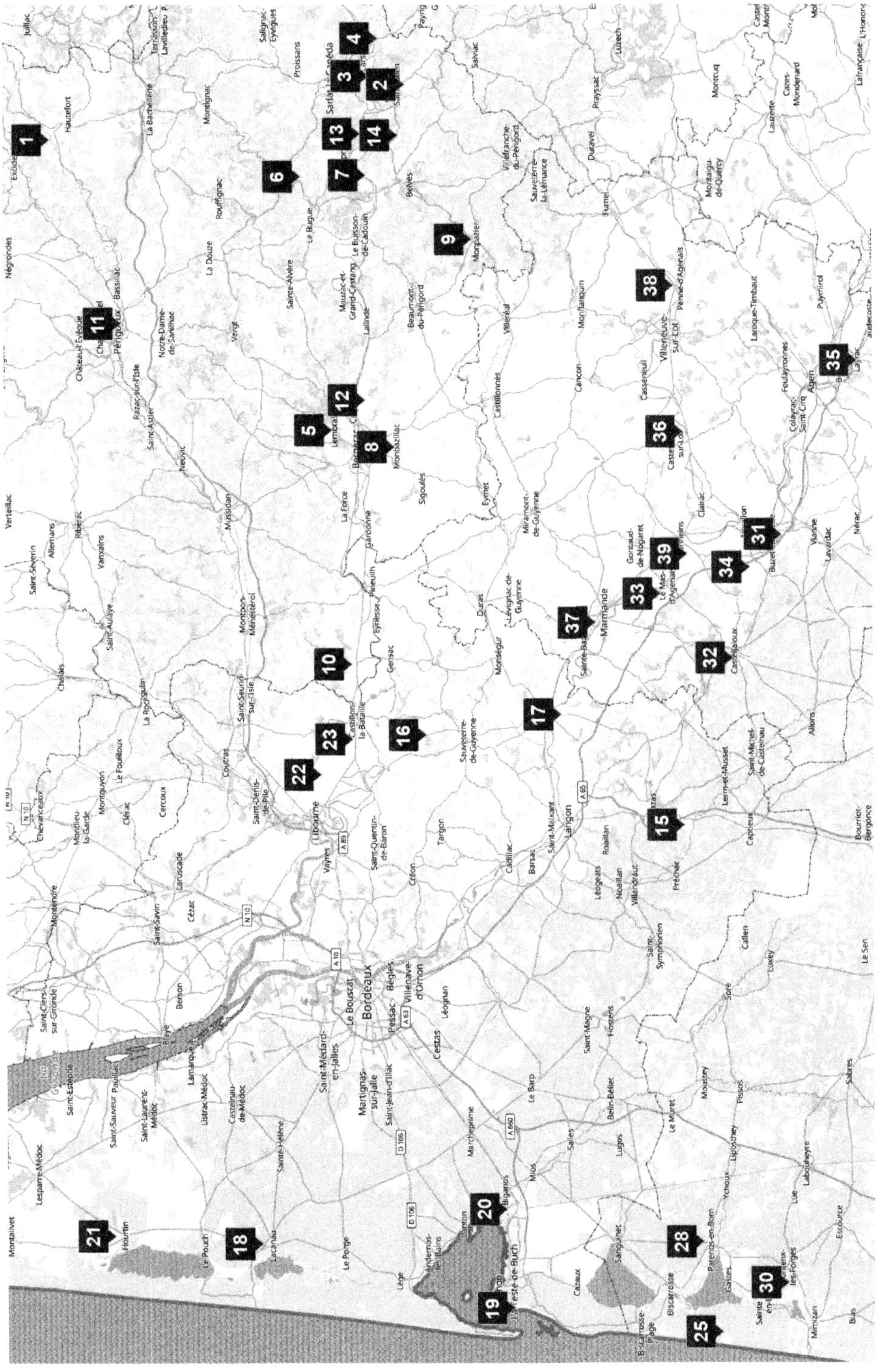
1
2
3
4
5
6
7
8
9
10
11
12
13
14
15
16
17
18
19
20
21
22
23
25
28
30
31
32
33
34
35
36
37
38
39
Bordeaux
Libourne
Bergerac
Marmande
Agen
Langon
Périgueux
Arcachon
Villeneuve-sur-Lot
Casteljaloux
Castillon-la-Bataille
Sarlat-la-Canéda
Monpazier
Lacanau
Hourtin
Biganos
Cestas
Pessac
Le Bouscat
Bazas
Sainte-Bazeille
Castelmoron-sur-Lot
Sauveterre-de-Guyenne
Saint-Médard-en-Jalles
Blaye
Pauillac
Ribérac
Mussidan
Lalinde
Le Bugue
Belvès
Fumel
Nérac
Biscarrosse
Parentis-en-Born
Mimizan

24 DORDOGNE

ANGOISSE

ADDRESS: LE POINT DU JOUR, D704 **TYPE OF AIRE:** PRIVATE
FACILITIES: WATER /GREY & BLACK DRAIN/ RUBBISH/ WIFI/ ELECTRIC
LOCATION: RURAL **NO. OF SPACES:** 8
PRICES: PARKING: FREE **SERVICES** 3€ WATER or ELECTRIC
OPENING TIMES: 01/04 -31/10 **GPS:** N45.43291 E01.14346
DIRECTIONS: From ANGOISSE take D704 NORTH 800m & AIRE is 50m on LEFT.
SITE DESCRIPTION: *A little private aire, located 800m to the north of the village, in the grounds of a private residence where 8 level spaces are found in a grassy area accessed off a gravel track with some shade but no lighting. Spaces are well set back from the road, separated by low hedges, each with ehu's & wifi. Artisanal service point with platform drain.*
REVIEW: *The aire is located in the pleasant rural environment of a private small holding, just off the D704 road with ample level parking for 8 vehicles. Fairly quiet with hook up, wifi, picnic tables & bbq plus boules pitch. No charge for parking but jams & fruit/ veg for sale, bread can be ordered for next morning. Grocers shop in village as well as tabac, bar/ restaurant & Poste but few other services/ attractions. Tel/ Text: 0622754334*

CENAC ET ST JULIEN

ADDRESS: RUE DU PORT , OFF D46 **TYPE OF AIRE:** PRIVATE
FACILITIES: WATER /GREY & BLACK DRAIN/ ELECTRIC/ WIFI
LOCATION: RURAL/ RIVER **NO. OF SPACES:** 11
PRICES: PARKING: 10 – 12€/ 24HRS **SERVICES**: INCL
OPENING TIMES: ALL YEAR **GPS:** N44.80434 E1.20472
DIRECTIONS: From NORTH take D46 SOUTH to CENAC, cross RIVER & 1st LEFT
SITE DESCRIPTION: *This private aire is on the north side of the village within a short walk of the centre in a small parking area with 11 individual spaces on gravel backing onto grass areas. The aire is fenced & within 50m of the Dordogne river. Euro-Relais service point with drainage platform, wifi & ehu's, access by automatic barrier.*

REVIEW: *A modern, well maintained aire – fully automated with automatic barrier. Spaces a bit small but have some shade & are quiet with hook ups, wifi & hut with a washing machine. Parking rate varies depending on season. Beach on river with canoes & 300m to village shops/ eating places with a market on Tuesday mornings.*

DOMME

ADDRESS: LA PRADAL, D46E **TYPE OF AIRE:** MUNICIPAL
FACILITIES: WATER /GREY & BLACK DRAIN / ELECTRIC / TOILETS
LOCATION: SEMI-RURAL **NO. OF SPACES:** 20
PRICES: PARKING: 10€/ 24 Hrs **SERVICES**: 2€ WATER or ELECTRIC
OPENING TIMES: ALL YEAR **GPS:** N44.80183 E01.22154
DIRECTIONS: From VITRAC take D46E SOUTH towards DOMME, ½ km before town turn sharp LEFT & AIRE is 100m on RIGHT.
***SITE DESCRIPTION**: Situated on the eastern outskirts of Domme in a large tarmac car park, with marked spaces, lit & shaded by trees in places. A quiet spot close to open countryside & woodland, but still only ½ km to the town centre. A Raclet service point with drainage grid. Parking is illuminated at night & picnic tables available.*

REVIEW:** A good, quiet location close to the town but spaces quite short. Domme is well worth a visit with good eating places, old houses & fine views from the top of the old town, Thursday is market day. Parking fees are payable either 10am – 7pm or 7pm – 10am by credit card.* ***Note: When coming from Sarlat, head towards Vitrac & follow signs for "Bus Parking". avoid coming from Cenac – it is impossible for large vehicles.

GROLEJAC

ADDRESS: VILLAGE CENTRE, D704 **TYPE OF AIRE:** MUNICIPAL
FACILITIES: WATER /GREY & BLACK DRAIN/ ELEC./ TOILETS/ RUBBISH
LOCATION: SEMI-RURAL **NO. OF SPACES:** 14
PRICES: PARKING: FREE **SERVICES**: 2€ ELECTRIC or WATER
OPENING TIMES: ALL YEAR **GPS :** N44.82088 E01.28965
DIRECTIONS: Approaching GROLEJAC from SOUTH on D704, turn LEFT at R/bout
***SITE DESCRIPTION:** A modern municipal aire located behind the superette in the centre of this small village, where there are 14 level spaces on gravel, shaded a little by trees on one side & separated by grass verges & next to large grass area. Raclet service point with platform drain & toilets nearby*
***REVIEW:** Short walk to shops/ services, pleasant quiet spot with cycle track & Dordogne river nearby. Spar superette (adjacent), butcher, boulangerie, restaurant & bar in village.*

LEMBRAS

ADDRESS: OFF RTE DE PERIGUEUX, D936 **TYPE OF AIRE:** MUNICIPAL
FACILITIES: WATER /GREY & BLACK DRAIN/ RUBBISH/ ELECTRIC
LOCATION: SEMI-URBAN **NO. OF SPACES:** 10
PRICES: PARKING: FREE **SERVICES**: 6€ ELECTRIC
OPENING TIMES: ALL YEAR **GPS:** N44.88343 E00.52523
DIRECTIONS: From EAST on D936E to LEMBRAS, turn LEFT just after CHURCH.
SITE DESCRIPTION: *The aire is situated on the edge of the small rural village of Lembras, behind the school. The parking is in medium size gravel parking areas offering 5 double motorhome spaces bordered by grass areas with some shade at the eastern end. Artisanal service point & drainage platform with separate ehu's.*

REVIEW: *A very pleasant, well maintained spot, near to a river walk. Adjacent to farmland/ woods but only a short walk into nice village where there is a grocer, boulangerie, tabac, restaurant & bar/ café/ Poste. Individual hook ups are 12 hours for 1 jeton, water/ parking is free, jetons from shops.*

LES EYZIES DE TAYAC SIREUIL

ADDRESS: PROMENADE DE LA VEZERE **TYPE OF AIRE:** MUNICIPAL
FACILITIES: WATER /GREY & BLACK DRAIN/ TOILETS
LOCATION: URBAN/ RIVERSIDE **NO. OF SPACES:** 40
PRICES: PARKING: 6€/ 24 Hrs **SERVICES**: 2€ WATER
OPENING TIMES: ALL YEAR **GPS:** N44.93873 E01.00919
DIRECTIONS: From NORTH take D47 over river & turn 1st RIGHT to AIRE.

***SITE DESCRIPTION**: A good position, close to the village centre & alongside a river in a large parking area, pitches are mainly on hard standings, with many trees providing shade. Public toilets & a Raclet service point with drainage platform are adjacent.*

REVIEW: *Alongside the Vezere River, a lovely location; easy to access, all pitches are large, shaded, marked by hedges & no cars are allowed into the parking area. The aire is clean & well kept with plenty of room to park. A nice old village with a prehistoric museum, shops/ eating places but busy in summer. Fee is collected by counil official.*

MARNAC

ADDRESS: LES TERRASSES DU MERCULOT **TYPE OF AIRE:** PRIVATE
FACILITIES: WATER /GREY & BLACK DRAIN / TOILETS/ ELECTRIC/ WIFI
LOCATION: RURAL **NO. OF SPACES:** 6
PRICES: PARKING: 10€/ 24HRS **SERVICES**: INCL
OPENING TIMES: 13/03 – 31/10 **GPS:** N44.84225 E01.03387
DIRECTIONS: From MARNAC take minor road to MERCULOT & follow signs.
SITE DESCRIPTION: *This small private aire is located about 3kms north of the small rural village of Marnac in the hamlet of Merculot where there are 6 level spaces on gravel in the grounds of a farm. The spaces have no shade but have far reaching views over the Dordogne river. The aire has wifi available as well as hook ups, laundrette & showers with an artisanal service point.*

REVIEW: *A pleasant location in a very quiet spot, facilities include covered picnic area, laundry, wifi, hook up, table tennis as well as the availability of fast food. The fee includes water, wifi, a hook up & use of laundry. Restaurant nearby & the historic town of St Cyprien is about 5 kms away where there is a good range of shops & supermarket. Tel/Text: 0680858609*

MONBAZILLAC

ADDRESS: DOMAINE DE LA LANDE, D13 **TYPE OF AIRE**: PRIVATE
FACILITIES: WATER / GREY & BLACK DRAIN/ TOILETS
LOCATION: RURAL **NO. OF SPACES:** 10
PRICES: PARKING: FREE **SERVICES**: FREE
OPENING TIMES: ALL YEAR **GPS:** N44.78827 E00.49609
DIRECTIONS: From MONBAZILLAC take D13 SOUTH & AIRE is on RIGHT.
SITE DESCRIPTION: *This private aire is situated on the farm of the wine producer 'Domaine de la Lande' in a rural location, just south of village, ample parking on grass with good views over the vineyards & some small trees providing a little shade. Artisanal service point with drainage grid & toilets.*

REVIEW: *An excellent stop, extremely quiet, in the middle of open countryside surrounded by vineyards. Picnic tables with wines available to taste & buy. Very friendly welcome from the owner Monsieur Camus, a producer of red & rosé wines. Château & church in the village are worth visiting & there is also an epicerie, restaurant & Poste there.*

MONPAZIER

ADDRESS: OFF D660 **TYPE OF AIRE:** MUNICIPAL
FACILITIES: WATER /GREY & BLACK DRAIN/ TOILETS/ RUBBISH
LOCATION: URBAN **NO. OF SPACES:** 10
PRICES: PARKING: FREE **SERVICES**: FREE
OPENING TIMES: ALL YEAR **GPS:** N44.68505 E00.89402
DIRECTIONS: AIRE is behind 'POMPIERS' (Fire station) in village.
SITE DESCRIPTION: *The aire is located on the northern side of the village, next to the village fire station where there are level spaces on grass, shaded by mature trees with picnic tables. Artisanal service point with toilets nearby.*

REVIEW: *A quiet but popular location 200m from the centre of this pleasant old village, one of the 'Most Beautiful Villages' & one of the best preserved 13th C bastides in the region. Many old buildings, the arcades of the central square & an ancient market hall with a market day on Thursday & a good selection of shops/ restaurants in the centre.*

PERIGUEUX

ADDRESS: RUE DES PRES **TYPE OF AIRE:** MUNICIPAL
FACILITIES: WATER /GREY & BLACK DRAIN/ RUBBISH
LOCATION: URBAN/ RIVERSIDE **NO. OF SPACES:** 40
PRICES: PARKING: 7€/ 24 Hrs **SERVICES**: INCL
OPENING TIMES: ALL YEAR **GPS:** N45.18760 E00.73086
DIRECTIONS: Follow signs for AIRE in town to avoid narrow & one-way streets.
***SITE DESCRIPTION**: A good position for visiting this large town, the parking is in a large tarmac parking area next to the river & 400m from the town centre. Pitches are on hard standing bordered by grass areas but have little shade. AireServices service point with large platform drain.*

***REVIEW:** Nice modern aire on the south bank, overlooking the river, it is spacious and is popular with other motorhomes. Picnic tables & play area. Quiet & very convenient for the large range of shops, restaurants & amenities as well as the cycle path along the river. Interesting town with many old parts to it, a cathedral & Roman remains. Former winner of 'Aire of the Year'.*

SAINT GERMAIN ET MONS

ADDRESS: RUE RENE GUERIN, D21 **TYPE OF AIRE:** MUNICIPAL
FACILITIES: WATER /GREY & BLACK DRAIN/ ELECTRIC/ WIFI
LOCATION: SEMI-RURAL **NO. OF SPACES:** 20
PRICES: PARKING: 8€/ 24Hrs **SERVICES**: INCL
OPENING TIMES: ALL YEAR **GPS:** N44.84782 E00.59306
DIRECTIONS: From ST GERMAIN take D21 NORTH & AIRE is on RIGHT after 300m.
***SITE DESCRIPTION:** The aire is located about 300m north of the village, where there are 20 dedicated parking spaces on tarmac bordered by grass with little shade but lit at night. Access into the aire is by an automatic barrier operated by credit card. The aire is within 400m of the Dordogne river, close to a residential area & farmland. Artisanal service point with drainage platform, individual 6A hook-ups & wifi.*
***REVIEW:** A modern, purpose-built aire with good services, ehu's, wifi, picnic table, bbq & boules pitch. 3 spaces for long vehicles. Possible to stay for just 4 hours. Aire is a bit remote from village & no shops or services in village but there are shops, pizzeria & Spar grocer 300m north of aire in Mouleydier.*

ST VINCENT DE COSSE

ADDRESS: LA FERME DE PORTE D'ENVEAUX **TYPE OF AIRE:** PRIVATE
FACILITIES: WATER /GREY & BLACK DRAIN
LOCATION: RURAL/ RIVERSIDE **NO. OF SPACES:** 35
PRICES: PARKING: FREE **SERVICES**: FREE
OPENING TIMES: ALL YEAR **GPS:** N44.82677 E01.09814
DIRECTIONS: From BEYNAC take D703 4KM WEST & turn LEFT to PORT D'ENVEAUX (signed CANOES).

***SITE DESCRIPTION**: A private aire located on a farm on the banks of the Dordogne river with ample parking spaces on grass accessed off a gravel track in an orchard giving good shade but no lighting. The farm also has an Auberge offering meals with an outdoor eating area. Local farm produce (mainly duck products) for sale. Artisanal service point.*

***REVIEW:** An excellent, quiet location at the Ferme with well shaded spaces (low branches) on grass, on the banks of the Dordogne & with easily accessible services. The little restaurant offers good meals & you can also hire canoes here – a mini-bus takes*

you along the Dordogne & you can then paddle back. Fast food bar/ restaurant (seasonal) nearby & next to the river, picnic tables, nice walks along the river bank..

VEYRINES DE DOMME

ADDRESS: RTE DES MILANDES, FALGUEYRAT **TYPE OF AIRE:** PRIVATE
FACILITIES: WATER /GREY & BLACK DRAIN
LOCATION: RURAL **NO. OF SPACES:** 6
PRICES: PARKING: FREE **SERVICES**: FREE
OPENING TIMES: 01/04 - 30/09 **GPS:** N44.82055 E01.10363
DIRECTIONS: From VEYRINES take D53 NORTH & follow signs to 'Château de Milandes' & then BOUTIQUE.
SITE DESCRIPTION: *This private aire is located in the grounds of the 'Boutique des Bois d'Enveaux', a farm shop 1/2km from the Château de Milandes. The aire is in a quiet rural location close to the river with fine rural views where parking is on gravel/ grass bordered by lawns & next to the farm shop. Artisanal service point.*

REVIEW: *A nice quiet, very rural spot close to the Dordogne with ample spaces but not much shade. Meals available & the shop sells truffles, nuts, wine, cakes, foie gras & jams. The Chateau de Milandes – the former home of the famous 1940's cabaret dancer Josephine Baker, is nearby. Tel: 0553292445*

33 GIRONDE

BERNOS BEAULAC

ADDRESS: ROUTE GRANDE, N524 **TYPE OF AIRE**: MUNICIPAL
FACILITIES: WATER /GREY & BLACK DRAIN/ RUBBISH/ TOILETS
LOCATION: RURAL **NO. OF SPACES:** 10
PRICES: PARKING: 4€/ 24 Hrs **SERVICES**: 2€ WATER
OPENING TIMES: ALL YEAR **GPS:** N44.36945 W00.24315
DIRECTIONS: From BERNOS-BEAULAC take N524 SOUTH & AIRE is on LEFT.
SITE DESCRIPTION: *This purpose built aire is located 150m south of the small village of Beaulac, just east of the N254 passing through the village. Parking is on tarmac next to a small lake & a river with woodland adjacent, a little shade & lighting at night. UrbaFlux service point with drainage platform.*
REVIEW: *A lovely, quiet aire on the banks of the Ciron river with 10 places (slight slope), toilets with sinks & a bbq. Canoes can be rented in season on the river. There are a few shops; epicerie, pharmacy, bar, boulangerie, restaurant & a 16th C church in Beaulac.*

Bernos Beaulac

BLASIMON

ADDRESS: CHATEAU LA PEYRAUDE, BLEURETTE **TYPE OF AIRE:** PRIVATE
FACILITIES: WATER /ELECTRIC/ TOILETS/ WIFI/ GREY & BLACK DRAIN
LOCATION: RURAL **NO. OF SPACES:** 20
PRICES: PARKING: FREE **SERVICES**: 5€ WATER & ELECTRIC
OPENING TIMES: ALL YEAR **GPS:** N44.73463 W0.09942
DIRECTIONS: From BLASIMON, take D236 EAST & then D670 SOUTH. CHATEAU is signposted off D670.
SITE DESCRIPTION: *This rural aire is located south of Blasimon, in the hamlet of Bleurette, on the property of a wine producer with ample parking on grass, near to the property & next to the vineyards with some shade under trees. Artisanal services with water, wifi & electric plus toilets adjacent. The aire is in a secure gated area, which is locked at night.*

REVIEW: *A perfect stopover for a motorhome, very peaceful with good walks/ cycling around the area. Warm welcome from owners with meals & wine tasting available. Bbq, picnic tables & toilets . Free parking & services are also free if you buy 20€ of wine, ring if gate closed. Tel/Text: 0688020976*

FONTET

ADDRESS: BASE NAUTIQUE **TYPE OF AIRE:** MUNICIPAL
FACILITIES: WATER /GREY & BLACK DRAIN/ ELEC./ TOILETS/ RUBBISH
LOCATION: RURAL/ CANALSIDE **NO. OF SPACES:** 25
PRICES: PARKING: 10€/ 24Hrs **SERVICES**: INCL
OPENING TIMES: ALL YEAR **GPS:** N44.56103 W00.02266
DIRECTIONS: BASE DE LOISIRS & AIRE are signposted jn village.

SITE DESCRIPTION: *This excellent aire is located in the Base de Loisirs, just east of Fontet in a very pleasant location next to a small basin on the Lot-et-Garonne canal. The individual spaces are on gravel/ grass & separated by hedges, each having hook-up points with water taps adjacent to the pitches – access to the Base is via a gated entrance accessed by an entry code. There is ample shade under mature trees & there are also showers/ toilets available in high season. The Base has a small café/ bar (seasonal), a childrens play area, picnic area & a swimming lake with beach. Artisanal service point with drainage platform.*

REVIEW: *This is more like a small campsite than an aire, having a good range of facilities in season & being extremely well maintained. The location is very quiet at night, centred around a canal basin, with well shaded & private pitches - each with their own hook up & water supply. The aire is about 500m from Fontet but the village has only a boulangerie & a tabac, it is possible to cycle or walk along the 'Voie Verte' cycle path that follows the canal to Hure (4kms) where there are a few shops, a Poste & an English pub with meals. The aire is very secure with access via gates – opened with a code provided at reception when open or from the Marie when closed.*

GUJAN MESTRAS

ADDRESS: AVE DES LOISIRS, OFF D652 **TYPE OF AIRE:** PRIVATE
FACILITIES: WATER /GREY & BLACK DRAIN/ ELECTRIC/ WIFI/ TOILETS
LOCATION: SEMI-RURAL **NO. OF SPACES:** 76
PRICES: PARKING: 14 – 18€/24Hrs **SERVICES**: INCL
OPENING TIMES: ALL YEAR **GPS:** N44.61818 W01.09815
DIRECTIONS: Follow signs for AQUALAND, AIRE is behind it.

SITE DESCRIPTION: *The private aire here is located just off the A660 autoroute, on the southern edge of the town of Gujan Mestras, 3kms from the centre & opposite the Aqualand theme park. Access is via an automatic barrier operated by credit card. The parking is on grass accessed by gravel tracks, next to grass areas with a little shade next to pine trees, lit at night with CCTV. The aire is a modern construction with a Sanistation service point & 2 platform drains. Marked spaces are 50m² with ehu's & wifi.*

REVIEW: *A good modern, clean & well maintained aire with good facilities including 6A ehu's, wifi, laundrette, shop, fast food & bike hire. Large spaces, quiet apart from some noise when Aqualand is open, & 3kms to beach. Shops/ services available in town. Voted 'Aire of the Year 2016'.*

HOURTIN

ADDRESS: AVE DU LAC, D4 **TYPE OF AIRE:** MUNICIPAL
FACILITIES: WATER /GREY & BLACK DRAIN/ TOILETS/ RUBBISH
LOCATION: SEMI-RURAL **NO. OF SPACES:** 30
PRICES: PARKING: 7 - 12€/ 24Hrs **SERVICES**: 2€ WATER
OPENING TIMES: ALL YEAR **GPS:** N45.18150 W01.08178
DIRECTIONS: Take D4, AVE.DU LAC to HOURTIN PORT, & AIRE is on LEFT.
***SITE DESCRIPTION**: Within a short walk of a good beach & the port, this aire is found in a large parking area; individual spaces are on shaded hard standings divided by grass & accessed by a tarmac road. Open all year, fees are seasonal but free from Oct till March. WC block (for use of motorhomes only), rubbish bins & a mini Flot Bleu borne with a drainage grid, entrance via an automatic barrier.*

***REVIEW:** An extremely comfortable aire, quiet (don't park near skate park!) yet only a 10 minute cycle ride into Hourtin. Parking is under trees, the aire is at the edge of a forest, close to the beach, a marina, a play area & some shops. Good level cycle routes, bicycle hire & mini-golf nearby. Well maintained with a warden on site.*

LACANAU

ADDRESS: ALLEE DE SAUVIELS, LE HUGA **TYPE OF AIRE:** MUNICIPAL
FACILITIES: WATER /GREY & BLACK DRAIN/ RUBBISH/ ELECTRIC
LOCATION: SEMI-RURAL **NO. OF SPACES:** 50
PRICES: PARKING: 14€/ 24 Hrs **SERVICES**: INCL
OPENING TIMES: ALL YEAR **GPS:** N45.00581 W01.16528
DIRECTIONS: From LACANAU OCEAN take D6 WEST to LE HUGA & AIRE is on LEFT (next to Heliport).
SITE DESCRIPTION: *A slightly remote location in a very large parking area where pitches are on sand/ gravel hard standings with hook-ups, separated by a few hedges in places & with trees giving a little shade around the edges. Next to the Civil Protection Helicopter Base, the aire is about 3km from Lacanau Ocean & 10km from Lacanau. Artisanal borne with platform drain – hook ups are on separate terminals.*
REVIEW: *The aire is 3km from an excellent beach & is well laid out with shade in places. There is a cycle route to Lacanau village. The fees are paid at a ticket machine & a council employee comes round in morning to check you have paid. There is a market in Lacanau on Saturday mornings & one in Lacanau Ocean on Friday mornings.*

Lacanau

LA TESTE DE BUCH

ADDRESS: RUE GUYNEMER, CAZAUX **TYPE OF AIRE:** PRIVATE
FACILITIES: WATER /GREY & BLACK DRAIN/ ELECTRIC/ RUBBISH
LOCATION: RURAL/ LAKE **NO. OF SPACES:** 30
PRICES: PARKING: 14€/ 24Hrs **SERVICES**: INCL
OPENING TIMES: ALL YEAR **GPS :** N44.53168 W01.16020
DIRECTIONS: Take D112 SOUTH to CAZAUX & follow signs for Camping & AIRE.

SITE DESCRIPTION: *This aire is located outside the campsite "Camping du Lac", in Cazaux, 8kms south of La Teste, where there are 30 level spaces, lighting & shaded in places on gravel close to a large lake. Access is via an automatic barrier operated by credit card. Euro-Relais service point with drainage platform & 6A ehu's on each space.*
REVIEW: *A pleasant, quiet aire next to a large campsite (open April – September) where there is a laundrette, restaurant/ fast food plus showers & wifi (extra charge). Nice lake 300m away with good cycle routes. A few shops/ pizzeria in the adjacent village of Cazaux & a Carrefour supermarket in La Teste.*

ST EMILION

ADDRESS: CHATEAU DE ROL **TYPE OF AIRE:** PRIVATE
FACILITIES: WATER /GREY & BLACK DRAIN/ RUBBISH
LOCATION: RURAL **NO. OF SPACES:** 8
PRICES: PARKING: FREE **SERVICES**: FREE
OPENING TIMES: ALL YEAR **GPS:** N44.90889 W00.16290
DIRECTIONS: From ST EMILION take D243 WEST then 3rd RIGHT & 1st RIGHT.
SITE DESCRIPTION: *This private aire is located on the farm of a wine producer about 2kms to the north west of St Emilion where there are 8 spaces on gravel hard standings overlooking the surrounding vineyards. Artisanal service point with drainage grid.*

REVIEW: *The farm is part of the France Passion scheme but allows any motorhomes to stay here, there are a good selection of wines available to purchase. Picnic tables & grass areas but little shade, a very quiet rural location. St Emilion is an incredible 'open-air museum' with underground galleries covering more than 70 ha and a church, dug out of solid limestone. Town has numerous wine caves, shops, services & restaurants.*
Tel: 0557247038

ST PEY D'ARMENS

ADDRESS: CHATEAU GERBAUD, off D936E7 **TYPE OF AIRE:** PRIVATE
FACILITIES: WATER /GREY & BLACK DRAIN/ ELECTRIC
LOCATION: RURAL **NO. OF SPACES:** 20
PRICES: PARKING: 5€ /24Hrs **SERVICES**: 3€ ELECTRIC
OPENING TIMES: ALL YEAR **GPS:** N44.85167 W00.10667
DIRECTIONS: From ST PEY D'ARMENS follow signs for "CHATEAU GERBAUD".
SITE DESCRIPTION: *A private aire, in the grounds of a wine producer/ Chambre d'Hotes where there is ample parking on grass or gravel accessed by a gravel track, under trees & surrounded by the vines. The aire is about ½ km south east of the small village of St Pey & 150m south of the farm. Artisanal service point with drainage grid & ehu's.*
REVIEW: *A pleasant rural aire with good walks in the vineyards or the small woods & nice wines to buy from the farm, handy location for visiting St Emilion (6kms). Very quiet location with all services provided or free if you buy some wine. Visit to the 'Cave', wine tastings & purchase of wines are available but few facilities in village.*

St Pey

40 LANDES

CAPBRETON

ADDRESS: OFF AVE DES ALOUETTES **TYPE OF AIRE:** MUNICIPAL
FACILITIES: WATER /GREY & BLACK DRAIN/ ELECTRIC/ TOILETS/ WIFI
LOCATION: BEACHSIDE **NO. OF SPACES:** 100
PRICES: PARKING: 8-16€ / 24 Hrs **SERVICES**: INCL
OPENING TIMES: ALL YEAR **GPS:** N43.63575 W01.44683
DIRECTIONS: In CAPBRETON follow signs for PLAGE DE L'OCEANE & AIRE.
SITE DESCRIPTION: *The aire is in a large tarmac car park close to the beach, parking spaces are marked, lit at night but there is no shade here. It is also about 1.5km to the town centre & its shops, etc. Raclet service point with platform drain.*

REVIEW: *A good beach aire set amongst sand dunes, quiet, very large with little problems parking & close to the beach in Capbreton (on the south side). It can be quite exposed in bad/ windy weather. The boulanger calls each morning (in high season only) with bread & pastries, & there is a free shuttle bus to the town. Agent calls each morning for fee (possible to pay by credit card), electric, water & wifi included.*

GASTES

ADDRESS: AVENUE DU LAC **TYPE OF AIRE:** MUNICIPAL
FACILITIES: WATER /GREY & BLACK DRAIN/ TOILETS/ WIFI/ RUBBISH
LOCATION: SEMI-RURAL/ LAKESIDE **NO. OF SPACES:** 50
PRICES: PARKING: 9€/ 24 Hrs **SERVICES**: INCL
OPENING TIMES: ALL YEAR **GPS:** N44.32844 W01.15237
DIRECTIONS: From SOUTH take D652 to GASTES, at R/bout take 1st exit into AVE DU LAC & then LEFT at 2nd R/bout to AIRE.

SITE DESCRIPTION: *Next to a large lake & a yacht marina with parking spaces on grass in a large open area with access via automatic barrier & a tarmac track. Trees provide shade in places and the aire is lit, about 400m from the village centre. Artisanal service point & drainage grid with a small WC.*
REVIEW: *Quiet, pleasant aire next to a lake & a forest where shaded parking is on grass with easy to access services, small toilet block but regularly cleaned. Fishing is possible in the lake with a small beach about 50m away, play area & good walks in the forest. Shops/ eating places in village, market on Tues, boulanger calls each morning, cycle track to Mimizan & Biscarosse.*

LABENNE OCEAN

ADDRESS: OFF D126 **TYPE OF AIRE:** PRIVATE
FACILITIES: WATER /GREY & BLACK DRAIN/ ELECTRIC/ WIFI
LOCATION: SEMI-RURAL **NO. OF SPACES:** 90
PRICES: PARKING: 13- 15€/ 24Hrs **SERVICES**: INCL
OPENING TIMES: ALL YEAR **GPS:** N43.59632 W01.45495
DIRECTIONS: Take D126 WEST to LABENNE OCEAN, as you enter turn RIGHT at "PARC AQUATIQUE" sign & AIRE is 100m on LEFT.
SITE DESCRIPTION: *This large aire is run by the CampingCarPark company & is located to the east of the small seaside village of Labenne Ocean, where there are 90 spaces on hard standings/ grass shaded under pine trees, all with 6A ehu's. Near to the Aquatic park & not too far from the sea, access is by automatic barrier – CCP card required. Euro Relais service point & drainage platform.*
REVIEW: *A pleasant, shaded aire close to an aquatic park & 1.5km from the ocean, spaces with ehu & wifi. Quiet but some noise from the adjacent campsite in the school holidays, long leads needed for some ehu's. Level walk into Labenne Ocean where there are shops/ restaurants (seasonal) & 3kms of beach.*

Labenne Ocean

LEON

ADDRESS: ROUTE DU PUNTAOU, D409 **TYPE OF AIRE:** MUNICIPAL
FACILITIES: WATER /GREY & BLACK DRAIN/ TOILETS/ WIFI
LOCATION: RURAL/ LAKE **NO. OF SPACES:** 150
PRICES: PARKING: 11€ / 24 Hrs **SERVICES**: INCL
OPENING TIMES: ALL YEAR **GPS:** N43.88349 W01.31797
DIRECTIONS: Take D652 SOUTH to LEON, at R/bout take D409 2kms to AIRE.
SITE DESCRIPTION: *The aire is west of Leon, on the shore of the large Etang de Leon with spaces on grass shaded under the pine trees, lit at night & accessed off a tarmac road. An artisanal service point with a large platform drain, toilets & wifi.*

Leon

REVIEW: *About 100m from the lake; a very large, pleasant aire with picnic tables that is easy to find, practical with good shade & in a quiet location. Some seasonal shops & restaurants nearby with more shops in Leon – 2km away. Fishing, swimming & pedaloes on the lake in the summer & there is a daily market in town during July & August. Open all year & free in winter but no services then.*

MONT DE MARSAN

ADDRESS: AVE DE VILLENEUVE **TYPE OF AIRE:** MUNICIPAL
FACILITIES: WATER /GREY & BLACK DRAIN/ ELECTRIC/ WIFI
LOCATION: SEMI-RURAL **NO. OF SPACES:** 45
PRICES: PARKING: 6-9€ / 24HRS **SERVICES**: 1€ WATER or ELECTRIC (4hrs)
OPENING TIMES: ALL YEAR **GPS :** N43.88998 W00.475660
DIRECTIONS: Entering town from EAST on D1, AIRE is signposted on RIGHT.
SITE DESCRIPTION: *The aire is 900m east of the town centre, in a large wooded parking area with spaces on grass, lit at night & having shade. A pleasant location with access via an automatic barrier operated by credit card, a tarmac track accesses the parking spaces. UrbaFlux service point & double drainage platform with ehu's.*

REVIEW: *Quiet, shaded spots in a former campsite, level walk to town centre where there is a good range of shops/ services. Bbq, children's play area & wifi on site. Animal Park adjacent. Good level cycle track that goes into town, bus stop 50m away. Well signposted in town.*

PARENTIS EN BORN

ADDRESS: RTE DES CAMPINGS **TYPE OF AIRE:** MUNICIPAL
FACILITIES: WATER /GREY & BLACK DRAIN/ ELECTRIC/ TOILETS
LOCATION: SEMI-RURAL/ LAKESIDE **NO. OF SPACES:** 20
PRICES: PARKING: 9€/ 24Hrs **SERVICES**: INCL
OPENING TIMES: ALL YEAR **GPS:** N44.34417 W01.09893
DIRECTIONS: From PARENTIS take RTE DU LAC to LAKE & turn RIGHT.
SITE DESCRIPTION: *The aire has a large hard standing parking area bordered by pine trees with adjacent grass areas, next to the Municipal campsite in a semi-rural location, about 100m from the beach & about 2km south west of Parentis. Euro-Relais service point with platform drain & ehu's, toilets nearby.*
REVIEW: *A good sized, quiet aire with some shaded places on gravel surrounded by woodland with hook-ups (but only 16 for 20 pitches) & services included in rate. Access is by automatic barrier. Restaurant / bar, & good lake beach nearby. Supermarket in Parentis.*

Parentis en Born

SOUSTONS

ADDRESS AVENUE DE LA PETRE **TYPE OF AIRE:** MUNICIPAL
FACILITIES: WATER /GREY & BLACK DRAIN / ELECTRIC/ TOILETS
LOCATION: RURAL/ LAKESIDE **NO. OF SPACES:** 80
PRICES: PARKING: 10-16€ /24 Hrs **SERVICES**: INCL
OPENING TIMES: ALL YEAR **GPS:** N43.77495 W01.41070
DIRECTIONS: Exit R/bout on D652 for SOUSTONS PLAGE & follow AVE DE LA PETRE to AIRE at end of road.
SITE DESCRIPTION: *Between the sea & a picturesque lake, parking is on gravel/ grass with shade provided by mature trees but little lighting. Access is via automatic barrier. Euro-Relais borne with drainge platform, toilets & 16A ehu's.*

REVIEW: *A good aire situated next to a lake & 500m from the sea in a verdant location, quiet at night with shaded pitches. The lake is nice to cycle or walk around and there is also a beach, which is about 200m from the aire with golf & tennis nearby. Unfortunately the nearest shops are 2kms away although there is a nearby bread shop but only open in high season.*

STE EULALIE EN BORN

ADDRESS: ROUTE DU LAC, **TYPE OF AIRE:** MUNICIPAL
FACILITIES: WATER /GREY & BLACK DRAIN / TOILETS
LOCATION: RURAL **NO. OF SPACES:** 40
PRICES: PARKING: 5€ - 8€ / 24 Hrs **SERVICES**: INCL
OPENING TIMES: 01/04 - 30/10 **GPS:** N44.30638 W01.18210
DIRECTIONS: Take D652 NORTH from STE EULALIE & turn LEFT @ WATER TOWER, follow this small road to AIRE on LEFT.
***SITE DESCRIPTION**: The aire is next to the Camping du Lac campsite & the large Biscarosse lake, where pitches are on grass, fairly level and some shaded by mature trees. There are outside cold showers, WC's (handicapped) & an artisanal service point.*

***REVIEW:** One of the nicer aires in this area; quiet and next to a small marina, the spaces are grassy and shaded and the aire is very clean & quiet. There is direct access to a sandy beach on the lake but no shops in the vicinity apart from a snack bar (seasonal). Wifi & laundrette available at campsite (pay here).*

47 LOT-ET-GARONNE

BUZET SUR BAISE

ADDRESS: PORT DE BUZET, OFF D12 **TYPE OF AIRE:** PRIVATE
FACILITIES: WATER/ GREY & BLACK DRAIN/ TOILETS/ ELECTRIC/ WIFI
LOCATION: SEMI-RURAL/ CANAL **NO. OF SPACES:** 6
PRICES: PARKING: 8€/ 24 Hrs **SERVICES**: 2€ WATER or ELEC. or SHOWER
OPENING TIMES: ALL YEAR **GPS:** N44.25664 E00.30695
DIRECTIONS: From BUZET take D12 NORTH, cross CANAL & AIRE is 1st RIGHT.
***SITE DESCRIPTION:** This small aire is located to the north of Buzet next to the canal marina where there is a small tarmac parking area having level spaces on tarmac/ grass with picnic tables, lighting & shade in places. The aire is between the canal & a river where there is a toilet block in the Capitainerie with showers & laundrette. Euro-relais service point with drainage platform.*

REVIEW: *A very pleasant, quiet canal-side aire with pitches next to the port offices. The aire benefits from wifi as well as showers/ toilets & a small laundrette. Short walk (350m) into small village, which has a Spar grocer, boulangerie, pharmacy, tabac/ presse, a couple of restaurants & a pizzeria. Parking is free from 1/11 till 31/03. Jetons from the port or from a machine.*

CASTELJALOUX

ADDRESS: CASTEL CHALETS, OFF D933 **TYPE OF AIRE:** PRIVATE
FACILITIES: WATER /GREY & BLACK DRAIN/ ELECTRIC/ WIFI/ TOILETS
LOCATION: RURAL/ LAKE **NO. OF SPACES:** 25
PRICES: PARKING: 18-23€ /24Hrs **SERVICES**: INCL
OPENING TIMES: 01/ 04 – 30/10 **GPS:** N44.29292 E0.07365
DIRECTIONS: Take D933 SOUTH out of town, at R/bout take last exit signposted "Casino/ Lac" & AIRE is outside campsite.
SITE DESCRIPTION: *The aire is in a parking area under pine trees, outside a private campsite, with large spaces on gravel. Parking is about 1.5km south from the town centre and is in a quiet position next to a large leisure lake. There is an artisanal service point with a platform drain, ehu's, wifi & access to the campsite toilets/ showers.*

REVIEW: *A well-equipped but expensive, quiet, lakeside aire with hook-ups, free wifi & access to the campsite facilities. Remote from the town where there is a good range of shops/ services. Peak parking rate applies in July & August. Casino nearby, play area, lake with beach & swimming pool adjacent, walks / cycling around lake. Closed in winter.*

CAUMONT SUR GARONNE

ADDRESS: CANAL, OFF D143 **TYPE OF AIRE:** MUNICIPAL
FACILITIES: WATER /GREY & BLACK DRAIN/ ELEC./ RUBBISH/ TOILETS
LOCATION: SEMI-RURAL/ CANALSIDE **NO. OF SPACES:** 9
PRICES:PARKING: FREE **SERVICES**: 2€ WATER OR ELECTRIC
OPENING TIMES: ALL YEAR **GPS:** N44.44180 E0.17905
DIRECTIONS: Take D143 EAST to CAUMONT, cross CANAL to AIRE on RIGHT.
SITE DESCRIPTION: *A dozen spaces under mature trees, lit at night & next to the Garonne canal passing through this village. Parking is on gravel facing the canal, close to the village with an Artisanal borne, toilets & platform drain. Jetons from Mairie or Poste.*

REVIEW: *Aire is well shaded and tranquil next to canal & near to the Garonne river with picnic table & a cycle path adjacent. Short walk into village but no shops or facilities there apart from a takeaway food bar that is only open in the summer.* ***NOTE: Access road is narrow & long vehicles may have to reverse into the aire spaces.***

LAYRAC

ADDRESS: ROUTE DE CAUDECOSTE, D129 **TYPE OF AIRE:** PRIVATE
FACILITIES: WATER /GREY & BLACK DRAIN/ ELECTRIC/ WIFI/ TOILETS
LOCATION: RURAL **NO. OF SPACES:** 4
PRICES: PARKING: 11€/ 24Hrs **SERVICES**: 3€ ELECTRIC
OPENING TIMES: ALL YEAR **GPS:** N44.13642 E0.66443
DIRECTIONS: Entering LAYRAC from EAST on D129, AIRE is on LEFT at D17 junction.
SITE DESCRIPTION: *This private aire, 'Le Moulin', is on the east side of town with 4 spaces in a small gravel parking area in the enclosed grounds of a mill, about 300m from*

the town centre & its' shops. Access is via an automatic barrier, with CCTV for security. There is shade here & an artisanal service point with ehu's, wifi, bbq, toilets & platform drain.

REVIEW: *A nice, friendly little well-equipped aire next to the river in the grounds of an old mill with 4 level spaces overlooking the river, each with shade & a picnic table. 3A electric & wifi included in price but supplement of 3€ if you need 6A. Road noise but quiet at night. Visit to the hydro-electric mill is possible. Small range of shops & restaurant in town as well as a small Municipal aire. Tel: 0553871537*

LE TEMPLE SUR LOT

ADDRESS: OUTSIDE CAMPING LE BOSC, OFF D911 **TYPE OF AIRE:** PRIVATE
FACILITIES: WATER /GREY & BLACK DRAIN/ RUBBISH/ELECTRIC/WIFI
LOCATION: SEMI-RURAL **NO. OF SPACES:** 16
PRICES: PARKING: 6.5€/ 24HRS **SERVICES**: INCL
OPENING TIMES: ALL YEAR **GPS:** N44.38149 E00.53656
DIRECTIONS: From village, take D911 EAST & turn RIGHT @ 'CAMPING' sign.

SITE DESCRIPTION: *The aire is located 500m east from the centre of the village where there is an artisanal service point with platform drain, ehu's, wifi & bins. The aire is lit at night & has some shade - it has 8 x 50m² parking spaces on gravel & 8 on grass, surrounded by farmland. Access is via an automatic barrier operated by credit card.*
REVIEW: *An excellent, well-maintained aire outside a 3* campsite (open 01/ 04 – 04/11), on the edge of this small rural village. Large spaces with individual electric points, bbq, wifi & picnic tables, light road noise. Restaurant & a couple of shops in village. Campsite bar, restaurant, shop & pool open in July & Aug. InterMarche in St Livrade (7kms). Small municipal aire in village.*

MARMANDE

ADDRESS: RUE DE FILHOLE **TYPE OF AIRE:** MUNICIPAL
FACILITIES: WATER /GREY & BLACK DRAIN/ ELECTRIC
LOCATION: RURAL **NO. OF SPACES:** 50
PRICES: PARKING: 10€/ 24Hrs **SERVICES**: INCL
OPENING TIMES: 01/04 – 31/10 **GPS:** N44.49505 E00.16268
DIRECTIONS: AIRE is just SOUTH of the town, well signposted.
SITE DESCRIPTION: *The aire is on the south side of the town, in a wooded & grassy area where there are 50 level spaces, lit at night & shaded by mature trees on grass accessed by automatic barrier & a tarmac track. Aire is in a secure fenced area with 6A ehu's, an artisanal service point & drainage grid.*

REVIEW: *A large, well maintained & managed aire, clean with friendly management. A pleasant quiet spot with shade under trees & parking on grass (soft in wet weather). The aire is secure & safe, barriers being locked from 10pm till 8am. Short walk into town where there is a good variety of shops/ eating places & a Tuesday market. Play area, mini golf nearby.*

ST SYLVESTRE SUR LOT

ADDRESS: ALLEE DU PORT **TYPE OF AIRE:** MUNICIPAL
FACILITIES: WATER /GREY & BLACK DRAIN / TOILETS
LOCATION: URBAN/ RIVER **NO. OF SPACES:** 12
PRICES: PARKING: FREE **SERVICES**: FREE
OPENING TIMES: ALL YEAR **GPS:** N44.39593 E00.80521
DIRECTIONS: From SOUTH on D103, cross RIVER into town & turn 1st LEFT.
SITE DESCRIPTION: *Located next to the Lot River with parking in a medium sized tarmac car park, lit at night with shade in places backing onto a grass area. An artisanal borne & narrow platform drain next to the petrol station with a WC block nearby.*

REVIEW: *A 'car park' aire but the location is fine; on the edge of the river, quiet, level & a lovely outlook. There is a small market here on Wednesday morning as well as an InterMarche (with laundrette) adjacent as well as a small campsite, with other small shops / restaurants within 300m. Walks alongside the Lot river. Busy during day but quiet at night.*

VILLETON

ADDRESS: NEXT TO MUSEUM, D120 **TYPE OF AIRE:** MUNICIPAL
FACILITIES: WATER /GREY & BLACK DRAIN/ TOILETS
LOCATION: SEMI-RURAL/ CANALSIDE **NO. OF SPACES:** 4
PRICES: PARKING: 6€/ 24Hrs **SERVICES**: INCL
OPENING TIMES: ALL YEAR **GPS:** N44.36397 E0.27273
DIRECTIONS: Take D120 WEST towards VILLETON & turn RIGHT immediately before the CANAL, to AIRE next to MUSEE (signposted).
SITE DESCRIPTION: *The aire is in the centre of the hamlet & has 4 spaces for motorhomes with additional parking shared with cars and a restaurant nearby. There is shade here, lighting at night & a mini Flot Bleu service point with platform drainage. Pay at ticket machine.*

REVIEW: *The aire is officially for 4 motorhomes but there is room for a dozen here. A nice, quiet shaded aire next to the Canal de Garonne & outside the local museum (a collection of agricultural machines & equipment) with a picnic area & pizza restaurant but no shops. Cycle path along canal with cycle hire depot.*

64 PYRENEES-ATLANTIQUES

ACCOUS - LHERS

ADDRESS: HAMEAU DE LHERS, OFF D339 **TYPE OF AIRE:** PRIVATE
FACILITIES: WATER /GREY & BLACK DRAIN/ ELECTRIC/ TOILETS/ WIFI
LOCATION: RURAL **NO. OF SPACES:** 20
PRICES: PARKING: 9€/ 24Hrs **SERVICES**: 4€ ELECTRIC
OPENING TIMES: ALL YEAR **GPS:** N42.91025 W0.61939
DIRECTIONS: From ACCOUS take D339 to LHERS, AIRE is signposted.
SITE DESCRIPTION: *The aire is located a few kms south of the small hamlet of Lhers at 1,100m alt. where there is a large level, gravel parking area (unshaded) with fine views of the surrounding mountains. The aire is next to some gites /a small campsite & shares their facilities – toilets, showers & laundry. The pitches have hookups & wifi. Artisanal service point with drainage grid.*

REVIEW: *An excellent aire in a magnificent tranquil location, welcoming owners & meals available, fresh bread in morning, hot showers, washing up area, clean toilets, play area, bbq & laundrette. Good walking area. Restaurant, bar & pizzeria in Accous.* ***Note: The aire is remote, at the end of a long track so best to check for spaces, pay by cash only. Tel/ Text: 0670204586***

ORRIULE

ADDRESS: LABARRAQUE, RTE DE NARP, D30 **TYPE OF AIRE:** PRIVATE
FACILITIES: WATER /GREY & BLACK DRAIN/ ELECTRIC/ WIFI
LOCATION: RURAL **NO. OF SPACES:** 9
PRICES: PARKING: 10€ /24Hrs **SERVICES**: INCL
OPENING TIMES: ALL YEAR **GPS:** N43.41088 W00.85054
DIRECTIONS: From NARP take D30 NORTH, AIRE is on LEFT just after ORRIULE turn.
SITE DESCRIPTION: *This aire is on the property of a beef farm, in a medium size parking area, close to the farm & about 400m from the hamlet centre. There are individual spaces on gravel separated by grass with fine panoramic views, lighting but no shade. Artisanal borne with drainage platform & ehu's.*

REVIEW: *Nice owners & a very quiet spot with excellent views of the Pyrenees but quite remote & no facilities in the nearby hamlet of Orriule. Hook-ups, wifi, picnic tables & bbq, pay by cash. 'Voted Aire of Year' by CamperContact. Tel/ Text : 06 47 01 86 84.*

SALIES DE BEARN

ADDRESS: CHEMIN DU HERRE **TYPE OF AIRE:** MUNICIPAL
FACILITIES: WATER /GREY & BLACK DRAIN/ ELECTRIC
LOCATION: URBAN **NO. OF SPACES:** 20
PRICES: PARKING 8€/ 24Hrs **SERVICES**: INCL
OPENING TIMES: ALL YEAR **GPS:** N43.47302 W0.93399
DIRECTIONS: From WEST in town on D17 take 1st RIGHT & then 2nd RIGHT.
SITE DESCRIPTION: *The aire is on the western edge of the town, each location is delimited by a timber barrier and connected to an ehu, on level gravel surfaces. Lit at night but little shade. Artisanal service point with drainage platform, access controlled by an automatic barrier & ticket machine.*

REVIEW: *A well designed, quiet aire, in a pleasant environment with views of the Pyrenees yet only a short walk to town centre with countryside in the opposite direction. Thermal spa town with a medieval quarter, shops, eating places & a supermarket.*

SEVIGNACQ MEYRACQ

ADDRESS: AIRE DU GAVE D'OSSAU **TYPE OF AIRE:** PRIVATE
FACILITIES: WATER /GREY & BLACK DRAIN / ELECTRIC
LOCATION: SEMI-RURAL **NO. OF SPACES:** 20
PRICES: PARKING: 10€ /24 Hrs **SERVICES**: 2€ ELECTRIC, 3€ WATER
OPENING TIMES: ALL YEAR **GPS:** N43.10712 W0.41192
DIRECTIONS: From SEVIGNACQ take D934 SOUTH to AIRE (signposted RIGHT).
SITE DESCRIPTION: *The aire is in a large 'park like' setting, with pitches on grass/ gravel, under mature trees, & accessed by a gravel track. Laundrette, ehu's & artisanal service point with drainage grid.*

REVIEW: *A beautiful aire; quiet, with views, well shaded pitches, green & peaceful on the banks of a river with ehu's, but long leads required. Nice welcome from the owners - locally produced foods as well as drinks & ices can be bought on site, order bread for morning, restaurants & shops in Arudy.*

ST JEAN PIED DE PORT

ADDRESS:CHEMIN D'EYHERABERRY, OFF D301 **TYPE OF AIRE:** MUNICIPAL
FACILITIES: WATER /GREY & BLACK DRAIN/ ELECTRIC/ RUBBISH
LOCATION: URBAN **NO. OF SPACES:** 30
PRICES: PARKING: 10€/ 24 Hrs **SERVICES**: INCL
OPENING TIMES: ALL YEAR **GPS:** N43.15893 W01.23773
DIRECTIONS: Take D301 SOUTH (sign St Michel) out of town & AIRE is on LEFT.
SITE DESCRIPTION: *The aire is in a section of the Municipal campsite, on the south side of the town, where there are about 30 spaces mainly on hard standings with lighting at night & grass areas, it is about 300m from the town centre. There are trees giving good shade & an Artisanal service point with drainage grid & ehu's*

REVIEW: *There are 2 aires in this old fortified town but this is much nicer than the other, being in the grounds of the campsite with good size shaded spaces with ehu's bordered by grass. Quiet location, close to the good range of shops, eating places, OT & an InterMarche supermarket. Pay at ticket machine.*

AUVERGNE

Auvergne region is made up of 4 departments;
Allier (03), Cantal (15), Haute-Loire (43) & Puy-de-Dome (63)

Auvergne Map

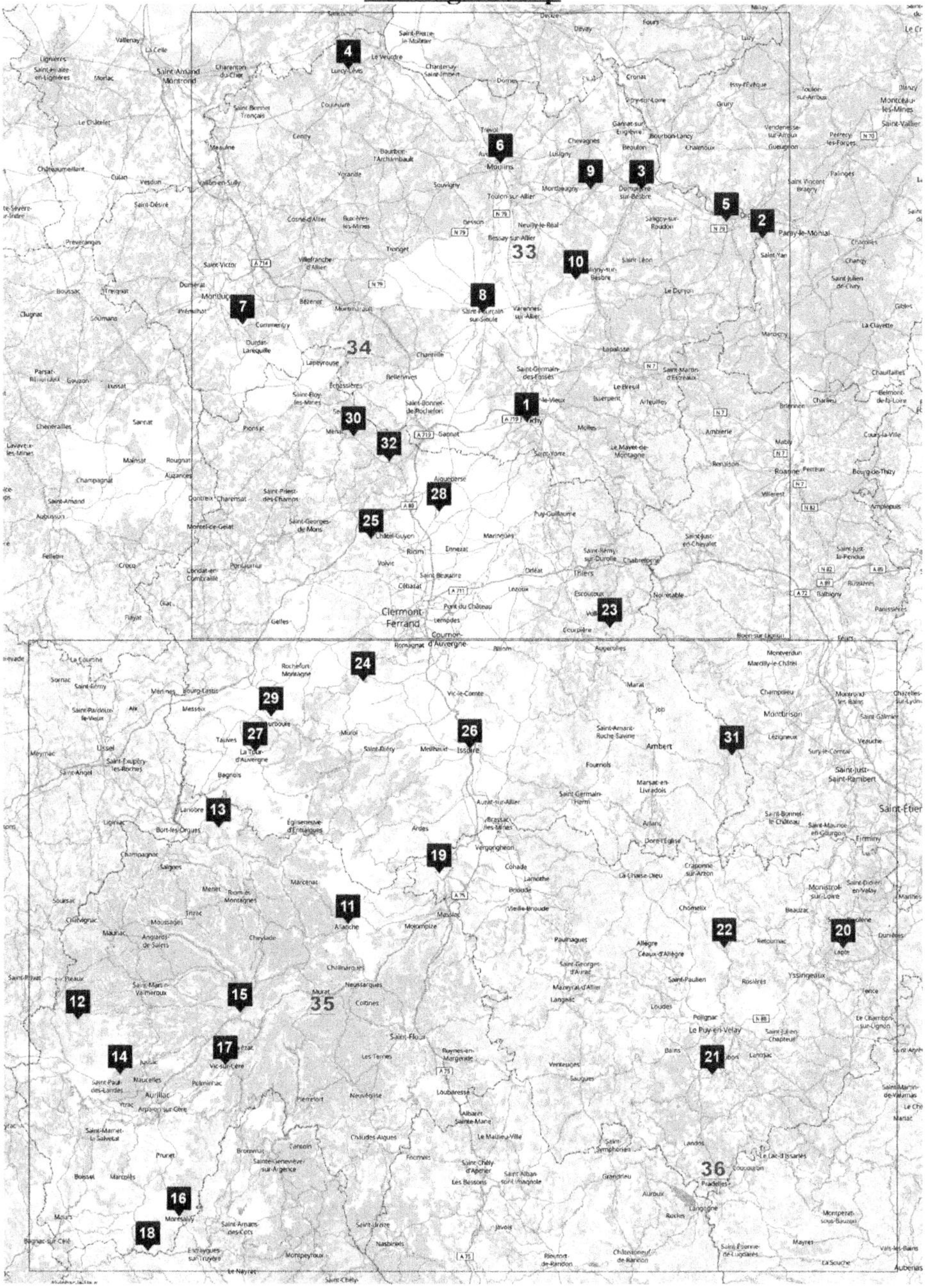

See next 2 pages for enlarged maps & key

<u>Key to enlarged Auvergne Maps (below)</u>

Former campsites that are now aires are noted in ***bold***

1) BELLERIVE SUR ALLIER – 2) CHASSENARD – 3) DOMPIERRE SUR BESBRE
4) LURCY-LEVIS – 5) MOLINET – ***6) MOULINS*** *– 7) NERIS LES BAINS*
8) ST POURCAIN SUR SIOULE *– 9) THIEL SUR ACOLIN – 10) TRETEAU*
11) ALLANCHE – 12) ARNAC – 13) CHAMPS SUR TARENTAINE – 14) CRANDELLES
15) MANDAILLES ST JULIEN – 16) MONTSALVY – 17) VIC SUR CERE
18) VIEILLEVIE – 19) ***BLESLE 1*** *& 2 – 20) LAPTE –* ***21) SOLIGNAC SUR LOIRE***
22) VOREY – 23) AUBUSSON D'AUVERGNE – ***24) AYDAT***
25) CHARBONNIERES LES VARENNES – 26) ISSOIRE – 27) LA TOUR D'AUVERGNE
28) LE CHEIX SUR MORGE – ***29) MURAT LE QUAIRE*** *– 30) POUZOL*
31) ST ANTHEME – 32) ST PARDOUX – ***33) ST GERARD – 34) LOUROUX***
35) MURAT *– 36) PRADELLES*

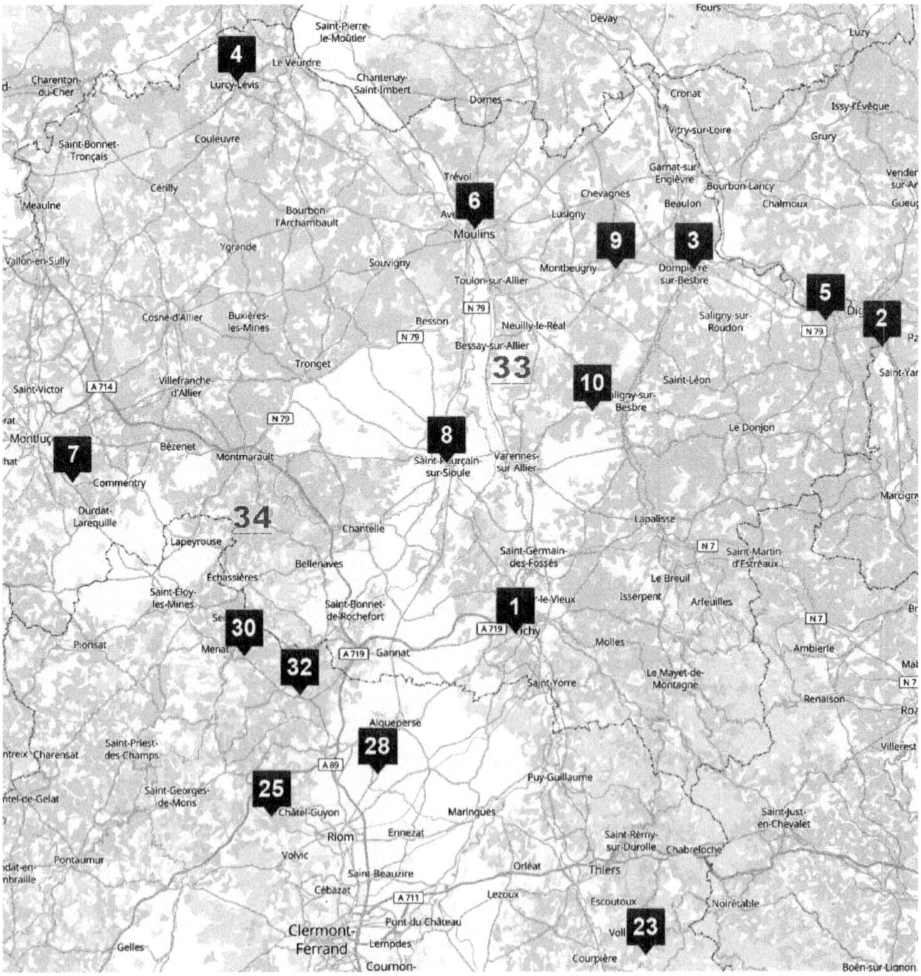

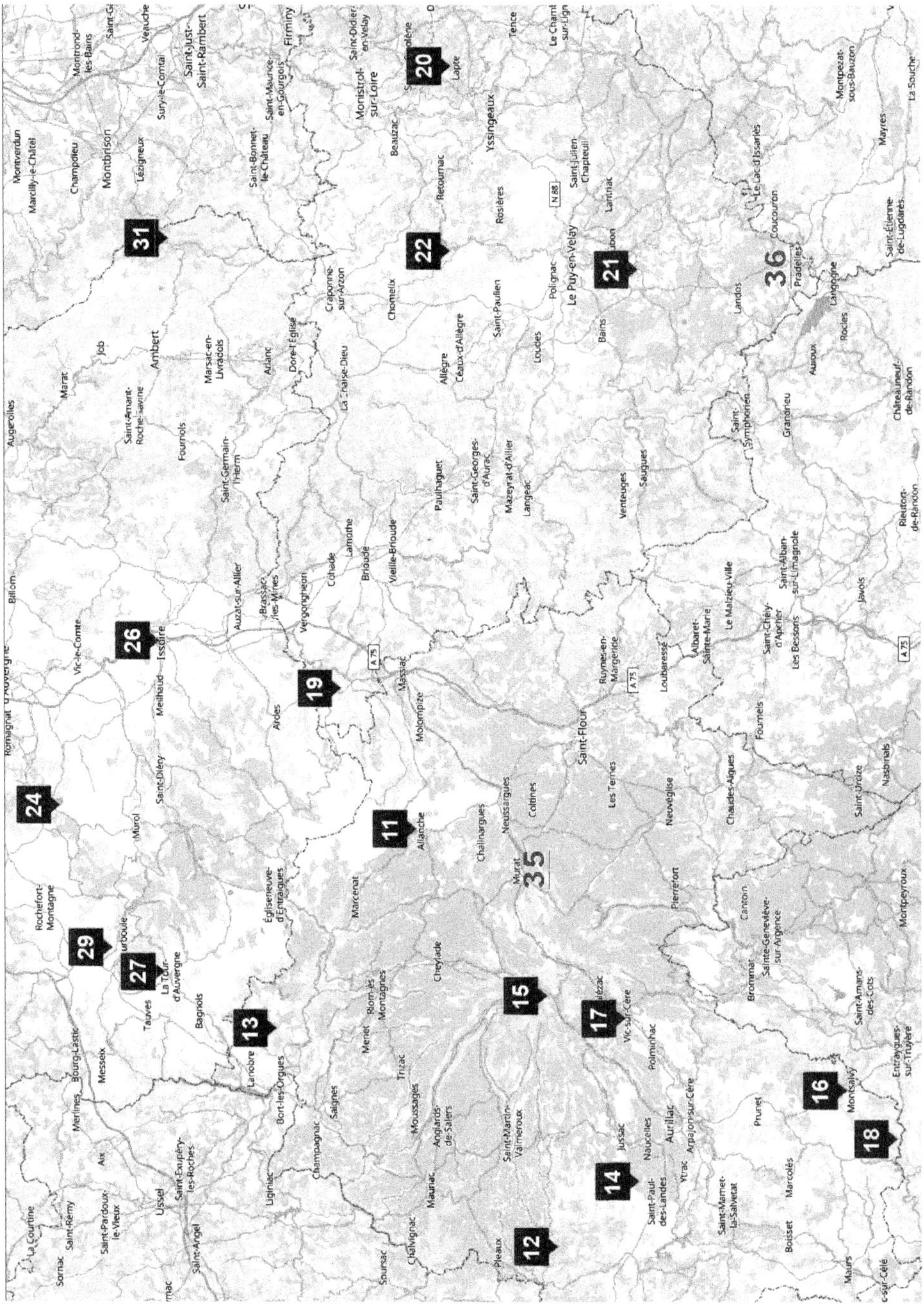
24
26
31
29
27
13
19
11
22
20
21
35
36
15
17
14
12
16
18
Issoire
Montbrison
Ambert
Saint-Flour
Murat
Le Puy-en-Velay
Brioude
Massiac
Allanche
Aurillac
Vic-sur-Cère
Bort-les-Orgues
Ussel
Yssingeaux
Langogne
Pradelles
Montsalvy
Saint-Just-Saint-Rambert
Firminy
La Chaise-Dieu
Langeac
Saugues
Pierrefort
Chaudes-Aigues
Riom-ès-Montagnes
Salers
Mauriac
A 75
N 88

03 ALLIER

BELLERIVE SUR ALLIER

ADDRESS: RUE CLAUDE DECLOITRE **TYPE OF AIRE:** PRIVATE
FACILITIES: WATER /GREY & BLACK DRAIN/ ELECTRIC/ TOILETS
LOCATION: RURAL/ RIVERSIDE **NO. OF SPACES:** 45
PRICES: PARKING: 12€/ 24Hrs **SERVICES**: INCL
OPENING TIMES: ALL YEAR **GPS:** N46.11539 E03.42998
DIRECTIONS: From SOUTH on D131, follow 'Berges de l'Allier' camping signs.
SITE DESCRIPTION: *This pleasantly located private aire is situated on the west bank of the Allier river about 1.5km east of the town centre, on the banks of the river & close to the Beau Rivages campsite with its facilities. The aire has level spaces (lighting with shade in places) on gravel/ grass accessed by a gravel track & bordered by trees, entry via an automatic barrier operated by a credit card. Artisanal borne with drainage platform, toilets & ehu's.*

REVIEW: *A well-managed private aire run by the adjacent campsite, a quiet spot, 100m from the river. Heated toilets (dated) with sinks & shower, ehu's. A bit remote from the large town but there are good cycle tracks along river plus restaurants within 100m & a supermarket. 37 space, 4* campsite adjacent with shop, snack bar, laundrette, wifi & bar (open 01/ 04 - 08/ 10).*

CHASSENARD

ADDRESS: LA CROIX ROUGE, D169 **TYPE OF AIRE**: MUNICIPAL
FACILITIES: WATER /GREY & BLACK DRAIN / RUBBISH/ TOILETS/ ELEC.
LOCATION: RURAL/ CANAL **NO. OF SPACES:** 6
PRICES: PARKING: FREE **SERVICES**: 2€ WATER or ELECTRIC
OPENING TIMES: ALL YEAR **GPS:** N46.41438 E03.97415
DIRECTIONS: From CHASSENARD head SOUTH on D169. Upon crossing CANAL after 2kms – AIRE is immediately on LEFT next to CANAL.
SITE DESCRIPTION: *The aire is in a small gravel parking area bordered by grass areas next to the Canal de Roanne, about 2kms south of Chassenard. The aire is next to the small canal marina & is surrounded by open fields with lighting & shade in places. A modern Euro-Relais borne with drainage platform & adjacent toilets.*
REVIEW: *A very pleasant, quiet, small aire in a canal side setting, limited parking on hard standing but also possible to park on grass. Well equipped with toilets, a covered picnic table, grass areas & walks along the canal banks. Remote from the small village of Chassenard where there is just a restaurant/ pizzeria/ bar. Digoin is 5kms away where there are shops, etc.*

Chassenard

DOMPIERRE SUR BESBRE

ADDRESS: CHEMIN DES PERCIERES, OFF D779 **TYPE OF AIRE:** MUNICIPAL
FACILITIES: WATER /GREY & BLACK DRAIN/ TOILETS/ ELECTRIC
LOCATION: URBAN/ RIVER **NO. OF SPACES:** 6
PRICES: PARKING: FREE **SERVICES**: FREE
OPENING TIMES: ALL YEAR **GPS :** N46.51841 E03.68505
DIRECTIONS: Entering town on D779 from EAST, turn 1st LEFT after RIVER, AIRE is on LEFT.
SITE DESCRIPTION: *A Municipal aire located on the eastern side of this small town, 300m from the centre, where the modern Euro-Relais service point with drainage platform has a small toilet block adjacent. There are 6 individual spaces in this gravel parking separated by shrubs, lit at night & having shade under trees.*

REVIEW: *Reserved riverside motorhome parking, quiet with shaded level spaces, popular in summer, a short walk from town centre. Services clean & free including ehu's, picnic table & modern clean toilets adjacent, more parking nearby. Reasonable range of shops in town & a Super U supermarket with a market Sat. mornings. Park, play area & walks adjacent. 67 space campsite on opposite bank of river.*

LOUROUX DE BOUBLE

ADDRESS: ROUTE DE BOIS MAL, D129 **TYPE OF AIRE:** PRIVATE
FACILITIES: WATER /GREY & BLACK DRAIN/ ELECTRIC/ WIFI/ TOILETS
LOCATION: RURAL/ RIVER **NO. OF SPACES:** 26
PRICES: PARKING: 9 -12€ /24HRS **SERVICES**: INCL
OPENING TIMES: ALL YEAR **GPS :** N46.23007 E02.99888
DIRECTIONS: From VILLAGE take D129 NORTH - AIRE is on LEFT after 2kms.
SITE DESCRIPTION: *This 'Camping Village' aire managed by the CampingCarPark company is located 2kms north of the village, next to a forest, & is in a large grass former campsite 'La Graviere' with farmland to the south. Good shade, pitches on grass accessed by a gravel track, entry via an automatic barrier, CCP card required. Euro-Relais service point with drainage platform. Large pitches each with individual 6A ehu's & wifi.*

REVIEW: *Quiet spot but not very handy for the village, next to a large forest. Large unmarked parking spaces with shade under trees & all services. Toilets/ showers with sinks on site but closed Oct – April. Boulangerie, Proxi superette & restaurant in village.*

LURCY-LEVIS

ADDRESS: NEXT TO LAC SEZOT **TYPE OF AIRE:** MUNICIPAL
FACILITIES: WATER /GREY & BLACK DRAIN/ ELECTRIC/ TOILETS
LOCATION: RURAL/ LAKE **NO. OF SPACES:** 10
PRICES: PARKING: FREE **SERVICES**: 3€ WATER or ELECTRIC
OPENING TIMES: ALL YEAR **GPS:** N46.73805 E02.94067
DIRECTIONS: From NORTH take D951 SOUTH & D1 to LURCY-LEVIS. As you enter town turn LEFT to LAKE & AIRE.

SITE DESCRIPTION: *The aire is located next to a large lake to the north of this small town (Pop.2,000), in a rural setting surrounded by farmland. The parking is on gravel bordered by grass areas with little shade but lighting at night, there are also picnic tables, a play area, boules pitch, toilets (incl. disabled) & fishing is possible in the lake. AireServices borne with platform drain.*

REVIEW: *A quiet, clean & well maintained aire next to a lake with 10 spaces on hard standing bordered by grass. Jetons from the tabac/ bar in town opposite the church. There are shops & services in Lurcy-Levis as well as a supermarket & there is also a motor racing circuit in town, but fortunately it is to the south of town.*

MOLINET

ADDRESS: ROUTE DE MOULINS, D779 **TYPE OF AIRE:** MUNICIPAL
FACILITIES: WATER /GREY & BLACK DRAIN/ ELECTRIC/ TOILETS
LOCATION: SEMI-RURAL/ CANAL **NO. OF SPACES:** 12
PRICES: PARKING: FREE **SERVICES**: 2€ WATER or ELECTRIC
OPENING TIMES: ALL YEAR **GPS :** N46.47055 E03.94149
DIRECTIONS: From NORTH take D779 to MOLINET, AIRE is on LEFT before Roundabout.

SITE DESCRIPTION: *This purpose built modern aire is located 500m north of the centre of this small rural village, next to the Loire canal & opposite the canal marina, where there are 12 individual level spaces for motorhomes, parking on hard standing with adjacent grass areas. The aire has little shade but is lit at night & there are picnic tables available. Flot Bleu service point with drainage platform & toilets.*

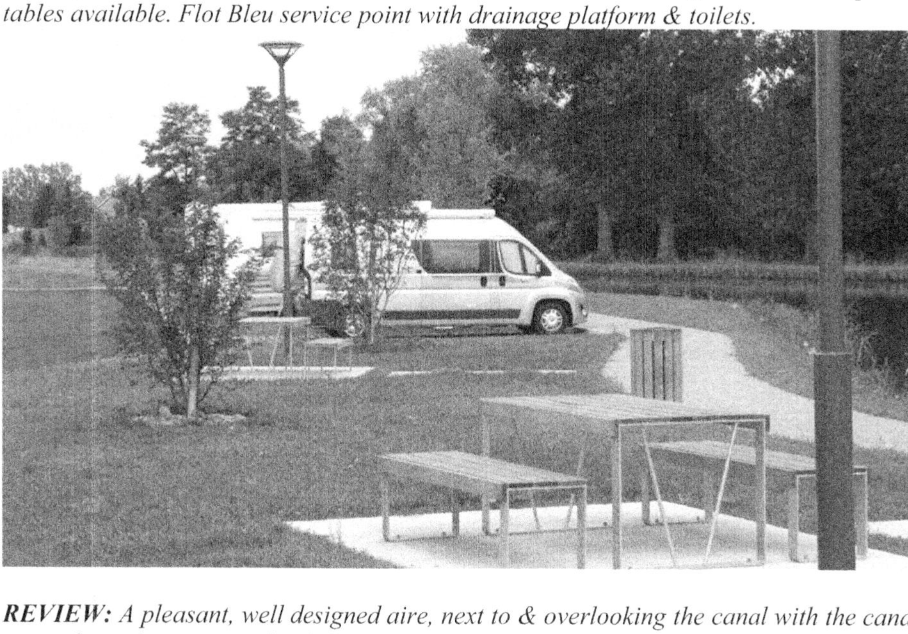

REVIEW: *A pleasant, well designed aire, next to & overlooking the canal with the canal towpath on the opposite bank for walks/ cycling to Digoin. Self-cleaning toilets, picnic tables, slight road noise from adjacent road & a level walk to the village centre where there is a supermarket, café /tabac, pharmacy, pizzeria & Poste with a wider range of services in Digoin (3kms).*

MOULINS

ADDRESS: CHEMIN DE HALAGE **TYPE OF AIRE:** MUNICIPAL
FACILITIES: WATER /GREY & BLACK DRAIN/ ELECTRIC/ RUBBISH
LOCATION: URBAN/ RIVER **NO. OF SPACES:** 80
PRICES: PARKING: 0.1€/Hr **SERVICES**: 2€ WATER or ELECTRIC
OPENING TIMES: ALL YEAR **GPS:** N46.55832 E03.32453
DIRECTIONS: Entering MOULINS from WEST on D945, turn RIGHT at R/bout just before river & then take next LEFT to AIRE (signposted).
***SITE DESCRIPTION**: A very large aire located on the west bank of the Allier River just across from the city of Moulins. The aire is in the former municipal camping where there are numerous level pitches on grass accessed by tarmac tracks, some shaded & some in the open, all lit at night. A Flot Bleu service point with a drainage platform & ehu's, jetons available from machine at entrance. Parking paid at automatic barrier on exit – all by credit card.*

***REVIEW:** An excellent, cheap & very popular aire, awarded 'Aire of the Year 2014', in the former municipal campsite. There are many quiet, pleasant pitches most with nearby ehu's, overlooking the Allier river yet only a short level walk across the bridge to the centre of Moulins where there are all the shops, services & eating places that you need. 3 museums in town including a restored 19th C 'time capsule' town-house, an old 'quarter' as well as the Cathedral to visit. Aire is well signposted in town. Walks along river & cycle path. Local shops & InterMarche supermarket within 150m of aire.*

NERIS LES BAINS

ADDRESS: OUTSIDE CAMPING DU LAC, D155 **TYPE OF AIRE:** MUNICIPAL
FACILITIES: WATER /GREY & BLACK DRAIN/ ELECTRIC/ TOILETS/ WIFI
LOCATION: SEMI-URBAN **NO. OF SPACES:** 6
PRICES: PARKING: 9€ /24Hrs **SERVICES**: INCL
OPENING TIMES: ALL YEAR **GPS:** N46.28667 E02.65227
DIRECTIONS: In NERIS on D2144, turn WEST at R/bout & follow signs for "CAMPING" & AIRE.
***SITE DESCRIPTION:** The aire is located outside the 3* Municipal campsite, about 500m west of the town centre, where there are individual spaces separated by hedges on gravel for up 6 motorhomes in a small tarmac parking area. The parking has little shade, is lit at night & is about 50m from a large leisure lake with tennis courts adjacent. Raclet service point with drainage platform & toilet.*

REVIEW: *A nice quiet spot, well maintained by the campsite. Toilet block adjacent with shower, 10A electric included in price, wifi available by the hour. Reasonable range of shops/ services in town & a supermarket. Thermal spa town with walks in area, cycleway along old railway track to Montlucon & Roman remains in town. Campsite is open 14/04 – 31/10, aire is free when campsite is closed but no electric/ wifi.*

ST GERAND DE VAUX

ADDRESS: RTE DU LAVOIR **TYPE OF AIRE:** MUNICIPAL
FACILITIES: WATER /GREY & BLACK DRAIN / ELECTRIC
LOCATION: RURAL/ LAKE **NO. OF SPACES:** 40
PRICES: PARKING: FREE **SERVICES**: 2€ WATER or ELECTRIC
OPENING TIMES: ALL YEAR **GPS :** N46.38389 E03.39897
DIRECTIONS: Entering village from WEST on D32, turn 1st LEFT (sign 'Etang') to AIRE.
SITE DESCRIPTION: *This aire is located about 600m to the north of this small rural village on the site of the former Municipal campsite, pleasantly situated next to a large fishing lake & surrounded by farmland. Parking is on grass/ hard standing, shaded by mature trees. Euro-Relais service point with drainage platform.*

REVIEW: *A quietly situated aire next to a nice lake, ample parking with plenty of shade, picnic tables & play area. Restaurant 'Le Cheval Blanc' in the village with good menu & takeaway plus bread available, also sell jetons for borne (as well as the Mairie). Not much in village apart from Château to visit. Walks around lake & fishing.*

ST POURCAIN SUR SIOULE

ADDRESS: RUE DE LA MOUTTE **TYPE OF AIRE:** MUNICIPAL
FACILITIES: WATER /GREY & BLACK DRAIN / TOILETS / ELECTRIC
LOCATION: SEMI-RURAL/ RIVERSIDE **NO. OF SPACES:** 70
PRICES: PARKING: FREE **SERVICES**: 4€ WATER or ELECTRIC
OPENING TIMES: ALL YEAR **GPS:** N46.31212 E03.29654
DIRECTIONS: From SOUTH on D2009, in town, cross BRIDGE & turn RIGHT into RUE DE LA MOUTTE to AIRE.
SITE DESCRIPTION: *The large aire here is on the banks of the River Sioule & close to the Municipal campsite. Pitches are located on grass/ gravel underneath willow trees or next to the river with a tarmac access road, illuminated at night. A quiet location with shops & town centre within 400m. The service point has a Flot Bleu borne on a central plinth with a double platform drain allowing motorhomes to use it at once. There are separate terminals for 6A ehu's & an information board at the entrance. The aire is well maintained & managed by the adjacent campsite.*

REVIEW: *A pleasant & peaceful location, on the side of the Sioule river with a good selection of shops /eating places in town less than 5 minutes walk – a very nice facility where parking is free with ample spaces but not enough ehu's. Previous winner of 'Aire of the Year'.*

THIEL SUR ACOLIN

ADDRESS: RUE DE LA MOTTE, OFF D12 **TYPE OF AIRE:** MUNICIPAL
FACILITIES: WATER /GREY & BLACK DRAIN/ ELECTRIC
LOCATION: SEMI-URBAN **NO. OF SPACES**: 11
PRICES: PARKING: FREE **SERVICES**: 2€ WATER or ELECTRIC
OPENING TIMES: ALL YEAR **GPS:** N46.52274 E03.58778
DIRECTIONS: From village centre take D12 EAST, turn LEFT at CEMETERY to AIRE.
SITE DESCRIPTION: *The dedicated aire here is located on the eastern edge of this large village, next to the cemetery where there is a gravel parking area reserved for motorhomes with 11 level spaces separated by shrubs, bordered by grass areas, shade in places & lit at night. 3 bornes each with 4 electric hook up points & an AireServices service point with drainage platform.*
REVIEW: *A modern purpose-built aire with large separate spaces & farmland adjacent. 500m walk to just a boulangerie & Proxi superette in village (no bar) & not much else. Quiet spot with picnic area adjacent.*

Thiel

TRETEAU

ADDRESS: NEXT TO LAKE, RUE DU ROSIER **TYPE OF AIRE:** MUNICIPAL
FACILITIES: WATER /GREY & BLACK DRAIN/ ELECTRIC/ TOILETS
LOCATION: RURAL/ LAKESIDE **NO. OF SPACES:** 15
PRICES: PARKING: 4€/ 24 Hrs **SERVICES**: 2€ WATER or ELECTRIC
OPENING TIMES: ALL YEAR **GPS:** N46.36812 E03.51784
DIRECTIONS: From SOUTH on D163 in TRETEAU, turn 1st LEFT after CHURCH.
SITE DESCRIPTION: *An aire, located next to a lake & about 400m west of the small village, where the parking is on gravel or grass, overlooking the lake & accessed by a gravel track with shade under trees in places. Euro-Relais junior service point with drainage grid & toilets.*

REVIEW: *A very pleasant, quiet position, next to a large lake (where you can fish) with a walk around it, a play area & within a short distance of the village centre with a few shops; boulangerie, café & restaurant. Fee collected by official in pm.*

15 CANTAL

ALLANCHE

ADDRESS: STATION PARKING, OFF D9 **TYPE OF AIRE:** MUNICIPAL
FACILITIES: WATER /GREY & BLACK DRAIN/ RUBBISH
LOCATION: SEMI-URBAN **NO. OF SPACES:** 25
PRICES: PARKING: FREE **SERVICES**: FREE
OPENING TIMES: ALL YEAR **GPS:** N45.22945 E02.93163
DIRECTIONS: Take D9 EAST into ALLANCHE& LEFT to the STATION/ AIRE.
***SITE DESCRIPTION**: The aire is in the large gravel & grass parking area of the former railway station (to the west of the town) in a pleasant location with open fields to the west. Many level pitches that are either on grass or gravel, no lighting & not much shade but a quiet situation with views over the town & beyond. Euro-Relais service point with drainage platform.*

***REVIEW:** Excellent aire, ample room, very quiet, open location, very close to town & shops. Interesting old town with a reasonable range of shops, bars & eating places. The tourist office is located in the adjacent old station building & the railway is now a Velorail. Nice walks around the town where there is an ancient fortified church & the remains of the towns ramparts. Just the Tourism tax of 0.8€ pp to pay in OT.*

ARNAC

ADDRESS: NEXT TO MAIRIE **TYPE OF AIRE:** MUNICIPAL
FACILITIES: WATER /GREY & BLACK DRAIN/ ELECTRIC/ TOILETS
LOCATION: SEMI-RURAL **NO. OF SPACES:** 2
PRICES: PARKING: FREE **SERVICES**: 2€ WATER or ELECTRIC
OPENING TIMES: ALL YEAR **GPS:** N45.06020 E02.23387
DIRECTIONS: Take D42/ D61 NORTH to ARNAC, pass thru village & AIRE is next to MAIRIE.
***SITE DESCRIPTION:** The aire is next to the Mairie at the northern end of this very small (pop 180) rural village, where there are 2 spaces on tarmac in a park like area with picnic tables & a playground adjacent. The spaces have adjacent grass area with trees. Euro-Relais service point with drainage grid & toilets nearby.*
***REVIEW:** A pleasant & quiet location but very rural. There is a bar/ restaurant in the village & the nearby 'Village de Vacances' has an epicerie that is open May – Sept. Large lake to north of village.*

Arnac

CHAMPS SUR TARENTAINE

ADDRESS: ROUTE DE BORT, D679 **TYPE OF AIRE:** MUNICIPAL
FACILITIES: WATER /GREY & BLACK DRAIN/ TOILETS/ RUBBISH
LOCATION: URBAN **NO. OF SPACES:** 5
PRICES: PARKING: FREE **SERVICES**: FREE
OPENING TIMES: ALL YEAR **GPS:** N45.39449 E02.55795
DIRECTIONS: Take D679 EAST to the village, the AIRE is on LEFT (signposted) behind wall before Garage.
SITE DESCRIPTION: *The aire is well located on the western side of the village, a short walk to the centre where there is a small selection of shops. The aire is located next to the D679 but shielded from it by a high stone wall, where level parking is on grass under small trees. Euro-Relais service point with a large platform drain.*

REVIEW: *A quiet location on the outskirts of this pleasant, large village in a wooded valley & close to the river. Reasonable range of shops including a mini-mart, boulangerie, butchers, petrol station, bars, etc & there is also an open air swimming pool, next to a pleasant municipal campsite. Good modern service point with toilets adjacent.*

CRANDELLES

ADDRESS: PARKING NEXT TO LAC **TYPE OF AIRE:** MUNICIPAL
FACILITIES: WATER /GREY & BLACK DRAIN /RUBBISH
LOCATION: SEMI-RURAL/ LAKE **NO. OF SPACES:** 10
PRICES: PARKING: FREE /24HRS **SERVICES**: 3.5€ WATER
OPENING TIMES: ALL YEAR **GPS:** N44.95891 E02.34272
DIRECTIONS: AIRE is behind CHURCH & next to LAKE.
SITE DESCRIPTION: *The aire here is on a gravel parking area accessed by a tarmac road, next to a large lake – with good views over it. An excellent location with services & parking spaces easily accessible. Little shade, but a quiet position on the edge of the village, with a nice walk around the lake. Raclet service point / drainage grid.*

REVIEW: *A beautiful aire in a lovely quiet spot where there is a playground nearby, bathing in the lake as well as a nearby café/ bar that also sell bread. Dogs are not allowed around the lake. Jetons from the bar/ Mairie.*

MANDAILLES ST JULIEN

ADDRESS: VILLAGE CAR PARK **TYPE OF AIRE:** MUNICIPAL
FACILITIES: WATER /GREY & BLACK DRAIN
LOCATION: SEMI-RURAL/ RIVER **NO. OF SPACES:** 5
PRICES: PARKING: FREE **SERVICES**: 4€ WATER
OPENING TIMES: ALL YEAR **GPS:** N45.06933 E02.65650
DIRECTIONS: From SOUTH on D17, in village, cross RIVER & turn LEFT to AIRE.
SITE DESCRIPTION: *The aire is on the west side of the small village in a large tarmac car park, the individual spaces are separated by grass verges & are slightly sloping with a little shade. Euro Relais service point with drainage platform.*

REVIEW: *A good location for visiting Puy Mary, next to a river with fine views & very peaceful. Shop in village & jetons from either of the two restaurants.*

MONTSALVY

ADDRESS: OFF D19 **TYPE OF AIRE:** MUNICIPAL
FACILITIES: WATER /GREY & BLACK DRAIN / TOILETS / ELEC./ SHOWER
LOCATION: SEMI-RURAL **NO. OF SPACES:** 10
PRICES: PARKING: FREE **SERVICES**: 2€ WATER or ELECTRIC

OPENING TIMES: ALL YEAR **GPS:** N44.70785 E02.49666
DIRECTIONS: Take D920 SOUTH to MONTSALVY. In the centre of village turn RIGHT onto D19 – AIRE on left.
***SITE DESCRIPTION**: The aire here is in the small tarmac parking area on the western edge of the village, behind the village hall, with individual spaces separated by hedges/ grass verges, slightly sloping with no shade. The car park is next to open countryside with an easy to access Raclet service point, drainage grid & adjacent WC block (suitable for handicapped).*

***REVIEW:** A well equipped aire with spaces having good privacy & a modern WC block (cleaned daily) that also has a hot shower (for 1€), toilet & sinks with a boules pitch adjacent. Montsalvy is a very pretty medieval fortified village with shops/ restaurant near to the parking. The church here is worth a visit, built on the foundations of the old fortified walls with an 18th C tower. Aire was voted 'Aire of the Year 2018'.*

MURAT

ADDRESS: STALAPOS, OFF N122 **TYPE OF AIRE:** PRIVATE
FACILITIES: WATER /GREY & BLACK DRAIN / ELECTRIC / WIFI / TOILETS
LOCATION: SEMI-RURAL/ RIVER **NO. OF SPACES:** 120
PRICES: PARKING: 11-16€/ 24 Hrs **SERVICES**: INCL
OPENING TIMES: ALL YEAR **GPS :** N45.10266 E02.86528
DIRECTIONS: Follow signs off N122 in MURAT to AIRE/ CAMPING.

***SITE DESCRIPTION**: This 'Camping Village' aire is managed by CampingCarPark in the former Municipal campsite on the south side of Murat about 600m to the centre of town. There is good shade on many of the spaces & public toilets/ showers are nearby (open 1/05 - 30/09). There is an Artisanal service point with platform drain, ehu's & wifi*

as well as a play area, laundrette & recycling bins nearby. Access via automatic barrier, CCP card required.
REVIEW: *A very nice medieval 'Small Town of Character' with a well-situated & clean aire within easy walking distance of the town centre. Quiet rural spot with ample large grass or tarmac spaces each with ehu, next to the small river with walks nearby. Wifi has variable reception & toilets closed Oct till April. Good range of shops/ eating places in town & InterMarche near to aire.*

VIC SUR CERE

ADDRESS: AVE DES TILLEULS **TYPE OF AIRE:** MUNICIPAL
FACILITIES: WATER /GREY & BLACK DRAIN / ELECTRIC
LOCATION: SEMI-RURAL **NO. OF SPACES:** 10
PRICES: PARKING: FREE **SERVICES**: 3€ WATER or ELECTRIC
OPENING TIMES: ALL YEAR **GPS:** N44.98253 E02.63145
DIRECTIONS: From N122 turn EAST into RUE DU 14 JUILLET & then 1st LEFT into AVE DES TILLEULS – AIRE is 300m on RIGHT.
SITE DESCRIPTION: *The aire is situated next to the Municipal campsite in a medium sized tarmac car park on the eastern edge of the town, 300m to the centre, next to a small river & overlooking open countryside. Spaces are divided by grass verges with some shade provided by mature trees, lit at night & screened from the road by hedges. Euro-Relais service point & drainage platform, jetons from OT.*

REVIEW: *The aire is in a quiet location, about 500m from the town centre although there is an InterMarche supermarket adjacent. Good selection of shops in the town; boulangeries, restaurants, butchers, tabac & chemist, etc with free wifi at OT. Large park area opposite. Pleasant medieval town with many fine old houses & a mineral water spring. Nice walk nearby in the Pas du Cere.*

VIEILLEVIE

ADDRESS: OFF D141 **TYPE OF AIRE:** MUNICIPAL
FACILITIES: WATER /GREY & BLACK DRAIN/ ELECTRIC
LOCATION: SEMI-RURAL **NO. OF SPACES:** 6
PRICES: PARKING: FREE **SERVICES**: 2€ WATER or ELECTRIC
OPENING TIMES: ALL YEAR **GPS:** N44.64491 E02.41819
DIRECTIONS: Approaching from EAST on D141, AIRE is on LEFT in village centre.

SITE DESCRIPTION: *The aire is located in the centre of this small village where there is a purpose-built parking for motorhomes with 6 level spaces on tarmac separated by grass verges with high hedges. AireServices service point with drainage channel. Restaurant & grocery shop in village.*

REVIEW: *A very pretty little village with a nice little aire, well maintained & quiet. Individual spaces having good privacy separated by shrubs/ trees on the edge of village. Short walk to the Lot river & fishing, walks along river. Picnic table in aire & a picnic area adjacent with large grass area. Old château in village, a good stopover for visiting the historic village of Conques.*

43 HAUTE-LOIRE

BLESLE 1

ADDRESS: HOTEL 'LE SCORPION', D909 **TYPE OF AIRE:** PRIVATE
FACILITIES: WATER /GREY & BLACK DRAIN / ELECTRIC/ TOILETS
LOCATION: RURAL **NO. OF SPACES:** 20
PRICES: PARKING: 13€ / 24 Hrs **SERVICES**: INCL
OPENING TIMES: ALL YEAR **GPS:** N45.31215 E03.18679
DIRECTIONS: From BLESLE, take D8 EAST & D909 NORTH, HOTEL is on LEFT before Railway Bridge.

SITE DESCRIPTION: *The aire is in a small field behind the Hotel 'le Scorpion', with parking on grass, the pitches being shaded by apple trees & overlooking woods/ farmland with use of showers & WC's included in the price. Flot Bleu service point & ehu's.*
REVIEW: *A good, quiet location behind the Hotel Scorpion, a reasonable selection of meals are available in its restaurant which is open all year round & every day in the summer, closed on Tuesdays in winter. Blesle, one of the "Most Beautiful Villages", with its shops/ restaurant is 2km distant. Handy stopover 5kms from A75, Jcn 22. Also 6 motorhome spaces in Blesle village (no services) & a second private aire (see below).*

BLESLE 2

ADDRESS: OFF D8 **TYPE OF AIRE:** PRIVATE
FACILITIES: WATER /GREY & BLACK DRAIN/ ELECTRIC/ WIFI/ TOILETS
LOCATION: RURAL/ RIVER **NO. OF SPACES:** 44
PRICES: PARKING: 9-13€/ 24HRS **SERVICES**: INCL
OPENING TIMES: ALL YEAR **GPS :** N45.31203 E03.17279
DIRECTIONS: Approaching village from WEST on D125, turn 1st RIGHT to AIRE.
SITE DESCRIPTION: *This 'Camping Village' aire, run by CampingCarPark, is situated in the former municipal campsite 'La Bessiere', about 400m south of the village centre & next to the river Sianne. Pitches are on gravel/ grass (most shaded), each has 6A ehu & wifi with toilets/ showers & sinks (open 15/05-15/09). Artisanal service point with drainage platform. Access by automatic barrier, CCP card required.*

REVIEW: *A pleasant location next to the river, close to one of the 'Most Beautiful Villages in France' - quiet with play area, bbq's & good shaded pitches but some low branches. Toilets cleaned regularly but only open May- Sept. Grocer, butchers & restaurant in village as well as a museum, impressive church & beautiful old houses.*

LAPTE

ADDRESS: RUE DR.TASSY, D65 **TYPE OF AIRE:** MUNICIPAL
FACILITIES: WATER /GREY & BLACK DRAIN/ ELECTRIC/ RUBBISH
LOCATION: SEMI-RURAL **NO. OF SPACES:** 6
PRICES: PARKING: FREE **SERVICES**: 3€ WATER or ELECTRIC
OPENING TIMES: ALL YEAR **GPS:** N45.18443 E04.21339
DIRECTIONS: Entering LAPTE from WEST on D65, AIRE is immediately on RIGHT.
SITE DESCRIPTION: *The aire is located on the western side of this small rural village in a gravel/ tarmac parking area bordered by grass areas with picnic tables & surrounded by shrubs. The aire has little shade but is only a short walk (200m) from the village centre. Euro-Relais service point with platform drain. Jetons from shops.*

REVIEW: *A pleasant little rural aire with half a dozen spaces in a quiet situation next to the 'Via Fluvia' tarmac cycle track along a former railway line 20kms long. Grass area adjacent with picnic tables & play area. Short walk into village where there is a small range of shops; grocer, boulangerie, butcher, restaurant & a bar/ tabac. Leisure lake 5kms away.*

PRADELLES

ADDRESS: SALAISONS DE PRADELLES, N88 **TYPE OF AIRE:** PRIVATE
FACILITIES: WATER /GREY & BLACK DRAIN/ ELECTRIC/ RUBBISH
LOCATION: RURAL **NO. OF SPACES:** 70
PRICES: PARKING: FREE **SERVICES**: INCL, ELECTRIC 2€
OPENING TIMES: ALL YEAR **GPS :** N44.77540 E03.88753
DIRECTIONS: AIRE is next to RN88 just NORTH of PRADELLES (signposted).
SITE DESCRIPTION *This private aire is in a large grass parking area behind the butchery/ delicatessen business 'Salaisons', the parking is on grass accessed off a gravel track with picnic tables & shaded under trees. The aire is about 1km north of the small village, surrounded by open farmland but is also next to the main Route Nationale. 2 x Artisanal service points with drainage platform.*

REVIEW: *A pleasant aire with good facilities next to a butchery enterprise (produce available for sale) just north of Pradelles Quiet despite being close to the RN, quite secure – fenced & the gate to the parking is locked between 7pm & 7am. Quaint village -*

one of the "Plus Beaux Villages de France" with many old buildings, an old church & a museum as well as a Velo-Rail that runs for 18kms from Pradelles along the old railway line. Tel: 04 71 00 85 49

SOLIGNAC SUR LOIRE

ADDRESS: RUE DE L'IRIS, OFF D276 **TYPE OF AIRE:** MUNICIPAL
FACILITIES: WATER /GREY & BLACK DRAIN/ ELECTRIC/ TOILETS
LOCATION: RURAL **NO. OF SPACES:** 20
PRICES: PARKING: 12€/ 24Hrs **SERVICES**: INCL
OPENING TIMES: 01/05 – 31/10 **GPS:** N44.96478 E03.88037
DIRECTIONS: From village take D276 SOUTH, turn LEFT @ Aire sign to AIRE.
SITE DESCRIPTION: *The aire in this small village is located next to the village football pitch, in the grounds of the former campsite, on the south side of the village. The parking backs onto the football pitch & is surrounded by farmland, shaded by small trees & is 500m from the village centre. There are about 20 large grassy places accessed by a tarmac track, separated by hedges, each with ehu, entry is by automatic barrier operated by credit card. Raclet service point with drainage platform. Closed in winter.*

REVIEW: *A very pleasant aire in the village campsite, a bit remote from the village but very quiet. Well maintained & secure with a gate/ fence around. Small village with a few shops; boulangerie, grocer, pharmacy & a couple of bar/ restaurants. Cycle track to Le Puy en Velay.*

VOREY

ADDRESS: CHEMIN DE FELINES **TYPE OF AIRE:** PRIVATE
FACILITIES: WATER /GREY & BLACK DRAIN/ ELECTRIC
LOCATION: SEMI-RURAL/ RIVERSIDE **NO. OF SPACES:** 5
PRICES: PARKING: 2€/ 24Hrs **SERVICES**: 3€ WATER, 4€ ELECTRIC
OPENING TIMES: ALL YEAR **GPS:** N45.18679 E03.90469
DIRECTIONS: Entering VOREY from NORTH on D103, turn RIGHT to CAMPING before bridge over river & AIRE is 250m on LEFT.
SITE DESCRIPTION: *This private aire is outside the 3* campsite "Les Moulettes" on the western edge of the village, next to a small river with open countryside & forest to the west. There are 5 spaces on tarmac, in a cul-de-sac, separated by grass areas, in a*

pleasant position, lighting but little shade. Artisanal service point with drainage grid. The adjacent campsite has a pool, 2 sanitary blocks & a restaurant/ snack bar.

REVIEW: *A very quiet & pleasant private aire run by the village campsite. The aire is open all year, although the 39 pitch campsite is only open 01/05 – 15/09. Parking & jetons paid for at campsite reception or at 'Les Rives' restaurant when closed, no water in winter. Nice location overlooking a river & only a short walk into the village (250m), where there is a bakery, butcher, supermarket, wine 'cave', restaurants, bank, post office, an internet café & a pharmacy with a market on Sunday mornings.*

63 PUY-DE-DOME

AUBUSSON D'AUVERGNE

ADDRESS: LAC D'AUBUSSON **TYPE OF AIRE:** MUNICIPAL
FACILITIES: WATER /GREY & BLACK DRAIN/ RUBBISH/ TOILETS/ WIFI
LOCATION: RURAL/ LAKESIDE **NO. OF SPACES:** 25
PRICES: PARKING: 6€ /24Hrs **SERVICES:** INCL
OPENING TIMES: ALL YEAR **GPS:** N45.75319 E03.61187
DIRECTIONS: From SOUTH take D45/ 41 to AUBUSSON, AIRE is on RIGHT just after LAKE.

SITE DESCRIPTION: *This aire is located about 500m west of the small village in a large tarmac parking area outside the Base de Loisirs & about 200m from the shores of the large Lac d'Aubusson. The parking has little shade but is lit at night, there are toilets (handicapped) nearby. Artisanal service point with drainage platform (water available all year).*

REVIEW: *A very quiet spot surrounded by farmland & close to the lake. Not too far from village but no facilities. Fishing in lake & beach for bathing as well as walks around lake, a picnic area, play area & 5 bbq's. Pay for parking at 'Maison du Lac' where wifi is available, lake is popular in summer with families. Parking fee reduces in winter.*

AYDAT

ADDRESS: RUE DU STADE, OFF D90 **TYPE OF AIRE:** MUNICIPAL
FACILITIES: WATER /GREY & BLACK DRAIN / ELECTRIC / TOILETS/ WIFI
LOCATION: SEMI-RURAL / LAKESIDE **NO. OF SPACES:** 40
PRICES: PARKING: 11€ / 24 Hrs **SERVICES**: INCL
OPENING TIMES: ALL YEAR **GPS:** N45.66024 E02.97702
DIRECTIONS: In AYDAT, AIRE is between the CHURCH & the LAKE.

SITE DESCRIPTION: *This large well-appointed aire has spaces on grass accessed by a tarmac track – most pitches having shade, lighting & ehu's, 100m from the village centre. This is a former Municipal campsite that has been converted into an aire for motorhomes, pay at the machine for entry via automatic barrier. Modern Artisanal service point with a large platform drain, toilets/ showers & sinks for washing up.*

REVIEW: *This is a popular tourist area, especially with the French, so there are lots of activities on the Lac Aydat with plenty of eating-places around the lake (in season) & 20 mins drive to Puy de Dome. The aire is in a pleasant green location next to the lake, a children's play area adjacent, with lovely countryside & forests surrounding the village. There is an epicerie, tabac, pizza van in the village & a bread van calls in summer.*

CHARBONNIERES LES VARENNES

ADDRESS: ROUTE DE ST-GEORGES, D90 **TYPE OF AIRE:** MUNICIPAL
FACILITIES: WATER /GREY & BLACK DRAIN/ ELECTRIC/ RUBBISH
LOCATION: SEMI-RURAL **NO. OF SPACES:** 12
PRICES: PARKING: FREE **SERVICES**: 2€ WATER or ELECTRIC
OPENING TIMES: ALL YEAR **GPS:** N45.88467 E02.98008
DIRECTIONS: Take D90 EAST to PAUGNAT, AIRE is on RIGHT.

SITE DESCRIPTION: *This aire is located south of Charbonnieres, in the small village of Paugnat where there are several spaces on grass/ gravel on two levels, accessed by a gravel track, with some shade under trees, lit at night with information board. AireServices service point with drainage platform, jetons from shops.*

REVIEW: *In a green & wooded spot, on the south side of Paugnat, quiet parking with good shade 400m from the village where there is a butcher, bar/ news & boulangerie. Leclerc supermarket at Chatelguyon (10kms).*

ISSOIRE

ADDRESS: BVD ANDRE MALRAUX **TYPE OF AIRE:** MUNICIPAL
FACILITIES: WATER /GREY & BLACK DRAIN/ RUBBISH
LOCATION: URBAN **NO. OF SPACES:** 8
PRICES: PARKING: 6€/ 24 Hrs **SERVICES**: INCL
OPENING TIMES: ALL YEAR **GPS :** N45.54515 E03.24099
DIRECTIONS: From WEST take D996 into town, turn LEFT @ 1st R/bout & AIRE is 1st LEFT.

SITE DESCRIPTION: *The aire is located in a cul-de-sac, near to a Carrefour supermarket, where there are 8 individual spaces on hard standing, shaded by small trees & bordered by grass verges, lit at night. The aire is situated on the western side of this large town, about 400m from the centre. Separate Euro-Relais service point with drainage platform. Pay at machine.*

REVIEW: *A good, quiet aire for visiting the town & only 3kms from A75 (Jcn 13), with separate spaces in a side street behind flats, 50m from a Carrefour supermarket. Level walk into town where there is a large range of shops, OT & eating-places. Abbey, museum & old part of town to visit.*

LA TOUR D'AUVERGNE

ADDRESS: RTE DE BAGNOLS, D47 **TYPE OF AIRE:** MUNICIPAL
FACILITIES: WATER /GREY & BLACK DRAIN/ TOILETS/ RUBBISH
LOCATION: RURAL/ LAKESIDE **NO. OF SPACES:** 30
PRICES: PARKING: FREE **SERVICES**: 2€ WATER or ELECTRIC

OPENING TIMES: ALL YEAR **GPS:** N45.53275 E02.68212
DIRECTIONS: Enter village from WEST on D47 take 1st LEFT to AIRE.

SITE DESCRIPTION: *An aire overlooking a leisure lake in a rural location, not far from the town centre, with numerous spaces on grass/ tarmac in a terraced parking area, little shade but good views. Raclet service point with drainage grid.*
REVIEW: *Ample parking next to a lake, popular in summer, a very quiet location with good walks in the area, free wifi sometimes available at nearby sports hall. Reasonable range of shops/ eating places in the town.*

LE CHEIX SUR MORGE

ADDRESS: RUE DU FAUBOURG, D425 **TYPE OF AIRE:** MUNICIPAL
FACILITIES: WATER /GREY & BLACK DRAIN/ ELECTRIC/ RUBBISH
LOCATION: SEMI-RURAL **NO. OF SPACES:** 6
PRICES: PARKING: 5€/ 24 Hrs **SERVICES**: 2€ WATER or ELECTRIC
OPENING TIMES: ALL YEAR **GPS:** N45.95121 E03.17811

DIRECTIONS: From LE CHEIX take D425 SOUTH 600m & AIRE is on RIGHT.
SITE DESCRIPTION: *This purpose-built aire is located on the southern outskirts of this large village in a small hedged parking area with individual parking spaces for motorhomes on gravel hardstandings, separated by grass verges & lit at night. The aire is close to the village football field & a short walk from the village centre. Artisanal service point & drainage platform.*
REVIEW: *A well designed, modern aire in a quiet location yet only a short walk into the village where there is a small range of shops/ cafe. Good place for a stopover but a bit remote & little of interest in village apart from a Roman bridge.*

MURAT LE QUAIRE

ADDRESS: ROUTE BANNE D'ORDANCHE, D609 **TYPE OF AIRE:** PRIVATE
FACILITIES: WATER /GREY & BLACK DRAIN/ ELECTRIC/ WIFI/ RUBBISH
LOCATION: RURAL/ LAKE **NO. OF SPACES:** 37
PRICES: PARKING: 13€ /24Hrs **SERVICES**: INCL
OPENING TIMES: ALL YEAR **GPS:** N45.60278 E02.73778
DIRECTIONS: From MURAT, take D609 NORTH 1.5kms & AIRE is on RIGHT.

SITE DESCRIPTION:

The aire is located close to a lake, 1.5km north of Murat, managed by the CampingCarPark company & is in a medium size gravel/ grass parking area in a rural area. No shade but lit at night, access is via an automatic barrier operated by CCP card. There are 37 large spaces on grass separated by hedges, accessed by a gravel track. Urba Flux service point with drainage platform, pitches have access to 10A ehu's & wifi.

REVIEW: *A well-equipped & well-maintained aire in a former campsite, next to a large lake but a bit remote from the small village (restaurant/ shop) & 5kms from the town of La Bouboule. CCP card required. Slight road noise from nearby D609 & only 12 ehu's for 37 spaces, but otherwise pleasant with fine mountain views.*

POUZOL

ADDRESS: PONT DE MENAT, OFF D2144 **TYPE OF AIRE:** MUNICIPAL
FACILITIES: WATER /GREY & BLACK DRAIN/ ELECTRIC
LOCATION: RURAL/ RIVER **NO. OF SPACES:** 8
PRICES: PARKING: FREE **SERVICES**: 2€ WATER
OPENING TIMES: ALL YEAR **GPS:** N46.102198 E02.93197
DIRECTIONS: Take D2144 SOUTH to PONT DE MENAT, cross RIVER & 2nd LEFT

SITE DESCRIPTION: *A rural aire in a wooded location alongside the river where there are 8 spaces on gravel in a circular arrangement, each space is separated by grass areas & adjacent to large grassy areas with picnic tables & some shade from small trees. The aire is accessed off the main road by means of a gravel track. Flot Bleu service point with drainage grid.*

REVIEW: *A nice little aire next to the Sioule river with level spaces on hardstanding surrounded by grass & trees with a picnic table. Very quiet but a bit remote with no facilites in Pouzol – nearest shops are at Menat, about 3kms away. Canoeing & fishing .*

ST ANTHEME

ADDRESS: CAMPING, OFF D996 **TYPE OF AIRE:** MUNICIPAL
FACILITIES: WATER /GREY & BLACK DRAIN
LOCATION: SEMI-RURAL/ RIVERSIDE **NO. OF SPACES:** 30
PRICES: PARKING: 5€/ 24 Hrs **SERVICES**: INCL
OPENING TIMES: ALL YEAR **GPS:** N45.52321 E03.91436
DIRECTIONS: From ST ANTHEME take D996 WEST & turn 1st LEFT to AIRE.
SITE DESCRIPTION: *The aire is outside the village campsite, south of the village, next to a small river and a lake with ample parking spaces on grass, lighting & having some shade, accessed via a tarmac track. Artisanal borne with water & drainage grid.*

REVIEW: *A nice rural aire, the adjacent lake has a beach with picnic tables, swimming & pedaloes, whilst the village with shops/ bars is about 500m away. Plenty of walks in the area. Council official collects the fee.*

ST PARDOUX

ADDRESS: ETANG DE CAYERS, OFF D99 **TYPE OF AIRE:** MUNICIPAL
FACILITIES: WATER /GREY & BLACK DRAIN/ ELECTRIC
LOCATION: RURAL/ LAKESIDE **NO. OF SPACES:** 5
PRICES: PARKING: FREE **SERVICES**: 2€ WATER or ELECTRIC
OPENING TIMES: ALL YEAR **GPS:** N46.05931 E02.99056
DIRECTIONS: From ST PARDOUX take D2144 NORTH, then LEFT on D99.
SITE DESCRIPTION: *The aire is about 1km west of the village, next to a lake with 5 parking spaces on gravel in a small parking area, with some shade, lit at night & accessed via a tarmac track. Euro-Relais service point & drainage grid. Jetons from shops/ hotel in village.*
REVIEW: *A quiet & pleasant aire next to a lake with beach & fishing possible, in a rural setting, with spaces that overlook the lake and are bordered by grass with shade in places. Steep access. Village has just a butcher/ grocer and a boulangerie/ news.*

RHONE-ALPES

Rhone-Alpes region is made up of 8 departments;
Ain (01), Ardeche (07), Drome (26), Isere (38), Loire (42),
Rhone (69), Savoie (73), Haute-Savoie (74)

Rhone-Alpes Map

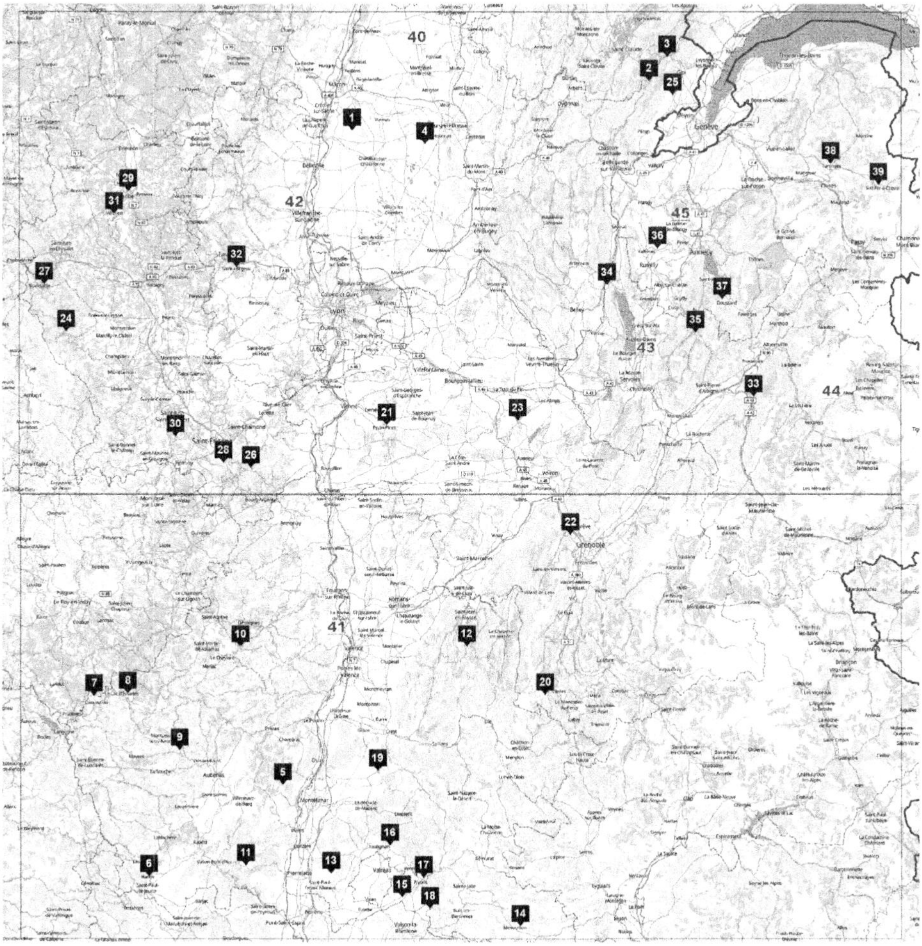

See next 2 pages for enlarged Rhone-Alpes maps & key

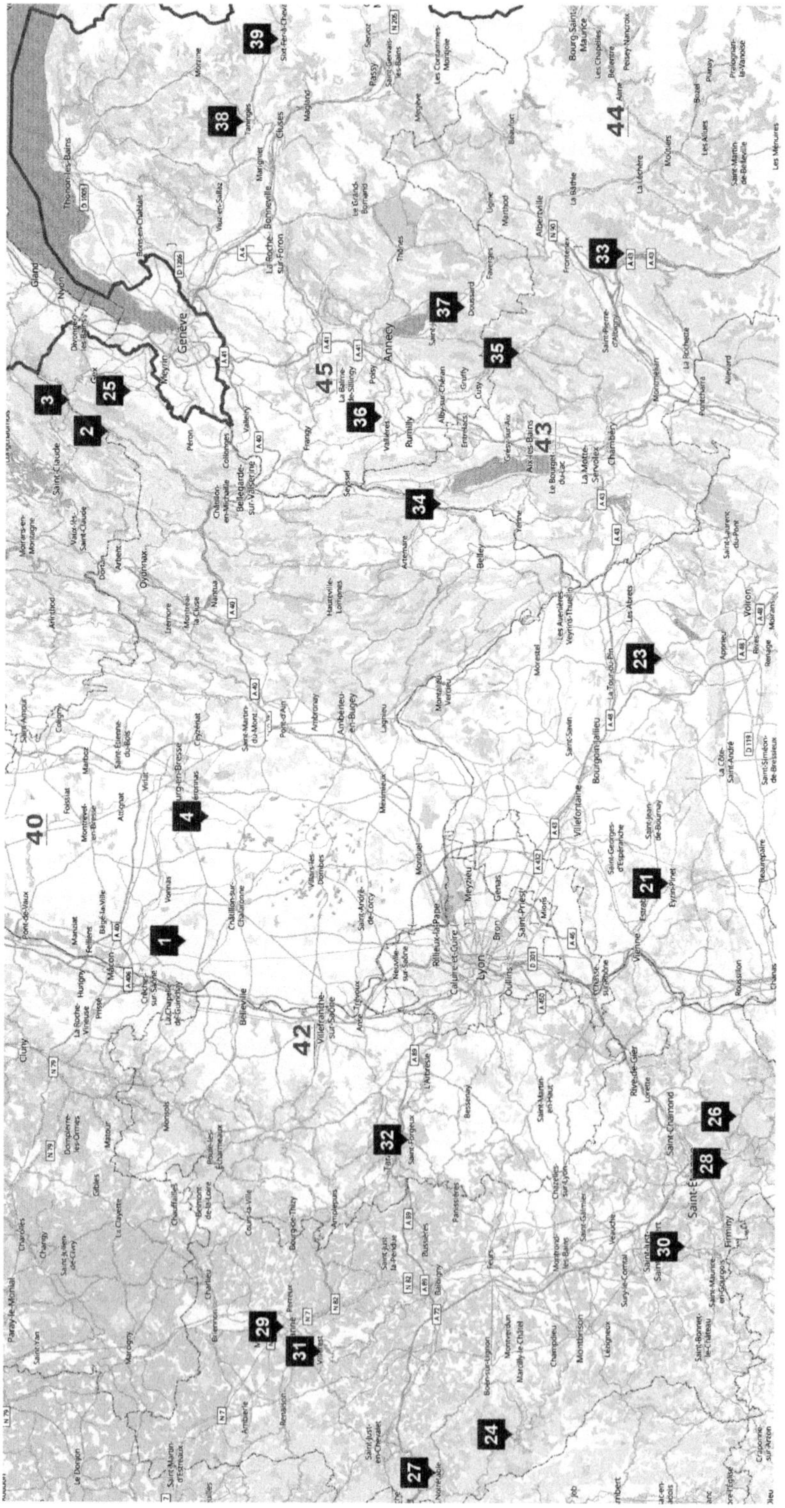
Genève
Annecy
Lyon
Chambéry
Aix-les-Bains
Villefranche-sur-Saône
Bourg-en-Bresse
Mâcon
Saint-Étienne

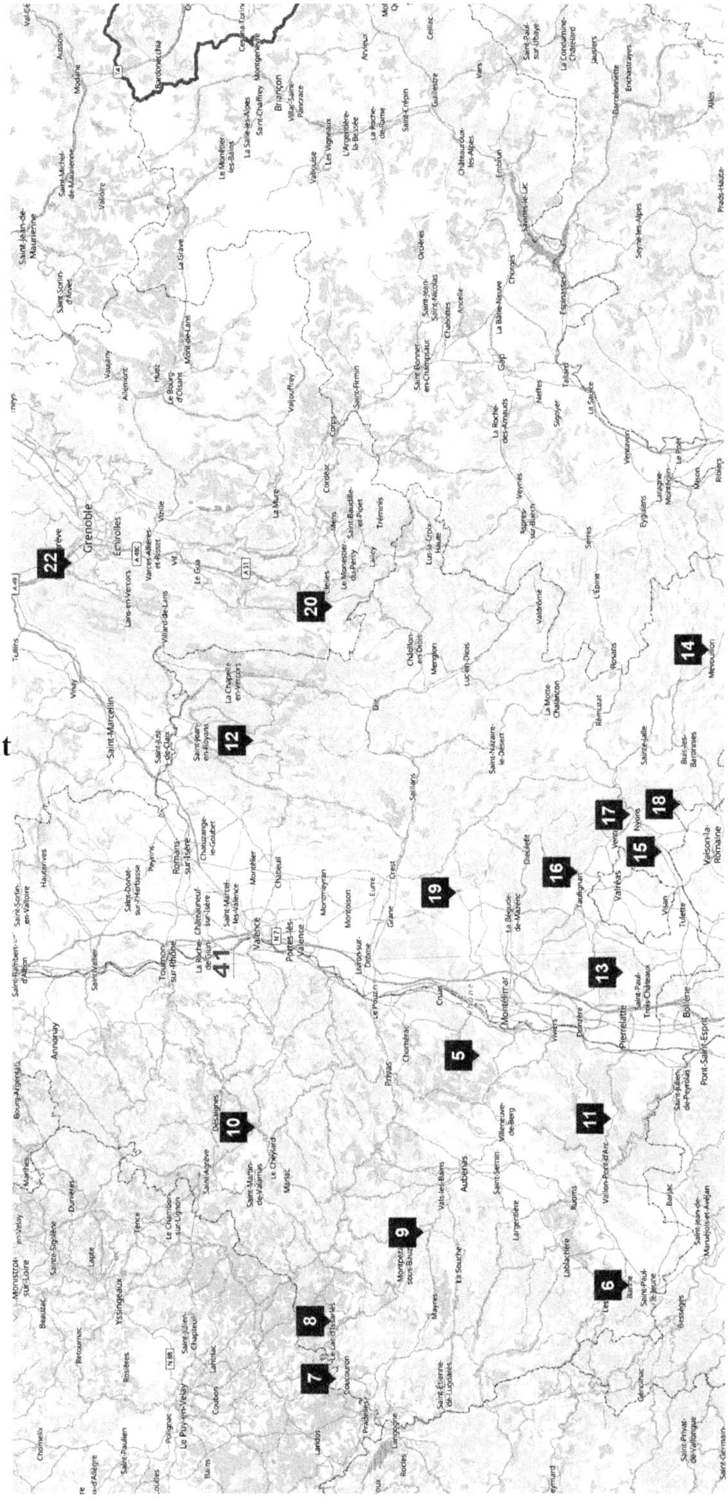

Key on next page

Key to enlarged Rhone-Alpes Maps (on previous 2 pages)
Former campsites that are now aires are noted in ***bold***

1) ILLIAT – 2) LELEX – 3) MIJOUX, - 4) ST ANDRE SUR VIEUX JONC
5) AUBIGNAS – 6) BANNE – 7) COUCOURON – 8) LE LAC D'ISSARLES
9) MEYRAS - 10) NONIERES – 11) ST REMEZE – 12) BOUVANTE – 13) CLANSAYES
14) MEVOUILLON – 15) MIRABEL AUX BARONNIES – 16) MONTBRISON-SUR-LEZ
17) NYONS1 & NYONS2 – 18) PIEGON – 19) PUY ST MARTIN – 20) CHICHILIANNE
21) EYZIN PINET – 22) SASSENAGE – 23) VIRIEU SUR BOUBE
24|) CHALMAZELLE – 25) CROZET – 26) LE BESSAT – 27) NOIRETABLE
28) PLANFOY – 29) ROANNE – 30) SAINT VICTOR SUR LOIRE – 31) VILLEREST
32) ST FORGEUX – 33) ~~AIGUEBELLE~~ – 34) CHANAZ – 35) LESCHERAINES
36) HAUTEVILLE SUR FIER – 37) LATHUILE – 38) TANINGES
39) SIXT FER A CHEVAL – ***40) MANTENAY - 41) LA ROCHE 42) VILLEFRANCHE***
43) AIX LES BAINS *– 44) MACOT LA PLAGNE – 45) LA BALME DE SILLINGY*

01 AIN

ILLIAT

ADDRESS: LAC D'ILLIAT (OFF D66A) **TYPE:** MUNICIPAL
FACILITIES: WATER /GREY & BLACK DRAIN /TOILETS/ RUBBISH
LOCATION: RURAL/ LAKE **NO. OF SPACES:** 4
PRICES: **PARKING**: FREE **SERVICES**: FREE
OPENING TIMES: ALL YEAR **GPS:** N46.18535 E04.88802
DIRECTIONS: From ILLIAT church, take D66A SOUTH. The AIRE is on LEFT, 300m from the village centre (signposted).
SITE DESCRIPTION*: This aire is in a pleasant open location on the southern outskirts of the small village of Illiat. Parking is next to a fishing lake on a small parking area, shaded, lit at night, with just 4 individual spaces on gravel, separated by hedges. Artisanal borne with a drainage platform & toilets adjacent.*

REVIEW: *A very calm & peaceful spot next to a lake, about 300m south of the small village. Restaurant within 100m. Well equipped aire with lighting, modern service point & good toilets (handicapped access) with washing-up sink. Fishing in adjacent lake (Mar – Nov).*

LELEX

ADDRESS: TENNIS COURTS, LA PELLIERE **TYPE OF AIRE**: MUNICIPAL
FACILITIES: WATER /GREY & BLACK DRAIN/ ELECTRIC
LOCATION: SEMI-URBAN **NO. OF SPACES:** 8
PRICES: PARKING: FREE **SERVICES**: WATER 2-5€ & ELECTRIC 4 – 8€
OPENING TIMES: ALL YEAR **GPS:** N46.30029 E05.93392
DIRECTIONS: From LELEX follow D991 South & bear RIGHT @ VVF signpost, AIRE is 250m on RIGHT.
SITE DESCRIPTION: *This Municipal aire is at the western end of this small ski station, where there are 8 level spaces (but more possible) available on tarmac, close to a VVF holiday village & backing onto trees, 400m to village centre. AireServices service point with drainage platform & ehu's, water & electric available all year round.*

REVIEW: *A modern aire pleasantly located on the outskirts of this small rural village, quiet with some shade but little lighting. Charge for water (10mins) & electric (24hours) varies from summer to winter (only 7 ehu's though). Picnic tables. Small range of shops & eating places in village though some are only open in winter.*

MANTENAY MONTLIN

ADDRESS: ROUTE DU MOULIN **TYPE OF AIRE:** PRIVATE
FACILITIES: WATER /GREY & BLACK DRAIN/ ELECTRIC/ WIFI/ TOILETS
LOCATION: RURAL/ RIVER **NO. OF SPACES:** 30
PRICES: PARKING: 9-14€/ 24HRS **SERVICES**: INCL
OPENING TIMES: ALL YEAR **GPS :** N46.42223 E05.09218
DIRECTIONS: From MANTENAY take Rte du Moulin towards river & turn RIGHT.
SITE DESCRIPTION: *This 'Camping Village' aire, run by CampingCarPark, is situated in the former campsite 'du Coq', about 800m west of Mantenay & alongside the river. Pitches are on grass (most shaded) separated each with 6A ehu & wifi with toilets (open 01/04-15/10). Euro-Relais service point with drainage platform. Access by automatic barrier, CCP card required.*
REVIEW: *A pleasant location on a small river, away from the village but quiet with large pitches, play area, picnic tables & good facilities but wifi variable. Refurbished toilets/ showers/ sinks regularly cleaned but closed in winter. Auberge in village but little else. Grocery & cheese vans visit aire.*

MIJOUX

ADDRESS: ROUTE DE LA COMBE, D50 **TYPE OF AIRE:** MUNICIPAL
FACILITIES: WATER /GREY & BLACK DRAIN /ELECTRIC
LOCATION: URBAN **NO. OF SPACES:** 20
PRICES: **PARKING:** FREE **SERVICES:** 4€ WATER OR ELECTRIC
OPENING TIMES: ALL YEAR **GPS:** N46.36965 E06.00229
DIRECTIONS: From the centre of MIJOUX, take D50, 500m towards LES ROSSES.
SITE DESCRIPTION: *This aire is in a pleasant open location on the outskirts of the small village of Mijoux, where there are a few shops & services. Parking is free on a large gravel parking area & with some spaces on grass, picnic tables, surrounded by pine forests & hills with very nice views. AireServices borne with drainage channel.*
REVIEW: *A very calm & peaceful spot but services expensive. The site can probably accommodate about 30 motorhomes. The aire is not very well signposted & is about 500m from village centre & shops.*

SAINT ANDRE SUR VIEUX JONC

ADDRESS: IMPASSE DES LYS **TYPE OF AIRE:** MUNICIPAL
FACILITIES: WATER /GREY & BLACK DRAIN/ RUBBISH
LOCATION: URBAN **NO. OF SPACES:** 5
PRICES: PARKING: 6€/ 24Hrs **SERVICES:** INCL
OPENING TIMES: ALL YEAR **GPS:** N46.15299 E 05.15195
DIRECTIONS: In village take road opposite Pizzeria & follow signs for AIRE.

SITE DESCRIPTION: *This municipal aire is located 400m from the centre of this small rural village in a small parking area with 5 individual parking spaces on tarmac, next to hedges/ small trees providing a little shade & with lighting at night. The artisanal services & large drainage platform are adjacent.*
REVIEW: *Pleasant, quiet aire located on the south side of the village, next to the football pitch. 5 large hard standing spaces separated by grass verges. Council official calls in evening to collect fee, water included in price, toilets next to football pitch. Not much in village apart from a boulangerie/ grocer, pizzeria/ restaurant & a bar.*

07 ARDECHE

AUBIGNAS

ADDRESS: PARKING OFF D363 **TYPE OF AIRE:** MUNICIPAL
FACILITIES: WATER /GREY & BLACK DRAIN/ TOILETS/ RUBBISH
LOCATION: SEMI-RURAL **NO. OF SPACES:** 5
PRICES: PARKING: 3€/ 24 Hrs **SERVICES**: FREE
OPENING TIMES: ALL YEAR **GPS:** N44.58707 E04.63188
DIRECTIONS: From SOUTH take D363 to AUBIGNAS, AIRE is on LEFT.
SITE DESCRIPTION: *This aire, at the southern entrance to the village, is in a medium sized gravel car park with a Raclet borne, drainage grid, rubbish bins & modern toilets. Nice position with good views, but little shade. A lovely medieval village, but unfortunately no shops.*

REVIEW: *A very interesting ancient village with narrow cobbled streets. An outstanding location, quiet & benefiting from a splendid panoramic view, grass areas & picnic tables, voluntary contribution for parking/ services. No shops in village but bread van passes Tues & Fri mornings.*

BANNE

ADDRESS: NEXT TO CHURCH **TYPE OF AIRE:** MUNICIPAL
FACILITIES: WATER /GREY & BLACK DRAIN /ELECTRIC
LOCATION: SEMI-RURAL **NO. OF SPACES:** 12
PRICES: PARKING: FREE **SERVICES**: 3€ WATER or ELECTRIC
OPENING TIMES: ALL YEAR **GPS:** N44.36511 E04.15689
DIRECTIONS: In the village, AIRE is next to CHURCH.

***SITE DESCRIPTION**: This aire is located in a small car park of this very interesting medieval hill village, parking next to the Church/ cemetery & close to the Château on a gravel surface. Pitches are on grass or gravel. Euro-Relais borne with drainage grid & an adjacent play area.*

REVIEW:** Aire is a bit basic but the location makes up for it, a medieval village with old sandstone houses, narrow lanes & its ruined château, very quiet, with magnificent panoramic views. Parking is either behind church or next to the adjacent cemetery, jetons available in the Mairie or shop (sells regional produce).* ***NOTE: Use D251 from west as D309 is very narrow, aire is not recommended for vehicles over 8m long.

COUCOURON

ADDRESS: CLOSE TO CAMPING **TYPE OF AIRE:** MUNICIPAL
FACILITIES: WATER /GREY & BLACK DRAIN/ ELECTRIC/ TOILETS
LOCATION: RURAL/ LAKE **NO. OF SPACES:** 25
PRICES: PARKING: 12€/ 24Hrs **SERVICES**: INCL
OPENING TIMES: ALL YEAR **GPS:** N44.801217 E03.96283
DIRECTIONS: At R/bout at village entrance on D16, turn WEST to LAKE & AIRE.

***SITE DESCRIPTION:** This aire is located outside the Municipal campsite, next to a large lake & about 500m west of the small village of Coucouron. Parking is on a large gravel parking area backing onto woodland, overlooking the lake with grass areas*

adjacent, some shade on one side of the area & lighting at night. There are toilets & a snack bar nearby & fishing is possible in the lake. Artisanal service point with drainage grid & ehu's.

REVIEW: *A lovely lakeside aire, very quiet parking (slight slope) with electric & walks around the lake (illuminated at night), swimming/ boating on the lake, with a small café (summer only) next to the beach (N. end of lake), showers are available in the adjacent camping. The aire is very popular in the summer but the Municipal campsite next door is not much dearer (open 01/05 - 30/09). Parking is free when camping is closed but no services available. Shops in the quaint village include; boulangerie, butcher, 8-8 supemarket, bars & eating places with a market on Wednesday morning.*

LE LAC D'ISSARLES

ADDRESS: OFF D116 **TYPE OF AIRE:** MUNICIPAL
FACILITIES: WATER /GREY & BLACK DRAIN /ELECTRIC /TOILETS
LOCATION: SEMI-RURAL **NO. OF SPACES:** 20
PRICES: PARKING: 13€/ 24 Hrs **SERVICES**: INCL
OPENING TIMES: 01/05 – 15/10 **GPS:** N44.81979 E04.06228
DIRECTIONS: From SOUTH on D116, enter village & AIRE is on the LEFT.
***SITE DESCRIPTION**: The aire is in a medium size gravel parking next to the tennis courts, close to & overlooking the village. Pitches are on grass/ gravel with lighting but little shade & separate ehu's. Artisanal service point with drainage grid, toilets (handicapped) & showers.*

REVIEW: *The aire is clean, well equipped, well located; close to the village /shops & lake yet very quiet. A council official comes at about 18.30 to collect the money, price includes electric, services, toilets & showers. The village is nice & the lake is beautiful. Butcher, Vival mini-mart, boulangerie, Poste, bars & restaurants in village.*

MEYRAS

ADDRESS: FOOTBALL STADE **TYPE OF AIRE:** MUNICIPAL
FACILITIES: WATER /GREY & BLACK DRAIN /ELECTRIC
LOCATION: SEMI-RURAL **NO. OF SPACES:** 15
PRICES: PARKING: 4€ /48Hrs **SERVICES**: 4€ WATER or ELECTRIC
OPENING TIMES: 01/04 - 31/10 **GPS:** N44.67959 E04 26897
DIRECTIONS: From N102, take D26 into village, AIRE is on LEFT next to FOOTBALL PITCH.

***SITE DESCRIPTION**: A modern aire, found next to the village car park, south side of village, with 15 spaces in open surroundings. Tarmac surface, nicely laid out with individual spaces separated by shrubs, some shade in places, lighting at night, fenced/ gated & good views. Adjacent grass areas with picnic tables. AireServices borne with a drainage grid – jetons from the Mairie, OT or shop.*

***REVIEW:** Excellent aire, very clean & quiet yet only a short walk into village centre. A pretty medieval thermal spa village with a château, a grocery shop, bars & eating places plus a pizza van on Friday evenings. Same price for 1 or 2 nights, official collects fee or pay at Mairie.*

NONIERES

ADDRESS: LES COLLANGES **TYPE OF AIRE:** MUNICIPAL
FACILITIES: WATER /GREY & BLACK DRAIN / TOILETS
LOCATION: RURAL/ LAKE **NO. OF SPACES:** 7
PRICES: PARKING: FREE **SERVICES**: FREE
OPENING TIMES: ALL YEAR **GPS:** N44.90909 E04.47208
DIRECTIONS: From NONIERES take D578 SOUTH, turn LEFT after 2kms (signposted "Base Aquatique"). Follow road to lake & AIRE at EAST end.

***SITE DESCRIPTION**: The aire is found 3kms south of Nonieres, in a small dedicated motorhome parking area next to & overlooking a large leisure lake. The 6 large individual pitches are on tarmac, separated by grass strips, with picnic tables but no shade or lighting. Modern artisanal service point with drainage platform & small toilet block.*

***REVIEW:** The aire is very well located, popular in summer, close to the large lake & very quiet. Nice parking spaces separated by grass verges with adjacent benches & a small toilet block. Remote from any facilities apart from the Base Aquatique which is 400m away (open in the summer) & has a large swimming pool, restaurant & snack bar. Nonieres is a small village with few facilities but Le Cheylard, 1km to the west, has a SuperU & a reasonable selection of shops/ eating places.*

ST REMEZE

ADDRESS: LES CHAIS DU VIVARAIS, D362 **TYPE OF AIRE:** MUNICIPAL
FACILITIES: WATER /GREY & BLACK DRAIN /RUBBISH

LOCATION: SEMI-RURAL **NO. OF SPACES:** 6
PRICES: PARKING: FREE **SERVICES**: FREE
OPENING TIMES: 15/03 – 30/11 **GPS:** N44.39535 E04.50571
DIRECTIONS: From D4 in ST REMEZE, take D362 NORTH to R/bout & AIRE.

***SITE DESCRIPTION**: The aire is situated in the tarmac parking area of the village wine cooperative, an open location on north side of the village, little shade but with good views of the surrounding farmland. Artisanal borne with a large platform drain.*
***REVIEW:** The aire of 'Chais du Vivarais' is basic but with a warm welcome from the Coop & with practical services. Parking on tarmac surrounded by countryside in a quiet location on the outskirts of this small picturesque Ardeche village – 5 mins walk to the village shops. Stay is limited to 48 hours & not possible during the grape harvest, mid Sept till Oct. Good walking area with the Madeleine Caves nearby (7km) as well as the Aven Marzel Museum/ Cave.*

26 DROME

BOUVANTE

ADDRESS: FONT D'URLE SKI STATION **TYPE OF AIRE:** MUNICIPAL
FACILITIES: WATER /GREY & BLACK DRAIN/ ELECTRIC/ TOILETS
LOCATION: RURAL **NO. OF SPACES:** 10
PRICES: PARKING: 7€/ 24Hrs **SERVICES**: 2€ WATER
OPENING TIMES: ALL YEAR **GPS:** N44.89792 E05.32202
DIRECTIONS: From VASSIEUX-EN-VERCOURS, take D76 WEST & follow signs for FONT D'URLE.
***SITE DESCRIPTION:** This very rural aire is located at the ski station of Font d'Urle, south of Bouvante, in a quiet mountain location with fine views where there is ample level parking on gravel bordered by large grass areas. There is a little shade but no lighting. Toilets/ showers & ehu's available, picnic tables. Euro-Relais service point with drainage grid.*

***REVIEW:** A mountain stop welcoming in verdant surroundings with panoramic views, good walks & a hotel/ restaurant adjacent with bread available. Ehu's incl in price.*

CLANSAYES

ADDRESS: AIRE DE TORONNE, D571 **TYPE OF AIRE:** PRIVATE
FACILITIES: WATER /GREY & BLACK DRAIN /TOILETS /ELEC. /POOL /WIFI
LOCATION: RURAL **NO. OF SPACES:** 25
PRICES: PARKING: 10€/ 24 Hrs **SERVICES**: 4€ ELECTRIC
OPENING TIMES: ALL YEAR **GPS:** N44.36975 E04.79778
DIRECTIONS: From CLANSAYES. take D571 SOUTH – the AIRE is signposted on LEFT after 2kms.
***SITE DESCRIPTION**: This private aire, in the grounds of a Chambre d'Hotes, is in a rural location surrounded by farmland, parking is on gravel hard standings shaded by small trees. Artisanal service point with a large platform drain, 6A ehu's, wifi, toilets & showers.*

***REVIEW:** In a pleasant & green but remote location, secure gated compound with tennis court, bbq & swimming pool. Pizza van calls on Saturdays. A pleasant, quiet spot with ample shaded spaces but probably 2km from the medieval village of Clansayes (an uphill walk).*

LA ROCHE DE GLUN

ADDRESS: RUE DE CRUSSOL **TYPE OF AIRE:** PRIVATE
FACILITIES: WATER /GREY & BLACK DRAIN/ ELECTRIC/ WIFI/ RUBBISH
LOCATION: SEMI-URBAN **NO. OF SPACES:** 38
PRICES: PARKING: 13€ /24HRS **SERVICES**: INCL
OPENING TIMES: ALL YEAR **GPS :** N45.00899 E04.84616
DIRECTIONS: From WEST take D222A over RHONE into town, follow 'Piscine' signs & AIRE is adjacent.
***SITE DESCRIPTION:** This private aire run by CampingCarPark is located 400m south of the centre of La Roche, in the former Municipal campsite. Good shade & lit at night, access is via an automatic barrier operated by a CCP card. Flot Bleu service point with drainage platform, the 38 level, gravel pitches all have access to ehu's & wifi.*
***REVIEW:** Nice, quiet spot on the edge of this small town, 200m from the Rhone & a short walk to the shops (boulangerie, bar/ tabac & a superette), swimming pool & pizzeria adjacent (seasonal). Large 35m² spaces on gravel separated by grass spaces with mature trees.*

La Roch de Glun

MEVOUILLON

ADDRESS: DOMAINE LE CLOS DE BRUIS, OFF D546 **TYPE OF AIRE:** PRIVATE
FACILITIES: WATER /GREY & BLACK DRAIN/ ELECTRIC/ TOILETS/ WIFI
LOCATION: RURAL **NO. OF SPACES:** 25
PRICES: PARKING: 13 - 18€ /24Hrs **SERVICES**: INCL
OPENING TIMES: ALL YEAR **GPS:** N44.22814 E05.50531
DIRECTIONS: The AIRE is at the D546/ D234 junction, 5kms EAST of MEVOUILLON.
***SITE DESCRIPTION**: Located on the edge of 3ha of forest, this private aire/ small campsite is in a rural environment with nice views & with large spaces on gravel/ grass, very quiet with some shade. The parking is arranged in tiers on a few levels, with bbq, washing-up sinks, artisanal service point, toilets, showers, ehu's & wifi. Small food shop on site.*

***REVIEW:** A very remote, quiet & rural location at the foot of the ruins of Fort Mevouillon with good facilities but quite expensive. Great uninterrupted views with walks, mountain biking, paragliding, horse riding & rock climbing. Shop adjacent selling grocery, fresh bread, etc.*

MIRABEL AUX BARONNIES

ADDRESS: ALLEE DES SOUPIRS **TYPE OF AIRE:** MUNICIPAL
FACILITIES: WATER /GREY & BLACK DRAIN /RUBBISH
LOCATION: SEMI-RURAL/ RIVERSIDE **NO. OF SPACES:** 16
PRICES: PARKING: FREE **SERVICES**: FREE
OPENING TIMES: ALL YEAR **GPS:** N44.31284 E05.09997
DIRECTIONS: From NORTH on D538, cross RIVER into village, take 1st LEFT & then 1st LEFT to AIRE.

***SITE DESCRIPTION**: This aire is in a large tarmac car park on the northern side of the village (Pop 1600) & next to the River Gaude, 150m from the shops. Parking is either on tarmac or grass with some shade in places. Large platform drain & artisanal borne.*

***REVIEW:** The situation is very good but not very well signposted. Aire is quiet, clean & services are well maintained, whilst the village is very picturesque. A pleasant little medieval village with ruined château & a variety of facilities: butcher, 2 bakers, mini-market, Poste, cafes & bars. Additional parking is also available next to the nearby tennis courts, off D160. The mill 'Vieux Moulin' is worth a visit, 50m away.*

MONTBRISON-SUR-LEZ

ADDRESS: VILLAGE CENTRE PARKING **TYPE OF AIRE:** MUNICIPAL
FACILITIES: WATER /GREY & BLACK DRAIN /ELECTRIC
LOCATION: SEMI-RURAL **NO. OF SPACES:** 5
PRICES: PARKING: FREE **SERVICES**: 2€ WATER or ELECTRIC
OPENING TIMES: ALL YEAR **GPS:** N44.43604 E05.01817
DIRECTIONS: AIRE is in village centre next to MAIRIE.

***SITE DESCRIPTION**: The parking for this aire is in a medium sized car park next to the Mairie in the very small village centre – next to & bordered by vineyards with some shade. The Raclet borne with drainage grid is easy to access, but is in a separate spot; located next to the football pitch south of the village.*

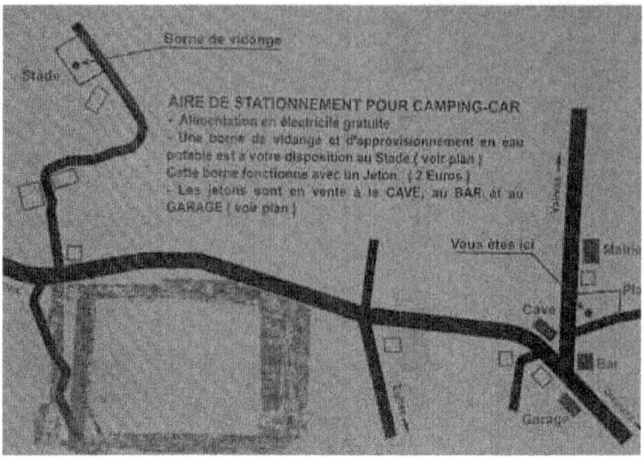

***REVIEW:** A very quiet aire in the middle of this vine growing area next to the village bar & wine cellar. A small village with a bar, restaurant, wine merchant, garage & shop. Aire has a small playground & picnic tables adjacent. Jetons available from the Cave, Garage or Bar. Parking is also available next to the service point, a pleasant rural spot with good views but quite remote.*

NYONS 1

ADDRESS: DOMAINE ROCHEVILLE, D538 **TYPE OF AIRE:** PRIVATE
FACILITIES: WATER /GREY & BLACK DRAIN/ WIFI/ ELECTRIC/ TOILETS
LOCATION: RURAL **NO. OF SPACES:** 6
PRICES: PARKING: 8€/ 24Hrs **SERVICES**: 4€ ELECTRIC
OPENING TIMES: ALL YEAR **GPS:** N44.36889 E05.11791
DIRECTIONS: From NYONS take D538 NORTH & DOMAINE is 1.5km on LEFT.
***SITE DESCRIPTION**: A private aire located on the property of a wine/ olive producer on the northern side of Nyons, next to the farm where there are 6 level spaces on grass, accessed by a gravel track & shaded by mature trees. Artisanal service point with drainage platform, small toilet block & ehu's. Tel: 0475263520*

***REVIEW:** A well maintained aire, fairly quiet & secure, away from road - behind farm, with good shade in places. Shop on site selling farm produce (olives, oil, wine, apricots & jams). Large spaces with hook-ups available as well as wifi & showers in summer, water & wifi included but electric is extra. A bit remote (2kms) from the town centre where there are all types of shops & bars/ restaurants. Pleasant town with unusual chapel on hill, château & medieval quarter.*

NYONS 2

ADDRESS: PROMENADE DE LA DIGUE **TYPE OF AIRE:** MUNICIPAL
FACILITIES: WATER /GREY & BLACK DRAIN/ RUBBISH/ TOILETS
LOCATION: URBAN **NO. OF SPACES:** 20
PRICES: PARKING: 10€/ 24Hrs **SERVICES**: INCL
OPENING TIMES: ALL YEAR **GPS:** N44.35811 E05.13861
DIRECTIONS: From SOUTH on D538, cross RIVER & turn LEFT @ R/bout to AIRE on RIGHT.
***SITE DESCRIPTION**: A Municipal aire located on the south side of Nyons, next to the river where there are 20 level spaces on gravel shaded by hedges/ mature trees. Access is via an automatic barrier which issues a card & you pay on leaving by credit card at a machine. Short walk to town centre with good range of shops/ services. Flot Bleu service point with drainage platform & toilets.*

REVIEW: *A pleasant well maintained aire, quiet despite being next to the road with good shade. Short level walk to town centre with all types of shops & bars/ restaurants. Good level walk/ cycle track adjacent that follows river. Free parking is also possible on the adjacent road but this suffers from road noise/ no shade & backs onto skate park. Free wifi available in the OT.*

PIEGON

ADDRESS: DOMAINE CHENE BLANC, OFF D516A **TYPE OF AIRE:** PRIVATE
FACILITIES: WATER /GREY DRAIN
LOCATION: RURAL **NO. OF SPACES:** 4
PRICES: PARKING: FREE **SERVICES**: FREE
OPENING TIMES: ALL YEAR **GPS:** N44.29533 E05.11678
DIRECTIONS: From MIRABEL DES BARONNIES take D516 then D516A SOUTH & follow signs for 'CHENE BLANC'.

***SITE DESCRIPTION**: This private aire is set amongst the vineyards of the wine/ olive oil producer 'Domaine du Chene Blanc' in a very quiet location. Parking is on grass & services are at the discretion of the owner but only water & grey drainage available.*
***REVIEW:** A nice stopover at a vineyard where the friendly Mr Grosjean offers a free stay for motorhomes. The aire is next to the D516A but very little traffic, so quite quiet. Surrounded by vines & pretty scenery, the aire is very rural with wonderful views, 3kms from Mirabel & 1km from Piegon. Wines/ oil for sale from the farm. Tel: 0475271201*

PUY ST MARTIN

ADDRESS: RUE DU TEMPLE **TYPE OF AIRE:** MUNICIPAL
FACILITIES: WATER /GREY & BLACK DRAIN/ RUBBISH
LOCATION: URBAN **NO. OF SPACES:** 18
PRICES: PARKING: 5€ /24Hrs **SERVICES**: INCL
OPENING TIMES: ALL YEAR **GPS:** N44.62790 E04.97506
DIRECTIONS: In village, follow signs for Parking, AIRE is behind Gendarmerie.
***SITE DESCRIPTION:** This Municipal aire is in a medium sized parking area reserved for motorhomes, pitches on grass bordered by hedges/ trees having shade in places, lighting at night & about 100m from the centre of town. Artisanal service point with large drainage platform.*

***REVIEW:** A very popular, pleasant little aire with individual spaces on grass, some separated by hedges, accessed by a gravel track. Quiet & secure spot next to the Gendarmerie, yet in the centre of this small town. SuperU express/ petrol station, tabac/ news & a boulangerie in town as well as a pizzeria, a restaurant & a bar. Honesty box provided.*

38 ISERE

CHICHILIANNE

ADDRESS: OFF D7B **TYPE OF AIRE:** MUNICIPAL
FACILITIES: WATER /GREY & BLACK DRAIN/ ELECTRIC/ TOILETS
LOCATION: SEMI-RURAL **NO. OF SPACES:** 15
PRICES: PARKING: 10€ (No time limit) **SERVICES**: 3€ WATER or ELECTRIC
OPENING TIMES: ALL YEAR **GPS :** N44.81242 E05.57459
DIRECTIONS: From CHICHILIANNE take D7B EAST & AIRE is opposite HOTEL.
SITE DESCRIPTION: *The aire is located opposite a hotel/ restaurant about 100m east of the village centre where there is a large tarmac/ grass parking area with spaces bordered by grass, shaded by mature trees & lit at night by adjacent street lamps. AireServices service point with drainage platform & toilets.*

REVIEW: *A pleasant aire set back from the road in a small park with play area, on edge of village with views of the mountains. The annual fee of 10€ allows unlimited stays & includes 1 jeton. Quiet spot & close to shops; bio boulangerie & bar/ restaurant, more shops at Clelles (6km). Good location for walking & cycling. Jetons from bar or Mairie.*

EYZIN PINET

ADDRESS: RUE DU STADE, D38 **TYPE OF AIRE:** MUNICIPAL
FACILITIES: WATER /GREY & BLACK DRAIN/ RUBBISH
LOCATION: URBAN **NO. OF SPACES:** 5
PRICES: PARKING: FREE **SERVICES**: FREE
OPENING TIMES: ALL YEAR
GPS: N45.47442 E04.99899
DIRECTIONS: From NORTH take D38 into town, AIRE 100m is on LEFT.
SITE DESCRIPTION: *The aire is located next to a small Proxi grocery shop about 100m from the town centre where there is a small gravel parking area behind the car park, with spaces for 5 motorhomes*

bordered by grass & shaded by mature trees, lit at night. Artisanal service point, drainage platform & rubbish bins.

REVIEW: *A pleasant modern little aire, in the town centre but set back from the road in a small park like area, on edge of small woods. Quiet spot & close to shops, grocery shop adjacent. Good location for walking & cycling. Various eating places in village. Château, lake & tower ruin in village.*

SASSENAGE

ADDRESS: RUE PIERRE COUBERLIN **TYPE OF AIRE:** MUNICIPAL
FACILITIES: WATER /GREY & BLACK DRAIN / RUBBISH
LOCATION: SEMI-RURAL **NO. OF SPACES:** 10
PRICES: PARKING: FREE **SERVICES**: FREE
OPENING TIMES: ALL YEAR **GPS:** N45.21348 E05.66871
DIRECTIONS: In town follow signs for "STADE", AIRE is next to football pitch.

SITE DESCRIPTION*: The aire is in a pleasant location alongside a minor road, close to a park area & the town sports complex on the north side of the town. Parking is in a small gravel parking area reserved for motorhomes with some shade in places, bordered by grass areas but only lit by nearby street lighting. Artisanal service point is opposite the aire in a lay-by in the road.*

REVIEW: *Very pleasant, quiet location close to a park & fishing lake, a popular aire that seems to fill up quite quickly so arrive early. Shops within a few hundred metres & café/ pizzeria in park. Tennis courts adjacent & 200m to Isere river. 12km level cycle path along river to Grenoble.*

VIRIEU SUR BOUBE

ADDRESS: RTE DE VAUGELAS, D17 **TYPE OF AIRE:** MUNICIPAL
FACILITIES: WATER /GREY & BLACK DRAIN/ TOILETS
LOCATION: SEMI-RURAL **NO. OF SPACES:** 5
PRICES: PARKING: FREE **SERVICES**: FREE
OPENING TIMES: ALL YEAR **GPS:** N45.48159 E05.47784
DIRECTIONS: From EAST on D17, as you enter VIRIEU - AIRE is on RIGHT.

SITE DESCRIPTION *The aire is located on the eastern edge of this small rural village, about 200m from the centre, in a small gravel parking with level spaces for 5*

motorhomes bordered by grass & shaded by mature trees but not lit at night. Site of an old sawmill with water wheel adjacent. Artisanal service point with drainage platform & toilets adjacent.

REVIEW: *A small well-maintained, shaded aire on the edge of this small village with toilets & washing-up sinks. Children's play area in village, château & picnic area nearby. Next to a minor road (D17) but not much traffic. Short walk into village where there is a small range of shops & a restaurant, market on Friday mornings. Lively village with distillery to visit/ tastings.*

42 LOIRE

CHALMAZEL

ADDRESS: LE PONT OUEST, OFF D6 **TYPE OF AIRE:** MUNICIPAL
FACILITIES: WATER /GREY & BLACK DRAIN /ELECTRIC
LOCATION: SEMI-RURAL/ RIVER **NO. OF SPACES:** 8
PRICES: PARKING: FREE **SERVICES**: 2€ ELECTRIC or WATER
OPENING TIMES: ALL YEAR **GPS:** N45.70298 E03.85294
DIRECTIONS: Entering CHALMAZEL from EAST on D6, turn LEFT @ CEMETERY & AIRE is 150m on LEFT.

SITE DESCRIPTION: *A modern aire situated on the east side of this small village, in a small tarmac parking area with 8 individual parking spaces, separated by low hedges & bordered by grass verges but little shade, close to the village centre. Flot Bleu borne with platform drain & separate point with 4 ehu's. Jetons from shops or OT. Second aire at the ski station.*

REVIEW: *A well designed aire in a quiet location next to a small river yet only a short walk to the quaint village centre where there is a château & a grocer, boulangerie, bar/tabac, bank, restaurant, hotel/bar. Good area for walking or alpine skiing in winter with 12kms of pistes & ski lift.*

LE BESSAT

ADDRESS: LA CROIX DU CHAUBOURET, OFF D8 **TYPE OF AIRE:** MUNICIPAL
FACILITIES: WATER /GREY & BLACK DRAIN /ELECTRIC/ RUBBISH
LOCATION: RURAL **NO. OF SPACES:** 4
PRICES: PARKING: FREE **SERVICES**: 2.5€ WATER or ELECTRIC
OPENING TIMES: ALL YEAR **GPS :** N45.36881 E04.52797
DIRECTIONS: From LE BESSAT take D8 EAST & AIRE is found 600m on LEFT.

SITE DESCRIPTION: *This aire is in a large tarmac car park on the east side of this small village, backing onto forest. There are large spaces separated by grass verges with little shade or lighting. Flot Bleu borne with platform drain & ehu's.*

REVIEW: *A pleasant spot at 1200m altitude, 600m from the village centre, set back from the adjacent D8 with 2 restaurants opposite. Jetons from shops for water or 6 hours* *of electric. Pleasant little village but only a grocer, 2 bar/ restaurants & boulangerie in village plus an Auberge. 4 allocated spaces with electric points but large parking opposite. Depart for way-marked walks & Nordic skiing.*

Le Bessat

LE CROZET

ADDRESS: LE BOURG, OFFD35 **TYPE OF AIRE:** MUNICIPAL
FACILITIES: WATER /GREY & BLACK DRAIN/ ELECTRIC
LOCATION: SEMI-RURAL **NO. OF SPACES:** 2
PRICES: PARKING: FREE **SERVICES**: 2€ WATER or ELECTRIC
OPENING TIMES: ALL YEAR **GPS:** N46.16927 E03.85725
DIRECTIONS: Take D35 EAST from village & bear RIGHT at the "AIRE" sign.
SITE DESCRIPTION: *This aire is located on the eastern side of this small rural village in a small gravel parking area bordered by grass areas, where there are 2 parking spaces & some trees providing shade. The parking is lit at night & is only 150m to the village centre. Artisanal service point with platform drain.*

REVIEW: *A nice, quiet aire within a short walk of the village but only 2 spaces (possibly 3) with a narrow access that has to be entered in reverse. Picnic tables. Quaint old medieval village with château tower & interesting old buildings but no shops, just a restaurant/ bar & OT.*

NOIRETABLE

ADDRESS: RUE DU PLAN D'EAU, D110 **TYPE OF AIRE:** MUNICIPAL
FACILITIES: WATER /GREY & BLACK DRAIN/ELECTRIC/ WIFI
LOCATION: SEMI-RURAL/ LAKE **NO. OF SPACES:** 7
PRICES: PARKING: FREE **SERVICES**: 3€ WATER OR ELECTRIC
OPENING TIMES: ALL YEAR **GPS:** N45.80755 E03.76945

DIRECTIONS: From NOIRETABLE take D1089 & D110 SOUTH, AIRE is on RIGHT.

***SITE DESCRIPTION**: The aire is in a large gravel parking area next to a lake, with individual spaces separated by grass verges but with little shade. 2 Flot Bleu bornes & a jeton machine - one borne is for electric & the other for water/ drainage with a platform drain, 800m to the centre of town.*

***REVIEW:** A green lakeside location with good views & practical services. 7 well separated spaces, very quiet & close to the lake with nice walks around it & a beach for bathing. Campsite adjacent & good range of shops/ eating places in town.*

PLANFOY

ADDRESS: CHEMIN DU VIGNOLET **TYPE OF AIRE:** MUNICIPAL
FACILITIES: WATER /GREY & BLACK DRAIN/ELECTRIC
LOCATION: RURAL **NO. OF SPACES:** 10
PRICES: PARKING: FREE **SERVICES**: 3€ WATER OR ELECTRIC
OPENING TIMES: ALL YEAR **GPS:** N45.37464 E04.44921
DIRECTIONS: Take D1082 SOUTH from PLANFOY, turn LEFT after 2kms at signpost 'STADE DU VIGNOLET'.

SITE DESCRIPTION: *Aire is in a small purpose built tarmac parking area with individual spaces separated by grass & sited next to the football field and a small wood. An open rural location with good views but a bit remote. 3 Flot Bleu bornes; 2 with with 4 electric sockets each & one for drainage/ water with a separate drainage grid, jetons from shops in village.*
REVIEW: *Aire is totally quiet, clean with well laid out with level pitches sited next to a sports field & some gites, lit/ shaded but not very convenient for the village. Nice walks in the woods, Planfoy is 2km north from the aire - a small village with a few shops including a boulangerie, epicerie, Poste, bars & restaurant.* ***NOTE: Access road can be difficult/ icy in winter; a steep slope & at 1,100m altitude.***

ROANNE

ADDRESS: QUAI DU CDT. FOURCAULT **TYPE OF AIRE:** MUNICIPAL
FACILITIES: WATER /GREY & BLACK DRAIN/ ELECTRIC/ WIFI
LOCATION: URBAN/ CANAL **NO. OF SPACES:** 10
PRICES: PARKING: 8€/ 24 Hrs **SERVICES**: 2€ WATER or ELECTRIC
OPENING TIMES: ALL YEAR **GPS:** N46.03817 E04.08317
DIRECTIONS: In town, follow signs for "Port de Plaisance" & AIRE is on EAST side.
SITE DESCRIPTION: *This Municipal aire is located in a large gravel parking area on the east side of town next to the Port de Plaisance, where there are individual spaces for motorhomes separated by grass areas (additional parking on grass), small trees offering a little shade & lit at night. Flot Bleu service point with drainage platform as well as a separate borne for electric & a machine for jetons.*

REVIEW: *A very pleasant & well equipped aire nicely located between the canal & the Loire river yet only a short walk into town. A quiet location overlooking the canal with good parking spaces & ehu's available. Toilets in the Capitainnerie & a play area nearby. The aire is about 450m from the town centre & its wide selection of shops & services.*

SAINT VICTOR SUR LOIRE

ADDRESS: PARKING BASE NAUTIQUE, D32 **TYPE OF AIRE:** MUNICIPAL
FACILITIES: WATER /GREY & BLACK DRAIN/ ELECTRIC /TOILETS
LOCATION: URBAN/ COASTAL **NO. OF SPACES:** 10
PRICES: PARKING: FREE **SERVICES**: 3€ ELECTRIC

OPENING TIMES: ALL YEAR **GPS :** N45.44833 E04.25667
DIRECTIONS: In ST VICTOR, AIRE is in BASE NAUTIQUE.
SITE DESCRIPTION: *The aire is situated in a tarmac parking area, at the Base Nautique in St Victor, overlooking the beach & about 450m north of the medieval village centre, on a promontory overlooking the Loire River. There are 10 allocated spaces separated by grass verges with a little shade as well as lighting. Flot Bleu service point with drainage grid as well as separate ehu's & toilets nearby.*

REVIEW: *An excellent aire with fine views over the Loire, a short walk from this interesting medieval village with a château. The large adjacent car park is busy during day & at weekends with visitors but quiet after 5pm for additional places to park. Water is free but electric is paid for by jetons either from Mairie or the adjacent snack kiosk (seasonal). Restaurant/ bar opposite (possible noise). Watersports on river as well as boat trips, walks/ cycling & play area adjacent.*

VILLEREST

ADDRESS: ROUTE DE SEIGNE, D18 **TYPE OF AIRE:** MUNICIPAL
FACILITIES: WATER /GREY & BLACK DRAIN/TOILETS/ELECTRIC
LOCATION: RURAL/ RIVERSIDE **NO. OF SPACES:** 20
PRICES: PARKING: 8€/ 24 Hrs **SERVICES**: 4€ WATER
OPENING TIMES: ALL YEAR **GPS:** N45.98607 E04.042984
DIRECTIONS: From EAST cross the LOIRE on D18 & immediately turn LEFT.
SITE DESCRIPTION: *The aire is in a large gravel terraced parking area next to a recreation space on the banks of the Loire river overlooking the river, but no shade. A small sanitary block with sinks & WC's, the village centre is about 1km distant. Artisanal borne with a large platform drain.*

REVIEW: *The aire is very pleasant, on the banks of a lake formed by a dam on the Loire river, a magnificent viewpoint & very quiet. A secure spot with a Gendarmerie adjacent. Fishing, bathing, sailing & mini-golf nearby as well as a beach & a cafe (seasonal). Council official collects fee, free in winter but no water. Shops & services in the medieval village of Villerest.*

69 RHONE

ST FORGEUX

ADDRESS: TENNIS COURTS, OFF D632 **TYPE OF AIRE:** MUNICIPAL
FACILITIES: WATER /GREY & BLACK DRAIN/ ELECTRIC/ TOILETS
LOCATION: SEMI-RURAL **NO. OF SPACES:** 6
PRICES: PARKING: FREE **SERVICES**: FREE
OPENING TIMES: ALL YEAR **GPS:** N45.85763 E04.47621
DIRECTIONS: In village follow signs "Le Tram" to SPORTS CENTRE & AIRE.

SITE DESCRIPTION: *The aire is located next to the village tennis courts, near to the cemetery & about 200m south of the village centre in a medium sized tarmac car park with level spaces having good shade. The aire is bordered by trees & surrounded by farmland but is not lit at night. Artisanal service point with drainage grid, 3 ehu's & toilets (black drain in toilets).*
REVIEW: *Small village with just a boulangerie, tabac/ bar/ news, & a café/ restauarant. Nice, quiet location, not far from village, clean toilets plus free electric with play area/ park. Additional parking next to cemetery adjacent. Handy stopover off A89 (Jcn 35) & the Route Nationale N7.*

VILLEFRANCHE SUR SAONE

ADDRESS: ROUTE DE RIOTTIER **TYPE OF AIRE:** PRIVATE
FACILITIES: WATER /GREY & BLACK DRAIN/ ELECTRIC/ WIFI/ TOILETS
LOCATION: URBAN/ RIVER **NO. OF SPACES:** 128
PRICES: PARKING: 14€ /24HRS **SERVICES**: INCL
OPENING TIMES: ALL YEAR **GPS :** N45.97253 E04.75207
DIRECTIONS: Exit A6 @ Jcn 31.2 & take D306 East - AIRE is on RIGHT just before RIVER.

SITE DESCRIPTION: *This very large 'Camping Village' aire is located on the south western edge of town, next to the Saone river, managed by the CampingCarPark company & is in a large grass former campsite in a residential area of the town with farmland to the south. Good shade & lit at night, access is via an automatic barrier, CCP card required. It is not too close to the town centre (1km) & its shops, lying to the southeast of the town centre. Euro-Relais service point with drainage platform. Large pitches, with tarmac access track, each with individual 6A ehu's & wifi.*
REVIEW: *Quiet spot but not very handy for town, next to the river & a lake with beach, seasonal restaurant nearby & a Lidl within 1/2km. Large parking spaces (80m^2) with shade under trees. Toilets/ showers on site but a bit small for 128 pitches & showers are closed Oct – April. Villefranche has a good range of shops/ services plus a market.*

73 SAVOIE

AIX LES BAINS

ADDRESS: RUE DES GOELANDS **TYPE OF AIRE:** PRIVATE
FACILITIES: WATER /GREY & BLACK DRAIN/ ELECTRIC/ WIFI/ RUBBISH
LOCATION: URBAN/ LAKE **NO. OF SPACES:** 86
PRICES: PARKING: 15€ /24HRS **SERVICES**: INCL
OPENING TIMES: ALL YEAR **GPS :** N45.69627 E05.88926
DIRECTIONS: In AIX, follow signs for "Aquarium" & AIRE is 200m North on RIGHT.

SITE DESCRIPTION: *This large private aire is located on the western edge of town, next to the Lac de Bourget, managed by the Campingcarpark company & is in the former Municipal campsite in a residential area of the town with the lake to the west. Good shade & lit at night, access is via an automatic barrier operated by CCP card. It is not too close to the town centre (800m) & its shops, lying to the NW of the town centre. Euro-Relais service point with double drainage platform. Large hard standing or grass pitches, with tarmac access track, each with individual 6A ehu's & wifi.*
REVIEW: *Quiet spot but fair walk to town centre, 100m from a large lake, 300m from the town leisure area & cinema. Large parking spaces (40m²) with shade under trees, 78 ehu's for 86 spaces. Building with washing-up sinks on site but closed Nov – April. CampingCarPark membership card required. Aix les Bains is a nice spa town with watersports on lake, beach & has a good range of shops plus a market.*

CHANAZ

ADDRESS: CHEMIN DE CAVETTAZ **TYPE OF AIRE:** MUNICIPAL
FACILITIES: WATER /GREY & BLACK DRAIN/TOILETS/ ELECTRIC
LOCATION: RURAL/ RIVER **NO. OF SPACES:** 20
PRICES: PARKING: 6€ /24Hrs **SERVICES**: 2€ WATER or ELECTRIC
OPENING TIMES: ALL YEAR **GPS:** N45.81289 E05.78729
DIRECTIONS: From CHANAZ take D921 NORTH over CANAL & take next LEFT.
SITE DESCRIPTION: *The aire is in a large gravel area bordering the Rhone river with parking on gravel under trees accessed by a tarmac track but no lighting. The aire is 500m north of the village, close to the campsite. AireServices borne with a platform drain is next to the campsite entrance, jetons from reception (open all year).*

REVIEW: *Nice, quiet location overlooking the Rhone & close to a canal with shade provided by mature trees, parking paid at a machine. Laundrette/ toilets in camping & restaurant opposite. The quaint riverside village is not too far with a Vival grocer, Poste, boulangerie, OT & wine shop. Level cycling & walking along the Rhone.*

LESCHERAINES

ADDRESS: BASE DE LOISIRS **TYPE OF AIRE:** MUNICIPAL
FACILITIES: WATER /GREY & BLACK DRAIN
LOCATION: RURAL/ LAKE **NO. OF SPACES:** 10
PRICES: PARKING: 6€/ 24Hrs **SERVICES**: 2€ WATER
OPENING TIMES: 15/04 – 30/09 **GPS:** N45.70325 E06.11105
DIRECTIONS: In village follow signs for Base de Loisirs/ Camping, AIRE is outside campsite.

SITE DESCRIPTION: *The aire is found in a small car park backing onto woodland, south of village, next to the campsite with 10 level spaces on gravel separated by grass verges with good shade. The village leisure area is adjacent with tennis courts & a lake. Euro Relais service point & drainage grid.*

REVIEW: *A quiet little aire outside the municipal campsite & the leisure lake with picnic area, playground, fishing & water-sports. Parking fee & jetons are payable at the campsite reception which has wifi & a laundrette. Village is 500m to the north where there is a boulangerie, Casino superette, butcher, café & bar/ restaurant with a seasonal restaurant within 200m.*

MACOT LA PLAGNE

ADDRESS:CARAVANEIGE DE PLAGNE VILLAGE **TYPE OF AIRE:** MUNICIPAL
FACILITIES: WATER /GREY & BLACK DRAIN/ELECTRIC/ RUBBISH/ WIFI
LOCATION: RURAL **NO. OF SPACES:** 40
PRICES: PARKING: 10 - 22€/ 24 HRS **SERVICES**: INCL
OPENING TIMES: MARCH – NOV **GPS :** N45.50879 E06.69225
DIRECTIONS: From LA PLAGNE follow signs for 'CARAVANEIGE'.

SITE DESCRIPTION*: An aire located 2kms from the ski village of la Plagne at an altitude of 1950m. The parking is reserved for motorhomes & has 40 spaces (8.5 x 4m) on gravel, securely arranged in 4 terraces with CCTV coverage. The spaces all have 16A hook ups, lighting at night but no shade. There is a Flot Bleu borne, with drainage grid & rubbish bins nearby. There is also additional parking (P1) at La Plagne 2100, the very large tarmac parking here is free, again no shade but lit at night & close to shops.*

REVIEW: *An extremely pleasant aire, very tranquil, next to the pistes with good mountain views, designed for skiers but also available outside the winter months at a reduced rate of 10€/ day. Spaces can be reserved online at www.parkinglaplagne.com. Spar grocer within 200m. Wifi available at extra charge, free shuttle buses to village.*

74 HAUTE-SAVOIE

HAUTEVILLE SUR FIER

ADDRESS: AUTRUCHELAND, CHEMIN DU MOULINET **TYPE :** PRIVATE
FACILITIES: WATER /GREY & BLACK DRAIN/ ELECTRIC/ RUBBISH
LOCATION: RURAL/RIVERSIDE **NO. OF SPACES:** 12
PRICES: PARKING: 10€ / 24Hrs **SERVICES**: 3€
OPENING TIMES: ALL YEAR **GPS:** N45.90464 E05.95885
DIRECTIONS: AIRE is signposted 'AUTRUCHES' from the centre of HAUTEVILLE.
SITE DESCRIPTION: *An aire in 'Ostrich-Land' - an Ostrich farm in a secure rural location, a couple of kms west of village, where parking is on a large level grass area accessed by a gravel track, surrounded by trees giving some shade & close to a river. Artisanal borne with a large platform drain & separate ehu's. Tel/Text: 0625872148*

REVIEW: *Access road to the farm is narrow but once you get there it is an extremely nice place with ostriches for company & the motorhoming proprietors are very hospitable. A quiet location, 50m from a pleasant little river where you can swim or fish for trout. Pitches liable to be soft in wet weather. Good range of local produce for sale, price includes electric & is reduced by 5€ if you spend 25€ in shop.*

LA BALME-DE-SILLINGY

ADDRESS: LAKE, ROUTE DES CARASSES **TYPE OF AIRE:** MUNICIPAL
FACILITIES: WATER /GREY & BLACK DRAIN/ TOILETS
LOCATION: RURAL/LAKESIDE **NO. OF SPACES:** 25
PRICES: PARKING: 6€/ 24HRS **SERVICES**: FREE
OPENING TIMES: ALL YEAR **GPS :** N45.97111 E06.03180
DIRECTIONS: From ANNECY take N508 NORTH to LA BALME-DE-SILLINGY. Go past the lake (on your LEFT) & then turn LEFT into ROUTE DES CARASSES.
SITE DESCRIPTION: *A lovely rural location nest to a large lake with good views, yet close (1/2 km) to a small village where there are shops including a boulangerie, bar-tabac, superette, butchers, garage & choice of restaurants. Parking is in a medium sized gravel car park with trees providing shade. The adjacent lake has good walks, boating, fishing, boules, a play area & picnic tables. There is an Artisanal borne with platform drain.*
REVIEW: *This is a superb, well placed aire (short distance from shops) next to a lake that you can walk around, in a quiet position & with fine views. Fishing & boating are possible in the lake but swimming is not allowed. There is also a 2nd aire in the village in the Zone Industrial de Lompraz.*

La Balme-de-Sillingy

LATHUILE

ADDRESS: RTE DE LA PORTE **TYPE OF AIRE:** PRIVATE
FACILITIES: WATER /GREY & BLACK DRAIN/ ELECTRIC/ WIFI
LOCATION: RURAL **NO. OF SPACES:** 25
PRICES: PARKING: 15€/ 24Hrs **SERVICES**: INCL
OPENING TIMES: 28/04 – 16/09 **GPS:** N45.79368 E06.20785
DIRECTIONS: From NORTH on D1508, turn RIGHT at 'Le Bout du Lac' to AIRE.
SITE DESCRIPTION: *A private aire located in a medium sized grass parking area, bordered by grassy areas, in a rural area, 1km north of the town, only a short walk from the Lac d'Annecy. The spaces are level, on grass accessed by a tarmac track - have a little shade but there is no lighting. Artisanal service point/ drainage grid, wifi & ehu's.*

REVIEW: *A well maintained & welcoming private aire with nice views but expensive, next to the proprietors farmhouse, hedged/ fenced all round with ehu's & wifi. Located between Lathuile & Chaparon but not very convenient for either. Level cycle track along the old railway line, Lake Annecy & beach within short distance with a large campsite adjacent. Farm produce for sale.*

TANINGES

ADDRESS: LE PRAZ DE LYS, SOMMAND **TYPE OF AIRE:** MUNICIPAL
FACILITIES: WATER /GREY & BLACK DRAIN/ ELECTRIC / RUBBISH
LOCATION: RURAL **NO. OF SPACES:** 70
PRICES: PARKING: 10€/ 24 Hrs **SERVICES**: 2€ WATER or ELECTRIC
OPENING TIMES: ALL YEAR **GPS:** N46.15927 E06.54948
DIRECTIONS: Take D308 NORTH & WEST to SOMMAND & turn LEFT to AIRE.
SITE DESCRIPTION: *This aire is located about 10kms north of Taninges, in the ski station of Sommand, about 300m from the ski lifts & has up to 70 spaces located in a large parking area of the ski station, entry by automatic barrier. Flot Bleu service point. There is also a 40 space aire just south of Praz de Lys (D308) where there are shops & restaurants.*

REVIEW: *A quiet spot (outside of the ski season) at 1,400m alt. with fine panoramic views of the mountains (including Mont Blanc), free in summer. Well maintained by a resident warden, with ehu's, no shops nearby but shuttle bus runs in winter.*

SIXT FER A CHEVAL

ADDRESS: ROUTE DU CIRQUE, D907 **TYPE OF AIRE:** MUNICIPAL
FACILITIES: WATER /GREY & BLACK DRAIN/ ELECTRIC / RUBBISH
LOCATION: RURAL/ RIVER **NO. OF SPACES:** 20
PRICES: PARKING: FREE **SERVICES**: 4€ ELECTRIC
OPENING TIMES: ALL YEAR **GPS:** N46.05677 E06.77968
DIRECTIONS: From SIXT take D907 200m EAST & AIRE is on RIGHT (signposted).
SITE DESCRIPTION: *This aire, located about 200m east of Sixt, has up to 20 level spaces located in a large tarmac parking area, edged with trees giving shade, lighting at night. Euro Relais service point with drainage grid.*
REVIEW: *A very quiet spot with fine views of the mountains., well maintained, just a short walk from the village centre where there is a Sherpa supermarket, boulangerie, 2 bars, OT & an auberge. Water is free, 16A ehu's give 12 hours of electricity/ jeton.*

MIDI-PYRENEES

Midi-Pyrenees region is made up of 8 departments; Ariege (09), Aveyron (12), Haute-Garonne (31, Gers (32), Lot (46), Hautes-Pyrenees (65), Tarn (81),Tarn-et-Garonne (82)

Midi-Pyrenees Map

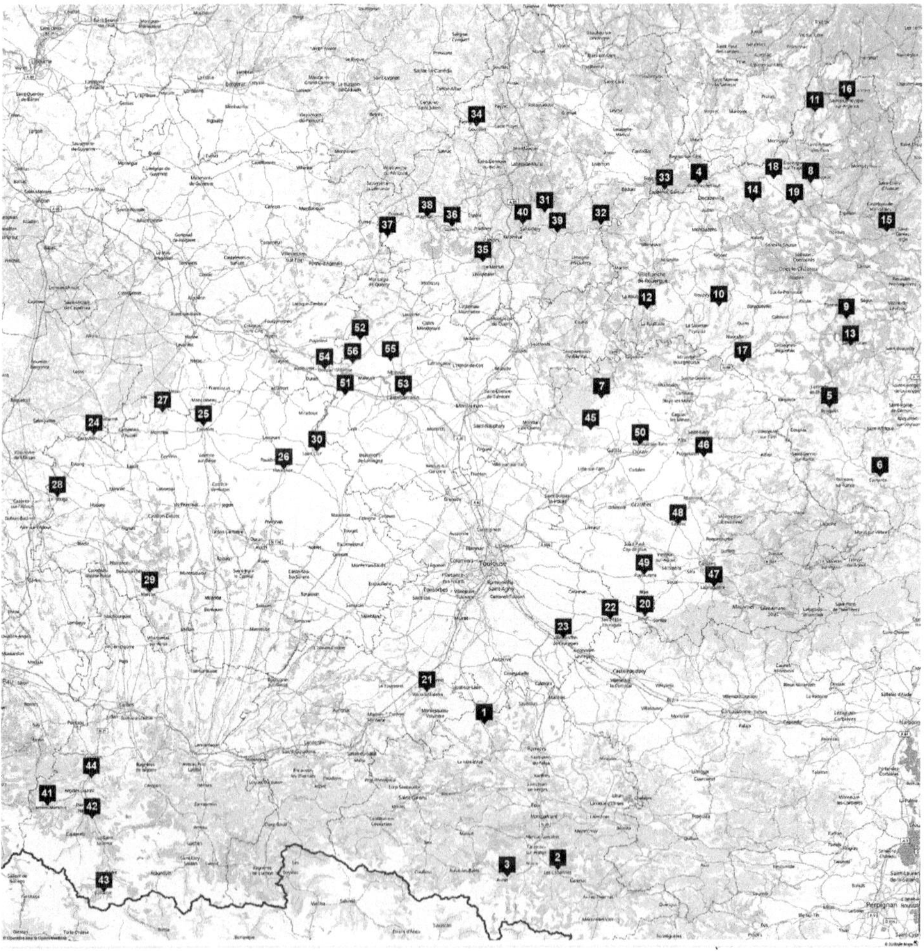

Key to enlarged Midi-Pyrenees Maps (next 2 pages)

Former campsites that are now aires are noted in ***bold***

1) LE FOSSAT – 2) LES CABANNES – 3) VICDESSOS – 4) BOISSE PENCHOT

5) BROQUIES – 6) CAMARES – 7) CAMPAGNAC – 8) CAMPUAC

9) CANET DE SALARS – 10) CASTANET – 11) LACROIX BARREZB – 12) MONTEILS

13) SALLES CURAN *– 14) ST CYPRIEN SUR DOURDOU – 15) STE EULALIE D'OLT*

16) STE GENEVIEVE SUR ARGENCE - 17)ST JUST SUR VIAUR – 18) SENERGUES

19) VILLECOMTAL *– 20) REVEL – 21) RIEUX-VOLVESTRE*

22) ST FELIX LAURAGAIS – 23) VILLEFRANCHE DE LAURAGAIS

24) CAZAUBON – 25) CONDOM1 & CONDOM2 – ***26)FLEURANCE***

27) FOURCES – 28) LE HOUGA – 29) MARCIAC – 30) ST CLAR – 31) BOUZIES

32) CAJARC – ***33) CAPDENAC GARE*** *– 34) GOURDON-EN-QUERCY*

35) LA BASTIDE MARNHAC – 36) LUZECH – 37) MAUROUX – 38) PRAYSSAC

39) ST CIRQ LAPOPIE – 40) VERS – 41) ARRENS MARSOUS – 42) CAUTERETS

43) GAVARNIE – 44) PIERREFITTE-NESTALAS – 45) CASTELNAU DE MONTMIRAL

46) FREJAIROLLES – 47) LABRUGUIERE – 48) LAUTREC – ***49) PUYLAURENS***

50) RIVIERES – 51) BARDIGUES – 52) CASTELSAGRAT – 53) CASTELSARRASIN

54) DONZAC – 55) MOISSAC – 56) VALENCE D'AGEN – 57) BOZOULS

58) LE NAYRAC *– 59) STE EULALIE DE CERNON*

60) VILLEFRANCHE DE ROUERGUE – 61) AUCH *– 62) ST MEDARD*

63) LAMAGDELAINE *– 64) MAULEON –* ***65) TOURNAY***

66) LA BASTIDE ROUAIROUX – ***67) BOURRET***

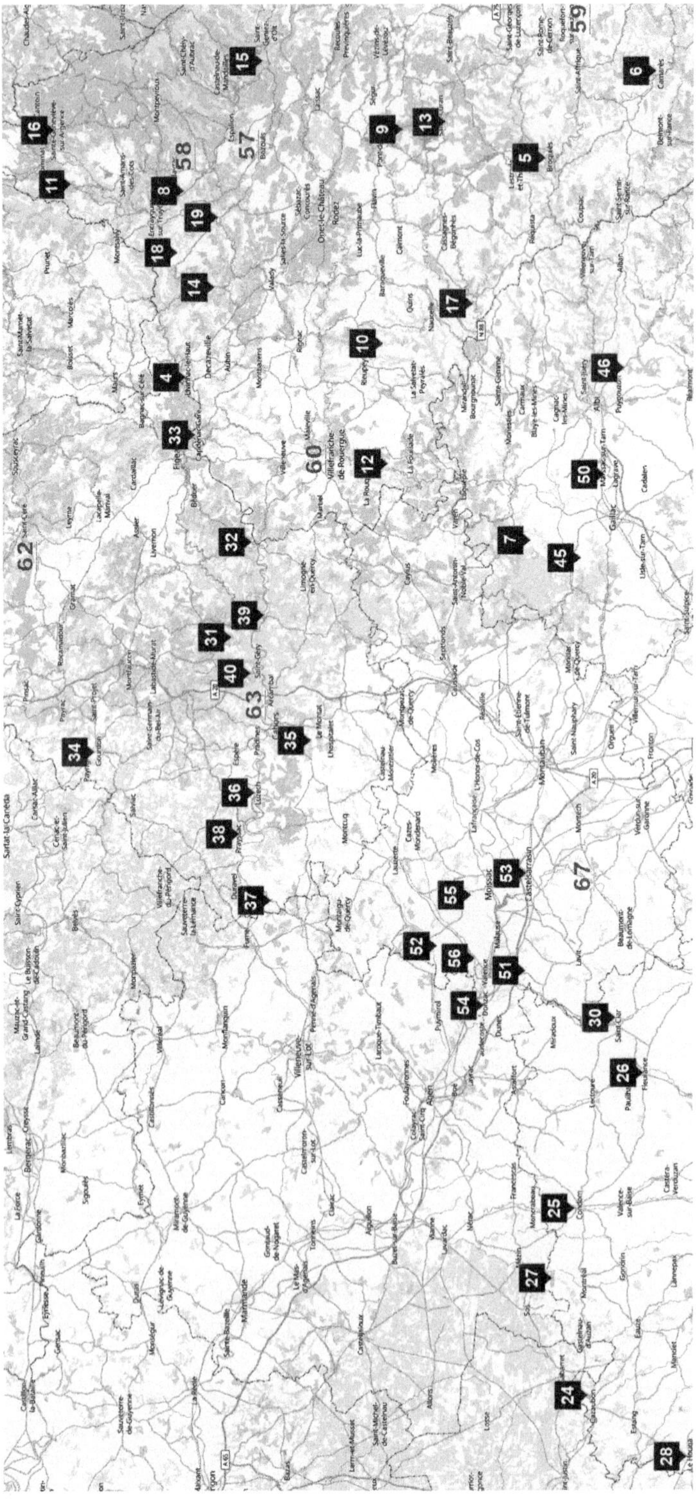

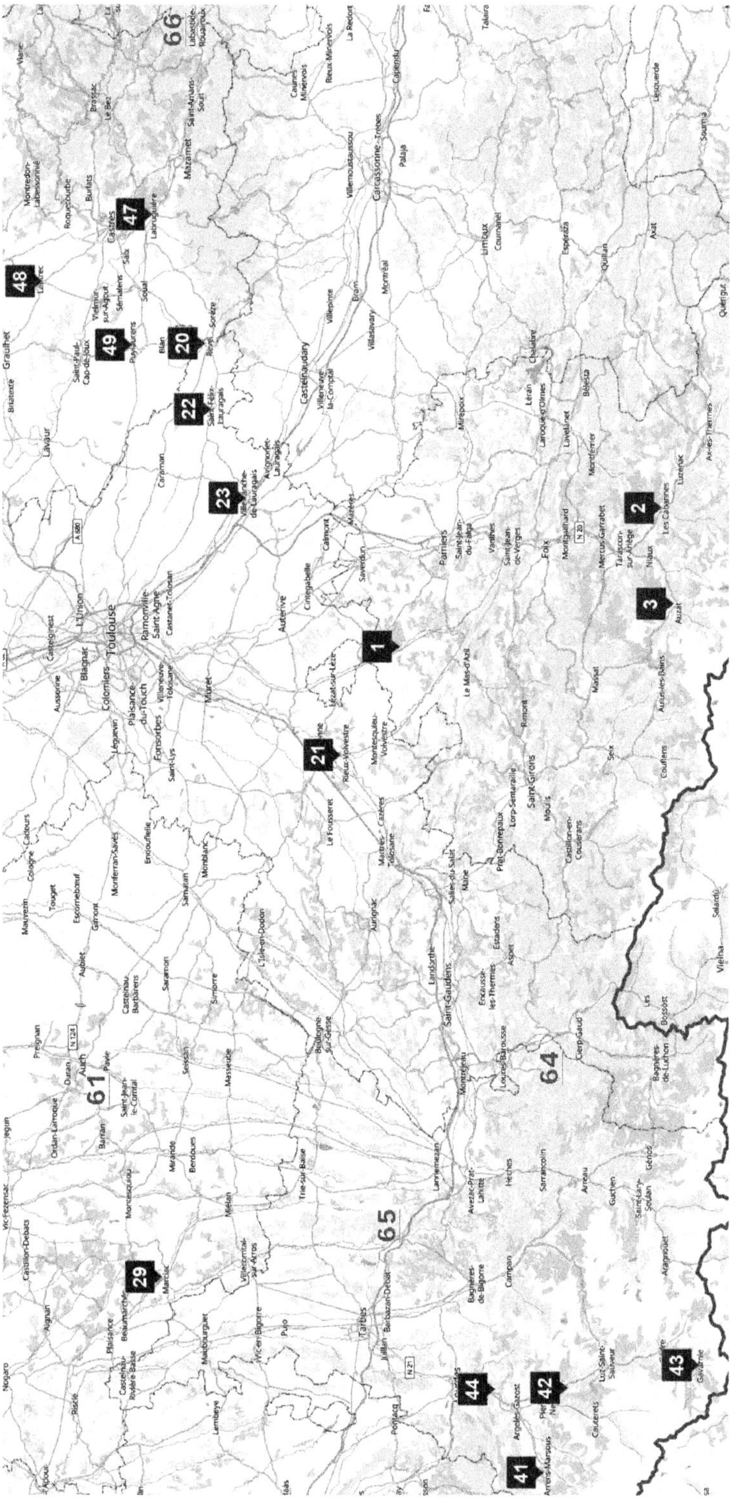
1
2
3
20
21
22
23
29
41
42
43
44
47
48
49
61
64
65
66
Toulouse
Blagnac
Colomiers
L'Union
Ramonville-Saint-Agne
Castanet-Tolosan
Muret
Auterive
Castres
Mazamet
Carcassonne
Castelnaudary
Pamiers
Foix
Mirepoix
Saint-Girons
Saint-Gaudens
Tarbes
Auch
Lourdes
Bagnères-de-Bigorre
Bagnères-de-Luchon
Montréjeau
Lannemezan
Vielha
Les Cabannes
Tarascon-sur-Ariège
Auzat
Lavaur
Graulhet
Caraman
Villefranche-de-Lauragais
Saint-Félix-Lauragais
Revel
Sorèze
Labruguière
Limoux
Quillan
Ax-les-Thermes
Lavelanet
Massat
Aulus-les-Bains
Seix
Couflens
Marciac
Mirande
Masseube
Trie-sur-Baïse
Argelès-Gazost
Cauterets
Luz-Saint-Sauveur
Gavarnie
Arrens-Marsous
Campan
Arreau
Saramon
Samatan
Lombez
L'Isle-en-Dodon
Boulogne-sur-Gesse
Le Fousseret
Rieux-Volvestre
Montesquieu-Volvestre
Cazères
Martres-Tolosane
Aurignac
Salies-du-Salat
Castillon-en-Couserans
Le Mas-d'Azil
Saverdun
Calmont
Cintegabelle
Belesta
Chalabre
Bram
Montréal
Villasavary
Palaja
Capendu
Nogaro
Aignan
Plaisance
Maubourguet
Vic-en-Bigorre
Rabastens-de-Bigorre
Pujo
Juillan
Barbazan-Debat
Pontacq

09 ARIEGE

LE FOSSAT

ADDRESS: NEXT TO CAMPING **TYPE OF AIRE:** PRIVATE
FACILITIES: WATER /GREY & BLACK DRAIN/ ELECTRIC/ TOILETS/ WIFI
LOCATION: SEMI-RURAL **NO. OF SPACES:** 20
PRICES: PARKING: 14€/ 24Hrs **SERVICES**: INCL
OPENING TIMES: 01/04 – 30/10 **GPS:** N43.17211 E01.41143
DIRECTIONS: In LE FOSSAT take D919 SOUTH past D14 turning & turn LEFT after 100m, follow road round to RIGHT & AIRE.
SITE DESCRIPTION: *This aire is located about 200m south of the village, next to the Municipal campsite, but is operated by a motorhome dealer. The individual pitches are on gravel hard standing separated by grass verges & shaded under trees in places, each pitch having an ehu. Artisanal service point with drainage platform. The aire also has access to the adjacent campsite showers & toilets.*

REVIEW: *The aire is well maintained with good sized, well spaced pitches, water, electric, warm showers & a toilet block – all enclosed, & supervised by the owner. In the village there is a boulangerie, 8 til 8 superette, café, pizzeria & a general store. The location is quiet being set back from the D919. Tariff reduces to 11€ on second day & is cheaper in winter without services.*

LES CABANNES

ADDRESS: NEXT TO GENDARMERIE **TYPE OF AIRE:** MUNICIPAL
FACILITIES: WATER /GREY & BLACK DRAIN / TOILETS
LOCATION: SEMI-RURAL **NO. OF SPACES:** 30
PRICES: PARKING: 5€ /24Hrs **SERVICES**: 2€ WATER
OPENING TIMES: ALL YEAR **GPS:** N42.78483 E01.68318
DIRECTIONS: From NORTH take D522 into LES CABANNES & turn RIGHT into RUE PRINCIPALE & then LEFT to AIRE (next to Gendarmerie).
SITE DESCRIPTION*: The aire is located in a large tarmac car park on the village southern outskirts, next to the Gendarmerie, & surrounded by hedges/ trees – giving shade in places but also having lovely far reaching views. There is a small public toilet*

block in the aire & no motorhome parking is allowed elsewhere in the village – only on the aire. Artisanal service point with a large platform drain.
REVIEW: *A good, large aire, very quiet with excellent scenery. Parking is paid for at a ticket machine by credit card, WC on site with a washbasin, securely located next to Gendarmerie. A small village of 400 inhabitants at an altitude of 530m, whose shops includes a superette, boulangerie, epicerie, tabac, petrol station, 3 restaurants & 2 bars, all 350m from the aire.*

VICDESSOS

ADDRESS: OFF RUE DU MOULIN **TYPE OF AIRE:** MUNICIPAL
FACILITIES: WATER /GREY & BLACK DRAIN / ELECTRIC / RUBBISH
LOCATION: RURAL **NO. OF SPACES:** 20
PRICES: PARKING: 10€ /24Hrs **SERVICES**: INCL
OPENING TIMES: ALL YEAR **GPS:** N42.76904 E01.50222
DIRECTIONS: From EAST on D8, at VICDESSOS cross over bridge & turn 1st RIGHT, then RIGHT again & LEFT to AIRE.
SITE DESCRIPTION: *The aire is next to the river, on eastern edge of the village, with ehu's, parking on grass having good shade under the trees, access by automatic barrier. The artisanal service point has a platform drain with a small toilet block.*

REVIEW: *This is a lovely village in the middle of the mountains with a river running through it. The aire is very peaceful apart from the sound of the river, with ample shaded, level parking. Fees are payable by credit card. Close to shops; bar & 8 til 8 superette.*

12 AVEYRON

BOISSE PENCHOT

ADDRESS: OFF RUE DU CHATEAU BAS, D42 **TYPE OF AIRE:** MUNICIPAL
FACILITIES: WATER /GREY & BLACK DRAIN/ ELECTRIC
LOCATION: RURAL/ RIVERSIDE **NO. OF SPACES:** 8
PRICES: **PARKING**: FREE **SERVICES**: 3€ WATER or ELECTRIC
OPENING TIMES: ALL YEAR **GPS:** N44.59188 E02.20592
DIRECTIONS: From SOUTH, follow D42 NORTH into village & turn LEFT to AIRE (next to Brasserie).

SITE DESCRIPTION: *The aire is in a small tarmac parking area on the west side of the village, alongside the Lot River with an adjacent landscaped park. There are 8 individual parking spaces with grass areas & small trees but little shade, lit at night & the aire is about 150m from the centre of the village. Raclet service point with 2 ehu's & a large drive thru platform drain, jetons from shops.*
REVIEW: *At the edge of the village, on the banks of the Lot, a superb stop on a well designed aire with 8 well arranged spaces on tarmac bordered by grass with picnic tables – quiet & lit at night. Restaurant & shops nearby, tennis courts/ swimming pool adjacent & fishing possible in the river.*

BOZOULS

ADDRESS: CHEMIN DE LA COMBE **TYPE OF AIRE:** MUNICIPAL
FACILITIES: WATER /GREY & BLACK DRAIN / ELECTRIC/ WIFI
LOCATION: SEMI-RURAL **NO. OF SPACES:** 35
PRICES: PARKING: FREE **SERVICES**: WATER & ELECTRIC: 2€
OPENING TIMES: ALL YEAR **GPS :** N44.46725 E02.72585
DIRECTIONS: From South take D998 to BOZOULS. As you enter town, turn LEFT (D581) & 1st LEFT to AIRE on RIGHT.
SITE DESCRIPTION*: The aire in Bozouls is in a large gravel car park on the southern* edge of the *village, next to open farmland, with spaces having some shade under trees also close to village centre. Euro-Relais service point (2€ coins only) with drainage platform & wifi. A good aire, practical, clean & quiet with level spaces having some shade with adjacent grass areas, petanque pitch & picnic tables nearby. Aire is 400m walk along footpath to village centre.*

REVIEW: *A nice village with reasonable selection of shops, InterMarché & market on Thursday mornings, a footpath also leads to the Bozouls canyon – a natural cirque, (400m wide & 100m deep) around which the village is encircled.*

BROQUIES

ADDRESS: RTE DE MAZIES **TYPE OF AIRE:** MUNICIPAL
FACILITIES: WATER /GREY & BLACK DRAIN/ ELEC./ TOILETS/ SHOWERS
LOCATION: URBAN **NO. OF SPACES:** 30
PRICES: PARKING: FREE **SERVICES**: FREE
OPENING TIMES: ALL YEAR **GPS:** N44.00510 E02.69389
DIRECTIONS: In village take D200E WEST towards BROUSSE LE CHATEAU, AIRE is on LEFT as you leave village.
SITE DESCRIPTION: *This municipal aire is situated on the western side of this small picturesque village, about 50m from the centre with fine views across the valley. The large tarmac parking area is next to the village boules pitch, having some shade along one side. There is an artisanal service point with drainage grid, 7 ehu's & a nearby toilet/ shower block.*

REVIEW: *Nice spot with ample spaces overlooking the Tarn, picnic tables & close to the village centre. Services & showers/ toilets are all free but you need a jeton from the Epicerie in village, donations box adjacent. The village has a few shops, bar/cafe, remains of its fortifications, a 17th C church & there are nice walks around the village with information boards. The nearby Tarn river has canoeing & kayaks available.*

CAMARES

ADDRESS: BASE DE LOISIRS **TYPE OF AIRE:** MUNICIPAL
FACILITIES: WATER /GREY & BLACK DRAIN / TOILETS / RUBBISH
LOCATION: SEMI-RURAL/ LAKESIDE **NO. OF SPACES:** 10
PRICES: PARKING: 5€/ 24 Hrs **SERVICES**: INCL
OPENING TIMES: ALL YEAR **GPS COORDS:** N43.81698 E02.87967
DIRECTIONS: In village, cross BRIDGE to EAST side of river & turn immediately RIGHT into CHEMIN DES ZIZINES. AIRE is on LEFT after 300m.
SITE DESCRIPTION: *The aire is in a recreation area next to the Dourdou river & a lake with parking spaces either on grass or gravel hard standings with large trees providing some shade. The basic artisanal services are provided by a small WC block –*

fresh water is from a tap inside, toilet cassettes are emptied in the continental toilet & a grey drainage grid is outside.
REVIEW: *A pleasant peaceful aire (below), next to an artificial swimming lake with beach, a childrens' playground, picnic tables & bbq, the parking is under large trees & there are toilets with washing up sinks. Shops & a biscuit bakery are 350m away.*

CAMPAGNAC

ADDRESS: NEXT TO CAMPING **TYPE OF AIRE:** MUNICIPAL
FACILITIES: WATER /GREY & BLACK DRAIN/ ELECTRIC
LOCATION: SEMI-RURAL **NO. OF SPACES:** 5
PRICES: PARKING: 3€ / 24 Hrs **SERVICES**: FREE
OPENING TIMES: ALL YEAR **GPS:** N44.41953 E03.08863
DIRECTIONS: From NORTH, enter village on D37 & AIRE is on LEFT.
SITE DESCRIPTION: *Aire is in a small purpose built tarmac parking area on eastern edge of the village, next to the Municipal campsite & behind the Gendarmerie. Individual spaces separated by grass verges & with shrubs/ trees giving varying degrees of shade. Parking is lit at night & there are picnic tables available. Parking is about 200m from the village centre. An artisanal service point with drainage channel.*

REVIEW: *A lovely aire with 5 spaces surrounded by greenery, a pleasant, quiet location, securely sited behind the Gendarmerie. Fee is payable at adjacent campsite (open 15/06 – 15/09), free when closed. Short walk into village where there is just a bar/ cafe/ boulangerie & a grocer.*

CAMPUAC

ADDRESS: OPP. CEMETERY, D46 **TYPE OF AIRE:** MUNICIPAL
FACILITIES: WATER /GREY & BLACK DRAIN / TOILETS / RUBBISH
LOCATION: URBAN **NO. OF SPACES:** 10
PRICES: PARKING: FREE **SERVICES**: FREE
OPENING TIMES: ALL YEAR **GPS:** N44.57018 E02.59168
DIRECTIONS: AIRE is just off the D46 thru village – opposite CEMETERY.
***SITE DESCRIPTION**: A small aire with parking on grass/ gravel on north side of the village, no shade or lighting, next to the village function hall. The artisanal service point with large platform drainage is next to a small WC building in the parking area, recycling bin adjacent.*

***REVIEW:** A well situated aire near to the middle of this nice little village but quiet at night & in a green environment. Parking is on grass or on concrete surfaces, services are easy to use. Just a snack bar in the village.*

CANET DE SALARS

ADDRESS: OFF D176 **TYPE OF AIRE:** MUNICIPAL
FACILITIES: WATER /GREY & BLACK DRAIN/ ELECTRIC
LOCATION: RURAL **NO. OF SPACES:** 15
PRICES: PARKING: 6€/24Hrs **SERVICES**: 2€ WATER
OPENING TIMES: ALL YEAR **GPS:** N44.23255 E02.74698
DIRECTIONS: . As you enter village on D176, AIRE is on RIGHT (signposted).

***SITE DESCRIPTION:** The aire is in a parking area on the south-west side of the village, with large adjacent grass areas. There are 6 parking spaces on tarmac with a dozen more on grass, accessed off a gravel track, with trees offering shade, lit at night & the aire is about 350m from the centre of the village. Artisanal service point with a large platform drain.*
***REVIEW:** A very quiet location set back from the road, next to football pitch, with level parking arranged in a circular arrangement, shade in places & lighting, short walk into*

village. Pay at bar or council official calls in morning to collect fee, which includes ehu, jetons required for water (from bar or garage in village). Play area adjacent. Bar/ tabac in village (next to church) sells grocery & there is also an Auberge/restaurant.

CASTANET

ADDRESS: CENTRE OF VILLAGE **TYPE OF AIRE:** MUNICIPAL
FACILITIES: WATER /GREY & BLACK DRAIN/ ELECTRIC/ RUBBISH
LOCATION: SEMI-RURAL **NO. OF SPACES:** 4
PRICES: PARKING: 8€ / 24 Hrs **SERVICES**: INCL
OPENING TIMES: ALL YEAR **GPS:** N44.27889 E2.28944
DIRECTIONS: AIRE is in village next to MAIRIE.
***SITE DESCRIPTION**: The aire is in a tree lined tarmac small parking area with reasonable shade next to the Mairie & the Salle des Fetes, bordered by a grass area where there are picnic tables. Spaces have individual electric hook ups for the 4 spaces provided & there are public toilets available in the adjacent village hall. Artisanal borne with a platform drain & rubbish/ recycling bins nearby.*

REVIEW:** A pretty aire with spaces shaded by trees, 4 places available each with an ehu. A very small picturesque village but no shops apart from a pottery, nearest shops are in Rieupeyroux, 6km north. Tourist info available at the Mairie where you can pay or put fee in letterbox if closed.* ***Note - not suitable for +8m vehicles.

LACROIX BARREZ

ADDRESS: OFF D505 **TYPE OF AIRE:** MUNICIPAL
FACILITIES: WATER /GREY & BLACK DRAIN/ ELECTRIC
LOCATION: SEMI-RURAL **NO. OF SPACES:** 10
PRICES: PARKING: 4€/24Hrs **SERVICES**: INCL
OPENING TIMES: ALL YEAR **GPS:** N44.77789 E02.63148
DIRECTIONS: Well signposted in village, next to Football Pitch.
***SITE DESCRIPTION**: This municipal aire is located on the western side of this large rural village, next to the football pitch, where there are 10 spaces with ehu's on grass, shaded by trees, in a large, level, hedged field accessed by a gravel track, 300m from village centre. A mini Flot Bleu service point with platform drain are in the road outside.*
***REVIEW:** A very quiet & peaceful aire, well maintained, about 10 mins walk from the shops, bar & restaurant in village. Hook-up & water included in the nightly rate, payable at Mairie – leave in letterbox if closed. Lake & picnic area within 300m, marked walks in area.*

Lacroix Barrez

LE NAYRAC

ADDRESS: RTE DE LA PLANQUE, OFF D97 **TYPE OF AIRE:** PRIVATE
FACILITIES: WATER /GREY & BLACK DRAIN/ ELECTRIC/ WIFI/ TOILETS
LOCATION: RURAL/ LAKE **NO. OF SPACES:** 26
PRICES: PARKING: 12-14€/ 24HRS **SERVICES**: INCL
OPENING TIMES: ALL YEAR **GPS :** N44.60444 E02.66824
DIRECTIONS: From village take D97 SOUTH, turn LEFT to AIRE after 1km.
SITE DESCRIPTION: *This 'Camping Village' aire, run by CampingCarPark, is situated in the former municipal campsite 'la Planque', about 800m south of the village centre & next to a large lake. Pitches are on gravel/ grass (some shaded), separated by hedges, each has 6A ehu & wifi with toilets/ showers/ sinks (open 01/07-31/08). Artisanal service point with drainage platform. Access by automatic barrier, CCP card required.*

REVIEW: *A pleasant location next a lake, remote from the village centre but quiet with level pitches. Toilets cleaned regularly but only open July & Aug. Play area, boules & tennis courts adjacent. Epicerie, cafe/ bar in village as well as petrol station. Close to Estaing, one of the 'Most Beautiful Villages in France'.*

MONTEILS

ADDRESS: NORTH OF VILLAGE, OFF D47 **TYPE OF AIRE:** MUNICIPAL
FACILITIES: WATER /GREY & BLACK DRAIN
LOCATION: SEMI-RURAL **NO. OF SPACES:** 4
PRICES: PARKING: FREE **SERVICES**: FREE
OPENING TIMES: ALL YEAR **GPS:** N44.26711 E01.99695
DIRECTIONS: Entering the village from NORTH on D47, the AIRE is on the RIGHT.
SITE DESCRIPTION: *The aire is in a modern purpose built parking area with 4 individual spaces on gravel hard standing & separated by grass verges, it is located on the northern edge of the village, backing onto farmland but only 100m to the village centre. The aire is surrounded by mature trees providing a little shade in places, it is next to the road but in a quiet spot with good walks in area. Artisanal service point with platform drain.*

REVIEW: *In a pretty village, a good free aire bordering a small stream in a green place with 4 quiet spaces bordered by grass. The small village has a boulangerie, a bar/ tabac/ news, an epicerie, a café & a restaurant.*

SALLES CURAN

ADDRESS: OFF D243, LAC PARELOUP **TYPE OF AIRE:** MUNICIPAL
FACILITIES: WATER /GREY & BLACK DRAIN/ TOILETS/ ELECTRIC
LOCATION: RURAL/ LAKESIDE **NO. OF SPACES:** 70
PRICES: PARKING: 12€ /24Hrs **SERVICES**: INCL
OPENING TIMES: 01/05 – 31/10 **GPS:** N44.20025 E02.77570

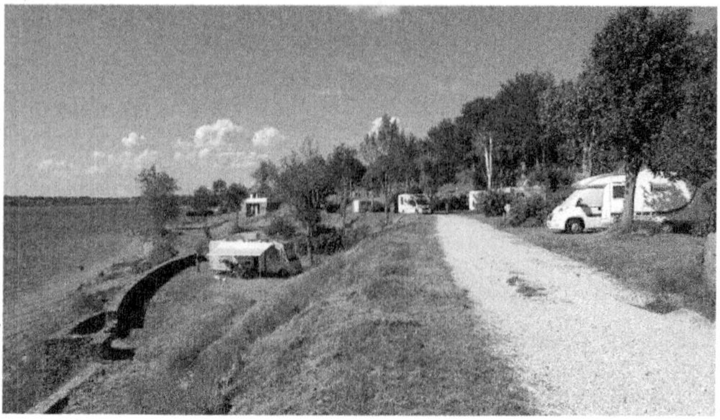

DIRECTIONS: From SALLES-CURAN take D993 NORTH & then D243 to AIRE.
SITE DESCRIPTION: *The aire here is located in the former Municipal campsite in a pleasant situation overlooking the Lac de Paraloup. There are 70 level spaces on grass on 3 levels with ehu's, some*

shaded, accessed by a gravel track/ automatic barrier. A mini Flot Bleu service point & double platform drain with toilets nearby.

REVIEW: *A quiet & clean aire close to the large artificial lake with a nice beach – fishing, swimming & boating allowed in season. Basically a Municipal campsite at a good price that includes electric, services, toilets & showers – fee collected daily by a council official. Close to the small hamlet of Les Vernhes but about 3kms from Salles-Curan where there are shops/ services. Walks around lake. Voted 'Aire of the Year 2017'.*

SAINT CYPRIEN SUR DOURDOU

ADDRESS: RTE DE RODEZ, D901 **TYPE OF AIRE:** MUNICIPAL
FACILITIES: WATER /GREY & BLACK DRAIN/ ELECTRIC/ RUBBISH
LOCATION: SEMI-RURAL **NO. OF SPACES:** 12
PRICES: PARKING: FREE **SERVICES**: WATER 2€, ELECTRIC 1€
OPENING TIMES: ALL YEAR **GPS:** N44.55217 E02.41078
DIRECTIONS: From NORTH on D901, AIRE is on RIGHT, 300m before VILLAGE.

SITE DESCRIPTION: *This aire is in a medium sized purpose built grass & tarmac parking area with grass areas adjacent, lighting but little shade. It is a quiet location where there are 12 level tarmac spaces with ehu's separated by grass areas. There is a Flot Bleu service point with a large drainage platform – easy to access. Previous winner of 'Aire of the Year'.*

REVIEW: *A well built, modern aire just north of this pleasant village (Pop 550), next to the campsite & football pitch. Large pitches in a quiet location despite being alongside the road. Shops & bar in village.*

STE EULALIE DE CERNON

ADDRESS: NORTH OF VILLAGE, OFF D77 **TYPE OF AIRE:** MUNICIPAL
FACILITIES: WATER /GREY & BLACK DRAIN / TOILETS/ ELECTRIC/ WIFI
LOCATION: SEMI-RURAL **NO. OF SPACES:** 20
PRICES: PARKING: 10€ /24HRS **SERVICES**: INCL
OPENING TIMES: ALL YEAR **GPS :** N43.98531 E03.13833
DIRECTIONS: Entering village from EAST on D77, turn 1st RIGHT @ AIRE sign.

SITE DESCRIPTION: *The aire in Ste Eulalie is in a modern medium sized gravel parking on the northern outskirts of the village (400m from centre) where there are ample level spaces in an enclosed area controlled by an automatic barrier which is operated by a credit card machine. The aire has toilet (handicapped) & shower. There is* *good shade with grass areas & it is close to the ancient village centre. Flot Bleu service point with platform drain & ehu's/ wifi for each space.*

REVIEW: *An excellent aire in a lovely setting, quiet, well maintained & secure with a helpful resident caretaker who lives adjacent. 16A hook-ups included in the rate as well as wifi & use of the toilets/showers. Aire is a short walk into village where there is a grocery shop, bar & restaurants in village. Beautiful little village with Knights Templar Commandery, church & remains of fortifications with walks/ cycle path nearby.*

SAINTE EULALIE D'OLT

ADDRESS: OUTSIDE CAMPING **TYPE OF AIRE:** MUNICIPAL
FACILITIES: WATER /GREY & BLACK DRAIN / TOILETS/ ELECTRIC
LOCATION: SEMI-RURAL/ RIVERSIDE **NO. OF SPACES:** 15
PRICES: PARKING: 10€ /24Hrs **SERVICES**: INCL
OPENING TIMES: ALL YEAR **GPS:** N44.46468 E02.94963
DIRECTIONS: Entering town from SOUTH on D597, turn 1st RIGHT before BRIDGE & follow road round. AIRE is signposted to RIGHT.

SITE DESCRIPTION: *The aire is in a modern medium sized gravel area on the western outskirts of the village (250m from centre) where there are over a dozen level spaces in an enclosed area controlled by an automatic barrier which is operated by credit card. The aire is next to a small campsite, which offers use of the toilets, sinks & showers. There is a little shade here & it is close to the shops. Artisanal service point with platform drain & ehu for each space.*

REVIEW: *An excellent little aire, well maintained & secure with a resident caretaker on the adjacent campsite. 16A ehu's are included in the rate as well as use of the toilets/showers. Aire is next to River Lot & a short walk into village where there is a small range of shops, bar, café & restaurant with a supermarket 2kms away. Beautiful little village classed as "One of the Most Beautiful in France".*

SAINTE GENEVIEVE SUR ARGENCE

ADDRESS: RUE DE L'ARGENCE **TYPE OF AIRE:** MUNICIPAL
FACILITIES: WATER /GREY & BLACK DRAIN/ ELECTRIC/ TOILETS
LOCATION: SEMI-URBAN **NO. OF SPACES:** 20
PRICES: PARKING: FREE **SERVICES**: 2€ WATER or ELECTRIC
OPENING TIMES: ALL YEAR **GPS:** N44.80197 E02.76199
DIRECTIONS: Entering village from the SOUTH on D900, take 2nd RIGHT after large lake. AIRE is 200m on LEFT.
SITE DESCRIPTION: *This Municipal aire is on the eastern edge of the village, next to the river & adjacent to fields, in a large gravel parking area – having little shade but lit at night. Flot Bleu service point with drainage platform, 4 ehu's & toilets nearby. Jetons from the Mairie, shops or café opposite.*

REVIEW: *At the heart of the small town, a pleasant stopover next to a small river. Town has a small selection of shops, a couple of eating places & a 15th C church. Ehu's only operate from 10pm till 7am.*

SAINT JUST SUR VIAUR

ADDRESS: LA FABRIE, D352 **TYPE OF AIRE:** MUNICIPAL
FACILITIES: WATER /GREY & BLACK DRAIN/ TOILETS/ ELEC./ RUBBISH
LOCATION: SEMI-RURAL **NO. OF SPACES:** 4
PRICES: PARKING: FREE **SERVICES**: FREE
OPENING TIMES: ALL YEAR **GPS:** N44.12381 E02.37528
DIRECTIONS: From EAST on D532, AIRE is on LEFT 300m before bridge over river.
SITE DESCRIPTION: *This aire is in a medium sized tarmac car park, in the hamlet of La Fabrie, 1km east of St Just, with a modern WC block & services, in a semi-rural location bordered by forest & farmland but little shade. There is a small playground adjacent, WC block has sinks for washing & there is a Raclet service point with a large drainage platform/ 2 ehu's. St Just is a very small village (Pop 250) at an altitude of 305m.*

REVIEW: *Well equipped aire with bbq, toilets, electric, washing up sinks & picnic tables – all next to a river in lovely surroundings. A very peaceful place, clean & well maintained – donation box for services.*

SENERGUES

ADDRESS: AUTRUCHES DE CONQUES, LA BESSE **TYPE OF AIRE:** PRIVATE
FACILITIES: WATER /GREY & BLACK DRAIN/ ELECTRIC/ TOILETS
LOCATION: RURAL **NO. OF SPACES:** 5
PRICES: PARKING: FREE **SERVICES**: FREE
OPENING TIMES: 01/04 – 30/11 **GPS:** N44.58970 E02.48242
DIRECTIONS: From SENERGUES take D242 SOUTH & LEFT onto D137 & then next LEFT to FARM & AIRE (signposted).
SITE DESCRIPTION*: This is a small private aire on an Ostrich farm, 2kms south of Senergues, in a very rural spot where there are spaces for up to 5 motorhomes, with level parking on grass – each having hook-up & picnic tables. There is an artisanal service point with drainage grid & toilets next to the farm building. Tel: 0565698395*

REVIEW: *A bit remote but the aire is very clean & quiet with far reaching views, no shade or lighting. All free but you are expected to pay to visit the farm, farm produce for sale in the shop.*

VILLECOMTAL

ADDRESS: LE FOIRAIL, OFF D904 **TYPE OF AIRE:** MUNICIPAL
FACILITIES: WATER /GREY & BLACK DRAIN/ ELECTRIC/ RUBBISH
LOCATION: SEMI-RURAL **NO. OF SPACES:** 30
PRICES: PARKING: FREE **SERVICES**: FREE
OPENING TIMES: 01/ 04 – 30/10 **GPS:** N44.53611 E02.56477

DIRECTIONS: From SOUTH entering village on D904, AIRE is on LEFT, immediately after Centre de Secours.
SITE DESCRIPTION: *Situated on the southern edge of this small rural village, bordered by farmland, the aire is in the former Municipal campsite with 30 spaces on grass, separated by hedges & mature trees providing shade. The village centre is only a short walk away & the Artisanal services are next to a small WC building in the car park*

REVIEW: *Excellent aire in the old Municipal campsite with 30 dedicated motorhome spaces on hard standing, accessed by a tarmac road, each having ehu's. Quiet location, good shade, well maintained & organised – unfortunately not open in winter. 300m walk to village centre with its small range of shops, restaurant, café & bar. Interesting old medieval village in red/ grey stone with many old houses, château, etc. Donation box for services.*

VILLEFRANCHE DE ROUERGUE

ADDRESS: OFF AVE DE LA LIBERATION, D47 **TYPE OF AIRE:** MUNICIPAL
FACILITIES: WATER /GREY DRAIN/BLACK DRAIN/ ELECTRIC/ WIFI
LOCATION: SEMI-URBAN **NO. OF SPACES:** 60
PRICES: PARKING: 9.5€/ 24 Hrs **SERVICES**: INCL
OPENING TIMES: 15/04 – 31/10 **GPS :** N44.34230 E02.02613
DIRECTIONS: In town follow "CAMPING DU ROUERGUE" signs to AIRE.

SITE DESCRIPTION: *The aire is located on the south west edge of the town, in part of the municipal campsite 'Camping du Rouergue', next to the town sports ground where there are ample shaded spaces on grass, lit at night & accessed by tarmac tracks. The*

pitches are separated by tall hedges, each with a water tap, ehu & wifi (in certain areas), access is via an automatic barrier. Flot Bleu service point with a large platform drain.
REVIEW: *A comfortable aire in a large section of the town campsite with good size (100m^2) level pitches in a quiet, shaded location. Close to the Aveyron river & about 15 mins level walk from the town centre - a medieval bastide with cobbled streets & old houses, many having arcades at ground level. There is a 15th C church & a 17th C chapel together with a good selection of shops plus a market on Thursday mornings.*

31 HAUTE-GARONNE

REVEL

ADDRESS: MOULIN DU ROI, OFF AVE J. NOUGUIER **TYPE OF AIRE:** PRIVATE
FACILITIES: WATER /GREY & BLACK DRAIN/ ELECTRIC/ WIFI
LOCATION: URBAN **NO. OF SPACES:** 28
PRICES: PARKING: 13€/ 24Hrs **SERVICES**: INCL
OPENING TIMES: ALL YEAR **GPS:** N43.45373 E02.01392
DIRECTIONS: From town centre, follow signs for PISCINE/ STADE & AIRE.
SITE DESCRIPTION: *This CampingCarPark aire is located on the eastern side of the town, in a pleasant location next to the campsite & swimming pool, where there are 28 spaces on gravel, lit at night with small trees but little shade. Access via an automatic barrier (CCP card required). Artisanal borne with drainage platform.*

REVIEW: *A nice quiet location, bordered by grass & overlooking the town sports centre., tennis courts & pool, having plenty of spaces, wifi (but with only 16 ehu's) & picnic tables plus a bbq - a cheaper rate applies in low season. Well maintained & designed, but about 1km distant from the town centre; a 14th C bastide town with covered market, medieval houses, museum, arcades, shops & eating places.*

RIEUX-VOLVESTRE

ADDRESS: ROUTE PLAN D'EAU **TYPE OF AIRE:** PRIVATE
FACILITIES: WATER / GREY & BLACK DRAIN/ ELECTRIC/ WIFI/ TOILETS
LOCATION: SEMI-RURAL/ RIVER SIDE **NO. OF SPACES:** 12
PRICES: PARKING: 12€ /24Hrs **SERVICES**: INCL
OPENING TIMES: ALL YEAR **GPS:** N43.26915 E01.17838
DIRECTIONS: From RIEUX-VOLVESTRE follow signs for PISCINE & AIRE.
SITE DESCRIPTION*: The aire, run by CampingCarPark, is next to the town leisure area & swimming pool, in a small tarmac/ gravel parking area, lit at night with shade provided by trees & adjacent grass areas. The aire is accessed by automatic barrier*

(CCP card required) & is located about 2 km north of the town centre & shops. Artisanal service point with 6A ehu's, wifi & drainage platform, modern toilet block adjacent.

REVIEW: *This is one of CCP's smallest aires but probably one of their best. Very quiet location with plenty of spaces, good facilities/ services, 50m from the river & backing onto a wood. but quite remote from the town. Toilet block with showers. Swimming pool (indoor & outdoor), leisure area & Municipal camping (open 01/04 – 31/10) adjacent with 66 spaces overlooking the Garonne river. Interesting medieval town with a cathedral, many fine buildings, shops & Sunday market.*

ST FELIX LAURAGAIS

ADDRESS: NEXT TO LAC DE LENCLAS **TYPE OF AIRE:** MUNICIPAL
FACILITIES: WATER /GREY & BLACK DRAIN/ TOILETS
LOCATION: RURAL **NO. OF SPACES:** 20
PRICES: PARKING: FREE **SERVICES**: FREE
OPENING TIMES: ALL YEAR **GPS:** N43.42684 E01.89857
DIRECTIONS: From ST FELIX take D67 SOUTH to Lac de Lenclas, & AIRE.

SITE DESCRIPTION: *The aire is located next to the Lac de Lenclas, 4kms south of village, in a very rural & remote location, the parking is in a large gravel car park next to the lake where there is also an adjacent restaurant. Spaces are shaded under mature*

trees with lighting at night. The services are as follows: Grey drainage in grid in car park, black drainage in adjacent toilets, fresh water tap outside toilet block.
REVIEW: *Excellent spot but not a 'true' aire, total tranquillity next to a lake with walks around it, fishing & with a restaurant / toilets although the services are very basic. Quite remote with no shops or services nearby apart from the restaurant, although the quaint medieval bastide village of St Felix has some shops.*

VILLEFRANCHE DE LAURAGAIS

ADDRESS: 10 CHEMIN DES MAGNAUQUES **TYPE OF AIRE:** PRIVATE
FACILITIES: WATER /GREY & BLACK DRAIN/ TOILETS/ ELECTRIC/ WIFI
LOCATION: URBAN **NO. OF SPACES:** 12
PRICES: PARKING: 13€ /24Hrs **SERVICES**: INCL
OPENING TIMES: 01/03 – 30/11 **GPS:** N43.39671 E01.70932
DIRECTIONS: From VILLEFRANCHE take D622 WEST & turn LEFT after Restaurant to the AIRE.
SITE DESCRIPTION: *This private aire is on the western side of the town, in a small parking area where there are 12 spaces on hard standing with a little shade & adjacent grass areas bordered by hedges. A nice residential position 500m from the town centre & shops. Artisanal service point & drainage platform. Tel/ Text: 0664954788*
REVIEW: *A well maintained, clean & quiet aire (owned by motorhomers) with good facilities; showers, picnic tables, toilets, ehu's, laundry & wifi. On outskirts of the town in residential area but just a 20 min. level walk into centre, with a SuperU within 10 mins. A medieval bastide town with many old buildings & good range of services. Canal du Midi nearby with walks along it.*

32 GERS

AUCH

ADDRESS: OFF RUE DU GEN DE-GAULLE **TYPE OF AIRE:** MUNICIPAL
FACILITIES: WATER /GREY & BLACK DRAIN/ ELECTRIC/ WIFI
LOCATION: URBAN/ RIVER **NO. OF SPACES:** 45
PRICES: PARKING: 12€/ 24HRS **SERVICES**: INCL
OPENING TIMES: ALL YEAR **GPS :** N43.63602 E00.58828
DIRECTIONS: Entering town from SOUTH on N21, as you enter town, turn RIGHT into RUE GEN DE-GAULLE turn RIGHT after 200m to AIRE.

SITE DESCRIPTION: *The aire is in the former Municipal campsite, on south side of town, on an island in the river, with spaces on grass separated by hedges, with mature*

trees providing some shade - shops nearby & centre of town about 500m distant. Access via an automatic barrier, Euro-Relais service point with drainage platform, wifi & ehu's.
REVIEW: *Quiet at night despite proximity of road, shaded parking spaces. Good selection of shops/restaurants in town including Carrefour & Leader-Price supermarkets. Footpath leads to centre of town from camping (20mins). Interesting medieval town with museums & château, aire is next to the green lane/ cycle route.*

CAZAUBON

ADDRESS: LAC DE L'UBY, LA MONTJOIE **TYPE OF AIRE:** MUNICIPAL
FACILITIES: WATER /GREY & BLACK DRAIN/ ELEC./ TOILETS/ RUBBISH
LOCATION: RURAL/ LAKE **NO. OF SPACES:** 49
PRICES: PARKING: 11€ /24Hrs **SERVICES**: INCL
OPENING TIMES: ALL YEAR **GPS:** N43.93433 W00.03233
DIRECTIONS: From CAZAUBON take D626 & N524 NORTH, turn RIGHT to LAC. AIRE is on RIGHT after campsite.
SITE DESCRIPTION: *Located on the north side of Lake l'Uby near to a campsite, in a gravel parking area with some shade from the many trees. There are toilets here & an artisanal borne with platform drainage & all services, together with good walks around the lake. The aire is locked & access is by a key from the OT (closes at 18.00) or campsite.*

REVIEW: *An agreeable aire in a green & shaded location on the banks of a lake with walks/ cycling, fishing or swimming, there is also a good swimming pool 500m distant. The aire is not near to any amenities apart from the campsite, it being approximately 3.5km to Cazaubon. Popular with people using the thermal spas at Barbotan (2.5km).*

CONDOM 1

ADDRESS: FERME DE PARETTE, OFF D930 **TYPE OF AIRE:** PRIVATE
FACILITIES: WATER /GREY & BLACK DRAIN/ ELEC./ TOILETS/SHOWERS
LOCATION: RURAL **NO. OF SPACES:** 10
PRICES: PARKING: 13€/ 24 Hrs **SERVICES**: INCL
OPENING TIMES: ALL YEAR **GPS:** N43.98702 E00.34938
DIRECTIONS: From CONDOM take D930 NORTH & turn LEFT after 4kms to AIRE.
SITE DESCRIPTION: *This private aire is on a farm about 4kms north of Condom, with 10 level spaces on grass & mature trees providing good shade. The aire is next to the farm & its shop selling local produce. Artisanal service point with drainage grid, toilets/ showers, laundry, sinks & hook ups. Tel: 0562281939*
REVIEW: *Remote from Condom but a very quiet rural location in a garden type setting, with good range of services. Shop on site selling farm produce – mainly poultry products.*

Facilities are a bit dated but all function ok as well as a washing machine, meals are also available. Also a good Municipal aire in Condom, see below.

CONDOM 2

ADDRESS: CHEMIN DE L'ARGENTE, OFF D931 **TYPE OF AIRE:** MUNICIPAL
FACILITIES: WATER /GREY & BLACK DRAIN/ RUBBISH
LOCATION: URBAN/ CANAL **NO. OF SPACES:** 12
PRICES: PARKING: 3€/ 24 Hrs **SERVICES**: FREE
OPENING TIMES: ALL YEAR **GPS:** N43.94849 E00.36340
DIRECTIONS: From town head SOUTH on D931, turn LEFT at Tennis Courts.
SITE DESCRIPTION: *This modern aire is in a large parking area on the south side of Condom, with little shade, next to the Municipal campsite & 900m from the centre of town. Aire is lit at night with 12 large spaces separated by grass on hard standings accessed by a tarmac track. Artisanal service point with drainage platform.*

REVIEW: *A quiet, pleasant location with parking on tarmac spaces bordered by grass areas, short walk from the canal & the swimming pool. Foot/ cycle path leads to town centre following canal & river. Picnic tables on site with ample room between pitches. Good selection of shops in town including supermarket 500m away & restaurant nearby. Swimming pool & 3* Campsite with wifi adjacent (open 01/ 04 – 30/09).*

FLEURANCE

ADDRESS: CHEMIN CARRERASSE, OFF D953 **TYPE OF AIRE:** MUNICIPAL
FACILITIES: WATER /GREY & BLACK DRAIN
LOCATION: SEMI-URBAN/ LAKE **NO. OF SPACES:** 40
PRICES: PARKING: FREE **SERVICES**: 2€ WATER or ELECTRIC
OPENING TIMES: ALL YEAR **GPS:** N43.84742 E00.67203
DIRECTIONS: From EAST on D953, AIRE is on LEFT just before RIVER.
SITE DESCRIPTION: *The aire is located on the eastern side of town, in a large parking area that was the former campsite, lit at night with mature trees providing good shade, bordered by a lake & farmland. Spaces are large, unmarked & either on hard standing or grass. The centre of town being about 350m distant, the aire is just off the D953 road thru town but is quiet at night. Mini Flot Bleu sevice point with drainage platform.*
REVIEW: *An excellent aire - a free campsite, relatively quiet here at night, well shaded parking spaces between a lake & the river. Jetons from OT or at petrol stations. Good selection of shops in town including Champion & Leader Price supermarkets, swimming*

pool & tennis courts adjacent to aire. The town is a medieval bastide with an ancient market hall & 13th C church.

Fleurance

FOURCES

ADDRESS: OFF D114 **TYPE OF AIRE:** MUNICIPAL
FACILITIES: WATER /GREY & BLACK DRAIN/ TOILETS
LOCATION: SEMI-RURAL **NO. OF SPACES:** 15
PRICES: PARKING: 7€/ 24 Hrs **SERVICES**: FREE
OPENING TIMES: ALL YEAR **GPS :** N43.99412 E00,22932
DIRECTIONS: From WEST on D114, cross RIVER to FOURCES & turn 1st LEFT.
SITE DESCRIPTION: *The aire is in a large parking area to the north of the village with mature trees providing good shade, lighting & centre of village is about 150m distant. Artisanal service point with drainage platform & toilets nearby.*
REVIEW: *A very pleasant, quiet aire having ample shaded level spaces with picnic tables on grass accessed from a circular gravel track. Short walk into the medieval bastide village which is one of the "Most Beautiful in France" with medieval buildings, arcades, a 15th C château, museum, ancient clock tower & churches. Small selection of shops & auberge in village.*

LE HOUGA

ADDRESS: LA FERME AUX CERFS, D6 **TYPE OF AIRE:** PRIVATE
FACILITIES: WATER /GREY & BLACK DRAIN/ ELECTRIC/ TOILETS
LOCATION: RURAL **NO. OF SPACES:** 10

PRICES: PARKING: 5€/ 24 Hrs **SERVICES**: 3€ ELECTRIC
OPENING TIMES: 15/02 – 31/12 **GPS:** N43.78267 W00.20399
DIRECTIONS: From LE HOUGA take D6 WEST for 1km & FARM is on LEFT.

***SITE DESCRIPTION**: This private aire is found in a quiet location on a deer & wild boar farm/ auberge with ample spaces on grass/ gravel shaded by trees & surrounded by open farmland. A basic artisanal borne & WC block, ehu's available on request.*
***REVIEW:** A really nice place with parking in a large car park next to the restaurant & is quiet with ample spaces. The farm has its' own shop selling venison, wild boar, paté, wines, liqueurs & preserves, there is also a small restaurant on site together with a park area for the deer & other animals. The owner of the farm is very pleasant & they produce good meals in the restaurant which is closed Sunday evening & Monday.*
Tel: 0562089697

MARCIAC

ADDRESS: CHEMIN DE RONDE, D3 **TYPE OF AIRE:** MUNICIPAL
FACILITIES: WATER /GREY & BLACK DRAIN/ RUBBISH/ ELECTRIC
LOCATION: SEMI-RURAL **NO. OF SPACES:** 40
PRICES: PARKING: 3€/ 24 Hrs **SERVICES**: 3€ ELECTRIC or WATER
OPENING TIMES: ALL YEAR **GPS:** N43.52726 E01.15864
DIRECTIONS: From MARCIAC take D3 NORTH 100m & turn LEFT into AIRE.
***SITE DESCRIPTION**: Conveniently located for the town centre, 150m away, this large aire is in a large tarmac parking with marked spaces on the northern edge of town close to open farmland, lit at night but has little shade. The Flot Bleu service point with platform drain & 8 ehu's available. Parking is reserved during the town Jazz Festival from 30/7 – 15/8. Jetons from a machine.*

REVIEW: *Parking is level & quiet at night, the aire is convenient for the town shops / eating places & is also close to a large leisure lake with large grass areas/ woods.*

ST CLAR

ADDRESS: CHEMIN DE RONDE, OFF D13 **TYPE OF AIRE:** MUNICIPAL
FACILITIES: WATER /GREY & BLACK DRAIN/ TOILETS/ SHOWERS
LOCATION: SEMI-RURAL **NO. OF SPACES:** 10
PRICES: PARKING: FREE **SERVICES**: FREE
OPENING TIMES: ALL YEAR **GPS:** N43.89104 E00.77239
DIRECTIONS: Entering village from NORTH on D13 take 1st LEFT into AIRE.
SITE DESCRIPTION*: The aire is located in a purpose built parking area on the eastern edge of the village, backing onto open farmland, just off the D13 road into the village. Parking is on grass/ gravel with small trees providing some shade & access via a gravel road, the aire is about 200m from the centre of the village. A basic artisanal service point with toilets & showers plus 2 sinks for washing up.*

REVIEW: *A very pleasant aire with good views, tranqil, practical services & a green location yet not far from the shops & the village. St Clar is a medieval bastide with many old buildings, a couple of interesting squares, an old covered market building & a School Museum. There are several shops in village; boulangerie, newsagent, supermarket, etc & a couple of restaurants/ pizzeria plus a market on Thursday morning.*

46 LOT

BOUZIES

ADDRESS: HALTE NAUTIQUE, P2 **TYPE OF AIRE:** MUNICIPAL
FACILITIES: WATER /GREY & BLACK DRAIN/TOILETS/ ELECTRIC
LOCATION: SEMI-RURAL/ RIVER **NO. OF SPACES:** 10
PRICES: PARKING: 6€/ 24 Hrs **SERVICES**: 2€ WATER or ELECTRIC
OPENING TIMES: ALL YEAR **GPS:** N44.48422 E01.64477
DIRECTIONS: Entering BOUZIES from ST CIRQ on D40, turn 1st RIGHT to AIRE.
SITE DESCRIPTION: *This modern aire is located in a medium sized grass/ gravel parking area (P2) on the northern edge of the village, next to the river Lot. The parking*

is level, has good shade & is bordered by grassy areas, about 200m from the village centre. Euro-Relais service point with drainage grid, modern toilets & washng-up sinks.
REVIEW: *A very pleasant location with good shaded parking spaces next to the Lot river. Quiet spot, only a short walk from the village centre where there is an epicerie, boulangerie, tabac & a couple of restaurants. Picnic area within 100m & beautiful walk along the Lot river towpath.* ***NOTE: The aire is best approached via St Cirq as the bridge over the river at Bouzies is only 2.3m wide.***

CAJARC

ADDRESS: RUE DU CUZOUL, OFF D662 **TYPE OF AIRE:** MUNICIPAL
FACILITIES: WATER /GREY & BLACK DRAIN/ RUBBISH
LOCATION: SEMI-URBAN **NO. OF SPACES:** 14
PRICES: PARKING: 7€/ 24Hrs **SERVICES**: INCL
OPENING TIMES: ALL YEAR **GPS:** N44.48318 E01.83915
DIRECTIONS: From WEST on D662, turn 1st RIGHT, as you enter town, to AIRE.
SITE DESCRIPTION: *The aire is situated next to the football pitch & campsite in a large gravel/ grass parking area, close to the Lot River & about 200m from the centre of town. There are 14 level spaces on gravel separated by grass verges with some young trees offering a little shade. Artisanal service point with a platform drain.*

REVIEW: *A quiet spot on the edge of the town, short walk into centre where there is a small range of shops & eating places. Parking fee is payable at a machine by cash or card. Cajarc has houses dating from medieval and Renaissance times with a circular boulevard built where the ramparts were.*

CAPDENAC GARE

ADDRESS: BVD P.RAMADIER, D86 **TYPE OF AIRE:** PRIVATE
FACILITIES: TOILETS/ WATER /GREY & BLACK DRAIN/ ELEC./ WIFI/ SHWR.
LOCATION: SEMI-URBAN/ RIVER **NO. OF SPACES:** 50
PRICES: PARKING: 11- 13€ /24Hrs **SERVICES**: INCL

OPENING TIMES: ALL YEAR **GPS:** N44.57308 E02.07305
DIRECTIONS: From WEST on D840, cross river into CAPDENAC LE GARE & take 1st RIGHT to AIRE.
SITE DESCRIPTION: *This former campsite is managed by CampingCarPark & is situated next to the river in a large grass parking area, 300m from the centre of the town. Most of the level spaces benefit from shade from the trees & all have 6A ehu's & wifi. Access via automatic barrier, CCP card required. Euro-Relais service point with drainage platform, toilets, sinks & showers (only open July/ Aug).*

REVIEW: *A pleasant aire, quiet & shaded, with good modern facilities, play area, fishing, next to the Lot yet only a short walk into town where there are restaurants/ shops & an InterMarche supermarket. Near to Capdenac le Haut, an interesting fortified village with panoramic views, one of the 'Most Beautiful Villages in France' that also has a nice free overnight parking area on grass, but no services except toilets.*

GOURDON-EN-QUERCY

ADDRESS: AVE J.ADMIRAT **TYPE OF AIRE:** MUNICIPAL
FACILITIES: WATER /GREY & BLACK DRAIN/ ELECTRIC/ RUBBISH
LOCATION: URBAN **NO. OF SPACES:** 8
PRICES: PARKING: FREE **SERVICES**: 2€ WATER & ELECTRIC
OPENING TIMES: ALL YEAR **GPS:** N44.73420 E01.38535
DIRECTIONS: From SOUTH take D673 thru town (one way), turn RIGHT @ AIRE sign & follow signs to AIRE.

SITE DESCRIPTION: *The aire is in a medium size parking area on south side of the town where there are 8 allocated spaces for motorhomes on concrete – each space has an ehu & a water tap. Electric & water are available by payment at a central payment machine. Spaces are well shaded in a quiet location about 200m from the town centre. Artisanal service point with a small drain.*

REVIEW: *The large spaces are bordered by grass in a quiet location but some slight noise during day from nearby train line. Hostelry close to the aire, short walk into the historic area of this bastide town where there are many interesting buildings & a ruined château plus a good range of shops, services & restaurants, very popular in summer.*

LA BASTIDE MARNHAC

ADDRESS: BEHIND MAIRIE, OFF D67 **TYPE OF AIRE:** MUNICIPAL
FACILITIES: WATER /GREY & BLACK DRAIN/ RUBBISH
LOCATION: SEMI-RURAL **NO. OF SPACES:** 10
PRICES: PARKING: FREE **SERVICES**: FREE
OPENING TIMES: ALL YEAR **GPS :** N44.38606 E01.39754
DIRECTIONS: AIRE is next to MAIRIE in village.

SITE DESCRIPTION: *The aire is in a large gravel car park on the southern edge of the village, with ample parking spaces, a little shade & some lighting from nearby street lights. The parking is at the side of the Mairie & tennis courts. Artisanal service point with platform drain & rubbish bin.*

REVIEW: *Quiet spot with good rural views on the edge of this small rural village where there are several spaces bordered by grass areas with picnic tables. Few facilities in the village apart from a combined bar /restaurant /grocery / bread shop.*

LAMAGDELAINE

ADDRESS: RTE DE CAHORS, D653 **TYPE OF AIRE:** PRIVATE
FACILITIES: WATER /GREY & BLACK DRAIN/ ELECTRIC/ WIFI/ TOILETS
LOCATION: SEMI-RURAL/ RIVER **NO. OF SPACES:** 29
PRICES: PARKING: 11-17€/ 24HRS **SERVICES**: INCL
OPENING TIMES: ALL YEAR **GPS :** N44.46603 E01.48486
DIRECTIONS: In village, AIRE is off Roundabout, opposite Mairie.

SITE DESCRIPTION: *This 'Camping Village' aire, run by CampingCarPark, is situated in the former municipal campsite, about 200m south of the village centre & next to the river Lot. Pitches are on gravel/ grass (most shaded) accessed by a gravel track, each has 6A ehu & wifi with toilets/ showers & sinks (open 01/07-01/08). Artisanal service point with drainage platform. Access by automatic barrier, CCP card required.*

REVIEW: *A pleasant location next to the Lot, quiet with large shaded pitches but some low branches, expensive in July & August. Toilets cleaned regularly but only open July & Aug. Shop & a couple of eating places in village but little else, handy for visiting Cahors (3kms).*

LUZECH

ADDRESS: LES BERGES DE CAIX, OFF D9 **TYPE OF AIRE:** PRIVATE
FACILITIES: WATER /GREY & BLACK DRAIN/ ELECTRIC/ TOILETS/ WIFI
LOCATION: RURAL **NO. OF SPACES:** 18
PRICES: PARKING: 14€/ 24Hrs **SERVICES**: INCL
OPENING TIMES: ALL YEAR **GPS:** N 44.49094 E01.29487
DIRECTIONS: From LUZECH take D9 NORTH to CAIX, AIRE is on RIGHT.

SITE DESCRIPTION: *The aire is situated a couple of kms north of Luzech, on the western side of the hamlet of Caix, in a large gravel parking area next to the river Lot. The aire has plenty of space, ehu's, wifi, lighting & some shade in places, it is 50m from the centre of Caix & is within 100m of the river. Artisanal service point with drainage grid & toilets nearby.*

REVIEW: *A very rural & picturesque location close to a leisure area on the north bank of the Lot river with a bar/ restaurant nearby (open 01/06 – 30/09). Toilets/ showers, only cold & a bit dated. Watersports, canoeing, bathing, play area, bbq & park nearby. There are few facilities in Caix but there is a good range of shops & restaurants in Luzech. Parking is free October till March but no water.*

MAUROUX

ADDRESS: LA GARENNE, D5 **TYPE OF AIRE:** MUNICIPAL
FACILITIES: WATER /GREY & BLACK DRAIN/ TOILETS
LOCATION: RURAL **NO. OF SPACES:** 12
PRICES: PARKING: FREE **SERVICES**: FREE
OPENING TIMES: ALL YEAR **GPS:** N44.45217 E01.04796
DIRECTIONS: From SOUTH take D5 to MAUROUX, AIRE is on LEFT before R/bout
SITE DESCRIPTION: *Located in a small wooded area with good shade from mature oak trees, where there are a dozen level spaces on grass/ gravel accessed by a gravel track. The aire is on the south side of this very small rural village. Artisanal borne with a drainage grid & toilets adjacent.*

REVIEW: *A basic but very pleasant aire in a shaded location with picnic tables, benches, a bbq & a play area. Service point is practical with a small toilet & sinks. Possible problems for very large vans manoeuvring around trees/ low branches. Short walk into village (200m) where there is a bar & restaurant. Good walks in area.*

PRAYSSAC

ADDRESS: AVE DES ACACIAS **TYPE OF AIRE:** MUNICIPAL
FACILITIES: WATER /GREY & BLACK DRAIN/ RUBBISH
LOCATION: URBAN **NO. OF SPACES:** 6
PRICES: PARKING: FREE **SERVICES**: FREE
OPENING TIMES: ALL YEAR **GPS:** N44.50372 E01.19194
DIRECTIONS: From EAST on D811 to PRAYSSAC, turn RIGHT to AIRE.

SITE DESCRIPTION: *This aire is situated in a small tree lined parking area on the east side of town, with parking on gravel bordered by grass, accessed by a gravel track, & shaded by mature trees – close to the town centre & its' shops. Artisanal service point with platform drain.*

REVIEW: *A pleasant small aire – quiet (at night), shaded & green with picnic tables nearby. The nice little town centre is a 5 min walk from here where you can find a range of shops & eating places, a Carrefour supermarket with fuel is within 2kms.*

ST CIRQ LAPOPIE

ADDRESS: BEHIND "CAMPING DE LA PLAGE" **TYPE OF AIRE:** PRIVATE
FACILITIES: WATER /GREY & BLACK DRAIN/ ELECTRIC/ SHOWERS/ TOILETS/ WIFI
LOCATION: RURAL/ RIVERSIDE **NO. OF SPACES:** 25
PRICES: PARKING: 7€ /24Hrs **SERVICES**: 2€ WATER or ELECTRIC
OPENING TIMES: ALL YEAR **GPS:** N44.47064 E01.68032
DIRECTIONS: From ST CIRQ take D8 EAST & then LEFT before BRIDGE to AIRE.

SITE DESCRIPTION: *This aire is an extension of the 4* campsite & is located just outside it in a large gravel car park with mature trees providing shade. A pleasant location between the campsite & the Lot river with a beach adjacent, but about 1km east of the village. The campsite has a snack bar/ takeaway & restaurant in high season & there is a small shop about 500m away over bridge. Campsite is open 13/04 - 29/09. A Raclet service point with a large platform drain.*

REVIEW: *The aire is located near to the river where there is a good beach, fishing & canoe hire, a very agreeable spot with plenty of greenery/ shade, picnic tables, wifi & free access to the campsite toilets but showers are extra (2€). An interesting old village perched on a cliff 100 m above the river, one of the 'Most Beautiful in France' with a few restaurants & shops – popular with artists & quite touristy. Warden collects fee, parking is free when campsite is closed.*

SAINT MEDARD DE PRESQUE

ADDRESS: NEXT TO D30 **TYPE OF AIRE:** PRIVATE
FACILITIES: WATER /GREY & BLACK DRAIN/ TOILETS/ ELECTRIC/ WIFI
LOCATION: RURAL **NO. OF SPACES:** 6
PRICES: PARKING: 10€/ 24HRS **SERVICES**: INCL

OPENING TIMES: ALL YEAR **GPS :** N44.87126 E01.84441
DIRECTIONS: From WEST on D30, AIRE is on LEFT, opposite turn to village.
SITE DESCRIPTION: *This small aire is in a gravel parking area of a private residence, 35m² pitches bordered by large grass areas, lit at night with some shade, located north of the village, close to a small river. Aire is in a rural location but not close to any amenities. Artisanal service point with drainage platform, toilets, ehu's, wifi & laundry.*

REVIEW: *Quiet location with pleasant proprietor, 6 level spaces, picnic tables, price includes services & use of laundrette. Bike hire available as well as a small shop. Close to the 'Most Beautiful Village' of Autoire with its waterfall & the cave at Padirac.*

VERS

ADDRESS: OFF RUE MONTOIS, D662 **TYPE OF AIRE:** MUNICIPAL
FACILITIES: WATER /GREY & BLACK DRAIN/ RUBBISH/ TOILETS
LOCATION: URBAN/ RIVER **NO. OF SPACES:** 10
PRICES: PARKING: 6€ /24Hrs **SERVICES**: INCL
OPENING TIMES: ALL YEAR **GPS:** N44.48585 E01.55495
DIRECTIONS: From EAST on D662, in VERS, turn 1st LEFT to AIRE (sign for CAMPING).

SITE DESCRIPTION: *The aire is next to the tennis courts & close to the river with shaded spaces on grass & hot showers/ toilets (at campsite) included. Campsite is open 01/05 – 30/09. Artisanal service point with a large platform drain & separate taps.*
REVIEW: *A comfortable aire situated alongside the Lot river, easy to find & practical, only a short walk from the shops & eating places. Quiet at night with picnic tables, no electric but all other facilities including showers & toilets. The village centre with 3 restaurants, boulangerie, tabac/ news & an epicerie/ butcher is about 200m from the aire, several good walks in the area.*

65 HAUTES-PYRENEES

ARRENS MARSOUS

ADDRESS: NEXT TO D918 **TYPE OF AIRE:** MUNICIPAL
FACILITIES: WATER /GREY & BLACK DRAIN/ RUBBISH/ WIFI
LOCATION: SEMI-RURAL/ RIVER **NO. OF SPACES:** 10
PRICES: PARKING: FREE **SERVICES**: 2€ WATER or ELECTRIC
OPENING TIMES: ALL YEAR **GPS:** N42.95838 W00.20733
DIRECTIONS: From EAST on D918 take 2nd turning LEFT in village to AIRE.
SITE DESCRIPTION: *The aire is next to the municipal campsite about 500m east of the village centre. Parking is on tarmac or grass next to grassy open areas but with little shade, small river runs past the parking area. Modern Euro Relais service point with drainage platform (not shown on photo below).*

REVIEW: *A quiet location with excellent views of the surrounding mountains, nice area for walking. Small village with a few shops; boulangerie, butcher, newsagent, pharmacy & a Proxi superette close to the aire & a heated swimming pool nearby.*

CAUTERETS

ADDRESS: AVE DE LA GARE, OFF D920 **TYPE OF AIRE:** MUNICIPAL
FACILITIES: WATER /GREY & BLACK DRAIN/ ELECTRIC/ RUBBISH
LOCATION: URBAN **NO. OF SPACES:** 30
PRICES: PARKING: 12€ / 24 Hrs **SERVICES**: INCL
OPENING TIMES: ALL YEAR **GPS:** N42.89355 W0.11291

DIRECTIONS: Take D920 SOUTH to CAUTERETS & bear RIGHT to the AIRE.
SITE DESCRIPTION: *The aire is located in a large tarmac car park that enjoys good views, at the entrance to the town about 300m from the centre, with parking in marked spaces with lighting but no shade. Artisanal service point, drainage grid & 3A ehu's.*

REVIEW: *The town is in a great setting, surrounded by the Pyrenees & the large aire shares these views, is peaceful with a good variety of shops nearby, market on Friday & the ski-lift at 300m distance.*

GAVARNIE

ADDRESS: HOLLE, D923 **TYPE OF AIRE:** MUNICIPAL
FACILITIES: WATER /GREY & BLACK DRAIN
LOCATION: RURAL **NO. OF SPACES:** 25
PRICES: PARKING: 8€ / 24 Hrs **SERVICES**: INCL
OPENING TIMES: ALL YEAR **GPS:** N42.73908 W00.01955
DIRECTIONS: Take D923 SOUTH to GAVARNIE, the AIRE is 2km before village.
SITE DESCRIPTION: *The aire is 2km north of the village, spaces on either side of the D923 in two large gravel car parks surrounded by meadows & the mountains, but no shade. Artisanal service point with a drainage grid.*

REVIEW: *A very pretty village with magnificent views of the surrounding mountains, but unfortunately the aire is not very close to the village though walking there & back is not a problem. Exceptionally quiet at night with a nice walk to nearby waterfalls. Free in winter but no services. The village has restaurants, bars, souvenir shops, boulangerie & a mini-market.*

MAULEON BAROUSSE

ADDRESS: D925 **TYPE OF AIRE:** MUNICIPAL
FACILITIES: WATER /GREY & BLACK DRAIN/ ELECTRIC/ RUBBISH
LOCATION: SEMI-RURAL **NO. OF SPACES:** 6
PRICES: PARKING: FREE **SERVICES**: 3€ WATER or ELECTRIC (4 hrs)
OPENING TIMES: ALL YEAR **GPS :** N42.96105 E00.56852
DIRECTIONS: From NORTH take D925 to MAULEON. In village, AIRE on RIGHT.
***SITE DESCRIPTION**: A small aire sited just to the north of the village centre with 6 large spaces on tarmac bordered by grass areas & close to the river, little shade but with lighting at night. A Flot Bleu borne with platform drainage & 4 ehu's.*

***REVIEW:** A really nice little aire, well placed in a park-like setting in this pleasant village – 5 mins from the shops (mini-mart, boulangerie, cafe/ bar/ news), quiet with lovely views & there are plenty of walks or cycle routes in this area.*

PIERREFITTE-NESTALAS

ADDRESS: PLACE LAMARTINE, OFF D920 **TYPE OF AIRE:** MUNICIPAL
FACILITIES: WATER /GREY & BLACK DRAIN/ TOILETS/ RUBBISH
LOCATION: SEMI-URBAN **NO. OF SPACES:** 10
PRICES: PARKING: FREE **SERVICES**: 2€ WATER
OPENING TIMES: ALL YEAR **GPS:** N42.96035 W00.07742
DIRECTIONS: Take D920 WEST from town & AIRE is on RIGHT, 100m after R/bout.
***SITE DESCRIPTION:** The aire is sited in the towns leisure & picnic area, close to the town centre with parking on hard standings separated by grass in a circular arrangement & accessed by a gravel track, shaded with lighting at night. Picnic tables & toilets are provided as well as an Artisanal borne with platform drainage.*

REVIEW: *A good aire, well placed in a park-like setting in this nice village, 5 mins from the shops, quiet & secure with picnic tables & toilets. Lovely views of the mountains & there are plenty of walks or cycle routes in this area including a 17km long 'Voie Verte' path that runs from the village to Lourdes. Campsite nearby.*

TOURNAY

ADDRESS: RUE DU GABASTOU **TYPE OF AIRE:** PRIVATE
FACILITIES: WATER /GREY & BLACK DRAIN/ ELECTRIC/ WIFI/ TOILETS
LOCATION: RURAL/ RIVER **NO. OF SPACES:** 45
PRICES: PARKING: 12- 13€/ 24HRS **SERVICES**: INCL
OPENING TIMES: ALL YEAR **GPS :** N43.18774 E00.24165
DIRECTIONS: In village follow signs to 'Complexe Sportif' & AIRE.
SITE DESCRIPTION *This 'Camping Village' aire, run by CampingCarPark, is situated in the former municipal campsite, about 200m north of the village centre & next to the river. Pitches are on grass (most shaded) accessed by a gravel track, lit at night, each has 6A ehu & wifi with toilets/ showers/ sinks (open 15/06-15/09). Artisanal service point with drainage platform. Access by automatic barrier, CCP card required.*

REVIEW: *A pleasant location next to the sports complex/ tennis courts, close to the village centre & quiet with large shaded pitches. Sanitary block well maintained but only open June- Sept., wifi variable. Shops in village (15 min walk via footpath), Tuesday market as well as an open-air swimming pool & a train station (trains to Lourdes or Tarbes).*

81 TARN

CASTELNAU DE MONTMIRAL

ADDRESS: DOMAINE LES MIQUELS, OFF D964 **TYPE OF AIRE:** PRIVATE
FACILITIES: WATER /GREY & BLACK DRAIN/ ELECTRIC
LOCATION: RURAL **NO. OF SPACES:** 6
PRICES: PARKING: 10€/ 24 Hrs **SERVICES**: INCL
OPENING TIMES: ALL YEAR **GPS:** N43.96629 E01.80302
DIRECTIONS: From CASTELNAU. take D964 2km & turn LEFT to LES MIQUELS.

SITE DESCRIPTION: *An aire located next to a restaurant/ bed & breakfast, with individual spaces on gravel with grass surround next to open farmland with superb views. The pitches have their own hook ups/ water tap but no shade. Artisanal service point & drainage.*

REVIEW: *A good little site with a warm welcome from the owners, lovely views, peaceful & there is access to a swimming pool (in summer) as well as the restaurant (for breakfasts & evening meals). Bread & croissants are supplied in the mornings. Quite isolated but there are shops (epicerie, patisserie, pharmacy & Poste) in the medieval village of Castelnau (3km) & Gaillac (12km). Small market in Castelnau on Tuesdays.*

FREJAIROLLES

ADDRESS: LE GRAND CHENE, D74 **TYPE OF AIRE:** PRIVATE
FACILITIES: WATER /GREY & BLACK DRAIN/ ELECTRIC/ TOILETS/ WIFI
LOCATION: SEMI-RURAL/ LAKESIDE **NO. OF SPACES:** 10
PRICES: PARKING: 15€/24Hrs **SERVICES**: INCL
OPENING TIMES: ALL YEAR **GPS:** N43.86041 E02.24905
DIRECTIONS: From FREJAIROLLES, take D81 SOUTH 2kms & turn RIGHT onto D74 (sign 'Le Grand Chene') to AIRE on LEFT.

SITE DESCRIPTION: *The aire is located in a small campsite next to a lake, about 2km south of the village in a medium size gravel parking area. The campsite is run by the adjacent restaurant which is open all year round. The individual pitches are shaded by trees, lit at night, surrounded by grass areas & within 100m of the leisure lake, the site is surrounded by farmland.*

REVIEW: *A very well equipped aire in a peaceful rural location with ehu's, toilets/ shower (dated but clean & handicap access), wifi & laundrette, 2kms from Frejairolles & 12kms from Albi. Children's play area, walks around lake & large grounds, pedalos, electric bike hire & bar/ restaurant adjacent. Tel/ Text: 0688232279*

LA BASTIDE ROUAIROUX

ADDRESS: OFF AVE DE LA GARE **TYPE OF AIRE:** MUNICIPAL
FACILITIES: WATER /GREY & BLACK DRAIN/ RUBBISH
LOCATION: URBAN **NO. OF SPACES:** 3
PRICES: PARKING: FREE **SERVICES**: FREE

OPENING TIMES: ALL YEAR **GPS :** N43.47506 E02.63445
DIRECTIONS: Take D612 into town & turn SOUTH opposite Gendarmerie to AIRE.

SITE DESCRIPTION *The aire is located close to the town centre, about 150m south of the centre in a medium size tarmac parking area where the 3 spaces are separated by low hedges. The parking has little shade but places are surrounded by grass areas & are lit at night. Artisanal service point with large drainage platform & rubbish bins.*
REVIEW: *A good little modern aire, quiet & well maintained with reserved motorhome spaces & picnic table. Short walk into town where there are several restaurants, bars, shops & a textile museum. Green lane/ cycle path along valley is next to the aire.*

LABRUGUIERE

ADDRESS: RUE PARC DU MONTIMONT, OFF D60 **TYPE OF AIRE:** MUNICIPAL
FACILITIES: WATER /GREY & BLACK DRAIN/ ELEC./ TOILETS/ RUBBISH
LOCATION: SEMI-RURAL/ LAKESIDE **NO. OF SPACES:** 14
PRICES: PARKING: 8€/ 24 Hrs **SERVICES**: INCL
OPENING TIMES: ALL YEAR **GPS:** N43.53156 E02.25525
DIRECTIONS: From LABRUGUIERE take D60 WEST & turn LEFT before BRIDGE.
SITE DESCRIPTION: *The aire is located next to the towns park area & a lake, about 1km south of the town centre in a medium size gravel parking area where the spaces are separated by low hedges. The parking is shaded by trees in places surrounded by grass areas, lit at night & within 100m of the leisure lake which is surrounded by woods/ farmland. Artisanal service point with drainage platform & ehu's, entry via automatic barrier.*

REVIEW: *An excellent aire, quiet & well maintained. with 24hr electricity, water & drainage. A bit remote from the town but next to the leisure area with a fishing lake, play area, bbq, walks & picnic tables. Labruguiere is a reasonable size town (pop 5,500) with medieval centre & a good range of shops/ restaurants.*

LAUTREC

ADDRESS: RTE DE VIELMUR-SUR-AGOUT, D92 **TYPE OF AIRE:** MUNICIPAL
FACILITIES: WATER /GREY & BLACK DRAIN/ TOILETS/ ELECTRIC
LOCATION: RURAL **NO. OF SPACES:** 50
PRICES: PARKING: 8€/ 24 Hrs **SERVICES**: 2€ WATER or ELECTRIC
OPENING TIMES: ALL YEAR **GPS:** N43.70419 E02.13006
DIRECTIONS: From LAUTREC take D92 SOUTH 1 km to AIRE on LEFT .
SITE DESCRIPTION: *The aire is in a very large gravel parking area next to the Aquaval leisure area, about 800m from the centre of this small rural village. The parking area is bordered by grass areas but there is little shade, children's play area adjacent & the lake is surrounded by open farmland. Euro-Relais service point with grid & toilets adjacent, entry via automatic barrier.*

REVIEW: *Large aire in a pleasant location next to a water park, fairly quiet (slight noise from adjacent D92 road), only has shade on one side of parking unfortunately & no lighting. Modern toilets with outside sinks, picnic tables. 20 min walk to interesting medieval village with arcaded square & small range of shops. Jetons from Aquaval reception (from May-Sept) or OT during rest of the year.*

PUYLAURENS

ADDRESS: RUE ALBERT THOREL, OFF D84 **TYPE OF AIRE:** MUNICIPAL
FACILITIES: WATER /GREY & BLACK DRAIN/ RUBBISH
LOCATION: SEMI-URBAN **NO. OF SPACES:** 10
PRICES: PARKING: FREE **SERVICES**: FREE
OPENING TIMES: ALL YEAR **GPS:** N43.56843 E02.01172
DIRECTIONS: From PUYLAURENS take D84 SOUTH & last exit at R/bout to AIRE.
SITE DESCRIPTION: *Aire is situated in a medium sized gravel car park on the southern edge of this large rural village. Individual level spaces on gravel separated by grass verges with good views of the surrounding farmland & some shade. Artisanal service point with drainage platform.*
REVIEW: *A nice, quiet aire situated in the former Municipal campsite which is fenced all round & several spaces are well shaded under trees. Aire is in a residential area with*

farmland to east, 10 min walk to village centre where there is a large selection of shops/ bars & restaurants plus a small Carrefour supermarket & a market on Wednesdays. Swimming pool, lake with fishing, tennis 100m away.

RIVIERES

ADDRESS: LA COURTADE HAUTE **TYPE OF AIRE:** PRIVATE
FACILITIES: WATER /GREY & BLACK DRAIN / ELECTRIC/ WIFI/ RUBBISH
LOCATION: RURAL/ RIVER **NO. OF SPACES:** 6
PRICES: PARKING: 15€ /24Hrs **SERVICES**: INCL
OPENING TIMES: ALL YEAR **GPS:** N43.91086 E01.98876
DIRECTIONS: From RIVIERES take C2 EAST & D200 SOUTH then follow signs 'Chalets du Lac' to AIRE.

SITE DESCRIPTION: *The aire is located 2kms east of Rivieres in the small village of La Courtade Haute, next to the Tarn river, & has 6 spaces with 16A ehu's/ wifi on gravel, separated by grass spaces/hedges, partially shaded by small trees. Artisanal borne with drainage platform.*
REVIEW: *A quiet, rural location next to the Tarn & close to a leisure area with boat/ canoe hire, fishing, tennis & golf. Large spaces (88m²) each with good walks/ cycle rides in area, bread van calls each morning.*

82 TARN-ET-GARONNE

BARDIGUES

ADDRESS: RUE DE LA MAIRIE, OFF D11 **TYPE OF AIRE:** MUNICIPAL
FACILITIES: WATER /GREY & BLACK DRAIN/ RUBBISH
LOCATION: SEMI-RURAL **NO. OF SPACES:** 5
PRICES: PARKING: FREE **SERVICES**: 2€ WATER
OPENING TIMES: ALL YEAR **GPS:** N44.03849 E0.89239

DIRECTIONS: In village, from CHURCH take road EAST to AIRE on LEFT.
SITE DESCRIPTION: *A fairly modern purpose built, gated/ fenced aire with 5 individual parking spaces on tarmac separated by grass verges & having some shade*

under mature trees, surrounded by farmland, 300m from the centre of the village. A modern artisanal borne with platform drain & rubbish bins.
REVIEW: *The little aire is clean & quiet, next to the cemetery, with views on the eastern edge of the village. A small play area & an excellent auberge nearby but little else in the pretty village.*

BOURRET

ADDRESS: ALLEE DE LA GARONNE **TYPE OF AIRE:** MUNICIPAL
FACILITIES: WATER /GREY & BLACK DRAIN/ ELECTRIC/ TOILETS
LOCATION: SEMI-RURAL **NO. OF SPACES:** 11
PRICES: PARKING: 8€/ 24 Hrs **SERVICES**: INCL
OPENING TIMES: 01/04 – 30/10 **GPS :** N43.94449 E1.16899
DIRECTIONS: AIRE is next to FOOTBALL PITCH on NORTH side of the village.
SITE DESCRIPTION: *A modern purpose built aire with 11 individual parking spaces on grass separated by hedges/ grass verges accessed by a tarmac track - having some shade under mature trees & lit at night. The aire is on the northern edge of the village & in a quiet spot about 200m from the centre. A modern Artisanal borne with platform drain with ehu's & toilets, access by automatic barrier.*
REVIEW: *Superb, clean & quiet with toilets in a former Municipal camping, within a short walk of the Garonne river & the village centre where there is a boulangerie/ superette, cafe & a restaurant. Electric included in price but only 4 sockets for 11 pitches.*

CASTELSAGRAT

ADDRESS: RUE DU COUVENT **TYPE OF AIRE:** MUNICIPAL
FACILITIES: WATER /GREY & BLACK DRAIN/ RUBBISH
LOCATION: URBAN **NO. OF SPACES:** 10
PRICES: PARKING: FREE **SERVICES**: FREE
OPENING TIMES: ALL YEAR **GPS:** N44.18378 E01.94505
DIRECTIONS: Entering village from WEST on D28, turn 1st LEFT & AIRE.

SITE DESCRIPTION: *The aire is situated on the western edge of this small rural village, about 100m from the centre, in a large gravel parking area bordered by flower beds/ trees with lighting but little shade. AireServices borne & drainage platform. Jetons are free from the shops/ Mairie.*
REVIEW: *A pleasant, quiet position with open farmland to the north & west, parking is quite large with grass areas & picnic tables adjacent. Short walk to shops; boulangerie, fish merchant, butcher, grocer/ tabac/ news & bar/ restaurant. Nice little medieval bastide village with 13th C arcades.*

CASTELSARRASIN

ADDRESS: CHEMIN DES DEUX PONTS **TYPE OF AIRE:** MUNICIPAL
FACILITIES: WATER /GREY & BLACK DRAIN/ ELECTRIC/ RUBBISH
LOCATION: SEMI-URBAN/ RIVER **NO. OF SPACES:** 24
PRICES: PARKING: 4€/ 24 Hrs **SERVICES**: 2,5€ WATER or ELECTRIC
OPENING TIMES: ALL YEAR **GPS:** N44.02721 E01.11084
DIRECTIONS: From EAST take D45 into town, turn RIGHT just before river to AIRE.
SITE DESCRIPTION: *The aire is situated on the eastern side of town, about 200m from the centre, in a large tarmac parking area with shade & lit at night bordered by grass areas/ shrubs, next to the river. Artisanal service point & drainage platform with ehu's, payment at automatic barrier.*

REVIEW: *A pleasant & quiet position close to the shops in town. The parking is quite large with ample level spaces & ehu's at a reasonable price, a nice town between a canal & the Garonne river with a good range of shops, supermarkets & restaurants in town. Handy stopover off A62 (Jcn 9).*

DONZAC

ADDRESS: NEXT TO LAKE, OFF D30 **TYPE OF AIRE:** MUNICIPAL
FACILITIES: WATER /GREY & BLACK DRAIN/ RUBBISH
LOCATION: SEMI-RURAL/ LAKESIDE **NO. OF SPACES:** 20
PRICES: PARKING: FREE **SERVICES**: FREE
OPENING TIMES: ALL YEAR **GPS:** N44.11297 E00.82029
DIRECTIONS: Leaving DONZAC on D30 NORTH, turn 1st LEFT & AIRE is on LEFT.
SITE DESCRIPTION: *The aire is at the northern edge of the village, surrounded by farmland in a small lake/ park area with spaces on gravel having a little shade & lighting. Artisanal service point with drainage platform.*
REVIEW: *A very nice aire, next to a fishing lake & quiet at night with picnic tables, bbq & play area. Footpath leads 250m to the pleasant village where there is a boulangerie, tabac, epicerie, pizzeria & restaurant.*

Donzac

MOISSAC

ADDRESS: CHEMIN DE RHODE **TYPE OF AIRE:** MUNICIPAL
FACILITIES: WATER /GREY & BLACK DRAIN/ ELECTRIC
LOCATION: SEMI-RURAL/ RIVERSIDE **NO. OF SPACES:** 35
PRICES: PARKING: 8€/ 24 Hrs **SERVICES**: INCL
OPENING TIMES: ALL YEAR **GPS:** N44.09794 E01.09259
DIRECTIONS: Take D813 NORTH to MOISSAC, cross RIVER & turn RIGHT follow road alongside river to AIRE on LEFT.
SITE DESCRIPTION: *The aire is in a large gravel parking area on the north side of the Tarn river, within 50m of the river & 300m to the town centre. The parking is in a semi-rural location with individual double pitches, surrounded by a residential area & farmland, with the river adjacent. Artisanal service point with drainage platform & ehu's, entry by automatic barrier.*

REVIEW: *A quiet, pleasant location, parking is level with a little shade, lit at night, picnic tables with a view of the river. Very attractive town with Abbey buildings, UNESCO listed Romanesque cloisters & a canal that passes thru the town. Moissac is a large town (pop. 12,000) with a good range of shops, a covered market plus a farmers market on Saturday & Sunday in summer. Cycle track along river.*

VALENCE D'AGEN

ADDRESS: RUE GARONNE **TYPE OF AIRE:** MUNICIPAL
FACILITIES: WATER /GREY & BLACK DRAIN/ RUBBISH/TOILETS/SHOWERS
LOCATION: URBAN/ CANAL **NO. OF SPACES:** 10
PRICES: PARKING: 5€/ 24 Hrs **SERVICES**: 5€ ELECTRIC + WATER
OPENING TIMES: ALL YEAR **GPS:** N44.10546 E00.88575
DIRECTIONS: In town follow signs for "PORT CANAL" then signs for AIRE (over bridge).
SITE DESCRIPTION: *The aire is in a small tarmac parking area next to the canal in the south west corner of this rural town, 300m from the centre, with small trees giving a little shade in places but no lighting. Level spaces on tarmac bordered by grass areas. AireServices service point with drainage platform, toilets. Official collects fee (only Apr – Oct).*

REVIEW: *A good, modern, well maintained aire next to the canal in a quiet position with direct access to the cycle track along canal. The aire is at the end of a cul-de-sac with spaces alongside road. Water & electric paid for together. The canal marina is within 100m where there are picnic tables, bbq, toilets & showers available. Pleasant town that has a good selection of shops including a supermarket, boulangeries, butcher, pharmacy, etc & cafes/ restaurants.*

LANGUEDOC-ROUSSILLON

Burgundy region is made up of 4 departments; Aude (11), Gard (30), Herault (34), Lozere (48) & Pyrenees-Orientales (66)

Languedoc-Roussillon Map

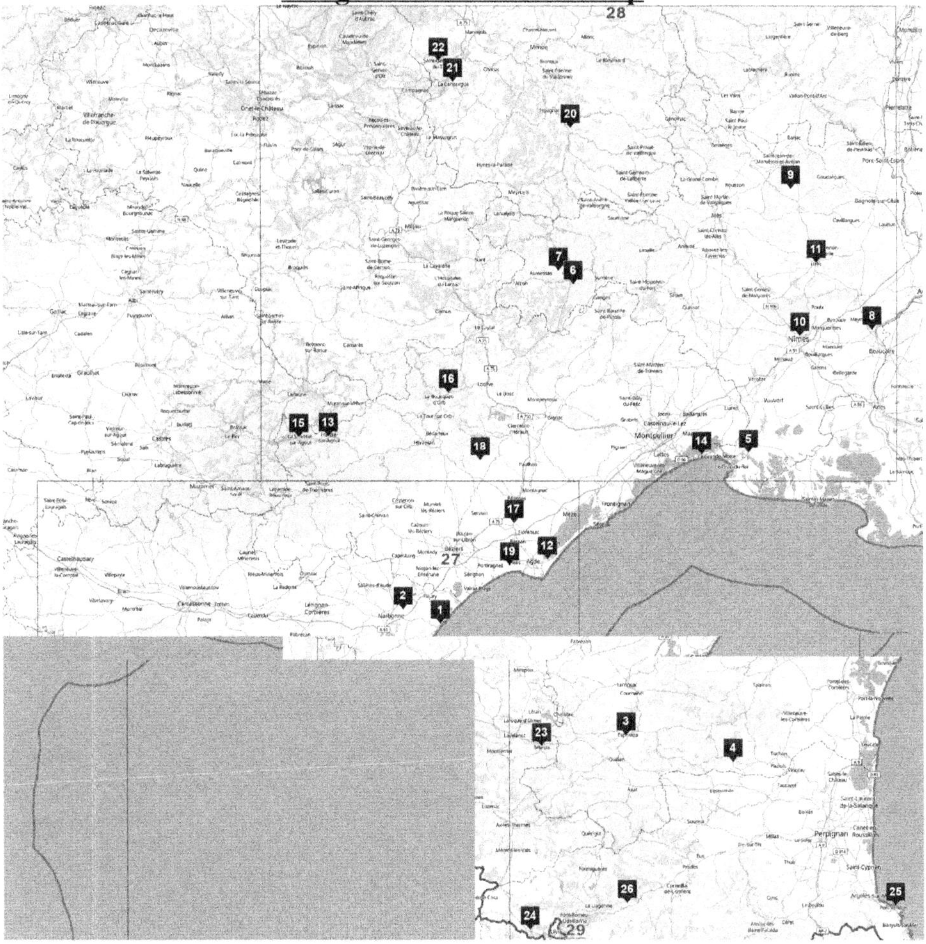

Key to enlarged Languedoc-Roussillon Maps (next page)

Former campsites that are now aires are noted in ***bold***

1) NARBONNE PLAGE – 2) VINASSAN – 3) ESPERAZA – 4) ~~DUILHAC SOUS PEYREPERTUSE~~ – 5) AIGUES-MORTES – 6) ~~AVEZE~~ – 7) BREAU ET SALAGOSSE
8) COMPS – 9) FONS SUR LUSSAN – 10) NIMES – 11) UZES – 12) AGDE
13) FRAISSE SUR AGOUT – 14) ~~LA GRANDE MOTTE~~
15) LE SALVETAT SUR AGOUT – 16) LUNAS – 17) ST THIBERY – 18) VAILHAN
19) VIAS – 20) FLORAC – 21) LA CANOURGUE – 22) ST GERMAIN DU TEIL
23) BELESTA – 24) ~~LATOUR DE CAROL~~ – 25) PORT-VENDRES
26) THUES ENTRE VALLS – 27) BEZIERS – ***28) AUROUX*** *– 29) FONT ROMEU*

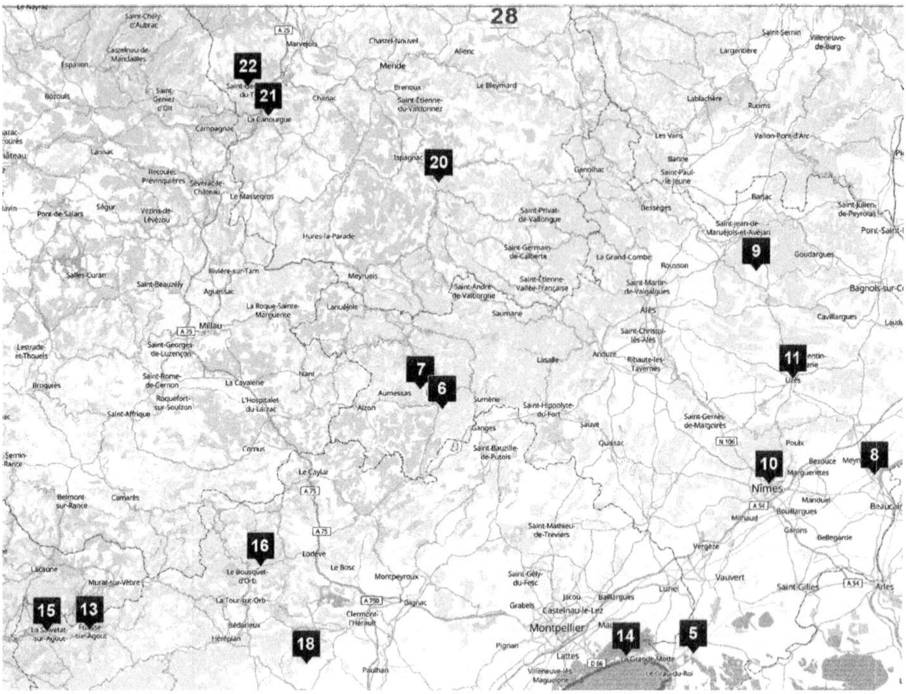
28
22
21
20
9
7
6
11
10
8
16
15
13
18
14
5
Marvejols
Mende
La Canourgue
Millau
Nant
Le Caylar
Lodève
Alès
Anduze
Ganges
Nîmes
Montpellier
Lattes
La Grande-Motte
Le Grau-du-Roi
Lunel
Vauvert
Saint-Gilles
Arles
Beaucaire
Uzès
Bagnols-sur-Cèze
Clermont-l'Hérault
Bédarieux
Pézenas

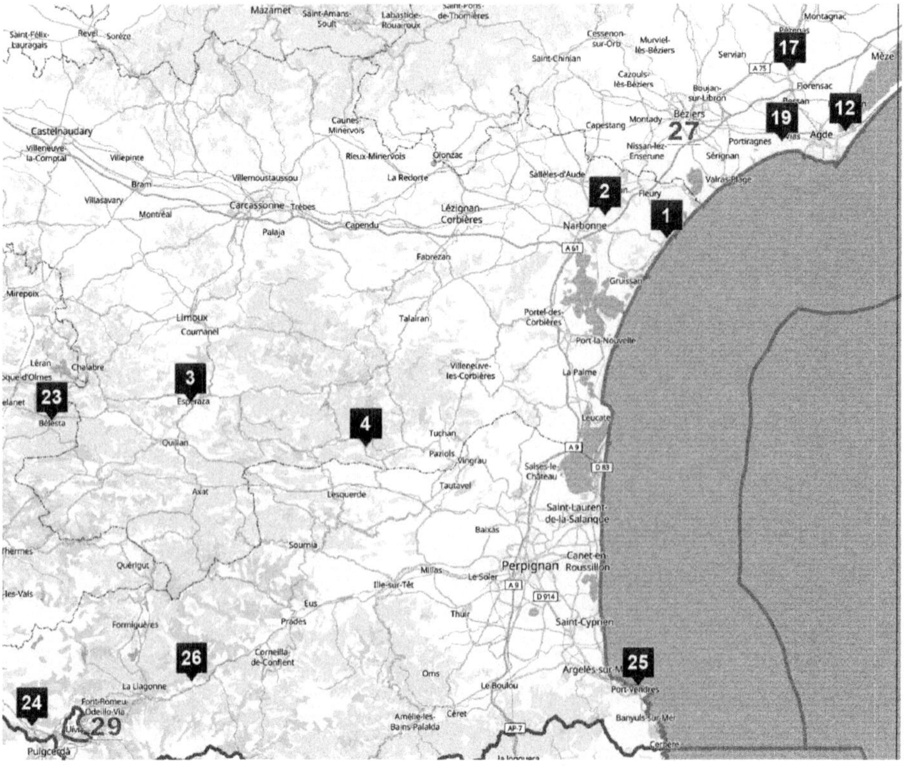
Mazamet
Castelnaudary
Carcassonne
Limoux
Narbonne
Béziers
27
Agde
17
19
12
2
1
3
4
23
26
25
24
29
Esperaza
Quillan
Gruissan
Port-la-Nouvelle
Leucate
Perpignan
Canet-en-Roussillon
Saint-Cyprien
Argelès-sur-Mer
Port-Vendres
Banyuls-sur-Mer
Cerbère
Prades
Céret
Puigcerdà
Font-Romeu-Odeillo-Via
Lézignan-Corbières
Capendu
Mirepoix
Bram
Trèbes

11 AUDE

ESPERAZA

ADDRESS: RUE VEDRINE **TYPE OF AIRE:** MUNICIPAL
FACILITIES: WATER /GREY & BLACK DRAIN/ RUBBISH
LOCATION: URBAN **NO. OF SPACES:** 20
PRICES: PARKING: FREE **SERVICES**: FREE
OPENING TIMES: ALL YEAR **GPS:** N42.93372 E02.21578
DIRECTIONS: In town take D46 NORTH to RIVER & turn LEFT just before BRIDGE. AIRE is on RIGHT (signposted).
SITE DESCRIPTION: *The aire is located on the south side of the river but close to the centre of this small town, just about 300m from the shops, parking borders the river but is also next to a minor road. There are ample parking spaces on gravel or grass, some with shade & lit at night. Large artisanal service point with platform drain.*

REVIEW: *A pleasant, quiet spot with picnic tables & play area alongside the Aude river (some traffic on adjacent road during day but none at night) - within a short walk of the town centre. Shuttle bus runs regularly to Carcassonne. Good range of shops/ restaurants in town & a large Sunday market as well as a Municipal camping (open 01/ 04 – 30/09). Attractions nearby include water sports on the river Aude which flows through the town & a Dinosaur museum. Many of the famous Cathar chateaux are only a short drive or cycle ride away.*

NARBONNE PLAGE

ADDRESS: CAMPEOLE PARK, D332 **TYPE OF AIRE:** PRIVATE
FACILITIES: WATER /GREY & BLACK DRAIN / RUBBISH / WIFI/ ELECTRIC
LOCATION: SEMI-RURAL/ BEACH **NO. OF SPACES:** 100
PRICES: PARKING: 13€ /24Hrs **SERVICES**: 2€ WATER or ELECTRIC
OPENING TIMES: ALL YEAR **GPS:** N43.14478 E03.14433
DIRECTIONS: Take D168 towards NARBONNE PLAGE. At R/bout near beach take 1st exit (D332 GRUISSAN) & AIRE is on LEFT at Campeole Park.
SITE DESCRIPTION: *The aire is located next to the beach (& the Aquatic Park) in a large tarmac car park, with plenty of spaces & some shade in places – about 1.5km to the centre of town & shops. Access via automatic barrier, a mini Flot Bleu service point .*
REVIEW: *A well looked after aire with good security (manned 7am– 7pm), flat & next to the beach but no ehu's. The large site is a bit exposed & wind can be a problem. Boulanger van calls each morning around 9am & a van selling fruit & veg calls in the evenings. A bit expensive considering electric / water are extra.*

Cycle path next to aire, walks nearby & next to water activity park. Nearby Narbonne is a labyrinth of medieval streets, Renaissance-style façades & a monumental Episcopal palace.

VINASSAN

ADDRESS: RUE DE LA FOND **TYPE OF AIRE:** MUNICIPAL
FACILITIES: WATER /GREY & BLACK DRAIN/ RUBBISH/ ELEC./ TOILETS
LOCATION: URBAN **NO. OF SPACES:** 16
PRICES: PARKING: 9€/ 24Hrs **SERVICES**: INCL
OPENING TIMES: ALL YEAR **GPS:** N43.20469 E03.07433
DIRECTIONS: In town turn WEST off D31 to AIRE (signposted).
SITE DESCRIPTION: *The aire is in a fenced, medium sized parking area on the north side of this small rural town, not far from the Mairie, where there are 16 level spaces on tarmac, well shaded by mature trees, lit at night. The aire is about 200m from the town centre & its shops. AireServices service point with platform drain & ehu's with toilets nearby.*

REVIEW: *A well-maintained, shaded, quiet aire yet close to the town centre where there is a small range of shops as well as a pizzeria & pub/ restaurant. Ample shaded parking places. Aire is accessed by an automatic barrier, electric included in price, pay by credit card. Walks around village.*

30 GARD

AIGUES-MORTES

ADDRESS: LES POISSONS D'ARGENT, D62 **TYPE OF AIRE:** PRIVATE
FACILITIES: WATER /GREY & BLACK DRAIN/ ELECTRIC/ WIFI
LOCATION: RURAL **NO. OF SPACES:** 120
PRICES: PARKING: 15€/ 24 Hrs **SERVICES**: INCL
OPENING TIMES: 01/ 03 - 31/10 **GPS:** N43.56332 E04.16390
DIRECTIONS: On D62, follow signs for 'CAMPING LA PETITE CAMARGUE'.
SITE DESCRIPTION *This aire is situated next to a 8 ha fishing lake where there are up to 120 spaces in a large, level, gravel parking area with little shade. Flot Bleu service point with drainage grid, ehu's & wifi available.*

REVIEW: *In a natural site of 20 ha, "Les Poissons d'Argent" has an adjacent fish farm, a restaurant (bread also available) & an aire welcoming120 camping-cars next to a lake but remote from town. Recommended for anglers, fishing included in price as well as water, wifi & electricity with bike hire available. Very quiet location, can get hot in summer & parking can be dusty.*

BREAU-ET-SALAGOSSE

ADDRESS: RIEUMAGE, OFF D272 **TYPE OF AIRE:** MUNICIPAL
FACILITIES: WATER /GREY & BLACK DRAIN/ TOILETS
LOCATION: RURAL **NO. OF SPACES:** 6
PRICES: PARKING: 2€/ 24 Hrs **SERVICES**: 2€ WATER
OPENING TIMES: ALL YEAR **GPS:** N43.99341 E03.56719
DIRECTIONS: From BREAU take D272 NORTH, AIRE is on LEFT after 500m.
SITE DESCRIPTION: *This is a peaceful location 500m north from the village centre, in a gravel/ grass parking area situated next to a river, with good shade here but no lighting at night. Artisanal service point with drainage platform.*
REVIEW: *A pleasant rural spot, very quiet but perhaps a bit remote from the village. Play area adjacent with picnic tables & bbq. 6 large spaces (6m wide). The small village is 1/2km away with just a boulangerie & a restaurant. Official collects fee.*

Breau et Salagosse

COMPS

ADDRESS: RUE DES ARENES **TYPE OF AIRE:** MUNICIPAL
FACILITIES: WATER /GREY & BLACK DRAIN/ TOILETS
LOCATION: SEMI-RURAL/ RIVERSIDE **NO. OF SPACES:** 20
PRICES: PARKING: 6€/ 24 Hrs **SERVICES**: FREE
OPENING TIMES: ALL YEAR **GPS:** N43.85404 E04.60785
DIRECTIONS: AIRE is well signposted in village.

***SITE DESCRIPTION**: Situated next to the Gardon river, on northern edge of the small village, the parking is in a large gravel area, accessed by a gravel track & mainly in the shade of large trees. There is ample space here & it is only 200m to the village centre. AireServices service point with a drive thru platform drain is on the north side of the parking.*

***REVIEW:** Very quiet, clean & peaceful in a pleasant well shaded location with fishing/ kayak/ swimming possible in the adjacent river, as well as a bbq & boules pitch. Some little shops in the village & a Thursday market. The Municipal Police or a council official call each morning for the parking fee. Handy spot for visiting Pont du Gard.*

FONS SUR LUSSAN

ADDRESS: PLACE DES ECOLES, OFF D187 **TYPE OF AIRE:** MUNICIPAL
FACILITIES: WATER /GREY & BLACK DRAIN/ELECTRIC
LOCATION: SEMI-RURAL/ RIVERSIDE **NO. OF SPACES:** 5
PRICES: PARKING: FREE **SERVICES**: 2€ WATER or ELECTRIC

OPENING TIMES: ALL YEAR **GPS:** N44.18494 E04.33175
DIRECTIONS: Entering FONS from SOUTH on D187 turn 1st RIGHT to AIRE.
SITE DESCRIPTION: *Situated next to a stream, the parking is in a medium size gravel area, accessed by a tarmac track on the eastern edge of this small rural village. There are 5 spaces here bordered by grass areas & it is only 200m to the village centre. Urba Flux service point with a platform drain.*

REVIEW: *A modern aire with 5 level spaces although there is room for 10, lit at night but no shade. Quiet location close to village centre where there is a grocer (sells fresh bread) & a restaurant/ bar (both sell jetons). Walks in area.* ***NOTE: D187 from north is quite narrow in places.***

NIMES

ADDRESS: DOMAINE DE FONTBESPIERRE, D907 **TYPE OF AIRE:** PRIVATE
FACILITIES: WATER /GREY & BLACK DRAIN/ ELECTRIC
LOCATION: RURAL **NO. OF SPACES:** 10
PRICES: PARKING: 14€/ 24 Hrs **SERVICES**: INCL
OPENING TIMES: ALL YEAR **GPS:** N43.87139 E04.27743
DIRECTIONS: From NIMES take D907 WEST. DOMAINE is signposted after 4kms.

DESCRIPTION: *Pleasantly situated in a very rural location about 4kms north west of Nimes, the parking is in a vast sandy/grassy, securely fenced & gated area, accessed by a long gravel track & mainly in the shade of trees with ample spaces. Artisanal service point with a drainage grid, ehu's.*
REVIEW: *A peaceful spot in a private weddings/ parties venue with a pleasant owner where there are several hard standing spaces for motorhomes but advance booking by*

phone is recommended. Parking is on sand/ grass with shade but no lighting with water & electric included. Also the option for use of showers, laundry, toilets & swimming pool for an increased fee. Access is between 8am & 9pm, intercom at gates for entry. Tel/ Text: 0614950390

UZES

ADDRESS: DOMAINE DE ST FIRMIN, RUE ST FIRMIN **TYPE :** PRIVATE
FACILITIES: WATER /GREY & BLACK DRAIN
LOCATION: SEMI-RURAL **NO. OF SPACES:** 5
PRICES: PARKING: FREE **SERVICES**: FREE
OPENING TIMES: ALL YEAR **GPS:** N44.01631 E04.42114
DIRECTIONS: In UZES follow signs "DOMAINE ST FIRMIN".
***SITE DESCRIPTION**: Located in the property of a wine producer, the parking is in a medium size gravel area, accessed by a tarmac track on the northern side of this rural town. There are 5 spaces bordered by the vineyards & it is only 400m to the interesting town centre. Artisanal service point with a platform drain. Tel/ Text: 0612314860*

***REVIEW:** A private aire, part of France Passion scheme, not far from the centre of this old bastide town with very friendly owners. Quiet parking on grass/ gravel amongst vines with a little shade from small trees. Aire is accessible 09.00 – 19.00 all week in summer but closed on Sundays in winter with a 1 night max stay. Small shop on site selling wines, olive oil & fruit/ veg in summer. Good range of shops/ services in town, a market on Saturdays & a good cycle track nearby.*

34 HERAULT

AGDE

ADDRESS: LES PEUPLIERS, D32E12 **TYPE OF AIRE:** PRIVATE
FACILITIES: WATER /GREY & BLACK DRAIN/ ELECTRIC/ TOILETS/ WIFI
LOCATION: RURAL/ RIVER **NO. OF SPACES:** 30
PRICES: PARKING: 12€/ 24 Hrs **SERVICES**: INCL
OPENING TIMES: 01/ 04 – 31/10 **GPS:** N43.29849 E03.45189
DIRECTIONS: From AGDE follow D32E12 SOUTH (west bank) towards coast, AIRE is on LEFT opposite Camping.
***SITE DESCRIPTION:** This private aire, owned by the campsite, is located in a large gravel parking area opposite to the campsite "Les Peupliers" where there are 30 level spaces with ehu's, lit at night & some shaded by trees. Access to campsite where there is a bar, snack bar, pool & laundry. Artisanal service point with drainage grid.*

REVIEW: *2km from the sea but only 50m from the Herault river, the aire "Peupliers" has level spaces on a semi-wooded site with basic toilets/ showers & wifi. Not too far from Agde town centre on the other side of the river with its good range of services.*

BEZIERS

ADDRESS: AVE FERNAND SASTRE **TYPE OF AIRE:** MUNICIPAL
FACILITIES: WATER /GREY & BLACK DRAIN/ ELECTRIC/ WIFI
LOCATION: URBAN/ RIVER **NO. OF SPACES:** 36
PRICES: PARKING: 8-13€ /24HRS **SERVICES**: 3€ WATER, 4€ ELECTRIC (24 hrs)
OPENING TIMES: ALL YEAR **GPS :** N43.33103 E03.22741
DIRECTIONS: In town follow signs for 'Parc des Sports Sauciers' & AIRE is next to it.
SITE DESCRIPTION: *The aire is managed by AireParkReservation, is 1.5km south of the town centre near to the sports stadium in a large tarmac parking area (marked spaces) with hedges / trees providing good shade in places, securely fenced & lit at night. A quiet location on an island between the Canal du Midi & the Orb river. AireServices service point with a platform drain, ehu's on each pitch, rubbish bins & wifi. Access is via an automatic barrier. Possible to reserve spaces online.*

REVIEW: *A very pleasant location (new in 2020) with nice walks/ cycling along the canal or the river, shops/ eating places nearby, 2kms from the Fonseranes locks & not too far from the town centre. A medieval 'Town of Art & History' with a Cathedral & many old buildings.*

FRAISSE SUR AGOUT

ADDRESS: RUE DES JARDINS, OFF D14 **TYPE OF AIRE:** MUNICIPAL
FACILITIES: WATER /GREY & BLACK DRAIN/ ELECTRIC/ TOILETS
LOCATION: SEMI-RURAL/ RIVERSIDE **NO. OF SPACES:** 10
PRICES: PARKING: 8€ /24Hrs **SERVICES**: INCL
OPENING TIMES: 01/03- 01/11 **GPS:** N43.60419 E02.79583
DIRECTIONS: From WEST on D14, in village turn 1st RIGHT to AIRE on RIGHT.

SITE DESCRIPTION: *Located on the banks of the river Agout & next to a picnic area, this aire has pitches on gravel/ grass with ehu's, accessed by a gravel track, with some shade under large trees. Mini Flot-Bleu service point/ drainage grid next to WC block.*

REVIEW: *This aire is quiet & shady with 10 spaces plus ehu's but you have to trail your lead across the access track. A very pretty village which has nice floral displays in summer & a good river for trout fishing. Aire is on south side of village, 150m from centre, where there is a boulangerie, grocer, butcher, restaurant & a bar/ cafe in village.*

LE SALVETAT SUR AGOUT

ADDRESS: CHEMIN DU REDOUNDEL **TYPE OF AIRE:** MUNICIPAL
FACILITIES: WATER /GREY & BLACK DRAIN/ RUBBISH
LOCATION: RURAL/ RIVER **NO. OF SPACES:** 6
PRICES: PARKING: FREE **SERVICES**: FREE
OPENING TIMES: ALL YEAR **GPS:** N43.60601 E02.69987
DIRECTIONS: In village follow signs for "STADE", AIRE is adjacent.

SITE DESCRIPTION: *This Municipal aire is located in a small parking area 400m north of the village centre, next to the football pitch where there are 6 individual level pitches on gravel separated by grass. There is good shade under trees, lighting & the aire backs onto open farmland. Drive-thru AireServices service point with drainage.*

REVIEW: *A quiet, shaded aire on the edge of the village next to the Agout river with picnic tables & bbq. Pleasant walk into village where there is a small supermarket, boulangerie, bar, restaurants & butcher.*

LUNAS

ADDRESS: BASE DE LOISIRS, OFF D35 **TYPE OF AIRE:** MUNICIPAL
FACILITIES: WATER /GREY & BLACK DRAIN/ RUBBISH
LOCATION: SEMI-RURAL/ LAKESIDE **NO. OF SPACES:** 50
PRICES: PARKING: FREE **SERVICES**: FREE

OPENING TIMES: ALL YEAR **GPS:** N43.70556 E03.18556
DIRECTIONS: Take D35 WEST from LUNAS & turn LEFT into BASE DE LOISIRS.
SITE DESCRIPTION: *Situated next to the villages' leisure area, the aire is in a very large tarmac & grass parking area, next to a large lake on the western outskirts of the village, 600m to village centre, but limited shade here. Artisanal service point with drainage grid & rubbish bins.*

REVIEW: *A well managed aire with spaces on grass & under trees next to a lake & a lovely quaint village with narrow roads, medieval buildings & excellent restaurants. A nice place, very popular in season & good for children with access to the leisure facilities (01/07 – 31/8); picnic area, swimming pool & snack bar.*

ST THIBERY

ADDRESS: DOMAINE DE LA VIERE, OFF D125 **TYPE OF AIRE:** PRIVATE
FACILITIES: WATER /GREY & BLACK DRAIN / ELECTRIC / TOILETS
LOCATION: RURAL **NO. OF SPACES:** 25
PRICES: PARKING: 10€ / 24 Hrs **SERVICES**: INCL
OPENING TIMES: ALL YEAR (0900 – 2200) **GPS:** N43.38244 E03.40183
DIRECTIONS: From BESSAN take D125 NORTH & 'DOMAINE/ MOTO-CROSS' is signposted off this road.

SITE DESCRIPTION: *Located 3km to the west of the small town of St Thibery, surrounded by olive trees, the aire is in a large, secure gravel parking area next to a wedding venue/ moto cross track. The parking is surrounded by small trees, providing some shade. There is an artisanal service point with drainage platform, toilets, showers, washing up sinks, bbq & separate ehu's. Fee collected by owner.*
REVIEW: *A well maintained aire & equipped with all facilities (toilets dated) in an enclosed private property but a bit remote from the town. Very quiet spot with some shade, lighting at night & 2 restaurants nearby, supermarket at 500m. Plenty of space for walking but best to avoid the days (2nd & 4th Sundays of month) when Moto-Cross meetings take place, due to noise.* ***Narrow access track off D125.***

VAILHAN

ADDRESS: NEXT TO CHURCH, D125E1 **TYPE OF AIRE:** MUNICIPAL
FACILITIES: WATER /GREY & BLACK DRAIN/ RUBBISH
LOCATION: SEMI-RURAL **NO. OF SPACES:** 6
PRICES: PARKING: 5€/ 24 Hrs **SERVICES**: INCL
OPENING TIMES: ALL YEAR **GPS:** N43.55531 E03.29885
DIRECTIONS: From VAILHAN take D125 NORTH, AIRE is next to CHURCH.
SITE DESCRIPTION: *The aire is located on the northern side of the village, in a large gravel parking area bordered by grass areas, next to the church with good views over the river & its valley. The aire is lit at night but has little shade, Artisanal service point with drainage platform.*

REVIEW: *An excellent little aire next to this small rural village, a quiet spot with good views & overlooking the large lake, walks nearby. There are picnic tables here & it is only a short walk into the village where there is a restaurant. Boulangerie van calls in morning.* ***NOTE: Best to approach village from south due to narrow roads from north.***

VIAS

ADDRESS: CHEMIN DE PORTIRAGNES, OFF D612 **TYPE OF AIRE:** PRIVATE
FACILITIES: WATER /GREY & BLACK DRAIN/ ELECTRIC/ WIFI
LOCATION: RURAL **NO. OF SPACES:** 20
PRICES: PARKING: 12€/ 24 Hrs **SERVICES**: INCL
OPENING TIMES: ALL YEAR **GPS:** N43.30997 E03.36216
DIRECTIONS: From VIAS take D612 WEST for 2kms & turn LEFT @ R/bout.
SITE DESCRIPTION: *A private aire located between Vias & Portiragnes where there are 20 spaces on grass or hard standing, bordered by hedges, lit at night but little shade. Artisanal service point with platform drain.*

REVIEW: *A well managed private aire with pleasant owners & prices vary with season, ehu's on each space & wifi. Handy for Beziers as well as beaches (2kms) & close to a nature reserve. Peaceful spot, a bit remote but near to campsite which has grocer/ boulangerie on site in season. Good selection of shops/ supermarket in Vias & Beziers.*

48 LOZERE

AUROUX

ADDRESS: OFF D988 **TYPE OF AIRE:** PRIVATE
FACILITIES: WATER /GREY & BLACK DRAIN/ ELECTRIC/ WIFI/ TOILETS
LOCATION: SEMI-RURAL/ RIVER **NO. OF SPACES:** 35
PRICES: PARKING: 9-13€/ 24HRS **SERVICES**: INCL
OPENING TIMES: ALL YEAR **GPS :** N44.75149 E03.72644
DIRECTIONS: In village on D988, turn opposite MAIRIE across river to AIRE.
SITE DESCRIPTION: *This 'Camping Village' aire, run by CampingCarPark, is situated in the former municipal campsite 'la Graviere', about 200m south of the village centre & next to the river. Pitches are on grass (most shaded) accessed by a gravel track, each has 6A ehu & wifi with toilets/ showers/ laundry & sinks (open 01/07-01/08). Picnic tables, play area, bbq & boules area. Artisanal service point with drainage platform. Access by automatic barrier, CCP card required.*

REVIEW: *A lovely location next to a small river, quiet with large shaded pitches but some low branches. Toilets cleaned regularly but only open July & Aug., wifi not very good. Pretty village with a chapel, 11th C church, a cafe/ baker, OT & a small market in square on Wednesday but little else. Nice walks in area.*

FLORAC

ADDRESS: NEXT TO CEMETERY, OFF D16 **TYPE OF AIRE:** MUNICIPAL
FACILITIES: WATER /GREY & BLACK DRAIN/ ELECTRIC
LOCATION: URBAN **NO. OF SPACES:** 20
PRICES: PARKING: FREE **SERVICES**: 4€ WATER or ELECTRIC
OPENING TIMES: ALL YEAR **GPS:** N44.32581 E03.59032
DIRECTIONS: Entering village from SOUTH on D16, AIRE is next to CEMETERY.
SITE DESCRIPTION: *Situated on the west side of the village, 400m from the centre, this aire is in a large tarmac parking area with marked spaces giving good views but little shade. Raclet service point with a platform drain & adjacent toilets.*

REVIEW: *The aire is clean, quiet & quite practical in a very pretty village with narrow streets, a château, small shops, mini supermarket & eating places. Spaces are a bit narrow & aire is well signposted but very popular in summer - arrive early.*

LA CANOURGUE

ADDRESS: AVE DU LOT, D998 **TYPE OF AIRE:** MUNICIPAL
FACILITIES: WATER /GREY & BLACK DRAIN
LOCATION: URBAN **NO. OF SPACES:** 40
PRICES: PARKING: FREE **SERVICES**: FREE
OPENING TIMES: ALL YEAR **GPS:** N44.43355 E03.21176
DIRECTIONS: From WEST take D998 into town & turn RIGHT into AIRE.
SITE DESCRIPTION: *The aire here is situated close to the centre of the town, on the western side, in a large gravel parking area with trees offering shade in places but no lighting. Artisanal service point with drainage platform.*
REVIEW: *A very pleasant, quiet aire set back from the road & only 200m from the town centre with its small range of shops/ services, well maintained with ample parking spaces but narrow access. Interesting town with market on Tuesday mornings.*

La Canourgue

<u>ST GERMAIN DU TEIL</u>

ADDRESS: BEHIND '8 to 8', OFF D52 **TYPE OF AIRE:** MUNICIPAL
FACILITIES: WATER /GREY & BLACK DRAIN/ ELECTRIC/ TOILETS
LOCATION: URBAN **NO. OF SPACES:** 10
PRICES: PARKING: FREE **SERVICES**: FREE
OPENING TIMES: ALL YEAR **GPS:** N44.47905 E03.17202
DIRECTIONS: From NORTH take D52 into village & turn LEFT at '8 to 8' SHOP.
SITE DESCRIPTION: *The aire is located in a large tarmac car park, behnd a superette, in the centre of this small rural village, with ample spaces but little shade. Short walk to the village centre & its shops. Artisanal borne with a platform drain, 2 ehu's & modern toilets adjacent.*

REVIEW: *A spotless aire, quiet & not far from the village centre with a nice view over the valley, next to a small play area & picnic table. It is situated behind the 8 to 8 mini-mart with several spaces for motorhomes. Small range of shops in village; mini-mart, butcher, boulangerie, chemist, café & bar, but nothing much to see in village unfortunately. Handy stopover on A75, Jcn 39.2).*

66 PYRENEES-ORIENTALES

BELESTA

ADDRESS: RUE DES LOISIRS **TYPE OF AIRE:** MUNICIPAL
FACILITIES: WATER /GREY & BLACK DRAIN/ ELECTRIC/TOILETS
LOCATION: RURAL **NO. OF SPACES:** 10
PRICES: PARKING: 5€/ 24Hrs **SERVICES**: 2€ WATER or ELECTRIC
OPENING TIMES: ALL YEAR **GPS:** N42.71575 E02.60759
DIRECTIONS: Entering BELESTA from the SOUTH on D21, turn 1st RIGHT to AIRE.
SITE DESCRIPTION: *The aire is situated on the south side of this small rural village, about 200m from the village centre. There are 10 level spaces on gravel separated by low hedges with small trees offering some shade. Flot Bleu borne with drainage grid & toilets nearby.*

REVIEW: *A pleasant, quiet spot with some shade & good views over the surrounding countryside. Short walk into this historic village with bar/restaurant/epicerie & museum but no shops although bread van calls each morning. Services include toilets/ hot showers (dated), boules, play area & bbq Official collects fee.* ***Note: Access is awkward for large vehicles.***

FONT ROMEU

ADDRESS: RUE 19 MARS, 1962 **TYPE OF AIRE:** PRIVATE
FACILITIES: WATER /GREY & BLACK DRAIN/ ELECTRIC/ WIFI
LOCATION: URBAN **NO. OF SPACES:** 28
PRICES: PARKING: 13€/ 24 Hrs **SERVICES**: INCL
OPENING TIMES: ALL YEAR **GPS :** N42.49738 E02.03685
DIRECTIONS: Approaching FONT-ROMEU on D10 from EAST, AIRE is on RIGHT.
SITE DESCRIPTION: *This private aire run by AirePark Reservation is located at an altitude of 1800m in the ski station of Font-Romeu-Odeillo-Via near to the Spanish border. The aire is on the south side of the town & has 28 pitches on tarmac, each with 16A ehu & wifi in a fenced parking area with CCTV surveillance, accessed via automatic barrier. AireServices borne/ drainage platform.*
REVIEW: *A modern aire in a quiet location with good views of the mountains & short drive from the ski slopes (45 runs with a total length of 43kms). Little shade but lit at night, short walk to shops/ eating places. Font Romeu is located in a National Park with many walking/ cycling trails. Possible to reserve a pitch online.*

Font Romeu

PORT-VENDRES

ADDRESS: PLAGE TAMARINS, ROUTE DE LA JETEE **TYPE :** MUNICIPAL
FACILITIES: WATER /GREY & BLACK DRAIN/
LOCATION: URBAN **NO. OF SPACES:** 20
PRICES: PARKING: 7-10€ /24 Hrs **SERVICES**: INCL
OPENING TIMES: ALL YEAR **GPS:** N42.51795 E03.11361
DIRECTIONS: Take D114 EAST to PORT-VENDRES, turn 1st RIGHT to QUAY / R/bout & 1st exit to AIRE.
SITE DESCRIPTION: *An aire with parking on gravel & mature trees providing good shade with lighting, toilets, an artisanal service point & drainage platform. Close to the beaches & the port / town centre are about 400m away.*

REVIEW: *A nice little aire in a pretty seaside town, quiet but only a short walk to the town centre / shops/ eating places & a supermarket nearby. Low branches on some of the pitches, Gendarmerie adjacent so hopefully safe. Police collect the fees at about 8.00am.*

THUES ENTRE VALLS

ADDRESS: RUE D'ENTRE VALLS **TYPE OF AIRE:** MUNICIPAL
FACILITIES: WATER /GREY & BLACK DRAIN/ TOILETS/ RUBBISH
LOCATION: RURAL **NO. OF SPACES:** 20
PRICES: PARKING: 10€/ 24Hrs **SERVICES**: INCL
OPENING TIMES: ALL YEAR **GPS:** N42.52381 E02.22448
DIRECTIONS: In THUES ENTRE VALLS, AIRE is opposite CHURCH.
SITE DESCRIPTION: *The aire is in a large parking area with spaces on gravel or grass, plenty of shade & tranquil, but access is narrow & can be difficult for large vehicles. Artisanal service point with toilets, access by automatic barrier.*

REVIEW: *Located in the tranquillity of the Gorges de Caranca, a very quiet & well maintained aire in a good walking area. There is a train station nearby with trips available on the famous "Little Yellow Train" through the 'Gorges' to the picturesque town of Villefranche de Conflent.*

PROVENCE-ALPES-COTE D'AZUR

PACA region is made up of 6 departments; Alpes-de-Haut-Provence (04). Hautes-Alpes (05), Alpes-Maritimes (06), Bouches-du-Rhone (13), Var (83) & Vaucluse (84)

PACA Map

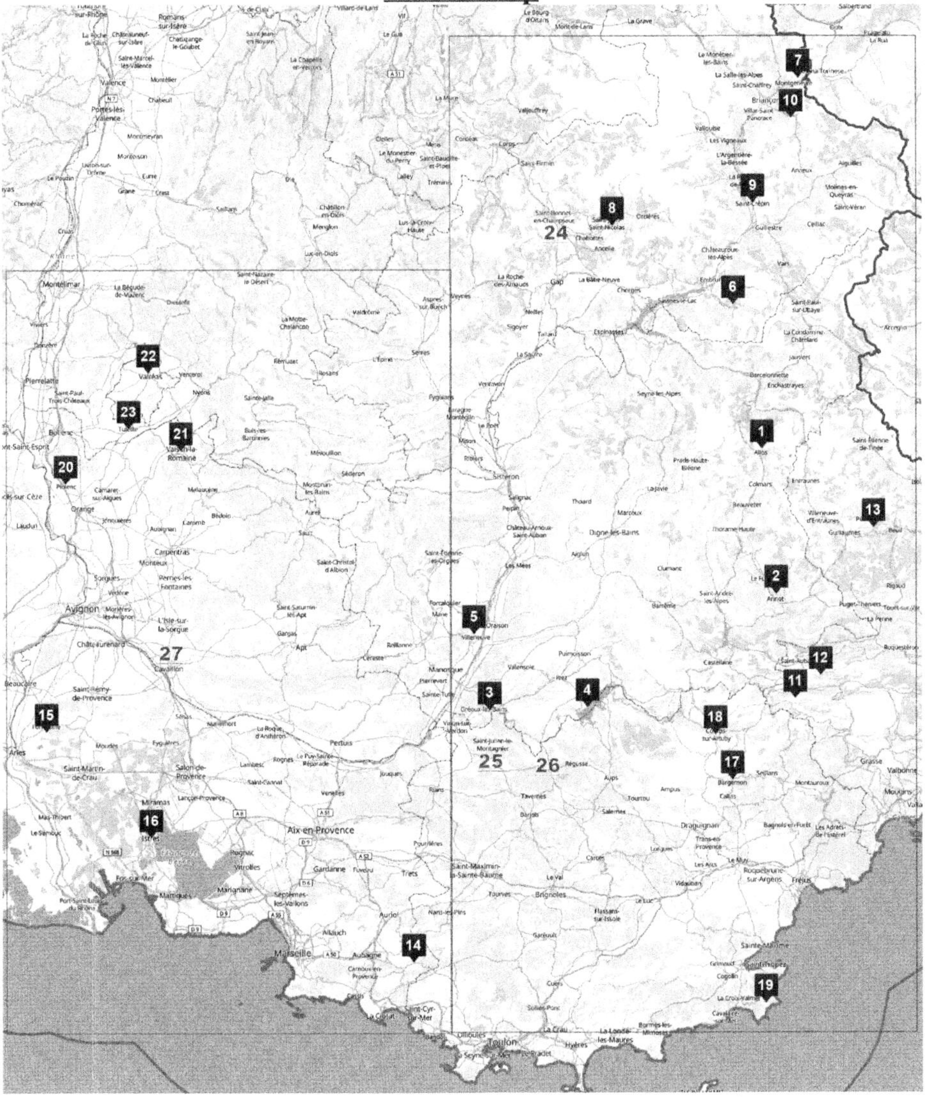

Key to enlarged PACA Maps (next 2 pages)

Former campsites that are now aires are noted in ***bold***

1) ALLOS – 2) ANNOT – ***3) GREOUX LES BAINS*** *– 4) STE CROIX DE VERDON 5) VILLENEUVE – 6) LES ORRES – 7) MONTGENEVRE –* ***8) PONT DU FOSSE***

9) ST CREPIN – 10) ST VERAN – 11) CAILLE – 12) THORENC – 13) VALBERG
14) CUGES-LES-PINS – 15) FONTVIEILLE – 16) ISTRES – 17) BARGEMON
18)COMPS SUR ARTUBY – 19) RAMATUELLE – 20) PIOLENC
21) VAISON-LA-ROMAINE – 22) VALREAS – 23) VISAN & VISAN2
*24) ST BONNET – **25) ST JULIEN** – 26) MONTMEYAN – **27) CAVAILLON***

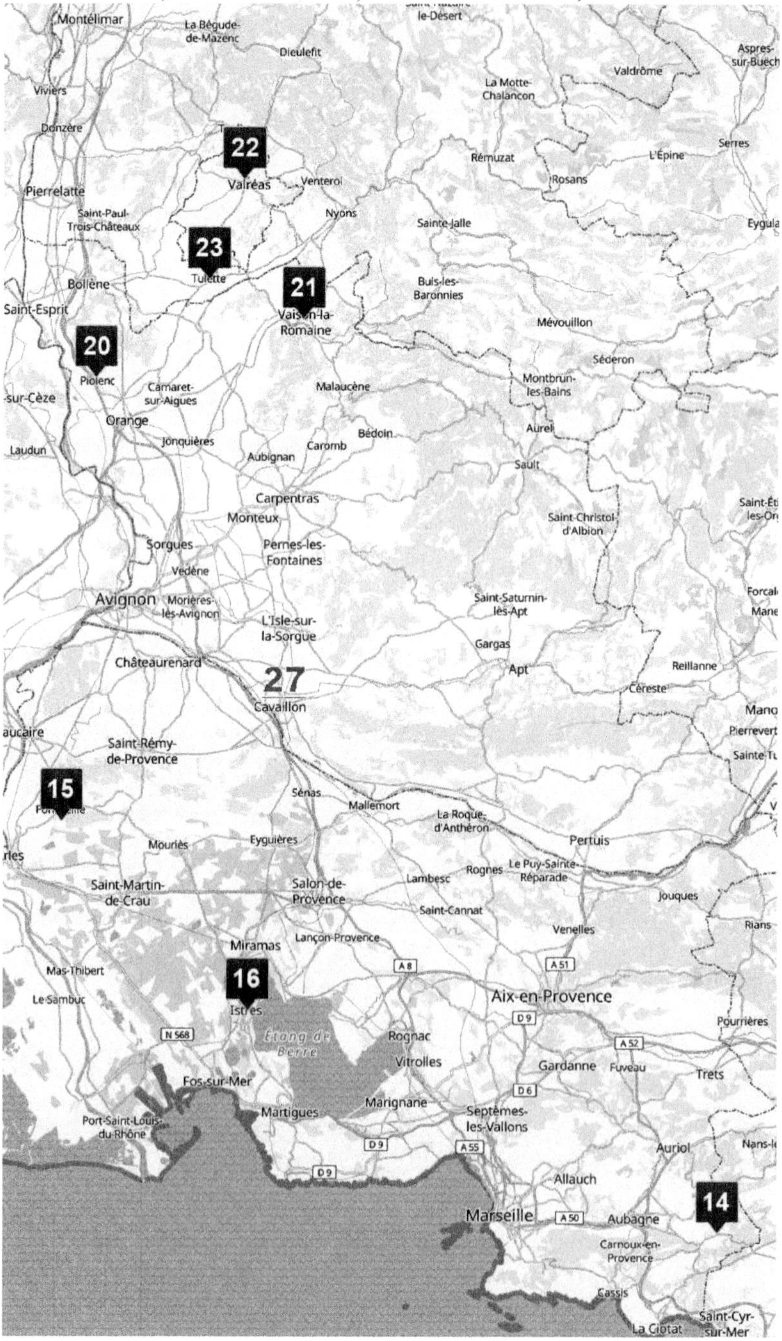

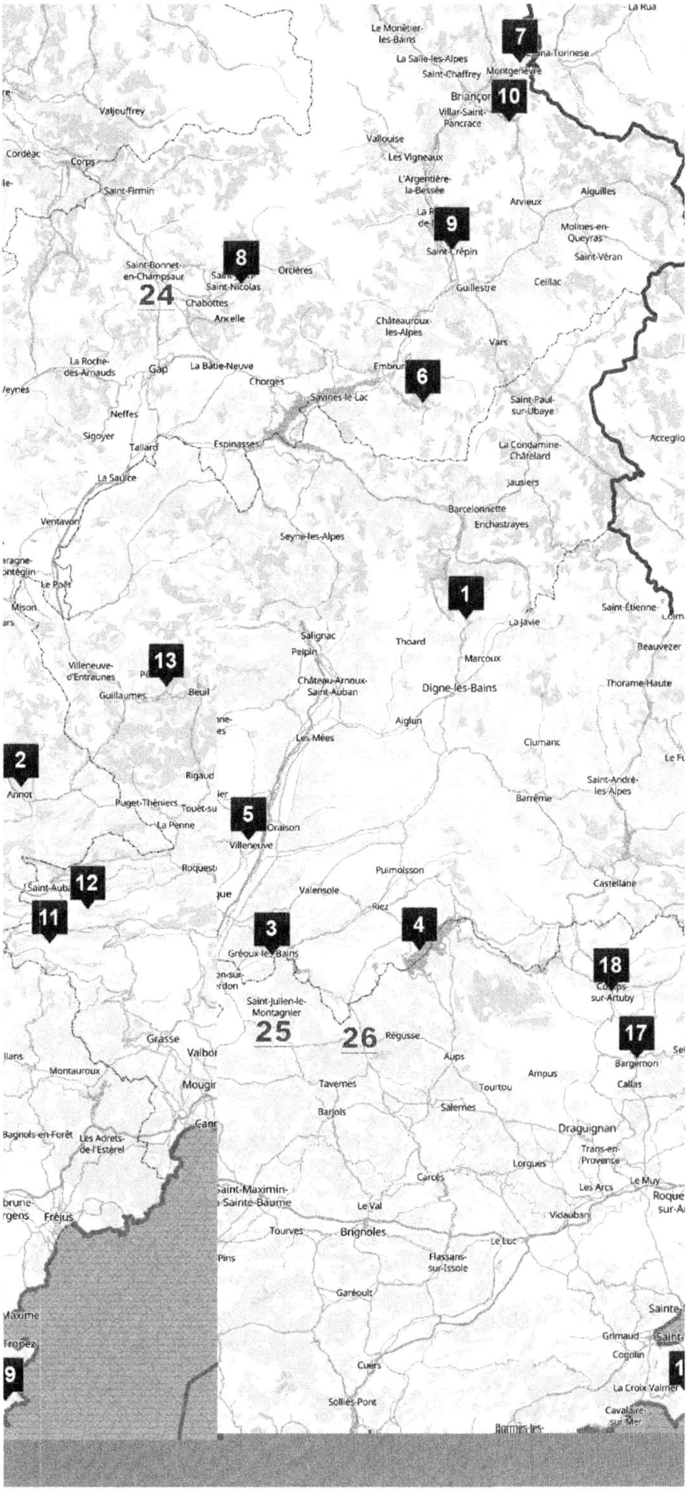
Le Monêtier-les-Bains
La Salle-les-Alpes
Saint-Chaffrey
Montgenèvre
7
10
Villar-Saint-Pancrace
Vallouise
Les Vigneaux
L'Argentière-la-Bessée
Arvieux
Aiguilles
9
Saint-Crépin
Molines-en-Queyras
Saint-Véran
Guillestre
Ceillac
Valjouffrey
Cordéac
Corps
Saint-Firmin
8
Saint-Nicolas
Orcières
Saint-Bonnet-en-Champsaur
24
Chabottes
Ancelle
Châteauroux-les-Alpes
Vars
La Roche-des-Arnauds
Gap
La Bâtie-Neuve
Chorges
6
Savines-le-Lac
Saint-Paul-sur-Ubaye
Neffes
Sigoyer
Tallard
Espinasses
Acceglio
La Condamine-Châtelard
La Saulce
Jausiers
Barcelonnette
Enchastrayes
Ventavon
Seyne-les-Alpes
Le Poët
Mison
1
Saint-Étienne-
La Javie
Salignac
Thoard
Peipin
Beauvezer
13
Marcoux
Villeneuve-d'Entraunes
Château-Arnoux-Saint-Auban
Guillaumes
Beuil
Digne-les-Bains
Thorame-Haute
Aiglun
Les Mées
Clumanc
2
Annot
Rigaud
Saint-André-les-Alpes
Puget-Théniers
Touët-su
5
Oraison
Barrême
La Penne
Villeneuve
Roquest
Puimoisson
12
Saint-Aub
Castellane
Valensole
11
Riez
3
4
Gréoux-les-Bains
18
sur-Artuby
Saint-Julien-le-Montagnier
25
26
Régusse
17
Grasse
Bargemon
Aups
Montauroux
Ampus
Callas
Mougin
Tavernes
Tourtou
Salernes
Barjols
Draguignan
Bagnols-en-Forêt
Les Adrets-de-l'Estérel
Trans-en-Provence
Lorgues
Carcès
Les Arcs
Le Muy
Saint-Maximin-la-Sainte-Baume
Le Val
Fréjus
Vidauban
Tourves
Brignoles
Le Luc
Pins
Flassans-sur-Issole
Garéoult
Grimaud
Cogolin
Cuers
La Croix-Valmer
Solliès-Pont
Cavalaire-sur-Mer

04 ALPES-DE-HAUT-PROVENCE

ALLOS

ADDRESS: NORTH of VILLAGE, OFF D908 **TYPE OF AIRE:** MUNICIPAL
FACILITIES: WATER /GREY & BLACK DRAIN/ ELECTRIC/ TOILETS
LOCATION: SEMI-RURAL **NO. OF SPACES:** 30
PRICES: PARKING: FREE **SERVICES**: 2.5€ WATER or ELECTRIC
OPENING TIMES: ALL YEAR **GPS:** N44.24250 E06.62267
DIRECTIONS: Take D908 SOUTH to ALLOS (1400). Just before village turn RIGHT immediately after BRIDGE to AIRE.
SITE DESCRIPTION: *The aire is in a large tarmac car park in the small ski station of Allos 1400, about 400m north of the village centre & 300m north of the Allos lake & Base de Loisirs. The parking backs onto wooded areas & the river but has little shade. There are public toilets adjacent & a Flot Bleu service point with drainage grid & 2 separate electric points. There is also a second aire at Foux d'Allos 1800 where there are 10 spaces & a Flot Bleu borne in the Quartier des Etoiles.*

REVIEW: *A well maintained & equipped aire but only 8 ehu's. Short walk into village & ski lifts are next to car park. There are also free shuttle buses to the other Allos (1500 & 1800) villages where there are more facilities. There are restaurants/ hotels in the village, a Poste, pharmacy, bank & OT (open all year).*

ANNOT

ADDRESS: CHEMIN DE LA COLLE BASSE **TYPE OF AIRE:** MUNICIPAL
FACILITIES: WATER /GREY & BLACK DRAIN/ RUBBISH
LOCATION: SEMI-RURAL **NO. OF SPACES:** 25
PRICES: PARKING: FREE **SERVICES**: FREE
OPENING TIMES: ALL YEAR **GPS:** N43.96313 E06.66465
DIRECTIONS: In village turn WEST over river onto CHEMIN COLLE BASSE.

SITE DESCRIPTION: *The aire is in a large, mainly hard standing, open parking area to the west of the large village with some trees providing shade, the parking is surrounded by open countryside. The aire is sloping/ uneven in many places & ramps are required. Artisanal service point with platform drain.*
REVIEW: *A very relaxing spot close to the small medieval village on the river Vaire with buildings dating from the 12th C. Some shade at the aire & plenty of spaces although it is difficult to find a level spot. Good selection of shops in village (300m away) including a Proxi supermarket. There are several terrace cafés, with plenty of huge, shady chestnut trees. Saturday market with mainly clothing, & a general market on Tuesday. Good area for walks & popular with climbers as well as a good base to see the Verdon Gorges. There is also a campsite "La Ribiere" (with wifi), ½ km north of the village off D908, open 02/03 – 17/11.*

GREOUX LES BAINS

ADDRESS: CHEMIN DE LA BARQUE **TYPE OF AIRE:** MUNICIPAL
FACILITIES: WATER /GREY & BLACK DRAIN/ ELECTRIC/ WIFI
LOCATION: URBAN **NO. OF SPACES:** 75
PRICES: PARKING: 11€/ 24Hrs **SERVICES**: INCL
OPENING TIMES: ALL YEAR **GPS:** N43.75500 E05.89011
DIRECTIONS: Take D952 into GREOUX, take D8 (dir. St Julien) & turn LEFT.

SITE DESCRIPTION: *This Municipal aire is on the site of the former Municipal campsite & is located on the south side of the town about 100m from the river, 400m from the town centre. The parking spaces are on hard standings accessed off a tarmac track, many of the spaces having good shade under mature trees with hook ups available. The service point is in a separate location, to the west of the town, off the D952 (Vinon) road, next to the sewage works where there is an artisanal service point with drainage platform.*
REVIEW: *An excellent facility, well maintained by this Thermal spa town with it's museum & casino plus a good selection of shops/ services. A quiet shaded spot, close to the town centre with 6A ehu's available on each space (incl. in price) & in a secure location – access by automatic barriers (open 24/7). A convenient spot for visiting the Verdon Gorges (12 kms).* ***NOTE: Not suitable for vehicles over 3.5T or over 8m long & camping-cars are prohibited from the car parks in town.***

STE CROIX DU VERDON

ADDRESS: ROUTE DU LAC **TYPE OF AIRE:** MUNICIPAL
FACILITIES: WATER /GREY & BLACK DRAIN / TOILETS

LOCATION: SEMI-RURAL/ LAKE **NO. OF SPACES:** 25
PRICES: PARKING: 8€ /24Hrs **SERVICES**:2€ WATER or ELECTRIC
OPENING TIMES: ALL YEAR **GPS:** N43.76111 E06.15103
DIRECTIONS: In STE CROIX take D111A towards LAKE & AIRE on RIGHT.
***SITE DESCRIPTION**: The aire is in a large tarmac car park with marked spaces, ample shade under mature trees, lit at night & near to the Lac Ste Croix on the outskirts of this village. The aire has uninterrupted views over the lake & is a quiet spot, a short walk to shops/ services. Artisanal service point with a platform drain, toilets & sinks.*

***REVIEW:** An excellent aire with lovely views of the lake, but very popular in summer - very clean & well maintained, ladies/ gents WC & sinks. The centre of the village is only 200m away where there are shops, restaurants, etc. Lac Ste Croix (14km long) is a wonderful spot for families with its well equipped beaches and the many activities offered whilst the old village has some lovely houses and pretty public squares.*

VILLENEUVE

ADDRESS: CHEMIN DES OLIVIERS **TYPE OF AIRE:** MUNICIPAL
FACILITIES: WATER /GREY & BLACK DRAIN / RUBBISH
LOCATION: URBAN **NO. OF SPACES:** 12
PRICES: PARKING: FREE **SERVICES**: FREE
OPENING TIMES: ALL YEAR **GPS:** N43.89583 E05.86110
DIRECTIONS: AIRE is next to the CEMETERY, well signposted in the village.
***SITE DESCRIPTION**: Aire is located on the north side of the village in a residential area; parking is in a gravel surfaced area with lighting, good shade under mature trees & nice views over the Durance valley/ Plateau of Valensole. Sufficient spaces for up to 12 motorhomes & only a short walk to the village. An artisanal service point with a platform drain.*

REVIEW: *A very simple, quiet & free aire in a good location close to the shops, etc near to the centre of the historic village surrounded by olive groves. The village has retained its historic past with narrow streets at the heart of the old village as well as beautiful houses built around a domed church with a belfry and bell-tower.*

05 HAUTES-ALPES

LES ORRES

ADDRESS: PARKING, HAMEAU DE PRAMOUTON **TYPE :** MUNICIPAL
FACILITIES: WATER /GREY & BLACK DRAIN/ ELECTRIC/ TOILETS
LOCATION: URBAN **NO. OF SPACES:** 40
PRICES: PARKING: FREE **SERVICES**: 3€ WATER or ELECTRIC
OPENING TIMES: ALL YEAR **GPS:** N44.49998 E06.55750
DIRECTIONS: In LES ORRES, proceed to LES ORRES 1550/ PRAMOUTON, the AIRE is located in the large CHAMP LACAS parking area
SITE DESCRIPTION: *The aire in Les Orres is in a large tarmac car park (Champ Lacas) with direct pedestrian access to the ski areas & there is also a free shuttle bus to the village centre (running until 18.30). There are toilets nearby in the Salle Hors Sac (Left Luggage) & a Flot Bleu service point, jetons from Left Luggage or shops.*

REVIEW: *The aire is large & although it is busy during the day (ski season); it is empty between 1730 & 0930, the borne is not in the parking area so is always accessible. Good walks in area. Les Orres is a small mountain village, with just one historical monument, the 16th C yellow stone church with a Romanesque bell tower.*

MONTGENEVRE

ADDRESS: PARKING DE L'OBELISQUE, OFF N94 **TYPE OF AIRE:** MUNICIPAL
FACILITIES: WATER /GREY & BLACK DRAIN / ELECTRIC/ WIFI
LOCATION: URBAN **NO. OF SPACES:** 200
PRICES: PARKING: 9€-17€/ 24 Hrs **SERVICES**: INCL
OPENING TIMES: ALL YEAR **GPS:** N44.93388 E06.73417
DIRECTIONS: Take the main N94 road thru MONTGENEVRE towards ITALY & the AIRE is located just after the OBELISK.

***SITE DESCRIPTION**: The aire is in a very large car park (slight slope) next to the RN94 road on the east side of the village, ample spaces with ehu's in an open location with good views but no shade. Entry to the parking is via an automatic barrier (pay on exit). Artisanal service point with platform drainage & a heated chalet with water taps.*
***REVIEW:** A very good aire with lovely panoramic views but there are only 80 x 10A ehu's for 200 spaces. Fairly peaceful & a very good place for winter sports/ skiing, close to the pistes with shuttle buses in winter, very popular at weekends. Several shops in the village mainly catering for skiers, but there is also a boulangerie, tabac, a couple of mini-markets & a butcher. Price varies according to season.*

PONT DU FOSSE

ADDRESS: LE CHATELET, OFF D944 **TYPE OF AIRE:** PRIVATE
FACILITIES: WATER /GREY & BLACK DRAIN/ ELECTRIC/ WIFI
LOCATION: RURAL **NO. OF SPACES:** 49
PRICES: PARKING: 11€/ 24Hrs **SERVICES**: INCL
OPENING TIMES: 01/04 – 15/11 **GPS:** N44.66785 E06.23487
DIRECTIONS: From EAST take D944 towards PONT DU FOSSE, 200m before VILLAGE turn LEFT to AIRE.
***SITE DESCRIPTION:** This former Municipal campsite is managed by CampingCarPark & is situated on the east side of the village alongside the river Drac. Access via automatic barrier, CCP card required. Euro-Relais service point with drainage platform. Pitches are on grass, level, with shade in places, each with 6A ehu & wifi but no lighting, good views. Village is about 300m from aire via a footpath alongside river.*

***REVIEW:** A very large, excellent aire in a wooded location, quiet with good facilities – picnic tables, bbq, boules pitch, ehu's & services. Shaded pitches on grass accessed by a gravel track. Pitches not marked - so not very well controlled & ground liable to flooding in wet weather. Short walk into nice village where there are a few small shops, bank, Poste plus restaurants/ pizzeria.*

ST BONNET EN CHAMPSAUR

ADDRESS: AVENUE PREMONGRIL **TYPE OF AIRE:** MUNICIPAL
FACILITIES: WATER /GREY & BLACK DRAIN / RUBBISH
LOCATION: URBAN **NO. OF SPACES:** 10
PRICES: PARKING: FREE **SERVICES**: FREE
OPENING TIMES: ALL YEAR **GPS :** N44.67684 E06.08219
DIRECTIONS: As you enter VILLAGE, follow signs for 'Cente Aquatique' & AIRE.

SITE DESCRIPTION: *The aire is in a large tarmac car park on the south west side of this small village (alt.1,025m), 10 marked spaces in a reserved motorhome area next to the swimming pool car park, lit at night with a little shade, 300m from village centre. Artisanal service point with drainage platform,*

REVIEW: *A pleasant aire, 15kms from Gap, in a mountain village on the famous Route Napoleon (RN85), with fine views of the mountains. Very quiet, slight slope, short walk into quaint medieval village where there is a small range of shops, bank, Poste & eating places. Nice old village with covered market, narrow streets & old houses. Good area for walking, skiing & mountain biking.*

SAINT CREPIN

ADDRESS: NEXT TO MUNICIPAL CAMPING **TYPE OF AIRE:** MUNICIPAL
FACILITIES: WATER /GREY & BLACK DRAIN/ ELECTRIC
LOCATION: RURAL **NO. OF SPACES:** 20
PRICES: PARKING: 8€/ 24Hrs **SERVICES**: 4€ ELECTRIC
OPENING TIMES: 01/05 – 30/09 **GPS:** N44.70510 E06.60029
DIRECTIONS: Exit N94 @ ST CREPIN & take D138 WEST towards river, AIRE is on LEFT, just after BRIDGE & CAMPSITE.

SITE DESCRIPTION: *This aire is located close to the Municipal campsite on the west side of the river Durance & village, next to a small aerodrome. The aire has use of the showers & toilets of the campsite, as well as swimming pool, with ehu's available (at an extra charge). Pitches are on grass, level, with shade in places, good panoramic views. Village centre is about 1/2km from aire, services at the artisanal borne with platform drain are free, situated outside the camping.*

REVIEW: *A good tranquil spot next to the river with shade in places, aerodrome opposite but not busy. Fee is collected by the campsite manager, electric is extra but water is free.*

SAINT VERAN

ADDRESS: PARKING,OFF D5 **TYPE OF AIRE:** MUNICIPAL
FACILITIES: WATER /GREY & BLACK DRAIN/ RUBBISH/ TOILETS
LOCATION: RURAL **NO. OF SPACES:** 20
PRICES: PARKING: 6€/ 24Hrs **SERVICES**: INCL
OPENING TIMES: ALL YEAR **GPS:** N44.70466 E06.86083

DIRECTIONS: From NORTH take D5 SOUTH to ST VERAN. As you enter village, parking & AIRE are on LEFT, before you enter village (signposted).

SITE DESCRIPTION *The aire is in a large gravel car park on the north west side of this small linear village (alt.2,000m), 20 spaces that are lit at night but no shade, 300m from village centre. Artisanal service point with grey drain & small toilet block,*
REVIEW: *Wonderful mountain location with fine uninterrupted views over the valley. Ample spaces – ramps needed here but quite a popular spot, council official calls each day to collect fee. Very quiet, short walk into quaint village (traffic not allowed) – the highest inhabited village in Europe & one of the 'Most Beautiful in France' where there are a few shops (tabac/ news, grocer, bars, gift shops) & eating places. A popular winter sports location with wood/ stone chalet houses & slate roofs.*

06 ALPES-MARITIMES

CAILLE

ADDRESS: RUE ST PONS **TYPE OF AIRE:** MUNICIPAL
FACILITIES: WATER /GREY & BLACK DRAIN/ ELECTRIC
LOCATION: SEMI-RURAL **NO. OF SPACES:** 4
PRICES: PARKING: FREE **SERVICES**: 4€ WATER or ELECTRIC
OPENING TIMES: ALL YEAR **GPS:** N43.77790 E06.73256
DIRECTIONS: Turn EAST off D79 into CAILLE & AIRE is at eastern end on LEFT.

***SITE DESCRIPTION**: The aire is in a very small tarmac parking area with a surrounding fence (no shade), bordered by open fields – with far reaching views of the mountains. Village centre is within walking distance & there is an adjacent play area. A quiet position with a Flot Bleu borne & drainage grid.*

***REVIEW:** A very nice spot; small but clean & quietly placed on the eastern edge of this little village – a good spot for cycling or walking. A few shops in the village; Proxi superette, butcher, auberge & boulangerie.*

THORENC

ADDRESS: ROUTE DE CASTELLANE, D2 **TYPE OF AIRE:** MUNICIPAL
FACILITIES: WATER /GREY & BLACK DRAIN/ ELECTRIC/ TOILETS
LOCATION: RURAL/ LAKE **NO. OF SPACES:** 12
PRICES: PARKING: FREE/ 24Hrs **SERVICES**: 5€ WATER or ELECTRIC
OPENING TIMES: ALL YEAR **GPS:** N43.79935 E06.80840
DIRECTIONS: From EAST on D2, continue 600m past village turning & turn LEFT to Lac Thorenc & AIRE.

***SITE DESCRIPTION:** This aire is next to the Lac de Thorenc where there are a dozen spaces in a tarmac parking area with shade under adjacent trees. The parking backs onto grass areas with open countryside/ forest, next to the large fishing lake & about 900m south from the centre of the village & its shops. Flot Bleu service point with drainage grid & small toilet block.*

***REVIEW:** A pleasant lakeside aire with picnic tables in a quiet rural location, close to a restaurant/ pizzeria (open all year). Plenty of spaces, 20min walk to the nice village with small selection of shops/ eating places. Various places to visit nearby including a 15th C fortified manor & remains of the medieval village of Castellaras (access only on foot).*

VALBERG

ADDRESS: ROUTE DE LA ROUYE **TYPE OF AIRE:** MUNICIPAL
FACILITIES: WATER /GREY & BLACK DRAIN/ TOILETS/ ELECTRIC
LOCATION: SEMI-RURAL **NO. OF SPACES:** 20
PRICES: PARKING: 10€ / 24 Hrs **SERVICES**: INCL
OPENING TIMES: ALL YEAR **GPS:** N44.09638 E06.93667
DIRECTIONS: In VALBERG, follow signs to STATION DE VALBERG & AIRE.

***SITE DESCRIPTION**: The aire is situated in a triangular shaped tarmac parking area with individual marked spaces bordered by grass next to the ski lifts, in a quiet position with good views of the mountains, lit at night & a little shade in places. Artisanal service point with platform drain but only one tap, ehu's on each space.*

***REVIEW:** This is a nice quiet aire in a beautiful location with some shops about 500m walk away from the aire & some good walks or cycle rides in the area. Valberg is one of* *the largest ski resorts in the Southern Alps; there is a small range of shops, bars & eating places in village.*

Valberg

13 BOUCHES-DU-RHONE

CUGES-LES-PINS

ADDRESS: LA RIBASSEE **TYPE OF AIRE:** MUNICIPAL
FACILITIES: WATER /GREY & BLACK DRAIN/ TOILETS
LOCATION: SEMI-RURAL **NO. OF SPACES:** 20
PRICES: PARKING: 5€ /24Hrs **SERVICES**: INCL
OPENING TIMES: ALL YEAR **GPS:** N43.28167 E05.70583
DIRECTIONS: From CUGES-LES-PINS, follow RUE DU DR. GASTINEL for 500m NORTH & AIRE is on LEFT.
SITE DESCRIPTION: *The aire is located in a large parking area with spaces on hard standing or grass & under the shade of large pine trees. A quiet location to the north of the village surrounded by forest/ countryside & looked after by an attendant. Access is by automatic barrier & the parking is arranged in terraces. Artisanal service point with platform drain.*

REVIEW: *This is a good aire that is quiet at night, fenced, gated & there is ample shade from the surrounding trees, but it does tend to get busy in high season. Nice walks in area with some starting from the aire. 1km from Cuges where there is a good range of shops/ services & a Carrefour supermarket.*

FONTVIEILLE

ADDRESS: AVE DES MOULINS, D33 **TYPE OF AIRE:** MUNICIPAL
FACILITIES: WATER /GREY & BLACK DRAIN
LOCATION: RURAL **NO. OF SPACES:** 40
PRICES: PARKING: 7€/ 24Hrs **SERVICES**: 2€ WATER
OPENING TIMES: ALL YEAR **GPS:** N43.71955 E04.71137
DIRECTIONS: From SOUTH on the D33, AIRE is on RIGHT as you approach village.
SITE DESCRIPTION: *The aire is located about 500m south of Fontvieille, in a large tarmac/ gravel car park with ample spaces & a little shade but no lighting, near to a wooded area with grassy spaces Urba Flux service point with drainage platform.*

REVIEW: *A quiet spot although there is slight road noise from the adjacent D33 road. Access controlled by automatic barrier. Aire is next to historic windmill/ museum with walks in forest & a footpath leads to the picturesque town with its old buildings & a good selection of shops/ restaurants plus an InterMarche supermarket. Free wifi at nearby OT.*
CAUTION – aire is liable to flooding in heavy rain & some areas can be muddy.

ISTRES

ADDRESS: CHEMIN DU CASTELLAN
TYPE OF AIRE: MUNICIPAL
FACILITIES: WATER /GREY & BLACK DRAIN/ RUBBISH
LOCATION: URBAN/ SEASIDE **NO. OF SPACES:** 12
PRICES: PARKING: 8€ /24Hrs **SERVICES**: INCL
OPENING TIMES: ALL YEAR **GPS:** N43.51549 E04.99285
DIRECTIONS: Head for MAIRIE, then take CHEMIN DU CASTELLAN to AIRE.

***SITE DESCRIPTION**: A modern aire located in a medium size tarmac parking area near the centre of this large town, the aire here is close to the sea, being well placed – only 10mins on foot to the old town centre. There are 12 individual spaces reserved for motorhomes & a modern artisanal borne with platform drain, lit at night but little shade.*
***REVIEW:** A quiet position next to a lake with beach & not far from the sea. Short walk to the centre of this busy seaside town with an old quarter, parks /gardens, a good range of shops/ eating places.*

83 VAR

BARGEMON

ADDRESS: RTE DE SEILLANS, D19 **TYPE OF AIRE:** MUNICIPAL
FACILITIES: WATER /GREY & BLACK DRAIN/ ELECTRIC
LOCATION: RURAL **NO. OF SPACES:** 6
PRICES: PARKING: FREE **SERVICES**: 5€ ELECTRIC
OPENING TIMES: ALL YEAR **GPS:** N43.62472 E06.55047
DIRECTIONS: From BARGEMON take D19 NORTH & AIRE is on RIGHT.

***SITE DESCRIPTION:** The aire is located about 400m north of the centre of this small town, just off the D19 road in a medium size tarmac parking area with level spaces on tarmac/ grass & next to a large wooded area. Drive thru Euro-Relais service point, ehu's & platform drain. Jetons from shops.*
***REVIEW:** A pleasant, modern aire set amongst olive groves on the edge of this picturesque town with good views, lighting but no shade. Quiet at night & a short walk into the old town where there is a Proxi superette, butcher, boulangerie, restaurant. Ramparts, chateau & old prison in town.*

COMPS SUR ARTUBY

ADDRESS: OFF D955 **TYPE OF AIRE:** MUNICIPAL
FACILITIES: WATER /GREY & BLACK DRAIN/ TOILETS

LOCATION: RURAL **NO. OF SPACES:** 16
PRICES: PARKING: FREE **SERVICES**: 3€ WATER
OPENING TIMES: ALL YEAR **GPS:** N43.70583 E06.50667
DIRECTIONS: From COMPS take D955 SOUTH, AIRE is on RIGHT after 300m.
SITE DESCRIPTION: *The aire is located about 400m south of this small (pop.300) rural village, just off the D955 in a medium size parking area with spaces on gravel, separated by sleepers, under mature trees & lit at night. The parking is next to a large grass area with picnic tables & is surrounded by open countryside, there is a small toilet unit with an adjacent artisanal service point & platform drain. Jetons from shops/ pizzeria.*

REVIEW: *A pleasant, shaded aire with good views, a bit remote from the village, quiet but possible road noise during day. There are a few shops in the village as well as a pizzeria. This picturesque village is at the entrance to the Gorges de Verdon & is a popular stop for walkers, there is a fortified 12th C church built by the Templars in the village.*

MONTMEYAN

ADDRESS: OFF D13 **TYPE OF AIRE:** PRIVATE
FACILITIES: WATER /GREY & BLACK DRAIN/ ELECTRIC/ WIFI
LOCATION: SEMI-RURAL **NO. OF SPACES:** 12
PRICES: PARKING: 9€/ 24 Hrs **SERVICES**: INCL
OPENING TIMES: ALL YEAR **GPS :** N43.64433 E06.06394
DIRECTIONS: Entering town from SOUTH on D13, take 1st EXIT @ R/bout & AIRE is 100m on RIGHT.

***SITE DESCRIPTION**: This modern aire is managed by AirePark Reservation in a medium sized tarmac/ gravel car park on the eastern outskirts of village, next to D13 with 12 spaces bordered by grass areas, lighting & some shade. The location is 500m from village centre & shops & there is an AireServices service point with a platform drain, ehu's & wifi. Access is via automatic barrier with credit card, also possible to reserve a space online.*

***REVIEW:** A good well-equipped aire, in a semi-rural area next to farmland with 12 spaces (but only 8 x16A ehu's) & easy to access. 500m from the medieval village centre where there is a small range of shops, lake with beach, museum & a ruined château/ ramparts. 6 km from the Gorges du Verdon & 14 km south-west of lake of Sainte-Croix.*

RAMATUELLE

ADDRESS: RTE DE BONNE TERRASSE **TYPE OF AIRE:** MUNICIPAL
FACILITIES: WATER /GREY & BLACK DRAIN/ RUBBISH/ TOILETS/ WIFI
LOCATION: RURAL / BEACHSIDE **NO. OF SPACES:** 100
PRICES: PARKING: 12€ / 24Hrs **SERVICES**: INCL
OPENING TIMES: ALL YEAR **GPS:** N43.21139 E06.66257
DIRECTIONS: From ST TROPEZ take D93 SOUTH, turn LEFT after 6km onto CHEMIN DES PRES & turn LEFT to AIRE.

***SITE DESCRIPTION**: The large aire is situated in a large sandy/ earth parking area about 150m from a nice sandy beach & 4km east of Ramatuelle, surrounded by bushes/ vegetation but no shade. Artisanal borne with drainage platform, toilets/ shower & sinks. Official collects fee.*

***REVIEW:** A reasonable aire by this region's standards, mainly due to its location next next to a nice beach but a bit too far from village & there is no shade. Facilities here are quite rustic, there is a restaurant nearby & a naturist beach, parking is cheaper in low season. Bread van calls April till Oct. The touristy village has ancient stone houses, narrow streets, shops & restaurants, shuttle buses to St Tropez.*

ST JULIEN LE MONTAGNIER

ADDRESS: BEHIND FOOTBALL PITCH, OFF D69 **TYPE OF AIRE:** PRIVATE
FACILITIES: WATER /GREY & BLACK DRAIN/ ELECTRIC/ WIFI/ TOILETS
LOCATION: SEMI-URBAN **NO. OF SPACES:** 35
PRICES: PARKING: 10-14€/ 24HRS **SERVICES**: INCL
OPENING TIMES: ALL YEAR **GPS :** N43.69605 E05.91276
DIRECTIONS: From NORTH on D69 turn LEFT @ 'Camping' sign to AIRE.

***SITE DESCRIPTION:** This 'Camping Village' aire, run by CampingCarPark, is situated in the former Municipal campsite, about 300m north of the village centre & next to the football pitch/ tennis courts. Pitches are on grass (most shaded) accessed by a* *gravel track, lit at night, each has 6A ehu & wifi with toilets/ showers/ sinks (open 01/06-30/09). Artisanal service point with drainage platform. Access by automatic barrier, CCP card required.*

REVIEW: *A pleasant location next to farmland on edge of village but close to the village centre & quiet with large shaded pitches. Sanitary block well maintained but only open June- Sept., wifi only works near entrance. Nice old village with medieval ramparts & shops/ eating places, Close to a large lake & the Verdon river with good hiking trail.*

84 VAUCLUSE

CAVAILLON

ADDRESS: AVENUE BOSCODOMINI **TYPE OF AIRE:** MUNICIPAL
FACILITIES: WATER /GREY DRAIN/BLACK DRAIN/ ELECTRIC/ WIFI
LOCATION: SEMI-URBAN/ RIVER **NO. OF SPACES:** 22
PRICES: PARKING: 11-16€/ 24 Hrs **SERVICES**: INCL
OPENING TIMES: ALL YEAR **GPS :** N43.821067 E05.03735
DIRECTIONS: In town follow signs for HIPPODROME/ CAMPING to AIRE.
SITE DESCRIPTION: *The aire, managed by AireParkReservation, is in a large parking area with individual spaces on grass/ concrete, lighting & shade in places - located next to the campsite, to the south of town. Pitches have ehu's, water, wifi & hedges on each space – maintained by the APR company. The aire is about 1.5km from the town centre but also close to the Durance river. AireServices service point with drainage platform. Can reserve online.*

REVIEW: *A good aire for this part of France, quiet (although near to the town horse track) with good services (22 spaces but only 17 ehu's) - a reasonable range of shops in town plus several restaurants with an InterMarche supermarket near to the aire & a Monday market. Nice old town with a Cathedral & Roman remains.*

PIOLENC

ADDRESS: AIRE DE LA GRAPPE, D43 **TYPE OF AIRE:** PRIVATE
FACILITIES: WATER /GREY & BLACK DRAIN/ ELECTRIC/ WIFI
LOCATION: RURAL **NO. OF SPACES:** 6
PRICES: PARKING: 10€/ 24 Hrs **SERVICES**: INCL
OPENING TIMES: ALL YEAR **GPS:** N44.18453 E04.79953
DIRECTIONS: From PIOLENC take D43 EAST, AIRE is next to D11 Roundabout.
SITE DESCRIPTION: *The aire is 3kms east of Piolenc, in the medium size gravel parking area of a fruit & vegetable shop with large separate spaces, divided by shrubs/ hedges, ehu's/ wifi & some shade. Secure location, locked at night. AireServices service point with drainage grid.*

REVIEW: *A pleasant aire in a quiet rural location in the grounds of a large fruit/ veg/ wine/ cheese retailer, friendly owners, aire is open all year but the shop is only open Mon-Sat from April till Oct. Quiet spot but remote from anywhere (supermarket 4kms away) although handy for visiting Orange (5kms). Tel/ Text: 0610564565*

VAISON-LA-ROMAINE

ADDRESS: AVE A.COUDRAY **TYPE OF AIRE:** MUNICIPAL
FACILITIES: WATER /GREY & BLACK DRAIN/ RUBBISH
LOCATION: URBAN **NO. OF SPACES:** 30
PRICES: PARKING: 9€ /24Hrs **SERVICES**: INCL
OPENING TIMES: ALL YEAR **GPS:** N44.24649 E05.07419
DIRECTIONS: At R/bout opposite AMPHITHEATRE, turn onto AVENUE ANDRE COUDRAY, turn LEFT at end & AIRE is on LEFT.
SITE DESCRIPTION: *The aire is on the northern edge of the town surrounded by farmland in a large gravel car park with little trees but no real shade & about 600m from the town centre. A well constructed artisanal borne with a large platform drain & 2 sinks for washing up. Council official collects the fee in pm.*

REVIEW: *A good size aire bordered by hedges in a quiet location & well located for the very interesting town centre having some of the best Roman remains in France (audio guides in English available) as well as a museum, art galleries, a chateau, cathedral, shops /services & a large market.*

VALREAS

ADDRESS: DOMAINE DE LUMIAN, OFF D941 **TYPE OF AIRE:** PRIVATE
FACILITIES: WATER /GREY & BLACK DRAIN/ ELECTRIC/ WIFI
LOCATION: RURAL **NO. OF SPACES:** 6
PRICES: PARKING: 3€/ 24 Hrs **SERVICES**: FREE
OPENING TIMES: ALL YEAR **GPS:** N44.39412 E04.96329
DIRECTIONS: From VALREAS take D941 WEST to 1st R/bout take 2nd exit, keep LEFT to AIRE.
SITE DESCRIPTION: *The aire is in a large gravel parking area close to the farm buildings of this wine producers' vineyard, with some shade provided by small trees. A very rural location surrounded & overlooking the vineyards, about 2km from Valreas. A good artisanal borne with platform drain, rubbish bins & electricity. Also a CCP aire in village but not as nice & more expensive.*

REVIEW: *A lovely place with picnic tables, nice views, a very friendly welcome from the owners, wine tastings in the evening & local produce is available for sale – honey, oil, wine, juices & seasonal vegetables. Accessible for all sizes of motorhome, no charge if buying produce. Village has a ruined château, 12th C church, shops & a museum. Tel/ Text: 0608099686*

VISAN 1

ADDRESS: DOMAINE DE LUCENA. OFF D20 **TYPE OF AIRE:** PRIVATE
FACILITIES: WATER /GREY & BLACK DRAIN/ ELECTRIC/ WIFI

LOCATION: RURAL **NO. OF SPACES:** 10
PRICES: PARKING: 5€/ 24 Hrs **SERVICES**: FREE
OPENING TIMES: ALL YEAR **GPS:** N44.31612 E04.98352
DIRECTIONS: From VISAN take D20 EAST, after 2km turn LEFT for 2km to AIRE.
SITE DESCRIPTION: *The aire is amongst the vineyards of the wine producer "Domaine Lucena", 3kms east of Visan, where there are 10 spaces on gravel near to the farm separated by some small trees, with views over the vines & olive trees. Artisanal borne with separate taps, ehu's & a large platform drain.*

REVIEW: *In the middle of vines & olive trees, an extremely tranquil aire with a warm welcome from the owner, guided visits & wine tastings available. Remote from any shops/ services. Tel: 0490287122*

VISAN 2

ADDRESS: DOMAINE DES LAURIBERT **TYPE OF AIRE:** PRIVATE
FACILITIES: WATER /GREY & BLACK DRAIN/ ELECTRIC/ TOILETS
LOCATION: RURAL **NO. OF SPACES:** 20
PRICES: PARKING: FREE **SERVICES**: 3€ / ELECTRIC
OPENING TIMES: ALL YEAR **GPS:** N44.34889 E04.97055
DIRECTIONS: From VALREAS take D976 SOUTH, after 3km turn LEFT for 1km.

SITE DESCRIPTION: *The rural aire is in a large gravel car park, overlooking the vineyards of the wine producer "Domaine Lauribert" where there are some small trees providing shade & an adjacent grass area, about 5km from Valreas & 5km north of Visan. Artisanal borne (with separate taps) & a large platform drain. Tel: 0490352682*
REVIEW: *An excellent, well maintained aire in a quiet, very rural position with spacious parking (slight slope), far reaching views, ehu's, very nice family owners & good wine to taste/ buy. Remote from any shops/ services.*

CRIT'AIR SCHEME

Since 2017, motorists, including foreign ones, have been subject to a €68 fine if they don't display their Crit'Air anti-pollution sticker on their vehicles, whilst driving in certain parts of France.
The stickers were only obligatory in Paris and most of the capital's surrounding suburbs, Lille & Strasbourg in the North, Lyon and Villeurbanne in central France, Toulouse in the south west and Grenoble in the south east. However since 2020, Crit'Air stickers are now obligatory in an additional 22 towns and cities across the country.
Signs on the road side will let you know you are in a Zone of Restricted Circulation (ZCR) but there are also Zones of Air Protection (ZPA) which are not permanent & come into effect during periods of peak air pollution.
The stickers indicate how environmentally friendly the vehicle is according to a colour code. The criteria is based on how old and how polluting the car is.
For those of you who are heading to France this year and have just realised they need to get hold of a sticker, you can do so by visiting this website: www.certificat-air.gouv.fr.
Stickers cost around €5 (inc p&p) & can take up to 30 days to arrive, the website has an English translation.
Note that all motorized vehicles need one, including motorbikes and scooters.
The stickers are essentially aimed at cracking down on pollution, with authorities able to ban the oldest and most polluting cars from driving at peak pollution times.
Note that in Paris vehicles that are classed "level 5" – the most polluting are banned from driving in the city from Monday to Friday 8am to 8pm.

What colour sticker should I have?

There are six categories and colours, depending on the year of the vehicle's registration, its energy efficiency, and the vehicle's emission quantity.

Crit'Air-Classification

Image table©Crit'Air.fr/Green-Zones GmbH

Crit'Air-Class	Two-, three- and light motorized four-wheelers	CARS	Light Utility Vehicles < 3,5 t	Big Trucks, Lorries and Busses
	Hydrogen – and Electric Vehicles			
	Gas powered vehicles Rechargeable Hybrid Vehicles			

Crit'Air-Classe	First registration date or Euro standard						
	Two-, three- and light motorized four-wheelers	Cars		Light Utility Vehicles < 3,5 t		Big Trucks, Lorries and Busses	
		Diesel	Petrol	Diesel	Petrol	Diesel	Petrol
	EURO 4 starting 01.01.2017 for Motorcycles and starting 01.01.2018 for Mopeds	-	EURO 5 and 6 01.01.2011	-	EURO 5 and 6 01.01.2011	-	EURO 6 starting 01.01.2014
	EURO 3 from 01.01.2007 until 31.12.2016 for Motorcycles and up to 31.12.2017 for Mopeds	EURO 5 and 6 starting 01.01.2011	EURO 4 from 01.01.2006 until 31.12.2010	EURO 5 and 6 starting 01.01.2011	EURO 4 from 01.01.2006 until 31.12.2010	EURO 6 starting 01.01.2014	EURO 5 from 01.10.2009 until 31.12.2013
	EURO 2 from 01.07.2004 until 31.12.2006	EURO 4 from 01.01.2006 until 31.12.2010	EURO 2 and 3 from 01.01.1997 until 31.12.2005	EURO 4 from 01.01.2006 until 31.12.2010	EURO 2 and 3 from 01.10.1997 until 31.12.2005	EURO 5 from 01.10.2009 until 31.12.2013	EURO 3 and 4 from 01.10.2001 until 30.09.2009
	No class for all types from 01.06.2000 until 30.06.2004	EURO 3 from 01.01.2001 until 31.12.2005	-	EURO 3 from 01.01.2001 until 31.12.2005	-	EURO 4 from 01.10.2006 until 30.09.2009	-
	-	EURO 2 from 01.01.1997 until 31.12.2000	-	EURO 2 from 01.10.1997 until 31.12.2000	-	EURO 3 from 01.10.2001 until 30.09.2006	-
No Crit'Air	No class for all types until 31.05.2000	EURO 1 and before until 31.12.1996	EURO 1 and before until 31.12.1996	EURO 1 and before until 30.09.1997	EURO 1 and before until 30.09.1997	EURO 1, 2 and before until 30.09.2001	EURO 1, 2 and before until 30.09.2001

List of aires by Department

Former campsites that have been converted to aires are noted in ***BOLD***

01 AIN

ILLIAT - LELEX - ***MANTENAY*** *- MIJOUX, - ST ANDRE SUR VIEUX JONC*

02 AISNE

BELLICOURT - CHATEAU THIERRY - COUCY LE CHATEAU AUFFRIQUE LE NOUVION EN THIERACHE – MALZY - NEUILLY ST FRONT - ROZOY SUR SERRE - ST GOBAIN

03 ALLIER

BELLERIVE SUR ALLIER – CHASSENARD - DOMPIERRE SUR BESBRE - ***LOUROUX*** *– LURCY-LEVIS – MOLINET -* ***MOULINS*** *- NERIS LES BAINS–* ***ST GERARD - ST POURCAIN SUR SIOULE*** *–THIEL SUR ACOLIN – TRETEAU*

04 ALPES-DE-HAUT-PROVENCE

ALLOS – ANNOT - ***GREOUX LES BAINS*** *- STE CROIX DE VERDON – VILLENEUVE*

05 HAUTES-ALPES

LES ORRES – MONTGENEVRE - ***PONT DU FOSSE*** *- ST BONNET ST CREPIN - ST VERAN*

06 ALPES-MARITIMES

CAILLE – THORENC – VALBERG

07 ARDECHE

AUBIGNAS – BANNE – COUCOURON - LE LAC D'ISSARLES - MEYRAS NONIERES - ST REMEZE

08 ARDENNES

MONTHERME – MOUZON – ROCROI - ***SEDAN***

09 ARIEGE

LE FOSSAT - LES CABANNES – VICDESSOS

10 AUBE

AIX EN OTHE - DIENVILLE - MESNIL ST PERE

11 AUDE

ESPERAZA - NARBONNE PLAGE – VINASSAN

12 AVEYRON

BOISSE PENCHOT – BOZOULS – BROQUIES – CAMARES – CAMPAGNAC CAMPUAC - CANET DE SALARS – CASTANET - LACROIX BARREZB – ***LE NAYRAC*** *MONTEILS -* ***SALLES CURAN*** *- ST CYPRIEN SUR DOURDOU - STE EULALIE DE CERNON - STE EULALIE D'OLT - STE GENEVIEVE SUR ARGENCE - ST JUST SUR VIAUR – SENERGUES –* ***VILLECOMTAL*** *–* ***VILLEFRANCHE DE ROUERGUE***

13 BOUCHES-DU-RHONE

CUGES LES PINS – FONTVIEILLE – ISTRES

14 CALVADOS

CLECY - COLLEVILLE - NOTRE DAME DE COURSON - PONT D'OUILLY – PORT EN BESSIN - STE HONORINE-DES-PERTES - ST VIGOR LE GRAND

15 CANTAL

ALLANCHE – ARNAC - CHAMPS SUR TARENTAINE – CRANDELLES MANDAILLES ST JULIEN – MONTSALVY - ***MURAT*** *- VIC SUR CERE – VIEILLEVIE*

16 CHARENTE

AIGRE -MONTMOREAU ST CYBARD - ST SIMON – SEGONZAC - TOUVRE

17 CHARENTE-MARITIME

CLERAC - LEOVILLE – ***LA ROCHELLE*** *- LA TREMBLADE – MIRAMBEAU - MORTAGNE SUR GIRONDE - SAUJON - ST GENIS DE SANTONGE – SOUBISE -* ***TONNAY CHARENTE***

18 CHER

HUMBLIGNY - NEUVY LE BARROIS – SANCOINS - ST AMAND MONTROND - VAILLY SUR SAULDRE – VILLEQUIERS

19 CORREZE

CHAMBOULIVE *– DAMPNIAT – OBJAT – TREIGNAC – TURENNE – UZERCHE*

21 COTE D'OR

FONTAINE FRANCAISE - LAMARCHE SUR SAONE - HEUILLEY SUR SAÔNE ***SEURRE***

22 COTES D'ARMOR

CHATELAUDREN - ILE GRANDE – LANFAINS – ***PLANGUENOUAL*** *–* ***PLEHEDEL*** *ROSTRENEN*

23 CREUSE

AURIAT – FELLETIN – JARNAGES - ROYERE DE VASSIVIERE ST JUNIEN LA BREGERE

24 DORDOGNE

ANGOISSE - CENAC ET ST JULIEN – DOMME – GROLEJAC – LEMBRAS LES EYZIES DE TAYAC SIREUIL -MARNAC – MONBAZILLAC – MONPAZIER PERIGUEUX - ST GERMAIN ET MONS - ST VINCENT DE COSSE VEYRINES DE DOMME

25 DOUBS

BAUME LES DAMES – NANCRAY – NANS SOUS STE ANNE - ORNANS VILLERS LE LAC

26 DROME

BOUVANTE – CLANSAYES – ***LA ROCHE*** *- MEVOUILLON - MIRABEL AUX BARONNIES – MONTBRISON-SUR-LEZ – NYONS1 & 2 – PIEGON - PUY ST MARTIN*

27 EURE

BROGLIE – CORMEILLES – GISAY LA COUDRE

28 EURE-ET-LOIR

COURVILLE SUR EURE – MARBOUE

29 FINISTERE

BOURG BLANC – GOULVEN – KERLOUAN – LAMPAUL GUIMILIAU – LAMPAUL PLOUARZEL - ***LANDERNEAU*** *- PLOUARZEL – PLOUMOGUER SANTEC - ST THEGONNEC*

30 GARD

AIGUES-MORTES – BREAU ET SALAGOSSE – COMPS - FONS SUR LUSSAN_ NIMES – UZES

31 HAUTE-GARONNE

REVEL - RIEUX-VOLVESTRE - ST FELIX LAURAGAIS VILLEFRANCHE DE LAURAGAIS

32 GERS

AUCH *- CAZAUBON – CONDOM 1 – CONDOM 2 –* ***FLEURANCE*** *– FOURCES*
LE HOUGA – MARCIAC - ST CLAR

33 GIRONDE

BERNOS BEAULAC – BLASIMON – FONTET – LACANAU - LA TESTE DE BUCH
GUJAN MESTRAS – HOURTIN - ST EMILION - ST PEY D'ARMENS

34 HERAULT

AGDE – BEZIERS - FRAISSE SUR AGOUT - LE SALVETAT SUR AGOUT - LUNAS
ST THIBERY – VAILHAN - VIAS

35 ILLE-ET-VILAINE

COMBLESSAC – FOUGERES - HIREL – ***LE PERTRE – LE VIVIER*** *- MESSAC*
PAIMPONT – SAINS - ST BRICE EN COGLES – ***ST MALO*** *- TINTENIAC*

36 INDRE

GUILLY – LUANT – MARTIZAY - NEUILLAY LES BOIS - ***REUILLY***

37 INDRE-ET-LOIRE

AMBOISE – AVOINE – GENILLE – GIZEUX - NOUANS
ST EPAIN - STE MAURE DE TOURAINE

38 ISERE

CHICHILIANNE - EYZIN PINET – SASSENAGE - VIRIEU SUR BOUBE

39 JURA

JEURRE – THOIRETTE

40 LANDES

CAPBRETON – GASTES - LABENNE OCEAN – LEON – ***MONT DE MARSAN***
PARENTIS EN BORN - SOUSTONS - STE EULALIE EN BORN

41 LOIR-ET-CHER

ANGE – AZE - LA FERTE BEAUHARNAIS – ***MONTHOU - MONTRICHARD***
PONT LEVOY - TOUR-EN-SOLOGNE - VERNOU EN SOLOGNE

42 LOIRE

CHALMAZELLE – CROZET – LE BESSAT - NOIRETABLE – PLANFOY – ROANNE
SAINT VICTOR SUR LOIRE – VILLEREST

43 HAUTE-LOIRE

BLESLE 1 & ***BLESLE 2*** *- LAPTE – PRADELLES -* ***SOLIGNAC SUR LOIRE*** *- VOREY*

44 LOIRE-ATLANTIQUE

CHATEAUBRIANT - LE POULIGUEN - ***PREFAILLES***

45 LOIRET

CHATILLON SUR LOIRE - ***LA CHAPELLE ST MESMIN*** *– LAILLY-EN-VAL*
SULLY-SUR-LOIRE

46 LOT

BOUZIES – CAJARC – ***CAPDENAC GARE*** *- GOURDON-EN-QUERCY*
LAMAGEDELAINE *– LA BASTIDE MARNHAC - LUZECH – MAUROUX –*
PRAYSSAC - ST CIRQ LAPOPIE – ST MEDARD - VERS

47 LOT-ET-GARONNE

BUZET SUR BAISE – CASTELJALOUX - CAUMONT SUR GARONNE
LAYRAC - LE TEMPLE SUR LOT – MARMANDE - ST SYLVESTRE SUR LOT –
VILLETON

48 LOZERE

__AUROUX__ - FLORAC - LA CANOURGUE - ST GERMAIN DU TEIL

49 MAINE-ET-LOIRE

__BOUCHEMAINE__ – BRIOLLAY – __CHENEHUTTE__ - CHENILLE CHANGE
__DAMPIERE SUR LOIRE__ - LA DRAGUENIERE – POUANCE – VALANJOU
__VAL DU LAYON__ - VILLEVEQUE

50 MANCHE

ARDEVON – BRICQUEBEC – CERENCES – FERVACHES – GRANVILLE
LE MONT ST MICHEL - LE MONT ST MICHEL/ BEAUVOIR – LESSAY
SOURDEVAL - TREAUVILLE

51 MARNE

BEAUNAY - GIFFAUMONT CHAMPAUBERT - LA CHEPPE - MAREUIL SUR AY
MUTIGNY – ST IMOGES - VILLENEUVE-CHEVIGNY

52 HAUTE-MARNE

BOURBONNE LES BAINS – CHAUMONT - COLOMBEY LES DEUX EGLISES
CORGIRNON – FRONCLES – JOINVILLE - STE LIVIERE

53 MAYENNE

AVERTON – __BOUERE__ - DEUX EVAILLES - __ST JEAN SUR MAYENNE__
VILLIERS-CHARLEMAGNE

54 MEURTHE-ET-MOSELLE

FAVIERES – MILLERY - PONT A MOUSSON – RICHARDMENIL – __THIAUCOURT__
VAL ET CHATILLON

55 MEUSE

__CHARNY__ - COMMERCY - DIEUE SUR MEUSE - DUN SUR MEUSE – HAIRONVILLE
HEUDICOURT - LES ISLETTES - LIGNY EN BARROIS
NONSARD LAMARCHE – STENAY

56 MORBIHAN

ARZON – BADEN – PENESTIN – PLOUHARNEL – __QUESTEMBERT__
ST AIGNAN - __SURZUR__

57 MOSELLE

AMNEVILLE – BITCHE - HOMBOURG HAUT – NIDERVILLER – RHODES
WALSCHEID

58 NIEVRE

CHAUMOT – IMPHY – ROUY – __ST PIERRE__

59 NORD

BANTEUX – BOUSSOIS – CAUDRY – COMINES – ESTAIRES - HAUTMONT
MARCOING – WATTEN

60 OISE

__BEAUVAIS__ – MORIENVAL – SERIFONTAINE - SONGEONS

61 ORNE

ATHIS DE L'ORNE – __LA FERRIERE AUX ETANGS__ - LONGNY AU PERCHE
MORTAGNE AU PERCHE - ST FRAIMBAULT

62 PAS-DE-CALAIS

AVION - EMBRY – ESCALLES – LONGFOSSE – MERLIMONT
NUNCQ-HAUTECOTE – RICHEBOURG – TARDINGHEN

63 PUY-DE-DOME
*AUBUSSON D'AUVERGNE – **AYDAT** - CHARBONNIERES LES VARENNES*
ISSOIRE - LA TOUR D'AUVERGNE - LE CHEIX SUR MORGE
***MURAT LE QUAIRE** - POUZOL - ST ANTHEME - ST PARDOUX*
64 PYRENEES-ATLANTIQUES
ACCOUS/ LHERS - ORRIULE - SALIES DE BEARN - SEVIGNACQ MEYRACQ
ST JEAN PIED DE PORT
65 HAUTES-PYRENEES
ARRENS MARSOUS - CAUTERETS - GAVARNIE – MAULEON
*PIERREFITTE-NESTALAS - **TOURNAY***
66 PYRENEES-ORIENTALES
BELESTA – FONT ROMEU
PORT-VENDRES - THUES ENTRE VALLS
67 BAS-RHIN
HARSKIRCHEN - ROTHAU
68 HAUT-RHIN
COLMAR – MUNSTER – ORSCHWIHR - UNGERSHEIM
69 RHONE
*ST FORGEUX – **VILLEFRANCHE SUR SAONE***
70-HAUTE-SAONE
CORRE - FAUCOGNEY ET LA MER - GRAY - SCEY SUR SAONE
71 SAONE-ET-LOIRE
CHAROLLES - GERMAGNY - LOUHANS - ST CRISTOPHE EN BRIONNAIS - ST
*GENGOUX DE SCISSE - ST GENGOUX LE NATIONAL – **TOULON SUR ARROUX***
72 SARTHE
BRIOSNE - MAMERS - PRUILLE L'EGUILLE
73 SAVOIE
***AIX LES BAINS** - CHANAZ – LESCHERAINES – MACOT LA PLAGNE*
74 HAUTE-SAVOIE
HAUTEVILLE SUR FIER – LA BALME DE SILLINGY - LATHUILE – TANINGES
SIXT FER A CHEVAL
76 SEINE-MARITIME
CLERES – ETOUTTEVILLE - GRIGNEUSEVILLE – HERTEAUVILLE - INCHEVILLE
LA MAILLERAYE SUR SEINE – MONTVILLE – NEUFCHATEL-EN-BRAY
ST ROMAIN DE COLBOSC - ST WANDRILLE RANCON
77 SEINE-ET-MARNE
*PROVINS - ST CYR SUR MORIN – **SOUPPES SUR LOING***
79 DEUX-SEVRES
*BOUGON - MAUZE SUR LE MIGNON – **MELLE** - NIORT - ST AMAND SUR SEVRE*
ST-MARTIN DE SANZAY
80 SOMME
***CAPPY** - CONTY – LONG - QUEND - ST VALERY-SUR-SOMME*
81 TARN
CASTELNAU DE MONTMIRAL - FREJAIROLLES – LA BASTIDE ROUAIROUX
*LABRUGUIERE - LAUTREC - **PUYLAURENS** - RIVIERES*

82 TARN-ET-GARONNE
*BARDIGUES – **BOURRET** - CASTELSAGRAT - CASTELSARRASIN - DONZAC*
MOISSAC - VALENCE D'AGEN

83 VAR
*BARGEMON - COMPS SUR ARTUBY – MONTMEYAN - RAMATUELLE – **ST JULIEN***

84 VAUCLUSE
***CAVAILLON** - PIOLENC – VAISON-LA-ROMAINE – VALREAS – VISAN 1 – VISAN 2*

85 VENDEE
LA BARRE DE MONTS - LA GUERINIERE - LE CHAMP ST PERE – L'EPINE
*LUCON - LA MEILLERAIE-TILLAY – MAILLE – **MOUILLERON***
*ST JEAN-DE-MONTS - ST VINCENT SUR JARD - **SEVREMONT***

86 VIENNE
***CHATEAU LARCHER** - LATHUS-ST REMY - NIEUIL L'ESPOIR – ROMAGNE*
***ST SAUVANT** - THURAGEAU*

87 HAUTE-VIENNE
FROMENTAL - JAVERDAT - LAC DE VASSIVIERE – PAGEAS – SEREILHAC
ST LAURENT SUR GORRE - ST PRIEST TAURION

88 VOSGES
BULGNEVILLE – CHARMES - MIRECOURT - MONTHUREUX SUR SAONE
PLAINFAING – ST DIE - THAON LES VOSGES

89 YONNE
GRON – GURGY - ST PRIVE

90 BELFORT
BELFORT

ABOUT THE AUTHOR

A keen motorhomer for many years and with numerous motorhoming holidays enjoyed in France, Alan Russell and his wife Sue eventually decided to relocate to that beautiful country. Drawn to the magnificent Auvergne region, they bought a property amongst the extinct volcanoes of the Cantal department in 2008, where they currently run a gite. Alan is also the creator and owner of the website www.motorhomingfrance.co.uk, that has been online since 2006.

OTHER BOOKS AVAILABLE FROM AMAZON:

Historical Tours in France by Motorhome

The Historical Tours in France guide covers the 19 former regions of France, from Brittany in the north west to Provence-Alpes-Cote d'Azur in the south-east. These 45 history themed tours have been researched and planned for a motorhome, visiting locations that I hope you will find interesting & picturesque whilst transporting you back to a France of yesteryear. The tours range from times as recent as WWII, back through Napoleonic times to the middle ages & on to the Roman occupation of France.

----

50 Great Motorhome Tours in Northern France
50 Great Motorhome Tours in Souhern France

The 50 Motorhome Tours Guides visit each of the regions of picturesque France. The tours vary in length from 1 to 8 days with suggested locations for a stopover each night – in each instance either at an aire or a campsite. The aires, for which the majority are free to stay, have full details together with description, services available, GPS coordinates and prices whilst alternative nearby campsites are listed with opening times and location. Every tour has information on places to see, museums, monuments and local attractions at each location visited as well as full directions, a road map and photographs.

- Tours in each of the Regions of France
- 1 to 8 Days in length with over 200 Photos
- Stopovers at either Aires or Campsites
- Road Map for each Tour
- Full directions & GPS Coordinates

Best Places to Visit & Stay by Motorhome in S.France

Best Places to Visit & Stay by Motorhome in N.France

Most Beautiful Villages & Towns in France by Motorhome

The award of '*Plus Beaux Villages de France*', the 'Most Beautiful Villages in France', has been given to over 150 villages throughout France where each village has fewer than 2,000 inhabitants & has a 'rich natural heritage' with at least 2 listed monuments. Whilst the title of '*Petites Cités de Caractère de France*' - 'Small Towns of Character', is awarded to small municipalities boasting a high-quality architectural heritage & who undertake to preserve this heritage.

The **'Most Beautiful Villages & Towns in France by Motorhome'** guide covers the 19 former regions of France visiting the listed Villages & Towns in these regions as well as UNESCO World Heritage sites, a total of **275 locations**. These visits having been researched and planned for a motorhome, with suggested stopovers for each location. Unfortunately the majority of campsites in France tend to open only during the summer months, with some of the Municipal campsites only opening in July and August. This would tend to restrict the timing of these visits, so they have primarily been planned using all-year-round aires as stopover places – with alternative campsites suggested, if preferred (and if they are open). As some 'motorhomers' may never have stayed at an Aire de Services, there is a chapter explaining their facilities and how to use them.

The guidebook has detailed descriptions of each location visited together with tourist information, location maps, photos & GPS coordinates. Full information is given on each aire visited as well as a review, facilities, prices, opening times as well as alternative nearby campsites. The book also includes details of aires (not on, but) near to the motorway junctions that can be used as a stopover en-route to your destination.

Printed in Great Britain
by Amazon

82350189R00241